The Person

Also by Theodore Lidz

The Family and Human Adaptation
(1963)

Schizophrenia and the Family
(1967)
(WITH S. FLECK AND A. CORNELISON)

Training Tomorrow's Psychiatrist
(1970)
(M. EDELSON, CO-EDITOR)

The Origin and Treatment of Schizophrenic Disorders
(1973)

Hamlet's Enemy
(1975)

The

PERSON

His and Her Development
Throughout the Life Cycle

(REVISED EDITION)

Theodore Lidz

Sterling Professor and former Chairman

Department of Psychiatry

Yale University School of Medicine

Basic Books, Inc., Publishers   New York

Library of Congress Cataloging in Publication Data

Lidz, Theodore.
  The person, his and her development throughout the
life cycle.

  First published in 1968 under title: The person: his
development throughout the life cycle.
  Includes bibliographies and index.
  1. Developmental psychology. 2. Personality.
I. Title.
BF713.L52 1976   155.2'5   76-22745
ISBN: 0–465–05540–0

To Ruth, my love

CONTENTS

PART I

The Setting

PART II

The Life Cycle

PART III

Patterns and Perspectives

PREFACE TO THE
REVISED EDITION

DURING the eighteenth century many leading biologists were convinced that the person existed completely preformed within the ovum as a microscopic homunculus. A number of eminent scientists disagreed. They insisted that the animalcule resided in the spermatazoa and not in the ovum. The inordinately intricate step-by-step differentiation of the organism from the fertilized germ cell could not be grasped, nor even observed, because of rationalistic and religious judgments of what made sense. The understanding of personality development and integration has been deterred by similar preconceptions. An individual's personality traits were long ascribed primarily to his ancestry. Aberrant behavior could readily be attributed to inheritance, for it clearly runs in families. One of my teachers could lightly dismiss an unmarried mother or a child who was a slow learner as being made of "poor stuff." Constitutional psychopathic inferiority was a proper diagnosis but a few decades ago, when delinquents were born and not made; and most psychiatrists continue to accept as axiomatic that persons suffering from schizophrenic disorders are genetically blighted.

Appreciation of the complexity of personality development has emerged slowly. Even the most dynamic orientation to the study of personality functioning and malfunctioning, psychoanalytic psychology, long assumed that the infant would develop into a well-integrated and highly adaptable individual unless an inherent defect, a severe emotional trauma in early childhood, or gross maternal neglect induced a fixation of libidinal investment during childhood. The many factors that enter into personality development and the many requirements that must be supplied by the nurturing persons and the enveloping social system could be overlooked because all viable societies must provide for the essential needs of their offspring and, because the primary child-rearing agency, the family, is so essential that it is universal and many of its critical functions have been taken for granted.

This book presents a psychodynamic description and conceptualization of personality development and functioning from birth to death. After presenting the fundamentals of the biological and cultural endowments with which infants enter the world, we shall carefully consider each phase of their life cycle, and the cardinal issues and tasks they must surmount to be properly prepared to enter into and accept the challenges and opportunities of the next phase that comes with the inevitability of the passage of time. The mastery of the tasks of each developmental phase of childhood is not simply an end in itself but is directed toward the attainment of a cohesive identity and a workable integration by the end of adolescence. The course of the life cycle will be followed past adolescence, for each period of adult existence requires reorientation and reorganization of the personality. We shall be following persons, not as isolates, but within the interpersonal, social, and cultural settings in which they live and from which they gain support and direction.

A major change in this book from the original edition is symbolized in the change in the title to *The Person: His and Her Development Throughout the Life Cycle.* I believe that the reader will find the change not simply symbolic but indicative of a thoughtful and pervasive reconsideration of female development and the female life cycle, of an awareness that currently women face critical new problems as their lives change in response to their higher education, fertility control, overpopulation, and the changing nature of the family. As always, freedom means choice, choice requires decision, and making decisions creates problems. The book seeks to elucidate many of the critical issues that now confront girls and women at the different phases of their lives. Not only the times, but my concepts, have changed in the nine years since the first edition was written. My horizons were expanded by the opportunity to study, together with Dr. Ruth Lidz, the family structure including the roles of men and women in various South Pacific cultures. In Papua/New Guinea where the various societies are extremely male dominated, we became acutely aware of the men's envy of women's inherent creative capacities. I am resigned to the likelihood that this new edition will not be entirely satisfactory to those liberated women who, in Alice Rossi's words, are given to "the view that marriage is passé, homemaking a drudgery, and children a drag." Still, I trust that it will become clear to the reader why I believe the family is an essential institution, marriage a potential source of fulfillment and strength, and why most persons, male and female, will continue to desire and cherish children, as troublesome as they can be and often are.

Numerous changes have been made in the book, aside from those concerned with female development, to encompass both the new knowledge and perspectives that have emerged over the past decade as well as my own increased knowledge and understanding. In response to suggestions from readers, the sections on the middle years and old age have been expanded markedly.

My original purpose in writing *The Person* was to provide medical students with a guide for learning about the persons who will be their patients. I had thought that the book could also serve the needs of those training to become clinical and social psychologists, social workers, counselors, college-trained nurses, and even attorneys, as well as others who require a comprehensive understanding of people. As I had sought to reorganize current knowledge to achieve a conceptualization which is not only internally consistent but which is also compatible with both the biological and the behavioral sciences with which personality theory must interdigitate, I believed that it might also be of interest to those seeking to bring order to the confused and confusing state of personality theory. The extensive use of the book in teaching various disciplines and its popularity with, and apparent value to, persons simply interested in "the proper study of mankind," as well as its translation into German, Italian, and Spanish provided sufficient incentive for me to undertake the necessary revision.

The developmental psychology of dynamic psychiatry and medicine evolved relatively independently of the remainder of psychology. Indeed, many academic psychologists and psychiatrists approach the study of personality so differently that they can scarcely communicate with one another and some have virtually ceased trying. Medical psychology developed out of therapeutic needs and has had strong leanings toward seeking the origins of disturbed behavior in how the genetically endowed infant unfolds in interaction with his interpersonal environment. It has been interested in learning how emotionally disturbed persons came to be the way they are, how such adverse developments might have been prevented or modified, and how personality functioning can be altered therapeutically. It has not been as interested in basing its theories on experiment or in obtaining statistically significant findings as it has been in gaining meaningful insights from work with patients and in achieving therapeutically useful knowledge.

This psychodynamic psychology received much of its impetus, its concepts, and its hypotheses from the genius of Sigmund Freud, who, by linking various psychiatric syndromes to repressed unconscious motivations and residual influences of childhood sexuality, directed attention to the critical importance of childhood experiences to mental illness. A new grasp of personality development and functioning arose out of the study of the pathological, for only when the smooth flow of normative development is disrupted can many of its intricacies be appreciated. Although long neglected in medical as well as in academic psychology circles, Freud's insights gradually gained wide attention not simply because of their therapeutic value but because they provided new depths to understanding humans and to human understanding.

It may have been advantageous for psychoanalysis to develop as it did, outside of the universities, free of the academicians who need to deal with measurable data; or who might prefer to experiment with rats because of the relative simplicity of such subjects and then make generalizations about human psychology, forgetting that man is not a monkey and even much less a rat; or who wish to avoid the complexities of human motivation and decision making even though they are of the essence of human psychology. Although psychoanalysis now permeates the thought and art of Western man, serious difficulties have arisen within psychoanalysis as a science and in relationship to other sciences where clarity and precision of concepts are necessary.

Under attack for many years because of the emphasis of psychoanalysis upon infantile sexuality and the importance of the sexual drive and unconscious motivation, analysts closed ranks and rightly regarded most of the attacks upon Freud and themselves as due to efforts to deny the pertinence of these topics. Many continued to believe that later criticisms by persons who were just as interested as they in unconscious processes and in infantile sexuality were still basically resistance rather than attempts at constructive criticism. Gradually the advantages of freedom from the academician were lost in a domination by a kind of scholasticism—a limitation of the search for knowledge and truth to within the confines of concepts that had been transformed into tenets or axioms. The world's resistance to accepting Freud's discoveries led to a counterresistance by psychoanalysts (Benjamin, 1950) to the inclusion of the findings of other sciences and scientists into psychoanalytic psychology.

As a result, no general theory of psychoanalysis exists that is internally consistent or adequately compatible with the remainder of science, but only an array of more or less related theories.* This is not the place to examine the various inconsistencies between these part-theories, particularly as I consider that many of them derive directly or indirectly from some fundamental deficiencies in understanding the nature of human beings and their adaptive capacities.†

Any developmental psychology must appreciate and give due consideration to the unique nature of the adaptive capacities of human beings—their ways of coping with the environment and surviving its hazards. The emergence of *Homo sapiens* depended upon the evolution of a brain and

---

* Careful study of the monumental labor of the late David Rapaport (1960), who was among the foremost psychoanalytic scholars, clearly reveals his inability to achieve a satisfactory integration of psychoanalytic theories. Similarly, the efforts of Merton Gill (1963), one of the most brilliant contemporary psychoanalysts, to achieve an integrated theory did not, I believe, turn out felicitously; and a related effort by J. Arlow and C. Brenner (1964) has added as many problems as it has managed to clarify.

† It might be useful to some readers, however, if I noted briefly how the book differs from various widely accepted psychoanalytic concepts. The purpose of the book, however, is not to offer a divergent or a modified theory, but rather an internally consistent approach that is in accord with established findings of both the biological and the behavioral sciences. Several salient differences will, however, be noted. (1) Those aspects of psychoanalytic theory that depend upon Lamarckian concepts of the genetic transmission of acquired characteristics, as also those that invoke a closed energy system for a biological organism, can, of course, have no place in a contemporary approach. (2) Libido theory is omitted except as metaphor that can occasionally be useful. No evidence of a displaceable sexual energy has been found; it has led to an unnecessary complexity of theory and probably nothing has done more to confuse psychoanalytic thinking. It explains nothing that is not more readily understood in other ways. The renunciation of libido theory does not mean neglect of the importance of sexual drives in human motivation, though it leads to a different approach to infantile sexuality. (3) The conflict between the topographic and structural hypotheses—that is, between considering psychic organization in terms of levels of consciousness as against conceptualizing it in terms of an id, ego, and superego—is resolved simply by considering that levels of consciousness pertain to mental functioning whereas the id, ego, and superego are constructs concerned with the structure and functioning of the personality. (4) The oedipal situation is considered in terms of the critical transition during which the essential erotized attachments of the small child to the mother must be frustrated and transcended. (5) The "secondary process" of reality-oriented conscious thought is given more importance—as in psychoanalytic ego psychology—and "primary process" thinking is considered neither to be present in early infancy nor to be a constant precursor of rational thinking, but rather is regarded as a different type of mental process that goes on under different conditions.

The most significant differences concern, first, the concept of human organisms as social beings whose development into persons depends upon their growth into, and their internalization of, the instrumentalities of a culture and the institutions of a structured social system as well as upon identification with and internalization of significant persons who themselves have made such assimilations; and second, the emphasis upon cognitive development, which has been largely neglected in psychoanalytic theory.

neuromuscular system capable of using tools, and particularly that tool of tools—language. The consequences of the development of language will be set out in the first two chapters and developed throughout the book. As the orientation emphasizes the central position of language and thought in understanding human development and behavior, it rests upon Meyerian psychobiology as well as psychoanalytic observation and theory. Adolf Meyer taught that persons can be properly understood only as integrated at a symbolic level because what they think and feel influences their functioning down to the cellular and biochemical levels of integration (Lidz, 1966). To incorporate language and thought into the description and conceptualization of the person's development, the studies of Jean Piaget as well as those of M. M. Lewis and others have been utilized. Meyer did not, however, consider how the communicative aspects of symbolic activity led to the development of cultures and social institutions, as required to formulate an adequate "field" theory or comprehensive working theory for the study of human development and maldevelopment.

Some aspects of personality development are common to all humans, reflecting the basic similarities in their biological structure and functioning. The prolonged helplessness and dependency, the late puberty, the dependence upon language and upon learning adaptive techniques, the need to provide prolonged care for offspring, and many other such factors tend to produce common features in all peoples and set the sequential pattern of the phases in the life cycle. All societies must take into account the same basic needs of persons and the human ways of survival and adaptation. Nevertheless, there is considerable leeway in how the essential needs of individuals can be satisfied and even greater latitude in how human abilities can be utilized. Different ethnic groups essentially reflect the evolution of different cultural heritages—that is, of different sets of adaptive techniques for coping with the environment. Thus, some aspects of the presentation of personality development in this book can have pertinence to all persons, some aspects to many peoples, but other portions are relevant primarily to middle- and upper-class Americans. The limitations will usually be apparent to the thoughtful reader.

In closing the prefatory remarks, I wish to note some of the major influences entering into the book's orientation. The confluence of psychoanalytic and psychobiological approaches reflects my psychiatric training. I entered medicine in order to become a psychoanalyst after first reading Freud in 1928. My training in psychoanalysis was delayed by two circumstances that were not without benefit. I was directed for my residency training to Adolf Meyer at the Henry Phipps Psychiatric Clinic of the Johns Hopkins Hospital, who strongly discouraged concomitant psychoanalytic training. However, because of my prior interests in language and aphasia and in the philosophies of James and Dewey, Dr. Meyer's approach to psychiatry was particularly meaningful to me. Then, four years of military service intervened during which I assumed responsibility for extremely severe psychiatric casualties and took care of several thousand patients who formed a cross section of the young men of America. Concomitantly, I was brought into contact with two preliterate societies and a decadent culture. These experiences have had a pervasive influence upon me. Immediately after the war, I entered upon my psychoanalytic training. My clinical and investigative interests in psychosomatic disorders and in schizophrenic patients have required major theoretic reconceptualizations of theories based primarily on studies of neurotic patients.

Aside from Adolf Meyer, John Whitehorn, and Lewis Hill, my major teachers have been persons whose writings I have studied rather than persons under whom I studied. The influences within psychoanalysis and psychiatry are many, and those outside of psychiatry even more numerous. A number of such influences including those of Shakespeare, Goethe, and Samuel Butler will be apparent in the text, which is, of course, the product of such teachings as filtered through my own experiences and integrated into a new entity.

The preparation of this book was made possible and supported in part by the National Institute of Mental Health through my Career Investigator grant. I wish to take this opportunity to thank the Commonwealth Fund for the support of a sabbatical year during which a preliminary draft of the first edition of the book was prepared; and to the Center for Advanced Study in the Behavioral Sciences for providing a haven where most of the first edition of the book was written. Once again I express my warm appreciation to Harriette Dukeley Borsuch who devotedly prepared the manuscript for publication as she has for all of my books, assumed various responsibilities which lightened my work considerably and enabled the publication of the revised edition sooner than anticipated. I wish to thank Kenneth Keniston again for his careful reading of the manuscript of the first edition, Dr. Lynn Whisnant for suggestions that have been incorporated in the chapter on the juvenile and the section on early adolescence, and the many readers who have taken the trouble to send comments and suggestions. Ruth Wilmanns Lidz, my wife, coinvestigator, colleague, sometime informal therapist, and much besides, to whom the book is dedicated, has been a direct and indirect source of a great deal contained in this volume.

THEODORE LIDZ

Yale University
New Haven, Connecticut
April 1, 1976

REFERENCES

ARLOW, J., and BRENNER, C. (1964). "Psychoanalytic Concepts and the Structural Theory," Journal of the American Psychoanalytic Association, Monograph Series No. 13. International Universities Press, New York.

BENJAMIN, J. (1950). "Methodological Considerations in Validation and Elaboration of Psychoanalytical Personality Theory," American Journal of Orthopsychiatry, 20:139–156.

GILL, M. M. (1963). "Topography and Systems in Psychoanalytic Theory," Psychological Issues, vol. 2, no. 2, Monograph 10. International Universities Press, New York.

LIDZ, T. (1966). "Adolf Meyer and the Development of American Psychiatry," American Journal of Psychiatry, 123:320–331.

RAPAPORT, D. (1960). "The Structure of Psychoanalytic Theory," Psychological Issues, vol. 2, no. 2, Monograph 6. International Universities Press, New York.

REMARKS TO THE READER—
IF A STUDENT OF MEDICINE

THIS BOOK concerns the normative development, structure, and functioning of the human being. Its focus, however, does not fall upon the tangible structure of the body as learned by dissection or by peering through a microscope, or primarily upon the unity of the physiological processes and the homeostasis of the internal environment, but upon the human organism as the person with whom the physician or therapist relates in treatment—as a total person with an individual life history and with relationships to others that provide meaning to his or her existence. It deals with the intangible matters of thoughts and feelings and the continuity of personality over time. It will seek to follow the person's development from a helpless animal infant into a specific individual with relationships to the self, to others, and to events that influence an individual's physical makeup, physiological responses, and state of health. Our concern, then, will be with those attributes that are essentially human rather than simply animal and with persons' integrated behavior within the world in which they live, a human social world as well as a physical environment.

Although concerned with matters that are essential to the study of psychiatry, this book seeks to provide some fundamentals required for the practice of modern medicine in which the patient rather than the disease is the focus of attention, and to prepare for the trained use of the doctor-patient relationship which enters into all treatment and, more often than is realized, forms the core of it. No book, no course, no individual tutelage can seek to convey all that a physician needs to know about people in order to be a good physician. Doctors learn from their patients and the task can never be completed in a lifetime. Still persons learn more readily if directed toward what is pertinent and if provided a conceptual framework for organizing their experiences.

Good physicians have always known that the majority of their patients come to them because of emotional difficulties. People turn to physicians, the clergy, and attorneys for help with problems with which they cannot cope alone, but physicians are in a particularly difficult position. Patients come to them with physical complaints derived from emotional difficulties and problems in living of which patients are unaware because they seek to banish them from consciousness in order to retain their equanimity, but for which substitute physical symptoms appear. It is safe to say that the majority of errors committed by physicians involve failures to recognize the emotional origins of symptoms, and when it is a failure to recognize a serious depression it can be as fatal as a failure to diagnose a malignancy while still removable. However, medicine and medical science have changed and entered an era in which the understanding and study of personality problems have become essential to scientific advance in many areas. The virtual conquest of infectious diseases through antibiotics and immunization has directed attention to other types of illness and has also created new problems. Medicine has been left with many conditions that do not kill but cannot be cured, and with a number of serious diseases that are often termed "diseases of stress" because emotional factors contribute notably to their origins. Whereas infectious diseases could often be studied and mastered by work with laboratory animals, the utility of animals in studying diseases of stress, such as peptic ulcer, essential hypertension, hyperthyroidism, ulcerative colitis, and rheumatoid arthritis, is far more limited. It is not quite possible to reproduce in rats or even in anthropoids conflicts involving marital discord, frustrated ambitions, drug addicted children, or discrepancies between ethical standards and sexual drives. The resolution of many of these conditions would seem to require an ability to work with emotionally disturbed patients and to become able to understand what can cause such disturbances and how they can be ameliorated. Thus, not only the care of patients but also the proper scientific study of their diseases requires an understanding of psychodynamics.

Students enter medical school for a wide variety of reasons, and often for reasons of which they never become fully aware. Some identify with an admired physician parent; others are simply following the expectations of parents; some may be setting out to combat cancer that had robbed them of a parent, or are determined to solve the problem of schizophrenia that has incarcerated a sister in a mental hospital; they may be following religious beliefs, "of the most high cometh healing"; or have decided that if they cannot be great they can at least be useful. These and other such motivations are acceptable reasons for studying medicine, but among these manifold reasons there must be an interest in people and a desire to help them, a wish to stand with patients against the fates and help them avert tragedy, and when one cannot, to help provide the strength to bear it. If there is no such interest in people, a student cannot properly become a physician. The student can still become a medical scientist, for which there is great need, and become very helpful to mankind, but not a physician.

Most medical students enter medical school with such interests in people, usually avid interests in patients as individuals, and are keenly sensitive to suffering and reactive to the drama, the often tragic drama of the hospital. Yet, as has been documented, during the four years in medical school this dominant interest in people often declines. Some claim that medical schools inadvertently teach their students to become indifferent and even cynical. Others insist that students simply become more realistic in their understanding of people and the expectations held for them. There is, of course, an important difference between the two words: "cynical" connotes a disillusionment; "realistic," an ability to see people as they are—as human, and because they are human often with selfish and hostile motivations. The physician, however, is involved with human weaknesses and requires an ability to take care of people despite their frailties—or even because of them.

There is some truth to the charge that medical students become indifferent to patients. They enter medical school to learn to treat people, but in most schools are immediately confronted by a person—a dead person called a cadaver, which they dissect. For variety, they peer at very thin slices of other bodies through a microscope. In the second year the student progresses to study pathology; the subject is no less dead, simply more recently alive. They soon become accustomed to patients who are very passive indeed. They may consider that the only good patients are those who are anesthetized or, at least, do not disrupt the study of them by talking, and certainly do not disagree with the physician and express opinions about what is being done to them. Some schools now provide a less traumatic introduction to the study of medicine, and also foster an understanding of people throughout the curriculum. The physician's sensitivity to suffering and a constant awareness of what illness means to patients and their families cannot but cause pain. A physician has need for defenses against too great an involvement. The construction of such defenses often starts on the first day of school, when students call the body they dissect a "stiff," as if to deny that it had once been a person, and when they utilize "dissecting room humor" to blunt the grimness of the task and the place. Such defenses are proper, necessary, and valuable, but they become deleterious to the development of a physician when the protective shell turns to callus and the student withdraws from learning what is meaningful in the lives of patients. The study of patients and their personalities can be hampered by just such needs to erect and maintain defenses.

Withdrawing or becoming indifferent or callous is not the most useful way to withstand the stress and pain that are inherent in the practice of medicine. Here, as elsewhere, a little knowledge may cause suffering, whereas broader knowledge brings strength. With trained understanding of people and their ways of reacting, the physician can serve as a guide to the patient who is confronted by pain and suffering and is lost among troubles and the need to make critical decisions. Physicians can learn to realize how much illness and misfortune mean to patients and still not become personally caught up in their troubles. Physicians cannot become too involved personally and yet maintain the perspective and judgment they require to help their patients. When they can help, and they can often help simply by listening and understanding, they are not likely to become resentful toward a patient because they can do nothing to cure the illness or save the patient's life, and can leave the patient better off in some way for having been under their care.

The adage "Know thyself" is intimately related to "The proper study of mankind is man." Medical students are privileged for they will be given the opportunity to learn about individuals more intimately than persons in any other profession; and not simply as spectators but as active participants in the drama of people's lives. Self-knowledge is fostered and even provoked by knowledge of others and comparisons of the self with them. One cannot come to know very much about others, however, without learning to know oneself, how one's life fits together and how one defends against experiencing insecurities and anxieties. Such learning about the self is bound to produce some discomfort in anyone who dares be sensitive. All students of people, of themselves, must recognize that "norms" by which to measure and judge the self do not exist. There is no proper standard of normality, no proper way of life, but rather different types of workable integrations.

Everyone has defects, weaknesses, hidden shames and guilts, but they are usually offset if not balanced by assets. There is ample room in society for difference and divergence, and few persons are capable of understanding others who have not been made alert because of their own shortcomings and insecurities. Tolerance of others may well start with tolerance of the self. The only way to be completely stable is to become inert, and there is ample time for that. The processes of development, accomplishment, and creativity, the pursuit of goals and the involvement in the lives of others, are all stabilizing forces that serve to integrate and protect against the effects of personality deficiencies that may become disturbing when development and involvement with matters beyond the self come to a halt.

PART I

The Setting

CHAPTER 1

❀

The Human Endowment

WHEN THE INFANT EMERGES into the world from the mother's womb, a loud wail marks the entry of air into the lungs and the shock of exposure to the world. Without being asked, the child is committed to the world and the life that lies ahead. If reluctant, the obstetrician holds the infant by the heels and raps them sharply, for this is the moment of decision. The baby has given up the symbiotic existence within the mother, where nutriment came through the placenta by filtration of the mother's blood. Now the umbilical cord is cut and tied. The neonate, or newborn, appears puny and is helpless—among the most helpless of all creatures born into this world—and will require total care for a long time. Still, the infant is a member of the human species that has inherited the earth and gained mastery over all that inhabits it: the most far-ranging and adaptable species that has ever existed—creatures who increasingly change the environment to suit their needs and desires.

This is an awesome moment, and it is a rare obstetrician who, despite the hundreds of similar deliveries he or she has performed, has not marveled at the process of the unfolding from the fertilized ovum that has taken place, and wondered what the future will hold for this particular infant who has just been ushered into the world. After the cord is cut, the

3

obstetrician, with practiced eye, will examine the infant to see if it is properly equipped for the task that lies ahead. At this point of transition we too shall pause to review what human children bring into the world with them, considering certain essentials of what they acquire during the ten dark lunar months in the womb and then what they must assimilate in order to survive and develop into individuals.

THE DUAL HERITAGE OF THE HUMAN

The neonate is just sufficiently complete to survive with the help of a mothering figure. Despite the relative incompletion at birth, the neonate possesses a great deal. The organism contains an inborn directedness for further growth and the potentiality for the very special type of adaptation that human beings acquired at the end of a billion or so years of evolution from a unicellular organism. Within the mother's uterus the fetus recapitulated in a token fashion the emergence of the human through many prior evolutionary forms and the preparation, through evolutionary trial and error, for survival. Although human beings attained their present physical structures some thirty thousand years ago and their genetic makeup has changed little in essentials since then, their way of life and their adaptive capacities have altered enormously—to an extent that makes their pre–Stone Age progenitors seem closer to the anthropoid apes than to the astronaut.

Infants can grow up to become contemporary persons because they have a second heritage that they acquire after birth from those with whom they will live. It is a heritage that has accumulated over countless generations, and which had been made possible by the uniquely human capacity to use words to communicate and think. The newborns will acquire an organized filtrate of the ways their forebears had learned to cope with their environment and live together—that is, a culture and its instrumentalities. They will learn these ways slowly as they grow up, for the ability to acquire them is an essential part of their physical endowment and they cannot even survive and grow into adulthood without them. Not only is the newborn infant physically immature and incomplete, but the human's method of adaptation, in contrast to that of all other animals, rests upon learning essential techniques of adaptation during the long period of immaturity that is a necessary correlate of the development of the complicated cerebral cortex which permits thought, learning, and decision making to supplant inborn patterns of behavior essential for survival. Infants, then, are born with two endowments, or, more properly stated, with one and into one. They possess at birth a genetically determined biological endowment which is both common to all mankind and also uniquely individual and which has already been modified by interaction with the intrauterine environment. They will grow into and assimilate a cultural heritage that is a product of the cumulative experiences of the particular ethnic group into which they are born but which also will be somewhat different for each person. The two endowments will be inextricably intertwined as the child matures and develops. Unless both of these endowments and their fusion in the individual are taken into account, human development and integration can never be understood properly. All dynamic psychologies have been concerned, either explicitly or implicitly, with the growth of the biological organism in its interpersonal setting, varying in emphasis on the importance of the genetic endowment and environment in shaping the personality. Neglect of one or the other has led to gross distortions of understanding, and unawareness of the problem has led to many of the grievous errors that have plagued psychology and psychiatry.

Evolutionary Considerations

Questions concerning why human beings are constructed as they are, why their physiological processes function as they do, why their adaptation depends upon their capacities to use tools and language, why and how they developed a "mind" or "psyche," can be answered only in evolutionary terms—through an understanding of the emergence of the human being from a unicellular organism through countless forms of animal organization by means of innumerable genetic mutations. We can ask such questions as "What for?" and "What purpose does it subserve?" without embarrassment over teleological implications. The process of evolution promoted survival through selecting out through mating those mutations or recessive genes that permitted a new or improved means of adaptation to a segment of the environment. We can assume that a structure or process found in the organism subserves the preservation of the individual or species and is a modification of something found in prior evolutionary forms, or that it is vestigial from a structure that had been useful in a prior form.

When, to speak symbolically, our post-simian ancestors climbed down from their arboreal habitat to give up their monkey business and keep their feet on the ground—clutching a stick as a club instead of hanging to it as a branch, and calling to one another with words instead of through interjectional sounds of warning or passion—a new phase in the history of our planet had its primordial origins some three or four million years ago. Once the value and superiority of the new form of adaptation were established, man emerged by successive modifications until approximately thirty thousand years ago. Then, within the brief thirty thousand years of his existence *Homo sapiens* has changed the order of nature radically, interposing the switching system of the human brain into the sequence of events and even the selection of species until eventually—now—the question of how long life in any form may continue on this planet depends more upon what transpires in people and between people than upon the eventual dimming of the sun.

Let us note in summary fashion what is distinctive about human evolution and adaptation. All forms of life are variations of a single theme. They are different means of assuring survival and reproduction of the fundamental unit of life, the cell. The cell contains chromosomes composed of genes —chemical templates that reproduce themselves and then control the development, structure, and organization of the organism. Single-celled organisms can survive and reproduce only under very specific conditions and are dependent upon the immediate availability of essential chemicals in the environment in order to function, if not to survive. Increasingly complex organisms evolved which could exist under more varied conditions and with longer periods of self-sufficiency. Each new form of life had a somewhat different structure suited to interacting with a different segment of the environment. Changes in structure that permitted such changes in adaptation depended upon utilization of mutations in the germinal cells— chance failures of the genes to reproduce themselves precisely, so that the new genes gave rise to an organism that was different from the parents. Stated succinctly, at least as far as higher animals are concerned, there can be no question about the answer to the age-old riddle—the egg preceded the hen. For the hen to have attained attributes different from those of its non-hen parents, a change had to have occurred in the chromosomes of the fertilized egg from which it emerged.

Let us shift from a chicken to a finch—to take a classical example. Darwin's finches, which played an important role in the evolution of the theory of evolution, comprise a number of varieties of finches, all of which emerged from common ancestors who happened into the Galápagos Islands. They flourished and competed for the available food supply—they might occasionally peck a bug from the bark of a tree, but they could not survive only by eating bugs from beneath the bark. Some underwent an accidental mutation of the genes that provided a longer and sharper beak—and could now enjoy a diet other finches could not reach—and as the trait aided survival, it was retained by means of the mating of finches with this characteristic. Other finches gained an advantage from other modifications in structure—such as permitted them to suck nectar from flowers or to eat insects in flight. Each structure permitted a different way of competing and a better use of a different segment of the environment and fostered the ability to survive and produce eggs. Birds that lived in and used the same environmental niche tended to mate with one another, and eventually the new mutant traits replaced former physical characteristics and thus changed the finch into a new variety.

While the emergence through such means of the millions of different forms of life that have inhabited the earth may seem highly improbable, we must remember that mutations are very common, that a billion years is a long time, particularly for rapidly reproducing simple organisms, and that, as Simpson (1950), the renowned paleontologist, has pointed out, selective mating is a means of achieving a high degree of improbability.

Selective Mating and Evolution

The emergence of a new species—at least in more complex forms of life—does not occur by the selecting out of a single mutation through mating. It results by selecting out in mating those specific mutations which, from among the myriads that occur by chance, improve some particular attribute or set of attributes that bestows a greater chance of survival in a given environment as mutations improve this attribute over thousands or hundreds of thousands of generations. In herbivorous mammals, for example, increased neck length allowed a mutant group to eat leaves competitors could not reach—and continuing selecting out of improvements in neck length permitted better use than competitors of a different segment of the environment. Another line fed in the open plains and its chances were increased by developing the fur that permitted ranging northward—combined with strength and horns to defend itself in the open country. The mutation that gave rise to a trait that permitted moving into a different environment led to selecting out further improvements in this trait that increased chances of survival and reproduction in that environment.

Although this summary of the evolutionary process is a gross and perhaps a brazen oversimplification, I believe it will suffice for our purposes.

The Evolution of Human Attributes

The human species, of course, emerged in the same gradual way. We cannot here trace the many fascinating phases in our evolution, but it seems important to note that humans with their inordinately complex brains may have been able to emerge only from an arboreal ancestor who had developed an opposable thumb to aid in climbing, who could nurture only one offspring at a time because the infant had to cling to its mother while she jumped from tree to tree, and thereby was more amenable to education by example, and who lived in groups that were dependent upon the exchange of vocal signals for defense and was already rewarding through selective mating increases in brain size and intelligence as means of survival.

Tools and Language

When our ancestors, for whatever reason, returned to live on the ground, and left the protection of the rain forest, the direction of future evolutionary selection had been established. Out of the trees, these ape men must have been highly vulnerable. They had little in the way of physical characteristics to safeguard their existence: no body armor, horns, tusks, claws, or massive strength, special fleetness of foot, or protective coloring. But they were endowed with a brain that, even in its relatively rudimentary form, bestowed new attributes that were worth the sacrifice of other characteristics. They could use tools: the stick that their ancestors had grasped for millions of years now became an extension of their physical structure— disposable and replaceable extensions that could be used as a club or throwing stick, and later as a digging tool to root out foods; as material for a shelter, as a bit of fuel for fire; and as charcoal for drawing pictures. It was an extension of the self—but also one object with many uses, and many objects with the same use, and thereby something that had a symbolic connotation.*

The ability to use tools depended upon the evolutionary acquisition of a brain and neuromuscular system capable of exquisite voluntary movements that could be learned. It was a brain that also made possible the fine coordination of movement of lips, tongue, larynx, and facial and respira-

---

* The chimpanzee dips a stick into an insect hole and then eats the insects that collect on the stick (Goodall, 1963, 1965). This is a primitive use of a tool, but only for one specific purpose. Anthropoid apes are highly social animals with some capacity for symbolic functioning and teach a great deal to their offspring through example.

tory muscles that permitted the acquisition of another tool, that less tangible tool that faded into thin air as its waves spread out in widening circles —the word. Upon the importance of this abstract tool grown into language rested the further evolution of the hominid into the human—that is, upon the word which permitted protohumans to communicate explicitly in order to direct others, and eventually to direct themselves by reflective thinking.

The Human Brain

Over the ensuing several million years many changes in prehominid physical structure took place. Many varieties of protohuman species developed until one became dominant or the more successful lines fused. But the important characteristics selected out of the mutations that occurred were those which had to do with the increasing development of the cerebral cortex and particularly of those several areas of the brain as well as skeletal structure essential for language development and with the accompanying increase in nerve pathways that permitted inborn or instinctual patterns to be supplanted by learned ways, and permitted complex choice and decision.* Over these millions of years—that is, over more than twelve million generations—through the selecting out of the proper mutations the brain tripled in size until the human species came into existence about thirty thousand years ago. It is a species whose newborns are among the most helpless of all animals, depending upon parental protection and nurturance for a dozen or more years, and with little capacity for survival anywhere without being taught—that is, without learning the essential techniques of adaptation from those who raised them—yet a species that has spread out and flourished almost everywhere on earth, from tropic to pole, from beneficent islands nurtured by green plants to harsh brick and concrete canyons nourished by green paper.† Yet, despite this increase in the range of environments, the many changes in human techniques of adapting to them have occurred with very little, if any, basic alterations in physical struc-

* The Lieberman-Crelin hypothesis concerning the reasons why the Neandertal hominid died out approximately forty-five thousand years ago is of interest, even though it remains the subject of much dispute. Lieberman and Crelin believe that the Neandertals, in contrast to the more direct precedessors of *Homo sapiens*, were limited by a skull structure that prevented the development of the vowel sounds *a*, *i*, and *u* (as in "not," "see," and "to")—sounds important in all modern languages—and thus had more limited capacities to communicate verbally. (See G. B. Kolata, "The Demise of the Neandertals: Was Language a Factor?")

† Hartmann's (1939) concept that humans are born "to live in an average expectable environment" has gained wide popularity among psychoanalysts but misses the essence of the adaptive capacities of the human species—namely, the ability of people to adjust the environment to meet their limited inborn physiological capacities.

tures, including the brain. This is in complete contrast to all other living things. We can say that although the human as an animal has remained unchanged, the human as a person changes continually. In contrast to other animals in which changes in adaptive techniques await changes in physical structure, humankind continues to evolve without such changes. The completion of the human brain through genetic mutations did not imply the completion of the human mind. Indeed, it was only after the emergence of the human brain that the mind really began to develop. It is, I believe, through the contemplation of how this evolution without genetic change could take place that we may gain an understanding of human adaptation and of what we mean by the human mind.

What then was so valuable about this ability to manipulate tools, both tangible and symbolic, that it was selected out as a superior means of assuring survival, and led to the development of *Homo sapiens* and to a new type of evolution?

Some are skeptical that humans could evolve from a pre-Stone Age specimen to their present state without incurring changes in their brain capacity. But consider, we can observe a transition of almost this magnitude occurring today in but one or two generations. While living in a remote country, I worked with a well-trained physician and enjoyed conversing with his brother, a colonel who was skilled in the civilized techniques of killing with a tommy gun and bazooka—and yet their grandfather had gained prestige and position by his skill in wielding a solid club of wood and showed his good manners by using a specially carved fork rather than his fingers when eating the men he killed with his club. As the sons of the chief, my friends had been educated in England. But one need only wander about most sheltered university campuses to encounter scholars whose parents or grandparents lived in Stone Age fashion in Africa or New Guinea as had countless generations of their ancestors.

Let us, for purposes of clarity, examine separately two sets of consequences of the acquisition of language, even though they are in actuality inextricably linked: those derived from verbal communication and those arising from its internal counterpart, mentation.

Language, Communication, and Culture

All animals communicate through actions and odors, if not through sound. Communication is a major adaptive attribute. Two animals who can cooperate through communicating have abilities that far exceed the sum of their individual capacities. They can warn one another, signal the presence of food, mark out areas against intruders, inform the opposite sex of their presence at appropriate times, etc. Apes that live in bands—such as baboons—depend greatly upon group organization for protection and survival. Indeed, the young and injured adults have little chance of surviving for a day if separated from the band.

Further, all higher animals depend upon learning from their mothers to supplement inborn patterns of behavior. Even a squirrel must be taught how to run properly along a branch, and how to scurry for cover upon jumping to the ground; but such learning depends upon following direct and tangible examples. Humans, in contrast, could, by means of the language they had gradually constructed, communicate the fruits of experience to others without having to resort to direct illustration. They could convey what they had learned to the next generation and across generations. They might, for example, prepare their grandchildren to survive a flood by telling them to take to high ground when certain signs of danger appeared, or give directions where to find game in years of scarcity. Methods of coping, adapting, means of surmounting crises—experience in general—became cumulative. Gradually, each group of persons living in the same area built up sets of ways of coping with their environment and of living together cooperatively that formed their culture and its instrumentalities. These included the language itself and ways of perceiving, thinking, and experiencing, as well as the tangible tools they created to work upon nature.

A body of information, customs, sentiments became part of the human heritage. The newborn no longer started life from scratch, only acquiring knowledge of ways of surviving that could be learned during a lifetime, but rather children assimilated the ways of the people who reared them through the long years of their immaturity. The language itself is a central part of these acquisitions, for after infancy a person's learning depends largely upon language.

Unless we understand clearly that human infants are born with a dual heritage, we can never understand human behavior rightly. They have a biological inheritance that is transmitted through the genes from generation to generation, and a cultural heritage into which they grow and which they must assimilate to become persons. These cultural and social institutions form a new environment that engulfs all individuals as much as does the air they breathe, entering into the children and nourishing them into persons rather than animals, teaching them how to live and how to survive, as Aleuts or Zulus according to where they happen to have been born.

This assimilation of ways of living transpires so naturally that we are apt to accept much of it as part of the unfolding of a person's physical endowment. We may laugh when we read in Herodotus of how the Pharaoh Psammetichos learned to his chagrin that the Phrygians rather than the Egyptians were the original race. Unable to find out through inquiry from the sages, Psammetichos gave two infants to a herdsman and instructed him that they be fed by goats and that no one ever speak a word in their presence. Herodotus' informants specifically denied the canard that Psammetichos had the children raised by women whose tongues he had cut out. He wanted to learn what word the children would first articulate after the babblings of infancy were past. After two years both children clearly enunciated and then frequently repeated the single word "Becos," which, as we well know, is the word for bread in Phrygian. At least one ignorant commentator on Herodotus observed that if there were any truth whatsoever in the story, the children were probably imitating the bleating of goats.*

Yet, many of us are apt to believe in inborn ethnic or national personality characteristics. We may even have to check our credulity when we read of an infant who grew into manhood reared by apes, and who eventually became their leader by dint of his human intelligence; and of how, when a young and beautiful white woman inevitably was cast up by the sea, he revived her and gently carried her to his treehouse where he served her tea—for, after all, he was really a scion of English nobility and would not have done otherwise. Such childish credulity is scarcely greater than that of a biologist who wrote an article suggesting that we might soon be able to send fertilized embryos to colonize other planets and thus conserve space and weight in rocket ships. Apparently this scientist expects the offspring to emerge like Pallas Athena from the head of Zeus, fully educated and capable of perpetuating the human species on some distant planet.†

---

* Salimbene, a medieval chronicler, narrates in more detail a similar story about Frederick II, the scientifically curious despot who ruled the Holy Roman Empire in the thirteenth century. Frederick "wanted to find out what kind of speech and manner of speech children would have when they grew up if they spoke to no one beforehand. So he bade foster mothers and nurses to suckle the children, to bathe and wash them, but in no way to prattle with them, or to speak to them for he wanted to learn whether they would speak the Hebrew language, which was the oldest, or Greek, or Latin, or Arabic, or perhaps the language of their parents, of whom they had been born. . . . But he laboured in vain because the children all died. For they could not live without the petting, and joyful faces and loving words of their foster mothers." Although this is very likely a legend repeated about various kings, we have recently learned that Frederick's findings could have been accurate. Spitz (1945) found that infants raised in an orphanage under good hygienic conditions but impersonally and without stimulation gradually wasted and died, or became irrevocably mentally defective. (See Chapter 5.)

† Life, September 10, 1965, in an article entitled "Control of Life," shows Dr. E. S. E. Hafez of Washington State University holding a set of vials, which he says "could contain 'the barnyard of the future complete with the farmer.'" Hafez be-

What would the natural child be like—the child unaffected by a cultural and interpersonal environment? There are many tales of feral children aside from those of Romulus and Remus. None has been definitely substantiated. The most plausible account is found in Arnold Gesell's *Wolf Child and Human Child,* which contains the diary of an Indian, Reverend Singh, recording how he raised two girls saved in early childhood after having been reared by a wolf. According to the account, Kamala, the girl who survived for some years, remained more animal than human: she continued to crawl on all fours; ate only from the floor; and could never be taught to speak. We cannot advocate belief in the report, for most authorities contend that a child could not survive if mothered by an animal. However, in India infant girls were sometimes abandoned because they impose a grave financial liability upon a family. Still, the children simply may have been congenital idiots found soon after abandonment.*

THE CULTURAL ENDOWMENT

A culture, then, has become an essential part of the human endowment. To examine the influence of the culture upon personality development is not to continue an old conflict concerning the importance of cultural versus biological factors in personality formation, but simply to recognize that the biological nature of the human organism is such that it depends upon the assimilation of cultural instrumentalities to make possible survival and development into a person. The culture in which the child is raised serves as a mold to shape the rough outlines of the personality, delimit drives, and provide organization to the manifold ways of adapting to the environment permitted humans by their physical endowment. Although the repressive

---

lieves that his techniques are particularly suited to the space age, as a means of colonizing the planets. "When you consider how much it costs in fuel to lift every pound off the launch pad," he says, "why send fully grown men and women aboard spaceships? Instead why not ship tiny embryos in the care of a competent biologist who would grow them into people, cows, pigs, chickens, horses—anything we wanted—after they got there?" Why not, indeed? Perhaps because we might confuse the resultant humans with the pigs.

* It is of interest, however, that the measurements of the long bones of the arms and legs of these children did not conform to those of children who walk; the difference would be expected in children who only crawled, as the length of these bones is regulated to some extent by muscular usage. The inclusion of such details requires unusual sophistication from a person perpetrating a fraud.

and limiting influences of society have been bemoaned,* delimitation is essential to the realization of potential. A person cannot develop into a harmonious entity without it. Indeed, without the skills and customs provided by society, a child cannot become anyone at all.†

Culture and Human Adaptation

The accumulation of abilities to work upon nature; to control fire; to make clothing, tools, and shelters; to cultivate plants; to domesticate animals, diminished the sway that natural forces held over people. Such acquisitions increased, far beyond limits permitted by their innate physiological capacities, the range of environments in which people could live. The control of the temperature of the body, for example, no longer rested solely upon the physiological mechanisms of regulating heat loss through the dilation and constriction of peripheral blood vessels, and upon sweating, shivering, and muscular activity: these physiological mechanisms were augmented and often obviated by the use of fire, clothing, and housing. Eventually, the body's thermostatic control could be abetted by a person's sleeping under a thermostatically controlled blanket within a themostatically controlled house. Through humans' interference with the process of natural selection by selecting to their purposes, a minute wild grain was transformed into hybrid corn which, together with the domestication of the hog and cow, provides some groups of people with a constant surplus of food which they must be cajoled into buying lest the economy fail and some persons go hungry. While the fundamental needs for the sustenance of life have not altered, the means of satisfying them have.

The culture influences physiological functioning in a great variety of ways. What stimulates or abolishes appetite depends on the culture more than on physiology; swallow nest soup, ancient eggs, grasshoppers, termites, human flesh are all considered delicacies by some, though none of these is apt to arouse American appetites. Anger and fright are innate emotional states, but what enrages and what frightens vary greatly. Physique may be affected by preferred activities: the high-status Greek in ancient times cultivated his physical prowess, whereas the Talmudic scholar of eastern Europe was rarely of muscular athletic build.

---

* See S. Freud, "Civilization and Its Discontents," and the radical and untenable extension of the thesis in Norman Brown's book, *Love's Body*.

† "The vast proportion of all individuals who are born in any society always, and whatever the idiosyncrasies of its institutions, assume the behavior dictated by the society. Most people are shaped to the form of their culture, because of the enormous malleability of their original endowment"—Ruth Benedict (1934).

The ways of reacting to life situations vary profoundly and affect the total functioning of the person. The Hopi Indians, for example, believe that thinking and concentrating bring about manifestation—that is, cause something to happen (Whorf, 1939). Thus relatives and friends beseech a sick person to forgive any slights they may inadvertently have given, to have positive thoughts about living, to wish to live for their sakes. They seek to save a relative's life by having affectionate thoughts about the person and by collectively wishing for his or her recovery. Should such patients perversely persist in remaining ill and worsen, those around them become enraged and start berating them for being mean and disregarding the needs and wishes of their relatives and friends. Eventually they may even beat the sick person to force a change in attitude.* Further, in our society we feel sorrow or are supposed to feel sad when a friend or relative dies; we rarely feel rage, and if we do we try to repress such feelings. Tears are accepted if not expected. However, a Hopi found crying when a relative is dying would be stigmatized as a "witch," for only a person who had purchased one's own life at the expense of the life of the relative would cry.

Culture and Personality

It becomes increasingly clear that the manner in which children are raised in a society influences their personalities. Balinese mothers, for example, customarily indulge their children during their first few years of life while they are nursing, but after weaning will frustrate and tease children who seek closeness and affection and foster jealousy of younger siblings: the schizoid aloofness of the Balinese can virtually be seen developing in response to such treatment (Bateson and Mead, 1942). Hopi parents also indulge their children and avoid antagonizing them by punishment but rather threaten that the supernatural Kachinas will come and beat them if they are not obedient. Then if a child misbehaves, the parents act as if they are protecting the child, whereas in reality they have summoned relatives to come in disguise and whip the child, sometimes very severely. It is a case of Santa Claus in reverse. The children are deeply disillusioned when they eventually learn the truth, and this disillusionment helps foster the suspiciousness of the motives of others that is so characteristic of the Hopi. This character trait is also fostered by the Hopi belief that any close relative,

* Such ideas and behavior may seem ridiculous to us, and yet they involve insights and wisdom usually absent from our medical practice and concepts of the etiology of illness. Many psychologically minded medical researchers now appreciate how depressive feelings, wishes to die, and states of helplessness and hopelessness contribute to the onset and the worsening of disease. (See G. Engel, 1962, and Chapter 20.)

including the mother, might be a malevolent witch who will trade the child's life for her own. The relationship between a society's belief systems and child-rearing methods forms an extremely complex topic that extends beyond the scope of this book.*

The ways in which different ethnic groups have patterned their lives and the customs they pursue are amazingly diverse, and some are almost beyond the imagination of persons from other cultures. Still, amidst these extremely varied patterns there are some requisites that all cultures must fulfill. No society can long survive without taking into account the biological makeup of its members. It cannot, for instance, neglect the total dependency of its newborn, or the sequence of the biological maturation of the child, or the presence of two sexes. Some small societies have placed a ban on all sexual relationships but they have not lasted for long, somehow finding but few recruits from the outside. A society is not only essential to its members but it has an existence of its own, and its culture is its heart, which its members will defend with their lives because without it they are rootless and lost. As all societies must fill certain identical needs for their members, including preserving the society itself, some features are common to all cultures, so common that they are often taken for granted and their critical nature overlooked. Families and language are of the essence and will be examined in greater detail below.

This, then, is one of the advantages bestowed by the capacity for verbal communication. It enables the gradual acquisition of a cultural heritage that becomes an essential part of the human endowment. It enables children to be born into very divergent environments and acquire from those who raise them the techniques essential for survival and for adaptation to the physical and social environment in which they will live.

Language and Thought

We must now examine another consequence of the acquisition of symbolic capacities—that internal counterpart of communication that we term thought or mentation.

Words make reflective and conceptual thinking possible. Even though we think with visual symbols as well as with other sensations and perceptions, words are the switching points—the symbols that we can manipulate in order to shift from one associational trend to another. They are our symbolic tools. Thought and language are inseparable. The autobiography

---

* The reader is referred to E. Erikson (1950), B. Whiting (1963), D. Aberle (1951), and M. Carstairs (1957), and R. Lidz and T. Lidz (1976).

of Helen Keller and the accounts of her remarkable teacher, Anne Sullivan, make it clear that even this person with her extraordinary intellectual potential remained imprisoned in a world of diffuse impressions and feelings until she was released by the word, and particularly until she grasped that each word her teacher spelled into her hand meant something.* Even the congenitally deaf who use sign language may be impaired intellectually unless they learn to use words. Efforts are made to insist that they use an alphabet and preferably learn to lip read, not because it is esthetically and socially superior but because the sign language does not contain symbols that are sufficiently abstract for higher intellectual functioning.† If, as oc-

* After a month of intensive work Miss Sullivan had taught her seven-year-old deaf-blind pupil to spell some twenty words. Still, these spelled-out words had not attained the status of symbols. Miss Sullivan was seeking desperately to convey that these finger signs represented a category of things. Like a very young child, Helen Keller confused "mug" and "water" and could not learn that "doll" stood for a new doll as well as for an old one. Miss Keller wrote of the critical day in her childhood when she passed across the barrier: "Miss Sullivan had tried to impress it upon me that 'm-u-g' is mug and that 'w-a-t-e-r' is water, but I persisted in confounding the two. In despair she had dropped the subject for the time, only to renew it at the first opportunity. I became impatient at her repeated attempts and, seizing the new doll, I dashed it upon the floor. I was keenly delighted when I felt the fragments of the broken doll at my feet. Neither sorrow nor regret followed my passionate outburst. I had not loved the doll. In the still, dark world in which I lived there was no strong sentiment or tenderness. . . . She brought me my hat, and I knew I was going out into the warm sunshine. This thought, if a wordless sensation may be called a thought, made me hop and skip with pleasure. . . . Someone was drawing water and my teacher placed my hand under the spout. As the cool stream gushed over one hand she spelled into the other the word water, first slowly and then rapidly. I stood still, my whole attention fixed upon the motions of her fingers. Suddenly I felt a misty consciousness of something forgotten— a thrill of a returning thought: and somehow the mystery of language was revealed to me. I knew then that 'w-a-t-e-r' meant the wonderful cool something that was flowing over my hand. That living word awakened my soul, gave it light, hope, joy, set it free! There were barriers still, it is true, but barriers that could in time be swept away. . . . Everything had a name, and each name gave birth to a new thought. As we returned to the house every object which I touched seemed to quiver with life. That was because I saw everything with the strange new sight that had come to me. . . . It would have been difficult to find a happier child than I was as I lay in my crib at the close of that eventful day and lived over the joys it had brought me, and for the first time longed for a new day to come" (Keller, 1902).
The account is not a retrospective idealization. From that moment Helen Keller learned with avidity, her disposition changed profoundly, and her teacher's task changed from an ordeal of striving to break through a wall to one of teaching the words and supplying a picture of the world around Helen so that she could readily learn what the words meant. It may be important to note that "water" was one of the two words Miss Keller had retained of what she had learned before meningitis left her blind and deaf at the age of twenty months.
† The matter is now in dispute, as some evidence indicates that verbal facility is not essential to abstract thinking but that visual symbols can suffice. The current studies of teaching chimpanzees to communicate through sign language is pertinent to the problem, but chimpanzee use of language for communication and problem solving is still at a very limited level (Gardner and Gardner, 1971; Rumbaugh *et al.*, 1973).

casionally happens, a child is born with damage to one of the areas of the brain essential to symbolic activity—areas necessary for the comprehension and expression of words as symbols rather than for simply hearing and saying them—the child remains an idiot.

Let us return to that protohuman and the stick he was grasping so that we may examine the functions of words in thinking. The stick the individual was wielding as a club was important because it was a tool—a disposable, interchangeable extension of himself. The word "stick" was also important, for it not only meant that specific piece of wood used as a club but it also denoted other pieces of wood used for fuel, for building shelters, for making arrows, for charcoal with which to draw mastodon, for "digging sticks." The word had acquired an abstract meaning or categorical usage designating pieces of wood of a certain approximate shape. It was abstract in another related context: pivoting about the word were all of the individual's many experiences with sticks—those tossed into the river and floating, those breaking off the branches of a tree as it crashed to earth, those turning into flame, the feel of various sticks, their weight, their odor when freshly peeled or after a rain. These various experiences could shift back and forth, one leading to another, connecting a variety of experiences that were dissimilar except in that they involved sticks.

People could think about sticks: their uses in the past, current needs for them, and potential uses for them in the future. They could fragment their memories and utilize them selectively, drawing upon past experiences to construct a hypothetical future. They could anticipate that something they were told was made of "wood" would burn; that an object they had not seen but was termed an "arrow" could be used for shooting from a bow. The word contained a predictive value that helped them direct their behavior. We shall return to consider the importance of the categorizing and predicting functions of words when we consider the child's linguistic development and how it relates to his "ego" functioning (Chapters 5 and 6).

As John Dewey (1925) pointed out, by means of verbal tools people can "act without acting." They can go through trial-and-error performances imaginatively, without committing themselves to the consequences of an actual deed. A person could consider whether a certain stick would suffice to kill an animal or whether it would be better not to risk the encounter until obtaining a better weapon. An individual is freed from the need to act in order to learn whether an action will be advantageous or disastrous. A person can select between alternatives upon the basis of what the imagined outcomes will be.

By the use of symbols, a human can select out appropriate fragments of the past and project converging lines through the momentary present into an imagined future. Herein lies a momentous change from animal behavior that greatly increases the chances for survival. Persons are no longer bound to motivation by their immediate past experiences and their present impulses, drives, and wishes. They can strive to achieve future gains and objectives that they keep in their minds. We can say that the human is goal-directed as well as drive-impelled. Any increase in the ability to plan toward the future greatly enhances one's chances of surviving. Much of human behavior is directed toward a consciously projected future—to provide for needs of the morrow, the next year, or for a future generation. With such potentialities, people gain a sense of free will; for when we leave theological matters out of consideration, this is what we mean by free will: the ability to select from among alternative paths into the future on the basis of past experiences.*

We cannot attempt to consider the many ramifications of the human capacity to symbolize, primarily through the use of words. This capacity enables people to create a symbolized internal version of reality which they manipulate imaginatively in order to increase the predictability of events, to find means of controlling them, and to be prepared in advance to meet them—but also to create and re-create worlds of their own that have no existence except in their own minds. How a person behaves and learns no longer depends upon conditioning. According to Greek mythology, civilization started when Prometheus stole fire from the Olympians and bestowed it upon humankind—a first harnessing of nature to people's ends. Prometheus means "forward thinking," or foresight. With this attribute came an awareness of contingency and death that bred anxiety—perhaps like the vulture pecking at the liver of the enchained Prometheus—but also the ability to eradicate imaginatively the ultimacy of death if a person so wished.

These, then, are the characteristics—stated in bare outline—that permitted people to survive, flourish, spread out over the earth, and become masters of it; altering nature to serve their ends rather than simply living in

---

* As Freud noted, the sway of instinctual drives and unconscious memories upon the determination of behavior is great, and individuals are not as "free" as they believe when making decisions on the basis of remembered experiences. However, such considerations do not settle the problem of determinism versus free will, and in no way prove that all human behavior is "determined" by the past. The complexity of the neuronal switching systems and the memories "programmed" therein is so great that perhaps little more is meant by free will than that all factors involved in a decision can never be traced and numerous contingencies may be involved. In essence it is a theological problem that does not concern us here.

their natural environment. Humans can utilize symbols in order to think and plan ahead, and they do so by imaginatively creating a symbolized version of their worlds that they can manipulate; and they learn new techniques of mastering their environment which they transmit to others so that learning becomes cumulative, and each new generation can possess the knowledge of its forebears.

THE HUMAN MIND

Humans think and meet the future, anticipating what will come. But what do they think with? The possession of a human brain is, of course, the sine qua non of abstract thinking, but the structure and functioning of this brain determines only in part *how* we think, and virtually nothing of *what* we think. True, the body, through the mediation of the brain, demands that we direct attention to the basic needs for survival of ourself and our species. If we lack oxygen, water, food, warmth, sleep, salts, or sexual outlets, or if we are endangered, primitive drives—mechanisms that antedated the human species—direct us toward seeking relief and influence our thinking. Starving persons can think of little other than food and dreams of food pervade their sleep. But how we set about stilling such needs will vary with time and place. One hungering individual picks up a crossbow and seeks water buffalo; another picks up a harpoon, finds a hole in the ice, and waits for a seal; another balances her checkbook and drives off to a supermarket. Then, too, people because of their foresight may have long periods during which they can be occupied with other matters, relatively free from the direct dictation of basic drives.

We say, rather, that we think with our minds. Mind! The concept of "the mind" carries varying degrees of purposeful vagueness. It refers to something so complex and intangible that we prefer not to be pushed into a definition that we may be expected to defend. We speak constantly about the "unconscious mind" but are not clear at all what we mean by either conscious or unconscious mind. The term contains residues of countless variant philosophies and psychologies that continue to haunt us. Ever since people started to ponder about themselves, they have puzzled over that intangible attribute that permits them to direct their behavior; that distinguishes them, at times, from the beast; that bestows upon them the godlike ability to reorder nature and enables them to surmount the dull or aching reality through soaring fantasy, or to note the poignancy of their experience in poetry or song. They have been apt to consider their minds as separate from their bodies, and even as distinctive from matter. Descartes strengthened the mind-body dichotomy and achieved a long but restless peace with the church by considering the mind an attribute bestowed by God and influenced by the soul that funneled into the brain via the pineal gland; he claimed the body and matter for science and left the soul and the mind to the church and to philosophy.

During the past half century, the scientists of the mind, the psychologists, envious of the tangible physical and chemical foundations of the biological sciences, have sometimes insisted that the functioning of the mind could be understood in terms of the neural impulses in the brain. Some have convinced themselves that the mind and brain are synonymous. Some have studied man through the examination of lower animals and found no place for a "mind." Some have sought to solve the problem by maintaining that we have simply been caught up in antiquated prescientific religious and philosophical speculations in seeking to locate and define the mind. The very word "mind" disseminates a decadent odor, and any respectable scientist who uses the term must be out of his mind. We can outlaw the word; we can use other terms; we can chant daily in unison that "the body and the mind are one" so as to exorcise the dichotomy from our thinking, but somehow none of these maneuvers quite comes off. "Mind" is not an archaism; we have need for such a concept, whatever we may term it; and no serious thinker can encase the mind within the skull as part of the brain. We can well envy that nineteenth-century pundit who managed to make short shrift of the problem: "What is Mind? No matter! What is Matter? Never mind!"

Of course, in writing a book about the personality it would be possible to evade the issue by avoiding the term. Still, as a psychiatrist who spends his days and years contemplating the mind, I should know what it is I study. I can say, like Humpty-Dumpty speaking to Alice on the other side of the looking glass, "When I use a word—it means just what I choose it to mean—neither more nor less" (Carroll, 1871). This state of affairs may have been all right for Humpty-Dumpty, even though it left Alice somewhat perplexed, but on this side of the looking glass meanings are measured in terms of how they foster communication. If we wish to join hands in a scientific effort to learn about the nature of human beings and their development, we require a common understanding of what we are scrutinizing.

Surprisingly or not, I think I do know what we mean when we speak of "the mind." By means of our brains we manipulate symbols, and without these symbols we cannot think. What we term "mind" includes both the complex neural apparatus and the symbolized material gained from experience that it utilizes. As we have been noting, the nature of the brain is determined genetically, but the nature of the symbolic material varies widely. How we think is established partly by the structural organization and physiology of our brains and bodies. We cannot, for example, utilize supersonic vibrations as does the bat, or carry out calculations for hours as does an electronic computer; but how we think also depends upon our education. Scientific thinking, to take one example, is a relatively recent phenomenon, a disciplined method of thinking that has been utilized for only a few hundred of the tens of thousands of years of human existence.

The brain is the apparatus with which we think, but it must be programmed to become a mind even as an electronic brain must be programmed. There are, of course, vast differences between the brain and the most complex electronic computers aside from the size and rigidity of the machine. Among the many differences is the fact that the brain is part of a living person and is not passive but seeks out and takes in according to its drives, needs, desires. It programs itself to a large extent. The brain as part of an organism is influenced by passions and desire; and as part of a person it partakes of character. Still, there are interesting similarities. The machine also utilizes a language. It stores memories that can be recovered only by the appropriate symbol. It can serve as an executive organ which utilizes insignificant amounts of energy to direct and control activities expending vast quantities of energy—as when a computer directs a foundry. But it must be programmed, and it is incapable of learning:* the programmers must learn for it.

Enculturation—Programming the Brain

In the human mind, the basic programming is the process of enculturation—children's assimilation of the ways of the society in which they grow up. Children are taught and learn the verbal symbols essential for thinking, but they must also have experiences for which the words stand. Persons think with the memories of their experiences, but their experiences include what they have learned from others. They have available to them that collectivity of experiences which is their cultural heritage and which,

---

* The point is debatable, depending on what is meant by learning. Computers can be programmed to base solutions or responses on cumulative input—one might say to base responses on past experiences.

even though it is the product of human minds, has an existence outside of any single brain. In literate societies a large segment of the experience and knowledge of the culture is recorded in print and conserved in books which are repositories of other minds. Individuals may tap these repositories in order to add to their experiences and to expand the information with which they think. The particular mind which has assembled a particular set of experiences and utilizes a unique way of perceiving and understanding the world ceases to exist with the death of the individual. Books such as *The Making of the Modern Mind* (Randall, 1940) and *The Mind in the Making* (Robinson, 1921) are treatises not on the development of the brain, but on the gradual emergence of the body of ideas and the ways of thinking of contemporary man. The existence of brains, or rather of persons with brains capable of carrying on the tradition, is taken for granted. In the sense in which I am using the word "mind" the content alone is insufficient, for the word also encompasses the brain which utilizes the material.

A basic part of the process of enculturation concerns the acquisition of ways of thinking. People do not simply accumulate sensations or even experiences but require ways of perceiving and thinking about what they experience. Each cultural group has evolved its own system of meanings and logic,* and how people think and feel about events affects their physiological processes. The experiences that a person lives through, or which impinge upon a person, can be categorized and understood in countless ways. Each culture perceives its environment somewhat differently; and even the language we use, with its specific vocabulary and rules of grammar, sets limits and guidelines for our thinking.† One difference between

---

* Chomsky (1968) and other structural linguists argue that basic syntactic structure is set by brain structure, a view which stands in opposition to Whorf's (1956) papers concerning basic structural differences in languages such as Shawnee. Piaget (1971), in his book on structuralism, argues convincingly that linguistic syntactic structures are not inherent but develop—a constructivist approach.

† People cannot pay attention to everything that transpires about them but must be able to focus their attention. Each culture directs its members to what that particular ethnic branch of mankind considers important, what pertinent, and what can be neglected and what must be ignored. One important method by which such filtering and sorting is carried out is through language. The flow of experience must be divided into categories to be thought about, talked about, and even to be perceived. Each culture categorizes experience somewhat differently, and very divergent cultures categorize experience very differently. However, because all humans have the same basic structure and needs and all environments contain fundamental similarities, all languages must have a number of almost identical categorizations. The vocabulary of a language is, in essence, a catalogue of the culture's categories—which children learn as they learn to speak. This topic is considered further in the next chapter. There are other filtering devices and techniques. A neurophysiological system, the *reticular activating system*, has much to do with helping an individual maintain focal attention. Individuals also acquire filtering techniques in accord with their own experiences and emotional needs. As will be examined in some detail in later chapters, they learn not to perceive, to alter

English and German philosophy—indeed between the English and German mind—would appear to result from the linguistic sanction in German for the coinage of new words to fit approximate nuances, whereas in English we are disciplined to fit our thoughts to the common vocabulary. We can also note that scientific efforts in the Western world had to remain limited until contact with the decimal system invented in India and until abstract algebraic thought introduced through Moslem culture brought release from cumbersome numerical systems and concrete geometric conceptualizations. While our minds have always been our cardinal instrument for adaptation, a new era of human existence opened when we consciously recognized that through the use of the mind as a tool to understand nature we could begin consciously to alter nature for our purposes. This revolution in the use of the mind, which was first specifically promoted by Francis Bacon (1625), was more basic than either the industrial or atomic revolutions which were but outgrowths of it. The possession of a mind (at least what I—using my Humpty-Dumpty prerogatives—mean by the mind) is a human attribute dependent upon the genetic evolution of a brain with a unique structure that permits the use of symbols as tools for communication and thinking. These are distinctively human capacities that make possible an extraordinarily useful method of adaptation and assurance of survival. This brain with its large cerebral cortex allowed less rigid patterns of living by replacing built-in instinctive patterns with learned ways of coping with the environment. The ability of humans to live in many different ways in vastly different environments depends upon the cumulative transmission of what they have learned, their ability to plan for the future, and to work upon nature and alter it to their ends. Our individual minds consist of the internalized, symbolized representation of our world and the techniques for living in it which our brains enable us to assimilate and manipulate. We cannot understand the mind in terms of the physiological functioning of the brain any more than we can seek to understand a telephone conversation in terms of the telephone system: though some garbled phone conversations are due to defects in the apparatus, and others to the confusion of the speakers.

To understand the mind, we must understand the capacities afforded us by our anatomic structure and our physiological processes; and we must understand how our unique brain enabled us to symbolize, communicate, and build up social systems and cultures, and also to communicate with

---

perception, to repress feelings and drives and memories in order to avoid anxiety; that is, they develop "mechanisms of defense." The topic leads into the consideration of cultural taboos and unconscious mentation.

ourselves by utilizing the verbal symbols that our progenitors had gradually developed as their language. It becomes apparent that the human mind could increase in complexity as the culture and its language became enriched by the accumulation of experiences and learning. Mind, culture, and language are intimately related.

BIOLOGICAL DRIVES

We have been considering the essentially human capacities of adaptation that permitted humans to survive, spread out over the globe, and become masters of it. Although it is necessary to recognize that we humans are not monkeys and to study our development and behavior as integrated through the capacities bestowed by symbolization, it is equally important to realize that we are animals and are directed and impelled by biological drives that often hold sway over our intellectual capacities and that our survival as individuals and as a species depends upon biological processes that were firmly established even before our emergence as human beings.

Although we cannot review all of the inborn genetic endowment that influences personality development, we shall consider briefly the nature of our basic drives and the biological bases of our emotions. The basic drives can be divided into three, and perhaps four, groups: those deriving from the tissue needs indispensable to life; the sexual drives; the defensive drives; and somewhat less clearly, the impulsions to stimulation and activity. All furnish primary directives in personality development.

The Homeostatic Drives

As noted earlier in this chapter the continuation of life in the simplest unicellular organism depends upon maintaining its composition constant within the relatively narrow limits that permit the chemical processes fundamental to life. No living thing is a closed system but carries out a constant interchange with its environment, from which it obtains nutriment for its development and its vital processes and into which it excretes waste products. Simple organisms can exist only under fairly specific environmental conditions, and the evolutionary process involves providing new ways of assuring the chemical transactions essential to life in the face of competition and environmental change. More complex and highly integrated organisms became less dependent upon the immediate constancy of the external environment. Higher organisms developed an "internal environment" of tissue fluids that surround the cells with a relatively constant environment despite the changes that take place in the external world. Maintenance of the internal constancy of the cells of the organism provides a major motivating force in all living things. "Homeostasis," the term used to designate this maintenance of constancy, is a key word in the study of physiology and behavior. It refers to several things. The internal environment is highly buffered chemically, and filled with checks, balances, and feedback systems that resist change; the organism is provided with various means of regulating its interchange with its surroundings that help maintain its constancy; there is an impulsion to activity that furthers the necessary assimilation and excretion. Such activities are automatic in lower systems of integration but include volitional activities in higher forms.

With the increasing complexity that permitted ever greater freedom from reliance upon the constancy of the external environment, organisms required more involved systems for interchange with the environment and for inner regulation to assure the proper milieu for every cell.* The chemical processes essential for the existence of the unicellular organism are no less vital to the most complex forms of life, whose intricate integrations are, in essence, only a means of maintaining the environment necessary for the occurrence of these processes in the cells. However, when a brain that permitted decision making developed, those functions that are indispensable to the preservation of the animal and the species were not left simply to choice or chance.

In humans the executive system involving the cerebral cortex, which is concerned with the choice of alternatives and decision making, remains subject to powerful persuasion that directs attention to homeostatic needs. Centers sensitive to such needs are located in the hindbrain, which developed early in vertebrate evolution; these centers send out signals in response to chemical changes in the blood and to neuronal stimuli which, when necessary, can virtually dominate the thought and activity of the

---

* Special systems evolved for respiration, assimilation and digestion of food, and for excretion; a circulatory system for the internal transport of chemicals; sensory organs and systems for gaining information about the environment; metabolic organs for the breakdown and manufacture of essential chemical compounds and for the transformation of food, water, and oxygen into a variety of forms of energy—for example, heat, kinetic, bioelectric. To gain information as well as to integrate the bodily functioning, chemical messengers transported in the body fluids were abetted by nerve fibers that transmitted messages with great rapidity. The development of an integrative executive organ in the form of a brain permitted unity of action of the complex organism. This fragmentary sketch seeks only to remind the reader of the inordinately involved integration of any higher form of life.

individual. The person becomes preoccupied with the need to alleviate a state of tension or discomfort produced by the chemical imbalance in the tissues—and, in some instances, to gain a sense of pleasure achieved by supplying the need that restores the requisite balance.

The most imperative need is for oxygen. We live in air and cannot survive for more than a few minutes without it. A diminution of oxygen in the tissues* reflexly produces increased respiration; but cutting off the air supply, as by strangulation, sets off immediate frantic efforts to free the air passages. We can withstand thirst longer; but as tissue fluids become depleted, a craving for water dominates our thoughts, feelings, and dreams, and virtually forces us to direct our energies to obtaining water. Lack of food does not create as impelling a need in us, for stored reserves in the body can be mobilized but hunger preoccupies; and the need for food and the efforts to be secure that food supplies are always available form a major motivation of human behavior, individually and collectively. The force that starvation can exert in directing a life and upon the mood can readily be overlooked or forgotten in a land of abundance, but even existence on a semi-starvation diet can seriously influence the ethics and emotional health of the individual.† It is not clear whether a deficiency of specific chemical elements or compounds other than water produces a drive to obtain them. Lack of sodium, which is vital to maintaining a proper fluid balance, causes animals to make long migrations to salt licks, and groups of people living in areas where salt is sparse set up complicated trade channels to obtain it regularly. Children's craving for candy may be due to, or at least reflect, their need for large quantities of carbohydrates to supply their lavish expenditures of energy. However, it is well to remember that human beings are so constituted that despite the intensity of hunger as a drive, persons have starved themselves to death amid plenty for political or religious convictions.

---

* Actually an increase in carbon dioxide which is usually synonymous with a need for oxygen.

† Schiele and Brozek (1948), in a study of nutrition, placed a group of university student volunteers on a twelve-hundred calorie diet. After a few weeks they quarreled over the number of peas they received and became very irritable. Some broke the diet in minor ways and suffered severe guilt feelings, and several had to be withdrawn from the experiment because they had become emotionally disturbed, probably because they hungered in a setting where the major barriers to eating were their own pledges to maintain the diet. Soldiers starving to death in Japanese prisoner-of-war camps were likely to lose their usual ethical standards, and a man needed a buddy to guard his food when he was too ill to feed himself. Knut Hamsun's *Hunger* and Gottfried Keller's *Der grüne Heinrich* present excellent portrayals of the emotions and motives of a starving man.

However, chronic gradual starvation may elude the drive as apathy intervenes. Persons suffering from the psychogenic emaciation termed "anorexia nervosa" may not experience hunger and refuse to eat even when reduced to living skeletons.

The maintenance of an internal body temperature very close to 98.6°F. (37°C.) is essential for the bodily chemistry; and although the regulation of temperature is carried out reflexly, there are limits to the body's ability to dissipate and generate heat. The search for warmth, and sometimes for relief from excessive heat, can also become an imperative drive that takes precedence over almost everything else. When a person is freezing to death, apathy—as in starvation—may finally intervene and replace the drive.

Although the functions of sleep are still poorly understood, the need for it can become a dominant motivation. Though it seems difficult to think of the urge to sleep as a drive, it can also preoccupy, but usually it will simply occur despite efforts to remain awake. Prolonged sleep deprivation can lead to mental confusion. The men in an army unit which I studied in the South Pacific, after fighting for eight days and nights with almost no sleep, suffered from mass hallucinosis.

The excretion of urine and feces also is vital and the need to urinate can also be an impelling preoccupation. However, the problems are somewhat different from those of the tissue needs, as any need for prolonged delay in satisfying such urges is a result of social requirements.

In fulfilling the body's needs for food and sleep and to excrete wastes, the individual is not only motivated by a need to relieve tension or pain but also because the alleviation of the imbalance can be pleasurable. People enjoy eating and sleeping, and many gain some erogenous pleasure from urinating and defecating, as will be discussed in later chapters.* Indeed any of the vital activities of breathing, drinking water, eating, seeking or avoiding heat, sleeping, and excreting can sometimes become perversions in the sense of being carried to excess for emotional reasons rather than because of bodily need, and some clearly become erotized through becoming connected to the sexual drives.

The Sexual Drive

In the post-Freudian world it seems unnecessary to emphasize the pervasive importance of sexuality in human behavior, or to draw the attention of the reader to how sexual impulses furnish the themes around which fantasies are woven, or how desire populates the dream world and inserts

---

* The theory that pleasure could be equated with tension release was accepted by Freud and has played a critical role in psychoanalytic theory. Although "parsimonious" it does not fit the facts, and the investigations of Olds (1958) and Delgado et al. (1954) practically force us to accept the concept that evolutionary selection set a premium on reward through pleasure as a separate factor from release from tensions. Stimulation of certain areas in the brain evokes positive responses, and an animal will learn to press a lever or carry out an action in order to have the area stimulated.

itself between the pages of books one studies, seeking to replace the dull facts recorded on them, or how it heightens sensitivity and at times would seem to provide invisible antennae with which a person can detect the feelings and cravings of another person.

The reasons why the evolutionary process led to the elaboration of strong sexual drives seem apparent. All higher forms of life are divided into two genders. The need for a union between two germinal cells for propagation permits opportunity for the selecting out of favorable mutations and assures a constant reshuffling of genes that lessens the influence of harmful mutations. As the perpetuation of the germinal cells is the essence of life, after the separation into two genders the act of mating could not be left to chance or entirely to choice; a drive to procreate exists in some form in all creatures. In some species instinctive patterns almost completely control mating behavior. The life cycle may lead to procreation and then death as in some fish. In most mammals a rutting period exists when the sexual drives become dominant and may even take precedence over self-preservative drives. In response to the sexual impulsion, the male may neglect almost all else and even court death in combat for the female. Anyone who has seen the torment of a male beagle (about the most "highly sexed" canine, I am informed) if confined when a female in heat is nearby; or watched two otherwise docile and domesticated tomcats turn into miniature tigers and slash and bite one another for priority with a female feline who acts as if nothing concerned her less than which of her two overardent suitors triumphed—must be impressed by the power of the sexual drive. Anthropoids and humans do not have rutting seasons, even though sexual drives may well be influenced by the season. Humans can delay gratification of the drive and forgo the pleasurable reward indefinitely, perhaps aided by the capacity for masturbatory release from compelling tensions. But the drive toward sexual union is denied only with difficulty. The sexual act is impelled both by the need for relief from tissue tensions and by the reward of positive sensual pleasure: the pleasure is accompanied by heightening of tension that further impels, and the climactic orgasm becomes a goal and reward in its own right. Sexual union between people is often further motivated by desires for the interpersonal closeness and sharing involved in love, and including recrudescences of "attachment behavior" that will be discussed in Chapter 5. Nature has created strong impulsions and rewards to assure the continuity of the species.

Although sexuality exerts one of the most compelling forces in the lives of humans, it does not have the inexorable power over human behavior of the homeostatic drives. Only persons leading relatively sheltered lives in which water, food, and warmth are readily available and in which sexual drives are impeded by social conventions can consider sexuality more compelling.* Indeed, upon consideration we can realize that it is because sexual gratification is not vital to life, as well as because the satisfaction of the drive can be delayed, displaced, and sublimated into other types of outlets that sexuality forms a critical lever in the educational process and forms a significant force in shaping the personality. The topic will be discussed in subsequent chapters.

Sexuality and aggression are crucial forces in human motivation and personality development, not because they are the most fundamental drives but because they are modifiable and subject to socializing influences and also because both sex and aggression must be controlled and channeled lest they become disruptive of the family and the community upon which people depend so greatly for their survival and well-being. Aggression is one of another set of essential drives.

Defensive Drives

An array of physiological defenses against danger that concomitantly arouses fear or aggression can also dominate the organism's motivations and behavior. These built-in automatic defenses against danger, which arose early in the evolutionary process to implement the capacity to fight enemies, flee danger, and mobilize resources in emergencies, are only slightly less important to the preservation of the animal than the drives arising from tissue needs. As soon as danger is sensed the bodily processes alter almost instantaneously to prepare for flight or fight without the intervention of conscious decision. Such defenses are crucial to survival in a world filled with enemies and inanimate hazards. The shifts in the physiological processes convey an ability to run faster, jump farther, fight beyond the limits of endurance; and to sense more keenly, react more rapidly, and think more alertly; as well as to minimize the effects of injury. The human being is heir to these physiological responses, even though they may impede as often as they help in dealing with dangers in civilized societies; but, as we shall see, these defensive drives continue to exert a profound influence on both behavior and mental activities.

Fear and aggression are potent drives, either of which can change a

---

* The author, who studied survivors immediately after their release from three years of starvation in a Japanese prisoner-of-war camp in the Philippines, gained a lasting impression of the force of hunger and starvation as a drive. It was somewhat surprising, however, to observe that soldiers on isolated islands who were deprived of sexual partners for two or three years and lived on a monotonous but adequate diet regularly reported that gradually their "bull sessions" shifted from talk of women and sex to long discussions of the meals they would eat after returning home, and that dreams of food became more common than overt sexual dreams.

man's life in a split second, sweeping aside resolve, training, plans, judgment, and careful reasoning. The dreams of glory of many a youth have vanished and turned into self-hatred with the first bombardment by the enemy; or the tensions of pent-up hostility suddenly unleashed have carried persons into conflicts in which they were hopelessly outclassed. The two behaviors are intimately related both physiologically and emotionally: fear is not synonymous with cowardice, and aggression is one means of overcoming the dysphoria of fear*—and there is an old adage about those who fight and run away.

The automatic physiological changes may be initiated in response to some signal of impending danger that is not even consciously recognized. The autonomic nervous system, particularly the adrenal-neural system, is most clearly involved in these changes and employs many of the same mechanisms utilized in the preservation of the homeostatic needs, and can even interfere with the homeostatic functioning, as will be discussed in Chapters 8 and 20. The animal or person is first alerted and then prepared to save itself by fighting or fleeing; which of these responses will predominate varies with the species and the total development of its means of survival—a tiger is primarily prepared to fight and a doe to flee. In some forms, such as the human, it is possible that lesser stimuli to the adrenal-neural mechanisms prepare for flight while more intense and prolonged stimulation prepares for fighting. Epinephrine secretion tends to heighten fear, which increases alertness to danger; and norepinephrine secretion helps prepare for action, particularly aggressive action, and thus helps induce feelings of hostility. We will not, at this point, discuss the complexities of these automatic preparations for self-defense. They are not just dysphoric feeling states from which individuals seek to free themselves; they are accompanied by immediate pervasive changes in the physiological functions, such as speeding of the heart, sweating, changes in respiration and distribution of blood flow, as well as numerous less apparent alterations. (See Chapter 20.)

The capacity or proneness to experience fear and aggression is born into us, but aggressivity is not a quality that must find an outlet. It is a type of response to danger that can dissipate when danger passes and the physio-

---

* An essential part of the indoctrination of United States soldiers prior to their entering jungle combat during World War II consisted of impressing them that being fearful did not mean they were cowards and that even the most heroic men were likely to experience fear but managed to surmount the fear and its often very distressing physiological accompaniments. They also had to learn not to break the tension by becoming aggressive and giving away their positions by firing their weapons or dashing out of their foxholes. The "banzai" charges of the Japanese that were often so disastrous to them may well have been related to an inability on their part to withstand the need to do something to alleviate anxiety in the face of continuing danger.

logical processes resume their non-emergency functioning. Some persons may be innately more prone to aggressive feelings than others, but chronically aggressive individuals are more usually persons who grew up under conditions that trained them to respond readily to certain circumstances or people—such as authority figures—with defensive aggressivity.*

In humans, anxiety is a derivative of fear and is accompanied by much the same physiological manifestations. Anxiety is largely concerned with unconscious dangers, particularly those that could result from one's own

* Hitler, for example, was brutally beaten by his father almost daily, according to his sister Paula (Stierlin, 1975). I am specifically emphasizing that aggression is not a genetic characteristic that makes murder and warfare an expected characteristic of mankind and therefore to some an acceptable state of affairs because it is inevitable. Two books that express such views, Konrad Lorenz's On Aggression, which considers aggression a human instinct, and Robert Ardrey's The Territorial Imperative, have gained widespread acceptance even though their conclusions are unwarranted. Lorenz's work on "imprinting" phenomena in ground nesting birds (1952) has rightly won him a position as one of the world's leading scientists, but much of the material in On Aggression is outside his field of special competence, and he has chosen to omit an enormous amount of data and evidence that controverts his thesis. Ardrey's book concerning territoriality in animals and the idea that humans defend their national territory instinctively also omits much evidence that many mammals and anthropoids behave very differently; and, in addition, misses the point that peoples defend their culture, their way of life, and right to live it rather than primarily their territories.

I lived for a time among the Fijians, who with their taboo against ambition, self-advancement, and individual possessions were among the friendliest persons I have ever encountered. They could easily live off their bountiful volcanic soil and the fish that teemed in the ocean. These friendly and happy people—for I became convinced that as a people they were unusually happy—had not always been such. Just about one hundred years ago they lived in terror and were terrifying and treacherous. They were known among sailors as the most bloodthirsty, flesh-craving cannibals in the world, their islands to be avoided. The people themselves feared to venture alone into the bush, lest they be clubbed by members of a neighboring village and end up at a feast. They were savage and cruel in their constant internecine warfare. To the missionary the Fijis were no paradise, but rather a brief stopover en route to paradise via the cooking pot—a much sought-after assignment by the zealous as a certain route to martyrdom and heaven. Eventually, however, the Fijians were converted to Western medicine and the Christianity the medical missionaries taught. An enlightened British government, to whom the Fijian chief ceded his authority, put an end to interisland warfare and soon induced the Fijians to abolish cannibalism. Then, for the first time, the natives could enjoy their blessed islands. No longer fearing their neighbors, they could live in peace and became men of peace. If the accounts of the early missionaries and travelers can be trusted, a remarkable change in the Fijian personality occurred over the past few generations. They are now fully trustworthy rather than treacherous; they show no suspiciousness of others; they live and let live as only people of dignity and pride can; and they are sure of their enormous strength, enjoying both work and play—and perhaps not clearly differentiating between them. Their ferocity—easy to regard as the untamed ways of the savage—disappeared within two or three generations.

If the fearsome cannibals could change rapidly, once they no longer needed to fear their fellow man, when in fact their dictum was no longer eat or be eaten, there is a chance, at least, that we too may learn to enjoy the bounty available to us—not that from a teeming ocean or a productive volcanic soil, but from our teeming and productive minds.

impulses, and it is also concerned with anticipated future dangers rather than tangible matters that can be coped with through action. Aggression has the derivatives of hostility and resentment, which like anxiety are not usually relieved by overt action. These derivative drives or emotions play major roles in motivation and behavior, as will be discussed in various contexts throughout the book.*

Assimilatory Drives

The group of phenomena that we shall consider under this heading concerns the innate impulsions of the infant and child to seek stimulation and to carry out motor activity. Proper physical and intellectual development of the child appears to rest upon such needs to assimilate new experiences; and, as we shall see, a new type of experience in itself serves as a stimulus to the individual to seek its repetition. There is now ample evidence that the basic motivations of animals, including humans, arise not only from needs to reduce physiological tensions, but that the organism requires arousal for its well-being. The organism requires stimulation and seems motivated to seek it. Infants require stimulation beyond their own capacities to obtain it, and failure to provide it leads to the disastrous consequences that the Pharaoh Psammetichos and the Emperor Frederick II reputedly found. Absence of stimulation is also almost unbearable to adults who may lose their holds on reality when kept in solitary confinement or when subjects in a sensory deprivation experiment (Solomon *et al.*, 1961) in which they are shielded as completely as possible from any stimulation.

We shall also note that an impulsion to the use of the neuromuscular system seems to be a built-in part of the organism's means of survival. The child enjoys movement for its own sake, including the use of vocalizations. Such more or less spontaneous activity seems essential for gaining mastery over the sensori-motor apparatus and for explorations of the environment.†

---

* Aggression and hostility are so clearly defensive and protective drives or affects that it is difficult to understand how psychoanalytic theory has, at times, connected them with an inborn "death instinct" or self-destructive instinct. However, in humans hostility can readily turn against the self and become self-destructive, even as it can fuse with sexual impulses to become sadism. These theoretic problems need not be discussed at this juncture. The reader is referred to Robert Waelder's discussion of both sides of the question in *Basic Theory of Psychoanalysis*, pp. 130–153.

† How far this extends to an impulsion toward gaining mastery over tasks, thereby giving rise to a fundamental "drive for mastery," remains an open question (Hendrick, 1943).

Consideration of such innate motivation for assimilation of experience is fundamental to Piaget's theory of cognitive development which will be discussed throughout the early chapters of the book.

EMOTIONS

When mental activity and ways of relating to others are being considered, fear, aggression, sexual feelings and their related states such as anxiety, anger, and love are often regarded as emotions or affects rather than "drives." It is difficult to isolate emotions in pure form, to separate them from drives, or even to analyze their nature.

Emotions are diffuse combinations of physiological states and mental sets that pervade thinking and influence relationships and individuals' satisfactions with themselves and their sense of well-being. The list of human emotions is almost endless. The study of emotions has ever been highly controversial, and a discussion of emotions must remain unsatisfactory at the present time. Attention here is simply being directed to the fundamental role of emotions in behavior, to their relationship to the preservation of the individual and the species, and to their diffuse and pervasive character.

Emotions do not simply develop through experience. They have a physiological basis;* but what arouses various emotions, how emotions combine, and which are most readily and frequently aroused in individuals depend largely upon their experiences, and to a large extent the childhood experiences with parents and family that color the attitudes persons have and the ways in which they feel about life.

Several other basic emotions or moods aside from the emotional states related to drives require consideration. The quality of a person's feelings

* Certain diffuse states are organized into physiologic patterns in the limbic system of the brain which MacLean (1955) has termed the "visceral brain." It is the oldest portion of the cortex and the part which may well have directed a primitive animal to partially organized behaviors on the basis of olefaction, olefactory memory, and the arousal of drives. Oral drives (concerned with food and its acquisition), attack and defense, and sexual stimulation have centers of organization in the limbic cortex with connections to the hypothalamus, neocortex, reticular activating system, and other centers. The close neuroanatomical connections between centers concerned with sex, aggression, and orality are worth noting. Continuing studies of the "visceral brain," together with those of the areas that arouse feelings of "pleasure" or "unpleasure" when stimulated, are currently clarifying some of the fundamental neuroanatomical and physiological problems connected with drives and emotions.

ranges between depressed and elated states with euphoria, a feeling of well-being balancing between them.* Other affects mix with these rather basic moods. Depressive states may be due to loss of love or loss of self-esteem, or to resentment toward a loved person. Such states relate to the feelings of the small child when deprived of the mother. A sense of well-being and even elation may relate to the infant's pleasurable responses to closeness to the mother and proper nurturance. The infant's smile and pleasurable gurgling have a positive evolutionary value because they elicit positive maternal feelings that help assure the infant the necessary nurturant care (see Chapter 5). Elation may also accompany unexpected success which brings a heightened evaluation of the self or of those with whom one identifies—as when a team is victorious or a school is cited for an achievement: it also occurs as part of a pathological effort to deny misfortune or loss that more properly should evoke depressive feelings.

Apathy, which is often related to depression, is a means of withdrawal from stimulation when efforts to reduce tension or, in the child, the need for the mother, are chronically frustrated; it provides a way of conserving bodily resources rather than squandering them in futile, frantic, and repetitive efforts to gain relief.

Among the elementary affects we may include fear, anxiety, anger, rage, elation, depression, apathy, attachment feelings, and sexual erotic feelings. These blend with pleasure and unpleasure feelings, and with pain, a sensation that signals trauma. Other emotions may be combinations of these, as well as admixtures of them with thoughts, memories, and values derived from relationships. An analogy may be drawn to the sense of taste, which rests upon the four basic sensations of sweet, bitter, sour, and salt which are modified by odors into an infinite variety of tastes. Various emotions, such as anxiety, disgust, shame, guilt, depression, will be discussed in some detail in appropriate places in subsequent chapters.

We have been focusing upon some of the fundamentals of animal organisms that assure the continuity of the germinal cell and its carrier. The need to preserve the constancy of the cell in a changeable environment, the impulsion toward union of the germinal cells for procreation, the automatic preparations to defend against danger, attachment behavior that helps the animal infant secure nurturant care—all these persist to exert compelling

---

* *Euphoria* is sometimes improperly used for elation. Euphoria is pathological only when inappropriate; thus persons dying of tuberculosis or of multiple sclerosis sometimes are euphoric, despite their miserable states of health. In the case of multiple sclerosis the euphoria reflects the severe damage to the frontal lobes of the brain.

influences in the highest mammalian forms. They continue to direct attention to fundamentals amid the extremely complex processes of adaptation that a person carries out while living in a society. A dynamic adaptive approach to human personality development requires recognition of such basic motivating forces underlying behavior.

THE SEQUENCE OF MATURATION AND DECLINE

The organism has a predetermined sequence of development and decline: a period of growth when assimilation prepares for maturity; a period of maturity when metabolic processes primarily subserve maintenance, repair, and procreation; a period of decline when metabolic exchange lags behind the needs for renewal and leads to death. Death, which we tend to consider the negative of life, makes much life and variety of life possible. It permits evolutionary change by the sorting out of mutations. Because of the sequence of development, decline, and death, all living things possess a time factor and a directedness in time as well as in space. Experience is not repeatable, for any experience that may seem a repetition occurs at a different time in the life cycle and affects an organism that has been changed by the earlier experience. The time factor, including the inevitability of death, profoundly influences the behavior and motivations of the human, who alone among animals is ever aware of it (see Chapter 18).

MALE AND FEMALE

The differences in the physical makeup of the two sexes related to their very different procreative functions also gave rise to dissimilarities in their cultural heritages even within the same society and to divergent though complementary role assignments in all societies. Such physical differences and accompanying divisions of life tasks have led, at least until very recently, to dissimilarities in the personality development and life cycle of men and women. Here the two heritages of humans, the genetic and the cultural, are particularly difficult to untangle because the fundamental division of tasks between males and females antedated the emergence of the human species. The gender-linked roles have become so firmly ingrained that many personality traits accompanying them have been assumed to be innate characteristics of one sex or the other.

The two sexes clearly differ in physical characteristics that cannot but influence personality development. Here, I wish only to call attention to a few such physical attributes, leaving the consideration of others and the elaboration of the topic to subsequent chapters. The differences in primary and secondary sexual characteristics, average size, musculature and pace of physical maturation are obvious. The girl not only has a clear physical demarcation of her change from a child to an adolescent capable of bearing children, but also of when her life will take on a rhythmic periodicity with the menstrual cycle. The adolescent boy and the man may have a greater urgency for release from sexual tensions, and will have only a momentary participation in the conception of a child with no inherent need to nurture his offspring, which permits him a freedom of movement and sexual activity that the woman may envy as well as his erectile penis, symbolic of such prerogatives. The woman has the potential of having a baby develop within her and virtually as a part of her and through her capacity to nurse and nurture to become extremely important to her children, capacities which the man may envy.* Children become aware of their sex very early, and then of the future potentialities and expectations that accompany the state of being a boy or girl, and soon are subjected to familial and cultural forces that influence the desirability and even the acceptability of the inevitable or potential consequences of having been born male or female.

The origins of the basic male and female roles are apparent from the observation of some preliterate societies. When women of these societies are pregnant, nursing, or caring for a toddler (frequently all three states are simultaneous), they have a great need for protection and for persons who can move beyond the village to obtain essential supplies. It is the men who must carry out such instrumental tasks if the group is to survive. Many subsidiary roles developed as part of this major division of the tasks essential for the survival of individuals and the social unit.

Only with industrialization, the higher education of women, and, particularly, the development of secure contraceptives that enable women to decide just when, if at all, they will have children, have many of the male

---

* The male envy of various capacities of women has generally been overlooked. Bettelheim (1954) attributes the practice of subincision by Australian Aborigines to such envy and the desire of men to give themselves female sexual attributes. In New Guinea the men would seem to deny how minimal their participation is in procreation by the belief that babies are built up from womb blood and semen, the construction of a fetus thus requiring frequent acts of copulation.

and female role dichotomies become unnecessary. However, even though no longer essential, the customary roles may seem desirable to many women as well as men. Deeply rooted traditions provide guidelines for living without which people can become perplexed, insecure, and anxious. Moreover, decisions concerning child rearing and marriage (that are necessary if sex-linked roles are to be markedly altered) must be made without the adequate experience that permits people to gauge the ultimate outcome. As we shall examine later (Chapters 6–10), there are other reasons that derive from both male and female development that interfere with rapid and profound changes in the roles of men and women. There are ample reasons why, at this juncture in history, women's roles should change and perhaps must change; but there are also reasons, rooted both in our physical structure and in our traditions, that lead to controversy about such issues and limit the speed, if not the extent, of the role changes.

THE RACIAL PHYSICAL ENDOWMENT

Within the endowment of characteristics common to the human species, each infant has some racial traits and some still more specific characteristics that depend upon the genes carried by the parents. The influence of biological racial differences upon adaptation and personality development is difficult to assess. The direct influence of racial differences on personality development was formerly overemphasized because of the tendency of every group to regard outsiders as barbarians as well as to justify its mistreatment of other races while bolstering its own self-esteem. If contemporary man did not develop from a single type of protoman, and divergent types of protoman survived, it seems probable that they were absorbed into the dominant strain that gained supremacy. Groups which were cut off from interbreeding produced separate races, all of which are equally human. Aside from some possible advantage of dark or light skin for living at certain latitudes, no definable advantage of the innate equipment of any race over others has been established. Obviously, differences in the appearance of the races and their skin color persist. However, all races have blended with others, and gradations exist that blur the boundaries of where one race starts and another race leaves off.

In some instances a genetic mutation that was advantageous to the survival of persons living in a specific environment spread among them.

The "sickling trait" of red blood cells found in a small percentage of African blacks provides a concrete example. These cells become deformed, fragile, and may fragment when the oxygen tension in the capillaries is low; persons who have this trait are susceptible to a serious anemia, but it renders them more resistant to malaria, which formed a much greater threat to their survival. A few groups which have remained relatively isolated, such as the African pygmies, maintain distinctive characteristics. However, anyone who has not specifically been interested in human dispersion may have difficulty in appreciating the extent of the migrations that have brought a reblending of divergent strains.*

THE FAMILIAL BIOLOGICAL ENDOWMENT

Traits of both parental lines clearly show in the child's physical structure, often with features of one or the other parent dominating at different phases of the child's maturation. The genetic endowment of each person is unique, differing from all others except an identical twin. These individual physical characteristics influence children's reactivity to their environment, including their interaction with others, and thereby the personalities they develop.† As the parents usually raise their children as well as conceive

---

* It may be useful to cite some examples. The Polynesians left India in the remote past, picked up and left influences in Indochina, Indonesia, and New Guinea; eventually they reached Tahiti and then spread out across the expanse of the Pacific in their double canoes. They fused with the Japanese (who had already mingled with the Ainu and later with the Mongols) in Micronesia; with the Melanesians who had migrated from Africa across the Indian Ocean into the South Pacific; with the Maorori (wherever they had come from) in New Zealand; with the Eskimo (who had crossed the Bering Sea from Siberia into Alaska); and probably with the Incas and other Amerindians on the coasts of America and in the islands of the Pacific. We might also note the sweep of the Mongols across all of Siberia into Europe, Asia Minor, China, the periphery of India, and over into Japan; or of the Semite Mohammedans into Spain, Sicily, and Italy, and their further intermingling across the trade routes of the Indian Ocean that lasted from the early centuries of the Christian era until the sixteenth century (with Indians, Chinese and the inhabitants of cities on the east coast of Africa); and eventually into Indonesia and beyond. In recent times, of course, the union of races has gained increasing momentum through improvements in transportation and through global wars.

† The inheritance of certain mutant genetic traits, such as Amaurotic family idiocy or Huntington's chorea, virtually seals the infant's fate. Others, such as limitations in the ability to metabolize sugar as in the diabetic, can present serious impediments that influence individuals' ways of life and the attitudes they develop. Other hereditary characteristics, such as an unusually short or tall stature, an unusually long nose, an inability to perceive red and green or to recognize the pitch of sounds, may or may not influence personality development, depending on where and how a person is brought up.

them, it is often impossible to differentiate the relative importance of their genes and their interpersonal influence upon the personality traits that their children develop.

The precise physical structure of individuals does not depend upon their genetic makeup alone. The chromosomal structure directs, patterns, and sets limits within which the organism can develop as it grows in an environment. The phenotype of some insects will vary widely according to the locale in which they develop. A relatively constant environment during the critical phases of the unfolding of the fertilized germ cell is assured all mammals, but the newborn has already been influenced to some extent by the specific uterine environment. Disruption of the placental circulation or the occurrence of viral diseases such as German measles in the mother may, for example, produce anomalies. Abnormalities of the mother's metabolism can affect fetal development, as when a lack of iodine in her serum causes the infant to be a cretin; and her emotional state during pregnancy may influence the infant's reactivity even before birth. Even identical twins differ at birth, for the uterine environment is not identical for them. The environment continues to exert an influence after birth. Genetic endowments may set limits for the height or intelligence that individuals can attain but their actual height or intelligence also depends upon how they are raised. The increasing height of the American population over the past several generations reflects the change in nutritional conditions and probably the diminution in childhood illnesses more than a genetic selection.

Whatever the person's specific genetic endowment, it is a human endowment and forms the foundation upon which personality characteristics will develop through interpersonal experience. As with all biological phenomena each physical attribute will vary from person to person, and if graphically represented will be scattered along a bell-shaped distribution curve. Persons have different ranges of tone perception, lengths of arm, sensitivity to touch, rates of metabolizing glucose, pepsin secretion, visual acuity, and so on. The range of variance is slight for some attributes, marked for others. Most traits in a person will be close to the median of the distribution curve, perhaps with an occasional attribute falling toward the more extreme ranges of the curve. Many divisions of persons or their attributes into distinct groupings, such as into hyperactive, average and placid babies, or into asthenic, athletic, and pyknic physiques, are simply means of stressing placement along distribution curves. However, some attributes, such as iris color and skin color, have multimodal distribution curves. Little is known about the distribution curves for many human attributes and even less about the importance of the interrelationships of such curves for various attributes within a single individual.

The significance of such differences for personality development is more a matter of conjecture than of knowledge at the present time; but they clearly have importance. One mother will be more at ease mothering a placid baby, whereas another will gain more satisfaction from a lively, active infant. A parent's lifelong fantasies may be shattered by the birth of a brunet child rather than a blond one. A girl who starts to menstruate at nine will have a different early adolescence than a girl whose menarche occurs at sixteen. Such influences can vary with differing cultural settings. In the United States even twenty or thirty years ago, if a boy were shooting upward in adolescence past the six-foot-six-inch mark, his parents would very likely be concerned and might well have taken him to an endocrinologist because of his abnormal growth. His life might have been made miserable by the teasing and jibes of confreres, and girls might have avoided the "freak." Today the parents of such a boy may hope he will grow another inch or two to be assured of free college tuition, and girls may eagerly eye this high school basketball star. A person's precise shade of color is extremely significant on the island of Jamaica, where it forms a cornerstone of a social class system; whereas in the United States it is not so much the shade of color but the presumption of black ancestry that has importance. Various life settings may foster or lead to the neglect of certain inborn potentialities. Innate perfect pitch perception will have a different influence upon children depending on whether they are born into a musical or nonmusical family, or into a society devoid of music. The developing personality will depend to a greater or lesser extent, in ways that can only be surmised at present, upon these innate physical differences.

In this chapter we have considered in very general terms the endowments of the newborn infant. Unless we understand that humans are born with a dual endowment, a genetic inheritance and a cultural heritage, we can never grasp correctly their development and maldevelopment. The evolution of the human species rested to a great extent upon the selecting out of mutations that improved the capacities for tool bearing and symbolic communication; and then, because of the ability to communicate verbally and think abstractly, humans became capable of modifying the environment to suit the limits of their physiological capacities, and to transmit what they had learned to subsequent generations so that further genetic change was no longer necessary to enable human beings to change their ways of life and to increase their adaptive capacities.

Through their abilities to communicate verbally and to think, humans acquired cultures and minds, and became dependent upon their interpersonal relationships and their social environment for gaining the techniques needed for adaptation and survival. Even though the uniquely human techniques of adaptation rest on the ability to use language, to consciously choose between alternatives, and to utilize foresight, those bodily needs that are critical to survival, and which assure the perpetuation of the species, are not left entirely to conscious decision (and possible neglect), but gain the individual's attention and can unconsciously dominate a person's activities through the force of the basic drives.

Whereas the acquisition of the physical endowment is controlled by the chemical code of the genes, the assimilation of the cultural heritage cannot depend on any such biological mechanism. The cultural techniques that are transmitted cannot be rigidly predetermined, for they must be suited to the society in which the child will live, and yet their transmission cannot be left to chance. The well-being of individuals and the continuity of the culture which is essential to their development depend on their having a satisfactory agency for conveying the mores and instrumentalities of the culture to its new recruits, and to assure that they, in turn, will become adequate carriers of the culture. The major part of this task of transmitting the culture devolves upon the family in almost all societies. We must now turn to examine the family as the basic agency upon which societies depend for nurturing and enculturating their members. In the family the various elements of the child's genetic and cultural endowments converge.

REFERENCES

ABERLE, D. F. (1951). *The Psychosocial Analysis of a Hopi Life-History*. Comparative Psychology Monographs, vol. 21, no. 1, Serial No. 107. University of California Press, Berkeley.

ARDREY, R. (1966). *The Territorial Imperative: A Personal Inquiry into the Animal Origins of Property and Nations*. Atheneum, New York.

BACON, F. (1625). "The Great Instauration," in *Selected Writings of Francis Bacon*. Modern Library, New York, 1955.

BATESON, G., and MEAD, M. (1942). *Balinese Character: A Photographic Analysis*. New York Academy of Science, New York.

BENEDICT, R. (1934). *Patterns of Culture*. Penguin Books, New York, p. 235.

BETTELHEIM, B. (1954). *Symbolic Wounds*. Free Press, Glencoe, Ill.

BROWN, N. (1966). *Love's Body*. Random House, New York.

CARROLL, L. (1871). *Through the Looking-Glass*. Macmillan, London, 1963, p. 114.

CARSTAIRS, M. G. (1957). *The Twice Born: A Study of a Community of High-Caste Hindus*. Hogarth Press, London.

CHOMSKY, N. (1968). *Language and Mind*. Harcourt, Brace & World, New York.

DELGADO, J. M. R., ROBERTS, W., and MILLER, N. (1954). "Learning Motivated by Electrical Stimulation of the Brain," *American Journal of Physiology*, 179:587–593.

DEWEY, J. (1925). *Experience and Nature*. Open Court, London.

ENGEL, G. L. (1962). *Psychological Development in Health and Disease*. W. B. Saunders, Philadelphia, pp. 72–304.

ERIKSON, E. (1950). *Childhood and Society*. W. W. Norton, New York.

FREUD, S. (1930). "Civilization and Its Discontents," in *The Standard Edition of the Complete Psychological Works of Sigmund Freud*, vol. 21. Hogarth Press, London, 1961.

GARDNER, B. T., and GARDNER, R. A. (1971). "Two-Way Communication with an Infant Chimpanzee," in *Behavior of Nonhuman Primates*. A. Schrier and F. Stollnitz, eds. Academic Press, New York.

GESELL, A. (1941). *Wolf Child and Human Child*. Harper & Bros., New York.

GOODALL, J. (1963). "My Life Among Wild Chimpanzees," *National Geographic*, 124:272–308.

——— (1965). "New Discoveries Among Wild Chimpanzees," *National Geographic*, 128:802–831.

HAMSUN, K. (1967). *Hunger*. R. Bly, trans. Farrar, Straus & Giroux, New York.

HARTMANN, H. (1939). *Ego Psychology and the Problem of Adaptation*. D. Rapaport, trans. International Universities Press, New York, 1958.

HENDRICK, I. (1943). "The Discussion of the 'Instinct to Master'" (letter to the editor), *Psychoanalytic Quarterly*, 12:561–565.

HERODOTUS, EUTERPE, Book II, chap. 2.

KELLER, G. (1918). *Der grüne Heinrich*, in *Gesammelte Werke*. Rascher, Zurich.

KELLER, H. (1902). *The Story of My Life*. Dell, New York, 1964.

KOLATA, G. B. (1974). "The Demise of the Neandertals: Was Language A Factor?" *Science*, 186:618–619.

LIDZ, R. W., and LIDZ, T. "Male Menstruation: A Ritual Alternative to the Oedipal Transition." In press.

LORENZ, K. (1952). *King Solomon's Ring: New Light on Animal Ways*. M. K. Wilson, trans. Thomas Y. Crowell, New York.

——— (1966). *On Aggression*. M. K. Wilson, trans. Harcourt, Brace & World, New York.

MACLEAN, P. D. (1955). "The Limbic System ('Visceral Brain') in Relation to Central Gray and Reticulum of the Brain Stem," *Psychosomatic Medicine*, 17:355–366.

OLDS, J. (1958). "Self-Stimulation of the Brain," *Science*, 127:315–324.

PIAGET, J. (1971). *Structuralism*. C. Maschler, trans. Harper & Row, New York.

RANDALL, Jr., J. (1940). *The Making of the Modern Mind*. Houghton Mifflin, Boston. Rev. ed.

ROBINSON, J. (1921). *The Mind in the Making*. Harper & Bros., New York.

RUMBAUGH, D. M., GILL, T. V., and VON GLASERFELD, E. (1973). "Reading and Sentence Completion by a Chimpanzee," *Science*, 182:731–733.

SALIMBENE, cited in J. B. Ross and M. M. McLaughlin, *A Portable Medieval Reader*. Viking Press, New York, 1949, p. 366.

SCHIELE, B. C., and BROZEK, J. (1948). " 'Experimental Neurosis' Resulting from Semistarvation in Man," *Psychosomatic Medicine*, 10:33.

SIMPSON, G. (1950). *The Meaning of Evolution: A Study of the History of Life and of Its Significance for Man*. Yale University Press, New Haven, Conn.

SOLOMON, P., KUBZANSKY, P., et al., eds. (1961). *Sensory Deprivation*. Harvard University Press, Cambridge, Mass.

SPITZ, R. A. (1945). "Hospitalism: An Inquiry into the Genesis of Psychiatric Conditions in Early Childhood," *The Psychoanalytic Study of the Child*, vol. 1, pp. 53–74. International Universities Press, New York.

STIERLIN, H. (1975). *Adolf Hitler*. Suhrkamp Verlag, Frankfurt-am-Main, Germany.

WAELDER, R. (1960). *Basic Theory of Psychoanalysis*. International Universities Press, New York, pp. 130–153.

WHITING, B., ed. (1963). *Six Cultures: Studies of Child Rearing*. John Wiley & Sons, New York.

WHORF, B. (1939). "The Relation of Habitual Thought and Behavior to Language," in *Language, Thought and Reality: Selected Writings of Benjamin Lee Whorf*. J. Carroll, ed. MIT Press and John Wiley & Sons, New York, 1956.

——— (1956). *Language, Thought and Reality: Selected Writings of Benjamin Lee Whorf*. J. Carroll, ed. MIT Press and John Wiley & Sons, New York.

SUGGESTED READING

BARDWICK, J. M. (1971). *Psychology of Women: A Study of Bio-Cultural Conflicts*. Harper & Row, New York.

BENEDICT, R. (1934). *Patterns of Culture*. Penguin Books, New York.

BROWN, R. (1958). *Words and Things*. Free Press, Glencoe, Ill.

LANGER, S. K. (1957). *Philosophy in a New Key*. Harvard University Press, Cambridge, Mass.

LIDZ, T. (1963). "The Family, Language, and Ego Functions," in *The Family and Human Adaptation: Three Lectures*. International Universities Press, New York.

PIAGET, J. (1971). *Structuralism*. C. Maschler, trans. Harper & Row, New York.

SAPIR, E. (1949). *Selected Writings of Edward Sapir in Language, Culture and Personality*. University of California Press, Berkeley.

TAX, S., ed. (1960). *Evolution After Darwin*, vol. 2 of *The Evolution of Man: Mind, Culture and Society*. University of Chicago Press, Chicago.

VYGOTSKY, L. S. (1962). *Thought and Language*. E. Hanfmann and G. Vakar, eds. and trans. MIT Press and John Wiley & Sons, New York.

CHAPTER 2

❁

The Family

INTRODUCTION

THE PERSON'S DEVELOPMENT cannot be understood properly without consideration of the critical role of the family in the child's developmental process. Infants do not develop into competent adults simply through the unfolding of their genetic endowment; they require not only prolonged nurturant care but also direction and delimitation of their vast potential to develop into integrated individuals capable of living in a society together with their fellows. The early stages of the life cycle upon which all later development rests transpire in the nidus of the family and evolve favorably or unfavorably because of how the parental persons guide the child through them as much as, or more than, because of the child's innate characteristics. Attempts to study the child's development independently of the family setting distort even more than they simplify, for they omit essential factors in the process.

The family is, knowingly or unknowingly, entrusted by virtually every society with the task of providing for its children's biological needs while simultaneously transmitting the society's way of life and techniques of adaptation. Everywhere the family evolved gradually along with the culture, for it must be suited to the society in which it exists and capable of transmitting the society's ways to the new generation. However, in examining how the family carries out its child-rearing functions, we must realize that the rapidity of social and cultural change during the past century has seriously weakened the family's capacities for rearing competent, stable, and adaptable individuals.* As we shall consider later in this chapter, the extended family has been broken by migrations and industrialization into isolated units of parents and children which lack the support of kin; intermarriage between different ethnic groups has mixed up traditional marital roles and ways of child rearing; awareness of the ways of other cultural groups as well as scientific advances have led to a distrust of tradition as a guide into the future. Customs handed down by parents, religious tenets that served to guide behavior, and the traditional relationships between parents and children and husbands and wives have been questioned and disregarded. Currently, women's challenges to their traditional place in society have further shaken the stability of the family.

Although some observers, male and female, believe that the women's movement and its demands will fade, there are reasons to believe that women's newly expressed strivings and demands reflect the alterations in their position brought about by recent social changes, and represent requisite efforts to establish a new societal equilibrium. Women's position has changed for a number of reasons: their increased education and capacity to pursue careers; their need or desire to work outside the home; the threat of overpopulation that has diminished the desirability of large families; the advent of the "pill" and other reliable contraceptive techniques, as well as the legalization of abortion, which permit women to decide whether they will have children, when, and how many; the decrease in the years women spend in child rearing; women's realization that they have as great a capability for sexual pleasure as men, if not greater; women's new confidence that they can achieve on their own, rather than gain satisfactions primarily through the accomplishments of husbands and sons; their desire for an autonomy in which major gratifications will derive neither from caring for others nor from being cared for; the reasonable expectation that in the absence of household help the burdens and satisfactions of housekeeping and child care should be shared by spouses, particularly when the wife works outside the home; and because of still other ways in which women

* As the family is the basic social structure of society, the warp and woof of the social fabric, the disorganization of the family can presage the dissolution of a society. According to Zimmerman (1947) the Christian fathers appear to have been keenly aware that the deterioration of moral character as well as the general social disorganization during the decline of Rome were related to the decline of the family. It was for such reasons that they reinstituted the sanctity of marriage and placed a divine interdiction upon consorts, hetaerae, and homosexual liaisons, and banned the abortions and infanticide that had been rife since the days of Augustus.

seek a place in society equal to, though not necessarily similar to, that held by men. As mothers virtually always have been the major figures in providing or guiding children's care, we must appreciate the impact of women's changing roles upon the personality development of children.

As part of women's desire to change their identities as well as their roles, there have been efforts to obliterate the differences in the ways in which boys and girls are raised. Such practices will have profound and far-reaching effects that are difficult to envision, for the blurring of differences between men and women affects one of the most fundamental and pervasive factors that provide structure to both people and society.

Efforts to change the family and society in order to meet the needs and wishes of liberated women are complicated, because not all women wish the same sort of liberation. Then, too, some women prefer the security of more traditional relationships with husbands and believe that they can gain greater satisfaction from complementing the life of a husband and raising children than from a career. They wish girls to be girlish and boys to be boyish, and admit that they are very concerned about any vagaries in their children's gender identities. They know where they are and who they are in their traditional roles and turn away from all invitations to depart from them.*

Many men and women who believe that family life has stifled their development and kept them from realizing their potentialities now seek to achieve greater freedom for self-expression by finding substitutes for conventional marriage and family life. It has been easier to criticize the shortcomings of marriage and of the isolated nuclear family than to find substitutes that provide greater satisfaction for adults and adequate assurance that children raised in such new types of families, or substitutes for the family, will develop into functioning adults. Thus, as a result of such experimentation, the family may become even less stable in the future. Still, the old extended family cannot be reinstituted in contemporary society. In time—if there is time—a new stable pattern may evolve. We may be able to foster constructive change if we can ascertain what the essential functions of the family are, and hold them fast to assure their preservation despite change (Lidz, 1963b). In this chapter we shall consider the family's functions for child rearing and how it has carried them out in the past. How it will carry them out in the future is a matter for conjecture, but the

---

* University-educated women—and men—particularly from the East and West coasts may find it useful to read *The Total Woman*, the best seller by Marabel Morgan that advises women how to find fulfillment as devoted, supportive, religious and sexually fulfilled wives who thus know how to provide sexual fulfillment to their husbands and to manipulate them subtly.

presentation will seek to convey something of the complex issues involved, and, perhaps, enable the reader to assay the feasibility of various proposals for the future.

FAMILY FUNCTIONS

The family forms the earliest and most persistent influence that encompasses the still unformed infant and small child, for whom the parents' ways and the family ways are *the* way of life, the only way the child knows. All subsequent experiences are perceived, understood, and reacted to emotionally according to the foundations established in the family. The family ways and the child's patterns of reacting to them become so integrally incorporated in the child that they can be considered determinants of his or her constitutional makeup, difficult to differentiate from the genetic biological influences with which they interrelate. Subsequent influences will modify those of the family, but they can never undo or fully reshape these early core experiences.

Because the family, like the air we breathe, is ubiquitous, it has long been taken for granted, and many of its vital functions have been overlooked and remain unexamined. Indeed, the family is a universal phenomenon, because human beings are so constructed that the family is an essential correlate of their biological makeup. It is the critical institution that enables children to survive and develop into integrated, functioning persons by augmenting their inborn adaptive capacities. The prolonged helplessness and dependency of children necessitate that they be reared by parenting persons to whom the child's welfare is as important as, if not more important than, their own; and it is children's need for and attachment to such parental figures that provides major motivations and directives for their development into competent members of society. The family, as we shall examine, also subserves essential functions for the spouses and for society, functions inevitably interrelated with child rearing.

The structure and functioning of the family must meet two determinants: the biological nature and needs of humans, and the requirements of the particular society of which the family forms a subsystem and in which its offspring must be prepared to live. Therefore, families everywhere will have certain essential functions in common while also having some very discrepant ways of handling similar problems.

Child Rearing for Membership in a Society

Let us consider in very general terms how the family shapes the child to the societal patterns and conveys the culture's instrumental techniques as an integral part of providing the essential nurturant care before we examine various aspects of the process separately.*

Infants in our society are traditionally fed on a more or less regular schedule and may even be left to cry if they become hungry before feeding time; their mothers dress and feed them at the same time each morning, and place them in their own cribs in their own rooms for naps at about the same time each afternoon, and prepare them for bed according to schedule each evening. As toddlers, they spend time in playpens and soon learn what they can touch and what they must leave alone, and which toys are theirs and which their siblings'. In most Western societies infants and children are already being prepared to live in time—for scheduled living—and for existence as independent individuals with their own possessions, and eventual autonomy from their families of origin. But other little children are being prepared for a different way of life. Let us look at our friends the Hopi in

* Recently, various people have called for the abolition of the family because it inculcates the societal mores and ethos into the child and thus interferes with the spontaneous, uninfluenced development of the child, who therefore can never be truly free. Such individuals fail to appreciate that a child cannot grow up uninfluenced by adults, and that such undirected freedom can only lead to the child's death or at least to a non-human type of existence. The reasons given by Cooper in *Death of the Family* show a surprising disregard of essential aspects of human development. Indeed, the family is so vital that it has unknowingly been carrying out its complex tasks since the emergence of humans, and some even long before protoman appeareed on the scene. As the parents who usually provide the family environment also by and large transmit the genetic heredity, the child's personality traits have traditionally been attributed to heredity. It was obvious enough: intelligent parents usually had intelligent children; the ruling class provided most governmental leaders; artisans bred artisans; and laborers supplied most of the laborers. Children did not always live up to expectation, but that was due to some fault in the ancestral line of the spouse. Perhaps it required the opening of the New World for such "obvious" truths to be questioned, for in the gigantic reshuffling children began to differ from their parents in many significant ways. (This happened even more distinctively in Australia where, I understand, few boast of traits handed down from their ancestral settlers at Botany Bay.) True, some children were raised in institutions and most of these did not turn out particularly well; but, after all, with rare exceptions, these were children of the poor and little more could be expected of them. It has required the comparisons of the influence of child-rearing procedures in widely different societies, the study of children raised in institutions (Freud and Burlingham, 1944; Spitz, 1945; Whiting, 1963), the gradual realization that individuals who are seriously disturbed emotionally were almost always raised in very faulty family settings (Ackerman, 1958; Lidz, Fleck, and Cornelison, 1965), and even more recently the understanding that the child's cognitive development rests heavily on family influences (Brown, 1965; Lidz, 1963a) to draw attention to some of these essential functions of the family and to pose the proper questions that are always required before proper answers can be found.

considering education to live in a time-oriented scheduled world. Hopi children grow up in a relatively timeless world that traditionally was encompassed by the horizon surrounding the mesa on which they live. In this small world, which their ancestors had inhabited for countless generations, little changes from day to day or from year to year. Children do not learn to hurry lest something be missed or an opportunity be neglected—or to make every minute count on their way to amounting to something. They do not learn to do things to bring about innovations because there can be no innovation; the Hopi believe that everything already exists. Everything already exists, but some things have not yet become manifest. They learn that wishing and thinking for something, particularly collective concentration such as occurs during rituals, are means of having things become manifest. Thus, thought and wish have greater pragmatic value than activity, and among the Hopi a child's wishful thinking and daydreaming are not likely to be derogated as escape mechanisms that supplant effort. They do not grow up being oriented to do things to try to improve themselves and their world. The language they imbibe along with their mother's milk not only is suited to this orientation but prevents them from considering matters very differently because there are no tenses in the Hopi language.* There is no way of talking about the past, present, and future but simply about what has and what has not become manifest—and to say that something is not yet manifest is the same as saying it is subjective; that is, it exists only in the mind, which, of course, is the only place we experience the future. The Hopi also do not think or talk about tomorrow or the day after tomorrow, but rather about when day will return again or return for the second time. Such differences are more than different ways of expressing something; they reflect a divergent orientation to the nature of the universe and human experience.†

We might also consider the plight of benighted Fijian children who are brought up without gaining any notion of attaining possessions or amassing wealth, or of outstripping peers in achievement and preparing to gain power in order to bring prestige and pleasure to parents. Little wonder that

---

* This does not necessarily make the Hopi language the ideal of language students who may be bothered by the many tenses in Latin, Hebrew, or English. The complexity comes about in other ways, such as in the change in the form of the verb to tell how something is known—for example, because it is seen, or heard, or because someone has said so, or because it customarily happens.

† The illustrations are not necessarily accurate and should be taken as symbolic illustrations (as the author is not an ethnologist). See D. F. Aberle, *The Psychosocial Analysis of a Hopi Life-History*; L. W. Simmons, *Sun Chief: The Autobiography of a Hopi Indian*; and B. L. Whorf, "The Relation of Habitual Thought and Behavior to Language."

they continue to live in grass huts and play neither golf nor bridge. They do not learn in early childhood that if their father does not work the family will go hungry, be dispossessed, or go on relief and lose its self-esteem. There is no cajoling or tacit threat of loss of love if they do not exert themselves to learn enough to gain entry into a proper nursery school that will assure admittance to the private school that will open the gates to a college that will prepare them for graduate school to make it possible for them eventually to occupy prestigious positions in society. Fijian children do not even know the meaning of private possessions except in the limited sense of a few personal necessities. What relatives in the village possess is theirs. Indeed, a person's future security depends on giving and sharing rather than accumulating. So long as Fijians practice the custom of sharing with relatives and providing for them when custom requires, they can be certain that relatives, even distant ones, will provide for them, even in old age. Food is generally available without requiring much effort to grow or catch and is freely shared. When the hut is rotted by termites, the villagers gather and collectively build a new one. Aspirations are limited because there is a taboo on ambition and self-advancement.

By means of similar methods that are largely unconscious because they are simply part of the way people live, boys in our society—indeed in all societies—are prepared to become men and girls to become women.

SOME SPECIAL CHARACTERISTICS OF THE FAMILY

Although we are concerned with the family's child-rearing functions in this chapter, we must appreciate that the family also subserves essential needs of the spouses and of the society, for these affect how it raises its children. The family constitutes the fundamental social unit of virtually every society: it forms a grouping of individuals that the society treats as an entity; it helps stabilize a society by creating a network of kinship systems; it constitutes an economic unit in all societies and the major economic unit of some; and it provides roles, status, motivation, and incentives that affect the relationships between individuals and the society. In addition, the nuclear family seeks to serve the sexual and emotional needs, and to stabilize the lives of the spouses who married to form it. These three sets of functions of the family—for the society, for the parents, and for the children—are interrelated, and it is likely that no other institution could simultaneously fill these three functions without radical change in our social organization. It even seems probable that these three functions of the family cannot be carried out separately except under very special circumstances because they are so inextricably interrelated. Nevertheless, these functions can conflict, and some conflict between them seems almost inevitable. The society's needs can conflict with those of both the spouses and children, as when the husband must leave the home to enter military service, or even when taxes diminish the family income appreciably. Fulfilling parental functions almost necessarily conflicts with the marital relationship, and the failure to anticipate and accept such interference has destroyed many marriages.

Indeed, there is considerable difference between a marriage without children and a family. In a marriage the spouses can assume very diverse types of role relationships and find very different ways of achieving reciprocity, provided they are satisfactory to both, or simply more satisfactory than separating. They can both live in their parental homes, or gain sexual satisfaction from a third partner, and so forth. The various ways in which spouses relate are virtually countless. However, when the birth of a child turns a marriage into a nuclear family, not only must the spouses' ways of relating to one another shift to make room for the child, but limits are also set on the ways in which they can relate to one another and simultaneously provide a suitable developmental setting for the child.

Even though a marital relationship is a complicated matter it can be understood in terms of the interaction between two persons. A family, in contrast, cannot be grasped simply in interactional terms, for it forms a true small group with a unity of its own. The family has the characteristics of all true small groups, of which it is the epitome: the action of any member affects all; members must find reciprocally interrelating roles or else conflict or the repression of one or more members ensues; the group requires unity of objectives and leadership toward these objectives to function properly; the maintenance of group morale requires each member to give some precedence to the needs of the group over his or her own desires; groups tend to divide up into dyads that exclude others from significant relationships and transactions.* These and still other characteristics of small groups are heightened in the family because of the intense and prolonged interdependency of its members, which requires the family, in particular, to have structure, clarity of roles, and leadership to promote the essential unity and to minimize divisive tendencies. The family, moreover,

* T-Groups and similar consciousness-raising groups are pseudogroups because they lack many of these characteristics. A "leaderless group" is to some extent a solecism.

is a very special type of group, with characteristics that are determined both by the biological differences of its members and by the very special purposes it serves.

The nuclear family is composed of two generations whose members have different needs, prerogatives, obligations, and functions in the family. Although the spouses are individuals, as parents they function as a coalition, dividing the tasks of living and child rearing. They are properly dependent on one another, but parents cannot be dependent on immature children without distorting the children's development. They provide nurturance and give of themselves so that the children can develop, serving as guides, educators, and models for their offspring, even when the parents are unaware of it.

Children, in contrast to parents, receive their primary training in group living within the family and are properly dependent upon their parents for many years, forming intense bonds with them while developing through learning from the parents and assimilation of their characteristics. Sexual relations within the family are forbidden for them lest the intrafamilial bonds become too firm. The children must so learn to live within the family that they can eventually emerge from it into the broader society.

The nuclear family is also composed of persons of two sexes, which traditionally, at least, have had differing though complementary roles and functions. As the roles and functions are no longer clearly divided according to traditional sex-linked roles in many families, how the tasks of living and child rearing are shared requires conscious agreement—a solution that can create difficulty, as will be considered in subsequent chapters. However, traditional roles usually remain more or less a factor in the way parents achieve reciprocally interrelating roles. The fundamental functions of the mother derive from the woman's biological makeup and is related to the nurturing of children and the maintenance of the home needed for that purpose, which has led women to have a particular interest in interpersonal relationships and the emotional harmony of family members—an expressive-affectional or affiliating role.* The father's role, also originally related to physique, traditionally has been concerned with the support and protection of the family and with establishing its position within the larger society—an instrumental-adaptive role. Some such role divisions continue

---

* See Chapter 1. When wives, from the time of marriage to late middle life, were caring for children and the management of the household required very special skills, it was more important than at present to prepare boys and girls to carry out different functions. However, because of an innate difference, because of family dynamics, or because of the influence of tradition, women tend to be more nurturant and affiliating than men.

in most contemporary families—even though not essential—because tradition changes slowly, but also because it continues to meet the needs of many spouses.

These characteristics of the nuclear family, and corollaries derived from them, set requisites for the parents and for their marital relationship if their family is to provide a suitable setting for the harmonious development of their offspring.

THE FAMILY'S REQUISITE FUNCTIONS IN CHILD REARING

The family fosters and organizes the child's development by carrying out a number of interrelated functions, albeit often without knowing it, which we shall examine under the headings *Nurture, Structure,* and *Enculturation.*

Nurture

The nurture of the infant and child is the one child-rearing function of the family that has been specifically recognized by most developmental theories. As it forms a major topic of this book, we shall here touch upon only a few principles that are germane to the integrated functioning of the family and leave their elaboration to subsequent chapters.

Parental nurturance must meet children's needs and supplement their immature capacities in a different manner at each phase of their development. It concerns the nature of the nurture provided from the total care given the newborn to how parents foster the adolescent's movement toward independence from them. It involves filling not only children's physical needs but also their emotional needs for security, consistency, and affection; and it includes furnishing opportunities for children to utilize new capacities as they unfold. Proper nurturance requires parents to have the capacity, knowledge, and empathy to alter their ways of relating to a child in accord with the child's changing needs. The degree of protective constraint provided a nine-month-old is unsuited for a toddler, and the limits set for a fifteen-month-old would restrain the development of a two-and-a-half-year-old child. The physical intimacy a father might provide his five-year-old daughter could be too seductive for an early adolescent girl. The capacity to be nurturant, or to be maternal, is not an entity. Some parents can properly nurture a helpless and almost completely dependent infant, but become apprehensive and have difficulties in coping with a toddler who can no longer be fully guarded from dangers inherent in the surroundings; some mothers have difficulties in permitting the child to form the erotized libidinal bonds essential for the proper development of the infant, whereas others have difficulty in frustrating the erotized attachment of the three-year-old. However, unstable parents and grossly incompatible parents are often disturbing influences throughout all of the child's developmental years, and such panphasic influences are often more significant in establishing personality traits or disturbances in children than the difficulties during a specific developmental phase.

While the mother is usually the primary nurturant figure to the child, particularly when the child is small, her relationship with the child does not transpire in isolation but is influenced by the total family setting. The father is also an important nurturant person and becomes increasingly significant as the child grows older. Further, the mother requires support in order to invest her infant properly with her love and attention and needs to have her own emotional supplies replenished; and in most contemporary families there is no one other than the husband from whom she can gain such physical and emotional sustenance.

The attachments of children to parents that arise as concomitants of their nurturant care provide major directives and motivations for their development into social beings and furnish the parents with the leverage to channel their child's drives. Children's wishes and needs for their parents' love and acceptance and their desires to avoid rebuff and punishment lead them to attempt to conform to expectations. Through wishing to be loved by a parent, as well as to become someone like a parent, the child gains a major developmental directive through seeking to emulate and identify with one or both parents.

The quality and nature of the parental nurturance which children receive will profoundly influence their emotional development—their vulnerability to frustration, and the aggression, anxiety, hopelessness, helplessness, and anger they experience under various conditions. As Erikson (1950) has pointed out, it affects the quality of the basic trust children develop—the trust they have in others, and in themselves. It influences their sense of autonomy and the clarity of the boundaries established between themselves and the parental persons. It contributes to the child's self-esteem as a member of the male or female sex. It lays the foundations for trust in the reliability of collaboration and the worth of verbal communication as a means of problem solving. The child's physiological functioning can be

permanently influenced by the manner in which the parental figures respond to physiological needs. Hilde Bruch (1961) has pointed out, for
example, that the child needs to learn that the physiological phenomena
that occur with hunger are signs of *hunger* that can be satisfied by eating—
something which may never occur if a parent feeds the child whenever the
child cries for any reason, or in response to the parent's own hunger rather
than the child's. It is apparent from this brief survey of topics that will be
discussed in later chapters why so much attention has properly been directed to the parental nurturant functions and how profoundly they influence personality development.

Structure

Let us now consider the relationship between the dynamic organization
of the family and the integration of the personality of the offspring. Although the family organization varies from culture to culture and according
to social class within a society, it seems likely that the family everywhere
follows certain organizational principles. The family members must find
reciprocally interrelating roles, or distortions in the personalities of one or
more members will occur. The division of the family into two generations
and two sexes lessens role conflicts and tends to provide an area free from
conflict into which the immature child can develop, and which directs the
child into the proper gender identity. While all groups require unity of
leadership, the family contains two leaders—the father and the mother—
with different but interrelated functions that enable them to form the coalition required to permit unity of leadership. We may hazard that, in order
for the family to develop a structure that can properly direct the integration
of its offspring, *the spouses must form a coalition as parents, maintain the
boundaries between the generations, and carry out the fundamental functions related to their respective gender-linked roles.** These requirements
which sound simple are not easy to attain or maintain.

THE PARENTAL COALITION

As has been noted, all small groups require unity of leadership, but the
family has a dual leadership. A coalition between these leaders is necessary
not only to provide unity of direction but also to afford both parents the
support essential for carrying out their cardinal functions. The mother, for

---

* The functions need not be the traditional ones, but we do not know the consequences of attempts to obliterate completely the differences between maternal and
paternal roles. It seems likely that it would lead to confusions of gender identity in the
child, and interfere with many facets of development. The reasons for such concerns
will become apparent in subsequent chapters.

example, can better delimit her erotic investment in the small child to maternal feelings when her sexual needs are being satisfied by her husband. Coalitions are usually easier to achieve when spouses fill complementary rather than similar roles. The family is less likely to break up into dyads that create rivalries and jealousies if the parents form a unity in relating to their children; a child's wishes to possess one or the other parent for himself alone—the essence of the oedipal situation—are more readily overcome if the parental coalition is firm and the child's fantasies are frustrated and redirected to the reality that requires repression of such wishes. Children provided with adult models who treat one another as alter egos, with each striving for the other's satisfaction as well as for his own, are very likely, when they grow up, to value marriage as an institution that provides emotional satisfaction and security.

The child properly requires two parents: a parent of the same sex with whom to identify and who forms a model to follow into adulthood; and a parent of the opposite sex who serves as a basic love object and whose love and approval are sought by identifying with the parent of the same sex. However, a parent fills neither role effectively for a child if he or she is denigrated, despised, or treated as an enemy by the spouse. Parents who are irreconcilable are likely to confuse the child's development because the child derives contradictory internal directives from them. It is possible for parents to form a reasonable coalition for their children despite marital discord and to some extent even despite separation; they can agree about how children should be raised, and each parent can convey to the children that the other is a worthwhile person and parent even though the parents could not get along together. Some of the most destructive effects of divorce on children occur when one parent villifies the other to a child.

THE GENERATION BOUNDARIES

The division of the nuclear family into two generations lessens the danger of role conflict and furnishes space free from competition with a parent into which the child can develop. The parents are the nurturing and educating generation and provide adult models and objects of identification for the child to emulate and internalize. Children require the security of dependency to be able to utilize their energies in their own development, and their personalities become stunted if they must emotionally support the parents they need for security. A different type of affectional relationship exists between parents from what exists between a parent and child. However, the situation is complicated because of the intense relationship heightened by erogenous feelings that properly exist between the mother and her very young child and by the slow differentiation of the child from the original symbiotic union with the mother(see Chapters 5 and 6). The generational division helps both mother and child to overcome the bond, a step that is essential to enable the child to find a proper place as a boy or girl member of the family, then to invest energies in peer groups and schooling, and eventually to gain a discrete ego identity. The generation boundaries can be breached by the parents in various ways, as by the mother failure to differentiate between her own needs and feelings and those of a child; by a parent's use of a child to fill needs unsatisfied by a spouse; by a father's behavior as a rival to his son; by a parent's attempt to be more of a child than a spouse. Incestuous and near-incestuous relationships in which a parent overtly or covertly gains erotic gratification from a child form the most obvious disruptions of generation lines. When a child is used by one parent to fill needs unsatisfied by the other, the child can seek to widen the gap between the parents and insert himself or herself into it; and by finding an essential place in completing a parent's life the child need not—and perhaps cannot—turn to the extrafamilial world for self-completion. The resolution of the oedipal situation thus depends for its proper completion upon the child having a family in which the parents are primarily reliant upon one another or, at least, upon other adults (Chapter 7).

Failure to maintain the generation boundaries within the nuclear family can distort the child's development in a variety of ways, and is a major source of psychopathology.

SEX-LINKED ROLES

Security of gender identity is a cardinal factor in the achievement of a stable ego identity (see Chapters 7 and 10)* and a child's sex is among the most important determinants of personality traits. This statement refers primarily to a person's self-concept and self-esteem as a male or female and to his or her ways of relating to others and not to capacities to carry out various occupations. Today many parents do not wish to raise sons who will lack affiliational and nurturant qualities, or daughters who will be passively dependent and incapable of pursuing a career. A child does not attain sex-linked attributes simply by being born a boy or girl, but through gender allocation that starts at birth and then develops through role assumptions and identifications as the child grows older. The maintenance of appropriate gender-linked roles by the parents is one of the most significant factors in guiding the child's development as a boy or girl. Although in most contemporary families the parents need to share parental functions

---

* This may or may not include the secure acceptance of the self as a homosexual. There are reasons to doubt that a child can have a clear self-concept as a homosexual; and, in most contemporary societies at least, homosexuality would seem to involve a greater or lesser degree of ambiguity about gender identity.

and many wish to share various roles, some differences between mothers and fathers need to be maintained to direct a child's development. The problem is more subtle than the father's filling of the instrumental, and the mother's the expressive-affiliative, role. It is apparent that even in traditional settings mothers carry out instrumental functions in running the home and raising children, and fathers fill affectional-affiliative functions with their wives and children. However, fathers have had the major responsibility for supporting the family and mothers for the emotional harmony of the family and for rearing children. Though the functions of mothers and fathers are changing, clear-cut role reversals furnish the children images of masculinity and femininity that are culturally deviant. Moreover, as Parsons and Bales (1955) have pointed out, a cold and unyielding mother is more deleterious than a cold and unyielding father, whereas a weak and ineffectual father is more damaging than a weak and ineffectual mother. More explicitly, a cold and aloof mother may be more detrimental to a daughter who requires experience in childhood with a nurturant mother in order to attain maternal characteristics than to a son, whereas an ineffectual father may be more deleterious to a son who must overcome his initial identification with his mother and gain security of his ability to provide for a wife and family than to a daughter. Further, the child's identification with the parent of the same sex is likely to be seriously impeded when this parent is unacceptable to the other whose love the child seeks. Of course, other difficulties can interfere with a child's gaining a secure gender identity, such as the parents' conveying the wish that the boy had been born a girl or vice versa; still, when parents adequately fill their own gender-linked functions, and accept and support the spouse in his or her roles, a general assurance of a proper outcome is provided.

The relationship between the family structure and the integration of the offspring's ego development is a topic that is only beginning to be studied. Still, a little consideration leads us to realize that the family's organization profoundly affects the child through such matters as the provision of proper models for identification, motivation toward the proper identification, security of sexual identity, the transition through the oedipal phase, and the repression of incestuous tendencies before adolescence.

Enculturation

The family's function of enculturating the child may be more properly divided into socialization and enculturation. Socialization concerns teaching the child the basic roles and institutions of the society through the transactions between family members; whereas enculturation deals with that which is transmitted symbolically from generation to generation. However, there is considerable overlap, and the two functions cannot always be differentiated.

The form and functions of the family evolve with the culture and subserve the needs of the society of which it is a subsystem. The family is the first social system that children know, and simply by living in it they properly gain familiarity with the basic roles as they are carried out in the society in which they live—the roles of parents and child, of boy and girl, of man and woman, of husband and wife—and how these roles of the family members impinge upon the broader society and how the roles of others affect the family. Whereas roles are properly considered units of the social system rather than of the personality, they also are important in personality development, directing behavior to fit into roles and giving cohesion to the personality functioning. Individuals generally do not learn patterns of living entirely on their own, but in many situations learn roles and then modify them to their specific individual needs and personalities.

Children also learn from their intrafamilial experiences about a variety of basic institutions and their values, such as the institutions of family, marriage, economic exchange, and so forth; and societal values are inculcated by identification with parents, ethical teachings, example, and interaction. The wish to participate in or avoid participating in an institution —such as marriage—can be a major motivating force in personality development. It is the function of the family to transmit to the offspring the prescribed, permitted, and proscribed values of the society and the acceptable and unacceptable means of achieving such goals. Within the family children are involved in a multiplicity of social phenomena that permanently influence their development, such as the value of belonging to a mutually protective unit; the rewards of renouncing one's own wishes for the welfare of a collectivity; the acceptance of hierarchies of authority and the relationship between authority and responsibility. The family value systems, role definitions, and patterns of interrelationship enter into the children far more through the family transactions than through what they are taught or even from what the parents consciously appreciate.

The process of enculturation concerns the acquisition of the major techniques of adaptation that are not inherited genetically but are assimilated as part of the cultural heritage that is a filtrate of the collective experiences of a person's forebears. The cultural heritage includes such tangible matters as agricultural techniques and food preferences, modes of housing and transportation, arts and games, as well as many less tangible matters such as status hierarchies, religious beliefs and ethical values that are accepted as divine commands, or axiomatically as the only proper way of doing things, and are defended by various taboos. In a complex industrial and scientific society such as ours, the family obviously can transmit only the basic adaptive techniques to its offspring and must rely upon schools and other specialized institutions to teach many of the other instrumentalities of the culture.

Enculturation is a topic that has received increasing attention in anti-poverty programs, in which it is becoming apparent that the cultural deprivation of the children is almost as important as their social and economic deprivations. They cannot learn readily because they have not been provided with the symbolic wherewithal for abstract thinking and with the breadth of experience to reason adequately in guiding their lives into the future. Further, there is increasing evidence that a significant proportion of mental retardation derives from cultural deprivation rather than from biological inadequacy.*

The studies of disorganized families and their young children, predominantly white, by Pavenstedt, Malone, and their colleagues (1967) clearly indicated that many of the children were permanently crippled both intellectually and emotionally by the time they had reached nursery school.†

* An example, more amusing than malignant, of the handicaps imposed upon a child by cultural deprivation is provided by the following essay written by a London slum child evacuated to the country during World War II.

BIRDS AND BEASTS

The cow is a mammal. It has six sides, right and left and upper and below. At the back it has a tail on which hangs a brush. With this he sends flies away so they don't fall into the milk. The head is for the purpose of growing horns and so his mouth can be somewhere. The horns are to butt with and the mouth to moo with.

Under the cow hangs milk. It is arranged for milking. When people milk, milk comes and there never is an end to the supply. How the cow does it I have not yet realized, but it makes more and more. The cow has a fine sense of smell and one can smell it far away. This is the reason for fresh air in the country.

A man cow is called an ox. The ox is not a mammal. The cow does not eat much but what it eats it eats twice so that it gets enough. When it is hungry it moos and when it says nothing at all it is because its insides are full up with grass.

† Despite a pseudoprecocity concerning autonomy, such as wandering about alone or being able to go to the store and make simple purchases for their mothers, they were markedly delayed in their perceptual and cognitive development. Their language was impoverished and they could not generalize from one experience to another, or even name an object after it was hidden from view. Impulsivity and inability to delay gratification were obvious; and they could be almost paralyzed by anxiety. Not only were they distrustful of adults, but their inability to differentiate between one teacher and another frustrated their teachers' efforts to establish meaningful relationships with them. An older group of children from disorganized black and Puerto Rican families

We have already considered some aspects of the family's critical task of transmitting the culture's adaptive techniques to its children, and here we shall only consider the crucial family function of inculcating a solid foundation in the culture's language. Language is the means by which people internalize experience, think about it, try out alternatives, conceptualize and strive toward future goals rather than simply seeking immediate gratification. After infancy a person's ability to acquire almost all other instrumental techniques depends upon language, and most cooperation with others, which is so vital to human adaptation, depends upon the use of a shared system of meanings. Indeed, the capacity to direct the self into the future, which we shall term "ego functioning," depends upon a person's having verbal symbols with which to construct an internalized symbolic version of the world that can be manipulated in imaginative trial and error before committing himself or herself to irrevocable actions.

To understand the importance of language to ego functioning, we must appreciate that, in order to understand, communicate, and think about the ceaseless flow of experiences, people must be able to divide their experiences into categories. Experiences are continuous, categories are discrete. No one can start from the beginning and build up a totally new and idiosyncratic system of categorization. Each child must learn the culture's system of categorizing, not only in order to communicate with others in the society but also in order to think coherently. Each culture is distinctive in the way its members categorize their experiences, and its vocabulary is, in essence, the catalogue of the categories into which the culture divides its world and its experiences.

The proper learning of words and their meanings and of the syntax of the language is essential to human adaptation, but there is no assurance that the language will be taught or learned correctly. The correctness and the stability of what children learn rests upon their teachers, primarily upon members of their families. The language usage children learn depends largely upon the parents' meaning systems and the way in which they reason, and also upon the consistency of the parents' use of words and of their responses to the child's usage.* The topic of how children learn

---

in New York studied by Minuchin and his coworkers (1967) had had very similar problems. Basil Bernstein (1974) drew attention to the serious limitations of lower-class children in London because of the paucity of verbal communication in their homes.

* We know, for example, from direct observation of family interaction and tests of family members individually and collectively that the styles of communication and meanings in families with schizophrenic offspring are strikingly vague and idiosyncratic. The verbal and nonverbal cues, punishments, and rewards of one parent are apt to be inconsistent and those of the two parents conflicting.

language and its importance to them will be amplified extensively as we follow the course of their development.

The enculturation of boys and girls has until now differed in all societies. Each sex has been taught a somewhat different array of skills and knowledge according to the society's gender-role divisions of the tasks of living. The priesthood, teaching in elementary schools, the practice of medicine, or raising vegetables may, for example, be predominantly male activities in some societies and female activities in others. However, child rearing and the maintenance of the home have been predominantly female functions in virtually all societies, whereas hunting and warfare rarely have been. Even words often have had different meanings for men and women: for a man, "pork chop" has meant something served on a plate, whereas for most women its meaning has included how it is purchased and prepared.*

FAMILY TYPES

The Family Type and Child Rearing

Within the limits set by the biological makeup of human beings, which divide the nuclear family into two generations and two genders and imposes certain functions upon the family, families exist in an endless number of forms, varying with the culture and subserving differing functions for the parents and children. Families can be classified in different ways—as patrilinear or matrilinear, patriarchal or matriarchal, patrilocal or matrilocal; as monogamous, polygynous, or polyandrous; as nuclear or extended; or according to various rules of exogamy that help direct the choice of partners. We shall first consider two general types of family organization that we commonly encounter in order to highlight some contemporary problems of family life.

The extended family with strong kinship ties will be contrasted with the more self-contained isolated nuclear family of parents and their children that is becoming increasingly prevalent in an industrial and highly mobile society.

THE EXTENDED KINSHIP FAMILY

We shall first take a model, an approximate model that is not specific to any society, of an extended kinship system common in societies with es-

---

* Women's current objection to the use of the masculine pronoun in referring to a single child or person when the gender does not matter derives from the implication contained in the usage that males are more significant than females.

sentially nonmigratory populations. It may be applied to some very different types of families, such as the Mexican village family, the Fijian family, and the Sicilian peasant family. However, it is of importance to us because many immigrant or second-generation families are emerging from this form of family life and continue to have values based upon it. Indeed, in a very modified form, extended families remain fairly common in contemporary urban populations. In the extended kinship system, the nuclear family is not clearly demarcated from the larger network of relatives. The various functions of a family are shared by the relatives. The parents have help in raising their children, who, reciprocally, have many surrogate parents. The influence of the eccentricities and deficiencies of the parents is minimized, and the impact of the individuality of parents upon children is also lessened. Advice and support are readily available to the parents. As at least one of the parents remains close to his or her family of origin, the couple are not completely dependent upon one another for tangible support and emotional complementation. Indeed, the husband and wife tend to live parallel lives rather than sharing mutual interests and functions. In a study of London families, Bott (1955) found that the women in modified extended families tended to spend much of their time with female relatives—sisters, sisters-in-law, mothers-in-law—whereas the men spent very little time in the home, making the pub the center of their nonoccupational activities. Persons who grow up in extended families have ample opportunity to observe and practice child-rearing techniques. Little girls often help care for children of relatives. Further, in communities where both parents are reared in a similar type of family and observe a number of other similar families intimately, the spouses enter marriage with relatively compatible ideas of the roles of husband and wife and of how children are to be raised. Particularly in nonindustrial rural communities, few new influences accrue to change the family pattern and parental roles from generation to generation. The family here is an organization which places emphasis upon the transmission of traditional ways of adaptation to the environment and upon the ways of living together that have evolved slowly with the culture.

The extended family tends to assure stability through furnishing clear patterns of how to live and relate to others. It has the disadvantage of retarding changes in adaptive techniques as required in a rapidly changing scientific era. The extended family breaks down with migrations and with the demand of industrial societies that their members, both labor and management, follow opportunities for employment. It would be erroneous to consider that the modified extended family is found only among the lower socioeconomic groups. The strength and power of some wealthy industrial and banking families have been heightened by kinship loyalties.

THE ISOLATED NUCLEAR FAMILY.*

For an ever-increasing number of American families the extended kinship ties have been broken by social and geographical mobility. A family pattern has evolved in which the couple is often on its own after marriage. Marriage, for many, marks the final achievement of independence from parents, and the marital partners are expected to be the heads of their own family. Marriages, particularly in cities, often cross ethnic and religious lines. This rapid reshuffling of ethnic influences and the fracturing of kinship ties enable each generation to raise its children differently rather than according to set patterns that become unsuited to changing needs.† However, there is little assurance that a family which arises from the joining of two dissimilar backgrounds, rather than through the trial and error of many generations, will be suited for rearing stable children.**

The atomization of family life into isolated nuclear families has placed many additional strains upon the family and its members. As Parsons and Bales (1955) have properly pointed out, the high divorce rates and even higher incidence of marital conflict do not bespeak a diminishing importance of the family, as has so often been assumed. Even though thirty-seven percent of marriages end in divorce, eighty percent of the millon people who are divorced in the United States each year remarry. The high divorce rate reflects not only the greater ease in obtaining a divorce, but also the greater strain due to the number of functions subsumed by the nuclear family and which must be carried out by the spouses alone. The wife, particularly during the years when her children are young, is not only overburdened but apt to lead a relatively isolated life at home. Her education for running a household and raising children is likely to be meager.

---

* In recent years a good deal has been written about the instabilities and unsuitability of the nuclear family when the *isolated* nuclear family is meant. "Nuclear family" simply means the parents and their children, an entity that exists everywhere, even within extended families, except, possibly, in a few societies.

† Differentiating so sharply between extended and isolated nuclear families serves to accentuate some of the problems confronting the family as an institution in the United States at the present time. In actuality a large proportion of families do not fit clearly into either category but are parts of modified extended families in which the spouses are the heads of their nuclear family but can expect support from their parents and siblings, particularly in emergencies.

** Overt and clear communication of needs, wishes, and expectations becomes increasingly important to intrafamilial harmony, as roles and role expectations become less definite and less implicitly understood by the family members. What had been implicitly understood in the family of origin may be misunderstood in the marital family. Such considerations enter into the efforts of psychiatrists and marital counselors to improve verbal communication between couples.

Caught up in cleaning, cooking, diapering, laundering, shopping, she thinks longingly of the days when she, too, left the home to work. The husband finds that when he returns from work his home is not a place for relaxation and romance but requires his presence as an auxiliary nursemaid, handyman, gardener, playmate for children. In most societies many of these functions are carried out by persons other than the spouses; and in many places couples do not necessarily expect companionship or even sexual gratification from one another. The discrepant expectations which spouses may have of one another because they come from different backgrounds has been aggravated by the notable shifts in the division of tasks between husbands and wives, with the need for conscious agreement about who will do what. In recent years, however, the stability of marriage probably has diminished, because more women, having only one or two children and the capacity to support themselves, are willing to accept or seek divorce than formerly. Further, fewer people seem willing to continue with marriages that do not provide personal gratification and continuing sexual pleasure.

Social and Ethnic Differences

No society is homogeneous and its component families reflect its subdivisions in their structure and functioning. Subdivisions exist according to social class, ethnic-religious groupings, and race. Although social class divisions are not as striking in the United States as in many other countries, they are still very significant; and the admixture of ethnic groups that have immigrated to America has resulted in a wide variation in family forms and practices. Children are raised very differently according to the social position of the parents and according to ethnic origins, particularly in families that have not yet been assimilated. The traditions taught, the expectations held, the role examples provided, and the intellectual atmosphere afforded the child vary from social class to social class. Even though great opportunity for upward social mobility exists in the United States, the classes tend to perpetuate themselves through the differing ways in which they rear their children.* The boy in a lower-class family will, in general, complete

---

* A conventional way of dividing the population according to social class is to subdivide each of the usual upper-, middle- and lower-class groupings into upper and lower subclasses. Families can be allocated into the six categories adequately according to a scale based on place of residence and the occupation and education of the parents (Hollingshead and Redlich, 1958). Although such categorization divides up a continuum, clear-cut differences in living patterns and child rearing typify the social class groupings; and the differences are fairly sharp between groups that are not adjacent in the scale—for example, the lower-upper class and the lower-middle class are notably different.

twelve years of schooling with reluctance and will have virtually finished his personality development by his mid-teens. The upper-middle and upper-class families will expect children to gain at least a college degree and continue to expand their horizons into their twenties, permitting them to remain more or less dependent upon parental support. Although the topic cannot be pursued here, the influences are far-reaching—affecting, for example, the prevalence of different types of physical and emotional illness in each social class (Hollingshead and Redlich, 1958).*

A relationship often exists between ethnic groupings and social class, as when one ethnic group is subjugated by another (as the African by the slaveholder) or when a displaced group finds a humble refuge in a new country. However, ethnic groups tend to perpetuate themselves because of their adherence to customs that afford their members a feeling of identity. The methods of child rearing which are unconsciously accepted as proper, and which are the only spontaneous methods that the parents know, promote the continuity. The people of the United States constitute an agglomerate of ethnic groups which are gradually shedding their prior cultural heritages to assume an American way of life—a culture of somewhat indefinite characteristics which is in the process of formation or constant reformation as it assimilates characteristics of different groups. Some ethnic groups such as the Mennonites, Hassidic Jews, and some Greek Orthodox communities, seek to guard against assimilation and try to maintain a strict hold over each new generation in order to preserve a separate identity. The customs of such groups are notably divergent from those of the general community. Other groups seek to become assimilated while maintaining some separate identity, whereas still others tend to lose the desire for separateness after one or two generations.

However, even after considerable assimilation has taken place, the way in which the family is structured and functions frequently contains many elements of Old World patterns which the parents continue to carry within them without knowing it. An understanding of children's development and the tasks they encounter requires recognition of such ethnic and religious differences. The Irish-American child may grow up influenced by the mother's tendency to treat her husband like a grown-up child, pretending to

---

* The lower-lower class has particular importance to the medical- and social-oriented professions because it is composed largely of persons who have sedimented out, so to speak, because of the emotional instability of the homes in which they were raised, and many members are no longer capable of forming families that can properly rear a new generation. Perhaps too little attention has been paid to the difference between lower-class families that have not yet had an opportunity to raise their positions, such as immigrant families or black families recently migrated northward, and those lower-class families that have fallen back or remained lower-lower class because of chronic emotional instability over several generations.

believe the fabricated tales he tells and admiring his ability to tell them; and while she seems to defer to her husband's authority, she holds the family reins tightly in her own hands, at the same time ceding to the church a superordinate authority which must not be questioned. The boys and girls in such families grow up with very different ideas and feelings about their respective roles and responsibilities, and with different reactions to male and female authority figures from those of children in those German-American families which retain the strict discipline of a stern father who is almost unapproachable to the child, but in which the mother acts as a go-between, knowing how to circumvent her husband by being deferential and concerned with his comfort while swaying him to yield to a child's wishes. Children with parents of southern Italian origins may be influenced by the expectation that they maintain strong ties to their extended family, and may be puzzled about their parents' seeming irreligiosity, for their attitude to the church is much more relaxed than that of the Irish children in the neighborhood and of the Polish priest, who is so rigid in his expectations of children. Jews, even after several generations in the United States, may be surprised to learn that some of their attitudes concerning health and education as well as a variety of family customs are not idiopathic to the family but clearly derive from customs of Eastern European Jews.*

The Afro-American Family

The situation of American blacks presents some special problems. In contrast to immigrant groups in the United States, most of whose members manage to emerge from lower-class status within one or two generations, blacks, because of their earlier status as slaves, their skin color, and the rural, uneducated background of many who recently migrated to cities, have not been able to become upwardly mobile as readily. A significant proportion are threatened with permanent lower-class status because of family disorganization in the inner-city slums. We are not considering here the ever increasing number of black families who are middle class,

---

* The anthropological and sociological reconstruction of the Eastern European Jewish communities wiped out by the Nazis, Life Is with People (Zborowski and Herzog, 1952), shows that, even though separated for several hundred years, such communities in different countries preserved identical customs, many of which are reflected in contemporary American-Jewish practices, value systems, and attitudes. A comparison of this volume with Thomas and Znaniecki's classic study, The Polish Peasant in Europe and America, offers a striking contrast of two cultures occupying the same physical environment—as striking as comparisons of the Navajo and Hopi, or the Fijians with the Indians living in Fiji. Italian-Americans can gain an appreciation of the origins of many of their family patterns by reading the novels and short stories of Varga (1953) or such books as Italian or American? The Second-Generation Conflict (Child, 1943).

even though their children are commonly confronted by serious problems because of their race. Many of the ways of life and of rearing children that have been considered characteristic of lower-class black families are simply attributes of lower-class families. The status of Afro-American and Latin American families in the New York inner city (Minuchin *et al.*, 1967) and of white, lower-class families in Boston (Pavenstedt, 1967) shows many basic similarities because all three are essentially without cultural tradition and similar types of disorganization are common to all. Relative lack of concern for the future, a high prevalence of broken homes, adolescent pregnancies, and premature reliance on older siblings to care for very young children are common. However, other factors bear consideration. The Afro-Americans brought to the Americas as slaves were largely cut off from their own ethnic groups, and their traditions were totally unsuited to life in slavery. Culture heroes and ideal figures who provide a people with models and self-esteem were forgotten. Frequently, slave owners paid little attention to family formation, couples were separated, and women were used for breeding slaves and as sexual objects of whites. Children were often raised without fathers, and the women had to take an unusual degree of responsibility for child rearing. The mother-centered family became a pattern that tends to persist, affording the boy an inadequate role model to follow into manhood.* Because of meager economic opportunities, the man has difficulty in achieving or maintaining adequate self-esteem. Problems such as these continue to aggravate those created by poor education and economic deprivation, and they obviously seriously influence the children's development.†

---

* In lower-class black families, sons are frequently rejected by their mothers, who prefer to have daughters. Such rejection is commonly accompanied by maternal domination, which increases the boy's lack of self-esteem as well as his hostility toward women. Grier and Cobb, in their book *Black Rage*, argue that black mothers purposely reject and emasculate sons to prepare them for their menial place in a white world. This is not what one hears from such mothers who gain little gratification from sons because they expect them to get into trouble and become a burden, and because the mother, as a child, had no father to give her affection, and, as a woman often has no consistent spouse to give her the love and support that would lead her to love his son. Without a stable and consistent father figure in the home the boy has no satisfactory male model to identify with and follow into adulthood, but only the model of a male intruder into the home, whom he resents. All too early, he follows the directives of peer groups, unchecked by a father he would like to emulate but only by the admonitions and punishments of a mother whose affectionate care is disrupted by the need to be a controlling and punitive figure. Here, as in many other family situations, a cycle has been established that tends to repeat itself from generation to generation.

† An excellent presentation of the background problems can be found in E. F. Frazier's *The Negro Family in the United States*. See also the Daedalus issue on "The Negro American," the U.S. Department of Labor report on *The Negro Family: The Case for National Action*, Comer's *Beyond Black and White*, and Myrdal's *American Dilemma*.

RECONSTITUTED FAMILIES

As over a quarter of all marriages in the United States are now second marriages, the topic of families containing a stepparent requires consideration. Eighty percent of the nearly one million persons who get divorced each year remarry, and increasingly such remarriages involve children.* Divorce in itself creates problems for developing children. Their security is diminished; the value of one parent as a model for identification and the other as a basic love object can be undermined, conflicts in loyalties occur, and many other functions of the family are affected. However, parental divorce may not be as injurious for children as living with parents who are seriously incompatible. The effects of divorce are accentuated when parents derogate their former spouses to their children and seek to turn the children against the other parent.

The reconstituted family, even when it provides a more favorable setting than the original family, almost always creates some significant difficulties for the children—a topic that we can only touch upon here. Commonly children are jealous of their parents' relationships to their new spouses, a situation aggravated for older children by their perception of the newly reweds' heightened sexual interests in one another. The chances of an adolescent girl's becoming pregnant increase shortly after her mother's remarriage (Fleck *et al.*, 1956). The child's obligation to conform with a parent's "visiting privileges"—decided by the parents themselves or by the court at the time of separation—interferes with the child's friendships and more natural schedule of activities. Each parent may seek to equal if not outdo the other in winning a child's affection and thus spoil the child, as when the child must go on vacation with each parent. Less fortunately, each parent resents the time and money he or she must give the child because of the disinterest of the other parent. The reshuffling of space, possessions, and affection with stepsiblings who live in the home or who visit in it creates difficulties. Stepparents are often reluctant to exert needed discipline. Parents become jealous of affection given to their children by

---

* In 1974 the parents of over a million children were divorced, involving approximately twice as many children as in 1965. A still larger proportion of second than first marriages end in divorce, a situation largely due to the fact that about eighty percent of second marriages in the lower socioeconomic segments of society break up. See L. A. Westoff, "Two Time Winners."

As every child knows from reading folktales about wicked stepmothers, reconstituted families were also common in the past. High maternal mortality in childbirth and infectious diseases created numerous widowers and widows—but remarriage after divorce differs from remarriage after the death of a spouse.

stepparents or of a child's preference for the stepparent. Then, too, the children, who are in many ways the persons most affected by a divorce, rarely have a say in their own disposition. The difficulties that ensue when one parent, usually though not always the father, simply deserts are, of course, still more serious.* Reconstituted families can, and often do, form good developmental settings for children, but it requires considerable understanding and effort on the part of all of the three or four parents involved.

SINGLE–PARENT FAMILIES

Currently one child in six is being raised by a single parent in the United States, a situation aggravated by poverty for about one of every ten children.† Almost a million children are being raised by fathers alone. Of course, one-parent families are nothing new. Widows, divorced persons, and unmarried mothers have managed to raise children by themselves successfully but rarely without considerable difficulty. Recently some women have preferred to have children and raise them without being married, and adoption agencies have given children to single parents of both sexes. Most single parents, particularly those who work, must rely heavily on neighbors, friends, babysitters, and care-taking agencies. We have already considered why a child properly needs a parent of each sex; but one competent parent is better than none. Here we must note that a parent also properly needs a partner to share the pleasures as well as the tasks and decisions involved in raising a child. Unless a person is not only highly motivated and very well organized but also capable of gaining considerable satisfaction from nurturing and being needed, he or she is likely to feel restricted, burdened, and, at times, overwhelmed by the task.**

* The problems are far from new, simply more common. Henry James sensitively considered the plight of an upper-class girl after her parents' divorce in *What Maisie Knew*.

† Figures are unreliable because welfare laws in the United States currently make it financially rewarding for some parents to live apart when the father's earnings are low. How many fathers simply live at other addresses but have not really deserted cannot be ascertained.

** The single-parent family, as many other topics in this chapter, is a complex subject that transcends the scope of this book. Unmarried adolescent mothers, particularly if black, usually remain in the parental home.

NEW FAMILY FORMS*

Over the past ten to fifteen years a number of persons who have been dissatisfied with the families in which they grew up or with their own marriages have suggested, and some have tried out, new types of marriage or substitutes for marriage which they believe will be more satisfactory for children as well as adults. The family, particularly the isolated nuclear family, is regarded as the source of all social evil, as the root of most individual unhappiness, and sometimes as an institution created by men to enslave women. The condemnations reflect an appreciation of the critical moment of the family in human affairs and the difficulties the contemporary family has in meeting the needs of spouses and children.

Various ways of living and rearing children have been suggested and carried out, such as: two or more couples living together, sharing housekeeping and child-care functions (and in some arrangements, sharing spouses); both spouses working half-time to enable one of them to be at home with the children; living in communes, with or without distinct individual marriages; contract marriages or non-marital relationships with a prior provision for separation; homosexual marriages; marriage only after the birth of a child; serial monogamy; etc. Some of these arrangements are attempts to avoid or diminish the commitments of marriage and at the same time to regain some of the dependency that was lost in separating from parents.

The communal forms of living are endeavors to retrieve advantages of the extended family. The desire for communal life, when not simply a wish to "drop out" of Western civilization, has been fostered by the Israeli kibbutz—though few, if any, communes have had the organization and discipline of the kibbutz—and also by the alluring picture presented in Skinner's *Walden Two*.† When effectively organized, communes permit

---

* Dual career marriages, in which serious efforts are made to enable the wife to continue her career and, when possible, not consider it secondary to her husband's, will be discussed in the chapter on marital adjustment.

† The Israeli kibbutz is a carefully planned and well-organized institution that seeks to fit into and be useful to the larger society, and in which members work hard to make the kibbutz economically viable. The kibbutz method of raising children collectively in nurseries and then in special children's units in accord with the kibbutz pioneers' socialist beliefs, has also been a means of making it possible for the women to work, as required by the circumstances, without permitting their absence to affect the children deleteriously. However, very careful attention is paid to providing adequate mothering and individual attention by substitute mothers. No effort is made to minimize the importance of the biological parents, who spend considerable time with the child after work each day, perhaps giving the child more of their undivided attention than parents in most

sharing of the tasks of living and can free the women for work outside the home. Sharing the care of children can lessen the ties of the child to the mother, which some people consider desirable. It is difficult to discuss the feasibility, advantages, and disadvantages of communal living because communes differ, because few people, as far as the author knows, remain in communes for more than a few years, and because insufficient time has elapsed to judge the outcome for children.*

The feasibility and practicality of various other types of family relationships depend very greatly on the persons involved.† It is clearly simpler to find the faults in the more traditional family life than find workable solutions. One can only hope that, with clearer conceptualization of the functions of the family, some successful innovations will emerge, as did the kibbutz.

Parental Personality and the Family

Whatever the form of the family, the personalities of the parents will be a major factor in how the family functions and what sort of child rearing it provides. How a family enculturates its children depends greatly upon how the parents grew up and internalized their culture. They transmit the cultural ways to their offspring through the language they use, their ways of relating, the taboos which they unconsciously hold, their value systems,

---

societies. The author, on a recent trip to Israel, found that many kibbutz women now wish to modify communal child rearing, by having the children sleep in their own homes, and also to return to more traditional activities of women. Tiger and Shepher (1975) believe such changes, which run counter to the ideology of the kibbutz movement and the wishes of the men, express the deep-seated wishes of women, perhaps reflecting something basic in women's makeup.

Walden Two is, as a careful reader will note, essentially a fantasy, for Skinner does not consider many basic problems that must be solved if such communes are to exist in reality.

* However, according to the book *The Children of the Counterculture* by Rothchild and Wolf, the misunderstanding of the capacities and needs of children, the neglect of them, and cruelty toward them is widespread in both rural and urban communes, and resembles in some ways the treatment of children in urban slums by adolescent parents who cannot invest or "cathect" their children because of their own intense dependency needs.

† Some types, such as the O'Neills' "open marriage" (O'Neill and O'Neill, 1972) seek certain benefits by sacrificing some of the fundamental advantages of marriage (see Chapters 13 and 14) and do not solve critical child-rearing problems. Others seem almost bound to fail because they do not meet many of the family's child rearing functions that have been considered in this chapter. One common problem is that a marital relationship is difficult enough to maintain, and when couples live together in multiples, whatever the type, the difficulties are apt to be multiplied rather than alleviated unless boundaries between couples are maintained and a firm organization exists—conditions that many persons living in groups seek to avoid.

and their role assumptions and expectations more than they do through
what they consciously teach to their children. Family ways that reflect the
individuality of the parents and how they interrelate transcend ethnic, religious, and social class origins. One child may, for example, grow up in a
home filled with talk in which the mother happily recites nursery rhymes to
her totally uncomprehending infant, gives a cloth picture "book" as one of
the first playthings, and later reads the baby a story each night as part of
the bedtime ritual. The father in such a family may take the child on trips
and patiently respond to endless questions. Another child has a mother
who cannot be close and is annoyed when her child interrupts the fantasy
life that sustains her, and has a father who, like the child, feels excluded by
his wife and who has found refuge in his profession and rarely relates to
the child. Such differences will be referred to repeatedly in subsequent
chapters.

Not only is the family the setting in which the child's personality development takes place, but the parents' personalities and interactions as well as
the transactions of the family as a whole profoundly influence the child's
development and who the child becomes. In a sense, the parents' ways and
personalities enter into the child's makeup as much as do their genes.

The child requires not simply nurturance of inborn directives to achieve
a mature and workable personality, but positive direction and guidance in a
suitable interpersonal environment and social system. The positive molding
forces have been largely overlooked, because they are built into the institutions and mores of all societies and into the omnipresent family which
everywhere has knowingly or unknowingly been given the task of carrying
out the basic socialization and enculturation of the new generation. The
biological makeup of the human being requires that a child grow up in a
family or a reasonable substitute for it, not only for protection and nurturance but in order to be directed into becoming an integrated person who
has assimilated the techniques, knowledge, and roles required for adaptation and survival.

As we study the various essential functions of the family for the child,
we realize that studies of child rearing as well as much advice given to
parents have largely neglected the influence of the family as a unit upon the

child. Emphasis has been placed upon what parents should do for the child and with the child—the influence of natural childbirth, nursing, cuddling, weaning, bowel training, love, stimulation, etc., all of which are important and will be considered in the ensuing chapters. But perhaps it has been so obvious that it has been taken for granted and then often forgotten that what counts most of all is who the parents are, how they behave, how they relate to one another, and what sort of family they create, including that intangible—the atmosphere of the home.

REFERENCES

ABERLE, D. F. (1951). *The Psychosocial Analysis of a Hopi Life-History*, Comparative Psychology Monographs, vol. 21, no. 1., Serial No. 107. University of California Press, Berkeley.

ACKERMAN, N. (1958). *The Psychodynamics of Family Life*. Basic Books, New York.

BERNSTEIN, B. (1974). *Class, Codes and Control: Theoretical Studies Toward a Sociology of Language*. Schocken Books, New York.

BOTT, E. (1955). "Urban Families: Conjugal Roles and Social Network," *Human Relations*, 8:345–384.

BROWN, R. (1965). "Language: The System and Its Acquisition," in *Social Psychology*. Free Press, New York.

BRUCH, H. (1961). "Transformation of Oral Impulses in Eating Disorders," *Psychiatric Quarterly*, 35:458–481.

CHILD, I. (1943). *Italian or American? The Second-Generation Conflict*. Yale University Press, New Haven, Conn.

COMER, J. P. (1971). *Beyond Black and White*. Quadrangle Press, New York.

COOPER, D. (1971). *Death of the Family*. Pantheon, New York.

Daedalus, journal of the American Academy of Arts and Sciences; issue on "The Negro American," Fall, 1965.

ERIKSON, E. (1950). *Childhood and Society*. W. W. Norton, New York.

FLECK, S., *et al.* (1956). "Pregnancy as a Symptom of Adolescent Maladjustment," International Journal of Social Psychiatry, 2:118–131.

FRAZIER, E. F. (1939). *The Negro Family in the United States*. University of Chicago Press, Chicago.

FREUD, A., and BURLINGHAM, D. (1944). *Infants Without Families*. International Universities Press, New York.

GRIER, W., and COBB, P. M. (1968). *Black Rage*. Basic Books, New York.

HOLLINGSHEAD, A. B., and REDLICH, F. C. (1958). *Social Class and Mental Illness*. John Wiley & Sons, New York.

JAMES, H. (1897). *What Maisie Knew*. Penguin Books, New York, 1974.

LIDZ, T. (1963a). "The Family, Language, and Ego Functions," in *The Family and Human Adaptation: Three Lectures*. International Universities Press, New York.

——— (1963b). *The Family and Human Adaptation: Three Lectures*. International Universities Press, New York.

LIDZ, T., FLECK, S., and CORNELISON, A. (1965). *Schizophrenia and the Family*. International Universities Press, New York.

MINUCHIN, S., *et al.* (1967). *Families of the Slums*. Basic Books, New York.

MORGAN, M. (1974). *The Total Woman*. Fleming H. Revell, Old Tappan, N.J.

MYRDAL, G. (1962). *American Dilemma*. Harper & Row, New York.

O'NEILL, N., and O'NEILL, G. (1972). *Open Marriage*. Avon Books, New York.

PARSONS, T., and BALES, R. (1955). *Family, Socialization and Interaction Process*. Free Press, Glencoe, Ill.

PAVENSTEDT, E., ed. (1967). *The Drifters: Children of Disorganized Lower-Class Families*. Little, Brown, Boston.

ROTHCHILD, J., and WOLF, S. (1976). *The Children of the Counterculture*. Doubleday, New York.

SIMMONS, L. W. (1945). *Sun Chief: The Autobiography of a Hopi Indian*. Yale University Press, New Haven, Conn.

SKINNER, B. F. (1960). *Walden Two*. Macmillan, New York.

SPITZ, R. A. (1945). "Hospitalism: An Inquiry into the Genesis of Psychiatric Conditions in Early Childhood," *The Psychoanalytic Study of the Child*, vol. 1, pp. 53–74. International Universities Press, New York.

THOMAS, W., and ZNANIECKI, F. (1927). *The Polish Peasant in Europe and America*. Alfred A. Knopf, New York.

TIGER, L., and SHEPHER, J. (1975). *Women in the Kibbutz*. Harcourt Brace Jovanovich, New York.

U.S. DEPARTMENT OF LABOR, Office of Policy Planning and Research (1965). *The Negro Family: The Case for National Action*. U.S. Government Printing Office, Washington, D.C.

VARGA, G. (1953). *Little Novels of Sicily*. Grove Press, New York.

WESTOFF, L. A. (1975). "Two Time Winners," *New York Times Magazine*, August 10, pp. 10–15.

WHITING, B., ed. (1963). *Six Cultures: Studies of Child Rearing*. John Wiley & Sons, New York.

WHORF, B. L. (1939). "The Relation of Habitual Thought and Behavior to Language," in *Language, Thought, and Reality: Selected Writings of Benjamin Lee Whorf*. J. Carroll, ed. MIT Press and John Wiley & Sons, New York, 1956.

ZBOROWSKI, M., and HERZOG, E. (1952). *Life Is with People: The Jewish Little-Town of Eastern Europe*. International Universities Press, New York.

ZIMMERMAN, C. (1947). *Family and Civilization*. Harper Bros., New York.

SUGGESTED READING

ANTHONY, E. J., and KOUPERNIK, C. eds. (1974). *The Child in His Family*. Wiley-Interscience, New York.

BELL, N., and VOGEL, E., eds. (1960). *A Modern Introduction to the Family*. Free Press, Glencoe, Ill.

LIDZ, T. (1963). *The Family and Human Adaptation: Three Lectures*. International Universities Press, New York.

MINUCHIN, S., et al. (1967). *Families of the Slums*. Basic Books, New York.

PARSONS, T., and BALES, R. (1955). *Family, Socialization and Interaction Process*. Free Press, Glencoe, Ill.

PAVENSTEDT, E., ed. (1967). *The Drifters: Children of Disorganized Lower-Class Families*. Little, Brown, Boston.

ROSSI, A. (1972). "Family Development in a Changing World," *American Journal of Psychiatry*, 128:1057–1066.

SIMPSON, G. (1960). *People in Families*. Thomas Y. Crowell, New York.

PART II

The Life Cycle

CHAPTER 3

❁

The Life Cycle

INTRODUCTION

IN THE ENSUING CHAPTERS we shall follow the child through the life cycle, the infant's course from the emergence from the mother's womb along the circuitous route until, weighted by years and with dimming memory, the person returns to the earth, the mother of all living things. No two persons are alike, and the path one follows is never the same as another's, for we are part of the infinite variety of an inexhaustible nature. The course of life that we intend to follow will be an abstraction that is no one's, but that of Everyman and Everywoman containing the essentials of all.

Despite the uniqueness of each individual and the different ways and varied environments in which we are raised, all of us are endowed with physical makeups that are essentially alike and with similar biological needs that must be met. In common with all living things our lives go through a cycle of maturation, maturity, decline, and death. In common with all human beings each of us goes through a prolonged period of dependent immaturity, forms intense bonds to those who nurture us, and never becomes free of our need for others; and we mature sexually relatively late as if the evolutionary process took into account our needs to learn how to live and how to raise our offspring. Each of us requires many years to learn adaptive techniques and become an integrated person, and we depend upon a culture and a society to provide our essential environments; we rely upon thought and foresight to find our paths through life and therefore become aware of the passage of time and our changing position in the life cycle. From an early age we know that the years of our lives are numbered; at times we bemoan the fact and at times we are glad of it; but in some way we learn to come to terms with our mortality and the realization that our lives are one-time ventures in a very small segment of time and space. These and many other such similarities make possible the generalizations and abstractions necessary for the scientific study of personality development.

THE PHASIC NATURE OF PERSONALITY DEVELOPMENT AND THE LIFE CYCLE

The development of the personality* and the course of the life cycle unfold in phases, not at a steady pace. The process is not like climbing up a hill and down the other side, but more akin to a Himalayan expedition during which camps must be made at varying altitudes, guides found, the terrain explored, skills acquired, rests taken before moving up to the next level, and the descent is also made in stages. Children go through periods of relative quiescence and then undergo another marked change as they move into a new phase of life, which opens new potentialities, provides new areas to explore, and poses new challenges for them to master and requires them to learn new sets of skills and abilities. Thus, when infants learn to crawl and can move toward objects that attract them, a new world opens before them that enables them to channel their ebullient energies in new ways, permits a new zest to become manifest, and opens up opportunities for new learning. But it also alters their mothers' lives and the relationships between mother and child, and they will have to learn to relate differently, expect rewards for different types of performance, and gain greater control of their own behavior before achieving a new relative equilibrium. Whereas

---

* In discussing the life cycle we follow a convention whose purpose is to lessen confusion by using the word *maturation* when referring to biological unfolding and physical growth, and *development* when referring to personality functions.

their parents had always been delighted with any display of new activities, now they seek to restrain or somehow limit behavior, and a child has difficulty in adjusting to such changed attitudes. Similarly, a child may have settled down into a reasonably stable relationship with family and peers, and found a suitable pace and place in the school world, when the sudden spurt of growth that precedes puberty alters the proportions of the body, almost making it unfamiliar to its owner, and then the surges of sexual feelings aroused by hormonal changes must be managed; and a period of relative calm and security has ended.

The phasic nature of the life cycle derives from several interlocking factors.

1. The acquisition of certain abilities must wait upon the maturation of the organism. The infant cannot become a toddler until the nerve tracts that permit voluntary discrete movements of the lower limbs become functional. However, even after maturation permits the acquisition of a new attribute, gaining the skills and knowledge to develop it is a very lengthy procedure, but is amenable to specific training and education. The amount of practice required before children can properly use their hands and learn to measure space three-dimensionally is enormous; but because much of it seems random movement or play, the quantity is rarely appreciated. Adequate mastery of simple skills must precede their incorporation into more complicated activities.

In a similar way phasic shifts in the physical equilibrium of the organism initiate new phases in the life cycle. The metamorphosis of puberty furnishes a prime example of how new inner forces provoke change without regard to prior developmental progress.

2. The individual's cognitive development plays a significant role in creating phasic shifts. The capacity to assume responsibility for the self and the direction of one's own life depends upon the increasing abilities to think, to communicate, and to know the nature of the world and of the people with whom one lives. The child's cognitive development does not progress at an even pace, for qualitatively different capacities emerge in rather discrete stages.

3. The society, through the child's parents, peers, and the roles it establishes for persons of differing ages, sets expectations that promote shifts in life patterns. At the age of five or six, for example, a child is moved into the role of the schoolchild which includes many new demands as well as new privileges. Becoming a married person involves socially set expectations such as an ability and willingness to rescind areas of independence to care for and consider the needs of a spouse. But, in order for any society to

remain viable, the expectations and roles it establishes must be compatible with people's capacities and needs at each period of life.*

4. The child gains attributes, capacities, roles, and, particularly, capacities for self-control and self-direction by internalizing parental characteristics. Little children clearly need "surrogate egos" in the form of one or both parents to direct their lives. The internalization of these directive influences also takes place in stages in relationship to children's physical, intellectual, and emotional development and the expectations established for them.

5. The passage of time is, in itself, a determinant of phasic changes, not only because there is a need to move into age-appropriate roles, but also because changes in physical makeup require changed attitudes and self-concepts, as when people reach middle life and realize that their life story is approaching a climax.

THE EPIGENETIC PRINCIPLE

The epigenetic principle maintains that the critical tasks of each developmental phase must be met and surmounted at the proper time and in the proper sequence to assure healthy personality development. Psychoanalysis adopted the principle from embryology, in which the proper unfolding of the embryo depends upon each organ's arising out of its anlage in the proper sequence and at the proper time, with each development depending upon the proper unfolding of the preceding phase. If something happens that disturbs one aspect of the sequence, a series of maldevelopments follow in chain. Some such aspects of personality development are obvious: a child who does not gain adequate autonomy from the mother prior to going to school will have difficulty in remaining in school, learning there, and relating to classmates. Personality development is not, however, as

---

* Differences in societal institutions and role allocations create variations in some aspects of the life cycle in different societies and even in subsystems of the same society— including differences in just when some phasic shifts occur in the life cycle. Thus, the Okinawan child is expected to have very little capacity for self-direction before the age of five, but is given considerable responsibility, particularly for siblings, soon thereafter. Adolescence differs in societies in which sexual intercourse occurs freely at or before puberty from those in which adolescents are warned that intercourse before they are full grown will endanger their lives (Newman, 1965). Old age differs from the period in the United States in societies where people are aged at forty-five and very few live beyond fifty or sixty.

rigidly set as embryonic maturation; and even though development is impeded or altered when a developmental phase is not properly mastered, compensations are possible, and deficiencies can sometimes even be turned into strengths, which is not the case with the embryo. We once again recall Helen Keller, who did not learn to use language and remained very immature emotionally until she was seven, as an outstanding example of such plasticity in personality development.*

Progression, Fixation, and Regression

The course of any life contains a series of inevitable developmental crises that arise out of the need to meet the new challenges that are inherent in the life cycle. Through surmounting these crises the individual gains new strength, self-sufficiency, and integrity. The avoidance of challenge leads to stagnation. Each person meets each developmental crisis somewhat differently but similarities exist in the ways people meet similar developmental problems, and there is likely to be something repetitive in how the same individual surmounts various crises in life.

There is often a pause before a child achieves the confidence to venture into the strange uncertainties of a new phase of life. The need for emotional security sets limits upon the pace of development. The child constantly faces in two directions and is prey to opposing motivations. There is an inner impetus to expansion and the mastery of new skills and situations, a desire for greater independence and new prerogatives, and a wish to become more grown up like the parental figures the child seeks to emulate; but movement into new areas brings insecurity, inability to manage the new situation creates frustrations, and greater independence requires renunciation of the comforts of dependency. The ensuing anxieties tend to direct the child toward regaining the security of shelter and dependency and to renounce for a time further forward movement, or even to fall back to gain greater dependency.

Children need support and guidance to progress properly. In some instances, they may need to be restrained from unbridled and untutored use of new capacities, as when they first walk or when they first mature sexu-

---

* Perhaps Helen Keller was enabled to reach her unusual emotional and intellectual capacities because she had the brilliant Miss Sullivan constantly interpreting the world to her—a compensatory advantage that perhaps no other person has ever had. Another notable example is Monica, a girl with a gastric fistula studied by Engel and Reichman (1956) who despite a severe retardation in her development related to hospitalizations and a lengthy period of depressive apathy in early childhood has married and become a competent mother (Engel, 1974).

ally; whereas in other circumstances they may need help or even some prodding to move into the next phase, as when reluctant to leave the familiar home to attend school. The developmental hazards lie on both sides: too much support can lead the child to become overly dependent; too little can leave the child stranded or struggling to keep afloat.

The failure to master the essential tasks of a developmental phase leaves the child unprepared to move forward into the next phase. Emotional insecurity, lagging physical maturation, and premature pressures upon the child to cope before attaining the necessary skills and emotional mastery are among the major reasons for such failures. The child gives up and ceases to progress developmentally, or, more usually, moves ahead in some spheres but squanders energy in repetitive efforts to cope with old problems. Children who do not receive enough gratification during infancy may continue to suck their thumbs, seeking the gratification needed then; or school-age children who never gained adequate security in the home continue to seek maternal protection when their peers are secure with one another. Such developmental arrests are termed *fixations*. The movement backward to an earlier developmental phase in which the individual felt secure is termed *regression*;* and paradoxically regression is part of developmental progress, for all children will, at times, regress in order to regain security. They may fall back to regain stability after a forward thrust or when some external threat upsets their equilibrium and makes them anxious. Small children progress with security when they feel that parental protection can be found at the center of their expanding worlds, when needed.

Although fixations and regressions are means of maintaining or regaining security, they create insecurities in turn if they are not simply temporary expediencies. The child remains improperly prepared to meet the developmental tasks of the next phase of the life cycle and is unable to accept its opportunities and challenges.

Even though children are pulled in two directions and the desires to remain secure can be powerful, the motivations to move forward are greater. Children are carried along by their growth, by impulsions for stimulation and new experiences, by drives, by needs for approbation and affection from significant persons, by desires for companionship with peers,

---

* Regression is said to occur to points or levels of fixation. Freud (1916–1917) used the analogy of an advancing army leaving troops at strongholds along its line of march; this "fixation" of troops at the strongpoints progressively weakens the advancing contingents but provides a secure line to which to retreat if the army experiences a setback. However, it seems more suitable to consider fixation as repetitive attempts to resolve old unsolved problems or tasks, and regression as the gaining of relief from anxiety by returning to a period of security or to former ways that do not arouse anxiety.

by the body's yearning for another, by the needs of survival, by the roles provided by the society, by desires for progeny, by awareness of mortality, and by other such influences which we shall examine in the ensuing chapters.

THE STUDY OF PHASES
OF PERSONALITY DEVELOPMENT

The descriptions of the various stages of personality development that will be presented in this book evolved to a very large degree from four rather different approaches to understanding the phasic emergence of personality attributes: those of Freud, Sullivan, Erikson, and Piaget. As familiarity with these approaches is essential to understanding the literature and language of personality development and psychopathology, the orientations and the essential contributions of each of these theorists will be included in the presentation of various developmental stages even when they differ from, or even run counter to, the conceptualizations of the writer. In the following paragraphs only brief orienting material will be offered to provide a perspective concerning the emergence of the phasic and epigenetic approaches to personality development and an overview of these several orientations.

Freud's Phases of Psychosexual Development

Consequent to his epoch-making studies of childhood sexuality, but based primarily on his analytic studies of adults, Freud conceptualized five phases of psychosexual development between birth and maturity: the oral, anal, phallic or oedipal, latency, and genital phases.

In a strict sense Freud was not proposing stages in personality development but tracing the vicissitudes of the sexual energy which he posited and termed *libido* and deemed a prime motivating force in all human behavior. He considered that the libidinal investment (cathexis)* of the oral, anal,

---

* The German word *Besetzung* was unnecessarily translated by a neologism created from the Greek—*cathexis*—which has come into common usage not only in psychoanalysis but in many related fields. "Cathexis" connotes the charge that attaches the libidinal energy to something, analogous to a positive or negative charge in electricity. Actually, *Besetzung* can properly be translated by the term *investment*, in the sense of an army investing a stronghold, and "invest" or "investment" will be used in this

and phallic zones in turn was an inherent part of physical maturation. The origins of these concepts are significant because as foundations of psychoanalytic theory they continued—and continue—to exert profound influence upon the subsequent development of the theory.*

Freud also used the phases of psychosexual development in a broader sense, and when the concepts of the various postulated phases of childhood development were divested of such metaphysiological speculations, or when less attention was given to these concepts of energetics, they served to draw attention to important aspects of child development and the parent-child interaction. Thus, to note but a few examples, the critical importance of proper maternal nurturance during infancy to all future emotional security; the relationship between harsh and rigid bowel training to the development of obsessive-compulsive personality traits; the origins of certain adult sexual incompetencies in fixations during the oedipal phase—devolved from appreciation of the phasic nature of childhood development and the focusing upon the critical issues of each phase.

The oral phase is virtually equivalent to infancy, when the child's needs and energies focus upon nursing and close relatedness to the mother. It is a time of almost complete dependency, with intake at first largely passive but shifting to more active and aggressive incorporation as the infant matures. The lips and mouth are highly erotized and a primary source of sensuous gratification. Either too much or too little oral gratification or some innate predisposition to orality can supposedly cause fixation and unpreparedness to move into the subsequent phases.

The anal period follows, and attention was directed to it by the frequency of problems related to bowel functioning, by anal erotic practices in adults, and by certain character traits connected to withholding and letting go. Bowel training was considered a primary developmental task of the second year of life, and the anal zone a primary source of erotic gratification during the period. Fixations at the anal phase have been related to various character traits such as obsessiveness, stubbornness, miserliness, and many other related characteristics, as well as lasting erotization of the

---

book. The use of the word "cathexis" has become somewhat loose in much of the psychoanalytic literature.

* A theory, like a child, is permanently influenced by its early developmental phases, particularly if such early influences are relegated to the unconscious lest parental figures be offended. Freud had been considering that anxiety states were caused by a damming up of sexual fluids by inhibition or repression of sexual activity, and that neurasthenia was a resultant of excessive sexual activity. The idea of a sexual fluid playing a major role in the production of certain neuroses continued in the modified form of a libido that cathected the various erogenous zones, and that was at first autoerotically invested in the self and then in one or another external object.

anal orifice. The specific focus on the anal area would appear to have been due to the emphasis on strict bowel training in Freud's cultural setting.

In the *phallic* or *oedipal* period the primary erogenous zone has been considered to shift to the penis in the boy and the clitoris in the girl with an upsurge of sexual feelings toward the parent of the opposite sex. The boy's wish to possess the mother and be rid of the rival father, and the girl's desire for the father and jealousy of the mother—the oedipal situation—come in conflict with reality, create fear of retribution from the hated parent, and lead the child to repress his or her sexual feelings and possessiveness of the desired parent. Instead, the boy pursues the more realistic goal of ultimately becoming a person like his father who can possess a person like his mother, and the reverse occurs in the girl with variations and differences that will be elaborated in the presentation of the oedipal phase. The child gains strength by identifying with the previously hated and feared parent, internalizes parental controls, and becomes more oriented to reality.* Various problems inherent in the conceptualization, such as the idea that the boy always internalizes a hated and feared father, and the evidence that the girl's development is not a mirror image of the boy's, will be considered in Chapters 7 and 8. The "oedipal transition" is considered a central event in personality development and critical to the patterning of all subsequent interpersonal relationships.

Following the resolution of the oedipal conflicts the child enters the *latency* period—a period when sexual impulses are supposedly latent, either because of a biological subsidence of libido or because of the repression of the sexual impulses that seem to children to endanger them.

The *genital* phase starts with the upsurge of puberty, with an erogenous reinvestment of the phallus in the male but supposedly with a shift from the

---

* The oedipal complex was named by Freud after the mythical king of Thebes who unknowingly fulfilled his predicted fate by killing his father, Laius, and marrying his mother, Jocasta, after solving the famous riddle of the Sphinx. When eventually the incestuous nature of the marriage was revealed, Jocasta hanged herself and Oedipus blinded himself. Freud considered that the myth symbolized an unconscious wish in all men that had to be overcome in their lives, and that unresolved residua created problems for everyone but serious problems for some that explained much psychopathology. Freud did not invent the oedipus complex; he discovered it. The story of Oedipus is the myth of the hero found (in one variant or another) in virtually all parts of the world: the tale of the child supposedly put to death lest he eventually kill his father or some father-substitute but who grows up in a foreign land and returns unknowingly to kill his father and marry his mother. Among the most primitive versions are the very ancient myths of Uranus and Kronos, and among the most sophisticated variants that of Shakespeare's Hamlet (Lidz, 1975).

It should be noted that the Oedipus myth proper concerns a father who feared the rivalry of his son (reflecting his own feelings to his father) and a mother who was willing to commit infanticide for her husband's sake. Some myths hold that Laius introduced sodomy into Attica.

clitoris to the vagina in the girl. If individuals pass through all previous phases without undue fixations, they become capable of mature sexuality. The capacity for genital sexuality was originally equated with the achievement of emotional maturity.

The Orientations of Sullivan and Erikson

The modifications of psychoanalytic developmental theory formulated by Harry Stack Sullivan (1946–47) and by Erik Erikson (1950) have particular pertinence to the orientation of this book.

Sullivan emphasized the importance of the interpersonal transactions between parents and child and the child's development in a social system; and he thus became an important influence in bringing psychoanalytic theory into a working relationship with the behavioral sciences. He also directed attention to the importance of the juvenile period, and, rather than letting it remain the "latency phase," emphasized the influence of the school and peer groups on the child's development, and how they could offset the intrafamilial influences. He also considered the critical significance of the events of adolescence.

Psychosocial Phases of the Life Cycle

Erikson also opened new approaches by superimposing an epigenesis of psychosocial development upon the psychosexual phases, and by designating the critical psychosocial task of each phase that the individual must surmount in order to be prepared for the next stage. A developmental crisis, so to speak, is inherent in each phase, for the sequence of maturation and development presents new essential problems with which the person must cope. Erikson also went beyond the traditional psychoanalytic psychosexual phases that end with the "genital phase." He emphasized the critical moment of late adolescence, when the personality must gel and a person achieve an ego identity and a capacity for intimacy, and then continued to consider the critical tasks of adult stages of the life cycle. He has formulated eight stages of psychosocial development, focusing upon the specific developmental tasks of each phase and how the society meets the needs of providing essential care, promoting independence, offering roles, and having institutionalized ways of assuring children's survival, their proper socialization, and their emotional health. The critical tasks of each phase are handled more or less differently in each culture.

As Erikson's paradigms will be discussed when we consider the specific developmental periods, only a résumé will be presented here. In the oral phase of psychosexual development the psychosocial task concerns achievement of a *basic trust* in the self and others, with failures leading to varying degrees of *basic mistrust*; the "basic" is emphasized to convey that the task is not particularly conscious but blends into and forms an inherent component of the total personality. Emphasis in the second year of life is upon the attainment of muscular control in general rather than upon bowel control in particular. In learning self-control the child properly gains a lasting sense of *autonomy*, whereas loss of self-esteem and shaming in the process lead to a pervasive sense of *doubt* and *shame*. In the phallic period the resolution of the oedipal crisis leads to a heightening of conscience, and it is the time when the child needs to develop the prerequisites for masculine or feminine *initiative* or become prey to a deep and lasting *sense of guilt*. The latency period moves the child to school, where the gaining of admiration, approval, and affection depends upon achievement, and now the child must acquire a capacity for *industry* or become subject to an enduring sense of *inferiority*. Erikson then departs from emphasizing the relationship between genital sexuality and emotional maturity and focuses upon the attainment of an ego synthesis by the end of adolescence that affords a sense of *ego identity*, "the accrued confidence that one's ability to maintain an inner sameness and continuity is matched by the sameness and continuity of one's meaning for others" (Erikson, 1959); and if this is not attained the person is subject to *identity diffusion*. After achieving a sense of identity, young adults can move on to achieve a true *intimacy* with another with the concomitant capacity to *distantiate* the self from forces or people whose essence is dangerous to their own; failure almost inevitably leads to *self-absorption*. Then, an interest in producing, guiding, and laying the foundations for the next generation makes the capacity for *generativity* the critical issue in the next phase of adulthood, with *stagnation* the negative outcome. The final phase in the schema concerns the achievement of mature dignity and *integrity* through acceptance of "one's own and only life cycle" and responsibility for how it has turned out, whereas *despair* involves the feeling that this one chance has been wasted and has, in essence, been worthless.

The approach takes cognizance of the fact that the child grows into a social system and must assimilate its institutions and roles, and helps eliminate the untenable concept that civilization through requiring repression is inimical to man's freedom. The specific dichotomies utilized to characterize the critical issues of each phase sharpen the appreciation of the need to cope with tasks rather than simply to pass through a phase free of traumatic influence.* Still, the critical issues selected neglect other developmental tasks that seem just as vital, and some that are more important.

Piaget's Approach to the Study of Cognitive Development

Another extremely important approach to the study of the child's development is found in the monumental work of Jean Piaget and his school. The child's cognitive development forms the core of these studies. Piaget has sought to trace and conceptualize the epigenetic development of intelligence, language, reasoning, concepts of nature, and the emergence of the categories of time, space, causality, etc.; but his studies of the child's moral development and of the child's play and dreams have also provided new insights and stimulation. Piaget has given but passing attention to the child's emotional development and to interpersonal and social influences upon development, which leaves some serious deficiencies in his observations, explanations, and theory.†

As Piaget's work has been carried out in a totally different frame of reference from the analytically oriented approaches that we have been considering, and as those unfamiliar with his work may find it difficult to grasp his conceptualizations, a very cursory introduction to Piagetian concepts and terms is offered in the following paragraphs.**

* The orientation, however, remains attached to a system of psychosexual phases based on libidinal shifts, even though it places minimal emphasis upon libidinal concepts and more upon the observable unfolding of the individual in his cultural setting, somewhat in contrast to the formulations of the psychoanalytic ego psychology of Hartmann, Kris, and Loewenstein (1946), and others. Hartmann's important contributions are not discussed in this chapter, as they have greater importance to efforts to reorganize and revitalize psychoanalytic theory than to developmental psychology (Hartmann, 1958, 1964). Unfortunately, his initial emphasis upon the emergence and development of "autonomous ego functions" in social systems became enmeshed in efforts to adhere to libido theory with consequent concepts of neutralization of aggressive and libidinal drives, the positing of countercathexes, etc.

† Piaget has been interested primarily in epistemology and set out to investigate how people learn to know and the psychological foundations of knowing. His studies led to the discovery and description of a vast amount of knowledge about child development. In evaluating Piaget's work, we must realize his intentions and not criticize him for not studying what we wish he would have studied. However, Piaget follows the French intellectual tradition and Ariès has commented in his book *Centuries of Childhood* that until recently child development meant to the French the child's intellectual development.

** The uninitiated may find it difficult to find their way into the hundreds of articles and numerous books dealing with various aspects of Piaget's work. Fortunately, a number of useful introductions to it are now available. The reader is referred to *The Psychology of the Child*, which Piaget and Inhelder wrote in 1969 as a synthesis of their studies of cognition; and to J. H. Flavell's *The Developmental Psychology of Jean Piaget*, which provides a fairly comprehensive and highly useful introduction that permits the serious student to read meaningfully in Piaget's various works, particularly pages 41–67 for an introduction to the basic theory.

Piaget has traced the ever increasing scope of the child's abilities by the constant process of adaptation of the existing state of the organism to new experiences. Children cannot utilize experiences which their cognitive capacities are not yet ready to assimilate. The foundations for experiencing develop step by step through the expansion and reorganization of existing capacities as children take in new experiences, and thereby become prepared to react to and utilize more complex experiences. The process of cognitive development is, thus, a very active process in which the organism is, in a sense, ever reaching out to incorporate new experience within the limits permitted by its capacities and organization at that moment in its development. Piaget's theory posits a constant cognitive reorganization that is more dynamic than either associational psychology, learning theory, or operant conditioning psychology. His observations are of great importance to any conceptualization of the life cycle not only because they provide guides to how the child and adolescent regard the world and can think about it at each stage of development, but also because of the interrelationship between children's development of autonomy and their cognitive capacities.*

The reader is likely to be puzzled and even discouraged by the unfamiliar terminology that is an inherent part of Piagetian psychology. Terms such as "aliment," "assimilation," "accommodation," "schema," and "egocentricity" have specific and rather idiosyncratic meanings, and other terms such as "circular reactions" and "decentering" are unique to the system. They do not, however, pose too formidable a barrier. The *aliment* is new experiential food which furnishes the nutriment for cognitive growth. The aliment is *assimilated* by the cognitive processes insofar as they are prepared to do so, and the cognitive processes *accommodate* to include what has been assimilated, reorganizing and expanding in the process. The term *schema* is used primarily in describing the first developmental period, that of sensori-motor development.† A schema is a cognitive structure to which experiences are assimilated, and which reorganize in the process. There are "sucking" schemata, "visual," "grasping," "hearing," and other schemata. The organism, so to speak, repeats activities that have produced new experiences, setting up *circular reactions* in order to gain the reward of new aliment until the aliment is thoroughly assimilated into the schema that has accommodated to it. The development

---

* The interrelationship had been almost completely neglected in psychoanalytic theories of development and of psychopathology until recently. See Gouin Decarie (1966), Burgner and Edgcumbe (1972), and Blatt (1974).

† Schemata are, so to speak, the preverbal sensori-motor equivalents of a system of relations and classes. See Piaget, *The Origins of Intelligence in Children*, p. 385.

of the child's cognitive abilities through increasingly complex circular reactions will be described in subsequent chapters, which, it is hoped, will help clarify these basic concepts of Piaget's system.*

Piaget's Developmental Periods

Piaget has divided cognitive development into four major periods, which in turn are subdivided into a number of stages and substages. The *sensorimotor* period, which lasts from birth through the first eighteen to twenty-four months, essentially covers preverbal intellectual development. The development of the child's ways of interacting with the world is traced, step by step, from the primitive reflex sucking, hand movements, and the random eye movements of the neonate to the stage when the child uses internalized visual and motoric symbols to invent new means of solving problems at a very simple level. The *preoperational* period follows and lasts until about the time the child enters school. Children become capable of using symbols and language. They do not yet have the ability to appreciate the role of another and adapt what they say to the needs of the listener, to note contradictions, or to construct a chain of reasoning. During the period they move away from static ways of thinking as they gain experience and as words become symbols of categories.† The period of *concrete operations* approximates the years between the start of schooling and the onset of puberty, the so-called latency period. Children have acquired a coherent cognitive system with which they can understand their world and work upon it, and into which they can fit new experiences. The period of *formal operations* starts early in adolescence when youths become capable of thinking propositionally, of conceptualizing, and of using hypotheses. It

---

* One other major aspect of Piaget's orientation requires mention. The newborn is completely egocentric, apprehending only in terms of how a new sensation meets an existing built-in reflex. Development involves a progressive *decentering* until sometime in adolescence individuals place themselves in their universe and their time in history, and can fit their ideas into abstract systems of logic and thought. However, in each period children must learn to decenter from an "egocentric" use of their new capacities. Egocentrism means not only the placing the self in the center of experience, but also the failure to distinguish the subjective from the objective (Piaget, 1962, p. 285), and the distortion of reality to the point of view of the individual. In a more general sense it includes the overevaluation of cognitive solutions without adequate attention to actual solutions. Thus, in the preoperational stage children believe that their actions or thoughts influence inanimate nature, etc., and adolescents must gradually come to appreciate that the manipulation of ideas in fantasy is not the same as convincing others who have differing orientations and convictions. Problems of cognitive egocentricity at each developmental stage will be discussed in subsequent chapters.

† Piaget's studies of the early phases of the preoperational period are sparse, limiting their usefulness for clarifying the early development of language, but his studies of the later phases of preoperational development contain some of his most significant work.

may require considerable education to move through the stage of formal operations for only exceptional persons appear to master this stage on their own.

THE ORIENTATION TO THE PHASES
OF THE LIFE CYCLE

It is not always feasible to sum up the various tasks of a developmental phase under a common rubric, nor is it always wise, for it can convey an oversimplification of a very complex process. Various aspects of the personality develop at differing tempos, and it is essential to study each developmental line separately. As Anna Freud (1965) has emphasized, the interrelationships between the development of such essentials as separation and individuation from the mother, cognitive abilities, gender identity, object relationships, self-concepts, and ethical concepts require continuing study. Still, dividing the life cycle into a series of rather natural phases permits the comparison of the various developmental lines, and how an individual's development may be globally or partially impeded, fixated, or regressed at a given phase in development.

In following the life cycle we shall focus on the critical aspects of each phase of development, noting how the biological process of maturation provides much of the pattern by opening new potentials and setting limits for the child's capacities, but also on how the culture, through the society and particularly the child's parents, provides expectations, and how children develop other expectations for themselves that help establish the sequence of phases and the crucial issues of each phase. Although attention will be given to the epigenetic concept as a cornerstone of developmental theory, room for compensations and later restitutions will be included. The phases, as in Erikson's approach, are not simply important in themselves, but as part of the larger pattern of how the child grows into an integrated adult.

The Divisions of the Life Cycle

The division of the life cycle into developmental stages in this book follows fairly clear lines of demarcation. *Infancy* approximates the first fifteen months of life when babies can neither properly walk nor talk and are almost completely dependent on others to care for their essential needs, to provide a sense of security, and the stimulation required for their proper emotional and cognitive development. So much occurs that we may doubt the wisdom of considering it as a single developmental period.

During the first half, the baby's physical maturation is of dominant importance, whereas during the second half the beginnings of individuation and socialization require greater attention. In the *toddler* stage, as the baby begins to walk and talk, crucial problems arise over the imbalance between the new-found motor skills and the baby's meager mental capacities. The necessary control by parental figures and their increasing expectations of the child almost inevitably lead to conflicts over control and initiative. Some time around the age of two and a half or three, the child ceases to be a baby and becomes a *preschool* or "oedipal" child. It is a critical time when the child must rescind the erotized attachments to the mother as well as the baby's highly egocentric view of being the center of her existence, and find his or her own place as a boy or girl member of the family. By the end of the period the child properly will have completed the tasks of primary socialization and internalized parental directives sufficiently to be ready for school and to move into peer groups. During these few years children take a giant step toward becoming independent and self-sufficient persons, even though they do so through appreciating the long road ahead before they can attain adult prerogatives.

In the *juvenile* period the equilibrium children gained within their families is disrupted as they go off to school, where they will be judged by their achievements rather than by ascription (Parsons, 1964), and as they spend increasing amounts of time with neighborhood peer groups, where they must also find their places on their own. Although psychoanalytic theory considers this time of life as the latency period, it is apparent that these early school years are critical to the development of many personality characteristics. Children begin to crystallize a concept of the self in relation to the ways in which teachers and peers, as well as parents, relate to them. *Adolescence* involves the discrepancy between sexual maturation and incomplete physical maturity, and between the upsurge of sexual impulsions and the unpreparedness for adult responsibilities and parenthood. Adolescence will be divided into three substages: the period around puberty starting with the sudden spurt of prepubertal growth; mid-adolescence with its expansive strivings and the revolt against adult standards and controls and its conformity to peer-group values; late adolescence, when delimitation and the achievement of an ego identity are central issues and yearnings for intimacy become major motivations.

The *young adult* period is a time for commitments—to a course in life, to marriage, and to parenthood. If a person cannot make these commitments, diffusion of energies and interests ensues, as well as loss of the opportunity for meaningful interrelationships with others. The choices of occupation and spouse, as well as whether or not to become a parent, profoundly affect the further course of the person's life. The passage over the crest of life during the *middle years*—the moving toward and away from the peak years—is often a time of stock-taking concerning the manner in which the person's one and only life is passing. The turn involves a state of mind rather than some clearly demarcated shift in life roles or bodily state. A person becomes one of the older, responsible generation. For some it is a time of fruition, for others a time of regret, disillusion, and resentment toward those who seem to have frustrated. In *old age* physical abilities and mental capacities slowly become more limited, people retire from work, and sooner or later become more or less dependent on others to provide for essential needs. *Death* is the end of the life cycle and an inevitable outcome that brings closure to every life story. Because persons are aware of this eventuality from an early age, it profoundly influences how they live their lives.

Panphasic Influences on Personality Development

Factors in the developmental process that are not phasic must also be taken into account. Persistent attitudes and styles of the parental figures, and indeed of the social system, pervade all phases of the child's developmental years. It is true that a parent may be more capable of relating adequately to the child in one phase than another because of problems in the child or in the parent's own development, but many such influences are panphasic. The obsessive parent not only exerts a deleterious influence upon the child by perfectionistic and rigid efforts to overcontrol when the child is starting to ambulate and to use the "potty," but continues to teach a specific way of coping with life and its anxieties that helps shape the child's personality. The mother who needs to find her own completion through a child not only is likely to interfere with the process of individuation and boundary formation between the child and herself during the second year of life, but also impedes the attainment of a sense of autonomy during the oedipal transition, when the child leaves her to attend school, and when the youth seeks to gain intimacy with another person in adolescence.

We must also note that *identifications* that are a major factor in shaping the personality also transcend specific periods; and although major patterns of identification may be set during the oedipal transition, later shifts in identification can be of paramount importance. Then, as we mentioned in the chapter on the family, there are the crucial intrafamilial influences involving the parents' relationships with one another, the nature of the family they establish, the structuring influence of the specific family, and the enculturating capacities of the parents that impinge throughout child-hood and transcend any single phase.

The approach we shall take specifically differs from those that explicitly or implicitly consider that the infant will unfold into a mature and well-integrated person as a concomitant of physical maturation unless there is something innately wrong with the child, or unless the child is deprived of proper maternal nurture or seriously traumatized emotionally in the first years of life. Such factors are, of course, critical, but we must also consider the positive influences that go into inculcation of emotional stability, stable integration, coherent identity, intellectual development, and that provide familiarity with roles and institutions, and instill the instrumental techniques required for successful adaptation. Some of the fundamentals of this orientation were introduced when we discussed the family's requisite functions of nurturing, structuring, and enculturating the developing child.

TOPOGRAPHIC AND STRUCTURAL CONCEPTS

The Topographic Concept: Conscious and Unconscious Mental Processes

As part of the description of the dynamics of children's development we shall trace the slow organization of the mind, which is part of the personality but not synonymous with it. We shall note the intricate development of the foundations of children's concepts of the world during their first few years of life, and their gradual progression to conceptual thinking (Bruner et al., 1956; Flavell, 1963; Kagan and Moss, 1962; Vygotsky, 1962), and how this epigenesis of their cognitive development intermeshes with their total personality development. But attention will also be directed to the importance of unconscious mentation: how the unconscious processes differ from the conscious in the solving of problems; how they contribute to breadth of experience; how they utilize unverbalized and diffuse factors in decision making; and how they permit the dreams and fantasy without which persons are scarcely human. We shall also examine how drives and impulses that cannot be expressed directly lest they provoke punishment or loss of self-esteem still continue to influence behavior and thought unconsciously in various subtle ways.

The Structural Concept: The Id, Ego, and Superego

We shall also note the emergence of what is usefully termed an *ego*, a construct used to designate the decision-making, self-directing aspects of the self or of the personality. Ego functions depend upon the use of language to construct an internalized representation of the world which can be manipulated in trial-and-error fashion to weigh potential outcomes and to contain gratification of wish, drive, and impulsion in order to cope with "reality" and the pursuit of ultimate objectives. The ego has been conceived as mediating between *id* impulses—the pressure of the basic drives and their pleasure-seeking or tension-releasing derivatives—and the *superego*, a construct that designates the internalized parental directives and, to some extent, also the internalized parental figures who continue to seem somewhat outside of the self. Superego directives, like the parents in childhood, can provide conscious and unconscious support to the ego functions in the person's struggle against pressures from id impulsions. They can also punish, as would imagined parental figures. The id impulses can counter the superego directives sufficiently to force the ego to allow adequate gratifications. It is essential, at this point, to indicate that these are simply highly useful ways of conceptualizing the structure of the personality, to clarify conflicts, and to help explain why certain motives and thoughts are repressed and kept out of consciousness. There are other useful ways of conceptualizing the structure of the personality,* and grave difficulties arise if these abstractions are reified and considered as clearly differentiated parts of either the mind or the personality. These concepts will be presented in greater detail in Chapter 8 after more adequate foundations for their consideration have been established.

Now, as we are about to start the infant on his or her course through life, observing rather than guiding the process, we must be prepared for the countless dangers that beset the path. Children are sturdy, the product of millions of years of trial and error. During the first years, when they neither

---

* As, for example, in Fairbairn's (1952) psychoanalytic "object-relations" theory, which does not utilize concepts of the id, ego, and superego in this fashion.

know the way nor possess the necessary strength or skills, they will be guided by persons who cherish them, and predecessors have trodden trails for them to follow. None traverses the life cycle unscathed. A smooth passage through each developmental phase is neither possible nor even an ideal. The conceptualization provides a pattern against which to measure the actual. Parents and the society strive to provide a nontraumatic passage; they do not foster deviance because they know that it comes unbidden and despite all efforts to avert it. Overprotection or development in an extremely stable and homogeneous setting is likely to produce colorless individuals.* As everyday experience often shows, difficulty can strengthen a person; trauma can produce defenses that can serve well in later emergencies; deprivation can harden. It is not a matter of adhering to a norm, but one of balance and integration. A seed bedded in but a handful of soil on a boulder can sometimes grow into a large tree by sending roots down to the earth, roots that firmly wedge it onto the rock: and the sequoia, the greatest of trees, grows best when forest fires periodically threaten its existence; they often scar it deeply but assure the proper composition of the soil.

* See the study of R. Grinker et al. (1962) of middle-class, Midwestern students at a Y.M.C.A. college, whom he has designated as "homoclites," persons who are unimaginative and uninterestingly average.

REFERENCES

Ariès, P. (1962). *Centuries of Childhood.* Alfred A. Knopf, New York.
Blatt, S. (1974). "Levels of Object Representation in Anaclitic and Introjective Depression," *The Psychoanalytic Study of the Child*, vol. 29, pp. 107–157. International Universities Press, New York.
Bruner, J., Goodnow, J., and Austin, G. (1956). *A Study of Thinking.* Wiley, New York.
Burgner, M., and Edgcumbe, R. (1972). "Some Problems in the Conceptualization of Early Object Relationships," *The Psychoanalytic Study of the Child*, vol. 27, pp. 315–333. International Universities Press, New York.
Engel, G. (1974). Unpublished report.
Engel, G., and Reichman, F. (1956). "Spontaneous and Experimentally Induced Depression in an Infant with a Gastric Fistula," *Journal of the American Psychoanalytic Association*, 4:428–452.
Erikson, E. (1950). *Childhood and Society.* W. W. Norton, New York.
——— (1959). "Growth and Crises of the 'Healthy Personality,'" *Psychological Issues*, vol. 1, no. 1, Monograph No. 1. International Universities Press, New York, p. 89.
Fairbairn, W. R. D. (1952). *Psycho-Analytic Studies of the Personality.* Tavistock Publications, London.

FLAVELL, J. (1963). *The Developmental Psychology of Jean Piaget.* Van Nostrand, Princeton, N.J.

FREUD, A. (1966). *Normality and Pathology in Childhood: Assessments of Development,* vol. 6 of *The Writings of Anna Freud.* International Universities Press, New York.

FREUD, S. (1916–1917). *A General Introduction to Psychoanalysis.* Boni & Liveright, New York.

GOUIN DECARIE, T. (1966). *Intelligence and Affectivity in Early Childhood: An Experimental Study of Jean Piaget's Object Concept and Object Relations.* International Universities Press, New York.

GRINKER, SR., R., GRINKER, JR., R., and TIMBERLAKE, J. (1962). " 'Mentally Healthy' Young Males (Homoclites)," *Archives of General Psychiatry,* 6:405–453.

HARTMANN, H. (1958). *Ego Psychology and the Problem of Adaptation.* International Universities Press, New York.

———— (1964). *Essays on Ego Psychology: Selected Papers on Psychoanalytic Theory.* International Universities Press, New York.

HARTMAN, H., KRIS, E., and LOEWENSTEIN, R. (1946). "Comments on the Formation of Psychic Structure," *The Psychoanalytic Study of the Child,* vol. 2, pp. 11–38. International Universities Press, New York.

KAGAN, J., and MOSS, H. (1962). *From Birth to Maturity.* Wiley, New York.

LIDZ, T. (1975). *Hamlet's Enemy: Myth and Madness in Hamlet.* Basic Books, New York.

NEWMAN, P. (1965). *Knowing the Gururumba.* Holt, Rinehart & Winston, New York.

PARSONS, T. (1964). "The School Class as a Social System: Some of Its Functions in American Society," in *Social Structure and Personality.* Free Press, New York.

PIAGET, J. (1962). *Play, Dreams and Imitation in Childhood.* C. Gattengo and F. M. Hodgson, trans. W. W. Norton, New York.

———— (1963). *The Origins of Intelligence in Children.* M. Cook, trans. W. W. Norton, New York.

PIAGET, J., and INHELDER, B. (1969). *The Psychology of the Child.* H. Weaver, trans. Basic Books, New York.

SULLIVAN, H. S. (1946–1947). *The Interpersonal Theory of Psychiatry.* H. Perry and M. Gawel, eds. Norton, New York, 1963.

VYGOTSKY, L. S. (1962). *Thought and Language.* E. Hanfmann and G. Vakar, eds. and trans. M.I.T. Press and John Wiley & Sons, New York.

SUGGESTED READING

ERIKSON, E. (1956). "The Problem of Ego Identity," *Journal of the American Psychoanalytic Association,* 4:56–121.

———— (1959). "Growth and Crises of the 'Healthy Personality,' " *Psychological Issues,* vol. 1, no. 1., Monograph No. 1. International Universities Press, New York.

FREUD, S. (1933). *New Introductory Lectures on Psycho-Analysis.* Norton, New York.

PIAGET, J., and INHELDER, B. (1969). *The Psychology of the Child.* H. Weaver, trans. Basic Books, New York.

SULLIVAN, H. S. (1946–1947). *The Interpersonal Theory of Psychiatry.* H. Perry and M. Gawel, eds. Norton, New York, 1963.

CHAPTER 4

❀

The Neonate and
the New Parents

THE BIRTH OF THE BABY marks a long-awaited moment. The expectant parents have spent many hours wondering about their future child, whom it will resemble, its future accomplishments, and what their child will mean in their lives. However, the wife with the fetus growing within her has been particularly given to daydreams. Her reveries have recaptured the crucial turns in her own life that led to her marriage and her pregnancy, and her fantasies reach into the distant future of the life waiting within her. She awaits the affection she will give and receive; and her daydreams, now as always, seek to evoke compensations for the frustrations and disappointments in her own life. Days of comfort and expectant hope are interrupted by periods of discomfort and anxiety. Although the first-born are in a minority, they require our attention for they usually present a more critical experience to the parents, profoundly altering their lives, bringing new sensations and awareness, and creating problems and questions for which they seek more guidance.

THE EXPECTANT MOTHER

"Morning sickness," with nausea and occasional vomiting, often disturbs the first few months of the pregnancy; but if the woman is mature and happily married, the pregnancy soon turns into a period of blooming when she experiences a sense of completion and self-satisfaction. Even though the mother may have been happily pursuing a career, she now feels that she is fulfilling one of the significant ways of being creative open to her, a way given only to women. She finds a new sense of closeness and sharing with her husband that forms a new and strong bond between them. An appearance that reflects happiness and contentment augurs well for the course of the pregnancy and for the child. Gradually, however, the expectant mother usually turns inward, often from the moment when she first feels the fetus move and she knows that she has a living being in her womb. She experiences a self-sufficiency because the most important thing to her is within her, and her own life and her own needs have become secondary to perpetuating herself and the species through the baby. Her husband may feel excluded and neglected, for he is no longer the primary recipient of her emotional investment. Yet he is more important to his wife than ever, for she can relax properly and invest her emotions in the fetus only when she feels secure, protected, and supported by her husband.

As much as the woman may enjoy her pregnancy, she eventually grows impatient. Her increasing girth makes her feel awkward; her balance becomes insecure; often she tires more readily; the movement and kicking of the fetus are annoying; and after the baby's head descends and engages her pelvis, she must urinate more frequently. Both parents are impatient to know how it will turn out, properly experiencing some concerns—not so much for the mother, for maternal deaths have become a rarity, but wishing to know that the baby will be normal. (Anomalous developments are sufficiently common to justify some concern.) The parents have also been limited in their fantasies, for they cannot know the sex of the child. As many parents feel disappointed if the child turns out to be of the opposite sex from that awaited, they tend to hold their imaginations in check, or are willing to consider both alternatives until they are certain.

Prenatal Influences

The emotional problems of the pregnant woman can affect the course of the pregnancy and the fetus. The influence of emotional turmoil in causing spontaneous abortions and serious physiological disturbances in the mother, such as pernicious vomiting or toxemia, is beyond the scope of this book except as an indication that the fetus is not totally protected from physiological imbalances of the mother. The baby's development does not start at birth but with conception. It is responsive to its fetal environment. If the mother bleeds seriously or if there is a marked disturbance in her metabolic equilibrium, the fetus may develop an anomaly through interference with its maturation.* It has become clear, particularly through the studies of Sontag and his coworkers (Sontag, 1941, 1944), that the mother's emotional state can influence the fetus. We are not concerned with superstitions that a child develops a harelip because the mother saw a rabbit, or that Annie Oakley's mother was frightened by a shotgun. Even though no direct nerve connections exist between the mother and the fetus, there is a neurochemical bond through the placental circulation. The mother's internal secretions can produce changes in the fetal heart rate, in its bodily movements, and perhaps in its intestinal activity. Spelt's (1948) studies have shown that during its last two months the fetus not only responds to loud noises but that its heart rate can probably be conditioned. There is evidence that the newborn of disturbed mothers may tend to be hyperactive in their responsivity to stimuli, and have more labile heart action and gastrointestinal functioning (Sontag, 1941, 1944; Spelt, 1948). However, any tendency to consider such newborn as neurotic at birth constitutes a very dubious extrapolation of known facts. While reasonable evidence indicates that undue sensitivity in the neonate can be related to the mother's emotional state during the pregnancy, we must also realize that such mothers are also likely to remain upset after the delivery when the baby's well-being depends upon her conscious and unconscious attitudes toward her infant rather than directly upon her physiological processes.

---

* If the mother contracts German measles early in her pregnancy, the virus can affect the development of the fetus's brain. Marked thyroid or iodine deficiency in the mother can lead to the production of a cretin, a child with deficient thyroid development. Diabetic mothers tend to give birth to unusually large babies. Medication that may not be noxious to the mother may seriously damage the fetus, etc. The course of labor can be influenced by the mother's fears; and a difficult, prolonged labor can require considerable anesthesia that diminishes the neonate's reactivity for several days, thus influencing the baby's start in life, or interfere with the supply of oxygen to the fetus and with breathing after birth, which can lead to damage of the brain, usually, though not always, of a minimal if not insignificant degree (Association for the Aid of Crippled Children, 1964; Corah, et al., 1965).

The Newborn's Appearance

The obstetrician reassures the mother and informs her of the baby's sex immediately after the delivery, without waiting for any questions. Despite such reassurance, many parents must stifle some feelings of disappointment when they see their babies, and hesitate to express concerns that a new-born's appearance may arouse in an inexperienced parent. The newborn is not very prepossessing, and it may take all of the mother's maternal love not to be disappointed with the creature to whom she has just given birth. The infant possesses the many endowments and assets that have been reviewed in the preceding chapters, but most of them are not yet apparent. Let us now take a more careful look at the infant who has just started life in the world beyond the womb.

The average baby born at term weighs seven and a quarter pounds and is twenty to twenty-one inches long. With its knees flexed and body curled in its familiar fetal position, it seems very tiny indeed, particularly when the obstetrician or nurse skillfully holds it on a hand and wrist. Somewhat wizened, the baby may appear more like an elderly denizen of the world than a newcomer, for there is little fat—in particular, the fat pads that will fill out the cheeks are missing—and the jaws are unsupported by teeth. The hair may be dark and straight, coming low over the forehead and convey-ing a hairy appearance that deprives the infant of resemblance to any known relative within the last ten thousand generations. Such hair, when present, will soon be replaced by hair so fine that some babies appear bald to casual observation. The vernix caseosa, a cheesy material which covers the body, provides a protective coating for the skin. The skin is reddened, moist, and deeply creased. The "caput," or swelling formed by pressure during the passage through the birth canal, may have temporarily deformed the nose, caused a swelling about one eye, or elongated the head into a strange shape. The skull is incomplete, for the bones have not joined in two areas called the "fontanelles" where the brain is covered only by soft tissues. The external genitalia in both sexes are disproportionately large due to stimulation by the mother's hormones and will regress in size. The breasts may be somewhat enlarged for the same reason and secrete a watery discharge discouragingly termed "witch's milk." The irises are a pale blue, which does not indicate a resemblance to either parent, for the true eye color develops later. The head, even though its contents are not fully developed, is very large in proportion to the body, and the neck cannot support it; whereas the buttocks are tiny, creating an appearance that is very disproportionate in comparison with adult dimensions.

The Neonate's Physiological Instability

The baby is arbitrarily termed a "neonate" for the first several weeks when control of the physiological processes remains unstable. The regulation of the body temperature is imperfect and breathing is often irregular. The eyes wander and cross. The newborn can hear little during the first twenty-four hours until air enters the Eustachian tubes. The neonate seems to prefer its former home and acts as if it resents any stimulation. It will sleep about twenty hours a day, its slumber broken primarily by crying that signals hunger—it needs milk from six to eight times a day. The infant's primary needs are sleep, warmth, and milk to continue maturing outside the mother.

TOTAL DEPENDENCY

Despite the diffuse and unorganized nature of the neonates' feelings, which we can, of course, only surmise through observation of their reactions, these first weeks of life receive much emphasis in the study of personality development—perhaps more because of how the parents' attitudes toward their child are established than because of the direct impact of events upon the infant. Neonates are virtually helpless but also passively omnipotent, for all needs are provided for by others. Their comfort and well-being depend upon the ability of mothering persons to understand their needs and satisfy them. The baby's future emotional security rests to a very great extent upon the development of a mutuality between the infant and the mother that permits them to interact on a nonverbal basis during the first year and provides the mother with empathic feelings for its needs. Neonates have little tolerance for frustration and can do little toward directing their mothers' efforts except to signal discomfort, and it is up to the mother to adjust to the infant. The ability to give birth to a baby does not assure the ability to nurture and properly care for one. Maternal feelings may be stimulated hormonally, and inborn responsivity may be stirred by certain activities of the infant, but such feelings do not provide the necessary skills, nor are they adequately pervasive to overcome the emotional problems aroused in many women by the tasks of mothering.

THE NEONATE'S BEHAVIOR AND CAPABILITIES

Although we are apt to think of newborns as tiny creatures whose nervous systems are still too incomplete to react to anything other than their physiological needs or to relate to the world, the careful observer will note a fascinating variety of behaviors and a definite capacity to begin to build upon experiences virtually from the time of birth.*

It has, of course, been apparent that neonates possess important ways of interacting with the world about them. They can suck and will start to suck when a nipple or anything else is placed in their mouths. At birth, or soon thereafter, babies reflexly turn their heads to the side of a stimulus to the lips and start to suck. They cannot yet properly grasp the nipple with their mouths unaided. The lips and mouth are all-important to the neonate, and the oral area is highly sensitive, richly endowed with tactile sensory receptors. Indeed, a fetus will respond reflexly to stimulation of the oral zone long before birth. The neonate's hands tend to be held closed, and if something rubs the palm, particularly if the area between thumb and forefinger is stroked, the hand reflexly clenches it and holds on with a strength that suffices to support the baby's weight if both hands are grasping. This innate "grasp reflex" serves no apparent purpose in the human infant but was of utmost importance in the last prehuman phase of evolution when the infant had to cling to its mother's hair. The grasp reflex lasts from four to six months until the forebrain matures and the nerve fibers that conduct impulses to the upper extremities are covered by a sheath of myelin which permits babies to begin to use their hands to make voluntary discrete movements. If the baby is dropped, or is suddenly jerked downward, or is startled by a loud noise, an immediate reflex change from the usual curled posture occurs as all four extremities are flung out in extension and the infant starts to cry. This "startle" or "Moro" reflex may have served to help a simian mother catch a falling infant by causing it to spread out to a maximal extent. Playful dropping motions that excite and please an older child terrify the young infant.

Several other reflexes require note. For some weeks after birth, a baby, if held erect with toes touching the ground, will make reflex stepping movements. However, they do not indicate that this is an extraordinary young-

---

* There were, however, few, if any, careful observers until Wolff (1966) studied four infants from the moment of delivery through their fifth day of life by continuous observation for sixteen to eighteen hours a day. He brought a new understanding of neonatal behavior by drawing attention to how it varies with the infant's differing states of sleep and wakefulness.

ster, prematurely ready to learn to walk, any more than the swimming movements the baby makes when properly suspended warrant a try at swimming. Stroking the outer side of the sole of the foot to test the "plantar" reflex causes a fanning out of the toes and an upward movement of the big toe, termed a "Babinski" response or reflex. It is an abnormal response in adults but indicates in infants that the pyramidal tracts of nerve fibers, essential for voluntary muscular control, are not yet covered by the myelin sheaths necessary for their proper functioning. Until the Babinski response disappears toward the end of the first year of life, the baby cannot voluntarily control the lower parts of the body. The upper extremities can be controlled sooner than the lower, and the infant will be able to start practicing finger control before becoming six months old. Thus the infant's ability to handle things, maintain balance, talk, walk, and control sphincters awaits the maturation of the nervous system, rather than practice and training alone.

Sleep

During their first days of life neonates spend about three-quarters of the time sleeping. The irregularity of the sleep and the baby's sudden startles during it may puzzle and even disturb some parents. Neonates have two or three rather distinct types of sleep. In *regular* sleep, their breathing is smooth and even but with spontaneous startle reactions (mostly of the extensor, Moro type), sometimes occurring every two minutes but with longer relatively undisturbed periods. In *irregular* sleep, startle reactions are much less frequent but breathing is irregular and erratic, and there are numerous muscular movements, including a variety of facial grimaces and mouth and tongue movements. At times, the infant falls into an intermediate state of *periodic* sleep, when bursts of deep and slow breathing alternate with very shallow breathing that may be almost imperceptible (Wolff, 1966, pp. 7–11).

Wakefulness

The neonate's waking life varies between states of drowsiness which are transitions between sleep and wakefulness, alert inactivity, waking activity, and crying (Wolff, 1966).

States of *alert inactivity* are of particular interest because it is during such states that infants begin to assimilate from the environment and we can note the beginnings of their cognitive development. States of alert inactivity occur most frequently when the infant is relatively free from tensions such as hunger. At such times the baby's face is relaxed, its eyes are open and have a bright and shining appearance, and there is little motor activity other than eye movement. Although periods of alert inactivity may not occur in the first day or two, or may last for only a few minutes, occasionally a newborn baby may be alert and inactive for over a half hour at a time. While in this state, if an object is placed in the neonate's field of vision long enough, the baby will follow it with its eyes as it is moved back and forth; and it will turn its eyes and head to the right or left when a sharp, clear noise is made, as if seeking the source of the sound. Although the human face does not lead newborns to fix their eyes any more than do inanimate objects, the child's ability to gaze at a parent seems to establish a relationship of a sort, and thus can be very meaningful to parents.

During periods of *waking activity*, neonates kick, mouth, suck their hands, and cry intermittently. At these times breathing is grossly irregular, the skin is flushed, and the eyes, though open, do not shine as during states of wakeful inactivity. Active waking states are more common before than after feedings. During the first week or two of life, if the infant should begin to pursue an object visually while in this state, activity stops; but by the end of the second week general bodily activity can go on together with visual pursuit movements.* Throughout the first month or so, infants pay attention to new or recently acquired patterns only when inactively alert, as if the assimilation required the involvement of their entire being. After the first week, it is possible to increase the duration of alert periods significantly by moving an object back and forth across the field of vision of the infant who is about to fall asleep. Clearly, neonates are already "interested" in stimuli that serve as "aliment" for their cognitive development.†

Crying

Crying is almost the only significant way in which very young infants can draw attention to their distress. The influence of different types of crying on parents is not as specific in humans as among some other species, and

* The importance of this change to understanding sensori-motor development will be considered in the next chapter, in the discussion of Piaget's observations and conceptualizations.

† Aside from such learning, recent evidence shows that the neonate can be conditioned in the first days of life (Connolly and Stratton, 1969), in contrast to earlier evidence to the contrary. Of particular interest is Reuben Kron's (1966) work showing that sucking behavior is amenable to "instrumental" conditioning, and thus suggesting that from the first day the reward of nutriment reinforces and accelerates sucking and, if sucking is unrewarded, the sucking reflex is gradually extinguished. We must, however, note that thumb sucking in older children does not become extinguished, even though it does not bring a nutritional reward.

parents' individual interest and experience rather than the type of crying may determine their response. However, three distinct types of crying can be distinguished, and often serve as guides even though the parenting person may not be aware of it (Wolff, 1969). The rhythmical cry is the basic pattern and is often set off by hunger.* Wolff noted that, whereas more experienced mothers might neglect such crying for a time, some would respond by feeding, and others by checking the diaper first. It is of interest that rhythmical crying can often be stopped by passing an object back and forth across the baby's visual field to evoke a state of alert inactivity, just as the drowsy baby can be aroused by the same maneuver. Similarly, a sharp sound and, after the second week, particularly a high-pitched voice, will alert the infant and bring a cessation of crying. Perhaps more important, if the neonate is picked up and held against a person's shoulder, it will become visually alert, stop crying, and start scanning—a means by which good "parenting" affords the neonate greater opportunity for environmental stimulation (Korner and Grobstein, 1966).

The *mad* or *angry* cry is more preemptory than the rhythmical cry and usually leads parents to stop what they are doing and check on their baby, even though they may not be alarmed by the expression of rage. Crying caused by *pain* usually leads parents to respond immediately and anxiously. It starts with a long cry followed by an extended period during which the breath is held in expiration, and may continue in this pattern.

When about three weeks old, the infant develops a new type of crying that seems to indicate a desire for attention. The crying is low in pitch and intensity and resembles long-drawn-out moans which occasionally become more clear-cut. Such crying, as other non-crying vocalizations, first appears when the baby is fussing but before actually starting to cry. The novel sound produced serves as aliment for a "circular reaction," which the baby practices when alert and thereby gains a new skill (Wolff, 1969). Thus, before infants are a month old they are acquiring ways of obtaining attention.

Laughing

Toward the end of the first month, the infant also displays a more affable way of relating. Many infants will chuckle and laugh when stimu-

* Rhythmical crying consists of a cry of perhaps a half to three-quarters of a second followed in turn by a brief silence, an inspiratory whistle, and another brief rest before the next cry begins. As the rest after the cry is shorter than the rest after the inspiration, one hears a unit as a cry followed by an inspiration rather than vice versa. Rhythmic crying is, at this period of life, accompanied by synchronous kicking.

lated in their armpits or on their bellies by gentle but firm and rapid finger movements, though not by tickling. However, here, too, neonates' responses depend greatly on their states of arousal. Parents can become quite confused by their infant's different responses to the same stimuli according to the state of arousal. Cooing and playing pat-a-cake, which produce a smile in the three-week-old when in an "alert inactive state," can provoke crying when the infant is showing mild discomfort by soft moans or diffuse activity; and the silent, nodding face that usually elicits a smile can lead a fussing infant to start to cry.

DIFFERENCES AMONG NEWBORN INFANTS

Even casual observation of the newborns in a hospital nursery reveals that they differ greatly in appearance and temperament. Some are fairly well fitted out and others appear somewhat premature. Some infants are naturally "cuddly" and easy to hold, whereas others are loose and sprawling, or rigid, when held. Some are placid, sleeping most of the time, and others are sensitive to stimuli and their needs are not so easily satisfied. Newborns, therefore, require somewhat different management of their needs, and start to experience the world on a somewhat different basis (Escalona, 1962).*

The parents, particularly the mother, soon after the child is born, adjust to the specific characteristics of their infant. A mother who may previously have interacted very well with a calm and docile first child may grow anxious when confronted with the care of a hypersensitive infant; or, on the other hand, a woman may grow concerned or even dissatisfied with a baby who is quiet and relatively unresponsive, needing greater reactivity in the child to stimulate and satisfy her. The innate characteristics of infants

* Some developmental defect, usually relatively trivial, exists in about one out of every sixteen infants. Some will create difficulties sooner or later and influence the course of personality development. Cardiac anomalies may require surgery during the first months or chronically impede physical development and activity. A prominent birthmark may have influence through parental attitudes and later through provoking self-consciousness in the child. The first weeks of life remain somewhat precarious, for even though infant mortality has been cut almost in half over the past thirty years, the death rate among neonates has declined only slightly. However, much of the danger to life arises because a certain number of babies are born without the essential equipment for survival. It is hoped that genetic counseling and reliable contraception will diminish the number. The properly formed and adequately mature neonate will survive without difficulty in contemporary civilized societies unless something untoward occurs.

can start a chain of interactional responses which may persist and greatly influence their development, or which may alter either as they change as they mature or in response to their parents' handling.

THE FAMILY MATRIX

The birth of a child, particularly the first child, produces a change in the parents' lives. Their lives and well-being are bound to the child's life for many years to come. The family unit undergoes a reorganization in order to provide room for the infant, and the roles of husband and wife alter to embrace the roles of father and mother. Although the mother is traditionally and rather naturally more involved in the care of the neonate, the relationship is too often regarded as if the two were living in a vacuum rather than as part of a family. The concentration of attention upon the mother and her child provides a useful focus, but often leads to neglect of highly significant influences affecting the relationship. The birth of a child, particularly the first, is a time of trial for many marriages. The division of tasks between parents shifts, and many mothers may give up, or at least suspend, their careers for a time. The family income is likely to diminish while expenses rise. Fathers who share the nurturant functions are, like mothers, more bound to the home and must forgo some recreational activities. Anger and irritation with the infant frequently reflect unhappiness in the marriage as hostility is deflected from the spouse onto the child. The father must be able to share the mother with the infant and not feel left out, and the mother cannot exclude her husband from her life and the child's. A couple who had purposely remained childless for five years in order to enjoy their own lives unhampered by parental responsibilities finally had a baby at the wife's insistence. The husband was a person who required constant bolstering of his self-esteem by admiration from women, and although promiscuous demanded his wife's complete attention. Soon after the baby was born, the mother found herself in a dilemma. When her husband was at home, each time she went to feed her son or paid attention to his cries, her husband would voice an imperative need and throw a tantrum if the infant's needs took precedence over his. He refused to forgo any social activities, and when babysitters were not available insisted that his wife bring the neonatal infant along to noisy drunken parties. As the son grew older, the father's jealousy and rivalry increased, and he constantly belittled his son's abilities while holding himself up as an unattainable model of masculine achievement. This mother could have provided adequate mothering only if she had broken off her marriage. Immature spouses are likely to behave even more immaturely when they become parents, particularly when they have married primarily in order to regain a parental figure to care for them and then cannot share their spouses with their children and accept parental responsibilities.

Fortunately, the infant usually creates new ties between the parents. They are united in their common product and become involved in experiences with their child that no one else can really share with them. The baby gives their lives new purpose and direction, and a sense of continuity with a new generation. The influence of children upon the lives of their parents will be discussed in Chapter 15.

When the new infant is not the first-born, brothers and sisters are not only affected, but their reactions impinge upon the neonate both directly and through the impact of their altered needs upon the parents. They are supposed to welcome the new sibling but almost always feel that the baby is an intruder who preempts the parents' attention and affection. The older child frequently regresses, unconsciously seeking the benefits of greater dependency, and requires more care and demonstrations of love than previously. The parents may become perplexed and frustrated in their efforts to provide for the infant while they are caught up in the obvious unhappiness of their older child. Many contemporary parents, aware of the jealousies aroused, seek to prepare the older children for the birth, consider their needs, permit verbal expression of hostility, and seek to compensate for the attention they give the infant and try to find ways of making the advent of the new child advantageous to the older children.

THE MUTUALITY BETWEEN MOTHER AND INFANT

Although the sharing of nurturant functions by both parents has become more prevalent, increasing the father's investment in the baby and making the mother's tasks less burdensome and more pleasurable, the mother almost always assumes the major role in caring for the infant and particularly the newborn infant. The infant properly needs to have an adult who intuitively knows its ways, and to whose ways the infant can learn to respond. The mutuality between mother and child which seems essential to enable the mother properly to empathize with the infant's needs and feelings, and to bestow love and tenderness, usually develops during the pregnancy rather than appearing suddenly after the birth. The fetus is part of the mother, and the love of the infant is properly partly a narcissistic love—not fully distinguishable from the woman's love and concern for herself and her pride in what she can produce and achieve. The pregnant woman's life, the investment of her thoughts and emotions encompass the fetus which gives a new and expanded meaning to her own existence. When properly developed, such investments continue to enfold the helpless infant, who continues to develop through the mother's care almost as completely as when within her womb. The differentiation of mother and child is a lengthy process for both, continuing over many years, as we shall examine in Chapter 5.

Although the mother seems to have a more natural unity with the infant, the sensitive father also becomes involved in the development of the fetus. He wonders what his wife's experience is like, feels her enlarging womb, thrills at the first signs of life, tries to ease her days as she grows awkward from her change in shape, and muses about what he will do with the boy or girl in the years ahead.

All sorts of interferences with the development of proper parental preoccupation with the developing infant can arise. Thus, a young and immature woman had married on the rebound and considered her husband inferior to her. She became infuriated when he did not idolize her and cater to her adolescent whims but expected her to assume responsibilities in their marriage. She had never really accepted the finality of the marriage, daydreaming that her former boy friend would realize his error, divorce his wife, and return to her. Her resentments welled up when she believed that her husband had purposefully impregnated her in order to hold her in the marriage. As the pregnancy progressed, unable to accept the reality, she spent more and more time lost in a fantasy of an imaginary life with her true love. She scarcely thought of the fetus within her and became annoyed by every movement or kick that encroached upon her daydreams, irritable and antagonistic to her baby before it was born. More tangibly perhaps, a woman already harassed by the care of six young children—a task amplified by her perfectionism and her concerns when they were out of her sight—finds that she cannot make room, emotional room within her, for the coming baby.

Even though the parents' fundamental emotional attitudes toward their baby involve their own personality development, their maturity as a man or woman, their happiness in their marriage, and other such factors that can scarcely be influenced by direct instruction, their insecurities over everyday, seemingly trivial matters of child care can create despair concerning their ability to care properly for and satisfy their infant. They must learn new techniques that sound so rudimentary and are so often taken for granted that they feel ashamed to admit their ignorance and seek help. The mother must, for example, if she breast feeds learn how to get her nipple into the baby's mouth and how to hold the infant securely. She does not know without instruction how long the baby should nurse or how frequently to feed. Diapering, cleaning, bathing, deciding how much the baby should be handled and how much left alone, and many other such items can provoke indecision. Sometimes nothing may seem to go right, usually because of the uneasiness and anxiety concerning her techniques and abilities that advice or instruction could dissipate. The turmoil can start family frictions, lead a wife to wish she had stuck to her career and eschewed motherhood and cause her husband to doubt his choice of a wife. Instruction in the elements of child care and making advice available to the young parents are particularly important in contemporary life, as traditional techniques are poorly conveyed and often mistrusted as old-fashioned and unscientific.*

The advice offered by those considered to be, or have considered themselves to be, authorities on how to raise children has changed several times in the past half century, adding to parents' confusion.† Recent teachings have urged parents and teachers to seek to meet children's maturational needs at each phase of their development—neither to place demands be-

---

* The millions of copies of Benjamin Spock's *Baby and Child Care* sold in many languages attest to the need. In New Zealand the Plunkett Society has specially trained nurses visit and advise every mother weekly at first and then with decreasing frequency until the child enters school—unless the parents specifically decline such help—and it also distributes carefully prepared literature to guide parents in the care of their children. The society also runs four special hospitals to which a mother and baby can be sent if either fails to flourish during the child's infancy.

† Behaviorist psychology, which dominated the scene in the decade preceding World War II, was one of the first major challenges to traditional child-rearing practices, and taught rigidly scheduled feeding and handling and early conditioning of bowel training to inculcate proper character training. A good mother was supposed to squelch her concerns and much of her maternal feelings for the good of the child; many mothers found this unnatural approach difficult, but only the more independent and secure mothers could flout the authorities and accept the guilt of raising their children improperly. Toward the end of the 1930s, a major shift in policy occurred under the growing impact of psychoanalytic teachings. Repression was considered the source of most emotional disturbances, but the advice to avoid unnecessary repressive measures was often misunderstood to mean abandonment of guidance and consistent firmness. Lately, there has been mistrust of scientific guidance, with an emphasis on bountifully supplying "love," often in the form of considerable handling and frequent nursing.

fore children are capable of meeting them nor, on the other hand, to restrain children from utilizing their abilities when they are ready either by continuing to do for them or by unnecessary restrictiveness.

Although differences of opinion exist concerning the older children's capacities and what might be expected of them, virtually all experienced persons agree that neonates can do almost nothing for themselves other than carry out their essential physiological processes, and that attention must be focused upon the parents' handling of the infant. Neonates have virtually no tolerance for frustration of their needs, and if they are born normally developed there is no need for them to experience repeated frustrations as the essential problems of the physical care of the newborn have been worked out.

MEASURES TO FOSTER MUTUALITY

During the past several decades, obstetricians and pediatricians have initiated various measures to improve the parents' security and knowledge, and to foster the development of a satisfactory mutuality between mother and infant (Stendler, 1950; Vincent, 1951).

Prenatal Courses

Expectant parents, particularly those awaiting a first child, are often offered *prenatal courses* in which they are taught the essentials of the physiology of pregnancy, of fetal development, and of childbirth so that they may overcome misconceptions and fears arising from ignorance. Here, too, parents learn about the infant's physical and emotional needs and how to provide for them. Such instruction, which usually includes an opportunity for free discussion, can help prevent mishandling of the baby as well as foster greater security in the parents. These courses also establish, even before the baby is born, a relationship between the parents and an expert, to whom they can turn if problems arise during the pregnancy or in caring for the baby.

Natural Childbirth

Many obstetricians promote the practice of "natural childbirth"—the conduct of the labor and delivery without anesthesia, or with minimal anesthesia—to permit the mother who is awake to participate in a process that properly constitutes one of the most important experiences in her life.* If a woman can relax during the labor and delivery and maintain the muscles of the pelvic floor in a reasonably relaxed state, labor is easier and less painful than when she is tense. Pain itself is bearable and often can be virtually ignored when it is not accompanied by fear. The woman who has gained confidence in her obstetrician and in herself, and who has been prepared by exercises that teach her to relax properly, can often cope with the pain experienced during a normal delivery without requiring narcotics and anesthesia. In a sense, "natural childbirth" has become feasible because of the advances of modern obstetrics that permit the mother to feel secure. Several types of anesthesia can also be used that permit the mother to remain awake and participate in the delivery. The essential mutuality is fostered, for she can immediately see and hold the infant she has brought into the world. The father now is permitted or even encouraged, in some hospitals, to be present during the delivery, to increase the meaning of childbirth to him and to implement his mutuality with both his wife and their child. Perhaps the effect upon the baby is almost as important, for if it has not absorbed a narcotic or anesthetic from the mother, the newborn is active and responsive, which fosters the establishment of a bond with the parents. The LaMaze technique, popular in France, seeks to ease the infant's entrance into the world by delivering in dim light and avoiding shocks such as the stimulation with cold water, etc. The value of the method is doubted by many and its safety challenged by some.†

"Rooming-In"

Many obstetricians have sought to foster the mother-infant bond by "rooming-in" programs, in which the newborn is kept in a bassinet along-

---

* The movement was started by an English obstetrician, Grantly Dick Read, whose book, *Childbirth Without Fear*, has exerted wide influence upon the practice of obstetrics. Read considered that most of the pain of labor is a product of civilization and that childbirth was simple and relatively painless among primitive peoples. Useful techniques can, upon occasion, derive from faulty assumptions. Indeed, many preliterate peoples fear childbirth, the women often experience considerable pain, and the high maternal and infant mortality rates can lead to reliance upon elaborate rites that may be almost as painful to an observer as to the mother because of their inefficiency.

† Although obstetricians have frequently been idolized by the women whose babies they deliver, in the past few years many women, particularly liberated women, have deeply resented the impersonal attitudes of many obstetricians, and the unfeeling manner in which they examine women, using a cold speculum and often talking to the woman only while examining her perineum; and women have sought out those rare persons—women obstetricians—as well as, increasingly, nurse-midwives.

side the mother's bed, where she can watch and take care of the baby herself. Mothers can often relax better with their babies close to them, secure that they are well. However, as most women now remain in the hospital for only two or three days, the importance of "rooming-in" has diminished.

Breast Feeding

There is an increasing trend to induce mothers to breast feed their babies. Breast feeding has many advantages (Aldrich, 1947). The mother's milk is rarely unsuited to the infant; it contains antibodies that help protect the infant from various infectious diseases; the suckling promotes contractions of the mother's uterus, aiding its reduction to normal size following the delivery. There are other practical advantages, such as freeing the mother from the need to prepare bottles; and contrary to expectation, breast feeding often permits greater freedom of movement, for the baby's food goes along with the mother. However, we are here interested in its promotion of a relatedness between mother and child. It is, for example, difficult to nurse a baby at the breast without holding it closely and providing the stimulation and the comfort of body contact, the mother's odor, and the mother's face upon which the baby fixes its eyes. Suckling also properly stimulates genital sensations in the mother which help establish an erotic component to the mother's attachment and can add to the pleasure of nursing. Unfortunately, some mothers become uneasy because they are sexually stimulated and believe that something is wrong with them and cease breast feeding. All in all, breast feeding assures that the infant will receive a reasonable amount of maternal attention and contact and during the first months spend much of the intervals between sleep in its mother's arms.

Some women, however, have a deep aversion to nursing, experiencing it as if a parasite were suckling at them, and others may have a strong sense of shame about its animal-like character. A baby can thrive very well if bottle-fed, and the mother may relate to her infant better while giving a bottle. Pressures toward breast feeding can be injurious if they make a mother feel guilty or unworthy because she is not for it. Fortunately with breast feeding the problem often takes care of itself, for fairly reliable studies indicate that mothers who do not really desire to nurse, or have unconscious blocks about it, do not succeed and must wean the child after a brief trial (see Chapter 5).

Well-Baby Clinics

The pediatrician seeks to provide guidance for the mother in child-rearing practices. Efforts are made to maintain regular contacts even when the child is well and thriving. The physical development of the infant and young child is followed, prophylactic measures such as inoculation recommended and provided, and discussions of any problems stimulated. The mother learns that she can discuss her own emotional difficulties which might interfere with the care she provides her offspring. The interest of the personal pediatrician, or of the clinic, lies in the total well-being of the child and in the mother-child relationship rather than in the child's physical health alone.

These various measures can all be effective and have been very worth while when they do not contain moralistic implications that set expectations, spoken or unspoken, beyond the mother's capacities, and provoke in her feelings that she is inadequate or rejecting of her baby.

The mother's security and spontaneity of feeling for her baby are usually more important than the precise techniques used in delivering and nourishing the infant. If the mother is happy during her pregnancy, if she consciously and unconsciously wants the baby, feels close to her husband, and has become caught up in the miracle going on inside of her, everything else is relatively secondary. Although she may experience difficulties, the chances are great that she will learn to overcome them and her positive feelings will win out over fears of labor or her inexperience in caring for an infant.

A good start is important, for absence of good relationships can make new infants fretful, and the parents' inability to satisfy the infant can nullify the enjoyment of having a baby and establish a pattern that may be difficult to overcome. Still, babies' primary needs during the first few weeks of life are food, sleep, and warmth—they are not extremely sensitive to their parents' inexperience. The atmosphere established is probably more important than the precise details of management. Babies are handled in very divergent ways in different cultures and in some places in a manner that to us would seem deleterious, and yet the infants survive and flourish. Parents' insecurities are alleviated by training and instruction and the various measures outlined, which can, at least, modify or blunt the edge of anxiety-ridden handling and cover difficulties in accepting the baby. Fortunately, parents' anticipated rejection of a baby often fails to materialize, because babies in their helplessness are very seductive and difficult to resist.

The Unwanted Infant

Although one likes to believe that the birth of a child is a happy event for the parents, it would be unrealistic not to recognize that a baby is often unwanted and that one or both parents are emotionally incapable of welcoming it. Such situations are important to those interested in child care because it is among such children that difficulties in physical and emotional health are more likely to arise. About seventy percent of pregnancies are unplanned, but this does not mean that most of these babies are unwanted or unwelcome. Many were simply not wanted at the specific time; and others, though undesired, are well accepted after the fact. Maternal rejection of a child and its serious effects have received much consideration in recent years. A variety of emotional and psychosomatic disturbances has been somewhat uncritically attributed to "maternal rejection" as if it were an entity. Whereas occasional mothers neglect their infants physically and emotionally and clearly do not respond to them properly, the matter is usually not this simple, for the mother's difficulties are less global and more specific. Some women fear pregnancy and labor because of residual childhood fears; often these are fears that have been banished from consciousness since childhood rather than having been reevaluated and overcome, such as ideas that the baby is born by an operation, or through the navel or the anus, and that they will be mutilated through childbirth. Some are fearful of being caught in a situation over which they have no control, such as the growth of the fetus within them and its birth. Yet they may desire and very much love the baby. On the other hand, a woman may enjoy being pregnant because of the attention and care she receives during it but have difficulties in being maternal to the baby because she seeks to be cared for as a child herself. A common cause of rejection of a child is the anger at being tied to an unhappy marriage, with the wife feeling that the husband *made* her pregnant—or, conversely, that a wife purposely became pregnant to prevent a divorce. Other women resent being kept from their occupations, which are more important to them than their marriages. Some women deeply resent their femininity, and can accept neither the pregnancy nor the baby which definitively challenges and destroys fantasies and self-deceptions of not being a woman. There are a wide variety of reasons, conscious and unconscious, why a woman can have problems with one or another phase of pregnancy, with childbirth, or with child rearing. Some who fear pregnancy or childbirth and have sought to avoid them may make excellent mothers after the child is born, having lived through their fears and found release from them.

Of course, one cause of "maternal rejection" is paternal rejection or disinterest in the baby and the refusal of the father to share the tasks of caring for the child. A woman may also resent an impregnation and its product that was more or less forced upon her by her husband.

We cannot here consider those pregnancies of deprived adolescent girls who want a baby as a doll to care for, but have no use for the child after it is old enough to require more than doll-like care; or who need to become pregnant to prove themselves or to satisfy a boy who must prove his manhood by having his girlfriend's belly "stick out."

More deep-seated emotional problems that involve the entire personality development of the parents are little influenced by instruction or techniques of improving a parent's relatedness to the child, and can even be very resistant to intensive psychotherapy. We have noted instances of such difficulties in the man who could not accept a child that interfered with the attention he needed from his wife, and in the woman who still sought to be mothered by her own mother and to be her husband's child.

The availability of very effective contraception and of therapeutic abortion when necessary are means of avoiding the births of unwanted children and particularly of children born to parents who cannot accept them or nurture them. Unfortunately, as we shall consider in the chapter on parenthood, reason does not always hold sway in such areas, and many people have children they are incapable of raising.

The Infant's Gender

The sex of the child is one of the most important factors that influences the parents' ways of relating to the child, regardless of whether they wanted a child of the given sex, are disappointed because of it, or truly had no preference. Even though boys and girls are cared for in much the same way while neonates, the child's gender stimulates subtle differences in parental handling and responses that are part of the covert training of the child to behave as a boy or a girl. We shall, however, defer considering the influence of gender upon the child's development until Chapter 7.

Often enough the gender of the child evokes disappointment in one or both parents—the father who wants an heir, or a boy he can raise to be a quarterback, or a son to take over his business; the mother who wants a daughter who will become more of a companion than her son, or who wants a boy to live out her fantasies of what life would have been like had she been a boy. A wife may feel rejected if she cannot produce a boy, even though she may consciously know that it is the husband's chromosomes that determine the sex of the offspring. She has such examples as the shah of Iran, who, despite the availability of excellent medical advice, divorced a wife because she produced daughters rather than the needed male heir.

STABILIZATION

The infant's physiological processes become considerably more stable by the end of its first month; breathing becomes regular, body temperature fluctuates less, and sucking becomes vigorous. The movements of the limbs become more or less symmetrical, but still random, though some infants can get their thumbs into their mouths to pacify themselves. The intervals between feelings of hunger have usually become more regular, but they are still brief and infants require five or more feedings every twenty-four hours. They enjoy a bath, its warmth, and the handling that goes with it, but protest if clothing is drawn on over the head—something to which infants seem to have an inborn aversion.

The nature of the neonate's world can only be reconstructed imaginatively. Although it seems to be dominated by the need for sleep and nutriment to foster growth and maturation, we have seen that, when in the proper state of arousal, the neonatal infant also assimilates sensations, and new stimuli can become more important than sleep. By the end of a month, infants' ways of reacting and relating have developed considerably from the reflex responses with which they were born. The mouth and lips—sucking and taking in—are central to infants' relatedness to the world in which they live; but almost imperceptibly their abilities have expanded through the use of sight, sound, and other ways of experiencing. Neonates do not distinguish between the self and the remainder of the world, including the nipple, whether flesh or latex, that comes and satiates and then disappears. Still, the baby is alive and responsive and in its undifferentiating way takes in sensations as well as milk—a satisfying closeness to the mother, her warmth, her feel, and her smell.

The lives of neonates differ from the onset. They are cleaned gently or roughly, bathed with confidence or trepidation, satiated or left tense and vaguely unhappy. Nurses familiar with neonates believe that they can often differentiate within the first weeks between babies who are content and those who are fretful in response to their mother's attitudes and handling. Many authorities believe that the mother's tensions are clearly conveyed to the neonate. Still, there are reasons to consider that newborn infants are not unduly sensitive to the manner in which they are handled, and, provided that their essential needs are met, the mother's emotional attitudes are important largely because of the patterns established and their consequences to the continuing mother-child relationship.

Neonates possess an omnipotence that they will never again possess. They but raise their voices and their needs are served. It is an omnipotence of helplessness; but they are fed, cleaned, cuddled, and kept comfortable. The feelings of undisturbed nirvana-like calm remain dimly within a person, and may serve as a retrogressive goal toward which individuals strive to return as they grow from it into a more demanding and disturbing world. All ill persons have a tendency to regress in order to regain care and protection, and the fetal position adopted by some schizophrenic patients is considered to derive from unconscious and unformed memories of the only period of bliss the patient has known. The neonate's helplessness diminishes gradually and the period blends into the remainder of infancy, but for many months the vital issues will continue to focus upon the parental persons' capacities to provide the total care that the young infant requires.

REFERENCES

ALDRICH, C. A. (1947). "The Advisability of Breast Feeding," *Journal of the American Medical Association*, 135:915–916.

Association for the Aid of Crippled Children. H. G. Birch, ed. (1964). *Brain Damage in Children*. Williams & Wilkins, Baltimore.

CONNOLLY, K., and STRATTON, P. (1969). "An Exploration of Some Parameters Affecting Classical Conditioning in the Neonate," *Child Development*, 40:431–441.

CORAH, N. L., ANTHONY, E. J., et al. (1965). *Effects of Perinatal Anoxia After Seven Years*. Psychological Monographs, vol. 79, no. 3.

ESCALONA, S. (1962). "The Study of Individual Differences and the Problem of State," *Journal of the American Academy of Child Psychiatry*, 1:11–37.

KORNER, A. F., and GROBSTEIN, R. (1966). "Visual Alertness as Related to Soothing in Neonates: Implications for Maternal Stimulation and Early Deprivation," *Child Development*, 37:867–876.

KRON, R. (1966). "Instrumental Conditioning of Nutritive Sucking in the Newborn," *Recent Advances in Biological Psychiatry*, 9:295–300.

READ, G. D. (1944). *Childbirth Without Fear: The Principles and Practice of Natural Childbirth*. Harper & Bros., New York.

SPOCK, B. (1968). *Baby and Child Care*. Hawthorn Books, New York. Rev. ed.

SONTAG, L. W. (1941). "The Significance of Fetal Environmental Differences," *American Journal of Obstetrics and Gynecology*, 42:996–1003.

—— (1944). "Differences in Modifiability of Fetal Behavior and Physiology," *Psychosomatic Medicine*, 6:151–154.

SPELT, D. K. (1948). "The Conditioning of the Human Fetus in Utero," *Journal of Experimental Psychology*, 38:338–346.

STENDLER, C. (1950). "Sixty Years of Child Training Practices," *Journal of Pediatrics*, 36:122–134.

VINCENT, C. E. (1951). "Trends in Infant Care Ideas," *Child Development*, 22:199–209.

WOLFF, P. H. (1966). "The Causes, Controls, and Organization of Behavior in the Neonate," *Psychological Issues*, vol. 5, no. 1, Monograph No. 17. International Universities Press, New York.

SUGGESTED READING

BENEDEK, T. (1956). "Psychological Aspects of Mothering," *American Journal of Orthopsychiatry*, 26:272–278.

BIBRING, G., DWYER, T. F., *et al.* (1961). "A Study of the Psychological Processes in Pregnancy and the Earliest Mother-Child Relationships: Some Propositions and Comments," in *The Psychoanalytic Study of the Child*, vol. 16, pp. 9–72. International Universities Press, New York.

BRODY, S. (1956). *Patterns of Mothering: Maternal Influence During Infancy*. International Universities Press, New York.

STONE, L. J., SMITH, H. T., and MURPHY, L. B., eds. (1973). *The Competent Infant*. Chaps. 1, 2, and 3. Basic Books, New York.

WOLFF, P. H. (1966). "The Causes, Controls, and Organization of Behavior in the Neonate," *Psychological Issues*, vol. 5, no. 1, Monograph No. 17. International Universities Press, New York.

CHAPTER 5

❀

Infancy

IN THE FIRST FIFTEEN MONTHS that we shall somewhat arbitrarily consider as the period of infancy, the helpless neonates turn into alert toddlers whose verve is fascinating, who actively explore their world, and who are learning how to gain some mastery over it by incessant experimentation. At some time around fifteen months of age, development leads to a focus on new tasks both for the infants and their parents; the children become ambulatory and can pursue objectives; they begin to try to direct their own behavior and yet do not have the capacities or the experience to do so, and the nurturing persons must set limitations for them.

These are a very long fifteen months. During no other period of life is the person so transformed both physically and developmentally. Yet what happens lies beyond the individual's recall, buried in the oblivion of wordlessness. At most some vague feeling, some amorphous recollection that eludes conscious memory may upon occasion flit in and out of an adult's awareness, perplexing or troubling as might a fragment of a dream. The inability to recollect our infancies sets limitations on our capacities properly to understand or depict the period. We depend largely upon observation and making presumptive connections between occurrences in infancy and characteristics that develop later in life. Still, because we recall nothing, there has been a tendency to discuss infancy in very global terms; sometimes primarily in terms of the infant's need for maternal love and of disturbances that ensue from lack of proper maternal nurturance or from frustration of oral needs. Yet these are the months when the foundations are laid, not only for future emotional stability, but also for basic though global character traits and for intellectual development. No part of life experience will be as solidly incorporated in the individual, become so irrevocably a part of a person, as infancy.

The clarification of how the various developments occur and how the profound transformation from neonate to toddler transpires has awaited direct, skilled, and detailed observations of infants.* Such direct observational studies, and particularly longitudinal studies that relate the events of infancy to subsequent personality functioning, are vital to assessing the importance of various influences affecting the infant and to clarifying the essentials of infant care.

During infancy profound maturational changes take place. The baby's weight triples by the end of the first year, and at fifteen months may be close to twenty-five pounds. With six teeth and the buccal pads filled, the face has rounded out. The nerves of the pyramidal tracts of the spinal cord that transmit motor impulses from the cortex have been covered by myelin sheaths and become functional, enabling the child to learn to stand, walk, and begin to gain sphincter control. The buttocks that were miniscule at birth have filled out, and body proportions have changed so that the head, while still relatively large, is balanced by the trunk and extremities.

THE NEED FOR TOTAL NURTURANCE

When we scrutinize the infant's developmental progress carefully, we find that so much occurs over fifteen months that we may doubt the wisdom of considering this span collectively as a single period. Indeed, so profound a

---

* Planned, scientific study of the infant's development has been carried out only during the past three or four decades. It has not always been obvious that the infant's personality development is a topic for scientific study. Direct observation of infants and children over the course of time probably started with Gesell's careful studies of maturation that established landmarks for comparison, and with Piaget's studies of the cognitive development of his own children in the service of epistemology. Currently, a variety of direct studies is expanding our knowledge of the period. Longitudinal studies through infancy and childhood are difficult to carry out, and many of them tend to focus on some specific facet of the problem to avoid a complexity that cannot be handled with scientific rigor. Only an occasional study is conducted in the infant's natural habitat, the home.

shift in behavior takes place some time between the sixth and eighth months that we shall divide the period in half, and subdivide it still further. However, infancy is unified by the extent of the children's dependency on others, by the inability to walk or talk except in halting and rudimentary fashion, and by the limitations of their intelligence.

Throughout infancy children are dependent upon the nurturant care provided by others. During the first several months when the predominant portion of their energies go into growth and they can survive only under carefully controlled conditions, the physical aspects of nurturant care are most important. Young infants require food, warmth, diapering, bathing, and care of their delicate skin to permit the long periods of sleep during which their organisms mature to become prepared for survival with better physiologic homeostasis than at birth. Then, as we shall discuss, the infant increasingly requires stimulating and socializing experiences to provide "aliment" for developing into a person. The lack of adequate physical care means death, wasting, or ill health; failure of socializing nurturance means distortion of emotional development and stunting of intellectual growth. The two aspects of nurturant care are obviously interrelated: the infant whose basic physiologic needs are not, or cannot, be satisfied remains in a state of tension that impedes the absorption of environmental stimuli, and it appears as if some infants make "friends with death for lack of love alone."*

During the first few months, physical nurturance is critical; even though affectionate care and cognitive stimulation are important, their neglect can probably be largely neutralized by subsequent attention. Disregard of such needs in the second half of infancy, however, leaves permanent impairments that can later be ameliorated but never undone. Whereas infants continue to require careful attention to their physical needs in the latter part of infancy, they are more resilient, which permits greater leeway in the manner in which physical care is provided. Still, it is a relative matter, for the socializing care provided during the first four months is very important even though not so essential as later. The mother who is pleased with herself and with having a baby brings a great deal of socialization to her small infant almost without realizing it. She cuddles her baby while she nurses, whether from breast or bottle; she holds her baby boy or girl closely for a moment after lifting the infant from the bassinet; she smiles at it, talks, and croons, while holding the baby in her lap or changing a diaper. She shakes her head up and down at him, shuttles him about gently as she raises him into the air to admire him at arm's length; she swishes

---

* Edna St. Vincent Millay, "Love Is Not All."

him about in the bath, drips water from the cloth onto his chest, scoops handfuls of warm water over him; she kisses his feet and holds his face to hers. Indeed, the mother is very likely to carry out a great deal of play, stimulation, and interaction with the infant simply as tangible expressions of her feelings toward her infant, her delight with her baby, and of her satisfaction with herself for having produced her boy or girl.

Mutuality Between Parents and Infant*

The provision of nurturance that fills the infant's needs is not always simple. Instruction and even firm tradition cannot take into account the marked differences among infants, or provide the mother with the "feel" that seems so important to establishing the proper mutuality between infant and mother. Although infants at a given stage of maturation are much alike, they also vary markedly within the range and patterns common to all. It is obvious that they look different and act and react diversely. Infants suck more vigorously, quietly, or apathetically; they take in different amounts of food and are satiated for longer or shorter periods; they are cuddly, sprawling, or resistant when held; their thresholds of alertness and sensitivity to discomfort vary; they vary from being very placid to hyperactive. Less apparent but just as surely, infants' physiological processes differ and influence their needs and how they mature and develop.

* We shall consider the importance of a mutuality between parents and infant largely in terms of the mother-child relationship, even though not all infants receive their primary care from mothers; and increasingly, fathers share the care of the infant and sometimes even fill the primary nurturant role. It seems advantageous, for reasons that will be presented, for the infant to relate to a single primary nurturing person with whose feel and ways of handling and relating the child can interact and who, in turn, is thoroughly familiar with the child and the child's preverbal signals. As considered in the previous chapter, the mother usually has a deeper sense of unity with the infant than does the father. Still, not all mothers are able to invest the baby adequately. A mother may be perfunctory and silent in handling the child, particularly if she is depressed following the birth, as occurs commonly enough. The infant may be nurtured more salubriously by the father or by an experienced, secure, and interested nurse than by the mother. Indeed, although the practice of leaving the essential care of the infant and small child to a nursemaid, once common among the well-to-do, has diminished greatly, many children are still raised in this manner. The mother, or both parents, can still form a good relationship with their infant by enjoying playful interactions with the child, or assume responsibility for those matters for which they feel secure and competent.

Under some circumstances, the infant may do best in a nursery that has a competent and devoted staff while the parents work—as in a kibbutz. The effects of multiple parental figures upon the child's development still remain unclear; but the care of multiple parental figures is clearly preferable to relative neglect or incompetent care.

In any event, it is virtually necessary to discuss parent-infant care largely in terms of the mother, because almost all studies aside from those of kibbutz child rearing have been concerned with the mother-child relationship.

We know that inborn characteristics will influence the sort of person a baby will become; but it is often difficult to ascertain just which traits come into the world within the infant and which appear in response to the type and quality of the nurture provided. In any case, the interweaving of inborn and environmental influences starts in the uterus and becomes increasingly complex during birth and thereafter. Some infants would present difficulties to any mother, but some mothers would create difficulties for any infant. At different periods in history or in different social settings the infant or the mother is more likely to be blamed: the baby is just impossible, or the mother is rejecting or emotionally unsuited to being a mother. Whatever the source of difficulty, we know that young infants can do nothing about their part in establishing a proper symbiosis with their mothers; and although we like to think that mothers could be different from what they are if they would only try, the most pertinent matters concern feelings and attitudes that are not readily influenced by conscious decision. We must try to accept both infants and mothers as they are, and hope that support, advice, or psychotherapy can help the mothers and that improved nurturance, perhaps more suited to infants' specific needs, will enable them to be more satisfied and easier to manage.

Some parents may find it easier to enjoy a placid infant, others a baby who is more alert and responsive or even hyperactive. One mother will feel more maternal because her infant has difficulties in nursing, but another will feel frustrated, tense, and angry. Problems can be compounded by the great changes which occur as infancy progresses and which require constant shifts in how the parents relate to their baby. To serve properly as a surrogate ego and meet the child's needs, a parent must not only empathize with the child but also with a child who is changing more rapidly than at any other time of life. Such shifts are made particularly difficult because infants can tell nothing; and parental figures must grasp how their infant feels, what it needs, what it may be able to do, and what it is that exceeds its abilities today, but may not next week. Clearly, experience, education, and conscious knowledge can help, but a great deal of interaction and decision making is carried out intuitively. Some mothers, presumably because of their own experiences during infancy and early childhood, have an earthy sensuous attachment to the infant; some have gained security, ease and knowledge from having helped raise younger siblings; and some simply gain so much pleasure from caring for their babies that the proper feelings follow. The care of the child is burdensome to some parents, for it seems like a very one-sided proposition with little reward. However, some parents, fathers as well as mothers, who had been reluctant to have a child, learn that having a baby need them, be dependent upon them, and be satisfied and happy because of them provides a deep sense of fulfillment and pleasure that the Japanese call *amaeru*, for which we lack a word in English (Doi, 1973). Indeed, many mothers feel that their infants give them a great deal: a sense of completion; relief from engorged breasts and the pleasure of having them sucked; focus to their lives; a source of interest and pride; a new bond to their husbands. Although the unit of mother and child is of primary importance throughout infancy, the pair are not living in isolation, and the mother's capacities to feel herself in a unity with the infant and the pleasure she gets in so doing reflect her relations to her husband and her other children as well as her own personality.

A proper empathy permits a consistency in responding to the infant's changing needs and ways which permits a type of nonverbal communication to become established between mother and child that eases the first year of life and greatly helps keep the discomforts and tensions of both mother and child minimal. But it also serves other important purposes. The mother's relaxation and comfort and also her tensions and irritability are conveyed to the infant through her handling. The relief of a mother's tensions may well be almost as important to infants as relief of their own needs. Perhaps the first leverage in having infants rescind instinctual efforts to gain immediate relief of tensions produced by hunger or thirst comes when they delay or modify their behavior in order to have the comfort of a relaxed mother. Such responsiveness on the part of infants can arise only when their mothers' ways of relating to them are sufficiently consistent to enable them to become conditioned to, or otherwise learn, signals and cues. Further, such responsivity to felt and observed cues by both mother and child provides the foundations upon which more clear-cut communicative signals will develop, and provides assurance that the infant will gain trust in the value of communication—including verbal communication—as a means of solving problems.

Basic Trust

A critical task and a central theme of infancy concerns the establishment of feelings of confidence in the world (Benedek, 1938). While completely dependent upon the care of others, children need to gain a sense that those upon whom they unknowingly depend, and who constitute their world, are dependable. As Erikson (1950) has aptly put it, the child attains a *basic trust* in others which will form the nucleus for achieving trust in the self, or the child is left with an enduring distrust. If children's essential needs are met when they are unable to provide anything for themselves, they gain a feeling that the world is trustworthy and adequately consistent to enable them to live in it with security. The provision of a firm foundation during infancy permits children to move into the next phase and invest their energies and attention in solving its basic tasks. They will have experienced and have established at the core of their personalities the security that when they were helplessly dependent, unbearable tensions had not been permitted to mount within them to provoke rage, nor had neglect led to the establishment of a pattern of apathy to defend against untenable tensions, nor had parental fears and anxieties been transmitted to them through the parents' ways of handling and responding to them. In contrast, deprivations during infancy interfere with progression as energy continues to be expended in a repetitive seeking after the satisfactions and security that were lacking. Such frustrations pave the way for tendencies toward regressive strivings for dependency and a hungering for affection in later life; or engender proclivities toward pessimistic hopelessness and to resentful rage when the individual is deprived.

A basic *trust in the self,* a pervasive sense of confidence that becomes an inherent characteristic in later life, rests upon *trust in others* during infancy because during much of infancy there is no clear boundary between the self and the remainder of the world, and infants cannot differentiate between how they feel and what others do that influences their feelings.

Infancy as the "Oral" Phase

Psychoanalytic psychology has termed infancy the *oral phase* of psychosexual development, thus emphasizing that the infant's life centers upon taking in nutriment through sucking and that the first critical relationships with others form while completely dependent upon them and receiving the vital nourishment from them.* In the process, a firm and enduring connection is established between affection and feeding, between a need for others and oral activity, and a basis is laid for later wishes, when overwhelmed by life's difficulties, to return or regress to such oral dependency. Infants are born prepared to maintain life by sucking and swallowing, which are their only organized way of relating to anything outside of themselves. The lips and their mucocutaneous junction areas are highly sensitive, and their

---

* Originally the concept of the oral phase, as noted in Chapter 3, connoted that the lips and mouth were the area in which the libido was primarily invested during the first year of life. It is not necessary to utilize this concept of a displaceable sexualized energy to explain the importance of orality in infancy and the erotization of the oral zone.

stimulation sets off the sucking reflex. They are not only sensitive but a source of sensuous pleasure which serves to assure—in evolutionary terms —that the infant will seek the stimulation that sets off sucking. The oral zone and the act of sucking are erotized in that sucking is pleasurable for its own sake, as is obvious if one watches babies suck their thumbs with lustful avidity, and because of the generalized gratification that accompanies nutritional and also non-nutritional sucking. Other types of sensual pleasure will be related to these oral satisfactions and connect orality to sexuality.

The period is "oral" also in the broader sense that infants' development rests upon assimilating stimuli from the environment to start the organization of their cognitive processes, and because their emotional security rests upon gaining feelings of security and well-being from those who nurture them.

The concept of orality, however, must not be taken too literally* as implying that how the child is fed is almost all that matters. Other sensations are also very important to the very young infant. Tactile sensations and skin erotism, as well as the totality of the handling, are significant in providing a sense of comfort and security in the infant.† The "oral" relatedness properly includes the relationship through touch, voice, odor, body position, warmth, and the visual connections to the mother's eyes and face that are an important aspect of nursing. Indeed, the infant's attachment to parenting persons depends as much on parental responsiveness to the baby's cries and how much social interaction with the infant is initiated as upon any other determinants (Schaffer and Emerson, 1964). The security, tenderness, and conviction with which the mother carries out her many maternal tasks enter into conveying the sense of inherent trust that is a cardinal

* Such literal concern with "oral libido" has led some to discuss problems of the period virtually in terms of the relationship between the mother's breast and the child's mouth. Melanie Klein and her followers have made significant contributions by drawing attention to the intensity of the infant's primitive feeling states and their influence on development, but they have neglected the state of the infant's cognitive development and attributed perceptions and concepts to it that are impossible at this period of life. The notions of the "good" and "bad" breast can be considered only metaphorically. See M. Klein, *The Psycho-analysis of Children*.

† Harlow (1958, 1966), in a classic experiment, demonstrated the importance of skin erotism in the infantile "oral" behavior of monkeys. He had rhesus infants nursed by artificial mothers of two types: one was constructed of wire and contained a bottle and nipple; the other was covered with terry cloth and did not contain a feeding device. The monkeys fed from the "wire mother"; but when frightened by a snakelike device that set off an inborn fear reaction, they ran to the "terry cloth mother" and clung to it, very much as baby monkeys cling to a real mother when frightened. Thus, the feeding did not lead the baby monkeys to turn to the wire device as a mother; the tactile quality of the terry cloth was more important. We shall refer to these experiments again for other important, though serendipitous, findings.

task of the period. However, the very young infant's sense of well-being and readiness to socialize rest on his proper nourishment, and we shall return to discuss feeding shortly.

OTHER MAJOR DEVELOPMENTAL TASKS

Although the attainment of an inherent sense of trust is a crucial task of infancy and critical to the future emotional well-being of the individual, it is far from the only fundamental task of infancy. In the first fifteen months the child traverses a great distance and establishes the foundations for many developmental accomplishments. However, such abilities and characteristics are potentials permitted by the process of physical maturation which the infant acquires under reasonable environmental conditions with greater or lesser facility, but they are not an inherent part of maturation. As careful studies of seriously deprived children have taught, without suitable nurturant care if not affection, and without environmental stimulation and an opportunity to use limbs and sense organs, very little developmental progress may take place—as will be discussed later in the chapter.

Even without considering the catastrophic results of gross neglect, it is apparent that what a baby will be like by the end of infancy depends upon the interplay of many factors. Erikson (1950) has stated that "while it is clear what must happen to keep a baby alive and what must not happen lest he be physically damaged or chronically upset, there is a certain leeway in regard to what may happen." This leeway permits different societies to utilize differing child-rearing procedures, each of which the members of the society consider to be the only proper method. One society will leave its infants to cry until the scheduled time for feeding; in another, mothers carry their babies in slings, positioned so that they can nurse at the breast when they desire; in a third, the newborn might be swaddled and left in covered cradles for months; and in still others, the baby might be handed to experienced wetnurses who nourish and nurture the child for the first year or two. Each method works but leaves its imprint on the developing personality. Indeed, the varying techniques are part of the way in which each society unknowingly prepares its offspring to become proper members.

The essential tasks of the mother are simplified in societies with definitive traditional directives for infant care. The mother can carry out her functions with a conviction and security that help impart an innate sense of trust to her child,* particularly since in such societies little if any connection between the child-rearing procedures and the child's future personality is appreciated. The situation of contemporary American parents is apt to be very different. They may mistrust the traditional and be very much on their own; and they are often burdened by an awareness that just what they do, how they feel, their own problems, etc., may be influencing their child's future. In considering the infant's development and the importance of the parents, it should be realized that an infant has considerable resiliency.

The Parents' Security

In general, the precise techniques for caring for babies and handling them are less important than having secure and consistent parents who can enjoy their infant and achieve a close mutuality with him or her. An overemphasis on the benefits of breast feeding or of prolonged breast feeding has at times been as brash as the behaviorist strictures of an earlier period.† And warnings of the dire consequences of relatively minor deficiencies in handling the young infant have been based upon theory and conjecture rather than definitive knowledge.** Fortunately, the infant seems very capable of tolerating the awkwardness of new and well-inten-

---

* This does not imply that the traditional techniques are always suited to instilling a basic trust; there are indications that the Balinese techniques described elsewhere in this book (see also G. Bateson and M. Mead, 1942) prevent the development of such trust, and sometimes a workable child-rearing pattern no longer exists—as perhaps during the Middle Ages after the Black Death and the Crusades so disrupted the structure of European society that in some localities only one out of every ten babies reached adulthood.

† Thus a psychiatrist who noted the paucity of anxiety states and combat neuroses among the Okinawans during the intense fighting for their island in World War II attributed their emotional stability to the fact that Okinawans were habitually breast-fed for three years (Moloney, 1945). He did not take other potential factors into account or realize that although Okinawans might be unusually mentally healthy on Okinawa, Okinawans living in Hawaii had mental illness rates as high as or higher than the remainder of the population, even though they too had been breast-fed for several years.

** There is no evidence that childhood schizophrenia, severe apathy, or serious mental retardation can be related to deficiencies in maternal care of the infant alone, unless it is a matter of severe neglect, maternal apathy, or brutality; and certainly there is no reason to believe that lack of cuddling, faulty holding, or inadvertent frustration lead to any such dire consequences.

Margaret Ribble's widely read book, The Rights of Infants, though properly drawing attention to the relief of tensions that can be accomplished by proper handling, feeding, etc., seems to have overstated the case to the extent of frightening some mothers and inadvertently creating the tensions in handling their babies that the author sought to have them overcome. Hilde Bruch's Don't Be Afraid of Your Child sought to reassure mothers of the sturdiness of their infants' emotional balance in order to offset such influences.

tioned mothers. Although mothers do not always know best, provoking guilt in a mother because her needs sometimes take precedence over her baby's, or because her personality difficulties make her anxious in caring for the baby, helps neither mother nor child. Personality problems are not solved by admonition or through warnings of dire consequences. Fostering security is usually far more important; the care of the baby can and should provide pleasure and become neither a chore that wears out the parents nor a source of constant concern.

THE NURTURE OF THE YOUNG INFANT

During the first few months the infant's feeding and sleeping are of central importance; and the parents' sleep as well as the child's depends greatly upon the feeding. The parents seek to furnish ample nourishment, to keep the baby clean and warm, to provide suitable conditions for sleeping. The infant can in these first months survive and even flourish with little socializing activity; but, after the first few weeks, stimulation, cuddling, and being talked at make a difference. A clear relationship exists between the amount of crying and the amount of nurturant care provided.* Indeed, parents often err in attributing their baby's crying to hunger. Even during the first few months a type of crying that seems to be related to a need for cuddling or activity can be quieted by rocking or walking with the baby (Illingworth, 1955). Still, because of the critical importance to the infant of proper nutrition, but also to help foster a proper mutuality between mother and child, breast feeding has been encouraged by many pediatricians and obstetricians during recent years, as has been discussed in the preceding chapter. However, we must realize that only a minority of mothers in the United States nurse their babies. When a mother breast-feeds willingly and without conscious conflict, breast feeding is very likely to be the most satisfactory method for both mother and baby; but there is nothing inherent in the process to insure gentleness, restfulness, or intimacy.† When a woman nurses from a sense of obligation or to prove to herself that she is a good mother, it is of dubious value. Indeed, it is likely that a mother who

* In a systematic study the crying of neonates was reduced by 50 percent by increasing nurturant care from 0.7 to 1.9 hours a day for each infant (Aldrich et al., 1946).
† Brody (1956) found by experimental observation that neither breast feeding, nor demand feeding, nor holding the baby while it was being fed would separately or collectively assure satisfaction in feeding.

does not really wish to nurse will have sufficient milk.* An impression has long existed that the milk of anxious or tense mothers may cause gastrointestinal upsets—which may be the reason a leading dairy firm advertises "milk from contented cows." However, the mother's tensions may be conveyed through the manner in which she handles the baby rather than through her milk. In any event, the manner in which infants take their food and how they digest it often reflects their mothers' handling,† and it is a matter that concerns attitudes and feelings that are not easily overcome by conscious effort or direct instruction, though instruction that serves to reassure and promote confidence can be very helpful.

Demand Feeding

The desire of pediatricians to see that their young patients receive adequate nourishment and oral gratification, and their recognition of the deleterious effects of frustration, have led many of them to recommend the practice of "demand feeding" (Aldrich and Hewitt, 1947).** According to this regimen, the infants are fed when they cry or otherwise show their hunger. The practice follows upon the realization that infants differ both in how much milk they can take at a feeding and also in how long it meets their needs. Little is gained by making infants wait for a scheduled feeding when they are becoming upset. A seriously frustrated and enraged baby has difficulty in nursing, and an upset child's gastric functioning may not be suited for digestion. The infant is incapable of learning to wait for a sched-

---

* Newton and Newton (1950) found that 74 percent of ninety-one mothers with a positive attitude about nursing before they delivered had enough milk by the fifth postnatal day, as against 26 percent with negative attitudes. Newton (1951) also reported a correlation between preference for breast feeding and the avoidance of rigid feeding schedules.

† Escalona (1945), in a study of infants of mothers in a reformatory, found that infants' refusals of food, sudden changes in preferences, and digestive upsets occurred in relation to the attitudes and behavior of the person who was feeding them, or to such factors as separation from the mother. In eight of ten infants who refused to take the mother's breast, the mothers were clearly high-strung and excitable; and six infants accepted a formula from another feeder on the same day on which they refused the same formula when offered by their mothers.

** "Demand feeding" also arose in reaction to the rigid scheduling that had been foisted upon mothers by pediatricians under the influence of behaviorist psychologists in the 1920s and 1930s. By this approach, a baby was to be trained—conditioned—almost from birth, and a mother who gave in to a child's needs for food at an unscheduled time was considered a bad mother who spoiled the child. Only reasonably self-sufficient mothers were likely to follow their own feelings and defy the authorities. A comparison of the 1938 and 1948 editions of the U.S. Children's Bureau bulletin *Infant Care*, published by the U.S. Government Printing Office, provides striking evidence of the vast change that occurred in these ten years concerning the child-rearing procedures advocated.

uled time during the first several months of life, and even later has little tolerance for delay. "Demand feeding" is a sensible approach, particularly when the mother can be adaptable in using it. If the mother can anticipate when her baby will become hungry and is not overly concerned about letting the child cry for a short time, a satisfactory feeding pattern can usually be established within a few weeks as the infant gains in physiological stability. Some mothers, however, who are insecure and overly conscientious interpret "demand" to mean that babies must be fed only when they cry and then as soon as they cry; mothers then can become enslaved to the task, often confusing the infant in the process, and her aggravation disrupts the mother-child harmony (Brody, 1956). When, as has been observed, a mother tries to nurse twenty or thirty times a day, a consistent signaling system cannot be established, and the child's socializing activities may be neglected.*

ATTACHMENT BEHAVIOR

The mere fact that a woman has become a mother provides no assurance that she will be maternal. The capacities to be properly nurturant involve basic factors in her own development and in her marriage which will be discussed in subsequent chapters. Still, there are biological factors in both mother and child that help establish an attachment between parents, especially the mother, and child. One potential benefit of breast feeding is that the pituitary hormone prolactin which stimulates the flow of milk may help foster feelings of receptive passivity and contentment in the mother (Benedek, 1949). We have noted that both the infant's lips and the mother's nipples are erogenous zones: sucking gratifies the baby independently of the satisfaction derived from food intake; and the baby's sucking properly provides the mother with sensuous pleasure, including genital stimulation. Bowlby (1969) has suggested that several forces induce "attachment behavior" between mother and child which he relates to "imprinting" phenomena in ground-nesting birds and the attachment of baby ungulates to their mothers. Although Bowlby may overstate the situation by the

---

* Disturbances in regulation of body weight, both obesity and pathological underweight, have been related to parents' feeding the infant and child in response to any indications of discomfort, thus preventing the child from establishing a connection between physiologically aroused sensations of hunger and the need for food (Bruch, 1961).

analogy, several factors of potential importance should not be neglected. It has become increasingly apparent that in the process of evolution infants became endowed with various means of fostering the attachment of parental figures to them, as well as for promoting their own attachments to specific persons. The mother's odor may, as in many animals, form a basic linkage between babies and their own mothers or mothering persons.* It has been suggested that the infant's crying may arouse some inborn response in adults. Whether the response is innate or not, most adults find the baby's wails sufficiently unpleasant to induce them to try to stop the crying through feeding, cuddling, or rocking the infant. The baby rapidly forms an auditory linkage to the parental figure: within a few days of birth a mother can pick out her child's cries from those of other neonates; and within a few weeks infants react specifically to their own mothers' voices. After the first month the infant's babbling usually evokes a vocal response from an adult, and a few weeks later a cooing or babbling interchange with the baby can be maintained for some minutes, particularly by the mother (Wolff, 1963). When the baby's eyes focus on a parent's face, and engage in eye-to-eye contact at about four weeks of age, a new phase in the mother-child relationship seems to start (Greenman, 1963). Wolff reports that mothers commented "Now he is fun to play with" and "Now he can see me" and began to spend more time with the child.

Smiling

The baby comes into the world equipped with the facility to smile, which by the fourth week develops into a social smile. The baby smiles on seeing the mother's face, which leads the mother to feel that her baby now recognizes her. Wolff (1959) has documented the observation that there is a noticeable rise in the amount of attention that the mother gives her child after the baby begins to smile at her. We must examine this slight but important event that so fosters the mother's attachment to her infant.

Within twelve hours of birth, neonates grimace in a way that suggests smiling (Wolff, 1959), and by the second week gentle stroking or a soft sound, particularly a high pitched voice, can elicit a fleeting smile in a

---

* The hypothesis is difficult to test in infants. However, older children can be noted to gain comfort and pleasure by inhaling the mother's odor, perhaps her genital odor, when they stand with head in the mother's skirt and sniff or breathe deeply. The relationship of the mother's odor to certain types of fetishist behavior and renifleur activities constitutes a complex and inadequately studied topic. Ainsworth (1967) noted that, when about six months old, infants in Uganda would bury their faces in their mothers' laps.

drowsy baby. Sometimes by the end of two weeks, and almost always by the end of a month, a soft human voice produces a definite smile in an alert baby, and may even change crying into smiling. Then, between the fourth and sixth weeks, the human face rather than the voice elicits the smile. The child searches the face and, when eye-to-eye contact is made, grins. Spitz's (1965) studies indicate, however, that babies innocently perpetrate a fraud upon their mothers by inducing them to believe that the smile is one of personal recognition. The baby does not really recognize the mother.* Any face will do, provided it is seen full, for a profile will not elicit the smile. According to Piaget, a singing and nodding full face will be most successful in eliciting the response at first. Spitz further found that the region of the forehead, eyes, and nose is the inducer of the response; it does not matter if the mouth is covered, but the smile is not elicited if any portion of the upper face is covered. Actually, it does not require a face; a crudely formed mask resembling the forehead and eyes suffices to elicit the smile when moved up and down.† However, the human face is a more effective stimulus. Although babies discriminate their mothers' voices by the fourth week, they smile at strangers as readily as at their mothers until the fourth month.

THE YOUNG INFANT'S WORLD

The infant's development starts slowly but accelerates during the third and fourth months. When the baby is about four months old the period of diffuse existence in which maturation and growth predominate is coming to an end, and the infant has become more of a social creature, with something of a distinctive personality. Babies have doubled their birth weight and are far more sturdy than they were at birth. Their lives no longer

---

* Although Spitz, who carefully investigated the smiling response, placed its appearance between the second and sixth *month*, it is now clear that it appears between the fourth and sixth week. Spitz studied institutionalized children, who were late in forming the response because of deprivation.

† It is possible that the early smiling response is an inborn response to a specific "releaser," the "releaser" consisting of a pattern resembling a human forehead, eyes, and nose, even as certain birds respond to a fixed pattern in the mother's coloring or in the appearance of a hereditary enemy—the smiling response here having an evolutionary survival value through fostering proper nurturant care. Ahrens (1954) found that a face-sized card with two black "eye" dots would suffice and that a card with six black dots was still more effective.

consist primarily of sleeping and eating, and they now are awake for fairly long periods, playing with their hands, looking and listening, and making cooing and gurgling sounds. They can now be propped into a sitting position and with the grasp reflex gone can clutch at things and play with their fingers, and they seem intrigued by dangling toys. They watch and listen and are alert to cues that signal what may happen next. Life has gained regularity through a pattern of an unbroken sleep of ten or twelve hours at night and reasonably regular feedings three to five times a day. When we study them closely they have gained many capacities and skills since they were born.

The slow start reflects not only the dominance of maturational needs during the first several months, but also the building of a foundation to which experiences can be assimilated. The newborn's mind may not be a "tabula rasa" (for it has a predetermined structure and organization), but it is bereft of experience with which to perceive its surroundings. However, the infants are far from passive recipients of experience, even though the stimulation must be brought to them. As Piaget has demonstrated (see Chapter 3), there is active assimilation of the external world, with concomitant reorganization and expansion of capacities, as the child's schemata accommodate to encompass what has been assimilated.

COGNITIVE DEVELOPMENT

A fine balance exists between what attracts and holds infants' attention or what they simply ignore, on the one hand, and what causes discomfort or even disorganizing fear, on the other. Unless a schema exists to which a new experience can be assimilated, babies pay no attention to a stimulus until it intrudes upon them. If a new sensation or action is assimilated to a schema, the child tries to repeat the experience (by means of circular reactions) until it has been accommodated into the schema—or we may say, the child has become habituated to it. Infants at all stages can be very alert and active in fostering such repetition, but when accommodation to it has been completed they seem bored by it, are ready to expand the schema by assimilating new pertinent experiences, and have a vigorous appetite for change of stimulus. A baby will examine a spot on the side of the crib with great interest over and over, but after a time act as if it no longer existed. However, when a stimulus that seems to fit into a familiar schema turns out to be distorted or somehow violates expectations it is likely to upset the child. Thus, after a mask of a face has been repeatedly presented to the child to elicit a smiling response, a mask with the eyes and nose turned sideway can provoke frightened crying. In an older child, if a person initially taken for the mother turns out to be a stranger, the child experiences anxiety.*

We must also appreciate that the "aliment" or stimulation provided by an object changes with experience. The thumb is, at first, simply part of a sucking schema, then later it is something to be looked at as part of a visual schema, and still later as something to poke into objects to explore their shapes, etc. Thus an object's meaning for a child and the relationships between objects change constantly as the child develops cognitively.

Let us consider some of Piaget's observations of how the infant acquires the abilities of a four-month-old baby by this gradual process of assimilation of new experiences, and the modification of existing schemata in the process.

Piaget's First Stage

Piaget terms the first two years *The Period of Sensori-Motor Development*. Its first stage, which approximates the first month, is simply called *The Use of Reflexes*, in which the innate sucking and grasp reflexes and the eye movements are modified slightly (Piaget, 1963, p. 23). As there is little accommodation to sensory "aliments," little expansion in what can be assimilated by the infant occurs. However, as noted in the preceding chapter, some assimilation starts on the first day of life, and changes in smiling and in response to sounds are apparent by the third week. Sucking is set off by an increasing variety of different stimuli to the lips; the head reflexly turns to the side on which the lips are stimulated; and some discrimination between non-nurturant and nurturant objects develops in that when infants are hungry they are apt to reject their fingers or any thing other than the nipple as an object for sucking.

The Second Stage

The second stage of sensori-motor development starts at the age of a few weeks and continues approximately through the fourth month. It is *The Stage of First Acquired Adaptations and the Primary Circular Reaction*.

* As Wolff (1963) notes, each repetition of a circular reaction alters behavior to some degree, sometimes almost imperceptibly, and change is cumulative rather than abrupt. Until repetition of an act no longer changes behavior, "the corresponding schema is said to be in a state of disequilibrium." The theory assumes that disequilibrium gives rise to a need to function, or a need to repeat action to the point of adaptation.

Now the innate reflex patterns begin to be modified. The changes in the sucking schema are most apparent and it is worth examining these seemingly trivial alterations, as they form the simplest example of the pattern of assimilation and accommodation that forms the core of Piaget's conceptualization of cognitive development. The tongue in the sucking schema accidentally licks the lips and thus receives a new type of sensation or stimulation—new sensory aliment. The sensori-motor schema repeats the activity that provided the new aliment and becomes circular in "seeking" to regain it. The innate reflex schema of sucking is now altered by the experience; the sensation of lips on tongue has been assimilated and the sensori-motor sequence accommodates to include it. In such fashion children begin to modify reflex patterns, build up schemata, and start their intellectual development and knowledge of the world.

The infant soon begins to bring the thumb to the mouth, originally by accident, but the behavior develops into a firm schema after frequent repetitions as a circular reaction; it is rewarded by relief of tension through sucking and by the erogenous pleasure of the act. Children follow objects that fall within the visual field during the first month, and soon spend much waking time staring at objects. They are not perceiving as yet,* but simply looking and assimilating, gradually organizing their visual schemata. Through a blending of visual schemata with sucking schemata, they will respond to the sight of the bottle by opening the mouth or by stopping their crying. Soon, aside from crying, children show a tendency to repeat sounds they make—blowing noises, little laughing sounds, etc.—and the sounds themselves serve as stimuli for their reproduction in circular reactions. Then some distinctions that begin to signal differing needs may be noted in the child's vocalization as well as cries. Such differentiation will depend upon the mother's consistency in responding to different sounds, which then leads the child to repeat the sound which is the first part of the circular reaction that leads to the effect. These simple accommodations of the vocalizing muscles to repeat sounds heard are important preliminaries of learning to speak. The schemata of hearing and vision begin to interpenetrate and accommodate to one another, and soon babies listen to what they see, and look at sounds.

Sucking activities are, of course, very much the center of the infant's life.

---

* Studies of congenitally blind persons whose sight was operatively restored in adolescence or adult life indicate how visual perception must be organized through experience. Patients reported that at first they experienced only new strange sensations or diffuse light. It took days to discriminate any differences between objects. These were persons who, in contrast to the infant, had already organized their surroundings through nonvisual perception—had an object concept and names for objects.

The mouth, at first, is virtually an organ of prehension, through which many things are sampled and experienced. However, starting in this second period, the grasp reflex diminishes and manual prehension develops rapidly. Piaget has studied the changes in prehension, carefully considering five substages that lead from the simplest circular reactions to the ability to look at what is grasped and to try to grasp what is seen.* This coordination between grasping and vision forms a notable step toward differentiating objects and relating to the world. Sucking and the visual-sucking schemata diminish in importance, whereas the coordination of vision and handling increasingly gain importance as a means of relating to and understanding the environment. Then, at about the end of the third month the child begins to coordinate vision, prehension, and sucking. Thus a child, looking at the mother's hand, grasps it, and draws it toward the mouth while looking at it.†

INTERACTIONAL ACTIVITIES

Although in these first months of life infants are primarily occupied with physical maturation, including the stabilization of their physiological processes, they have also prepared for the intense interaction with parental persons that will soon begin to take place. Infants can control their hand movements; differentiate sounds; respond to faces with a smile accompanied by arm waving, kicking, and babbling; anticipate sufficiently to stop crying at the sight of their mothers, a bottle, or the sound of mother's voice. They make a wide variety of sounds which they keep practicing by circular reactions. Still the mother is not yet a person, for there are no

---

* The sequence is as follows: (1) The innate grasp reflex is modified by primary circular reactions that lead to repetitions of touching and grasping of various parts of the body—bringing the hand to the mouth to suck, and a simple staring at the hands in the visual field. (2) The child not only carries whatever is grasped to the mouth, but also grasps whatever is placed in the mouth—a prelude to the future dominance of prehension over mouthing. (3) Looking at the hand in the visual field leads to an increase in hand movements, which suggests that causing a new sensation in the visual field leads to a circular reaction of repeating the hand movement that changed the visual sensations. Now, when the hand happens into the visual field, it can be held there. (4) The infant can grasp objects in the visual field. At about four months, for example, if the rattle and hand are *both* in the visual field, the infant can grasp the rattle. (5) The child looks at what is grasped and tries to grasp what is looked at, a tendency that can cause the mother considerable difficulty.

† J. Piaget, *The Origins of Intelligence in Children*, pp. 89–121. See also P. H. Wolff, "The Developmental Psychologies of Jean Piaget and Psychoanalysis."

persons. There is no proper distinction between the self and the environment, or between what is internal and external, or between objects and the sensori-motor patterns through which the infant interacts with them. Nevertheless, the mother is distinguished from others. Some children will, at eight weeks, cry if picked up by a stranger, and although four-month-olds will smile at anyone, the mother's face is apt to bring a more pronounced response. The parents begin to experience the pleasure of interacting with a very distinctive baby.

Even though unrecognized, the mother or some nurturing person is of utmost importance to the child. Mothers seek to provide for their babies' physiological needs and keep their physiological tensions minimal, and while providing stimulation protect them from disorganizing overstimulation. The infant can do little about reducing drive tensions except signal discomfort. The mother is not only providing conditions that will enable the child to gain a sense of confidence in the world, but promotes conditions under which he or she can best learn. Infants do not advance by resolving conflicts or learning how to rid themselves of tensions, for they have no such capacities. They learn because of an innate urge to assimilate new experiences. They are so constituted—their central nervous systems are so organized—that new experiences, including their own bodily movements, are rewarding sources of stimulation.

The parents' attempts to satisfy their child's needs are not always effective: indeed, the difficulties encountered lead some parents to the verge of despair. An occasional child is hypersensitive and difficult to satisfy. An illness may disturb the equilibrium of another. A satisfying feeding schedule or method of feeding cannot be established. Holding and cuddling do not seem to comfort another. Colic or bowel movements cause the child pain. The sleep of the child and that of the parents is intermittent. Most difficulties are short-lived and are resolved—perhaps with the aid of the pediatrician. How much derives from something in the child and how much from the nature of the nurturing care may remain unanswered. This is the time when disturbances in the parent-child relationship are apt to be reflected in physiological dysfunctions, particularly in feeding disturbances and gastrointestinal functioning.

FROM THE FOURTH TO THE EIGHTH MONTH

After the first four months a period of transition begins, during which infants' interests move away from themselves into their surroundings, and which leads up to the critical shift that takes place some time around the seventh month, when parents clearly become specific persons to their children and the babies become much more in the way of social beings—the time when the second major subphase of infancy starts.

A great deal occurs during the middle third of the first year as the baby increasingly becomes a lively character with a distinctive personality whose activities are intriguing. Indeed, this is often the heyday of the mother-infant relationship. The infant increasingly becomes a separate person who is eagerly responsive to parents, and parents respond by supplying affection and stimulation, and follow the child's changing ways. The child's care is increasingly less a one-sided affair and the baby's responsiveness often elicits warm and tender parental feelings. By about the seventh month, infants sit comfortably and without effort and can use both hands to hold things at the same time and perhaps pound them on the table or floor, enjoying both the movement and the noise. They can handle things, for the grasp reflex is virtually gone. In sitting they gain a new perspective on the world and greater freedom to use their hands. When prone, they begin to make crawling movements and may even manage to move a bit: they will not remain static much longer. They have found their feet and explore them with their hands and mouths. They can occupy themselves by using almost any object as a toy to manipulate, to wave, or to bang. They like to sit and watch other members of the household and may enjoy sorties beyond the house—gazing and learning. Now they babble endlessly, stimulated both by their own voices and by others talking to them. They are making sounds that prepare for almost any language, but soon they will move toward sounds of the language they hear. Certain noises become rudimentary signals of needs and wishes. Some frustration can be tolerated, and delays in signaling needs through crying can be noted, as when the child waits until hearing the mother in an adjacent room to convey hunger by crying. There is one new source of discomfort. The first teeth—the two lower incisors—are cutting through the gums. They cause pain and may provoke sudden outbursts of crying. The baby bites on the gums, seeking relief. The discomfort may interfere with sleep or eating, and the biting sometimes interferes with breast feeding. Although teething children can cause parents considerable frustration by their irritability and crying, they clearly require additional attention and cuddling to counter their distress.

Now that the infant is interested in the mother, comforted by her presence and stimulated by watching her, mothers are likely to keep their babies with them while they work in the kitchen or while the parents eat. Some children, in turn, clearly follow their mothers with their eyes and turn toward them when their mothers leave the room, and as they approach eight months may crawl after their departing mothers (Schaffer and Emerson, 1964; Ainsworth, 1967).

Piaget's Third Stage of Cognitive Development

This midportion of the year is the time of Piaget's third stage of sensori-motor development, to which he has given the lengthy but intriguing title *The Stage of Secondary Circular Reactions and Procedures Destined to Make Interesting Sights Last* (Piaget, 1963, pp. 122–180). As with the primary circular reactions, the infant repeats actions that accidentally produce a new experience, but these experiences are now primarily changes produced in the environment rather than changes related to bodily activities as in the earlier stage. Thus, a hand movement accidentally sets a hanging toy in motion and the infant then repetitively makes the hand movement that strikes the toy and swings it. Through such circular reactions babies begin to explore the world around them and gain means of influencing it. They assimilate sensori-motor units, for actions and objects are not yet clearly distinguished but remain part of a unified schema. In watching the child strike a swinging toy, one can note gradations in the intensity with which the toy is hit, and how the child slowly gains control over the amplitude of the swings. Eventually, a further modification occurs. A familiar object or situation may no longer set off the movement required for its activating the circular reaction, but the infant seems content to carry out only a fragment of the movement. It seems as though "the child were satisfied to recognize these objects or sights . . . but could not recognize them except by working, instead of thinking, the schema helpful to recognition . . . [that is] the secondary circular reaction corresponding to the object in question" (Piaget, 1963, pp. 185–186). These are precursors of purely contemplative recognition and symbolization.

The infant now also tends to assimilate new objects into old patterns or schemata. A new doll, for example, is put through the baby's repertoire of sensori-motor schemata set off by such objects: it is sucked, waved, fingered, rubbed against the bars of the crib, dropped to the floor. An interesting aspect of these secondary circular reactions is the use of "procedures for making interesting sights last." The child's behavior may seem very puzzling. The child sees something happen at a distance and then in order to get it to recur will go through a set of movements as if attempting to control the distant object by magic—by waving the arms, kicking feet, shaking the crib; but the baby is simply providing the first portion of a circular reaction that may have accidentally preceded the "sight," and then goes on to use its repertoire of sensori-motor schemata to try to activate the "sight." It is behavior that is semi-intentional; it is really still aimed at bringing about a repetition of something that happened accidentally. A significant aspect of these "procedures" concerns the substitution of sounds for actions, as when the baby smiles and says "aah!" when the door opens. The sound may be considered as an indication of recognition that someone is about to appear, or it may be understood as part of a secondary circular reaction—the first part of the procedure for making the "interesting sight" of a person appear again. In any case, it is part of the preparation for language.

THE SECOND HALF OF INFANCY

In the second half of the first year a new major subphase of infancy starts. Psychoanalytic psychology has emphasized a shift to an oral aggressive phase with teething, when the infant seeks actively to incorporate rather than assimilating more passively.*

Piaget has demonstrated that the infant now gains a more discrete concept of objects, including the mother; and Spitz emphasizes that a new organizing principle occurs when infants relate to their mothers as specific individuals.† In any event, infants now need specific parenting persons in order to feel secure, and are becoming social individuals for whom depriva-

---

* The pain of teething may stimulate tensions and conceivably aggressive feelings. The breast-fed infant who bites the nipple may be weaned, and weaning can engender frustration with marked aggressivity—as can clearly be observed in older children when abrupt weaning is enforced. However, at this time the infant can begin to go after things and becomes less passive.

† As we have noted, infants have a special relationship to their mothers that is apparent after the age of four or five months. Many of the child's sensori-motor schemata have been developing in relation to the mother and to her ways of handling and reacting to her infant. The infant is more relaxed and comfortable in the care of the mothering person. Although separation from the mother causes the baby to be upset, before the seventh or eighth month she can be replaced by another competent person without serious consequences.

tion of interpersonal stimulation becomes a serious handicap to their emotional and intellectual development. We shall consider the nature of this change.

The Mother as a Separate Object

Ever since A. Freud and D. Burlingham's (1944) pioneering observations of the traumatic impact on babies of separation from their mothers during World War II and Spitz's (1965) studies of institutionalized infants a great deal has been written about the importance to the small child of a continuing mothering person, and of how the loss of the mother disrupts the child's development and leads to depression and apathy. Although the evidence is not conclusive as yet, it appears that deprivation of the mother becomes particularly significant and highly traumatic some time between the ages of six and eight months. When younger infants are placed in a hospital they show strange behavior *after* they return home or when they are shifted to a new setting within the hospital. Schaffer (1958) has termed this the "global syndrome." On returning home the infant seems preoccupied with the surroundings, raising his or her head and scanning objects without focusing on anything, and even ignoring the mother. The blank expression or frightened look is naturally very disturbing to the mother, who finds her child very changed. However, such behavior lasts only for a few hours or occasionally for a few days.

By the sixth or seventh month, however, the development of the essential interaction with the mother culminates in clear-cut "stranger anxiety."* Instead of responding to a stranger's smile with a smile, the baby shows evidence of apprehension, tends to turn away and may start crying. The response is not to the mother's leaving but to the stranger's approach. It is as if the infant were upset at the dissonance from the familiar. Now strangers are tolerated best when they enter the scene unobtrusively and approach the child quietly, preferably when the child feels safe by being close to the mother or some other very familiar person. The mothering person has now become a specific source of security to the child, and her presence, as we shall see, seems essential to the baby's well-being.

During the second half of infancy, lengthy separation from the mother produces far more drastic results than those described by Schaffer in the

---

* See R. Spitz, *The First Year of Life*, pp. 150–162. Spitz termed the phenomena "eight month anxiety" but here, as elsewhere, he fixed the onset late because a large portion of his studies were conducted with deprived infants. However, the onset can occur any time after six months.

younger infant. The baby is stricken with a reaction similar to grief or depression which can progress to continued weeping, clinging, and disinterest, and to virtual loss of contact, apathy, and retardation, depending upon the duration of the separation and the quality of the substitute care that is provided.* It is difficult to sort out the differential impact of loss of the mother, loss of social stimulation, duration of the loss, and the quality of the substitute care. After the child and mother are reunited, the child displays a marked overdependence with excessive crying whenever the mother leaves, a clinging to the mother, and a heightened fear of strangers: behavior that lasts for several weeks or longer. Spitz in his study of infants of prison inmates noted that those children whose mothers had been more involved with them suffered more than those whose mothers had not related well and who, in addition, were able to accept substitute mothers more readily.† We shall consider the effects of more lasting deprivations later in the chapter.

We should also note that the retardation and lack of verve shown by infants who are institutionalized soon after birth become pronounced during the second half of infancy. Of course, the mother does not become more important to the older infant. The difference is that the baby now recognizes that objects, and particularly the mother, are separate entities. The infant now reacts to her loss, rather than simply experiencing the diffuse uneasiness or the physiologic upset that absence of the mother provoked at an earlier age.

Piaget's Fourth Stage of Cognitive Development

Piaget has clearly demonstrated that by seven or eight months of age the infant has an idea of an object as against the earlier inclusion of the object as part of a sensori-motor schema. The fourth stage of sensori-motor development has much to do with the differentiation of objects. It is termed

---

* The classic study is by R. Spitz and K. Wolf, "Anaclitic Depression: An Inquiry into the Genesis of Psychiatric Conditions in Early Childhood." See also J. Bowlby, "Grief and Mourning in Infancy and Early Childhood," and subsequent discussions by Anna Freud, Max Schur, and René Spitz, pp. 53–94.

† This indicates that the benefits of good maternal care can turn into a disadvantage if the child loses the mother. An experiment of Seitz (1959) furnishes similar evidence that what is advantageous depends on the conditions. He deprived some of the kittens in a litter of adequate nursing experience, leaving the remainder to nurse freely. The orally deprived kittens did not flourish as well as the others and were less placid. After weaning, he conducted a test in which the kittens, in order to obtain food, had to cross a platform on which they were shocked. The orally deprived ignored the shock and obtained food regularly, whereas the normally nursed kittens became upset, could not gain food, and developed rather typical animal neuroses.

The Coordination of Secondary Schemata and Their Application to New Situations. The idea of the object and intentionality are related. Thus, in seeking after an object, the baby retains the image or knowledge of the object even though it is partially hidden from view, and combines schemata in obtaining it. If a pillow is placed between a child and a ball the child will push away the pillow (one schema) and then grasp the ball (a second schema). Children's actions, at this stage, are now moving away from modifications of reflex acts to the pursuit of ends-in-view. They will begin to explore objects carefully, turning them over to look at the other side, feeling their shapes and looking at them from various angles. The objects seem to present them with a problem, and to some degree they recognize that there is an objective reality to which they must adapt themselves. As the period progresses, infants are less bound to testing procedures "destined to make interesting sights last." A child who sees a person ring a bell will push the person's hand toward the bell rather than go through a repertoire of sensori-motor schemata. An object is no longer something simply to be used as part of a schema, or for purposes of activity for activity's sake, but rather something to be mastered. This new relationship to the environment helps explain why separation from the mother becomes so traumatic at this phase of an infant's development.*

The Start of Locomotion and Speech

As infants move toward and past their tenth month, they not only are much more active but interact with members of the family, whom they draw into their lives. When a mother enters the baby's room in the morning she is apt to find the child standing holding on to the side of the crib, babbling away, and with toy-animal bedfellows tossed on the floor. The child begins to crawl, moving around the playpen, and may even be able to walk in tottering fashion if held by both hands. Babbling has moved toward the sounds of the language, and the baby may well please the parents by saying "da-da" or "ma-ma." These reiterative syllables are not yet real language, as will be discussed when we focus on early language development in the next chapter. The child may also have learned to imitate

---

* Another important development in children's ways of relating involves their responses to signals. Although they have shown recognition of anticipatory signals earlier, anticipatory responses now become much more consistent. A child may start to cry when seeing its mother putting on her coat. Many such responses are conditioned, but they are merging with intentional behavior. It seems quite intentional when a baby girl will open her mouth for the spoon when it comes from the fruit bowl but not when it comes from the cereal bowl.

waving "bye-bye" and awkwardly clap hands. There are still difficulties in using some newly gained skills: the child may pull up to a standing position but have difficulty getting down to the floor again, hesitant of landing with a thud, or may enjoy rolling or throwing a ball but be unable to release it at will.

During the remainder of infancy, babies are consolidating and improving their skills. They practice through endless play at gaining dexterity as well as at learning to judge size and distance. At about a year they may toddle if held by one hand and cruise by holding on to furniture; but they are most mobile on all fours. The number of words the child knows increases, and their use is becoming more specific. They are also likely to bestow little hugs and kisses to convey affection to members of the family. But now they are also beginning to show initiative, and parents can have difficulties in feeding children who seek to feed themselves, or gain the cooperation of infants insistent on continuing what they are doing. The problems engendered by the child's mobility and incessant exploratory curiosity will reach their crisis later, and will be discussed in the next chapter.

The Response to "No!"

The "ma-ma" and "da-da" are scarcely words and do not yet designate specific persons, but sometime during these last months of the first year a significant step takes place in children's language development and, indeed, in their ways of relating when they begin to respond to "no!" (Spitz, 1965, pp. 174–195). Perhaps it is a major step away from the unblemished innocence of childhood. The sharp "no-no!" of a parent at first simply frightens infants and causes a pause in their activities or makes them cry, but soon the interjection stops them from what they are doing. The control is limited, but it is control through verbal communcation that can be carried out from a distance; and it forms a sign that the child can internalize. It merges with children's growing awareness that displeasure in parents causes discomfort in them. However, it will be another five or six months before children use "no" themselves.

Self-Gratification

The child may have adopted a favorite blanket, sweater, or stuffed animal as a transitional object (Winnicott, 1953) and begin to display the phenomenon that Linus in the comic strip "Peanuts" has made so famous. It is a tactilely pleasant object that provides comfort and a sense of security in the mother's absence. It is a reflection of the skin sensuality that forms a part of the child's "oral" behavior. Children will clearly express displeasure when the "security blanket" or some other transitional object is missing, particularly at bedtime. As the child grows somewhat older it becomes increasingly difficult if not impossible to provide a substitute without provoking a serious upset. Thumb sucking, genital play, the need for a transitional object, are all means of providing for the self and of gaining comfort when the mothering person is not available. They are expected behaviors, and absence of genital play or thumb sucking may be as much a reason for concern as their presence. Efforts to deprive the infant and young child of such gratifications will result in frustration and increased insecurity. However, many parents are seriously concerned by these "habits" and are apt to take stringent measures to stop them.*

Weaning

Weaning, which often occurs between the ninth month and the end of infancy, may increase the frequency and intensity of thumb sucking. Infants need to gratify their oral sucking impulsions and there is evidence that insufficient sucking during feeding increases finger sucking; and, while too brief periods of nursing or too easy a flow of milk may lead to intensive finger sucking, well-gratified babies may be even more prone to prolonged thumb sucking. The determinants are not always clear and studies of the topic are in some respects contradictory (Klackenberg, 1949; Levy, 1928; Sears and Wise, 1950). Weaning traditionally has been considered a major frustration and potential source of emotional trauma. Abrupt weaning, particularly when accompanied by separation from the mother, can have serious consequences, but currently weaning does not usually cause notable frustration. If the baby is more than a few months old, additional foods including semisolids have been added to the diet and the child has become accustomed to taking food from a spoon or cup. If the child is weaned from the breast, a bottle may be substituted, and if the mother or nurse continues to hold and cuddle the baby, the shift from breast feeding can proceed smoothly. The desire to satisfy the oral needs of the child properly

* Even the leading pediatric texts of thirty to forty years ago advocated the use of arm braces to keep babies from sucking thumbs, and various physical restraints to stop masturbation in both male and female children. There is little, if any, evidence that thumb sucking causes irregular dentition. The common belief that masturbation leads to mental deficiency, insanity, or neurasthenia dies slowly and continues to be held by many parents. It is probable that the erotic quality of thumb sucking and the use of transitional objects as well as masturbation is disturbing to many adults, partly because it reawakens their own childhood fears, guilt, and shame.

had led some to delay weaning from a bottle until the child is older, but ideas that prolonging breast feeding into the second or third year makes weaning easier have no clear foundation.*

Twelve to Fifteen Months

As the child's first birthday forms a major occasion to the parents, there is a tendency to consider that the period of infancy or the "oral phase" terminates at this turn of the calendar. It seems more appropriate, however, to include the first fifteen months in infancy, for at about fifteen months the child is no longer just tottering but usually can toddle about; and the phase of sensori-motor development is drawing to a close, for the use of words and the greater comprehension of language markedly changes children's intellectual capacities and increasingly permits them to direct themselves.

Piaget's Fifth Stage

It is worth scrutinizing some of senior infants' techniques more closely in order to appreciate the limitations as well as the capacities of their minds as they are about to be graduated into the next phase of life. Piaget terms the fifth period of sensori-motor development that extends from about the twelfth to the sixteenth month *The Tertiary Circular Reaction and the Discovery of New Means by Active Experimentation* (Piaget, 1963, pp. 263–330). The child now clearly differentiates the self from the object, and the object from the act. The exploration of objects that had occupied the infant earlier now turns into explorations of how objects act and how they can be manipulated. The child is now experimenting, so to speak, to see what happens, rather than simply repeating experiences. The experi-

---

* The interesting studies of Sears and Wise (1950) indicate that weaning frustration increases with the duration of breast feeding. However, many variables require further attention and study. It seems possible that weaning came to be considered so traumatic because of the difficulties in weaning older children, as well as the manner in which it had been done before the practice of gradually introducing other foods early. Even in primitive societies the process can be so difficult that it is sometimes carried out with the help of such procedures as anointing the nipple with a bitter substance, or by painting the breast to make it look frightening. In some societies the mother leaves the community for several weeks, thus forcing the weaning process but adding problems caused by loss of the mother's presence. It may be simpler to wean from the breast before the mother becomes a highly significant object to the child or before the child develops a conscious memory.

Bowel training commonly is started toward the end of the first year and can create many difficulties, but is better deferred until later in life. This topic will be discussed in the next chapter.

mental trial and error still begins with something that happens by chance; it is still a "circular reaction" but of a higher type. The difference between repeating the fortuitous and active experimentation is narrow. The child drops an object accidentally, repeats the action, and continues noting the deviations that occur each time, and thus experiments with different ways of dropping an object. And now the object is differentiated from the action, and thus the action can be tried with different objects. A child may, for example, learn to pull a string in order to get a toy attached to it by means of numerous trial-and-error experimentations which started with the chance appearance of the toy after the cord was pulled. Once the child has learned with one toy, the schema or knowledge rapidly becomes generalized. From here it is only a small step to the next stage when foresight based on a related experience leads to insightful action without trial and error.*

If an object the child wants is placed under a cushion where the baby finds it and it is then placed under a different cushion, the child will now look directly under the second cushion rather than repeat the previously successful act as would a somewhat younger child. Nevertheless, limitations of the senior infant's cognitive powers can be noted in the way in which an object is still apt to be tied to the circular reaction of which it had been a part. Thus, a thirteen-month-old girl rolls a ball under a chair and successfully retrieves it. Then she rolls it under the sofa where she cannot see it and cannot reach it. After trying unsuccessfully to reach under the sofa she returns to the chair and seeks the ball under it. She is repeating the act that had previously been rewarded by retrieval of the ball, and seems to expect to find it even though she has seen the ball roll under the sofa.†

---

* Thus one of Piaget's daughters at just thirteen months of age, upon seeing an orange peel, turns it upside down and makes it rock; apparently she was able to foresee the possibility from the shape. (See J. Piaget, *The Origins of Intelligence in Children*, p. 328.) It is of interest that this same child who could use foresight to this degree still employed a much more primitive *secondary* circular reaction some five months later. After obtaining a toy by dislodging it by shaking the chair on which it was resting, after it had been removed to another part of the room she continued to try to get the toy by shaking the chair.

† Similarly one of Piaget's daughters at fifteen months of age sees her father approaching in the garden and smiles at him; but when her mother asks, "Where is Papa?" she turns and points at his office window, carrying out a customary (and probably an emotionally rewarded) response to the mother's question. Even when this child was over two years old, when she was walking with her father in the garden and heard a noise in his office, she said to him, "That is Papa up there." (See J. Piaget, *The Construction of Reality in the Child*, p. 59.)

Piaget's Sixth Stage

Piaget's sixth and final stage of sensori-motor development is not part of infancy, extending as it does from the sixteenth or eighteenth to the twenty-fourth month, though some manifestations of the stage may be present at fifteen months. The child becomes capable of inventing new means for solving problems through mental combinations without requiring tangible trial and error. Such behavior requires the use of symbols and the internalization of symbolic acts. Piaget notes that verbal symbols may not be necessary at this level of complexity, for the child may use motoric "signifiers" in carrying out such acts. For example, Piaget's daughter used the gesture of opening her mouth wider and wider to help master the opening of a matchbox. However, as the child now understands many words, it is difficult to assess just how much the child is using verbal symbols even though she does not speak them. While this sixth stage forms the culmination of the sensori-motor period in which familiar sensori-motor schemata are applied to new circumstances, it also marks the beginning of a new major phase in which the child begins to use the human attributes of verbal symbols and foresight in solving problems (Piaget, 1963, pp. 328–330).

EARLY DETERMINANTS OF PERSONALITY TRAITS

As children reach and pass their first birthdays, they assume certain more definite and distinctive characteristics—some of which seem to foreshadow what sorts of persons they will become. Still, there will be time for many revisions and time for significant changes in the way in which parents relate to them as they grow older, and time for exigencies of trauma, illness, or for months or years of fair weather to alter radically the way in which development is progressing.

However, careful observation may reveal to an experienced observer that the child is beginning to favor and develop certain adaptive mechanisms and may also be utilizing some precursors of specific defensive mechanisms. Children may be making the most of some innate attribute such as unusually good intellectual endowment or motor coordination, or may unknowingly be reacting to some particular way in which the parents have responded to them. By this time each mother-child combination develops a highly characteristic pattern of interaction. The pattern whether satisfactory or not tends to persist at least for the next few years.* It is difficult to differentiate between innate tendencies and those that develop in response to the nurturant care, and virtually impossible unless the child had been studied carefully since shortly after birth. We might consider, however, an infant who displayed superior motor coordination in his first months of life. His mother and father, both of whom are athletically inclined, take pleasure in his motor activity. They play with him by swinging him by his arms, turning him in somersaults, encouraging swimming and stepping movements. However, when he begins to throw things from his crib and will not desist, his mother considers him contrary and disobedient and slaps his hands; when he crawls and knocks over a lamp, she smacks him sharply. "No's" punctuate the air and startle the active baby into inactivity. The mother is afraid he is becoming wayward like her brother who is in a reformatory. Her impulsive slapping of the child starts loud quarrels with her husband, which in turn cause the baby to cry frantically. His movements become more crude and the anticipated excellent motor coordination fails to develop. Instead, he seems to become perplexed and given to more impulsive actions. In contrast, a little girl's motor dexterity develops into coordination of fine movements as her parents spend time with her playing with simple puzzles and construction toys, and enjoy seeing her use crayons. In similar fashion, we can note children develop verbal skills either because of a particularly keen ability to discriminate sounds, or through being with older persons who talk with them or at them a great deal, or because their mothers like to sing to them and stimulate responsive recitation.

The child may also be showing more diffuse patterns of reactivity, such as a geniality that reflects the developing innate sense of trust; or, in contrast, something of a disinterest in people, turning from them to play with toys, which may seem to reflect the mother's preoccupation with other matters when with the child, or the mother's compulsive ways of handling her child,† or, as in the case of another child, in reaction to the mother's need not to have her flow of fantasies disrupted by her child's moves toward companionship.

---

* Bowlby (1969, pp. 343–349) cites the careful observations of the French workers M. David and G. Appell that can be found in translation as "Mother-Child Relations" in J. Howells, *Modern Perspectives in International Child Psychiatry*.

These workers found that the magnitude of the differences between mother-child pairs can hardly be exaggerated. Simply in the amount of interaction with disregard of the quality, one mother interacted with her daughter almost continuously while the child was awake, another mother virtually ignored her year-old daughter, a mother and son spent much time together silently, each engaging in activities alone, etc.

† See S. A. Provence, "Some Aspects of Early Ego Development," for an example of the infantile precursors of the use of intellectualization as a major adaptive technique.

These more subtle relationships between inborn capacities, parental interests, parents' emotional problems, and the family atmosphere are now first coming under careful scrutiny; and the long-term influences upon the emerging personality are still somewhat conjectural. Currently, we can only consider some of the grosser and more obvious influences, and even then it becomes increasingly apparent that the number of variables is so great that they are difficult to assess clearly.

Some Developmental Disturbances

Children approaching fifteen months can be, and usually are, beings filled with vitality, curiosity, and with a push toward exploring their expanding worlds and finding ways of mastering them. Frustrations are inevitable and cause outbursts of anger, but they are short-lived. However, not all children flourish in this manner. Some have become quiet, apathetic, and do not emit any glow; many others show evidence of being troubled; and some have not reached anticipated levels of intellectual capacity. Even though we are not concerned with pathology in this book, it seems useful to consider some of these less fortunate outcomes in order to demonstrate and accentuate the importance of the interpersonal environment to the developmental process, even during infancy.

The Effects of Emotional and Social Deprivation

The observations made by Spitz (1945) of children raised in a foundling home are among the most dramatic and tragic.* The babies had developed normally during their first three months while cared for and breast fed by their own mothers or by substitute mothers. Then the mothers were removed and the babies retained in the foundling home, where they received adequate physical care, good food and medical attention, and lived under very hygienic conditions. Each nurse took care of from eight to twelve infants who were left in cribs separated by opaque partitions almost all of the time where they received little handling or personal attention. The infants soon showed a progressive deterioration and by six months were notably retarded, lying supine and almost immobile, unable to turn themselves over, in contrast to the usually active ways of the child at this age. Gradually their faces became vacuous and their expressions imbecilic. They developed bizarre, uncoordinated movements. Despite the food provided, some developed marasmus—a wasting from malnutrition—and

* See also A. Freud and D. Burlingham, *Infants Without Families*.

about thirty percent died within the first year. Of the survivors many—or most—were unable to stand, walk, or talk at the age of four. These children had not only been deprived of affectionate care and the attention that usually goes with it, but they had received extremely little stimulation of any type, being thus deprived of the fundamental experiences required as "aliment" for learning.

While there are no other reports of *series* of children who did as badly as those reported by Spitz, other studies, and notably those of Provence and Lipton (1962), have documented the severe retardation of institutionalized infants that grows progressively worse during the second half of infancy. The children studied by Provence and Lipton were seriously impaired in their motor control; and their interests and interactions with people and toys as well as their language development were impoverished; even self-exploration and autoerotic activities such as thumb sucking and genital manipulation became minimal. Moreover, they were dull and disinterested, "the light had gone out," or, as an observer remarked about the child that stood out as being the least handicapped, "If you crank his motor you can get him to go a little, he can't start on his own."[*]

The effects of maternal deprivation are complicated, even during infancy.[†] They vary with the time of onset of the separation, the duration, the quality of the mother's care prior to the separation, the individual endowment, and the quality and quantity of the substitute care provided, so that different difficulties and deficiencies can result. At present, relatively little is known about the interplay of these various factors. Now, raising an infant in the family does not, of itself, insure against emotional and social deprivation. Indeed, a pediatrician is apt to see some children who are not just deprived and neglected but grossly mistreated, all too frequently an infant that has been beaten and battered for crying and thereby disturbing

---

[*] Provence and Lipton's comparisons of the best endowed and best cared-for institutionalized child in the study with an average child who was reared by his parents at home is very much worth reading.

The follow-up studies of some of these children who had been placed in families when they were about a year and a half old showed that they improved very rapidly and made up for much of the lost time, but careful examination revealed that they continued to suffer serious deficiencies, such as impairments in the capacity to delay when frustrated that interfered with their abilities to solve problems; a failure adequately to generalize what they learned; an undue concreteness in thinking; and failure to expect and seek help from adults that limited learning; and a continuing superficiality in their relationships to others. It appeared unlikely that certain attributes that should be acquired in the first year of life can be properly acquired later, which provides further evidence of the importance of the ontogenetic sequence during the first year that has been emphasizd by Piaget.

[†] For evaluative efforts of such studies see M. S. Ainsworth, *Deprivations of Maternal Care: A Reassessment of Its Effects*.

an immature and unstable parent. Even some well-intentioned parents can provide little because of economic necessity when the baby is left in the care of a completely disinterested sibling or incompetent child. Immature parents with little self-control are likely to be very impatient with their babies. Frequently difficulties arise because parents do not realize infants' limitations. One mother suddenly slapped her young infant for being impudent when he stuck out his tongue at her; a father cannot understand why the baby will not eat the food given her without messing her clothes, etc. One encounters depressed or apathetic mothers who cannot do anything for or with the child beyond providing food and hygienic care accompanied by little if any fondling, play, or talk. Such situations, particularly after the first four to six months, can create serious impairments and emotional disturbances.

The full effects of infantile deprivation on personality functioning in later life are still unknown. Thus, when Harlow (1958, 1966) raised baby monkeys on "wire" and "terry cloth" mothers, it seemed at first that they did well on such impersonal mothering. However, they later became asocial in various ways, and eventually it became apparent that they were uninterested in mating and did not know how to mate. However, some of the females were successfully impregnated, but after giving birth to offspring they were completely lacking in maternal behavior, refused to permit the baby to approach and cuddle against them, and often attacked the baby so that it sometimes became necessary to remove the offspring from the mother's cage lest she kill it.

The Hospitalized Infant and Small Child

Such studies have forcefully drawn attention to the necessity of providing for the infant and small child's emotional and social needs when they are hospitalized for illness or surgery. Indeed, it is only during the past few decades that hospitals have considered that the baby has critical needs other than strictly medical attention.* Young children need their mothers with them a good deal of the time, particularly in strange surroundings, or good substitute care must be provided. The disturbances caused by separation have often been confused with the effects of an illness or with difficulties in recovering from an operation. Most modern hospitals now realize

---

* Thirty years ago in one of the foremost pediatric centers, babies were tied down when they were about a year old, lest they fall out of the cribs; and mothers could not stay with the baby at night, and were even treated as nuisances who interfered with the nursing routine when permitted to visit during the day.

the importance of providing for the emotional needs of young children as well as their physical care. Surgeons have recognized that speed of recovery and even post-operative mortality rates can depend upon the emotional climate of the unit. With more prolonged hospitalization the child's intellectual and social needs require attention, and good pediatric services now have nurses who play with the children and maintain nursery school-like playrooms in which the children spend their time whenever feasible.

THE INFLUENCES OF INFANTILE PATTERNS ON THE ADULT PERSONALITY (ORAL TRAITS)

The long-term problem has received attention in psychoanalytic literature through consideration of the "oral" character and the effects of fixations at the oral stage of development. The term "oral character" is loose and has varied connotations that cannot be defined too closely. Psychoanalytic theory has tended to divide "oral" characters into two major types which supposedly reflect frustrations in the two halves of infancy. The "oral incorporative" character consistently seeks to get from others passively, wishing to be cared for as a dependent child. Such persons fear being abandoned and starved and have little faith in the world unless they have someone to feed and care for them, and lack confidence in their ability to manage for themselves. "Oral aggressive" characters retain strong needs for care from others but do not feel they can obtain what they need without being grasping and hurting others in the process. In adult life they may drive themselves intensely while exploiting others to obtain security. Another dichotomy that has been formulated concerns excessive indulgence as contrasted with deprivation in infancy. Those indulged excessively as infants acquire a lasting and inappropriate optimism that prevents them from providing for themselves as they feel certain that others will look out for them. Those who have been deprived and frustrated have a deep-seated pessimism, becoming hostile and resentful when their needs are not met, and they tend to give up easily.

However, these are oversimplifications of a complex problem.* Few

* The difficulties can also be considered in terms of a child's failure to overcome the infantile attachment to a parent, a failure of the process of separation-individuation that will be discussed in the next chapter; or in terms of so-called narcissistic fixation, in which a person continues to hold childhood magical beliefs that an omnipotent parent can satisfy all of the person's needs, which leads to expectations that parents

adults can be characterized in terms of oral tendencies that are the resultants of infantile experiences alone. Other developmental periods will be affected by whatever gave rise to the oral problems, and the child is usually raised by the same parents who contributed to the oral problems of infancy. It seems more useful to speak of oral characteristics that enter into the shaping of the personality. Such oral characteristics may be of such dominant importance that they prevent the development of a mature person, or may simply consist of traits that can sometimes be turned into assets as well as create handicaps. The term "oral traits" need not be an epithet but simply a useful term to help describe a personality. Oral characteristics can be highly useful, as in the case of some authors who boundlessly take in and then pour forth words. Thomas Wolfe, for example, could not contain his "orality" but incorporated vast chunks of life and had difficulty limiting the flow of words in his writings, and had a prodigious love of food. Indeed, in one short story he has the hero make love to his girl in terms of food, with his passion centering on the girl's ability to cook and provide food. A more aggressive type of orality may be considered evident in the love of words shown by George Bernard Shaw, who displayed a "biting wit" that contained considerable hostility.

"Oral" Character Traits in an Adult

The relationship between food and affection is often very noticeable. Of course, many mothers consider providing food as an essential manifestation of their love, and some offer food as a substitute for affection.* The relationship between affectional needs and food requires consideration when a physician prescribes a diet; for when persons addicted to food are placed on a stringent diet, they may become seriously depressed. The striving to amass wealth because of the fear of being left without resources can motivate industrialists.

The interrelated "oral" problems of love, food, insecurity, dependency are apparent in the history of a man suffering from a peptic ulcer: a history which will also demonstrate some of the difficulties inherent in any attempt to sort out the salient factors in their development.

A man in his mid-thirties was flown to a medical center because of a recurrence of bleeding from a peptic ulcer. He had never previously left his

---

and other significant persons can never meet. See H. Kohut, *The Analysis of the Self*, pp. 42–56.

* The relationship of such maternal traits to obesity in the offspring has been studied and documented by H. Bruch and G. Touraine (1940).

hometown and the vicinity of his mother. The first episode of ulcer symptoms and bleeding had occurred while he was awaiting induction into the army and was apprehensive about leaving home. He was a highly intelligent man who worked at a job far below his capacities. It was a secure job in which he felt underpaid, but on the several occasions when he had made plans to take a job of greater interest and potentiality, he would start to overeat markedly, become apprehensive, and decide that the risk of changing positions was too great. He would then become resentful because he was not properly appreciated, feel like telling off his employer, but could never dare to show his hostile feelings. He would then suffer from indigestion, which led him to believe that he was not healthy enough to assume greater responsibility in a new job. He had married at the age of thirty, finding a widow who not only was a mothering sort of person but also had sufficient independent income to allay his concerns about his ability to support a wife. Indeed, he realized that he had married only because his mother was growing old and might soon die.

Although his infancy and early childhood could not be reconstructed accurately some thirty-five years later, it was known that his mother had been a very apprehensive woman who sought to remedy her son's supposed frailty by pouring food into him. Food had been important to her as a token of security. The patient had become obese in childhood. The patient considered that a traumatic childhood experience had a lasting effect on him. When the patient was four years old, in the days prior to social security, his father lost his job and could not find another. The family ran out of food; the mother baked a cake with the remaining flour and told the patient to eat well as she did not know when they would be able to buy food again. He became acutely anxious, fearing that the family would starve to death. The father soon found employment and the family was never again in such desperate straits.

Although the patient felt that his parents were unusually devoted and had provided for him as well as they could, his wife disagreed. She believed that her husband's parents had brainwashed him into believing in their beneficence by telling him of their many sacrifices for him. She found them penurious people, chronically fearful of the future, who transmitted their insecurities to their son and who had discouraged him from attempting to seek better employment. She offered, as an example, an episode that had occurred when the patient was a young adolescent. He had worked hard all summer to earn the money to purchase a bicycle he very much wanted. His parents encouraged the project; but when he had enough money, they insisted that he buy a new suit instead of the bicycle. Although he had considered leaving his hometown to find employment in a city, he developed severe motion sickness when he rode on a train, and even when he drove an auto beyond his town limits.

It seems very likely that this man's distrust of the world and his own capacities started in infancy, but later experiences certainly contributed to it, amplifying rather than helping him overcome his lack of confidence; and his insecurities clearly reflected the attitudes of both of his insecure parents.

The concepts of oral fixation and regression have been highly useful despite their diffuseness. However, they are not fully sufficient to explain the personality problems and deficiencies that follow upon infantile deprivations; for, as we have seen, a number of other developmental tasks aside from satisfying "oral needs" must be surmounted in infancy to lay the foundations for stable personality development. As these foundations need to be laid down in association with the physical maturation of the child, later experiences can never fully compensate for the deprivations experienced in infancy.

The first fifteen months of life have a unity as a developmental period because throughout them the child is completely dependent on others for nurture: for the food and bodily care essential for survival and healthy physical maturation; for the affectionate attention required for security and freedom from untenable tensions; for the experiential stimulation that is necessary for cognitive development. The infant undergoes a profound physical transformation during these months and the foundations are laid down upon which future personality development will rest. If infants' essential needs are filled and untoward tensions do not repeatedly arise within them, they will have established at the core of their beings a basic trust in the world and those who inhabit it, upon which a confidence in themselves and in their capacities to care for themselves can develop. A great deal more than gaining a basic trust and the satisfaction of oral needs must take place during infancy if the person is to develop properly. We have followed infants' slow emergence from the undifferentiated state in which they started life, to the formation of intense attachments to others upon whom they depended, and with whom they began to interact meaningfully. We have noted how, as infants differentiate, they have a great need for specific mothering figures, and how separation from such persons can have disastrous effects upon them.

Now children enter a new phase, walking, chattering a jargon mixed with words, more definitely understanding language, moving about on their own, exploring and getting into things; their parents' tasks in caring for them also change. Parents can no longer be concerned only with satisfying their children's needs and wishes, providing experience and socialization, but must now also limit their activities so as to assure their safety and the integrity of the household. Children, in turn, now must learn self-control and delimitation to be capable of exercising some sovereignty for themselves.

REFERENCES

AHRENS, R. (1954). "Beitrag zur Entwicklung des Physiognomie- und Mimikerkennens." *Z. exp. Angew. Psychol.*, 2:412–454.

AINSWORTH, M. S. (1962). *Deprivations of Maternal Care: A Reassessment of Its Effects.* Public Health Papers No. 14. World Health Organization, Geneva.

———. (1967). *Infancy in Uganda: Infant Care and the Growth of Love.* Johns Hopkins University Press, Baltimore, Md.

ALDRICH, C. A., and HEWITT, E. (1947). "A Self-Regulating Feeding Program for Infants," *Journal of the American Medical Association*, 135:340–342.

ALDRICH, C. A., et al. (1946). "The Crying of Newly Born Babies: IV. Follow-up Study After Additional Nursing Care Had Been Provided," *Journal of Pediatrics*, 28:665–670.

BATESON, G., and MEAD, M. (1942). *Balinese Character: A Photographic Analysis.* New York Academy of Sciences, New York.

BENEDEK, T. (1938). "Adaptation to Reality in Early Infancy," *Psychoanalytic Quarterly*, 7:200–215.

———. (1949). "The Psychosomatic Implications of the Primary Unit: Mother-Child Relatedness," *American Journal of Orthopsychiatry*, 19:642–654.

BOWLBY, J. (1960). "Grief and Mourning in Infancy and Early Childhood," *The Psychoanalytic Study of the Child*, vol. 15, pp. 9–52. International Universities Press, New York.

———. (1969). *Attachment and Loss.* Vol. 1: *Attachment.* Basic Books, New York.

BRODY, S. (1956). *Patterns of Mothering: Maternal Influence During Infancy.* International Universities Press, New York.

BRUCH, H. (1952). *Don't Be Afraid of Your Child: A Guide for Perplexed Parents.* Farrar, Straus & Young, New York.

———. (1961). "Conceptual Confusions in Eating Disorders," *Journal of Nervous and Mental Diseases*, 133:46–54.

BRUCH, H., and TOURAINE, G. (1940). "Obesity in Childhood: V. The Family Frame of Obese Children," *Psychosomatic Medicine*, 2:141–206.

DAVID, M., and APPELL, G. (1969). "Mother-Child Relations," in *Modern Perspectives in International Child Psychiatry.* J. Howells, ed. Oliver & Boyd, Edinburgh.

DOI, T. (1973). *The Anatomy of Dependence.* J. Bester, trans. Kodansha International, Tokyo.

ERIKSON, E. (1950). "Growth and Crises of the 'Healthy Personality,' " in *Symposium on the Healthy Personality*, vol. 2: *Problems of Infancy and Childhood*. M. J. E. Senn, ed. Josiah Macy, Jr., Foundation, New York.

ESCALONA, S. (1945). "Feeding Disturbances in Very Young Children," *American Journal of Orthopsychiatry*, 15:76–80.

FREUD, A., and BURLINGHAM, D. (1944). *Infants Without Families*. International Universities Press, New York.

GREENMAN, G. W. (1963). "Visual Behavior of New-born Infants," in *Modern Perspectives in Child Development*. A. J. Solnit and S. Provence, eds. International Universities Press, New York.

HARLOW, H. (1958). "The Nature of Love," *American Psychologist*, 13:673–685.

HARLOW, H., and HARLOW, M. (1966). "Learning to Love," *American Scientist*, 54:244–272.

ILLINGWORTH, R. S. (1955). "Crying in Infants and Children," *British Medical Journal*, 1:75–78.

KLACKENBERG, G. (1949). "Thumbsucking: Frequency and Etiology," *Pediatrics*, 4:418–424.

KLEIN, M. (1937). *The Psycho-analysis of Children*. A. Strachey, trans. Hogarth Press, London.

KOHUT, H. (1971). *The Analysis of Self: A Systematic Approach to the Psychoanalytic Treatment of Narcissistic Personality Disorders*. International Universities Press, New York.

LEVY, D. M. (1928). "Fingersucking and Accessory Movements in Early Infancy: An Etiologic Study," *American Journal of Pediatrics*, 7:881–918.

MOLONEY, J. C. (1945). "Psychiatric Observations in Okinawa Shima: The Psychology of the Okinawan," *Psychiatry*, 8:391–399.

NEWTON, N. R. (1951). "The Relationship Between Infant Feeding Experience and Later Behavior," *Journal of Pediatrics*, 38:28–40.

NEWTON, N. R., and NEWTON, M. (1950). "Relationship of Ability to Breast-Feed and Maternal Attitudes Toward Breast Feeding," *Pediatrics*, 4:860–875.

PIAGET, J. (1954). *The Construction of Reality in the Child*. M. Cook, trans. Basic Books, New York.

———. (1963). *The Origins of Intelligence in Children*. M. Cook, trans. W. W. Norton, New York.

PROVENCE, S. A. (1966). "Some Aspects of Early Ego Development: Data from a Longitudinal Study," in *Psychoanalysis: A General Psychology*. R. Loewenstein, L. Newman, M. Schur, and A. Solnit, eds. International Universities Press, New York.

PROVENCE, S. A., and LIPTON, R. C. (1962). *Infants in Institutions: A Comparison of Their Development with Family-reared Infants During the First Year of Life*. International Universities Press, New York.

RIBBLE, M. A. (1943). *The Rights of Infants: Early Psychological Needs and Their Satisfaction*. Columbia University Press, New York.

SCHAFFER, H. R. (1958). "Objective Observations of Personality Development in Early Infancy," *British Journal of Medical Psychology*, 31:174–183.

SCHAFFER, H. R., and EMERSON, P. (1964). "The Development of Social Attachments in Infancy." Monographs of the Society for Research in Child Development, vol. 29, no. 3, pp. 1–77.

SEARS, R. S., and WISE, G. W. (1950). "Relation of Cup Feeding in Infancy to Thumb-Sucking and the Oral Drive," *American Journal of Orthopsychiatry*, 20:123–138.

SEITZ, P. (1959). "Infantile Experience and Adult Behavior in Animal Subjects: II. Age of Separation from the Mother and Adult Behavior in the Cat," *Psychosomatic Medicine*, 21:353–378.

SPITZ, R. (1945). "Hospitalism: An Inquiry into the Genesis of Psychiatric Conditions in Early Childhood," in *The Psychoanalytic Study of the Child*, vol. 1, pp. 53–74. International Universities Press, New York.

————. (1965). *The First Year of Life: A Psychoanalytic Study of Normal and Deviant Development of Object Relations.* International Universities Press, New York.

SPITZ, R., and WOLF, K. (1946). "Anaclitic Depression: An Inquiry into the Genesis of Psychiatric Conditions in Early Childhood, II." *The Psychoanalytic Study of the Child,* vol. 2, pp. 313–342. International Universities Press, New York.

WINNICOTT, D. W. (1953). "Transitional Objects and Transitional Phenomena: A Study of the First Not-Me Possession," *International Journal of Psycho-Analysis,* 34:89–97.

WOLFF, P. (1959). "Observations on Newborn Infants," *Psychosomatic Medicine,* 21:110–118.

————. (1960). "The Developmental Psychologies of Jean Piaget and Psychoanalysis," *Psychological Issues,* vol. 2, no. 1, Monograph No. 5. International Universities Press, New York.

————. (1963). "Observations on the Early Development of Smiling," in *Determinants of Infant Behavior,* vol. 2. B. M. Foss, ed. Wiley, New York.

SUGGESTED READING

BOWLBY, J. (1969). *Attachment and Loss,* vol. 1: *Attachment.* Basic Books, New York.

BRODY, S. (1956). *Patterns of Mothering: Maternal Influences During Infancy.* International Universities Press, New York.

GESELL, A. (1940). *The First Five Years of Life: A Guide to the Study of the Preschool Child.* Harper & Bros., New York.

PIAGET, J., and INHELDER, B. (1969). *The Psychology of the Child.* H. Weaver, trans. Basic Books, New York.

SPITZ, R. (1965). *The First Year of Life: A Psychoanalytic Study of Normal and Deviant Development of Object Relations.* International Universities Press, New York.

STONE, J., SMITH, H., and MURPHY, L. (1974). *The Competent Infant: Research and Commentary.* Basic Books, New York.

CHAPTER 6

❀

The Toddler

CHALLENGES AND TASKS

As babies emerge from infancy and start to walk and talk, they enter a phase in which the crucial problems involve the imbalance between their new-found motor skills and their meager mental capacities. They are driven by impulsions to use their new abilities and to explore their surroundings, but their verbal and intellectual abilities lag far behind their motor development. They are also caught between their needs for their mothers and their wishes to separate from them and have more autonomy. Limits must be placed upon these little children for their own safety and for the preservation of their family possessions. They have little, if any, ego of their own; the past and future are nebulous, and parenting persons must now, more than at any other time, function as surrogate egos for them. But toddlers do not understand; they are only beginning to tolerate delay and frustration; it is not possible to talk things over with them. Children now find themselves in a different sort of relationship with their parents than previously. During infancy their parents had nurtured them, provided for their needs, and encouraged their expansiveness: but now they must be delimited. The parents expect their babies to respect limits and renounce immediate gratifications in order to maintain a satisfactory relationship with them. Parents now set expectations for the toddlers to meet. It is not a simple transition for an unreasoning and unreasonable baby to make.

The baby has emerged from the passivity of infancy, and now seems both driven by an inner impulsion to activity and pulled by the attraction of new stimuli in the surroundings—by a need to gain mastery over his or her body and to explore the environment. Whereas during the first year much of the infant's food intake went into physical maturation, now an increasing amount goes into fuel for the physical activity that reaches prodigious proportions by the middle of the second year. Gains in height and weight slow down markedly. The annual increments in weight are less between two and five than at any other time before the attainment of adulthood.

The baby is now moving away from the need for complete care and a symbiotic existence with a mothering person. It is a phase that is critical to the establishment of a basic *trust in the self* and a *sense of initiative.** Children are in the process of establishing boundaries between themselves and their mothers, both physical boundaries and a sense that they can do things as separate individuals. But in this process of separation and individuation they increasingly recognize that parents are separate persons from them and their vulnerability inevitably evokes anxieties. They cannot yet come to feel that they can care for themselves.

The dangers, as always, lie on both sides. Children cannot yet really be responsible for themselves, and they are far from being independent. Indeed, toddlers' venturesomeness depends upon having close at hand the shelter of a parent's arms and lap to which they can retreat when they overreach themselves. A mother who finds too anxiety-provoking those activities of her child that lead into a world full of very real dangers—stairways, gas burners, lamps that topple, car-filled streets—may overlimit and

---

* Erikson (1950) considers this period in the child's life vital to the development of *autonomy*, with the negative trend being the development of a lasting sense of shame and doubt, and he considers "initiative" vital to the subsequent phase. The child is clearly beginning to establish autonomy and as Margaret Mahler (1975) has demonstrated the processes of separation and individuation from the mother are a major task of these years. However, I believe that the problems of autonomy reach their zenith in the next developmental phase, and that the achievement of initiative precedes the capacity really to move toward autonomy. The difference is partly a matter of word meanings as well as of emphasis. There is always a danger in using single phrases to epitomize the involved tasks of a complex developmental period. The reasons for my not focusing on "autonomy" will become apparent (I trust) in the way we shall consider the oedipal period. However, I wish to stress that other, crucial tasks arise and require resolution in this stage of life—particularly certain aspects of language learning and their impact on cognition and ethical development.

surround the child with gates, fences, and a barrier of "no's" that stifle initiative and self-confidence. Parents who have little confidence in their abilities to guide and control their child are apt to project such feelings and magnify the child's incapacity to care for the self. Parents who cannot tolerate disorder, or who overestimate babies' capacities to conform and regulate their impulses, can convey a sense of "being bad" to the child, and thereby provoke a sense of guilt or shame that undermines feelings of worth and self-trust. The child may be led into an overconformity that satisfies the parents but covers hostile resistance and stubbornness.

In psychoanalytic theory, this period of life is the *anal phase* of psycho-sexual development in which the investment of the child's libido has shifted from the oral zone to the anal region. The child now gains erogenous pleasure from passing or withholding bowel movements that stimulate the libidinized anal mucosa. Giving or withholding, compliance or stubbornness, and related behaviors become important and influence character formation. For many children in Western societies, the conflicts that arise because of the need to conform and comply with the wishes of others, in contrast to infancy when needs were satisfied by parental figures, can focus on bowel training, particularly on premature bowel training. The demands for bowel control can epitomize all of the requirements imposed by early socialization—the need to rescind gratification and the freedom to give in to impulsions and accept a need to control the self. Ever since Freud published his essay "Character and Anal Erotism," it has been recognized that there is a clear connection between anal erotic gratification, conflicts over bowel training, and certain configurations of personality traits. However, bowel training need not take place during the second year; it is neither a biological nor a social necessity. Certain of the problems conventionally associated with anal erotism and bowel training seem more clearly related to the developmental tasks pertaining to conflicts between initiative and conformity.* Therefore, the anal aspects of the period will be discussed after the broader developmental characteristics have been considered.

The period will terminate toward the end of the third year, when children have gained sufficient vocabulary and adequate syntax to comprehend

---

* Erikson's observations of the Yurok Indians cannot be passed over casually. The Yuroks place great emphasis upon the acquisition of wealth, holding on to possessions, rituals for controlling nature obsessively, etc., which, according to psychoanalytic theory, would carry with it an expectation of unusual emphasis on anality and rigid bowel training. Yet there seems to be only the most casual type of bowel training. On the other hand, there are ritualized regulations about eating and obtaining food that demand premature self-control from the child.

much of what is said to them and when they have become reasonably separate individuals. Their linguistic abilities and knowledge will help them brook delays, because they can anticipate future goals and benefits. They can now maintain a mental image of their parents and emotional bonds to them during separations that are not lengthy. They will have internalized enough of their worlds to understand expectations, to begin to reason, and to listen to reason.

Although a smooth passage from fifteen to thirty-six months is not impossible, it is unlikely. The toddler's developmental situation almost inevitably creates difficulties for both child and parents. The extent and nature of the problems, and just when they arise, vary with the child, the parents' sensitivities, and the child-rearing practices they utilize. Although the more manifest problems usually involve difficulties in control and the expectations for self-control of some form of behavior—bowel training, eating, or physical initiative—and the child's reactive temper outbursts, resistance, and negativism, the less apparent anxieties about separation from the mothering person also create difficulties. However, another critical task of the period that has received far less attention in the literature demands attention. It concerns linguistic development—how it is influenced by children's interactions with their parents and how parental and cultural value systems become involved in the process. There is a contrapuntal-like development of these two themes—the increasing physical capacities and the slower acquisition of language. Both involve the child's expanding abilities. The developmental phase ends when a reasonable equilibrium between the two is established.

THE TODDLER'S CAPACITIES AND BEHAVIOR

Sometime before fifteen months the baby really walks, even though in a stumbling, wobbly manner. Although skills increase rapidly, it will take more than a year for walking to become fully automatic. As toddlers progress through their second year into their third, they can be a delight to watch as they move with earnest intent from one activity to another. They are sources of constant interest as new abilities and skills follow one another rapidly and they become increasingly responsive to verbal exchange. The babyish speech is still amusing, for no more is expected from the toddler. They are venturesome and venture constantly but still remain babies who enjoy giving and receiving demonstrable affection. They are unfolding to become individuals with ways of acting and expressing themselves that are distinctively their own. As they approach two the pace quickens and, typically, they are into everything. They begin their "love affair with the world" (Greenacre, 1957). Anything precious or potentially harmful must be kept out of their way. While intriguing to watch develop, toddlers, particularly boys, can also readily become sources of despair to the mother, whose energy and wits are taxed to the limit as she tries to keep up with her little boy and find ways either to control him or to arrange the surroundings for him. A toddler girl can also be highly exasperating in her innocence, for in the flash of an unguarded moment she can light into something forbidden, turn the living room into a shambles, or vanish from sight. The impulsion to activity outruns not only mastery of the body, but even more the child's knowledge of what he or she can do or may do.

Motor Skills

The toddler is a strange admixture of grace and awkwardness; the graceful and well-proportioned body somewhat comical in its rapid stumbling movements, body tilted slightly forward, ankles somewhat stiff, and both arms waving in extraneous movements. Until the child is well past two, arm movements are apt to accompany many activities, and when one hand is used the other accompanies it until unilateral differentiation of muscular control is well established. When the small child pounds on a pan with a block held in one hand, both arms will be in movement. The gross movements of the arms and legs are mastered long before fingering, which requires a great deal of practice. The toddler is apt to carry small objects tucked under the arm rather than in the hand. It takes practice to time the release of objects, as in throwing or rolling a ball, perhaps to the annoyance of the father who wishes to start training his son to be a ball player as soon as he emerges from the cradle.

Through play which appears to be so random, the child is gradually learning muscular coordination and is exploring one item after another as is necessary to gain understanding of the surrounding world. Even movements that seem completely natural to adults require lengthy practice before they can be carried out automatically and without concentration. A girl of two sitting down in a chair appropriate for her size takes care and expends effort. She may climb into it laboriously and then let her feet down, or she may carefully measure the distance by sighting through her legs and then let down her rump while still watching herself. Skills do not come simply through maturation but through countless repetitions that go on day after day and which are necessary to enable children to learn coordination and to measure the space in which they live.

Cognitive Capacities

Similar considerations apply to perceptual and cognitive development. The child is endowed with organs that register sensations, but must learn to organize the sensations that impinge upon them, utilizing the concordance of various sense modalities and sensori-motor schemata to build the sensations into perceptions, and then with the help of words learn what are discrete things, and what various things are. Children of this age are very distractible, as their attention shifts from one stimulus to another, taking the body along with it. To some observers the child's naïveté seems surprising. A little boy may, for example, try to grasp the line made by a crack in the floor and reach for things well beyond his range. It is a very new world that distracts from any continuity of effort. A girl leaves a toy to touch a kitten, only to move toward the sound of her mother in the next room, but she may be waylaid by the carpet sweeper in the hall that demands her attention. Still, they learn very rapidly and as they gain skills they will be fascinated by repeating over and over again what they are mastering. The circular reactions of the sensori-motor period are still major means of learning (see Chapter 5). A toddler will place one block on another and repeat it, and can keep amused piling colored rings on a stick until such tasks are thoroughly assimilated and become so simple that they are meaningless, and then are part of the schema that is ready to assimilate more complex activities. Attention becomes firmer, bringing a period of relative calm until still greater skills enable the child to move more rapidly about the house and to a wider range of exploration. Parents unconsciously become alert to the sound of their child's activities and chatter; they learn that silence must be investigated because it may well indicate that something new has attracted and held the child, who is likely to be exploring something that is potentially dangerous, or to which the child is a danger.

Routines can become time-consuming and try the parents' patience. Children develop their own ideas about what should be done, their own interests, their own pace. They can refuse to be hurried as they messily feed themselves and become more interested in play than in food. Hands may be too occupied to be lifted into the armholes of an undershirt or sweater. The mother must exert ingenuity to keep the toddler either interested or distracted while being fed, bathed, and dressed. The toddler is attentive to songs and soon likes to listen to simple stories, even though they may not be understood. The crib ceases to confine as the child learns to clamber out of it; and even though everyone else in the house may be thoroughly fatigued by bedtime, the child may be reluctant to end the day. On the other hand, if things have gone well, toddlers are usually delighted and full of laughter when others pay attention to them and participate in some activity with them.

Gradually, children keep themselves occupied for longer periods, but preferably with a parental figure close at hand. They may happily play with a couple of pots, listen to a phonograph record repeat itself, or page through a picture book, occasionally glancing at the mother while she works in the kitchen. Water often holds a particular fascination for toddlers, who can keep busy pouring it from pot to pot, filling containers in the sink, or playing with the contents of the bath. They imitate more and more, and like to "help" their mothers with household chores if the mother can goodnaturedly and appreciatively accept the interfering aid. Left without a parental figure, the child is apt to lose ebullience and turn inward. Both boys and girls identify with the mother at this stage, picking up her ways of doing things, her intonations, and her likes and dislikes. Of course, a child will also enjoy being with the father and share his work of tinkering with the car or gardening. Often less alert than the mother to the child, a father may suddenly realize that the child is no longer at his side and become shaken when he locates the two-year-old climbing a tree, or stumbling along carrying a pruning knife, oblivious to the danger.

Control and Conflict

As children's motor abilities and their urges to use them have temporarily outrun their comprehension and experience, parents must provide the guidance and set the limits. The parents' own contentment, the prerogatives of other children, and the preservation of the household, as well as the child's safety, must be taken into account when judging what latitude can be permitted the child. Providing the proper guidelines always presents problems to parents. Babies' logic at eighteen months is composed largely of their impulses to carry out their desires; life consists of the present, and they are bereft of foresight. As we have seen, "no" is learned before "yes," and it can become a major tool in the effort to preserve prerogatives. The child takes over from parents their use of "no" to refuse to comply with demands. Too much limitation, too frequent negations deprive children of

a sense of initiative and enjoyment, and can lead them to become negativistic.

There are ways of avoiding collisions of wills and frequent clashes of
temperament without having the family become enslaved to the baby's
whims and without squelching the child. Insofar as possible an area of the
house is cleared for action with all dangerous and valuable things removed
but with enough left to permit interesting exploration. Children's energies
are channeled into nondestructive activities. Toddlers are highly distractible, and drawing attention to some new activity can often serve better
than a "don't" or a physical restriction. The parents are bolstered by a
realization that the phase will pass. Still, this is not a time for offering
lengthy explanations or alternatives. Somewhat older children can be given
choices, but at this stage firm, pleasant, and patient guidance free from
indecision solves the important matters, whereas latitude is permitted in
areas that do not matter.

Now, as throughout early childhood, the mutuality between parent and
child forms a major guide. It requires the indefinable judgment of a person
who knows and empathizes with the child. It involves permitting children
to use their abilities as they develop but not setting demands beyond their
capacities. It requires a consistency from the parent that enables the child
to learn how to have a pleased parent. The need for a comfortable parent,
as has been noted, serves as a major directive to the child and a reward for
which to relinquish immediate gratification. Still, the most devoted mother
is human and has her limits and moods. These young dynamos can wear
out their mothers faster than themselves and mothers cannot always be
wise, consistent, and pleased.

Any attempt to consider the process of child development only in terms
of an unattainable ideal is unrealistic. The parents' moods and limits require recognition as well as do the child's needs. Just as in infant feeding,
the trend in setting controls has shifted from early training in obedience
and conformity to a "permissiveness" that has sought to minimize frustration and the repression of self-expression. "Permissiveness" has too often
been interpreted by educators as well as by parents to connote that any
restriction of children will distort their personality development. Parents
have often had the notion that restricting a child indicates the presence of
rejecting qualities derived from unconscious hostility to the child. The
ensuing inhibition of self-expression in the mother, who often cannot admit
her frustration and weariness even to herself, can produce an unnatural
atmosphere in the home and a false front that has a more deleterious
influence in the end. The general atmosphere created, the comfort and

security of the parents in feeling that what they do is correct, and the meaningfulness of the restrictions that must be imposed are far more important than temporary parental upsets and losses of patience. Somehow the child can usually accept what the parents are convinced is proper.

SEPARATION-INDIVIDUATION

Children are now moving away from the symbiotic union with the mother while still having her close to provide for their needs—becoming members of a family rather than primarily members of a mother-child unit. The process involves both separation and individuation (Mahler, *et al.*, 1975). Separation concerns the child's disengagement and differentiation from the mother. Individuation involves the development of a stable inner representation of the mother, a time sense, a capacity for testing reality, and an awareness that others have an existence discrete from the child's. We have already examined the first stages in which the infant differentiates and tentatively moves away from the mothering person.* As children become toddlers they may seem rather independent of the mother as long as she is near. However, when left without the mother or some other very familiar person they take less interest in the surroundings, their activities slow down, and they appear preoccupied. If the child becomes upset, an unfamiliar person has difficulty in comforting the child, but when the mother returns the "toned down" state terminates, though sometimes only after a brief spell of crying (Mahler *et al.*, 1975, p. 74).

Then, as children grow more clearly aware of their mothers' separateness, they may seem to regress and seek more attention from her and greater closeness to her. In this *"rapprochement* phase" they are apt to

---

* Mahler distinguishes four subphases: *differentiation,* which starts at about the fourth month, when the infant moves from an autistic, self-contained phase into symbiosis with the mother; the *practicing* period, which lasts from around the eighth to the fifteenth month, when the child can crawl and then begin to walk away from the mother; the *rapprochement* period, which lasts until the child is about two; and an open-ended period, during which the baby is "on the way to object constancy." The phases concern a sequence rather than specific time periods and their duration varies from child to child. Mahler's work has greatly furthered our knowledge of child development even though done in a nursery rather than in the children's homes. At home among familiar surroundings, the little child's relations with the mother are likely to be rather different and temporary absences of the mother are not as likely to upset the child as much. The findings and inferences were also influenced by the absence of the father and by the paucity of information concerning the parents' relationships and the family transactions.

follow their mothers about, "shadowing" them and wanting the mothers to play and interact with them. A mother might become annoyed with her child's increased demands and the apparent recrudescence of babyishness. However, the children have not regressed but are now forming a more real relationship rather than simply requiring their mothers' presence. Children now want to do things together with a parent rather than just play near them. Now the mother's absence usually leads to greater rather than diminished activity; it seems as though active play can help the child master the separation anxiety. However, in the nursery school, it does not always suffice for a child to realize that an absent mother is nearby where she can be found or that she will soon return. A child may cling to a teacher and become too miserable to play. When a teacher seeks to provide comfort, the child may become drowsy or even fall asleep, withdrawing from the unhappy situation, or may complain and reject everything the teacher (or babysitter) does to distract and comfort the child.*

As improvement in children's linguistic and cognitive capacities enables them to communicate better with persons other than family members and to understand parental assurances, as well as to retain relationships with absent parents, both their separation anxiety and the insistence of their demands diminish. Children begin to have ambivalent feelings toward the same person rather than, as formerly, "split" the mother into a "good" and a "bad" mother according to the feelings the mother arouses at the time, as we shall consider later in the chapter. Now, too, children begin to fear loss of a parent's love rather than simply the loss of the parent, and behavior becomes more consistent in order to maintain the parents' love—a topic we shall pursue further in Chapter 8 when considering superego formation.

FAMILY MEMBERSHIP

The home is the center of toddlers' lives and in this sheltered environment they try themselves out, gain the feel of their bodies and how to use them, and acquire confidence in themselves. Although children can do well in nursery settings and even nursery schools before the age of three, they

* Other methods of coping with separation were: sitting in the chair mother had sat in; going into the cloakroom, which formed a transitional place between home and nursery; eating large quantities of cookies, i.e., replacing the feeder with food; being read to or looking at books to distract themselves or to place themselves in a relationship similar to a usual relationship with the mother (Mahler *et al.*, 1975, p. 100).

usually develop more comfortably when they learn to relate to others through experiences with family members before the need to interact with others becomes of primary importance. Even within the home the child is constantly moving against the limits that are safe and into conflicts with the rights of others. Children properly learn the essential delimitations of behavior under the aegis of parents who seek to foster their welfare and cherish them, who know their ways and can tolerate their trespasses, and who comfort them when they overreach themselves. Their intense bonds with their mothers and their need for their mothers meliorates the restrictions that are placed on them tolerantly and lovingly. The onus of delimitation is offset by the satisfaction of pleasing the mother. Theoretically, at least, they live in tolerant and understanding homes in which the consistency of the parents leads to consistency in themselves. Behavior that would produce a rebuff from outsiders is not only acceptable but is expected within the home. Here temper outbursts need cause no lasting shame and tears no loss of face as they will when the children move into the world of childish compeers.

Although the home and the family are the center of children's lives, they increasingly move into contact with new places and persons. They go walking with their parents and get into things on the way. There are important things that they cannot resist exploring and examining until they learn to anticipate the more intriguing goal of a playground or store. While they may refuse to ride in their strollers, feeling grown up enough to walk just like their mothers, they can, at first, use the support of pushing the stroller along and are glad to have it as a vehicle when they tire.

PEER RELATIONSHIPS

In one way or another a child meets other children and at first may simply regard them as objects to be explored, and so the child feels, pats, and pushes them. Even later, toddlers will not play together but go about their own activities, enjoying the presence of others. The solitary play of several two-year-olds in the same room or yard will be broken by sudden, silent tugs of war or outbursts of screams and tears as one encounters the outrage of another who wants to use the same toy or space. At home, unless there are siblings of similar age, toys are the child's own possession. In another few months children will engage in parallel play in which two or more play at the same thing but still not with one another. The presence of other children of the same age is important to the child as he or she passes the age of two. A child will watch another play, enjoy observing briefly, and may then imitate the other. The boundaries of the self are still far from clear, emotionally as well as physically, and the exuberance, laughter, or tears of one child may become infectious to another. An older toddler may empathize with, and seek to comfort, a crying child.

Activities with other children provide new essential experiences through which they learn their role. They gain new perspectives of themselves through seeing other children, and eventually begin to see themselves through the eyes of other children, which is a very different matter from seeing the self only as a child in an adult world in which one is small, relatively helpless, and unequal to what others can accomplish.

As children approach three they begin to move beyond the confines of the home where they are the center of attention, and into the world with others. Even though it will be a very protected world for another few years, how a child fits into it depends upon the security and initiative gained at home. A basic trust in the self provides the foundation for relating to other children, including the freedom to express and assert oneself and the tacit assumptions of finding friendliness.

Toddlers are now rapidly expanding the range of their activities and their knowledge of the world, but the expansion has necessitated delimitation by their parents. Learning what is permissible and what is forbidden, what pleases and what displeases parents, is part of the process of socialization. The child is becoming more of a social creature through the limitation of drives and desires. There is an unfortunate element of confusion in the process. Some activities are prohibited simply because they are dangerous to a baby and not because they are otherwise unacceptable, whereas some behaviors are banned because they are contrary to the mores. Unless parents distinguish between what a child must or must not do for the child's safety, the societal rules, or the parents' passing feelings, the child's ethical development may become confused.

LEARNING LANGUAGE

Concomitantly, babies are learning to talk. They are now acquiring the adaptive technique that is uniquely human. It constitutes a major expansion of their capacities and a major aspect of the process of enculturation, but it also presents difficulties and frustrations as well as pleasures to little children. The delimitations in using language that the parents impose upon children are not as apparent as the bounds they set upon their actions, and they are not as likely to create feelings of frustration, but they are very real.

During the first year and a half, the baby's cognitive capacities develop essentially by progressive expansion of sensori-motor schemata, as has been outlined in the preceding chapter. The nurturing persons play a part primarily through keeping the child's tensions and emotional upsets minimal and by supplying gratifying stimulation and opportunities for new experiences. Learning language, however, is a very different matter. It involves the acquisition of an existing complex system of sounds, meanings, and syntax through interaction with tutors, primarily the family members. Although it depends upon the prior elaboration of sensori-motor schemata, it is not a direct continuation of this earlier type of cognitive development. Learning language requires the assimilation of schemata that have been built up by others. The development of verbal communication requires a new start, so that language will at first play a relatively small part in directing the baby's behavior.

In learning language, children not only are learning to communicate verbally but are also assimilating the culture's system of meanings and its ways of thinking and reasoning. As noted in an earlier chapter, each society categorizes experience somewhat differently, and the vocabulary of its language forms a catalogue of the categories it uses in perceiving, thinking, and communicating. We have also noted that the family is the society's major enculturating agency. Babies are extremely dependent upon parental tutors, particularly their mothers, to mediate between them and the language of the society. Parents, as we shall see, interpret the baby's primitive words into words of the language and also interpret the language to the child. It is a lengthy and involved process and we shall be able only to touch upon some of the highlights. Thus, at this phase of life when toddlers are gaining greater initiative and strive to do more and more things for themselves, they become very dependent upon the mother, or some other person who is very familiar with them, for verbal comprehension. In order for babies to gain the language facility essential for the development of good intelligence, they need someone who is thoroughly familiar with their behavior, and who can interpret their needs, gestures, and primitive usage of words with reasonable accuracy and teach them, albeit often unknowingly, how these things can be conveyed linguistically, patiently working with them to build up their language. The consistency of the tutor's interaction with the child is extremely important, as also is the tutor's ability to suit the teaching to the child's capacities. More is involved than the speed and fluency of linguistic development; the child must now develop a trust in the utility and reliability of verbal communication and thereby a trust in the value of rationality. We will amplify this topic in the next chapter. As we examine a few salient aspects of the process by which the child acquires language, the importance of the mothering person or persons will become apparent.*

The Origins of Words

The foundations upon which the acquisition of language is built are laid down in the first year along with the mutual understanding between child and parents of needs, wishes, feelings, and intentions. The capacity to develop speech is an innate human attribute and all infants start to babble. However, the babbling must be reinforced by hearing it, and the deaf child soon stops babbling. The sounds that children make stimulate them to repeat the sounds and then to vary them. In Piaget's terms the sounds are aliments that stimulate circular reactions (see Chapter 5), and the vocalizations of others also stimulate the child's babbling and vocal experimentation. Infants' babblings gradually shift to resemble the sounds used in the language being spoken to them and around them. However, M. M. Lewis (1964, p. 33) believes that there are six archetypal nursery words—a type of basic baby language—that are used everywhere, varying but slightly from place to place. These are repetitions of the vowel "ah" with different consonants—"dada," "nana," "mama," "baba," "papa," and "tata." Babies repeat these or closely related sounds as circular reactions to their own sounds and to their parents' modified imitations of them. Certain of the repetitive sounds such as "mamama" or "dadada" are selected out and repeated by parents and are thus reinforced. The persons around the child respond to given sounds when they are used under certain circumstances, which lead to their repetition as part of particular action patterns or circular reactions. Still, the child's early use of "mama" is far from giving a name to the mother.

---

* Piaget can be followed only in part. Piaget's studies of intellectual development between the end of the sensori-motor period and the later preoperational period when the child is three and a half or four are very meager. His studies seem to consider the period very much as he did the sensori-motor period, with a relative lack of appreciation of words as carriers of categories developed by the culture and of the interactional nature of the learning process. His theories of the period of preoperational intelligence are more suited to the later portions of the period when the child is between three and seven. Fortunately, M. M. Lewis (1964) has collated many of the studies made of children's language between one and three years and has furnished numerous observations of his own.

The word "mama" begins to fill an instrumental function for children when they are about a year old. When, for example, the infant drops an object from the crib, fails to reach it, and says "mama" while reaching for it, mother sizes up the situation and hands her baby the object. It also has a declarative value; after being fed, a little girl gazes at her mother and contentedly says "mamama," which induces her mother to hug her. The repetition of the syllable thus produces a response. Now we find that a generalization of the "word" occurs and it is used in a wide variety of manipulative and affective contexts. It will require another ten to twelve months until "mama" is gradually limited to a designation for the mother. Thus, Piaget recorded that his son said "mummy" at fourteen months in surprise or appreciation when his mother was swinging her body; at fifteen months he used it to indicate that he wanted something, even when appealing to his father; and at sixteen months to get his father to light a lamp, when he saw his mother's clothing in a closet, and also when his mother gave him something. Eventually, the child learns the meaning because of the consistency of the mother's response to the word, because she and others apply the term to her, and because of other such social interactions.

The baby's speech starts with the archetypal sounds used by infants everywhere that are reinforced by the parents and made to denote something by them. The baby's language is then expanded by "words" that form a transition between the "basic baby language" and conventional words. They are two-syllable repetitions such as "tata" for "good-bye," "nana" for nurse or grandmother, etc., and then "bye-bye," "bow-wow," and other such words that the baby learns from adults who are adapting their speech to the baby's capacities.* The toddler cannot learn to say "mother" but only "mama" or some such similar simple utterance. "Mom" or "mommy" can then be assimilated to "mama," etc. The parents, then, are speaking baby language to the child as if they were aware that the baby can at first only imitate and learn words that they have transformed into two simple syllables. Then, in accord with the child's development, they gradually move toward using sounds that more closely approximate the real word.

The Origins of Meanings

It seems likely that each new word the child learns during this period goes through a phase of expansion before it becomes narrowed down to a usage that is approximately appropriate. Thus, Piaget (1962, p. 216) found that soon after his thirteen-month-old daughter learned "bow-wow,"

* The child is not only learning meanings but also to accommodate his vocal sensori-motor schemata to pronouncing words.

she pointed to a dog while standing on her balcony and said "bow-wow,"
and thereafter the word was used for anything seen from her balcony—
including horses, baby carriages, cars, and people; and not until three
months later was "bow-wow" reserved for dogs.

Let us look further at the process of expansion and contraction of word
meanings. Expansions are difficult to follow. "Wawa" meaning water may
be learned for a glass of water and then be used for the glass as well as the
water, and then for all shiny objects, before being narrowed down to the
fluid; and it may go through other such false expansions at the time it is
applied to running water in a bath, and again when water is seen in an
ocean. Lewis (1964, pp. 50–57) has provided an example of how the
expansion and limitation of a word occurred. His son, when twenty months
old, said "Tee" (Timmy) for the household cat and then, at twenty-one
months, for a small dog. Soon thereafter he used "Tee" for a cow and then
for a horse. At twenty-two months he learned "goggie" for his toy dog and
soon also used this word instead of "Tee" for a small dog. Then he learned
"hosh" for horse, and stopped using "Tee" for cat as he had learned
"pushie," but he continued to use "Tee" for cow until he learned "moo-ka"
when a little over two years old. A St. Bernard dog was rather understandably termed a "hosh" until he learned that it was a "biggie-goggie." Thus,
over a period of about three months, the "Tee" which had been used for a
variety of animals was replaced by words that classified animals in a
manner that was reasonably similar to that used in the culture. He learned
such differentiation through experiments in establishing communication by
extending and contracting the applications of these sounds under the "responsive guidance of those who share in his experiences" (Lewis, 1964, p.
57).

The word gradually gains a discrete meaning and becomes a symbol as it
comes to designate the unity and identity of the object as perceived from
different perspectives and in differing situations; and also when different
objects with the same critical attributes are categorized together by being
denoted by the same word. The first of these ways of achieving a stable
meaning is obviously simpler for children. When they, at about a year and
a half of age, say "mama," they are symbolizing their mothers' identity for
them under various conditions. It is much simpler to use "bow-wow" for a
toy dog under all circumstances than to learn what objects are properly
denoted by the word. The meanings of words continue to develop, narrowing to precision of meaning and broadening to include an ever increasing
number of experiences with the word and whatever it designates. Although
the meanings of common words become fairly definite during childhood,

they will continue to change throughout life. The word "mother" has different meanings for a person when a small child and when a college student, and a still somewhat different meaning when a psychiatrist.*

Early Syntactical Development

The single word used by the baby at eighteen or twenty months has a diffuse meaning, and in its diffuseness it often expresses a sentence which the mother who knows her child can understand. The baby's "mama" can mean "I am hungry" or "Give me my ball" or "I love you, Mother"; and the mother, sizing up the situation, responds as if a complete sentence had been expressed. In the process, she will often also expand the child's verbalization by saying "Tommy hungry" or "Tommy want ball?" which is part of the lengthy process of teaching language to the child, even though she knows that it may be months before the child will be able to use the expanded expression.

Then when the children are about two years old, they begin to use two- to four-word expressions which, despite their simplicity, greatly increase the specificity of the communication. These are expressions such as "Mommy come," "Papa go bye-bye," "Nice doggie." The words are almost always in the proper sequence (Brown & Bellugi, 1961). It is not clear whether the child can "program" only such simple expressions because of the immaturity of the nervous system or because they are a step in gradual assimilation and accommodation.† Here again, the parental persons are in a position to guess the meaning from the situation, or they know how to behave or question the child in order to find out. The communication is between child and parent and not between child and any person in the community. Outsiders can understand only a small fraction of what the child seeks to convey. Brown has observed that mothers will, virtually without realizing it, expand the two- or three-word sentences for the child by adding a few crucial words. They do not usually expand them into complicated sentences but judge how far the child's comprehension may exceed his capacities for expression. For example, a little girl says "Mama lunch," and the mother judges whether she means "Mother, give me

* Miss Sullivan's major concern in teaching Helen Keller was to convey the knowledge that words stood for categories of things and not single objects. The reader may also be interested in the ingenious manner in which Dr. Itard in 1797 taught the wild boy "Victor" that words stood for categories, and the limited success he attained.

† As Brown (1965) points out, the words used are "contentives"—that is, words with content that can be used to designate things or actions; and the words left out are "functors"—articles and prepositions, and perhaps forms of "to be."

lunch," "Mother is eating lunch," "Mother is making lunch," etc. The mother then adds the words that make the distinction and, in the process, is teaching the rudiments of syntax.

Questions and the Naming Game

Sometime during the third year, varying from child to child, babies begin to ask questions, and then if they have proper respondents their vocabularies and comprehension expand rapidly. The questions are of several general types, each reflecting increases in children's intellectual capacities. Perhaps most notable are the naming questions that mount to a crescendo that strains the patience of many parents. The "What's this?" or "What's that?" may be stimulated by the parent's questions. Some of the questions are a game; it is a game that children can play as well as adults. Children ask some questions about names they know in order to have an adult turn the question back and permit the child to have the pleasure of answering correctly. Sometimes it is a means of gaining attention; sometimes a search for confirmation that the name applies to another object of the same category. It appears as if the child now realizes that everything has a name that must be learned and starts seeking this important knowledge. It will be recalled that the moment Helen Keller learned that objects have names constituted the turning point in her life. Knowing the name actually bestows a new power upon a toddler. The child needs the names in order to begin to learn through talking rather than through action and to internalize the environment symbolically so as to make possible its imaginative manipulation. Even at this early age the names permit a degree of predictability about the world. A little boy may learn that all balls roll simply by playing with them, but he cannot know what objects are "toys" and can be played with from their appearance, as toys come in very varied shapes; nor can he know what foods are "sweet" before tasting them—but the words let him know in advance (Bruner et al., 1956).

The child developed some appreciation of the constancy of the object during the period of sensori-motor development as illustrated by the searching for it after it disappeared. Such knowledge is often fostered by adults, who hide an object and ask the child where it has gone. At first such questions only produce action responses—the child seeks the missing ball or block—but eventually they produce verbal responses, such as "there," or even "stairs" meaning "upstairs in my room." The baby now clearly holds visual images of absent objects in memory, and from here it is not a very large step to references to the past and future. As the notion of the future is based upon expectations derived from past experiences, the child for some time remains somewhat confused about what is past and what future and so may, at times, say "yesterday" when meaning tomorrow, even when considerably older.

As the third birthday approaches, questions are apt to include inquiries about reasons, "Why?" and "What you doing?" At this age children do not have any real concept of cause and effect, as Piaget (1928) has pointed out, and even when they learn to reply to questions with "because" responses, they are only designating spatial or temporal juxtapositions. Still, it is a start, and, after all, the problem of causality is confusing even to philosophers and scientists.

By means of such step-by-step development that we have considered only in fragmentary form, the child's linguistic and intellectual growth gains momentum during the third year of life. By the age of three, and sometimes even by the age of two and a half, the child has acquired hundreds of words, and some children know more than a thousand by then. According to Brown (1965), children by then may use nearly all of the syntactical forms of the language in sentences of twelve to fifteen words. They really converse, and it is sometimes difficult for adults to realize the limitations in their usage of the words. Nevertheless, children can now begin to reason, to reason among themselves, to project a simple future, to play imaginatively, and to fantasy. With such mental abilities they pass into a new phase of development.*

We have seen that the child's language development depends greatly on

---

* Children spend time practicing using language very much as they repeat motor activities over and over until they are mastered and can be incorporated into more complex schemata. The linguist Ruth Weir (1962) studied the speech of her son while he was alone in his bedroom prior to falling asleep by making tape recordings of his productions at about two and a half years of age. The child's language development was somewhat precocious, as might be expected of the child of a linguist who was particularly interested in language development. As Roman Jakobson notes in the introduction to Weir's book, "Many of the recorded passages bear a striking resemblance to . . . exercises in text books for self-instruction in foreign languages: 'What color—What color blanket—What color mop—What color glass . . . Not the yellow blanket—The white . . . It's not black—It's yellow . . . Not yellow—Red . . . Put on a blanket—White blanket—and yellow blanket—Where's yellow blanket . . . Yellow blanket—Yellow light . . . There is the light—Where is the light—Here is the light' " (Jakobson, 1962). The recordings reveal many fascinating aspects of linguistic development.

Of course, some children say very little until they are two years old, or occasionally even older, and yet their language usage is not retarded when they start to speak. Such development is likely to occur most frequently when there are other young children in the family and the child hears a great deal of simple speech. One little boy, who had clearly comprehended a great deal but said very little, announced shortly after his second birthday, "I can talk now," and soon showed that he had assimilated a fairly extensive vocabulary and proper syntactical forms.

the parental tutors, particularly the mother who can understand the child's nonverbal communication and who interacts so constantly with her child. However, not all mothers understand intuitively, not all are patient or even interested, and many mothers nurture their babies in relative silence. It appears as if paucity of interchange affects children's linguistic and perhaps their intellectual development, but the topic is now first coming under scientific scrutiny. Children's dependency upon their mothering persons for verbal understanding is great, for no one else is likely to be able to communicate as effectively with the baby. It is one reason why removal of the child of two and three from the mother is so traumatic, for the child now needs a mothering person for many such reasons. Toddlers exist in states of dependency—they may be establishing boundaries between their mothers and themselves but they are still far from autonomous. They are not yet really separate from their mothers and if separated from mother for a lengthy period they lose much of their capacities for initiative and even for survival.

THE STRUGGLE FOR MASTERY

The struggle for mastery and control often reaches a peak between the ages of two and two and a half, when children struggle with conflicting impulses within themselves as well as against parental controls. In some instances, the increase in their abilities now that they communicate in two- to four-word expressions leads parents to overestimate their comprehension and their capacities for being reasonable. The child has now learned a good deal about the household rules and regulations but is not always motivated to rescind impulses or comply as much as parents expect. Children maybe heard muttering "no" to themselves as they begin to internalize parental rules. There may be tantrums when the child can neither decide to conform nor tolerate loss of affection. Periods of negativistic behavior occur when a child does not wish to comply with anything and regression to more infantile behavior may occur.

It is said that this is a time of notable *ambivalence*—that is, an admixture of opposing feelings toward the same person. However, not until children are near the age of three can they begin to contain opposite feelings at the same time. They often vacillate from one to the other, often to the bewilderment of their parents. The toddler is apt to consider the mother who gives and bestows love as the "good mother" and the frustrating mother as another person—the "bad mother." Similarly, the child may consider the self as two children: a good, pleasing child and a naughty, contrary one. The "good child" may wish to renounce responsibility for the "bad child." At about this time one may hear the child say "Now you my mommy" when the mother becomes pleasant after a set-to; or the "good child" will insist that not he, but the bad boy or a toy doll, had pushed the plate off the table. After all, the notion of the conservation of objects is not yet firm, and a person or object may not be recognized after changing a characteristic.*

Toilet Training

Many of the cardinal problems of this developmental phase may focus upon the process of toilet training, particularly when premature training imposes demands that the child cannot readily master or even understand before the age of two and a half or three. Toilet training places paradoxical demands upon the puzzled child who sometimes is supposed to give in order to please, and at other times to hold back in order to please. Continence and control are demanded just when conflicts over self-control are at a height. The struggle over who is to be the master, the parent or the child, can reach an impasse on this battlefield. Like the proverbial horse who can be led to water, the child can be sat on the potty but cannot be made to defecate. Here is one aspect of interaction in which children can stubbornly have their way—well, can almost have their way, for some parents will resort to suppositories and enemas, "for the sake of the child's health," and thus win the struggle on this front, usually only to lose it elsewhere.†

---

*We can note, for example, that Piaget's daughter, J., at two years and seven months, upon first seeing her younger sister, L., in a new bathing suit and cap, asked, "What's the baby's name?" Her mother explained that it was a bathing costume but J. pointed to L. herself and said, "But what's the name of that?" and repeated the question several times. As soon as L. had her dress on again, J. exclaimed very seriously, "It's L. again," as if her sister had changed her identity with her clothes. (See J. Piaget, *Play, Dreams and Imitation in Childhood*, p. 224.) At two years and four months in looking at a picture of herself as a younger child she asked, "Who is it?" When told it was she when she was small, she said, "Yes, when she [J.] was L."

† A young woman of eighteen, for example, was admitted to the hospital because of serious fecal impaction and for study of why she was unable to move her bowels. She related that she had never defecated spontaneously in her life. Soon after her birth her mother had used suppositories and, when these became ineffective, enemas. Enemas are likely to lead to other types of difficulties. For most children they are more painful than pleasurable and can stimulate sadistically toned fantasies of being controlled and attacked; others find the sensuous quality of the stimulation, and being controlled while passive, highly seductive.

Actually, there is no reason why bowel training should be attempted before the age of two and a half, or why it must present anything of a problem at all. Many parents have found that if they can be patient and unmoved by the condescension of neighbors who believe that their own children were perfectly trained at the age of a year or eighteen months, the child will eventually wish to use the toilet following the example of the other members of the family or the suggestion of the parents. Children trained in this manner may never know that having bowel movements can raise a significant issue or even that such a thing as constipation exists. It is also clear that when children are toilet trained before the age of eighteen months there are often recrudescences of soiling later. Further, virtually all children are bowel-trained by the age of three, the difference being that those who have been trained strictly will continue to have preoccupations and difficulties if not certain of the characterologic problems that will be discussed below.

ANAL EROTISM

If, however, the customary practice of starting bowel training early is followed, the ensuing conflicts can then provide very ample reasons why psychoanalytic theory has termed this the *anal phase* of development.* Paradoxically, virtually all of the literature on child rearing emphasizes the problems of toilet training in discussing the period, even though the major problems for which mothers seek help concern feeding and temper tantrums.

Psychoanalytic theory has hypothesized a shift of libidinal investment from the oral to the anal zone toward the end of the first year of life. There is little reason to continue to hold this concept. However, the area is highly sensitive, and its stimulation can produce erotic gratification. After weaning increased attention may be given to the pleasurable stimulation provided by the mother as she cleans the soiled child. The process provides the child with another source of intimate relatedness to the mother in which she is simultaneously caring for the child and providing sensory stimulation of a pleasurable nature. In addition, cleaning the child often requires cleansing and stimulating the genitalia.

Eventually the child must renounce obtaining such care and pleasure

---

* Parents' wishes to bowel train early have become less compelling since the institution of diaper services, washing machines, and disposable diapers.

from the mother. Actual control of defecation can be attained only after muscular control of the sphincters becomes possible through maturation of the nerve tracts in the spinal cord, and even then the achievement of coordination takes time. However, many infants are more or less conditioned to have bowel movements at a given time, perhaps after meals when the gastro-colic reflex that tends to produce evacuation after eating is activated. Perhaps it is more accurate to say that mothers are trained to set their babies on the pot when they are likely to have a movement, and then children become conditioned to do so. However, a child may find that all satisfaction derived from anal erotism need not be relinquished. Pleasure can be gained holding on to the feces until the release of the bolus stimulates the mucosa. Children can stimulate themselves while cleaning themselves, or wait until given enemas, which some children find pleasurable. In general, it has been considered that early bowel training with its premature demands and deprivation of gratification leads to a fixation at an anal level of psychosexual development and to perseverance of "anal" problems. It seems more in keeping with known facts that undue erotization of the anal area follows upon excessive maternal instinct in the problem and stimulation of the region. Many mothers continue to place considerable emphasis on proper evacuation throughout childhood and even into adolescence.* Some aspects of the problems attributed to anal fixation are more clearly reflections of the more general struggles of the period concerning initiative and control that so often focus on bowel training.

When training is carried out in a relaxed and noncompulsive manner, children come to feel that they can care for these essential needs by themselves. They gain a sense of trust in themselves and in their bodily equipment. The parents who distrust their children's capacities to care for themselves and their use of initiative in play are likely to be parents who cannot trust a child's body to function properly unaided, and those who are upset by the disorder the child creates in the house are likely to be disturbed by soiling and seek early bowel training.

Early Ethical and Aesthetic Influences

Now, bowel training is particularly likely to contain ethical and aesthetic implications that will influence character structure. The child is learning basic meanings which can be influenced by the process. Whereas soiled

---

* A set of seriously disturbed adolescent twins claimed that whenever one had a fight with their mother, she gave them both enemas simultaneously, insisting that they were "contrary" because they were constipated. The procedure was carried out in a highly ritualized and erotized manner. Both twins insisted that they had believed that "constipation" meant "being angry at mother."

diapers do not disturb infants or small children who seem to value their products and even enjoy the odor and feel, their parents regard the matter differently. Usually, mothers' behavior in cleaning soiled children is very different from their behavior when nursing or bathing them. They are not likely to gain pleasure from the act, and at best their attitudes are ambivalent. A mother is apt to show disgust in her facial expression; and as the child begins to understand, words such as "dirty boy," "shame," and "smelly baby" may accompany her discovery that the child is soiled. Before long the child will also say "dirty" or "shame" at such times. These are among the earliest aesthetic and ethical evaluations. Soiling and matters associated with defecation are considered shameful, dirty, and bad; and, by contrast, clean and good are equated. When children in negative moods toward their mothers soil themselves they are "bad" and feel ashamed of themselves—and such feelings spread to other contrary behaviors. A child learns to defend against such feelings by being overly clean—at least externally, particularly if feeling hostile and dirty inwardly.

"Anal" Characteristics

The problems arising from parental restrictiveness of the child's initiative, and paradigmatically from bowel training and the renunciation of anal erotism, transcend this developmental phase and influence character formation. Various groupings of traits related to the problems that are paramount during this critical stage of early socialization have been designated as *anal characteristics*. For example, it has been repeatedly noted that persons who are constipated may also be stubborn, showing covert hostility through withholding from others in a silent and determined fashion. Not infrequently there will also be varying degrees of miserliness, pettiness about details, meticulousness, and pedanticism. A person who is meticulously clean externally may be dirty or messy underneath, or perhaps fastidious in the way possessions are arranged on the surface while those things that are out of view are disordered. Such persons have problems about holding on and letting go, and about keeping for oneself or sharing with others both possessions and information about the self. There is ambivalence about love and hate which must be concealed and is clearly connected to obsessive-compulsive character disorders. The traits may be present in various combinations as well as hidden from the self and others by reaction formation—that is, by a tendency to undo such trends by going to opposite extremes. Such characteristics are, of course, not necessarily pathological unless they dominate the total personality, and some such trends exist to a greater or lesser degree in almost everyone. In moderate degree they can have very positive value as when they contribute to perseverance, thoroughness in work, and ability to save.

As these traits develop in relationship to the all-important parental figures when basic attitudes are first being established, they are likely to permeate later interpersonal relationships. Some persons who are "anal characters" may feel that others are always trying to get something from them, or that others will shame them if they express their natural feelings or needs. They learn to keep things to themselves and cannot be open or trusting. Paranoid individuals who fear attack from others often have strong anal characteristics. The essence of the matter seems to be that a child who has been overcontrolled at this critical phase is likely to become a person who must hide the hostilities and aggressions engendered and who unconsciously feels that if one's true feelings are found out one will be rejected, hated, and in danger. Such persons develop devious ways of preserving initiative or autonomy, but it is usually a constricted and withholding way of maintaining a semblance of self-assertion.

An "Anal" Character

One often sees persons much of whose way of life seems to have been determined by the events of this period but whose anal characteristics are not altogether pathological. For example, an excellent physicist who has made significant contributions to science has never been incapacitated by such characteristics but has turned them into assets that balance his limitations. Although a fine scientist, he is very slow in his work, carrying out his experiments with meticulous precision. Fortunately he had moved into a sphere of study concerned with physical measurement where such characteristics are highly advantageous. His colleagues know very little about what he does and his chief is often frantic because nothing seems to emerge from months of effort. If rushed, he becomes anxious and a negativistic streak appears which leads him to waste his time in unnecessary checking and endless recalculations. However, slowly and carefully his researches become productive. He is a tight-lipped man with a very pedantic manner, and even his wife knows little about what he thinks or does. At home he is constantly concerned about money, insisting upon paying the bills himself but in a manner that makes his wife frantic, as his tardiness embarrasses her with various shopkeepers. He spends hours going over the accounts and he has difficulty in making out checks. Quarrels in the home arise about matters of waste, for he insists that his wife never throw out any food, claiming that he prefers eating stale bread and drinking leftover coffee. He examines the refrigerator each night to make certain that nothing that might possibly have been used has been discarded. While he appears very neat in his dress, his wife has complained that "his drawers are a mess." These words unconsciously conveyed one of her reasons for being aggravated with him. She feels that despite his oversolicitous concern about her health and welfare, he is hostile to her in many little ways, never giving or really sharing; and responding to complaints by becoming more silent and withdrawn.

Feeding Problems

Problems of "orality" and difficulties with feeding are not confined to infancy. Feeding problems are a major reason why mothers consult pediatricians about their two- and three-year-olds. The contemporary emphasis upon the child's vitamin, mineral, and protein intake, particularly in television commercials, abets such concerns. However, mothers commonly unconsciously relate feeding with bestowing love and care. Food is something tangible they can give that enters into their children and fosters their growth. Some children learn very early that eating is a function that also enables them to assert their independence. A little boy can stubbornly refuse to open his mouth, avert his head, spit out food, and even vomit what has been put into him. If he has felt neglected, his dawdling or fussing about eating can provoke his mother and hold her attention. Feeding can become the arena in which the struggle for mastery and initiative takes place. Such conflicts are, of course, unnecessary. Children seek relief from the tensions produced by hunger, and soon learn to eat sufficiently if the food is removed when they begin to dawdle unduly or when they become negativistic. However, the mealtime is usually a social occasion for both child and parents, a time when they can relate happily and the child cannot be expected to consume meals in a playless mechanical routine.

When a mother conveys to her son that he will eat if he loves her, or that her little girl must eat to show her love, difficulties are very likely to ensue. Such patterns often last into late childhood, and mothers who continue to feel that an adult offspring is still a child may try to show their affection and concern through insisting that the child eat all they provide. Occasionally, serious disturbances arise because a mother does not follow the child's needs but her own emotional needs or insecurities in feeding her child. Hilde Bruch (1961) points out that the child must learn the relationship between the physiological indication of hunger and the ability of food to still such sensations. If a mother feeds her infant whenever the baby cries, and continues to act as if any unhappiness of the small child can be allayed by food, the child may never learn to recognize hunger, or learn that food is a means of satisfying hunger feelings rather than a way of coping with one's own or one's mother's unhappiness or anxieties.

The Influence of the Parents and Their Relationships

The parents' basic attitudes toward their child reflect their own personalities and upbringing and not simply their acceptance or rejection of the child. They are affected profoundly by their relationship with each other, by the satisfactions they gain from their marriage and their sexual fulfillment in it. A husband's behavior as a father cannot but influence his wife's behavior as a mother: must she protect the child from his jealousy or annoyance with the child; must she "cover up" for the child, or begin to cover up for the father to his children? The father is essentially the first intruder into the mother-child entity, and as such is probably always resented to some extent, but he can also be welcomed as someone who adds enrichment and enjoyment to the child's life.

The parents' ways of relating to their child and their basic attitudes about child rearing extend across the years rather than being limited to a single developmental phase—though almost all parents are likely to be more concerned about some developmental tasks and have greater problems in coping with one developmental phase than with others. A mother who could not feel that her milk would properly nourish was also afraid to bathe her son lest she drop him, later thought he needed frequent enemas to move his bowels, and could rarely let him play outside of a fenced enclosure; and when he was a schoolboy, she constantly sought additional help for him from teachers. However, some mothers who feel very insecure in handling a helpless, frangible infant become more relaxed with an older child; but, perhaps more commonly, mothers who are at ease as long as they can care for a child completely become apprehensive when the child begins to venture on its own. For such reasons the essential mother-child harmony is often disrupted during the period of early ambulation, and the anxieties provoked in the mother concerning the child's initiative and the dangers of the world are conveyed to the child. The anxieties may lead to regressive trends toward the securities of the oral phase accompanied by fears of venturing beyond attachment to a feeding and protecting mothering figure.

Some parents limit the child excessively not because of anxieties concerning physical harm but because they cannot tolerate the child's unknowing infractions of rules, which they consider expressions of innate evil that must be overcome before they become habitual. Many generations of persons in our society have been raised on the assumption that the basic evil in people must be countered by discipline and prayer. Such indigenous belief systems have tended toward the production of somewhat guilt-laden children who must either achieve salvation or demonstrate that they are one of the elect who will be saved through good deeds or achievement. In general, a moderate sense of guilt commensurate with the Protestant ethic is deemed desirable in our society. However, some parents, because of ignorance or impatience, seriously constrict and foster undue hostility in the child by reinforcing a barrier of "don'ts" with impatient grabs, slaps, and glances.* As children cannot win in overt conflict with parents, they find covert means of combat; but, as they are still closely identified with one or both parents, hostility and aggression toward a parent is always also aggression toward the self. And as children not only need their parents but also seek to love them, it is also often better to feel guilty and turn the hostility against the self.

A child's innate tendencies to be particularly active and explorative may aggravate such problems when one or both parents can cope well only with a quiet and conforming child. As boys are generally more active than girls, the difficulties between the boy toddler and his parents may be greater than the girl's unless the parents enjoy a child's outgoing activity.†

In discussing children's development between the ages of fifteen and thirty-six months, we have emphasized the problems that arise because of the imbalance between the toddlers' motor skills and their abilities to

---

* The author recently interviewed a mother who sought advice concerning her six-year-old who stammered severely. She brought her two-and-a-half-year-old with her, as he could not be trusted to remain in the waiting room with his older brother. The child sat quietly on her lap for ten minutes and then wiggled to get up. The mother shook him and impatiently exclaimed, "Can't you stop fussing about?" A few minutes later she apologized and put him down. As he walked to look out of the window, she called, "Stay away from the radiator, you'll burn yourself." When he put his hand on my desk to pick up a ruler, "Why do you always have to be a nuisance?" stopped him. Then his thumb went into his mouth, but his mother pulled it out saying, "Aren't you ashamed to let the doctor see you suck?" Then, as he climbed into a chair, she smacked him on his rear with a "Why can't you be still for a moment?" It seemed clear why his older brother stammered.

† Little boys apparently receive more attention from their mothers than do little girls, but it is not clear whether this comes about because boys are innately more active and thus stimulate mothers to provide more attention, or because their activity requires more attention, or because, in a general way, mothers are likely to lavish more attention on boys than on girls. Fathers, who are frequently harsher than mothers, often treat girl toddlers more gently and less punitively than they do boys.

communicate verbally, to understand, and to think. The parents must set limits on their children's impulsions to be active, to explore, and gain mastery over their world. The cardinal tasks of gaining a sense of initiative and of confidence in their own competence are likely to be countered by the manner in which children are controlled, which can foster inhibition of action and lack of self-confidence. Some struggle between child and parents over control is almost inevitable and often focuses on bowel training or feeding. The child's overt compliance and conformity is often accompanied by suppressed anger, heightened ambivalence to parental figures, covert resistance and stubbornness that can exert lasting influences upon the personality. The child is simultaneously acquiring the ability to use language, and we have sought to outline the beginnings of the complex process that will enable the child to communicate needs and wishes verbally, to acquire new knowledge from others, and to gain the cognitive abilities required to direct and control one's own behavior. At the end of the period a relatively good equilibrium has been established between the children's motor and linguistic abilities, and they are ready to gain a more definite autonomy from their mothers and find their places as members of the family. At this toddler stage children's lives interdigitate so closely with their mothers' that prolonged separation from the mother affects them profoundly, causing physiological and depressive disturbances, very much along the lines discussed in the preceding chapter. The reader may have noted that we have scarcely differentiated between the two sexes in this chapter; the differences between boys and girls have not been forgotten or disregarded. Indeed at this age the differentiation of the genders is becoming very clear. The topic has simply been skirted to permit a more focused discussion in the next chapter.

REFERENCES

Brown, R. (1965). "Language: The System and Its Acquisition. Part I: Phonology and Grammar," in *Social Psychology*. Free Press, New York.

Brown, R., and Bellugi, U. (1961). "Three Processes in the Child's Acquisition of Syntax," in *New Directions in the Study of Language*. E. H. Lenneberg, ed. MIT Press, Cambridge, Mass.

Bruch, H. (1961). "Transformation of Oral Impulses in Eating Disorders: A Conceptual Approach," *Psychiatric Quarterly*, 35:458–481.

Bruner, J. S., Goodnow, J., and Austin, G. (1956). A *Study of Thinking*. John Wiley & Sons, New York.

Erikson, E. (1950). *Childhood and Society*. W. W. Norton, New York.

FREUD, S. (1908). "Character and Anal Erotism," in *The Standard Edition of the Complete Psychological Works of Sigmund Freud*, vol. 9. Hogarth Press, London, 1959.

GREENACRE, P. (1957). "The Childhood of the Artist: Libidinal Phase Development and Giftedness," *The Psychoanalytic Study of the Child*, vol. 12, pp. 47–72. International Universities Press, New York.

ITARD, J. M. G. (1797). *The Wild Boy of Aveyron*. G. & M. Humphrey, trans. Century, New York, 1932.

JAKOBSON, R. (1962). Introduction to R. Weir, *Language in the Crib*. Mouton, The Hague.

LEWIS, M. M. (1964). *Language, Thought and Personality in Infancy and Childhood*. Basic Books, New York.

MAHLER, M., PINE, F., and BERGMAN, A. (1975). *The Psychological Birth of the Infant*. Basic Books, New York.

PIAGET, J. (1928). *Judgment and Reasoning in the Child*. M. Warden, trans. Harcourt, Brace, New York.

———. (1962). *Play, Dreams and Imitation in Childhood*. C. Gattengo and F. M. Hodgson, trans. W. W. Norton, New York.

WEIR, R. (1962). *Language in the Crib*. Mouton, The Hague.

SUGGESTED READING

BROWN, R. (1958). *Words and Things*. Free Press, Glencoe, Ill.

FREUD, S. (1905). "Three Essays on the Theory of Sexuality," in *The Standard Edition of the Complete Psychological Works of Sigmund Freud*, vol. 7. Hogarth Press, London, 1953.

LEWIS, M. M. (1964). *Language, Thought and Personality in Infancy and Childhood*. Basic Books, New York.

McCARTHY, D. (1946). "Language Development in Children," in *Manual of Child Psychology*. L. Carmichael, ed. John Wiley & Sons, New York.

MAHLER, M., PINE, F., and BERGMAN, A. (1975). *The Psychological Birth of the Infant*. Basic Books, New York.

SEARS, R., MACCOBY, E., and LEVIN, H. (1957). *Patterns of Child Rearing*. Row, Peterson, Evanston, Ill.

CHAPTER 7

❀

The Preschool Child

THE BASIC DEVELOPMENTAL TASKS

Sometime around the age of three, the child ceases to be a baby and becomes a preschool child. During the next two or three years the child passes through one of the most decisive phases of life's journey that has been termed the oedipal transition. The baby has required a close relationship with a mothering person, but now, in order to release attention and energies for investment beyond the family in school and with playmates, the child must relinquish the erogenous aspects of the relationship, albeit reluctantly and often painfully. The child must now complete the task of differentiating from the mother and become sufficiently secure as an autonomous boy or girl member of the family to begin to venture beyond its shelter.

How this transition transpires depends upon the process of separation and individuation that we have been examining, including the mother's ability gradually to frustrate her child's attachment to her, but it is fostered by other changes which accompany maturation. The child's movement toward increasing independence involves gaining the experience and cognitive capacities required for reality testing and self-guidance. It also involves the ability to cope with the frustrations and anxieties that inevitably arise as increasing autonomy brings insecurity and, in turn, fosters desires to regress to the shelter of mother's presence.

By the end of the period, children will have learned the lessons of primary socialization: to feed and dress themselves, and to control not only their bowels and urine but also their temper outbursts—at least most of the time. They will have attained considerable organization of their personalities, and the major lines of their future development will have been established. The start of coming to terms with reality as specific individuals in a social system takes place within the family, which forms a microcosm in which a patterning of ways of relating to others and of reacting emotionally is laid down. Here children must gain an appreciation and acceptance of themselves as boys or girls and achieve a firm gender identity. They find their places as members of the childhood generation with its limitations as well as prerogatives; they adjust to the competition of siblings for attention and affection; and they gain some realization of their families' position in society. A great deal must happen in these years to make possible the shift in their emotional relatedness to their parents, the oedipal transition, and to prepare them for school and participation in peer groups.

Freud first drew attention to the critical importance of the child's transition through the "oedipal" or "phallic" period. He believed that the investment of libido—sexualized energy—shifted to the penis in the boy and the clitoris in the girl, which led to an upsurge of erotic love for the parent of the opposite sex and desires to possess that parent sexually.* The guilt aroused by these oedipal strivings with ensuing anxieties of punishment by castration, death, or abandonment leads the child to give up or repress the love for the parent of the opposite sex and gain strength by identifying with the parent of the same sex, and in the process gain the capacity for self-control to replace the need for parental control. Freud considered that the way in which a child resolves these "oedipal conflicts" forms a major directive to personality development as well as a potential source of various types of developmental disturbances. The nature of this oedipal transition will be examined more explicitly later in the chapter. Even though contemporary understanding of child development requires profound alterations of the classic psychoanalytic theory of the oedipal transition, the reorientation of children's relationships to their parents at this developmental period—the essence of the oedipal transition—clearly forms a critical determinant of the course of further personality development.

Erikson considers the basic issues of the period to involve the balance

---

* Freud later modified his conceptualization of the girl's oedipal transition, as discussed later in the chapter.

between initiative and guilt: the initiative being concerned with the seeking of a parental love object and the efforts to become a person like a parent through identification with the father or mother; the guilt derives largely from rivalry with the father and siblings for the mother. From the ensuing anxiety over retribution, a conscience or superego develops that serves to regulate initiative, and by making children dependent upon themselves makes them dependable. These developments are fostered by the expansion of children's imagination permitted by their increased locomotor and linguistic capacities (Erikson, 1959).*

By the time they are three, children are beginning to emerge from the protected but confining shelter of their mothers' care, but they will require time and experience before they have the mental tools and emotional stability properly to comprehend their still small worlds and become able to guide themselves beyond their homes. Piaget has made us aware of the striking limitations of preschool children's language, reasoning, comprehension, and moral judgments. It seems essential to understand something of preschool children's cognitive abilities and limitations to be able to grasp properly the tasks confronting them and their means of coping with their problems. There are many aspects of this complex and crucial developmental period that require attention, each clamoring, so to speak, for priority. To bring order to the presentation, we shall adhere to the following sequence: a general description of oedipal children's capacities and behavior; cognitive development; development of gender identity, including the impact of fantasies about childbirth; sibling rivalries; the oedipal problem and its resolution. Last, we shall consider the influence of the nature of the oedipal transition upon personality functioning and malfunctioning.

CAPABILITIES AND BEHAVIOR

When their development has progressed reasonably well, three-year-olds are fascinating to watch as they tenaciously explore how things fit together and come apart, and question what things are and what they are for. No

* The reversal in this book of the periods in which the issues of initiative and autonomy are crucial does not indicate a basic difference concerning the essential tasks of these periods, but rather a difference in the use of terms as well as a somewhat different orientation concerning the nature of the transition the child is making. Here, as elsewhere, the use of an eponym to signify the crucial issues of a developmental phase has serious limitations.

longer toddlers, they tend to waddle as they move earnestly about, but they soon attain an angelic grace as the simple motor schemata that they acquired so laboriously become increasingly automatized and coordinated, and become subordinated to more integrated and purposeful uses which permit satisfaction from more sustained activities. Even the early stages of language mastery lead to a major inner reorientation. The parent and child can increasingly give directions to one another, and children are learning to direct themselves, in part, by talking to themselves. They gain a modicum of self-control, some orientation toward a proximate future rather than simply toward gratification of present needs and wishes, and can use fantasy as a means of gratification and amusement. Increasing periods of delay can be interposed between the stimulus and the response, and simple alternatives can be taken into account. Alertness to reward and punishment, even if they are only a matter of parental approval or disapproval, tempers behavior. The child becomes much more of a participant in social interaction. However, tolerance remains limited and frustrations can produce sudden outbursts of temper and aggression, which can pass as quickly as a cloud on a windy day unless the parent prolongs the storm.

By now children have gained control over their bowels, and accidents are rare; but although urination is controlled by day, they may still wet at night, or need to be picked up to urinate without actually waking. When preoccupied with play, they may occasionally wet themselves, much to their shame; and the parent or nursery teacher is alert to the little boy holding his penis or the girl wriggling though perhaps unaware of her discomfort. The boy is likely to enjoy urinating and now stands up and imagines that he is shooting a machine gun—"ack-ack-ack"—or hosing out a fire, gaining a feeling of masculine power. If the girl has watched boys she may now also wish to stand up to urinate and expresses feelings of deprivation, even though she is generally content with being a girl like mommy.

It is difficult to provide a brief and coherent description of what the child of three and four is like, not only because rates of maturation and development vary, and children are by now so distinctively different in their ways of relating, but also because boys and girls can no longer be encompassed by the same description. Although currently the differences between boys and girls have probably decreased and may diminish markedly in families in which parents make conscious efforts to relate similarly to a boy or girl, usually their ways are becoming increasingly different. The separation of the sexes may be more apparent in neighborhood play than in nursery school. When playing "family," the four-year-old boy becomes reluctant to fill a maternal role, even though the mother may be the more important and powerful parent. It is the boy who tends to exclude the girls as part of his way of overcoming his dependency on females, a trend that becomes more marked during the next developmental phase. The girl spends more time in the house and in her mother's company, and when she is with her friends, more time talking than doing. The types of activities in which the two sexes engage are already diverging.

Children by the age of three and, even more, when four become more in the way of companions to parents, but their efforts to participate in parents' activities can sometimes create greater difficulties for parents than the earlier needs to contain and control them. The homemaker, who has usually been the mother, has someone to converse with during the day, though perhaps primarily as a listener to the increasingly lengthy monologues in which the child talks of imagined activities and tells what he or she is going to do for mother when he or she grows up. At three and four years of age both the boy and the girl will participate with the mother as she works around the house. There is considerable movement toward behaving grown up in real activities as well as in play, both through imitation of the behavior of elders. However, as children do not yet have the knowledge or skills, they will engage in "symbolic play," in which they assimilate the activity to their own ideas about it and their capacities to engage in it. Still "symbolic play," which greatly helps children cope with their ineptitudes and feelings of inadequacy, develops slowly. Children of three may simply build blocks into something they can demolish, but at four they will laboriously make constructions that need not resemble very closely what they intend them to be. As they work at their play, children carry on monologues, even when no one is present. They are, in essence, thinking aloud and telling themselves what to do: "a block—one there—one there—a boat—boat—make a boat—Mommy will go in boat—another block," and so on. This *synpractic* speech will gradually be internalized, but will still be vocalized occasionally even after the child starts school (Vygotsky, 1962). At three, the child's imagination can transform almost anything into the object needed for play. A block becomes a boat in the bathtub, a train on the carpet, a hammer when the child is imaginatively constructing something. Having achieved sufficient motor control, the child is usually not as occupied with body mastery and exploration as with carrying out play that provides the satisfaction of achievement. A child will enjoy finger painting for the outlet it affords for smearing, but also for the pleasure of creation, though perhaps still free from the need to make a picture of something. A four-year-old girl responded to her parent's question of what she was painting: "How should I know? I haven't finished it yet!" but the younger child need not have anything other than the colored lines when finished. However, even the most abstract creations usually represent something to the child who will gladly explain just what it is. Children are likely to admire their productions, praising themselves and seeking the praise of an adult. Modesty is not yet part of their vocabulary or behavior, and self-aggrandizement seems to come naturally.

Play with Peers

Children's worlds are expanding even when they do not go to nursery school. They can care for themselves sufficiently to play with others in their yard, or in the park under supervision. A few props help the four-year-olds with their imaginative play; a purse turns a child into a mommy at the supermarket, a six-shooter into a cowboy; a space helmet into an astronaut. They have entered that wonderful period when fantasy need not yield too much to reality, and dilemmas can be solved simply by altering the way they imagine the world. They enjoy swings and jungle gyms, where they demonstrate their prowess with pride. Children begin to play with others; at first it is parallel play, in which they are pleased by the presence of others, but they do not play at the same thing; but it gradually shifts into imaginative role taking. Naturally, playing "house" and "family" predominate, for these are roles and activities the child knows best; such play often innocently reveals family characteristics that parents prefer not to recognize. Television has, of course, increased the range of activities that even very young children can initiate and elaborate upon. At this age, the child may suddenly shift from being a space pilot to become a snake wiggling along the floor; or, when fatigue mounts, may even turn into a baby sucking an imaginary bottle.

If we listen to children conversing when they are sitting together idly, or when they are engaged in some sedentary activity, we find that although the talk has the form of conversation it is very likely to be a dual or *collective monologue*. One child says something to the other and waits for a reply, then what the other child says has no connection with what the first child said, and so they continue, both voicing their own preoccupations or fantasies in turn. Many children at four virtually crave the company of other children, at least of another child. The little boy may awaken in the morning filled with energy and with plans of what he will do with his friend, impatient to be finished with breakfast and off on his adventures. Girls and boys usually enjoy the nursery school world of agemates in which adults remain in the background when possible. Some must be satisfied with imaginary companions, or prefer them as they are more amenable to direction and are less aggressive and competitive. An imaginary comrade may be quite fleeting, imaginary even to the imagining child, or may have the force of reality that must be taken into account in planning the day's activities. A mother may sometimes feel desperate when she must not only set the table for two but even serve food for two rather than one. One such child enjoyed playing catch with older boys but, unable to catch as yet, became very fond of Joe, invisible to others, with whom he could play flawlessly with an equally invisible ball. Transitional objects, dolls, or fuzzy toy animals are favored companions and may virtually be endowed with life, even as Christopher Robin shared his adventures with Pooh Bear (Milne, 1961); and the child cannot go to bed and face the dark and lonely night without them.

Even those fathers who have shown little interest in babies are now likely to find enjoyment in the child. He is an object of admiration; the son perhaps more than the daughter now wants to do things with him, and boasts of his father to other children. The girl, even before three, learns alluring ways of endearing herself to her father, who finds it easier to be tender and affectionate with a daughter than with a son. Whereas children commonly invoke authority with "My mommy says—"they seek status and prestige with "My daddy can—"; in both cases summoning up instrumental attributes. The father will, reciprocally, usually enjoy spending time with the child who provides such gratifications. The patterns of father-child interaction vary greatly from culture to culture, but in ours there has been an increasing tendency for the father to become an important figure to the child at an early age; and, as we shall examine, play a significant role in guiding the gender typing of the child by what behaviors of the boy or girl he cherishes or disapproves.*

Children are by now clearly members of families rather than simply the mother's child, and they often have difficulty finding their places in it. They are envious of older siblings and jealous of younger ones, and may resent the father's prerogatives with the mother or vice versa, as we shall examine later in the chapter. Nevertheless, in relationship to outsiders children have

---

* Such comments differ from commonly expressed ideas that many contemporary problems of child rearing derive from the father spending little time at home. Whereas it seems clear that some occupations and some men's ambitious strivings keep fathers out of the home a great deal, fathers in general seem to share responsibilities for their children and participate in play with them more than earlier in the century. The import of the weakening of paternal authority to the problems of contemporary society as expressed by H. Mitscherlich in Society Without the Father is a different issue.

a sense of belonging to their families. Each child has two names: a first name identifies the child within the family and a last name that identifies the child with the family. A four-year-old refused to return to nursery school on the day after his three-year-old brother first attended: it turned out that it was not a matter of rivalry or jealousy, but of his intense shame because *his* brother had made a puddle on the nursery school floor.

Anxieties

The period is not without blight. Indeed, it is a time when fears may mount to phobic proportions; when efforts to contain anxieties over desertion by parents can paralyze thought and activity; when fears of evil lurking in the bedroom corner propel the child into the parents' bed. Greater independence brings insecurity in its wake. Increased knowledge leads to awareness of more numerous dangers. Expanding fantasy conjures up menacing as well as benevolent persons and events. Concerns over death may begin; these are extensions of separation anxiety: the child's death and the mother's are almost equally anxiety provoking to the child, who does not and cannot understand what death really means. The television introduces murder and mayhem into the quiet of the playroom as well as incomprehensible scenes of passion that frighten as well as stir puzzling feelings in the child.

Jealousy of a new baby and wishes to be rid of the intruder may lead to fears of kidnappers who could, after all, kidnap the child as well as the baby. Concerns over retribution from the father, who the boy may ambivalently wish were dead, bring wolves or lions into the bedroom at night as the child projects similar wishes onto the father. The various intrafamilial "oedipal" and sibling rivalries bring masked fears of retribution that appear in dreams. Dreams and reality are not readily separable. A three-and-a-half-year-old girl who was afraid to sleep because of nightmares was assured that the tigers were not real but just pictures in her head. A few days later she started to cry when a fire engine with siren screaming stopped outside of the house, but she immediately reassured herself, saying, "Sissy [her younger sister] is having a bad dream about a fire engine." Many children now seek the comfort of the parents' bed in the middle of the night in order to feel safe; they feel secure from all harm as long as the omnipotent parents are tangibly close. Such concerns usually heighten as the child approaches five and the oedipal feelings become more intense, and we shall later note how the development of means of handling the anxiety will be a major force in directing personality development.

COGNITIVE DEVELOPMENT

We followed children's early acquisition of language until the age of two and a half or three, by which time they had acquired sizable vocabularies and had mastered the essentials of syntax. It is important to the understanding of preschool children to recognize the limitations of their intellectual capacities and their comprehension of their surroundings. As we followed children's emergence from the period of sensori-motor intelligence to the age of about three, their limitations were apparent; but after they become able to speak fairly fluently and begin to lead active lives, with a fair degree of self-direction and control, their capacities are readily overestimated. Indeed, as we read Piaget's many studies and experiments we are apt to be surprised again and again at the limitations on children's ways of thinking and conceptualizing reality well into the school years.

Reality and Fantasy

When children acquire language, they gradually become freed from the tangible sensori-motor schemata and the concrete present. They can internalize visual signs, recall them, rearrange them, and recombine them imaginatively with the aid of verbal symbols or words.* They become able to fragment the past in order to select appropriate memories and project a future toward which they can direct themselves. Ultimately such attributes will permit intelligent reflective behavior. However, the internalization of the environment symbolically also permits the development of imagination and fantasy, which need not be referred back to reality. For a time, at least, this capacity to manipulate symbols imaginatively will interfere with problem-solving behavior. It is patently simpler to solve problems in fan-

---

* Piaget considers that the child can learn to use language only after becoming capable of forming discrete stable motoric and visual symbols that can be recalled and "imitated." Words or verbal signs can then be attached to these symbols. These aspects of his theory are far from satisfactory, for nouns are necessary for the process of dividing experience into units, as noted in Chapter 1. However, I wish only to call attention to such problems; they need not be discussed or argued here. Piaget discriminates between *symbols*, which always remain bound to the tangible experience and are therefore personal, and verbal *signs*, which are socially learned and capable of communication, and eventually (but not in early childhood) become freed from the more concrete and specific symbols. However, in keeping with more common usage, in this text "symbols" will also be used to mean words, except when we are specifically discussing Piaget's concepts.

tasy than in reality. Children whose oral and anal drives have been frustrated, and who cannot gain the solace and personal attention they would wish, and who find that they cannot compete with elders, or control others, can gain or regain in fancy what they cannot in reality. Indeed, as we learn from patients in analysis, the three- and four-year-old is very likely to regress in fantasy to recapture oral and anal gratifications, particularly when going to sleep or in conjunction with masturbatory play. Such fantasies are usually deeply repressed and can be recovered only with difficulty. However, fantasy also serves other ongoing and more reality-oriented needs.

After all, it is difficult for young children to know what is reality and what is imagination. A little girl's experience is very limited and she hears about things that she can grasp but vaguely. She can go exploring for the North Pole at the end of her street—that is a very distant place where she has seen a pole, a telephone pole, in the snow. Let us consider the tales of a four-year-old whose father has been overseas in World War II for over three years. His mother has a great investment in this unknown figure whom he knows only by hearsay, and she constantly attracts attention by telling friends and relatives—and even the boy—about his father's experiences in the war. After a time, the child also has his "boys," his sons, overseas who are in and out of battles, in and out of hospitals, and who lose legs and regain them from day to day. These "boys" (all soldiers were "boys") were just as real to him as a father he had never known and who existed only in his mother's talk. Another four-year-old heard a great deal from his grandmother about how things were done in her native land. Soon he has his own Cocaigne, his Utopia, where he goes almost any night and which has the appropriate name of "Milkins." There, things are done properly, his way: the family has one very large bed in which they sleep together; he has his own automobile which he can drive, and when his mom is nice to him she can come to Milkins with him, sleep in the big bed, and he will give her a new car. Is "Milkins" any less real to him than Europe, or even New York, which he has never seen?

Children are not at all certain that they cannot change the world to suit their needs, or even to change themselves. Little boys can fully expect to become mommies when they grow up; and many little girls have believed they would turn into a boy, like the three-and-a-half-year-old Piaget reported who said, "I think the mountain [the mons] hanging here grows and turns into a little long thing with a hole in the end for water to come out, like boys have" (Piaget, 1962, p. 173), or like another girl who decided that she would go back inside of her father and when she came out she would be a boy. Naturally, mothers give birth to girls and fathers to boys. After all, her mother can grow a large tummy and even a new baby. It will take years before the facts are sorted out, and before the child learns that although fantasy can give pleasure and dampen the pain of frustrations, it does not change reality, or at the most can be but a prelude to acting upon reality.

Limitations of the Child's Comprehension

Words are the carriers of categories and contain a predictive value (as has been discussed in Chapter 1), but when the child first learns names for things they are almost only empty shells into which the members of the category or class will be fitted as the child gains experience. They are like labels on empty filing folders. The categorizing function of words is not a matter that can be pushed and rushed very much: mere instruction in word meanings and in the relationships between words divorced from experience or from a need to solve problems serves little. Meanings keep developing throughout life, and it is not until children are at least six or seven that they have learned enough to abstract from the tangible image and to form the superordinate and subordinate categorizations that are necessary for logical thinking—and even then it is still at a rather concrete and limited level. The little girl of four or five may well know that dogs, cats, and cows are animals, but is her stuffed bear an animal? Do animals think and talk? After all, in the stories that are read to the child, animals understand. Mickey and Minnie Mouse talk on television. Christopher Robin goes walking with Pooh, who does not say very much but is very understanding. In some respects, just as the mother modified sentences for the younger child's comprehension, parents and people who write stories for children fit the stories to the child's conception of the world. The successful writer for children properly grasps how the child thinks and views the world. The process tends to be circular. Children do relatively little thinking for themselves about the nature of the world. They rely upon the authority of their elders. If parents talk about what animals think, why then animals must think. However, as we shall see, there are other reasons why the child endows animals with language and thought and the inanimate world with feelings. Adults who read or tell imaginative tales that depart from reality are not perverting the child's notions of truth and falsehood, or of reality and fantasy. Usually, they are stimulating fantasy that can serve the child well. Children's manipulations of a fantasy world and its people in play and daydreams in accord with their own needs constitute a prelude to coping with the reality that cannot be so readily manipulated. It is an important stage in the process of mastery through the manipulation of symbols. A reality orientation will come to the child in time through the sorting out of his or her own tangible experiences of what works and what leads to further frustration, and in terms of how useful communications are in establishing a workable interaction with others.

Another difficulty arises because preschool children lack organized frames of reference into which they can fit what they learn. They have only their own limited experiences and the authority of their elders as to what constitutes reality and truth. They do not yet have the various systems developed by the culture, its measures of time and space, its ways of categorizing, its ethical code, and its value systems into which to fit and organize their experiences, and which provide them with bases for comparison and standards of evaluation. They do not know what their society considers worthy of attention and what can, or should, be ignored.* Persons cannot pay attention to all of the stimuli that encroach upon them, and each culture varies in what it finds significant but children are first learning such differentiations.†

Egocentricity

The preschool child's orientation, as Piaget repeatedly points out, is markedly *egocentric*. Piaget's use of the term has often been misunderstood, sometimes being confused with narcissism, another notable trait of early childhood.** Children can see things only from their own limited points of view and narrow perspectives. They do not realize or appreciate properly that other persons see things differently. For a time, they cannot even grasp that a person seated in another part of the room does not have the same view of things as they have. If asked what the other person sees, they are very likely to describe what they see themselves. Even seven- or eight-year-olds have notable difficulties in explaining something to another

---

* An interesting approach to the subject of how a culture establishes taboos in order to differentiate between things categorized as separate entities, and the functions of language in the process, is found in E. Leach, "Anthropological Aspects of Language: Animal Categories and Verbal Abuse."

† Stating the matter more in Piaget's terms, the child has not built up schemata to which many of his experiences, particularly those imparted to him verbally, can be properly assimilated, and the processes of accommodation and assimilation are temporarily out of balance.

** Because of such confusion, Piaget has, of late, used the expression "centering on the self" instead of "egocentric" (Piaget and Inhelder, 1969, p. 61, note), but "egocentrism" is too firmly established in Piaget's writings to eliminate now.

child, or in repeating a story so that another can understand it. They cannot grasp properly what needs to be explained, and may omit things they visualize in thinking of the story. Thinking is also egocentric in that a child believes that other persons, and also animals and inanimate objects, are motivated or activated in the same way as the self and one's own parents are. For example, the clouds move because they want to hide the sun; the water in a stream flows because oars push it; didn't the train (that was missed) know we weren't in it? (Piaget, 1962, pp. 245–291). Egocentrism, as we have noted, also concerns the overestimation of cognitive, subjective solutions over the objective.

Preoperational Intelligence

Children from about two and a half to six or seven are in Piaget's *preoperational* period of intellectual development. It constitutes a prolonged transition from the sensori-motor period to the period of concrete operational intelligence in which conceptual thinking begins, and retains marked residues of sensori-motor behavior, with language and thought remaining tied to concrete and specific visual images. The linguistic symbols refer to specific examples of the categories they designate rather than the abstract categories. Piaget has carefully analyzed the nature of preoperational intelligence.* The transition to the stage of *concrete operations* with the ability to deal with categories develops gradually and school-aged children are often thinking preoperationally—to some extent even up to the start of adolescence.†

---

* The period is sometimes subdivided into two stages at about the age of four to five; the first stage is that of *preconceptual* thought, and the second that of *intuitive* thought.
   The preconcept is characterized by incomplete assimilation since it is centered on a typical sample of a set rather than including all the elements of a set (which requires a further abstraction from concrete reality and visual symbols) and also by incomplete accommodation which is limited to evocation of the image of the individual example. The child cannot yet grasp transformations but only a series of static states, and these are irreversible—that is, the child cannot hold the original state in memory so as to refer back to it and follow the transformation (J. Piaget, *Play, Dreams, and Imitation in Childhood*, p. 284). Reasoning is *transductive*, neither inductive nor deductive but proceeding only from the particular to the particular (A = B; B = C; therefore A = C) and not generalizing from classes or developing class generalizations—that is, categories (*ibid.*, p. 234). *Intuitive thought* shows evidence of less "centration" on the image, a diminution of egocentric confusion between what is subjective and what objective, and movement toward concrete operations. The reader is referred to Chapter 10 of Piaget's *Play, Dreams, and Imitation in Childhood*.
   † Studies of the concept formation of adults by means of the Object Sorting Test show that the concept formation of many persons with less than a high school education remains very limited (Wild *et al.*, 1965).

Let us consider some of the preschool child's ways of thinking. We have already noticed the *animism*. Piaget's daughter J., when three years old, remarked that the clouds moved to hide the sun; and when she was five and a half that "the moon was hiding in the clouds, it's cold" (Piaget, 1962, p. 251). She not only bestows upon the moon the power to hide but also a motive. The child may be reluctant to pick a flower and hurt it. Aspects of nature are explained by *artificialism*. "Mountains are little stones that have grown bigger" (p. 248), or at three, "I think the sky is a man who goes up in a balloon and makes the clouds and everything" (p. 248). Names are an inherent part of an object and not something bestowed by people. At four Piaget's daughter L. was certain that the name of a mountain was "Soleve" and not "Saleve," insisting she could tell by looking at it (p. 256); and when over five and a half his daughter J. asked, "How did they find out the name of [the mountain] the Dent Blanche?" (pp. 255–256). Dreams are puzzling. The child believes that they have a tangible existence in the room, outside of the self; and may be uncertain whether or not someone else in the room might be able to see the dream, and is puzzled how it can be seen with eyes closed. Causality is also considered in animistic terms. An eight-year-old girl studied by Piaget still believed that she could make the clouds move by walking, that everybody could; and when asked if the clouds also moved at night, said that the animals walking about at night made them move. At an earlier age, the child may become involved in circular reasoning such as that the wind makes the trees move, and the moving trees make the wind that moves the clouds. As we might anticipate, rules of games are, like their names, something inherent in the game, or perhaps rules that God or the parents once made. Children of four or five may be able to understand and try to adhere to the rules, but are very likely to change them to suit their needs. Thus a four-year-old boy invented his own game and insisted that his brother and father play it with him, but they could not follow his rules until they grasped the one fundamental rule: that the four-year-old must always win.

It is apparent that preschool reasoning is very loose. Before the age of seven children's use of "because" is rare, and when it occurs in response to "why" it usually precedes an animistic or artificialistic explanation. Children are likely to join ideas together by using " 'n then" as a conjunction, relying upon sequence as a cause. Actually, it is difficult to analyze children's reasoning at this age because of its global, syncretic nature which is related to the absence of adequate categories or classes. When pushed a child can usually find some reason to connect things together.

In describing the preschool child's abilities we have noted the various characteristics of preoperational thought. It is egocentric as a result of the child's limited experience, absence of reference systems, and difficulties in differentiating the subjective from the objective. Fantasy and reality are intermingled, and reality gives way to fantasy in face of the child's needs. As word meanings are limited they do not supply the categories required for logical thinking. Thought is still tied to internalized visual signs, and the child is apt to *center* on a single aspect of the object and neglect other attributes and so distort reasoning, and also to center on a typical example of a category rather than a true abstraction. Thinking tends to be static because children cannot take into account the transformations from one state to another. It suffers from being irreversible because they cannot maintain an original premise while reasoning; and, similarly, there is difficulty in remembering the image with which they started and need for comparison with the end result.* Piaget stresses in many different ways the imbalance between assimilation and accommodation during this period of life.†

Piaget's analyses of children's intellectual processes and ways of experiencing during the preoperational stage are highly intriguing.** However, for our present purposes it may suffice to understand something of children's capacities and limitations and how they understand the world about them. Many of their limitations would seem to be understandable in terms of inexperience, which means that they will be egocentric; in terms of the fact that even though they have words it will take time and experience before words really designate categories; and that they have not yet gained the culture's ways of reasoning and systematizing. How much depends upon the immaturity of the nervous system, and how much upon the slow process of organizing the "mind," are not yet known.

There is some danger that emphasis on the limitations of young children's mental processes and egocentric views of the world can lead to gross

---

* See Chapter 9 for further discussion of these concepts.

† Piaget notes that in contrast to the sensori-motor period the child not only assimilates current experiences but must also try to handle internalized imagistic symbols and assimilate to these schemata as well as current ones. I believe this does not differ greatly from saying that the child must deal with material recalled from memory as well as with ongoing experiences. It is also essential to bear in mind that children do not yet have the schemata to which they can properly assimilate what they simply hear about. Piaget considers the imbalance between assimilation and accommodation to account for the child's pervasive use of *imitation*, in which there is a primacy of accommodation over assimilation; and of *symbolic play*, in which there is primacy of assimilation over accommodation. The reader must again be referred to Chapter 10 of *Play, Dreams, and Imitation in Childhood*, pp. 273–291.

** Studies of preoperational intelligence may serve to clarify many aspects of the thinking of schizophrenic patients. See Lidz, 1975, Chapter 2.

underevaluations of children's potentialities. Children's abilities vary with intelligence level and the social and intellectual milieu in which they are raised. After all, John Stuart Mill, as well as other child prodigies, could manage the syntax of Greek and Latin by the age of four to five. Far less remarkable children can manifest a strange admixture of primitive and complex thinking. The four-year-old who seemed to believe in the reality of his fantasy country "Milkins" could at the same time readily distinguish various makes of cars, including the models from different years under the proper brand names, and also categorize them according to the body style, irrespective of brand names. This constitutes a rather high level of category formation, and was related to a dominant interest as well as to the presence of an adult companion who went to considerable effort to help him learn the differentiations.

With experience and education children move beyond preoperational thought. With increasing socialization and under the subtle pressure to conform in order to gain acceptance, as well as to find relief from anxieties, children begin to repress unacceptable wishes and the fantasies and thoughts that accompany them. Much of the material will become unconscious and interfere less directly with reality-directed and reflective thinking. The nature of the unconscious processes and how they continue to influence behavior will be considered in the next chapter.*

The Development of Trust in Verbal Communication

Children of three or four are starting to assemble their major resources for conducting their lives through their abilities to use language. Their reality testing will depend upon the slow sorting out of experiences and the learning of what works and what does not that started during infancy; but this will, in turn, also depend upon the consistency and reliability of the behavior of their tutors, primarily the members of their families. Verbal communication assumes increasing importance as children emerge from

---

* The movement beyond preoperational thinking does not depend upon maturation alone. In various primitive societies persons depend upon animistic and artificialistic explanations of causality throughout life and tend to depend upon various types of magical thinking in dealing with matters beyond their own control such as fertility, weather, and the strength of enemies, in order to attain some control over the contingencies of life. One need not venture among primitive peoples to find adults who manifest similar phenomena. Palmists, astrologers, and faith healers abound in localities where the law does not forbid them. Magic potions, amulets, and love charms are readily available in most large cities. Physicians who take care of persons from the lower socioeconomic sectors and from various minority ethnic groups are likely to become aware that some of their patients are not placing all of their eggs in one basket and are relying upon various types of white magic as well as upon the physician.

their families. Family members had, through long experience, been able to understand and even anticipate many of their needs without the children's verbalizing them. Still, the child's trust in language—and what can be conveyed verbally and what responses words will elicit—develops in the home setting. Here the child learns how effective words will be: whether they concur with the unspoken communications; whether they are apt to match the feelings that accompany them; whether they subserve problem solving or are just as often a means of masking the existence of problems. The child's trust in verbal communication depends upon whether the words of the persons who are essential to the child help solve problems or confuse, whether they provide more consistent signals than nonverbal cues, and whether the child's use of words can evoke desired responses. Difficulty can arise when parents' words contradict their nonverbal signals, as, for example, when the mother's words of affection are accompanied by irritable and hostile handling of the child; or when the mother's instructions for the child to obey grandmother are accompanied by her obvious delight when the child disobeys and becomes a nuisance to the grandmother. The value of words is also diluted or negated when erroneous solutions are habitually imposed, as when a child who cries from fear is fed because all crying is interpreted as a sign of hunger. Predictive values of communication are undermined when promises rarely materialize. A disturbed young woman told how very early in life she had ceased to trust what her mother said, and virtually stopped listening to her incessant talk, for she had learned that her mother's tales of the wonderful things they would do together never materialized. It took her many years to learn that her mother was simply sharing the fantasies that sustained her.*

Interference with children's efforts to explore their surroundings and solve problems by themselves can also impede the development of language. Children who have been treated as passive objects for whom almost

---

* Persistent denial of the correctness of children's perceptions and understanding of what transpires about them can have a particularly malignant influence in promoting distrust of language and fostering distortions of meanings. The child is repeatedly placed in a "bind" because the obvious is negated, and the child is threatened with loss of approval or love if things are not seen the way in which a parent needs to have them seen. A mother keeps telling a little boy that he must love his father as she does, that father is very good to them; but father comes home drunk every other night, beats his wife, and usually gives his son a whack or two. Perhaps, less malignantly but more commonly, children are punished if they do not tell the truth, but cannot avoid hearing their mothers falsify why they cannot attend a church meeting or their fathers boast of how they concealed the truth in selling the old family car. Children may also learn that what people say is more important than what they do; and that what one does is less important than not being caught—common situations in families with delinquent children.

everything must be done have little need to speak. Discouragement of verbal play also hinders. Children need to try out words and expressions in a multitude of contexts and learn from the responses elicited. They often repeat what a parent says and does, imaginatively exchanging roles with the parent. "You tired, Mommy; sit here, Johnny reads you book." Through filling the reciprocal role in play, children expand their comprehension and use of words as well as developing through such identifications. Parents who cannot participate in such play, and who insist upon firm adherence to reality, discourage such exploratory problem solving. Sometimes, parents consider the child's "make-believe" to be lying, reprimand the child severely, and cut off all expressions of fantasy. The parents of an adolescent delinquent related that they were not surprised that he was in serious trouble, for he had been a difficult child from the start, already given to lying at the age of three—he had told them about playing with another boy when no one had been about, and of how he had helped mow the lawn when he could not yet push the lawnmower. They felt that they had been forced to make strenuous efforts to change his ways, but their punishments could not alter his inherent nature.

As Basil Bernstein (1974) has found, children in many lower-class families gain little linguistic experience in their homes, where there are few conversations and children are simply given abrupt orders, and much interaction is at the nonverbal, concrete level needed to carry out the fundamentals of life.

Here, discouragement and disparagement of a child's questions limit the verbal explorations essential for learning. Children's incessant questions can become a test of parental patience and provoke: "Why can't you shut up for a while?" "What difference does it make what it is called?" "It doesn't mean anything at all!" Sometimes punishment for what is simply the conveying of needs can lead to a vicious cycle of creating greater needs, more pressing attempts to communicate, and eventually to despair. A little girl of four who imparted her wish to be rid of her baby brother was told that she was wicked and severely admonished never to hurt the baby. Fearful of rejection, she called for her mother at night, only to be threatened that she would be sent off to a school for bad girls if she didn't let her mother sleep. The child stopped calling her mother at night because of her fears, but instead developed a severe pain in her head. The severe headaches then led to her hospitalization, which caused the girl to suffer acute separation anxiety. Parents can impede and distort the development of linguistic abilities in a great variety of ways. The examples presented should suffice to indicate how the child can fail to develop trust in the usefulness of language for communicating and as an instrument for solving problems.*

GENDER IDENTITY

Whether a child is a boy or girl has always been one of the most important determinants of personality characteristics. How much of the child's tendency to assume gender-linked personality traits is innate and how much is environmental are difficult to determine,† but in all societies children are consciously, and perhaps even more unconsciously, prepared for the functions they will carry out as adults. As most women in our contemporary society spend far fewer years rearing children than formerly, with a larger proportion of them engaged in careers outside the home, and as men come to share more of the child rearing and household tasks, boys and girls need to be prepared for less differentiated roles and functions than in the past. However, at least because of their different procreative functions, if not also because of different developmental problems as well as deeply rooted needs and traditions, some definite differences between males and females are unlikely to disappear. Freud could write with complete assurance some forty years ago, "Male and female is the first differentiation that you make when you meet another human being, and you are used to making that distinction with absolute certainty" (Freud, 1933). Now we can only say it is a distinction that you used to make with certainty. Nevertheless, the difference remains of the essence in human relationships, and the children's gender will, at least for some time to come, continue to determine much of the future pattern of their lives.

The influence of the child's gender on personality development has been so pervasive that until recently it has simply been taken for granted, and

---

* Disturbances in the child's language development are increasingly being related to impoverished self-control in childhood and to the development of serious psychopathology such as schizophrenia and delinquency in later life (Bateson *et al.*, 1956; Lidz, Cornelison, *et al.*, 1965; Singer and Wynne, 1965a, 1965b; Wynne and Singer, 1963a, 1963b).

† The various observations and experiments concerned with the psychological differences between the sexes have been assembled and reviewed in *The Psychology of Sex Differences*, by Eleanor Maccoby and Carol Jacklin. Judith Bardwick has examined the theories and evidence concerning how and why women's personalities differ from men's, perhaps with some bias toward the importance of biological factors, in *The Psychology of Women*. As we can here consider only the more salient and clear-cut influences, the reader must be referred to these sources for a more thorough evaluation and discussion.

little attention has been paid to the complex and subtle matter of the dynamics of the personality differentiation of the two sexes. Theories have often been rooted in culturally accepted beliefs rather than upon scientific evidence. Although many questions remain, the topic requires considera- tion before we turn to the oedipal transition proper, for the nature of the oedipal strivings and the way in which they are resolved depend upon the child's gender and the firmness of his or her gender identity. Further, the proper resolution of the child's oedipal problems solidifies the child's gender identity, and when the oedipal transition becomes confused, it can augment conflicts or even create new problems concerning gender identity.

Biological Factors

The child's sex is genetically determined, but, as we shall examine, biological factors only influence but do not determine the gender identity.

Let us now review very briefly some of the salient aspects of gender determination and what it may have to do with gender identity in humans. Whether the child is male or female depends upon the presence of an X or a Y chromosome in the fertilizing sperm that joins with the X chromosome in the ovum. The presence of the Y chromosome usually assures that at a critical phase in fetal development the testes secrete androgen which influ- ences the anlage of the genito-urinary tract to develop male internal organs and later to develop male external genitalia. It must be understood that neither gonads nor sex hormones are necessary for the development of infantile female external genitalia. It has now become fairly certain that in mammals, including monkeys, the male hormone also acts upon the un- differentiated brain to organize certain circuits in male rather than female patterns (Diamond, 1965; Young et al., 1964). The androgen acts upon the fetal brain to direct young males after birth to show more active and aggressive play and a tendency to sexual mounting behavior; and the ab- sence of such an androgen leads to female trends of interest in babies and greater interest in grooming behavior. The duration of such influences in primates is unknown, but they last for at least two years and start the baby in the proper gender role. Indeed, in Jane Goodall's (1963, 1965) studies of chimpanzees in their natural habitat, a young immature female was observed to try repeatedly to take a baby away from her mother to care for it herself: such behavior was not observed and would not be anticipated in young males.

Recent studies have shown that when androgens are given to pregnant monkeys, the female offspring of such pregnancies tend to show the male rather than the female behavior patterns in childhood. Such experiments cannot, of course, be conducted in humans. However, occasionally female fetuses are exposed to high levels of male hormone because of a defect in the production of adrenal hormones, resulting in oversecretion of genitally masculinizing hormones. Fifteen preadolescent girls suffering from this adrenogenital syndrome showed more interest in boys' toys and less in doll play and less satisfaction in being girls than did a control group, even though the excess secretion of male hormone was stopped medically in infancy (Ehrhardt, Epstein, and Money, 1968).* Another group of girls who had been exposed to progestins prior to birth, given to prevent their mothers from aborting, were between three and fourteen years old when studied. Progestins, even though female hormones, have a masculinizing effect. Nine were designated as "tomboys" by their parents or themselves, and showed a marked interest in boys' toys and team sports (Ehrhardt and Money, 1967). Such studies suggest that prenatal exposure to androgen has a masculinizing influence in humans as well as in other mammals. It may be possible that some pregnant women who are subjected to severe stress secrete sufficient androgen from the adrenal cortex to produce a masculinizing influence upon a female fetus. It seems unlikely that androgen secretion in the mother would induce *patterned* male behavior in human infants, but it might well influence the readiness of males and females to learn behaviors appropriate to their genders.† There are also indications that chromosomal abnormalities may influence gender-linked behavior in a very general way. Thus, men with Klinefelter's syndrome, an anomaly due to the presence of two X chromosomes and one Y chromosome, are not only sterile and weakly motivated sexually, but may tend toward confusions in gender identity. In contrast, men with two X and two Y chromosomes tend toward outbursts of aggressive behavior as well as being very tall, eunuchoid, and mentally retarded (Garcia *et al.*, 1967).

Gender Allocation

The studies by Hampson, Hampson, and Money of seventy-six pseudo-hermaphrodites and hermaphrodites of almost every known type require

---

* The critical nature of the study was, however, diluted, as seven of the fifteen girls had been thought to be boys at birth; and even though the erroneous gender allocation was corrected before seven months in age, the parents' knowledge of the genital masculinization may have influenced "their expectations and reactions" regarding their children's behavioral development.

† See D. Hamburg and D. Lunde, "Sex Hormones in the Development of Sex Differences in Human Behavior," for an excellent review of the literature on this topic. See also R. Green, *Sexual Identity Conflict in Children and Adults.*

thoughtful assessment in any theory of gender role determination.* In these
individuals various combinations of discrepancies existed between the assumed gender in which the person had been raised and the external genitalia, the internal organs, the chromosomes, and the hormonal secretions
after puberty. In only four of the seventy-six subjects was there any notable
inconsistency between the sex in which the person had been raised and the
gender role established despite the obvious developmental difficulties created for many of them by the uncertainties about their actual gender and
by various physical abnormalities. Thus, chromosomal males with gonadal
agenesis had almost always been thought to be girls, at least till puberty,
and they were clearly feminine in behavioral characteristics. In some diagnostic categories some children had been raised as boys and others as girls.
It is also significant that in twenty-five of the series there was a marked
contradiction between the appearance of the external genitalia and the
assigned sex, and yet all but a few had come to terms with the anomalous
situation and established a gender role consistent with the assigned sex and
rearing. The topic is extremely complex but the results of the study seem
sufficiently definitive to warrant the conclusion that the gender assigned
and in which the child is reared can outweigh chromosomal and hormonal
influences and the appearance of the genitals in determining gender identity. However, the investigators have now modified their earlier conclusions
that the human is born psychosexually neutral: that is, with gender-linked
sexual behavior developing only in accord with the way in which the child
is reared. The evidence now indicates that because of prenatal genetic and
hormonal influences, humans are predisposed at birth to a male or a female
gender orientation, but that such influences only predispose to a pattern
that can be modified greatly by subsequent life experiences.†

* The cases studied include females with virilizing adrenal cortical hyperplasia, simu-
lant females with testes, chromosomal males with gonadal agenesis and female physical
morphology, cryptorchid males reared as females, and others. There were contradictions
between chromosomes and the gender in which the child was reared in nineteen cases;
between the gonads and the gender in which the child was reared in twenty; between
hormonal sex and the gender in which the child was reared in twenty-seven postpubertal
cases; between appearance of external genitalia and the gender in which the child was
reared in twenty-three; and between internal accessory organs and gender rearing in
eighteen (Hampson and Hampson, 1961; Money, 1965; Money et al., 1957).

† "Our findings indicate that neither a purely hereditary nor a purely environmental
doctrine of the origins of gender role and orientation is adequate. Gender role and
orientation is not determined in some automatic, innate, or instinctive fashion by
chromosomes, gonadal structures, or hormones. However, sex of assignment and rearing does not automatically and mechanically determine gender role as there is a small
group of patients whose sexual outlook diverged somewhat from that of the sex to
which they had been assigned. It appears that a person's gender role and orientation
become established as that person becomes acquainted with and deciphers a continuous multiplicity of signs that point in the direction of his being boy or girl. Those

While such investigations are important in helping sort out the factors determining sexual identity as well as sex-linked behavioral traits, confusions concerning a child's gender are rare, and with occasional exception the physical appearance, chromosomes, hormonal secretions, and the assigned gender are in harmony. By the age of two or two and a half the identity of the child as a boy or girl is already well ingrained in the child's awareness and behavior. Indeed, the Hampsons and Money, on the basis of their experience with children whose gender assignment had been changed, believe that such changes after the age of two and a half are very likely to create serious problems for the child (Money *et al.*, 1957).

Although the child knows its gender by the age of two, the matter is not as clear-cut as one might imagine. If we remember the way in which the child thinks and fantasies between the ages of three and five, it becomes apparent that many inconsistencies can exist in the children's concepts of themselves. They know what they are but not what they might become. Many boys of three or four will openly express their belief or wish that they will grow up to be a mommy. A little girl may fully believe that when she grows older she will develop a penis. Both boys and girls may fantasy as well as fear that they may change sex when they grow up. It is necessary to appreciate the boy's initial identification with his mother to understand the foundations for many sexual aberrations and related psychopathological conditions.

Parental attitudes are very likely to differ according to the child's sex from the time of birth and influence the child's emerging behavior in many subtle ways. It is difficult to tell whether the boy usually becomes more active in response to a pattern evoked *in utero* by androgen secretion or in response to the manner in which he is treated.* Many mothers relate more actively with a son than with a daughter (Cohen, 1966). The father may often play a more crucial role than the mother in fostering gender-linked attributes. Whereas the mother may fill her nurturant role with the young

---

signs range all the way from nouns and pronouns differentiating gender to modes of dress, haircut, and modes of behavior. The most emphatic sign is the appearance of genital organs" (Money, *et al.*, 1957).

* Although many differences in the behavior of male and female neonates and young children have been reported, most studies have not been replicated. Moss (1967) found that neonatal girls seem to sleep more, and as boy neonates and young infants are more fussy and active they obtain more handling and fondling than girl neonates. However, a replication study failed to find significant differences in the sleep-wake cycle in boys and girls (Moss and Robson, 1970). Little boys are found to be more aggressive—or at least more active—than girls. Girls seem to show greater verbal ability and boys better visual-spatial ability and perhaps mathematical ability (Maccoby and Jacklin, 1974), etc., but the activity or "aggressivity" seems the most clear-cut and consistent finding.

child in very much the same way whether it is a boy or girl, the father may have more active physical interaction with a little son and feel freer to display affection and softness with a daughter. J. Kleeman (1971) noted that by one year the girl's coyness, flirting, and kiss-seeking behavior with her father and not with her mother may be striking. Fathers in turn note that their two- to three-year-old daughters are flirtatious, coy, and cuddling and like it, whereas they may frankly state that they cannot stand feminine traits in a son (Goodenough, 1957).* Fathers want sons to be boyish and girls to be feminine more decisively than do many mothers.

The establishment of a firm gender identity in the child is clearly a complex matter, for it depends upon a multiplicity of factors. The sexual organs are, of course, a major influence in contributing to the child's basic orientation as a male or female. Erikson considers that in addition to providing a general directive to both child and parents a boy, in response to the presence of his penis and the feelings it engenders, tends to become intrusively active, whereas a girl, responding to her external and internal sexual organs, feels receptive and even ensnaring. He considers that the girl develops feelings and ideas of an inner space, a creative space that profoundly influences her way of relating and her feelings about herself (Erikson, 1959). The sexual hormones may have influenced the fetus *in utero* and will also affect behavior in the adolescent but do not impinge upon the young child. Despite the importance of various biological factors, the gender assigned the child by the parents and the ensuing interactional patterns within the family can, as we have seen, outweigh all other considerations. The child's identification with the parent of the same sex is clearly important in guiding the child's development as a male or female, but the child does not initially take on behavioral ways of an adult man or woman. Parental preferences, encouragements, and prohibitions of certain types of gender-linked behavior are also significant. However, once the children clearly identify themselves as boys or girls some time before the age of two and a half, a more general factor may come into operation. Kohlberg (1966) considers that once gender identity is established children deduce what male and female behavior is supposed to be, and more or less seek to adhere to the stereotypes they have formed. At first such ideas are simple, based on a limited set of features that a child can grasp, and thus are both stereotyped and oversimplified. However, the concepts are not static but

---

* Ten out of twenty fathers described their two- to three-year-old daughters in terms such as "a bit of a flirt"; "arch and playful with people"; "a pretended coyness"; "I notice her coyness and flirting, 'come up and see me sometimes approach'" (Goodenough, 1957).

change as children grow older and their cognitive abilities permit them to appreciate more complex aspects of maleness and femaleness. In this way identification with peers of the same sex becomes very important as the child passes the age of four or five, as we shall examine in Chapter 9.

Children's Reactions to Sex Differences

What makes children boys or girls may not be obvious to the child. Some do not have an opportunity to ascertain the physical differences till later in childhood, but ignorance of the difference is more often due to an inability to see or to remember what has been seen and is upsetting. Children may pay more attention to the clothing than to the genitalia. A five-year-old, when asked while he was looking at a nude baby if it were a boy or girl, replied, "I don't know—it's hard to tell with the clothes off." However, the discovery that boys have penises whereas girls do not may have a critical effect upon the lives of some children. The little boy who believes that all children are born with penises but those of girls had been removed fears the loss of his; and some girls may blame their mothers for not providing them with a penis, as we shall discuss when considering the oedipal transition. The girl's feeling that she has been deprived, or that she was born with a penis which has been removed, has been considered a trauma common to all women by some psychoanalysts, but others attribute the so-called penis envy to resentment over the second-class role in society to which being a woman—and, therefore, deprived of a penis—assigns her. Freud rather strangely believed that the psychoanalysis of women could not progress beyond recognition and acceptance of such feelings of deprivation. However, Bettelheim (1954) has observed and emphasized that children of both sexes are likely to envy both the physique and the prerogatives of the other sex. His observation led him to study the practice of subincision among Australian Aborigines, which he considers is a means of partly assuaging men's envy of women's natural creativity.* Sometimes a little girl can become very much concerned or preoccupied with the absence of the handy little tool that she observed on a boy. Some will rebel and try to change the situation either in reality or imaginatively. The girl

---

* R. and T. Lidz (1976) studied the practice of male menstruation in New Guinea and similarly related it to male envy of women's natural creativity and closeness to nature as well as of women's capacities for self-purification through menstruation that eliminates the dangers of contamination by contact, particularly sexual contact, with men. Ritual male menstruation also plays a major role in eliminating the female influence of the mothers who raise them for the first eight to twelve years with little influence from the fathers.

may insist on standing up to urinate; or the parents may merely note references to her fantasies. Thus, a four-and-a-half-year-old had been a happy child until the birth of her brother. She was not only jealous of the attention the infant received but properly attributed the parents' delight with the baby to his sex. She began to stand up to urinate and insisted on wearing blue jeans, refusing to wear dresses. Her mother sought to ease the situation by explaining the advantage the girl had in being able to have a baby. The explanation included some information about how babies are made and grow in the mother. The girl then developed a severe phobia of contamination and refused to eat many foods, fearing she might ingest a "seed" and have a baby grow in her "stomach."

Such crises are unlikely to occur—or, if they do, are readily surmounted—when the girl can appreciate that the mother has self-esteem as a woman, and also that the father has esteem and affection for his wife as a woman. Being a girl who will grow into a woman can have many advantages over being a boy, as well as vice versa. In some societies little, if any, unhappiness over being female arises, because girls are raised to accept completely the female way of life. New Guinean women who are kept in a very inferior position have been known to say, "Let the men have their rituals and sacred objects if it makes them happy; after all we have the important things in life: the babies, pigs, and gardens." In our contemporary society, girls are likely to be rebellious about the lot in life that awaits them. It is hoped that, as they become freer to choose their way of life—to pursue a career, to become a housewife and mother, or to combine the two—the advantages of being female will increase and dissatisfaction with women's fate become less common. The choice can, of course, make the lives of young women more difficult, as we shall consider in Chapters 10–13.* Obviously not all little girls accept being female. A period of boyish behavior that lasts until shortly before puberty is common, and may be accompanied by unexpressed daydreams of being a boy. The eventual solution of the problem may hang in balance until some time in adolescence; but a proper resolution of the oedipal situation usually consolidates the acceptance of a feminine identity. The identification with the mother, fortified by the father's pleasure in having a daughter, usually wins out, directing the girl into feminine ways and satisfactions.

The little boy, in contrast to the girl, must shift from his initial symbiosis with his mother to identify with his father and brothers, and model himself

* We must, however, differentiate between dissatisfaction with the opportunities open to women in a society and unhappiness at being a woman, even though the two sometimes become confused in women's liberation literature.

after other boys. Little boys, as we have already noted, often have strong desires to become "mommies." The mother is apt to be for the little child the secure, protecting, and bestowing adult. The wish to become a man may not be as natural as Freud assumed; and perhaps society must make the goal of masculinity seem tempting to the little boy. The shift is fostered by his mother's admiration of his father as well as the societal evaluation of the male role. It may be enhanced by the pride the boy takes in his penis, and perhaps by his mother's conscious or unconscious pleasure in his having a penis. Boys usually start gaining pleasure by playing with their penises at a very early age, and solace by grasping the penis when in pain or emotionally upset. The boy can become very upset when he discovers that there are persons who have no penis. He may conclude that girls have had their penises cut off, and fear for his own intactness and male identity. Concern that the penis can disappear may be augmented by the fluctuations in its size. The concern may be so anxiety-provoking that the boy seeks to deny the potentiality, refusing to perceive or remember having seen anyone without a penis. He may imagine that his mother has simply hidden hers, or that his baby sister has not yet grown one. Such ideas and concerns were brought home to a mother very vividly when her five-year-old son asked where she kept her penis. She reminded him that she had told him that boys and men have penises but girls and women do not, that they have other organs instead. The boy then said, "Yes, I remember now, that's where someone axed you one!"

Freud considered castration anxiety to be a universal and a critical aspect of all male development that plays a major role in the oedipal transition. However, in homes where matters concerning sex and genitals are taken more casually than in Victorian times, anxiety over castration may not occur at all, and when it does be less of a central issue. However, the existence of castration concerns is very apt to be minimized because of the tendency to repress the childhood fear after the problem has been resolved. Castration anxiety occurs or is augmented, according to psychoanalytic theory, because the penile erotic masturbatory sensations stimulate erotic fantasies which in the little child are rather naturally connected to the mother and the bodily care she provides. Masturbation tends to continue unless the child is severely admonished or threatened with dire consequences unless he stops. Threats that the penis would fall off, or that the father would cut it off, unless the masturbating stopped were once common, and still occur in some families. Even without such threats, the connection between masturbation and fantasies about the mother may eventually lead to severe conflicts and guilt feelings, with fears of retribution from the father, which force the boy to suppress his autoerotic play. However, it has also become evident from the analysis of patients in whom castration anxiety has become a severe and enduring problem that such concerns are likely to reflect the individual's wish to be rid of his penis. Although such wishes may seem unlikely, a boy may fantasy retaining his identification with his mother, or he may become envious of the preroga- tives of sisters and feel burdened by the demands placed upon him for achievement because he has a penis. Severe anxiety here, as elsewhere, is very often related to fear that an ambivalent wish might materialize.* Psychoanalysis had, until recently, failed to consider seriously not only that some women envy men but that many men wish they could be women. Transsexual operations are sought far more frequently by men than by women.

By the age of four, boys and girls are beginning to move into separate groups. Although boys may act contemptuously toward girls—which has been taken to indicate their assimilation of the cultural devaluation of females, or of scorn for the "castrated" sex—evidence indicates that it is part of boys' efforts to gain distance from and become independent of feminine influence because they must overcome their initial identification with a woman as well as their wishes to be taken care of by a woman.

Security of Gender Identity

A child's comfort and security as a member of his or her own sex depend very greatly upon parental attitudes. As parents neither treat a child completely in accord with his or her sex, nor themselves provide fully consistent models as males or females, nor consistently reward masculinity in a boy or femininity in a girl, no child grows up to be purely masculine or feminine, which designations are, after all, only relative. As every psychia- trist knows, some of the most aggressive masculine behavior often covers intense feminine strivings or homosexual tendencies; and among the most ensnaringly seductive women are some who are incapable of attaining any sexual gratification. The Greeks in their mythology of the heroic and un- conquerable Heracles included an episode in which he exchanged roles

---

* A young man with severe castration anxiety, who could have his hair cut only by a woman barber and his teeth repaired by a female dentist because of unconscious derivatives of such fears, also had mild transvestite tendencies. He was markedly envious of his older sister, not because she enjoyed a favored place with their mother, but rather because his mother had such inordinate expectations that he live out the life she would have wished for had she been a male, and also that he recoup for her the position in select society that her father had lost for her family by being an alcoholic and a wastrel.

with Queen Omphale and lived with her as a woman. Parents who have had their hearts set upon having a child of a given sex may be unable to absorb their disappointment when the newborn turns out contrary to their hopes. Girls are more likely to feel unwanted, and according to tradition less often be of the sex that the parents wanted. In an effort to make up to her father for having disappointed him (as if it were her doing and not his) the girl may strive to become a boyish companion for her father.* Some mothers are unable to relate properly to a daughter, and may more or less consciously encourage the development of masculine traits. A husband may treat his wife so contemptuously that their daughter sees little advantage in a feminine role. Boys can also disappoint their parents and feel that they should have been girls. The male role may be dangerous in a home where an aggressive and dominant wife constantly belittles and cuts off her husband. An occasional mother may have her heart so set on having a daughter to provide companionship, or to whom she can give all the things that she lacked in childhood, that she feminizes the boy. A marine who suffered a combat neurosis after displaying exceptional heroism confided that he had joined the service to bolster his inadequate feelings of masculinity: he had been dressed as a girl until he was five, and had never been able to believe that he was really a male.†

When the development goes well, the emerging gender-linked roles fuse with the biological directives. The society, just like the evolutionary process, has a vital interest in seeing that children of both sexes assimilate whatever gender-linked roles are appropriate to the society and needed by it. As only girls can give birth to children and are likely to be the primary nurturant figure for the small child, it seems vital to foster at least some differences between the sexes. In the past at least, and to a great extent still today, the girl who is to become a mother, and who will have a vital interest in preserving the integrity of her family, is already becoming more interested in people and how they relate to one another. She is not as physically active as the boy. She is spending more time playing house and caring for her dolls. She is quieter and more passive, waiting upon the action of others, but she is also very likely to know how to make herself attractive to her father. The boy, who is to become a husband upon whom a wife and children can be dependent, is beginning to deny his dependency upon his mother and manifest feelings of superiority to girls. He is already

---

* A classic example of an extreme outcome can be found in Radclyffe Hall's novel *The Well of Loneliness*.

† There is now strong evidence that most male transsexuals were kept in very close physical proximity to their mothers, sleeping cuddled together, and their identification with the mother fostered by her without opposition from the father (Stoller, 1968).

moving out into the neighborhood and into a male competitive world. The trends start early; they need to be deeply rooted.

Since the gender identity and its accompanying roles are so dependent upon the ways in which parents relate to the child, interact with one another, and regard themselves, it becomes apparent that all sorts of variations in gender identity and in the security and stability of the gender identity can develop. Because the pattern of a person's relationships will be carried out in accord with his or her sex, the gender identity will have far-reaching repercussions, but here we must be concerned primarily with how it influences and is influenced by the oedipal transition.

KNOWLEDGE AND FANTASIES OF CONCEPTION AND CHILDBIRTH

Sooner or later, often in conjunction with the birth of a younger sibling, the child puzzles about the origin of babies. Stories about storks are likely to stretch the credulity of even a young child, particularly in a country where there are no storks. Simple explanations that the child grows within the mother and comes out through a special opening may satisfy for a time. Detailed explanations are beyond the child's comprehension and do not decrease misapprehensions. Children usually develop or expand theories on their own. The mystery of the origin of babies is one of the primal mysteries of childhood.

The young child is likely to believe that the seed is placed in the mother's mouth, or that it comes from eating a seeded food. The baby before birth may be envisioned as sitting in the mother's stomach with open mouth, ingesting the food she eats. How the baby gets out of the mother is an even greater puzzle. Obviously, the child is likely to believe that it emerges from the anus; but the navel, which appears to serve no other good purpose, is often selected. As mothers go to hospitals, the doctor may remove the baby by an operation. There are many potential sources of anxiety to the child, particularly to the little girl who cannot conceive of how she could produce a baby without incurring disastrous consequences to her body. However, in this regard as in many others, the child's attitude reflects the parents'; and if not given reasons to feel discomfort or concern, children usually accept their parents' explanation and ask when they wish to know more. The child's reasoning may be difficult to follow, as in the case of the four-year-old boy who, after puzzling over an explanation of how the baby grows in the mother, asked, "Now, before the baby is born, is the baby in the mother or the mother in the baby?"

SIBLING RELATIONSHIPS

Although it is simpler to consider the development of a single child growing up in relation to parents, it is unrealistic as the interactions between siblings are among the major formative influences. If a child does not already have siblings, a brother or sister is likely to appear before the child completes the oedipal phase. Sibling relationships are not only almost as important as the oedipal triangle of parents and child in directing and crystallizing a child's early development, but the oedipal transition is usually greatly influenced by the presence of other children. Even though a discussion of siblings will complicate an already complicated subject, it will permit a more rounded and realistic presentation.

Sibling rivalry has probably received far more attention than the advantages of sibling relationships. The hostility of brothers receives attention in the opening pages of the Old Testament in which Cain's fratricide—a crime relating homicidal impulses to fraternal jealousy—is considered second immediately after the original sin of Adam and Eve. The rivalry between brothers for a father's blessing led Jacob to drive a hard bargain with the starving Esau and cheat him, albeit with their mother's help. Jacob, in turn, was deprived of his favorite son when his ten oldest sons united to rid themselves of the precocious Joseph.

The arrival of a new baby can naturally provoke intense jealousy; a child's entire life is changed by it. The infant usually has priority for the mother's attention. Still, the child is often expected to take delight in the new arrival and share the parents' enthusiasm. A child who had been awaiting a baby brother with happy anticipation may now feel deceived: the little brother can't join in play, doesn't talk, and is little more than a nuisance. Children are not joking when they ask whether the parents can't give the baby back, or comment that a new puppy would have been preferable. A three-and-a-half-year-old girl with a one-year-old brother, when told that still another baby was expected, was disappointed to learn that her parents would not simply be, as with the family car, trading in her brother for a new and more preferable model. Despite parents' attempts to prepare their children and make them feel that the baby is theirs as well as the parents', this is a time of tribulation during which most children can be expected to show regressive behavior. A child may insist on returning to the bottle, or start soiling again. Being a baby and unable to care for oneself clearly has advantages. Tics or a stammer may appear, symptoms that reflect efforts to control aggression toward the baby.

Parents often sigh with relief after the baby is several months old and the older child has accepted the situation without obvious difficulties. However, problems are even more likely to occur when the infant emerges from the crib or playpen and gets into the older child's possessions. The mother must now divide her attention between two active children. The older child's aggressivity toward the baby or toddler may provoke the first real conflict with the parents, who must protect the younger child and cannot practice their customary tolerance. Children learn to conform in order to maintain the parents' approval but may do so by *reaction formation*. They repress hostility and become overgood or overdemonstrative toward the baby. The defense does not always work, and, a child may develop a disturbing slyness, appearing affectionate toward the baby when the parents are about but pinching, hitting, poking, or otherwise provoking the baby when no one is about.

Envy of Older Siblings

Whereas older children are given to jealousy of younger children, younger children are usually envious of children older who have many prerogatives and gain attention through their accomplishments. Their envy may spur children to activities beyond their capacities and lead to various frustrations. When the young child can somehow identify with the older and take pride in the older's abilities, things can go well; but if the child feels defeated and constantly left out, he or she may stop trying to emulate the older sibling and simply feel resentful. Here again, the older children are very likely to follow the parental example of being helpful to younger siblings if they do not feel deprived or constantly reprimanded because of the younger.

The rivalrous conflicts that are almost bound to occur, particularly among closely spaced siblings, create turmoil; and the noise of the friction, like a squeaking wheel, gains attention from the parents who seek means of lubrication to restore quiet and calm. The regressions of the older child, the turn from carefree happiness to sullen discontent, the hyperactive strivings to regain the center of the stage, cannot but disturb the parents. Their efforts to mediate and provide justice are not always compatible with a child's emotional needs. Punishment for attention-seeking tactics can read-ily leave the child feeling misunderstood and lead to new infractions.

Affection and Identification Between Siblings

The positive feelings between siblings and the great need and affection they often develop for one another can be overlooked because their fights attract more attention. Ambivalence is characteristic of good as well as poor relationships between young siblings. Most quarrels, even those that look as if they would end in fratricide, are quickly forgotten by the chil-dren, who make up wordlessly and resume their companionship while the parents are still pondering how they will manage the situation.

While difficulties in finding conflict-free space within the family and desires for affection provoke rivalries, the similarities in how they are raised and in their backgrounds can make siblings very much alike and quite understanding of one another, and they are apt to be closer to one another than to any other person. The siblings' similar ways of regarding situations, and similar superego developments, may enable them to under-stand what the other thinks and feels without any verbal exchange. Indeed, a sibling's values may be as important as the parents' in the formation of a child's superego directives. The need for a sibling's esteem and affection can take precedence over strivings for parental love. A child may cede priority with a parent rather than see a beloved sibling unhappy or endan-ger their relationship. One child may conceal or fail to develop some ability rather than move into an area in which the other has gained recognition. Siblings may divide roles between them as they find ways of sharing the living space to avoid conflict. The division of a single place within the family becomes most noticeable with identical twins who encounter the special developmental problem of differentiating from one another as well as from the mother (Kent, 1949; Koch, 1966; Lidz, Cornelison et al., 1958). Here, the sharing of ways of doing things and the reliance upon one another for support often create serious difficulties for the twins in learning to lead separate lives.

Ordinal Position and Development

The significance of the ordinal position of the child to various abilities, traits, and mental health has been studied in a variety of ways. Statistical studies have limited value to the understanding of the individual because of the variations in circumstances and parental attitudes from family to fam-ily. Apparently first-born children enjoy some advantages as far as achievement of intellectual superiority and eminence is concerned (Altrus, 1966). Oldest children clearly gain a different perspective from that of younger children, particularly in large families where they assume some responsibility for the siblings. The advantages may derive from the greater opportunity for contact with adults that they have while still small, and from their being the sole recipient of the parents' attention for a time. Whereas the first-born will often maintain a certain priority in the mother's affections, a youngest child may also have a special position in remaining her "baby" no matter how grown. Younger children benefit from the parents' experience with the older and from having an older sibling to provide an example. The middle child, particularly when all children are of one sex, is apt to be caught between the jealousies of the older and the envy of the younger who may form a coalition against the middle child.

When the parents are particularly eager to have a son, the appearance of a second daughter can create poorly concealed disappointments. A second daughter may respond by tending to become boyish in order to compensate the parents; though the third daughter does not usually follow suit. Still, the long-awaited arrival of a son after several daughters (as one father commented, "After three zeros, finally a digit!") does not always place the boy in an enviable position. The older sisters become jealous of the parents' delight in the presence of a son and heir, and may be particularly envious of his prized penis. Two sisters managed to make their four-year-old brother very self-conscious and ashamed of his penis. The boy may grow up under the aegis of three or four mothering figures, not all of whom are completely benevolent, and in a family that is more attuned to feminine than masculine patterns of behavior. He may be pampered but at the same time be expected to have the manliness to become his father's successor and the carrier of the family name. Some such boys become very envious of the girl's role, with its freedom from great expectations and acceptability of continuing dependency, and develop strong castration wishes. The position in the family does not of itself establish definite patterns. One may also see a youth with three or four older sisters whose masculinity and independence has been properly fostered and with a suitable father figure to emulate who feels very comfortable in his favored position.

Sibling Relationships and the Oedipal Transition

The sibling relationships, or more usually the parental attitudes toward the siblings, can decisively influence children's oedipal relationships as well as the firmness of their gender identities. A girl born into a family in which

the parents had become emotionally estranged prior to her birth was confronted by a difficult situation. Her mother deeply resented her birth, which
she felt held her in a marriage that she had decided to dissolve just before
she found herself pregnant. The mother, feeling neglected by her husband,
had become very much caught up in her relationship with her three-year-
old son, and could find no room for a daughter. The mother's own lack of
self-esteem as a woman contributed to her disinterest in a daughter. The
father moved into the gap, seeking to provide the mothering the girl
needed. The family soon divided into two hostile camps. The mother, not
caring for the father or the daughter, did not furnish a model with whom
the girl could identify nor did she impose any obstacles to the father and
daughter developing an intense relationship. The father, also feeling deprived, used the girl as a replacement for the mother and formed a close
and seductive relationship with her. The way was prepared for the continuation of an incestuously toned relationship into the girl's adolescence.

A girl who feels displaced by a series of younger siblings may become
fixated upon a need to regain the mother's love and never properly develop
oedipal strivings toward her father. She may prematurely decide that if her
mother has no room for her because of the needs of the younger children,
she will become her mother's helper, share the mother's tasks and woes,
and thereby gain her mother's approval and affection. She then tends to
become a little mother who never has a proper childhood. Some such
children continue to spend their lives seeking eventually to be appreciated
and loved by the mother, even remaining at home unmarried, waiting until
all the others have left.

The few illustrations that have been presented are intended only as
random examples of the diverse influences that sibling relationships can
exert on the oedipal situation. Common patterns may exist, but not many
have been clearly defined. Indeed, the whole question of the influence of
sibling relationships upon a child's development beyond the relatively simple problems of sibling rivalry and twin relationships has received insufficient attention.

Siblings present so many difficulties that a child may well wish he or she
were an only child, believing that life could unfold far more smoothly
without the competition. Yet, only children are often lonely and feel deprived of brothers and sisters. They do not have the opportunity to learn to
cope with jealousy and envy of rivals within the home; or to compromise
with siblings and share adult attention; or to erect and strengthen defenses
against feeling displaced. These may sound like very doubtful benefits, on
the order of hitting oneself over the head so as to feel good when the pain

stops, but they are important in the long run. The opportunity to share intimately in childhood, to know how someone close feels in various situations, to become familiar with the ways of the opposite sex, to assume responsibility for a brother or sister, to have a sibling show pride and happiness over what one accomplishes, are among the many benefits of having siblings. Basic experiences are properly gained within the shelter of the family.

THE OEDIPAL TRANSITION

We have been following the little child's gradual differentiation from the early symbiotic union with the mother; the assumption of a gender identity; the decrease in egocentricity with the expansion of cognitive capacities and experience; and the process of individuation as the child gains inner structure and increasing capacities for self-control and self-direction. The nebulous boundaries between child and mother have become more definite. The father has become, sooner or later according to the family style, an increasingly important nurturant figure. The initial symbiosis with the mother has broken up into two components: an identification in which the child seeks to be like the mother and take on her attributes, and an object relationship in which the child seeks to maintain a tender or erotized relationship with the mother. All of these developments have to do with the oedipal transition, a process that is not as clear-cut and circumscribed as originally conceptualized by Freud.

Many vagaries exist in the concept of the oedipal complex that may perplex the thoughtful student, who should be aware that many aspects of the oedipal process await clarification.

The term *oedipal attachment* usually refers to the child's erotized attachment to the parent of the opposite sex; and to the resolution of the oedipal complex—to the repression or resolution of the erotic components prior to the age of five or six—because of fear of retribution from the parent of the same sex as the child. As we shall see, such concepts are only tenable in part, and only under certain circumstances. In a more general sense, the oedipal transition has to do with the child's rescinding the erotized attachment to the mother and the feelings of being the mother's primary source of affection and interest, and finding and accepting a place as a boy or girl member of a family unit.

As we have seen, the little child's attachment to the mother contains strong erotic components. The little child had required erotically toned nurturant care from the mother, which stimulated sensuous oral, anal, and tactile feelings that generalized to color the child's feelings toward the mother. Genital sensations, perhaps more in the boy than the girl, became connected to fantasies about the mother, stimulating feelings of possessiveness and love. Young children consider themselves the center of their mothers' interest and affection, just as their mothers are central to their lives. We have noted the egocentricity of children's thinking, and nowhere are little children more clearly egocentric than in their view of their relationships with their mothers. The child seeks to avoid coming to grips with the changes in the relationship to the mother that the various developments in the child's life have fostered, but inevitably reality closes in and forces the child to terms. The child's renunciation of a priority with the mother and repression of the erotic components of the attachment to her—the resolution of the child's oedipal attachment—seem to be the pivot about which many changes in behavior, thought, and personality organization consolidate.

Just how the oedipal conflicts are resolved will exert a major influence upon the pattern of all future interpersonal relationships and the structuring of the personality. How it is resolved depends upon prior experiences, the particular makeup of the individual, the family members, and the configuration of the family. For better or for worse, decisive changes will take place by the time the child enters school and the next developmental phase.

The Classic Psychoanalytic Concept

Because Freud's discovery and exposition of the oedipal conflict and its resolution form a landmark in the history of man's struggle to gain an understanding of himself, and because the oedipal conflict is incorporated in psychoanalytic as well as many other theories of development, the classic psychoanalytic conceptualization will be presented, even though some aspects of the theory clearly require reformulation (Freud, 1916–1917). We shall then consider a broader approach to understanding the oedipal transition.

On the basis of his own self-analysis, the psychoanalysis of patients, and from his contemplation of Sophocles' *Oedipus Rex* and Shakespeare's *Hamlet*, Freud became convinced that the little child develops an intense sexualized love for the parent of the opposite sex; that the love arouses jealousy, guilt, and anxiety which lead the child to repress the feelings into the unconscious; and that in so doing the child comes to identify with the parent of the same sex, and gains a superego in the process. Freud understood the conflict and its resolution primarily in terms of the vicissitudes of the child's libido in accord with his concept that sexual or "libidinal" conflicts were at the root of all neuroses. After the anal phase of development passes, the child's libido becomes invested in the genitals—in the penis in the boy and the clitoris in the girl. The shift of libido to the genitals causes or accompanies an upsurge of sexual feelings in the child, often with a marked increase in masturbation. The sexual feelings of the boy attach themselves to the mother, and those of the girl to the father. Freud offered various explanations of the shift of the girl's attachment from the mother to the father.* The child seeks erotic gratification from the parent who is the love object, and fantasies possessing this parent in marriage. The other parent is resented as an intruder, someone unnecessary and superfluous in the child's scheme of things. Those children who have witnessed parental intercourse, or who have developed fantasies based on noises they have heard, wish to replace a parent in the act. The child now wants to be rid of the rival parent, wishes that parent would die, and may fantasy killing the parent. The child's hostile and aggressive impulses are then *projected* onto the parent; that is, the child believes the parent rather than the self is hostile. If the boy can wish to be rid of his father, the father can want to be rid of him. The child becomes anxious, and at night, when defenses are low and darkness and quiet foster fantasy, dreams and nightmares bring terror. The little boy who experiences the connection between his erotic fantasies and the sensations in his genitals may fear that his father will settle the matter by cutting off his penis. This "castration anxiety," Freud believed at times, was at the bottom of almost all anxiety, including anxiety over death. Unable to stand the anxiety he is experiencing, the little boy renounces his erotized wishes to possess his mother. Instead, he decides to grow up to become a person like his father who can gain the love of his mother. He now identifies with his father, seeks to take on his traits, and is impelled into a firmer masculine identity. The father's restrictions and prohibitions, whether real or imagined, are internalized and serve to bolster the ego's capacities to repress and to maintain the repression of the incestuous strivings. Freud considered that the superego is formed at the time of the resolution of the oedipal conflict by utilization of the "libidinal energy" that had been invested in the mother. With the li-

---

* See S. Freud, "Some Psychological Consequences of the Anatomical Distinction Between the Sexes" and "Female Sexuality."

bidinal energy utilized largely in the service of repressing erotic impulses, the child enters the latency period—a time relatively free from sexual strivings, preoccupations, and activities.

Freud was never quite satisfied with his understanding of the girl's oedipal situation and its resolution. He believed that the girl turns from seeking the mother as a love object because of inherent instinctual reasons; or because she becomes hostile to the mother, who she feels deprived her of a penis; or because she feels that the mother, who is also without a penis, is not a worthy object of her love. He finally emphasized that the girl's recognition of the anatomical differences between the sexes led her to desire a baby to compensate for the lack of a penis, and "with this purpose in view she takes her father as a love object. Her mother becomes the object to her jealousy" (Freud, 1925).* As the girl already feels castrated, she cannot suffer castration anxiety that forces her to renounce her desire to possess the father. However, she comes to fear the mother's jealousy, or her projections of her own jealousy onto the mother, and fears the mother will kill or abandon her. She then accepts her identification with her mother and strives to become a woman who can gain a man like her father. However, Freud recognized that the girl does not usually repress her desires for the father as completely as the boy represses his erotic feelings for his mother (Freud, 1933).

The question of the universality of the oedipus complex and, particularly, whether the boy's erotic attachment to his mother and the girl's to her father are inherent components of the human endowment became sources of considerable controversy. Understood in the terms just presented, it would be difficult to defend the omnipresence of the oedipal situation. We must recall that Freud was not only living in a strongly patriarchal society in which it was inconceivable that any boy might want to be a girl unless something were inherently wrong in his makeup, in which the father was or seemed to be the controlling, directing parent, in which virtually all upper-middle class children were cared for by nursemaids or governesses rather than their mothers, and in which there was little, if any, notion that both parents could share the nurturance of the child. Further, without evidence to the contrary, Freud could readily believe that there was an upsurge of sexual drive around the age of four or five because of the children's conscious and unconscious desires to possess their mothers.

---

* Freud thus regarded the oedipus complex as a secondary phenomenon in the female, and gave the impression that it played a less important role in female development (Freud, 1925; 1931).

There is, however, no evidence that the oedipal child experiences an upsurge of libido in the sense of an increased sexual drive such as occurs at puberty. The confusion of sensuous feelings with a sexual drive has created unnecessary theoretical complications. The child, particularly the boy, has shown genital masturbatory activity even earlier and, as we have previously noted, there are reasons why the child now tends to erotize if not sexualize his feelings toward his mother. Biochemical assays of the hormones as well as observation discount the hypothesis of an increased sexual drive (Tanner, 1961).* Oedipal children may be preoccupied with erotic and sensuous ideas and feelings but they are not being subjected to the same type of biological sexual impulsion that occurs in adolescence. However, despite the various reservations we have noted, and still others, the oedipal resolution can be understood as a way the child makes the transition from the initial and essential attachment to the mothering person to finding a place as a boy or girl member of the family.

A Reconceptualization of the Oedipal Transition

Children must overcome the intense bonds to their mothers that were essential to their satisfactory preoedipal development. There are several reasons why children rescind their erotized attachments to their mothers, which may or may not include the fear of the father. First, the mother gradually frustrates the child's attachment to her as part of the diminishing care she provides as the child becomes increasingly able to do things for the self (Parsons, 1964). She knowingly or unknowingly places greater distance between herself and the child. The process is often aided by the birth of a younger child who preempts much of her attention. Second, children suffer a serious narcissistic blow as their egocentric views of the world diminish. They learn that the parents do not consider a child's relationships to the mother in the same way they do. The mother's affectional attachments are divided between the child and her husband, and usually she gives love to other children as well. Children have difficulty realizing that love is not a quantity that is diminished by such division; the child wishes to feel central to the mother's life. The boy has wished to marry his mother, and may have confided his wish and hope to her. "When I grow up, I'm going to marry you," he tells his mother and it has seemed to

* Gonadotrophic hormones are not detectable in children of this age, and only appear in detectable quantities a few years before the onset of puberty. Between the ages of three and five, seventeen ketosteroids which are considered to reflect secretions of androgen cannot be found in the blood. Estrogen secretion as measured by bio-assay is also negligible (Hamburg and Lunde, 1966).

please her. Now, he realizes that she has not taken his wish seriously. She loves his father and the father has prerogatives that the child does not have. Although the child may be permitted in her bed, it is clearly a temporary matter whereas Father can stay. Mother will not wait for him to grow up to marry her. Indeed, she cannot, and will be as old as Grandma when he is old enough to marry. Children also begin to learn what marriage involves, and that parents have responsibilities as well as privileges, and children become concerned over their capacities to handle responsibilities in reality. Now, when children have become aware of their separateness from their parents and their own very real limitations, they experience their vulnerability. Nightmares may reflect anxieties over the vulnerability that accompanies the new-found independence as well as fears of a parent. These concerns are part of the sorting out of reality and fantasy that occurs during this period, and perhaps are a pivotal aspect of coming to terms with reality.

The blow to the child's self-esteem and sense of security may be severe. Wertham (1941) believes that the child's resentment toward the mother because of her rejection can reach matricidal proportions.* However, when children recognize that their mothers have other interests, most children develop defenses against the ensuing blow to their narcissism. The initial attempts take place while the child's understanding of the situation is very limited. As we have noted, the boy decides that he will marry his mother to retain her to take care of him and love him. The girl may turn to her father as a basic "love object" who will look after her. Whether these wishes are expressions of a child's "infantile sexuality," as Freud believed, or rather natural security operations remains debatable. Such fantasies properly fade as children recognize their parents' priority with one another, the generational differences and other such reality factors, which may be augmented by the dynamic that Freud emphasized: the child's fears of the jealousy of the father. At this juncture, the child develops a defensive pattern† to alleviate and prevent a recurrence of the insecurity and loss of self-esteem that would again evoke untenable feelings of anxiety, the empty and lonely feelings of loss, or the hostile resentment of depression.

One common defensive pattern in boys is that described by Freud. The boy fears his father's vengeance because he projects his own hostile feelings

---

* Wertham has designated the boy's enduring hostility toward his mother because of her withdrawal from him the "Orestes complex" after Agamemnon's son who killed his mother, Clytemnestra, to avenge his father's murder by his mother and her paramour, Aegisthus.

† For further consideration of defensive life patterns in contrast to mechanisms of defense see Chapters 19 and 20.

onto his father, and, fearing death or castration at the father's hands, gives up his desires for the mother, and so forth. However, the fear of the father is not simply projection. Often enough a father—and perhaps to some degree all fathers—feels displaced by the baby in his relationship with his wife. The intensity and duration of the boy's feelings will depend not so much upon the child's needs as upon the father's needs to be the center of his wife's attention, the mother's abilities to divide her interests and affection, the parents' capacities to feel secure in their relationship, and other such matters. When the father is jealous of his child, a son—or even a daughter—may have reason to fear the father, and a jealous father who seeks to keep his wife from the child and interferes with the mother-child relationship can, in turn, augment the child's wishes to be rid of his father and thus increase his guilt. However, when the father desires the child, gains pleasure from having a child, appreciates what his wife does for the child, and through participating in the child's care is a source of pleasure and security to the child, patricidal impulses are likely to be short-lived, if they arise at all. Instead, the boy learns that his mother loves him differently from the way he loves her, and perhaps that his father does not seriously consider the child to be a rival. Indeed, he appreciates that having a father has advantages.

If, then, the relationship between his parents is good, and his father's relationship to him is affectionate, the boy goes through a more felicitous oedipal transition than the classic version. He realizes that he must grow up before he can marry and he will wait for fulfillment in a relationship with a woman. He identifies with his father, seeking to become a man who can gain a love object like his mother, as could his father. He gains not only strength from the identification but also a model to follow into manhood. He regains or maintains his self-esteem by his identification with a person his mother admires. In contrast, when the boy represses his desires for his mother from fear of castration by his father and then identifies with his father, the boy identifies with a punitive and frightening figure and internalizes aggressive and sadistic characteristics. However, when a son identifies with a father who he feels is benevolent, he can feel that his achievements are extensions of those of his father rather than rivalrous efforts to supplant him, and he is not as likely to be inhibited in his strivings lest he surpass his father.

Although rivalrous, hostile feelings of a son for his father are more likely to predominate in settings in which the father is authoritarian and a distant, feared figure to the young child, as in Freud's Vienna, than they are in middle-class families in the United States, in which authority is shared by the parents and fathers are likely to be close to their children; fathers who are resentful of sons are common enough in the United States and probably in all societies.

With either pattern, the identification with the father may be said to strengthen the child's "ego" and also, through internalization of parental directives, the "superego." "Id" impulses are being confined and repressed, and no longer are permitted as much direct expression. With better self-control, improved reality testing, and less need for gratification from his mother, the boy is ready to move into peer groups where he must begin to make his way on his own.

Obviously, there are still other ways in which a boy can seek to defend against the anxieties and depressive feelings of losing his primacy with his mother. When the mother rejects the son, the boy's resentment, as we have noted, can be directed primarily toward the mother, and lead to lasting misogynistic tendencies. If the mother is contemptuous of the father or despises him, a son is not likely to seek to gain the love of a person like his mother by identifying with his father. If the boy feels engulfed and over-whelmed by a possessive mother, and has a weak father who does not intervene, he may never establish boundaries between himself and his mother or feel adequately masculine.* The ways in which the child resolves or fails to resolve the oedipal situation are many, and are not fixed in a single pattern. The differences do not depend primarily upon innate characteristics of the child, as Freud believed, or simply upon how the mother or the father relates to the child, but also upon how the parents relate to one another.

The Girl's Oedipal Transition

Although many of the considerations concerning how the parents' ways of relating to their child and to each other apply to the girl as well as the boy, the girl's oedipal transition, as Freud realized rather late in his life, cannot be conceptualized as a mirror image of the boy's. She, too, must

---

* The "oedipal transition" in some societies may be so different from the patterns described here that it seems erroneous to call it such. Thus, in Papua/New Guinean villages in which boys are raised primarily by their mothers, the movement away from the mother is accomplished through elaborate rituals in which the boys—as previously noted—are subjected to ritual bleeding or menstruation to rid them of their mother's blood, and in some places are symbolically reborn as males from male ancestor spirits, and identify with the collectivity of males more than with the father; and separation from their mothers is reinforced by stringent warnings that continued contact with women will interfere with maturation and may even kill them, etc. (Lidz and Lidz, 1976).

overcome her primary attachment to her mother in order to become a discrete individual. However, in contrast to the boy, she has the advantage of not needing to give up her identification with her mother, and often has in the mother a model with whom she is far more familiar than the boy is with his father. The continuation of the identification with the mother may account for the girl's greater stability and calm during the early school years. Freud, however, emphasized the girl's greater developmental difficulties because she must shift her choice of a basic love object from the mother to the father, which has led to difficulties in understanding feminine development. Whereas anger with her mother for not having created her a boy, or disappointment in the mother because she, too, is without a penis, may, at times, be significant in turning the girl's love from the mother to the father, but there are other important directives. As the girl emerges from her symbiotic existence with her mother and differentiates from her, she finds another love object within the family in the father, and is directed to him by his tendency to be close and affectionate with a daughter. She can be free of the primary bond with her mother and still have a love object within the family. As Freud eventually recognized, a girl first forms her "oedipal" attachment to her father at the time the boy is resolving his erotized attachment to his mother (Freud, 1916–1917) and she usually does not repress or rescind the attachment to her father until she approaches puberty. Although a girl may fear reprisal from her mother, either because of projected hostility or because the mother resents her daughter's closeness to her husband, experience shows that a girl is likely to retain fantasies of becoming her father's sexual choice over her mother at a rather conscious level. Fathers commonly gain considerable gratification from their daughters' adulation of them, and are likely to show overt affection for their daughters, which encourages the girls' fantasies. Unlike the child's initial attachment to the mother, the father-daughter bond is not primary and need not be frustrated so early in order to foster the girl's separation-individuation process. At about the time of puberty, however, she becomes frightened by the pressure of her desires and represses the erotic aspects of her attachment; or, as frequently happens, the father must place distance between himself and his nubile daughter. Many women feel and believe that they became unattractive to their fathers when they reached puberty because it was then that their fathers moved away from them. Indeed, it seems as if divorce occurs particularly often when a daughter is reaching puberty, and the daughter's sexual attractiveness to her father may be a factor in leading him to have an extramarital affair.

Thus, the girl's oedipal transition is very likely to occur in two stages:

the first occurs during the oedipal period proper, when she differentiates from the mother and shifts to make her father her "object choice"; and then, the prepubertal or early pubertal period, when anxiety forces her to repress her feelings for her father.*

The girl's ability to retain the father as a love object keeps her major emotional investment within the home longer than the boy's, and appears to serve to prepare her for her greater emotional involvement in the home in adult life. It may also help account for the tendency for girls often to select husbands who clearly resemble their fathers.

Family Integration and the Resolution of the Oedipal Conflict

The fate of the oedipal situation, then, depends upon a variety of factors, including some that are consequences of the child's maturation, some that depend upon the nature of the interaction between the child and one or both parents, and some upon the relationship between the parents. The dynamic structure of the family plays a major part in organizing the child's personality by guiding the way in which the oedipal conflicts are resolved. A properly structured family with a firm coalition between parents who maintain boundaries between the two generations and adhere to their respective gender-linked roles, however they are defined, enables the child to grow into a relatively conflict-free place within the family. The reader is referred back to Chapter 2 for a discussion of the importance of the family's structure to the personality development of its offspring. Here we are concerned only with the oedipal transition.

The desexualization of the parent-child relationship before puberty is one of the cardinal tasks of the family. It does not depend upon a subsidence of sexual drive as hypothesized in classic psychoanalytic theory, nor does it depend only upon the child's fear of retaliation from a parent, but primarily upon the child's coming to terms with the reality of the prerogatives of the parents and of the basic bond between them. A firm coalition between the parents does not permit the child's fantasies of separating the parents and gaining one for himself or herself to continue on a realistic basis. A parent who turns to a child for gratification of emotional or sexual needs instead of to the spouse or even extramaritally, moves the child across the generation boundaries. When there is a schism between the

---

* In his later writings on the subject Freud considered the girl's attachment to her mother to be preoedipal and part of the girl's early masculine character asociated with phallic (clitoral) sexuality. As the concept no longer seems satisfactory, the reader is referred to his writings (Freud, 1925, 1931) for further discussion.

parents, the child can move into the breach and seek to replace one parent in satisfying the needs of the other. In either case, as commonly happens, it becomes difficult to repress the oedipal erotic fantasies. When the parents are united as spouses and parents, and complement each other's roles and functioning, the child does not have an opportunity to fill an empty place in the wrong generation, but grows into the proper position as a childhood member of his or her sex. The child properly enters the "latency period" after establishing a position as a boy or girl in relation to the parents. When children can identify with the family as a unit and feel secure in their dependency upon it, they can venture into the broader world with energies free to form new relationships and to invest in learning.

A harmonious relationship between the parents, in which the father loves and respects his wife and supports her in her child-rearing functions and her career if she has one, enables the girl to develop a harmonious self-structure. The person with whom she identifies is desirable to the person who is her primary love object; and by following her maternal models she gains self-esteem in feeling that she can be loved and wanted as a woman. The same considerations apply to the boy. Unfortunately, such patterns are far more often an ideal rather than a reality. Not only are the majority of marriages far from fully satisfactory, but children in their oedipal jealousies can find flaws in parents and the parental relationships and readily magnify conflicts between parents.

Oedipal Fixations

There is an essential relationship between the oedipal situation and the incest taboo. While it has sometimes been assumed that the taboo which is virtually universal determines the resolution of the oedipal attachment, a need to evoke the taboo consciously is an indication that something is amiss in the family structure. The progression of the erotically toned child-parent attachment to an incestuous bond threatens the existence of the nuclear family, prevents the child from investing energies in extrafamilial socialization, and blocks his or her emergence as an adult.* If conscious avoidance of incest becomes necessary, the family transactions and the

---

* Overt incest between mother and son is very uncommon, and rarely occurs unless the mother is psychotic and with very rare exceptions the son becomes schizophrenic. Father-daughter incest, which is not subject to as intense a taboo, is far more common. The father usually has been deprived of his mother early in life, and often the wife seems to have handed the daughter over to the father as a substitute in order to permit the wife to evade her wifely responsibilities. Severe hysterical symptoms are common in women who have had incestuous experiences with their fathers.

personalities of the family members become further disturbed because spontaneous interactions become impossible, role conflict almost inevitable, and crippling defenses are often necessary. However, some transitory defenses against incestuous feelings' gaining consciousness are present in virtually all families; difficulties arise when defenses are necessary to stop overt activity.

Fixations of development at the oedipal stage come in many configurations and intensities. Disturbances in the resolution of the oedipal conflicts enter into a large proportion of all psychopathology. Fixations or serious difficulties in preoedipal development will also be reflected in oedipal difficulties. In a broad sense, the term "oedipal problems" refers to failures to overcome dependency upon the mother, to repress the sexual components in the love of the parent of the opposite sex, and to identify with the parent of the same sex. The common usage connoting a man's continuing dependency upon his mother often really refers to preoedipal oral dependency problems. The interference of sexualized feelings for a parent in later love relationships is a more central issue. Oedipal conflict is, as I trust has become clear, a normal aspect of development; it is the failure to find a suitable resolution of the conflict that creates ensuing developmental and personality disorders.

An Illustration of Unresolved Oedipal Problems

An excellent illustration of the disturbances that can ensue when oedipal problems persevere into adult life can be found in the melancholic Dane with whom we all have at least a passing familiarity. Hamlet had remained unmarried at the age of thirty; he was an only child whose mother lived "almost by his looks" (*Hamlet*, Act IV, Scene vii). He had identified strongly with his father, whose priority with his mother he had reluctantly accepted. When his mother remarried after his father's death instead of centering her attentions upon him, he was unable to accept the situation and became intensely depressed. When he then learns from his father's ghost what he has already unconsciously believed ("Oh, my prophetic soul, my uncle"—Act I, Scene v)—that his mother had been seduced by his uncle, who had then killed his father—he can no longer tolerate the situation. He feels life is empty and worthless. The narcissistic wound suffered in childhood when he could not displace his father is reopened; and the defensive pattern he developed to avoid further rebuff through identifying with his father, who could gain the love of a person like his mother, is shattered when he learns that his mother prefers his uncle to the father he had idealized. Although he has sworn to avenge his father by slaying his uncle, he cannot act. Freud believed that he could not kill his uncle because his uncle had only done what he himself had wished to do as a child—kill his father and marry his mother.* However, Shakespeare makes it apparent that Hamlet is enraged at his mother's betrayal of his father and of himself; and he is preoccupied with his mother's sexual activities with his uncle. He becomes intensely misogynistic, ranting at Ophelia and distrusting her for his mother's faults. If his mother is wanton, what woman can be trusted? It is only after he vents his rage upon his mother ("I shall speak daggers to her but use none"—Act III, Scene ii) and insists that she leave his uncle's bed, that he becomes free and can move toward action. Instead of informing his mother that his father had been murdered, he admonishes her, "Go not to mine uncle's bed—not—let the bloat king tempt you again to bed; pinch wanton on your cheek; call you his mouse . . ." (Act III, Scene iv). What sorts of thoughts Hamlet had been having about his mother and stepfather seem fairly clear from the "closet" scene. His jealousy of a father figure is also noted in his discourtesies to Polonius, the father of his beloved, and whom he kills by accident as he may have in fantasy. Ophelia, an only daughter of a widower father, then loses her sanity and commits suicide, for she, like Hamlet, who loved his mother, is caught in a insoluble conflict—now being forced to hate the person she had loved most because he killed her beloved parent.†

A realistic version of the plot of *Hamlet* was found in a young man with homosexual proclivities and a great fear of women. His mother had seductively showered affection upon him as she felt neglected by her husband, who was preoccupied by his affairs of state—the direction of a large industry. When his father died following surgery, the young man fantasied that his mother had plotted with the surgeon to kill his father so that they could marry. His illusion was only partially resolved when the surgeon paid no attention to his mother. Indeed, when he was in psychiatric treatment several years later he managed to distort the events surrounding his father's death, insisting that his father had died on the operating table when in fact his father had survived the operation for six months. He feared living alone with his widowed mother, at times (like Hamlet) fearing his incestuous impulses and at times his matricidal impulses. When his mother finally remarried, he made a serious suicidal attempt during the wedding recep-

---

* A theme elaborated by Ernest Jones in his famous essay *Hamlet and Oedipus*.
† The thesis is elaborated in the author's *Hamlet's Enemy: Myth and Madness in Hamlet*.

tion, feeling both abandoned by her and disillusioned with her for capitulating to her sexual desires.

The resolution of the oedipal conflict terminates early childhood. The need to rescind the wish to preempt a parent brings with it a reorganization of the child's world and a reevaluation of the child's place in it. Life will never again be viewed so egocentrically, and fantasy now yields priority to harsh reality. Children have now taken a giant step toward becoming independent and self-sufficient persons, even though they have done so by recognizing the long road ahead before they can expect adult prerogatives. They have found peace with both parents by repressing the erotic aspect of their attachments to one. Nevertheless the erotic attachment survives in the unconscious and will become a determinant of later relationships. The precise manner in which the oedipal situation—sometimes called "the family romance"—has been worked through is likely to set a pattern that will later be relived in different settings.

REFERENCES

ALTRUS, W. D. (1966). "Birth Order and Its Sequelae," *Science*, 151:44–49.

BARDWICK, J. (1971). *The Psychology of Women: A Study of Bio-Cultural Conflicts.* Harper & Row, New York.

BATESON, G., JACKSON, D., HALEY, J., and WEAKLAND, J. (1956). "Toward a Theory of Schizophrenia," *Behavioral Science*, 1:251–264.

BERNSTEIN, B. (1974). *Class, Codes and Control: Theoretical Studies Toward a Sociology of Language.* Schocken Books, New York.

BETTELHEIM, B. (1954). *Symbolic Wounds.* Free Press, Glencoe, Ill.

COHEN, M. B. (1966). "Personal Identity and Sexual Identity," *Psychiatry*, 29:1–14.

DIAMOND, M. (1965). "A Critical Evaluation of the Ontogeny of Human Sexual Behavior," *Quarterly Review of Biology*, 40:147–175.

EHRHARDT, A., EPSTEIN, R., and MONEY, J. (1968). "Fetal Androgens and Female Gender Identity in Early-treated Adrenogenital Syndrome," *Johns Hopkins Medical Journal*, 122:160–167.

EHRHARDT, A., and MONEY, J. (1967). "Progestin-induced Hermaphroditism: IQ and Psychosexual Identity in a Study of Ten Girls," *Journal of Sex Research*, 3:83–100.

ERIKSON, E. (1959). "Growth and Crises of the 'Healthy Personality,' " in *Psychological Issues*, vol. 1, no. 1, Monograph No. 1. International Universities Press, New York.

FREUD, S. (1916–1917). "Introductory Lectures on Psycho-Analysis," in *The Standard Edition of the Complete Psychological Works of Sigmund Freud*, vols. 15 and 16. Hogarth Press, London, 1954.

———. (1925). "Some Psychological Consequences of the Anatomical Distinction Between the Sexes," in *The Standard Edition of the Complete Psychological Works of Sigmund Freud*, vol. 19. Hogarth Press, London, 1961.

————. (1931). "Female Sexuality," in *The Standard Edition of the Complete Psychological Works of Sigmund Freud*, vol. 21. Hogarth Press, London, 1961.

————. (1933a). "The Psychology of Women," in *New Introductory Lectures on Psycho-Analysis*. W. W. Norton, New York.

————. (1933b). *New Introductory Lectures on Psycho-Analysis*. W. W. Norton, New York.

GARCIA, H., BORGANONKAV, D., and RICHARDSON, F. (1967). "XXYY Syndrome in a Prepubertal Male," *Johns Hopkins Medical Journal*, 121:31–37.

GOODALL, J. (1963). "My Life Among Wild Chimpanzees," *National Geographic*, 124:272–308.

————. (1965). "New Discoveries Among Wild Chimpanzees," *National Geographic*, 128:802–831.

GOODENOUGH, E. W. (1957). "Interest in Persons as an Aspect of Sex Differences in the Early Years," *Genetic Psychology Monographs*, 55:287–323.

GREEN, R. (1974). *Sexual Identity Conflict in Children and Adults*. Basic Books, New York.

HALL, R. (1928). *The Well of Loneliness*. Sun Dial Press, Garden City, New York.

HAMBURG, D., and LUNDE, D. (1966). "Sex Hormones in the Development of Sex Differences in Human Behavior," in *The Development of Sex Differences*. E. Maccoby, ed. Stanford University Press, Stanford, Calif.

HAMPSON, J. L., and HAMPSON, J. G. (1961). "The Ontogenesis of Sexual Behavior in Man," in *Sex and Internal Secretions*, vol. 2. W. C. Young, ed. 3d ed. Williams & Wilkins, Baltimore.

JONES, E. (1949). *Hamlet and Oedipus*. W. W. Norton, New York.

KENT, E. (1949). "A Study of Maladjusted Twins," *Smith College Studies of Social Work*, 19:63–77.

KLEEMAN, J. (1971). "The Establishment of Core Gender Identity in Normal Girls: I. (a) Introduction; (b) Development of the Ego Capacity to Differentiate," *Archives of Sex Behavior*, 1:103–116.

KOCH, H. (1966). *Twins and Twin Relations*. University of Chicago Press, Chicago.

KOHLBERG, L. (1966). "A Cognitive-Developmental Analysis of Children's Sex-Role Concepts and Attitudes," in *The Development of Sex Differences*. E. Maccoby, ed. Stanford University Press, Stanford, Calif.

LEACH, E. (1964). "Anthropological Aspects of Language: Animal Categories and Verbal Abuse," in *New Directions in the Study of Language*. E. H. Lenneberg, ed. MIT Press, Cambridge, Mass.

LIDZ, R., and LIDZ, T. (1976). "Male Menstruation: A Ritual Alternative to the Oedipal Transition," *International Journal of Psycho-Analysis* (in press).

LIDZ, T. (1973). *The Origin and Treatment of Schizophrenic Disorders*. Basic Books, New York.

————. (1975). *Hamlet's Enemy: Myth and Madness in Hamlet*. Basic Books, New York.

Lidz, T., Cornelison, A. *et al.* (1958). "The Transmission of Irrationality," in T. Lidz, S. Fleck, and A. Cornelison, *Schizophrenia and the Family*. International Universities Press, New York, 1965.

MACCOBY, E., and JACKLIN, C. (1974). *The Psychology of Sex Differences*. Stanford University Press, Stanford, Calif.

MILNE, A. A. (1961). *Winnie the Pooh*. Rev. ed. E. P. Dutton, New York.

MITSCHERLICH, H. (1969). *Society Without the Father*. Harcourt, Brace & World, New York.

MONEY, J. (1965). "Psychosexual Differentiation," in *Sex Research: New Developments*. Holt, Rinehart & Winston, New York.

MONEY, J., HAMPSON, J. G., and HAMPSON, J. L. (1957). "Imprinting and the Establishment of Gender Roles," *Archives of Neurology and Psychiatry*, 77:333–336.

MOSS, H. A. (1967). "Sex, Age, and State as Determinants of Mother-Infant Interaction," *Merrill-Palmer Quarterly of Behavior and Development*, 13:19–36.

MOSS, H. A., and ROBSON, K. S. (1970). "The Relation Between the Amount of Time Infants Spend at Various States and the Development of Visual Behavior," *Child Development*, 41:509–517.

PARSONS, T. (1964). "The Incest Taboo in Relation to Social Structure and the Socialization of the Child," in *Social Structure and Personality*. Free Press, New York.

PIAGET, J. (1962). *Play, Dreams, and Imitation in Childhood*. C. Gattengo and F. M. Hodgson, trans. W. W. Norton, New York.

PIAGET, J., and INHELDER, B. (1969). *The Psychology of the Child*. H. Weaver, trans. Basic Books, New York.

SINGER, M. T., and WYNNE, L. C. (1965a). "Thought Disorder and Family Relations of Schizophrenics: III. Methodology Using Projective Techniques," *Archives of General Psychiatry*, 12:187–200.

———. (1965b). "Thought Disorder and Family Relations of Schizophrenics: IV. Results and Implications," *Archives of General Psychiatry*, 12:201–212.

STOLLER, R. (1968). *Sex and Gender: On the Development of Masculinity and Femininity*. Science House, New York.

TANNER, J. (1961). *Growth at Adolescence*. 2d ed. Blackwell Scientific Publications, Oxford.

VYGOTSKY, L. S. (1962). *Thought and Language*. E. Hanfmann and G. Vakar, eds. and trans. MIT Press and John Wiley & Sons, New York.

WERTHAM, F. (1941). "The Matricidal Impulse: Critique of Freud's Interpretation of Hamlet," *Journal of Criminal Psychopathology*, 2:455–464.

WILD, C., SINGER, M., ROSMAN, B., RICCI, J., and LIDZ, T. (1965). "Measuring Disordered Styles of Thinking in the Parents of Schizophrenic Patients on the Object Sorting Test," in T. Lidz, S. Fleck, and A. Cornelison, *Schizophrenia and the Family*. International Universities Press, New York.

WYNNE, L. C., and SINGER, M. T. (1963a). "Thought Disorder and Family Relations of Schizophrenics: I. Research Strategy," *Archives of General Psychiatry*, 9:191–198.

———. (1963b). "Thought Disorder and Family Relations of Schizophrenics: II. A Classification of Forms of Thinking," *Archives of General Psychiatry*, 9:199–206.

YOUNG, W., GOY, R., and PHOENIX, C. (1964). "Hormones and Sexual Behavior," *Science*, 143:212–218.

SUGGESTED READING

BARDWICK, J. (1971). *The Psychology of Women*. Harper & Row, New York.

FREUD, S. (1908). "On the Sexual Theories of Children," in *The Standard Edition of the Complete Psychological Works of Sigmund Freud*, vol. 9. Hogarth Press, London, 1959.

———. (1916–1917). "Introductory Lectures on Psychoanalysis," in *The Standard Edition of the Complete Psychological Works of Sigmund Freud*, vols. 15 and 16. Hogarth Press, London, 1954.

LIDZ, T. (1975). *Hamlet's Enemy: Myth and Madness in Hamlet*. Basic Books, New York.

O'CONNOR, F. (1952). "My Oedipus Complex," in *Stories of Frank O'Connor*. Alfred A. Knopf, New York.

MACCOBY, E., and JACKLIN, C. (1974). *The Psychology of Sex Differences*. Stanford University Press, Stanford, Calif.

PIAGET, J. (1962). *Play, Dreams and Imitation in Childhood*. C. Gattengo and F. M. Hodgson, trans. W. W. Norton, New York.

CHAPTER 8

❀

Childhood Integration

THE CLOSING of the oedipal period brings a consolidation of the child's personality. The child now first achieves a fairly firm integration as an individual. It seems paradoxical to consider that the essential patterning of children's personalities takes place even before they start school. They have scarcely ventured beyond their homes and the protection of their families; they must still accumulate most of the knowledge they will require to guide their own lives, and they will remain dependent upon parental figures for support and guidance for many years to come. Yet, the Jesuits as well as the Communists have placed great emphasis upon these first six years of life, even venturing to say that if they can control these years they do not care who influences the child thereafter. Indeed, psychoanalytic psychology may convey the same impression because of its emphasis upon the events of childhood through the resolution of the oedipal conflicts and their pervasive influence upon all subsequent behavior. Even though personality development is far from completed at five or six and many significant influences will still accrue before a firm integration and a stable identity are achieved, we must examine the paradox and the nature and extent of the organization that has occurred.

THE FAMILY MATRIX

The fetus unfolds within the protected and relatively uniform intrauterine environment which helps assure its proper maturation. The child is born into the nexus of the family, and within it, where conditions are far less predictable and stable; the child's personality takes shape and the child is prepared to live in a specific society. Despite its shortcomings, the family forms a reasonably uniform social system that both shields the immature child from the larger society and also prepares the child to emerge into it. It forms a limited world, but the baby and small child are not ready to cope with complexity. The cast of persons with whom the child interrelates within the family remains fairly constant, which permits the child to develop expectancies and build up reasonably consistent behavioral patterns through reciprocal interactions. How children learn to maintain their emotional equilibrium and their sense of well-being within their families sets a pattern for their behavior outside their homes. They will, at first, expect reactions from persons outside the family similar to those learned from parents and siblings.* They will tend to change others into figures like their parents and to perceive them in familiar intrafamilial terms. Having managed to find their places within their homes, now at the age of five or six, children must move on to learn to live in the wider world, a less stable and benevolent place, where they do not occupy specially favored positions. The patterns acquired in the home form the foundations of their ways of interacting and will resist change: throughout their lives their perceptions of significant persons and their ways of relating to them will be compromises between the expectations they developed within their family milieu and the actual ways of persons they encounter.

As we have noted in the preceding chapter, the children's personalities gained considerable organization with the closure of the oedipal period. They became much more firmly grounded in reality by the necessity of accepting their childhood position in the family, by rescinding or repressing desires to possess the parent of the opposite sex as a love object, and by identifying with the parent of the same sex. In the process children gained long-term goals toward which to strive and models to follow into adulthood. The children's gender identities became reinforced through their

---

* Piaget (1962) notes that many subsequent interpersonal relationships will be assimilated to the schemata established in adaptation to the parents, particularly the affective schemata of interpersonal relationships. The transference relationships discussed in Chap. 21 rest on such foundations.

identifications with the parent of the same sex, and by becoming directed toward seeking a love object of the opposite sex. Their renunciation of hopes of actually possessing parental love objects permitted the children to come to terms with both parents and to find relatively conflict-free positions in relation to them. The transactions between the parents enter into their children's self-concepts and feelings of self-esteem. A boy whose father is loved and admired by his mother can gain a sense of worth in accordance with how he approximates his idealized father; and a girl can accept her worth more readily when the mother is desired and esteemed by her father. Children also gain a feeling of the value of being a father or mother, a husband or wife, as well as of being male or female, from the interactions of their parents.

DEVELOPMENT OF PERSONALITY STRUCTURE

Freud, in an effort to symbolize the nature of the intrapsychic conflicts of his patients, and particularly to clarify the sources of their anxieties, formulated his *structural theory* of the mind. He posited three mental realms or structures: the id, ego, and superego. Freud considered the *id* to be composed of the basic drives, particularly the libidinal drives and their derivatives, of chaotic, seething, unconscious impulses and their inchoate mental derivates that are not subjected to linguistic regulation or logic but seek to gain control of the person in the service of pleasure and sexual gratification.* The id, according to this theory, is the source of virtually all motivation. He conceptualized the *ego* as that part of the mind that has access to motility and has the function of decision making. He considered it as an offshoot of the primitive id, but with access to consciousness. The ego has the difficult task of mediating between the powerful pleasure-seeking, but potentially endangering id on the one hand, and both the reality that must be taken into account and the *superego*, a construct that designates the internalized parental directives. The superego, like the parents in childhood, can provide conscious and unconscious support to the ego in its struggle against pressures from id impulses and can also punish, as would

---

* Freud considered the *pleasure principle* a major directive in development and behavior. The organism is motivated to seek pleasure and avoid unpleasure (*Unlust*). Pleasure was, at times, equated with tension reduction, and tension—such as that created by "uncathected libido"—was equated with unpleasure. However, Freud also recognized that some pleasure was not simply the reduction of tension. The *id* seeks to follow the "pleasure principle," but the ego must modify its strivings in keeping with the demands of the superego and reality, or the "reality principle," for purposes of adaptation.

imagined parental figures. The id pressures can oppose the superego sufficiently to force the ego to allow adequate gratifications. In this manner
Freud conceptualized the dynamic conflict that went on within a person,
and symbolized how emotional disorders were the result of a failure in the
balance between id, ego, and superego. Too forceful an id would lead to
dangers, such as efforts to live out incestuous, oedipal desires. Too forceful
repression of the id because of superego demands would lead to constriction of the personality. Because the id can be denied expression only with
difficulty, when the ego is, so to speak, squeezed between the demands of
the id and superego the person can suffer anxiety lest the id impulses get
out of control. Neuroses were believed to result from various efforts to find
a way out of such dilemma, as we shall examine shortly.

We cannot here become concerned with the intriguing problems of the
origins of psychopathology, nor fully weigh the virtues and deficits of this
structural hypothesis. The dramatic conceptualization drew attention to the
vulnerability of humans in coping with their powerful primitive drives and
the demands of socialization, and has had a profound influence upon
twentieth-century thought and ethics. We must note, however, that the
structural concept is scarcely a description of the mind—at least of the
mind as described in Chapter 1—but seems closer to a way of conceptualizing the personality, at least of the motivating and regulating forces of
the personality.* Other difficulties with the structural concept derive from
the reification of the id, ego, and superego. Not only is such reification
basically untenable in scientific thinking, but it has lead to pseudo-solu-
tions of various problems concerning personality functioning and malfunctioning.

At this juncture we are concerned essentially with the forces that direct
and regulate children's behavior when they move beyond their families and
homes. Although their parents will continue to provide guidance and delimitation for many years to come, they can no longer be with their children to
serve as omnipresent counselors and protectors. It is clear that in order to
function effectively outside their families children need to have gained the
capacities to delay, moderate, or rescind the gratification of drives, impulses, and wishes and have learned the essentials of socialization; they

---

* As noted briefly in the Preface, considerable confusion entered psychoanalytic
theory when Freud sought to replace his "Topographic" concept of the mind; that is,
the division into Unconscious, Preconscious, and Conscious realms (which will be considered later in the chapter) with his structural concept. In so doing he endowed the
id with virtually all of the attributes he had previously given to the Unconscious. The
Structural and Topographic concepts, if not taken literally, do not conflict, for the
Structural theory is a way of conceptualizing the personality in a useful, simplified manner, and the Topographic theory is a useful concept of certain characteristics of the
mind or mental process.

must also have learned many basic techniques of adaptation, including a mastery of the fundamentals of language, and have internalized many parental directives and standards. Although they have been in conflict over the need to control erogenous longings for parents, the impact of sexual drives has not as yet subjected children to their imperious—or infernal— demands. The Structural theory is a highly useful way of symbolizing these various sets of influences that enter into self-direction. We can avoid the reification of the constructs of id, ego, and superego* that has so befuddled the psychoanalytic literature by speaking rather of id impulses, ego functions, and superego directives.

Id impulses, then, concern the influences of the basic drives produced by tissue tensions and serve to assure that the body's homeostatic needs, the sexual drives vital to the continuity of the species, and the aggressive drives that are important for self-defense will receive proper attention.

The tissue needs can be denied only with extreme difficulty, and ignoring them can lead to death. Still, it is possible to starve to death even among plenty for ideological reasons. However, the major concern of psycho-dynamic theory is with the sexual and aggressive drives which can be denied and displaced, and require delimitation and channeling lest they interfere with interpersonal relationships and the social systems that are essential for human existence. The child, as we have noted, has learned to delay the satisfaction of tissue drives such as hunger and thirst in accordance with the demands of reality and in order to gain parental approbation. Libidinal and aggressive desires and impulsions have also been repressed in varying degrees according to the standards of the culture and the parents.† Id impulses are obviously of vital importance but socialization depends upon their control and proper channelling.** Freud made

---

* Attempts to define these constructs very precisely and to allocate just what should be included under each, rather than utilizing them as useful terms, leads to confusion rather than precision. Rapaport (1960), who was one of the most scholarly, knowledgeable, and brilliant students of psychoanalytic theories, finally stated that the concepts were not indispensable to psychoanalytic theory and gave up his efforts to clarify the theoretic confusions involved in their usage.

† In some societies, as among the headhunters of New Guinea, the children are taught to be aggressively defensive at a very early age as is essential to their survival, but still it is aggression against enemies and not against fellow villagers that is condoned. The degree of sexual repression required also varies widely. Among some peoples, the young children masturbate openly and play at sexual intercourse, and in our society many parents seek to have the children refrain from masturbation only in public.

** In classic theory, the libido or sexualized energy was often considered the source of all "psychic" energy—and in extreme forms of theory, the ultimate source of all motivation. The untenable idea that such libido remained quantitatively constant, and that much of behavior and motivation was to be understood in terms of how quantities of this hypothesized energy were "cathected"—or invested in various parts of the body and in various objects (persons)—has been a major source of confusion in psychoanalytic theory.

us aware of how greatly our behavior and thought are influenced by sexual and aggressive drives even when impulses are controlled and kept out of our conscious awareness.

The *ego functions* have to do with self-direction, we may say with a person's capacities to direct the self into the future; we have been tracing the emergence of such capacities in children as they differentiate from their mothers, develop language, learn to understand the world about them, gain skills, and take on ways of parental-figures through identifying with them. Ego functioning depends very much upon the organization of an internalized, symbolized version of reality, in which imaginative trials can be made without committing the self to the irrevocable consequences of action. Self-direction, however, does not depend on reason or logic alone, and persons differ from one another, and in themselves from time to time, in how greatly passion sways, or in how current pleasure and future goals are balanced, or in how greatly parental or societal standards influence their behavior.

Children internalize some of their parents' ways as their own ways of living their lives—we may say, as part of their ego functioning—and in the process take on some societal directives. Some parental directives, however, are taken as a reference system of what behavior is prescribed, permitted, or proscribed, which we term the *superego directives*. That is, some behavioral standards are internalized as part of a person's basic ways of thinking, and some continue to be experienced as externally imposed standards to which a person conforms in order to remain at peace with the self, very much as the child had conformed with parental wishes and edicts. Superego directives are very much like the conscience but include positive as well as negative sanctions. Everyone probably conceptualizes and feels that certain parental and cultural ethical influences are added to one's own standards. Somehow, they do not seem to be quite fully incorporated into the self.

Many superego directives are unconscious. Many parental standards and societal sanctions are simply accepted as the ways in which persons should behave and have never been thought about consciously. People tend to feel euphoric when they have adhered to a proper way of life and dysphoric when they have breached the accepted and approved, and they may become self-punitive when they behave contrary to their parents' or their own ethical standards but may have no realization of what has affected their sense of well-being.

Just what self-direction should be considered part of a person's ego functioning and what as superego controls may be difficult to conceptualize and may be simply an academic matter. Indeed, the balance shifts as children grow older, feel less need for parental approval, become less concerned with parental censure, and have developed values of their own. Some ego syntonic standards become more completely integrated into the core of the self (Loewald, 1962). However, the concept of superego controls reflects a basic attitude about self-regulation. Some principles continue to seem externally imposed and are regarded as reference systems that serve to guide actions and feelings, and all persons probably continue to imagine throughout their lives of what their parents would disapprove and what would cause them happiness, even when they decide to improve upon or negate their parental values. The concept is very useful in work with patients, for it provides a simple means of symbolizing a major set of influences that enters into decision making and into feelings of self-esteem.*

Children followed parental directives and prohibitions from an early age; but as they become able to retain a stable image of absent parents, and they cease splitting parents into "good" and "bad" objects and maintain a more consistent concept of them, children also can more clearly direct themselves according to what they have learned will please or displease their parents. In the oedipal transition they take on the values as well as characteristics of parents with whom they identify.† Self-esteem rests greatly upon being someone whom a parent would love. Just as it is erroneous to think that the superego controls first appear at the age of five or six, it would be incorrect to believe that the child is now fully capable of self-regulation and that any shortcomings indicate a sociopathic future. Children may internalize parental directives but they remain extremely dependent upon parental standards of right and wrong, and still rely upon tangible adult authority. Their views are now less egocentric but they are still family centered. They lack judgment and tend to believe that rules are inherent parts of games or of life itself, and do not yet appreciate the more contractual nature of social behavior. God has ordained and the parents have taught what is right or wrong, and ethics are therefore likely to be considered in black and white terms. Such childhood rigor of evaluation is

---

* Thus, the inability of a person to permit himself any sensuous gratification can be considered in terms of the ego's conformity to superego demands formed in terms of childhood perceptions of paternal prohibitions: some hallucinations can be understood as externalizations of threats from the superego for incipient infractions; certain depressive reactions are concerned with superego punishment—usually for hostile feelings and resentment toward significant persons.

† Freud considered that the superego formed at the time of the resolution of the oedipal conflicts, at times as a precipitate of the oedipal situation, with the libidinal energy that had been invested in the parent of the opposite sex turned into the service of repression. Superego formation can be understood without resorting to such notions of shifts in libidinal energy.

apt to continue into adult life. On the other side, they will first learn much of social values and particularly of peer-group values in the years ahead. Fortunately, time for consolidation and modification of the superego remains before the impact of puberty adds powerful new stresses.

Children also have realistic reasons to relinquish immediate gratifications. They have been learning that the pursuit of future objectives often requires renunciation of present pleasures. For instance, if a little boy insists on dawdling in his mother's bed in the morning, he will miss going with his friend to the store. But children have also learned to forgo many erotic and aggressive wishes because they will bring disapproval or punishment, and they have even learned to keep such thoughts from others. Now they are also keeping thoughts and feelings out of their own awareness because they provoke feelings of guilt, shame, or anxiety. The more definitive development of the superego directives at this phase of life also involves the children's realization that they will not necessarily continue to receive affection and protection as an ascribed right, but that it also depends upon achievement—in the sense of retaining affection by adhering to parental moral values. The balance between ascribed and achieved approval will gain importance as children move beyond the family, as will be considered in the next chapter.

It is important to note that the term "ego ideal" has often been used as a synonym for "superego" in the psychoanalytic literature, but that it has also been given several other meanings, and thus just what "ego ideal" means in the literature depends upon the author and the context. One common and useful usage of ego ideal has been as the ideal image of what the child believes he or she should be, particularly in the form of the ideas the child forms of what the parents wish the child to be and to become. Children measure themselves by such standards and feel inadequate and perhaps depressed when they do not measure up to them. The ego ideal will usually contain large elements of the parent of the same sex whom the child wishes to resemble in order to become capable of gaining a love object like the parent of the opposite sex. Here again it becomes apparent that the organizing influences and the directive influences become confused when each parent negates the value of the spouse; or when they have conflicting values, standards, and ideals. A girl whose father was a philanderer and who frequently left his wife and child and whose mother was a conscientious wife and overly solicitous mother was caught between irreconcilable parents with very divergent values. She needed her mother, who was the only person upon whom she could depend, and sought to be a conscientious student and fastidious little girl, and when her mother chas-

tised her for masturbating, tried to suppress all sexual feelings. To satisfy
her handsome and dapper father who made life seem carefree and easy, she
fantasied becoming a woman like his attractive and sensuous mistress who
seemed better able to hold him than her mother. Becoming a woman like
mother seemed to have few advantages, and yet she needed her mother
upon whom she could depend. Alternative and contradictory superegos
formed that guided her into two different personality patterns, and eventually to an incipient dual personality.

UNCONSCIOUS MENTAL PROCESSES

An important aspect of children's increased organization concerns the sorting out of feelings, memories, perceptions, and ideas that are permitted to
enter consciousness; that is, what children let themselves think about. They
cannot tolerate the anxiety caused by ideas and feelings which are unacceptable to the internalized parental standards and which, if expressed,
would either produce rebuff or rejection by the parents, or loss of self-
esteem. It is safer not to permit temptation to arise than to be in danger of
giving way to it. Yet, much of the temptation arises from within, from
longings to have sensuous relationships and from impulses to give vent to
aggressive feelings, and from physiological drives that create tensions.
Children can keep from recognizing the nature of these tensions or, having
learned that such tensions are aroused by certain thoughts and perceptions,
can keep such ideas from intruding. It is necessary to examine how this
selection of what can enter consciousness occurs, and what happens to
thoughts that are excluded.

The explorations of the unconscious processes have been a major
achievement of psychoanalysis. Freud did not discover unconscious
thought, but he discovered the dynamic force of unconscious processes and
their far-reaching consequences; and through the study of dreams, the
neuroses, the associations of patients in psychoanalysis, and the meanings
of slips of the tongue, etc., went far in unraveling one of the most difficult
and diaphanous topics ever studied. However, it is essential to keep in
mind that the workings of the "mind" still present very much of a challenge, and many questions remain unanswered, if not, indeed, unasked.

In following children's cognitive development and the progress of their
linguistic abilities we have, for the most part, been examining the conscious

processes concerned with problem solving and adaptation to the environment. We have, however, considered the development of fantasy and the problems that arise because of the child's difficulties in differentiating between reality and fantasy. Much of the child's mental activities are carried out in the service of the *pleasure principle*—in seeking gratification more than in coping with reality—and in gaining pleasure in fantasy when reality requires renunciation. Sometime around the age of five or six much of the fantasy is recognized as unacceptable to others, and even to the self, as it runs counter to superego dictates. Much of the oral, anal, oedipal, and aggressive fantasies are shut out and pushed down into the unconscious. We say that they are *repressed*, a term we have used before, but which we shall now examine.

Origins of Unconscious Processes

Actually, from what we can determine, the oedipal child and young school child does not repress very effectively at first. Some of the forbidden material and fantasies are not unconscious but kept in separate compartments, so to speak, dissociated from everyday activities. They are permitted to emerge under fairly specific circumstances, such as when a little boy of seven is falling asleep and playing with his genitals he can have fantasies of seeing his mother undressed and putting his face against her breast. Another boy, while sitting on the toilet, has elaborate fantasies of an anal-sadistic and aggressive nature in which he imagines himself a superman bombing cities, visualizing the destruction of many little children each time his feces fall into the toilet. Such fantasies become more and more difficult to recall, and may eventually become "unconscious fantasies" that transpire automatically and cannot be recalled. Individuals may become aware retrospectively that time has passed during which they do not know what they were thinking. However, in psychoanalysis, many adults realize that fantasies have persisted in isolation since childhood. A woman who hated her husband but still gained much orgasmic pleasure from intercourse with him, realized that during intercourse she habitually fantasied sitting on an older man's lap and being masturbated—which she eventually traced to early childhood fantasies about her father.

Psychoanalytically oriented play therapy with children also indicates that many of their forbidden wishes and ideas have relatively simple access to consciousness. A six-year-old boy who started to stammer severely after a baby sister was born was watched playing with a family of dolls. He placed a baby doll in a crib next to the parent dolls' bed, and then had a boy doll come and throw the baby to the floor, beat it, and throw it into a corner. He then put the boy doll into the crib. In a subsequent session he had the father doll pummel the mother doll's abdomen, saying "No, no!" At this period of childhood, even though certain unacceptable ideas cannot be talked about, they are still not definitely repressed. Indeed, even in adult life what can enter consciousness varies with the circumstances. Death wishes for a boss who has refused a raise are permitted, but they create guilt and are repressed when the boss becomes ill and may die. Sexual thoughts and even practices are permitted with a call girl that cannot occur with a wife. Superego standards vary with time and place and so does the division between what can be conscious and what must not be.

One reason why unacceptable ideas can remain isolated, and can emerge in play and still not be clearly conscious, is that many of little children's sensuous feelings, desires, and thoughts, as well as their primitive hostile feelings, originated before language was well developed and they were never properly linked up with words; and some were never precise or in a form that could be communicated. Consciousness is related to verbal symbolization if not dependent upon it. There are no simple words for many of the diffuse ideas and fantasies that the child has felt, or symbolized visually, and they are not a topic for discussion by elders or with elders.* They remain very much of a private world, and are thought about in an amorphous combination of feeling states and mental images.

As children grow older they become more aware of which thoughts and impulses are acceptable. Very dependent on the protection and care of parents and other significant figures, children also become more sensitive to the possibility of losing them. Few children can reach the age of five or six without having experienced unbearable feelings of anxiety when parents have left, or the equally terrible depressed feelings that accompany their absence for a prolonged period. Efforts to avoid repetition of such feelings become fundamental motivations in a child's life. Superego directives help children seek to maintain themselves as persons whom the parents will want and will not abandon, and still later as persons who are satisfied with themselves and therefore can feel good. Such efforts require control of id impulses and of hostile feelings toward loved ones, and paradoxically, also finding ways of keeping out of consciousness awareness of parental behavior or traits that would make them less desirable, less protective, or less dependable—as, for example, recognition that Father might not come back

---

* In Piaget's terms affective schemata are not apt to be verbal schemata and new assimilations are made to them nonverbally. See also E. Schachtel, "Memory and Childhood Amnesia."

after one of the weekends he spends in another house with some woman other than Mother.

Children have been developing ways of maintaining their equilibrium and avoiding distress by disregarding reality or by altering their perceptions of it; these include ways of keeping id impulsions from becoming conscious. These ways are termed the *mental mechanisms of defense* against experiencing anxiety, and stated symbolically, help the "ego" to satisfy superego injunctions and withstand id impulses for immediate and unacceptable gratification. In the context of the physiological homeostasis of the organism, these mental mechanisms also protect the individual from the physiological impact of anxiety and depression which can have deleterious effects upon the body's functioning (see Chapter 20). There are many different mechanisms of defense that influence thought, behavior, and character formation, as we shall consider later in the chapter.

With the aid of various mental mechanisms of defense, various thoughts, impulses, and feelings that conflict with superego standards are banned from consciousness. Unconscious material cannot regain access to consciousness under ordinary conditions because defenses block associational pathways to it, or assimilation to schemata does not occur consciously; or, as we might put it in computer terms, the material "is programmed out." The material or the impulses are not extinguished but merely contained, shunted aside, or, sometimes, altered to more acceptable form. Thus sidetracked, the unconscious processes and materials do not enter directly into decision-making functions or reasoning, but they continue in a more primitive, nonverbal type of activity that can exert potent influences upon conscious thought and behavior. The unconscious processes exert their influence in disguised and roundabout ways in order to assert the demands of the body's drives, the desires for sensuous gratification, or the pressures of aggressive feelings. The analogy can be made to a subversive organization that goes "underground" when it is banned by the government. It awaits and ferrets out opportunities to assert itself and influence the governmental procedures in hidden ways. It often utilizes individuals and organizations that do not even know that they are being used. Just as the government pays the price of not knowing what goes on beneath the calm surface, individuals do not know what is festering in them unconsciously. If repression in the service of a rigid or harsh superego is extreme and permits little pleasure or satisfaction of the body's needs, the unconscious strivings may upset the equilibrium. Inexplicable irrational behavior erupts or ego functioning gives way to dissociated experiences or even to disorganized behavior.

The unconscious mental processes, then, do not generally serve reality testing and adaptation to social living, but *largely* the libidinal and aggressive drives that are unacceptable because they run counter to superego injunctions. They gain force from an individual's need for sexual outlets or for giving vent to unbearable feelings of hostility and aggression, and, in less demanding form from the intense desires to regain the sensuous gratifications and care of childhood that are denied to the older child and adult. Having renounced such impulses and desires, a person can no longer control their unconscious derivatives and the uses they make of perception and memories. The person is not free of them, for through influencing dreams, fantasies, and trends of associations, the unconscious processes often gain the upper hand. They may, so to speak, remain anonymous, but at the price of becoming the power behind the throne—that is, the person's thoughts and activities are influenced by, or even controlled by, the forbidden, but in a disguised form.

CONSCIOUS, PRECONSCIOUS, AND UNCONSCIOUS MENTATION

The mind, according to psychoanalytic psychology, is divided into three layers: the *conscious, preconscious*, and *unconscious*. The preconscious, however, consists of material that is not repressed and has ready access to consciousness but simply is not in focus, or the subject of attention at the moment. The conscious is limited to material which is being consciously thought about at the moment. The preconscious is not dormant but carries out activities in a fashion very much like that used by the unconscious, as will be explained presently.* Psychoanalytic psychology has been largely concerned with the dynamic unconscious—that is, the material that is denied access to consciousness. There are other sources of unconscious material. Ideas and ways of behaving that are inherent in the family or to the culture may be unconscious in that the individual never has reason to question them or even think about them. Egocentricity means, in a sense,

---

* Freud, at least at times, considered that the preconscious mind used "secondary process" thinking. Indeed, the preconscious is often included when one is talking about the conscious mind. However, "preconscious thought" is usually very different from conscious thinking.

unawareness that there are other, different ways of thinking or perceiving. Many of the unexpressed foundations of our belief systems and our way of life are unconscious.*

The Primary and Secondary Mental Processes

Freud designated the type of thinking that transpires unconsciously as the *primary process*, contrasting it with the *secondary process* thinking that is reality-oriented and seeks to regulate behavior in terms of the future welfare of the individual. The primary process has been studied largely in terms of dream processes, which may well differ from the primary process that goes on constantly during waking states. Freud tended to consider the primary process a forerunner of the secondary process. Secondary process rational thinking is a verbalization and syntactical organization of the diffuse primary process in accord with the demands of the superego directives and reality testing. However, it seems likely that the two types of thought processes which subserve different functions are carried out differently and that the secondary process does not simply reorganize more primitive material.† Transitional forms between the primary and secondary process are found in fantasies, semiwaking states, and in children's play.

Dreams are composed primarily of visual images. The *manifest dream* may derive from visual impressions of the preceding day and the associations they have unconsciously evoked translated into visual symbols. Thus,

---

* Another reason for maintaining material outside of conscious awareness requires mention even though it has received little if any attention in psychodynamic psychologies. As noted previously, each culture categorizes experiences differently. As experience tends to be continuous, what lies between these categories, between experiences and things that are recognized as entities and named—is kept from consciousness. Leach (1964) suggests that they are taboo; and as the separation of the self from the surrounding is particularly important, those substances that are ambiguously self and nonself or which have been self but become nonself, such as excreta, hair cuttings, semen, are particularly subject to taboo in most societies. The same reasoning can be applied to nursing and sexual relations that blur the boundaries between the self and another.

† Freud also described the functioning of the id in terms of primary process activity. When he formulated the *structural concept* (that is, the division of the mind into id, ego, and superego), he shifted much of his conceptualization of the unconscious as a division of the mind to the id, and thereby started the current confusions between the *topographical concept of the mind* (that is, the division of the mind according to layers of consciousness) and the structural concept.

Piaget has presented a different conceptualization of unconscious processes and suggests a continuity between what Freud has termed "primary" and "secondary" processes. His cogent critique of Freud's approach to cognitive matters warrants careful study (see Chapter 7 in *Play, Dreams, and Imitation in Childhood*).

a female college student who has been rather promiscuous, dreams of a young man she saw on the campus for the first time and thought attractive. In the dream she is lost in the country with him in an old auto. A sign points to her hometown fifteen miles in the direction opposite to that in which she is driving. The dream is somewhat akin to a charade, but the meaning is masked from the dreamer. As Freud showed in his study of dreams, it expresses a wish. She is on a date with the man who attracted her, and this is symbolized by driving with him in a car. The car also conveys much more; for, when asked to give her associations to various elements of the dream, she recalls that it is a car her family owned five years previously in which she first had sexual relations. She is lost in the country. She associates ideas of being a lost woman because of her promiscuity. She is fifteen miles from home. She had confided to a friend on the preceding day that she had had sexual intercourse with fourteen different men: the fantasy concerns a fifteenth. She is, so to speak, fifteen men away from home, and going further away. She is driving. She is the seducer rather than the seduced, a factor which introduces her wishes to dominate men. There is an element of anxiety about being lost in the dream. It involves her sexual drives and aggression that have led her to run away from home symbolically. These are her primary associations, and it is apparent that each trend can be followed further, and in this respect the dream symbolizes a great many past experiences, current wishes, and problems that converge in this brief dream fragment.

The young woman's dream has expressed a great deal, but much concerns matters that she prefers not to think about and motivations which she has hidden from herself. It condenses a wish for intimacy with a specific man, but it also includes residua from previous sexual experiences. It condenses time, for it mingles elements of experiences that took place five years earlier with a depiction of her current wish. Similarly, places are symbolic rather than actual; she could not go on a date with the young man fifteen miles from home, as she is at college two thousand miles from home. Such apparent contradictions are not contradictory, for we see that morally she feels she is fifteen miles from home. The wish may also arouse anxiety, for its fulfillment is not only counter to her superego but she feels it would further separate her from her parents. The manifest content of the dream, which consists simply of her driving in a car with an attractive young man, neither runs counter to superego dictates nor creates anxiety; but the latent content—that is, the associated material symbolized in the dream—contains many disturbing elements. In order to express all of the material symbolized in the dream, the young woman would have had to tell herself a lengthy story about her life and desires, and it would have to have contained the contradictions and irrationalities that constitute so much of human behavior but are difficult to express in language. We may assume that even though the latent content had been hidden from consciousness it might have influenced her behavior, or indicated that she was in the process of reassessing her behavior—for she had just decided to seek psychotherapy because of her concerns over her increasing promiscuity.

Attributes of Primary Process Mentation

The study of unconscious or primary process mentation is a complex matter and highly conjectural.* We must be content here to note some of the salient aspects of dreaming, and then to examine some of the effects of unconscious processes on behavior. The dream we have just examined briefly contained the following characteristics: thinking is carried out largely in visual symbols; the manifest content disguises and symbolizes a multitude of associations; it condenses many feelings and experiences and displaces ideas and feelings from one experience to another; it is timeless in the sense that old experiences have the same intensity as recent ones and connect to current experiences across time; opposites do not necessarily contradict but express a similarity between the apparent contradictions. The dream is also overdetermined; that is, the convergence of many related feelings and associations determines the actual manifest content of the dream.

It is not known how much of the dream is organized during waking hours at the time some passing thought or perception is repressed and then unrolls during the night when conscious censorship is in abeyance, and how much is composed during sleep.† For example, the young woman's dream may be composed largely of repressed associations that unconsciously went

---

* The reader is referred to Chapter 7 of Freud's *Interpretation of Dreams* and Lecture 10 in *A General Introduction to Psychoanalysis*. A different approach to the topic can be found in Chapter 7 of Piaget's *Play, Dreams, and Imitation in Childhood*. Erich Fromm's *The Forgotten Language* presents still another approach to the understanding of dreams.

† Currently, there are indications that dreaming is an essential physiological process, carried out largely during those periods of sleep when rapid eye movements are going on (REM sleep); and consistently depriving the sleeper of just this phase of sleep by awakening him when his eyeballs are moving causes emotional disturbances (Fisher, 1965; West et al., 1962).

on at the time when she saw the attractive man and a fleeting thought of trying to meet him and seduce him was repressed.

Unconscious Processes and Behavior

Let us examine another example which can illustrate something of the influence of unconscious mentation upon behavior. A medical student becomes acutely anxious during a physiology seminar and feels forced to leave. While crossing a bridge on his way home he fears that he might throw himself off of it. His anxiety increases and he hastens to the university psychiatrist, who manages to see him immediately. When he relaxes in the psychiatrist's office and tries to remember just what had been happening when he became so apprehensive in the seminar, he recalls that he had been looking at a fold in his trousers. The position of the fold led him to fantasy that he had a very large penis, and he went on to daydream of future sexual conquests. Then, with a shift in his position, the fold disappeared and the anxiety started. The trivial occurrence assumed importance because of the student's particular life situation. He had been crippled in early childhood and used crutches. He had been engaged to marry but his fiancée had died during the preceding year. Because of his disability he found it difficult to form intimate relationships with girls, and he had felt very lonely and sexually frustrated since the death of his fiancée. He recognized that his feelings of physical inadequacy included concerns that his penis might be too small. The immediate reasons for the onset of the attack of anxiety when the fold in his trousers collapsed had been clarified, but in the next visit the student recalled a related episode that will serve to illustrate the workings of unconscious processes.

The incident that disturbed him had occurred a few months earlier while he was spending a weekend on a farm where he had previously vacationed on several occasions. While walking along a quiet road he had a transient vision, almost hallucinatory, of a bear coming out of the woods and menacing him. He fantasied defending himself with a crutch. When asked to give his associations to the occurrence without censoring them, he recalled that after his fiancée died he had spent a few weeks at this farm; and finding one of her handkerchiefs in his pocket he had, in a sentimental gesture, buried it precisely at the spot where he later had the vision of the bear. The psychiatrist, noting a similarity in the student's pronunciation of "bear" and "buried," simply commented that it seemed as though the buried had returned. The student then told of his despair after his girl's death, and thought perhaps he had tried to overcome his grief by burying the handker-chief. He then felt impelled to speak of another incident, even though he did not know why. It was about his last date with his fiancée. They had gone to dine in a Russian restaurant which, he suddenly remembered, displayed a Russian *bear* on its sign. After they had sat down, his friend had complained of a headache and he went out and bought her some Bayer aspirin. After dinner they had gone to the girl's apartment, petted, and he had been *embarrassed* by the extent of her passion; as the psychiatrist suggested, *embarrassed* at being "bare-assed." The student went on to tell how they had undressed completely for the first time and he had been embarrassed by his deformity. Although a great deal more emerged, includ-ing concerns that his paralysis had been a punishment for masturbation, and that his girl had become ill because of their sexual activities, the material conveys how a series of associations about a bear—Russian bear, Bayer aspirin, embarrassed, bare-assed, buried—had unconsciously been organized and reappeared as a single symbol of a threatening bear; a symbol which the reader may be able to grasp stood for an entire sequence of painful memories and which related to his current loneliness and depri-vation, as well as to the feelings of genital inadequacy that had triggered his anxiety attack.

In the above illustration, one might consider that there is a type of logic in the associations that converged in the bear symbol. It had to do with connecting up a series of episodes about which the student felt guilt and for which he may have felt that he required punishment. He had tended to exclude these painful memories of his fiancée from his consciousness, but they clearly had been troubling him, and they became associated with the feelings of physical and sexual inadequacy that he had momentarily sought to resolve through fantasy during his seminar.

Preconscious Primary Process Thinking

The material that is subjected to primary process thinking may not be repressed but may be simply preconscious—that is, out of the focus of consciousness. Thus, a student who was reading Freud for the first time became convinced of the importance of unconscious mental activity by two episodes that happened in rapid succession while he was reading about unconscious determinants of behavior. Following an example in the book (Freud, 1901), he asked his roommate to say the first number that came to mind. He wished to see whether he could learn why his friend had selected that particular number. The roommate promptly said, "Forty-three," but insisted that he could offer no ideas why he had made this random selection. The student of Freud, however, said that he believed he could follow the reasons and wondered whether his roommate had actually had the thoughts he now attributed to him. He reminded his friend that half an hour earlier, the last time they had spoken, he had told his roommate that he had just mailed a dollar bill to a friend to whom he had lost a seventy-five-cent bet on a football game. Had his roommate not thought, "Why are you sending a dollar, four quarters instead of the three that you owe him?" His surmise was correct, for his roommate had thought just that. The second episode that impressed the student occurred a few minutes later. His roommate had asked him to check a letter he had written to a book dealer in Germany with whom he was having a dispute over a bill. He had found his roommate's German letter grammatically correct except for the closing phrase. His roommate had intended to write "*Hoch Achtungsvoll,*" meaning "(with) great respect," but inadvertently had written "*Hoch Verachtungsvoll,*" or "(with) great contempt," which of course came closer to expressing his actual feelings.

Primary process mental activity is not pathological or even less useful than the secondary process. It not only helps assure attention to basic needs by transmitting drives to the thought processes, but we are dependent upon such unconscious and preconscious types of thinking for much of our creativity. If persons cannot trust their unconscious, they can have little spontaneity, intuition, or empathy. Not only does artistic creativity rely heavily upon primary process organization,* but problem solving can also occur without conscious awareness. Thus, the mathematician Poincaré (1956) described how he resolved problems concerning Fuchsian functions that had defied his conscious abilities only after he had ceased trying. The answer came into his mind when he awoke in the morning; and subsequently another aspect resolved itself, so to speak, just as he was stepping onto a streetcar and was no longer consciously thinking of the problem. Awareness of problems can emerge in dreams in symbolic form, and answers to intellectual problems sometimes appear.† Some matters, such as with whom one falls in love, depend upon decisions that include factors

---

* Friedrich Schiller, in response to a friend's complaints of his (the friend's) lack of creativity, warned the friend that he would never be truly creative, rather than a critic, because he could not remove the guards at the gates of his consciousness.

† I am, of course, not referring to the selection of race horse bets through the use of dream books, but rather to such things as Kekulé's discovery of the formula for the benzene ring in a dream of two snakes each with the other's tail in his mouth.

that never even enter consciousness, as will be elucidated when we consider marital choice (Chapter 13).

The child relies upon primary process thinking far more than the adult, and the differentiation between the primary and secondary processes is not as yet so clearly drawn. Children are more intuitive in their likes and dislikes, more spontaneous in their decision making, and closer to their infantile experiences. The closing of the oedipal period does not suddenly block off access to ideas and feelings that are more clearly drive derivatives. As children grow older, just what material must be denied access to consciousness depends upon the nature of the superego injunctions and also upon the need to repress or exclude impulses that interfere with adaptive tasks. The screening or censorship occurs unconsciously and employs the various mechanisms of defense. Just how this sorting out occurs cannot be answered properly, but what answers can be given require consideration of the mental mechanisms of defense.

ANXIETY AND THE MECHANISM OF DEFENSE

Children experience anxiety and depressive feelings which are extremely unpleasant. They seek means of preventing the recurrence of such feelings. Anxiety and depression both contain physiological components. Alterations in bodily function that accompany anxiety or depression serve as warning signals. For example, the slight speeding of the heart or the tightening of muscles that accompanies fear or anxiety unconsciously becomes a signal. The warning signal throws a switch, so to speak, and unconsciously one or more mechanisms of defense are brought into operation that serve to alter the perception of the danger or block out some temptation. When the warning signals an external danger, the person becomes alert and may take measures to counter the danger. Properly speaking, an external danger evokes fear, not anxiety.* However, as so much of anxiety derives from internal danger—that is, from the danger that the person will give way to a forbidden desire—many defenses serve to block out awareness of the impulse, memory, or potentially dangerous train of associations.

---

* Soldiers in combat properly experience fear. When they can no longer tolerate the situation—the fear, deprivation, hostility to officers, etc.—they may begin to wish to be finished with it, even by letting themselves get killed. The real danger is then within the self and a soldier becomes *anxious,* and may then experience heightened danger by "projecting" the inner danger on to the enemy.

The use of a fragment of the physiological effects of anxiety as a warning is termed "signal anxiety." It takes effect without conscious awareness, and to some extent it is a matter of conditioning.

The mechanisms of defense are varied: some block out memories of disturbing experiences; some prevent the linkage of memories or experiences that would become disturbing if connected; some prevent emotions from linking with experience; some alter the perception of a drive or wish; some transform the drive into a form more acceptable to the superego (A. Freud, 1936). Certain mechanisms of defense are more common in childhood than other, more sophisticated defenses. An examination of some of the more significant mechanisms will serve to illustrate how profoundly they can affect thought, behavior, and personality development.

Repression, by which a drive or forbidden impulse is barred from consciousness, has already been discussed. It includes the barring or banishment of memories, perceptions, or feelings that would arouse the forbidden. Thus, in order to prevent rearousal of some childhood sexual experience or the discomfort of remembering sexual desires for a parent, the entire period of early childhood may be repressed. Repression is unconscious in contrast to suppression, which concerns conscious efforts to keep memories or feelings from intruding. Repression has been considered a central mechanism of defense and, in a sense, the cause of the "dynamic unconscious," which theoretically is composed of repressed materials. Repression often requires the collaboration of other defenses to maintain its effectiveness.

Isolation is another basic defense that we have noted in connection with the separation of childhood fantasies from the remainder of consciousness. Material may be available in consciousness but it does not become linked up with other associations, at least not with material that would arouse anxiety. Thus, in the story of the young man, the memory of burying the handkerchief had not been repressed, but it had been isolated from memories of other experiences that would have brought painful memories of his last evening with his fiancée. It is not always clear whether something has been isolated or repressed.

Regression has also been noted. It can be considered a mechanism of defense in which the child falls back to an earlier phase of development at which he or she felt secure—in particular, secure in being cared for and having others assume responsibility for the child. Some use of regression is a normal aspect of development—the falling back to regain security after overreaching for greater independence. It starts very early in life and is a major childhood adaptive technique. It can be anticipated in all persons who become physically ill and are no longer capable of taking care of themselves. It is almost a necessary accompaniment of placing oneself in the hands of a physician, and therefore it is important that all physicians recognize the phenomenon of regression and take it into account in caring for patients. Sick persons can readily be misjudged, for they are often more childish, petulant, demanding, than when well. Further, regression is so tempting and so thoroughly patterned in childhood that many patients try to counter their tendencies to regress by refusing to become properly dependent when ill; and, conversely, an inability to overcome such regressions and again face the problems of living often complicates recovery. Regression to childhood stages of development is a major source of psychopathology.

Fantasy formation has already been adequately discussed as a major adaptive mechanism and defense of childhood. Creative fantasy is usually an asset and may prepare the child for future reality-oriented behavior as well as dull the pain of reality. Of course, some children will turn their backs on reality to a degree that interferes with adaptation. When it becomes a strong mechanism of defense, fantasy is accompanied by isolation.

Sublimation is often considered to be a more sophisticated defense. The original meaning was borrowed from chemistry—the transformation of a solid into a gas without its going through a liquid state—and connoted the unconscious alteration of a drive into something more sublime such as poesy. However, it now has a much broader connotation. Sublimation is an essential part of a child's development. The child redirects drives and wishes into more acceptable channels but still has some outlet for them, as when aggression toward a sibling is transmuted into hammering on a toy, or when a wish to smear feces finds an outlet in finger painting. One might even say that a prizefighter who recognized in therapy that he had sworn as a child to beat his father to a pulp, had sublimated his aggression into a socially acceptable channel. Since the advent of psychoanalytic ego psychology the term *neutralization* has become important. It concerns the neutralization of a libidinal or aggressive charge with some counterenergy, thus permitting it to be used in the service of adaptation or intellectual functioning. The term bears a close relationship to sublimation. The concept of neutralization is useful and necessary only to those psychologists who are conceptualizing vicissitudes of libidinal energies. The cathexis of libido is neutralized by a *countercathexis*, and is then free for use for more constructive purposes.

Denial simply refers to the ability to deny the existence of something disturbing, such as one's own anger or sexual feelings. Children may insist that they are *not* angry, and we have noted the tendency and ability of a little boy to deny that creatures without penises exist. Most commonly it is a denial of one's own responsibility with *projection* of blame onto a parent or another child. *Reaction formation* may accompany denial: an unacceptable feeling is turned into its opposite. The jealousy and hate of the newborn sibling may be *denied, undone,* and turned into its opposite. Reaction formation is apparent in individuals who turn anal impulses into overtidiness or scrupulous cleanliness.

Projection and *introjection* are defenses that are particularly important in personality development and character formation. Projection concerns the attribution to another of one's own impulses or wishes. A little boy, for example, cannot accept or tolerate his feelings of hostility for a brother but instead believes that the brother is hostile to him. The defense is related to the physiological efforts to rid the body of something harmful as by vomiting or defecating—and, indeed, vomiting can symbolically represent efforts to be rid of an unacceptable feeling or wish. Projection is a complicated defense that enters into much of psychopathology and cannot be discussed adequately here.* The following is a clear-cut example of psychotic projection. A young soldier kept hearing a voice threatening "I'll kill you." At times he believed that a specific friend was threatening him. In therapy he recalled that he had started hearing the voice when his "buddy" had left him and become pals with another youth. Then his own inner voice had said, "Say I'm your best friend or I'll kill you." His homicidal impulse was untenable to him, and the threat was turned against himself by projection and the friend he wished to threaten seemed to become the one who did the threatening.

Introjection, which is related to identification, has more to do with the defense against disillusionment in a needed person. Children not only need their parents but need good parents. They may blame themselves, or attribute to themselves a parental trait, in order to preserve the worth of the needed love object, or object of his identification. In simplified terms, the child says, "It is not his fault, Father is not bad; I am." Or it may go, "They are not hostile to me, they do not take care of me because I am hostile to them, or because I am worthless."

Personality Constriction

There are many other mechanisms of defense, some of which will be presented in specific contexts in later chapters. It is important, however, to

---

* The use of projection can also indicate that a person has failed to establish adequate "ego boundaries," and still is unclear about what originates within the self and what originates in others. A child who is close to the original symbiotic tie with the mother will be apt to blame her for what upsets the child or what goes wrong with what the child plans—and it is not particularly pathological in a child.

note the more sweeping result of overstrict superego controls. The rigid restrictions imposed on a child by parents can become self-delimitations that require *constriction* of the personality and many defenses to maintain. The restrictions lead the child to *constrict* thoughts, feelings, activities in order to continue to feel desirable. Such children may be very good, overly good, but their inner lives become impoverished. The constriction usually occurs gradually and unconsciously. Children may grow up in homes in which parents believe that such overconformity and denial of impulses are the only proper way. However, occasionally constriction is more or less purposeful and seems the only means of preserving equilibrium and equanimity. Thus, a college girl who had grown up in a seriously disturbed home in which her parents were in constant discord, and whose only sibling had become psychotic, appeared to be reasonably well adjusted. However, she had given up having many friends, used few of her assets, and consciously strove to maintain acceptable relationships with both of her parents. She had taught herself not to think about her feelings toward her parents as well as never to express them, and indeed she had learned never to think back and recall disturbing events that had occurred during the day. She had learned that she could not tolerate having feelings, for they were almost always painful, nor could she have memories that would be certain to arouse hostility or despair. She maintained her emotional equilibrium but at the price of a relatively impoverished personality.

Mechanisms of Defense and Distortions of Perception

The various mechanisms of defense which we have been discussing may seem very complicated and beyond the capacities of a small child. In some respects we have outdistanced our slowly developing children in seeking to describe the organization of their personalities. Still, four- or five-year-olds commonly experience considerable anxiety, particularly at night, when wolves and tigers invade their dreams and projected hostilities harrow their fantasies. These problems are within the child who requires mental mechanisms to counter them. The various defenses help the child to maintain equanimity and prevent the intrusion of forbidden, unacceptable, or otherwise disturbing impulses and ideas into consciousness. In the process they limit and distort the perception of reality. They change the view of the self, of motives, and of the significant others, and thereby can create difficulties in adaptation. However, some degree of self-deception is probably necessary for survival. As Goethe reputedly wrote, "who destroys illusion in himself and in others, nature punishes tyrannically." As the same defenses or combinations of defenses tend to be used repeatedly by the same person, the defenses contribute to determining personality types and character. Whereas they help provide stability, they also create problems and foster some degree of neurotic behavior in everyone.

We have been reviewing how children's personalities became organized within the shelter of their families, and have been considering constructs useful in discussing personality functioning. Now children are about to enter school; new important influences will enter into shaping their personalities, and they will build upon structures already organized within the family. Children's abilities to function in new environments and the ways in which they will utilize what they encounter depend upon the emotional security and the intellectual equipment they have gained in the home. Although their parents will still provide, guide, and remain major formative influences for many years, children have by now become sufficiently well integrated to emerge into less sheltered environments and expand their horizons. They have achieved something of a self-concept (Mead, 1934) through reacting to and internalizing the attitudes of family members to each of them, but such concepts of the self are limited because they derive largely from interactions with parents in intrafamilial situations. Ego functions have developed along with linguistic and cognitive growth; and they have gained sufficient experience to begin to appreciate that others have somewhat different ways, including ways of understanding and believing, that must be taken into account in relating to others. They have completed their primary socialization and can control or contain wishes for sensuous gratification and outbursts of aggressivity. They are helped by their internalizations of parental standards and dictates which guide them when parents are not about, and by their identifications with parents. Concomitantly, cognitive and emotional development has been channeled into appreciation of what they can consciously perceive, recall, and think about —in part in order to maintain parental approbation and their own self-esteem, and in part because the language and the parents have conveyed what is taboo, what is inconsequential, what can be noted, and what it is vital to perceive.

The psychoanalytic "structural concept," which divides the personality into id, ego, and superego; the "topographic concept," which divides mental functioning into conscious, preconscious, and unconscious processes; and a presentation of various mental mechanisms of defense have been utilized in modified form to summarize the integrative processes. These concepts contain various shortcomings, whether they are presented in classical form or as modified in this chapter,* but they provide useful constructs for conceptualizing and discussing the inordinately complex process of integration; and the literature on personality development and functioning is scarcely intelligible unless the reader is familiar with them.

REFERENCES

ARLOW, J. A., and BRENNER, C. (1964). "Psychoanalytic Concepts and the Structural Theory," *Journal of the American Psychoanalytic Monograph Series*, No. 13. International Universities Press, New York.

FISHER, C. (1965). "Psychoanalytic Implications of Recent Research on Sleep and Dreaming," *Journal of the American Psychoanalytic Association*, 13:197–303.

FREUD, A. (1936). *The Ego and the Mechanisms of Defence*. C. Baines, trans. International Universities Press, New York, 1946.

FREUD, S. (1900). "The Interpretation of Dreams," in *The Standard Edition of the Complete Psychological Works of Sigmund Freud*, vols. 4 and 5. Hogarth Press, London, 1953.

————. (1901). "The Psychopathology of Everyday Life," in *The Standard Edition of the Complete Psychological Works of Sigmund Freud*, vol. 6. Hogarth Press, London, 1953.

————. (1916–1917). *A General Introduction to Psychoanalysis*. Boni & Liveright, New York.

FROMM, E. (1951). *The Forgotten Language: An Introduction to the Understanding of Dreams, Fairy Tales, and Myths*. Rinehart, New York.

GILL, M. (1963). "Topography and Systems in Psychoanalytic Theory," *Psychological Issues*, vol. 3, no. 2, Monograph 10. International Universities Press, New York.

GOETHE, J. W. VON (1782). "Die Natur," in *Schriften über die Natur*, pp. 15–17. Alfred Kröner Verlag, Leipzig, n.d.

LEACH, E. (1964). "Anthropological Aspects of Language: Animal Categories and Verbal Abuses," in *New Directions in the Study of Language*. E. H. Lenneberg, ed. MIT Press, Cambridge, Mass.

LOEWALD, H. (1962). "The Superego and the Ego-Ideal: II. Superego and Time," *International Journal of Psycho-Analysis*, 43:264–268.

MEAD, G. H. (1934). *Mind, Self and Society: From the Standpoint of a Social Behaviorist*. University of Chicago Press, Chicago.

PIAGET, J. (1962). *Play, Dreams, and Imitation in Childhood*. C. Gattengo and F. M. Hodgson, trans. W. W. Norton, New York.

POINCARÉ, H. (1956). "Mathematical Creation," in *The World of Mathematics*, vol. 4. J. R. Newman, ed. Simon & Schuster, New York.

RAPAPORT, D. (1960). "The Structure of Psychoanalytic Theory: A Systematizing Attempt," *Psychological Issues*, vol. 2, no. 2, Monograph No. 6. International Universities Press, New York.

SCHACHTEL, E. (1959). "Memory and Childhood Amnesia," in *Metamorphosis: On the Development of Affect, Perception, Attention, and Memory*. Basic Books, New York.

WEST, L., JANSZEN, H., LESTER, B., and CORNELISON, JR., F. (1962). "The Psychosis of Sleep Deprivation," *Annals of the New York Academy of Science*, 96:66–70.

* Three efforts to clarify psychoanalytic theory by leading psychoanalytic theoreticians serve to highlight the basic inconsistencies of psychoanalytic theory and the need for its thorough reorganization. See D. Rapaport (1960), M. M. Gill (1963), and J. Arlow and C. Brenner (1964).

SUGGESTED READING

BRENNER, C. (1955). *An Elementary Textbook of Psychoanalysis,* 2nd ed. International Universities Press, New York.

FREUD, A. (1936). *The Ego and the Mechanisms of Defence.* C. Baines, trans. International Universities Press, New York, 1946.

FREUD, S. (1900). "The Interpretation of Dreams," in *The Standard Edition of the Complete Psychological Works of Sigmund Freud,* vols. 4 and 5. Hogarth Press, London, 1953.

———. (1901). "The Psychopathology of Everyday Life," in *The Standard Edition of the Complete Psychological Works of Sigmund Freud,* vol. 6. Hogarth Press, London, 1953.

PIAGET, J. (1962). *Play, Dreams, and Imitation in Childhood.* C. Gattengo and F. M. Hodgson, trans. W. W. Norton, New York.

CHAPTER 9

❀

The Juvenile

THE CHILD'S DEPARTURE for school marks a long-awaited day. The mother turns her child over to the teacher at the classroom door or to the school bus driver, and breathes deeply to lighten the heaviness in her chest. She feels that she has handed her baby over to the world; she can no longer protect and offer her child guidance during the hours the child is away from home. Schoolchildren must manage on the integration they have achieved during the preceding years, and on the security they feel awaits them at home, which will still remain the center of their lives. The children are buoyed by pride in joining the schoolchildren and leaving the "babies" at home. They enter the classroom, where each feels somewhat lost among so many strange children, uneasy over the unfamiliar procedures and uncertain as they seek to follow the directions given by a strange woman. When the novelty wears off, some may decide that life at home was preferable.

THE CRUCIAL ISSUES OF THE JUVENILE PERIOD

The entrance into school is symbolic of the crucial issues of the period. Children now move into the world beyond the home and must begin to find their places in it, and in so doing their self-concepts, value systems, and cognitive capacities change. The equilibrium children gained at the closing of the oedipal period as they found their positions within their families is disrupted when they move off to school, where they will be judged on their merits, and into the neighborhood peer group, where they must find a place on their own. Neither the classroom nor the peer group forms a completely new environment. Most children have attended kindergarten, if not nursery school, and have played with children in the neighborhood. But new expectations accompany the role of schoolchild. They are no longer just children within their families but representatives of their families, and their parents would like to be proud of them. Children compare themselves with classmates and playmates and wish to measure up and be proud of themselves. A critical aspect of the transition concerns the shift from ascribed to achieved acceptance and status.

Within the family, the child's position was determined largely by biological determinants: each was a member of the childhood generation of a given sex, age, and sequential position. Basically, each was loved or accepted because he or she was his or her parents' child. In school and with peers it matters little that the child is a younger or older sibling, or a much loved or neglected child, except as such factors have influenced the child's personality and behavior. As part of a group of children of the same age, the child is often treated as part of the collectivity rather than with the individualized attention to which each became accustomed at home. The child must forgo many desires and mask idiosyncrasies in order to fit into the group. The teacher has an obligation to evaluate children on the basis of their achievement and, eventually, according to impersonal scales. Both in school and in the neighborhood confreres are rivals—sometimes harsh judges who are more likely to rub salt than salve in emotional wounds. In these altered circumstances, in these new environments, and in relation to new significant figures, the children's personalities will undergo considerable reorganization and they will develop new abilities to prepare themselves to live within the larger society rather than simply within a family.

Psychoanalytic psychology has relatively little to offer concerning the critical aspects of the period. Classic analytic theory considers the *latency period* a time of transition and consolidation between the closing of the oedipal period and the onset of puberty. Freud postulated that a biologically determined subsidence of libidinal drives or their effective repression permitted a period of relative calm. However, even as there is no evidence of a physiologically determined increase in sexual drive in the oedipal child, there is no reason to believe that a diminution in sexual drive occurs and accounts for the critical aspects of the latency period. There is little if any evidence that children have less impulsion to masturbation or that their sexual curiosity diminishes appreciably. However, children have come to terms with their positions in their families, repressed their sensuous desires for the mother, and internalized controls. Such repression of erotic interests may free energy for learning, as psychoanalytic theory postulates, or new experiences may stimulate children's cognitive appetites in accord with Piagetian theory. In any case, they will now be investing their interests outside the family, in peers and in learning. With their attachments divided between parents, teachers, and peers, and with their many new interests, there is often less turmoil at home. Then, too, children have completed their primary socialization and are less preoccupied with bodily functions, and require and obtain less sensuous gratification from their parents.

Many psychoanalysts have recognized the need to reconceptualize this developmental period and its importance in personality development. Harry Stack Sullivan (1953), in particular, placed considerable emphasis upon the juvenile period and particularly on the importance of children's finding their places in the peer group and in forming a close relationship with a "chum." He emphasized, too, that a relationship with a chum or some significant adult other than the parents could rescue a child from destructive intrafamilial influences.

Erikson (1950) has considered the development of a *sense of industry* the crucial theme of late childhood. Unless children acquire a sense of industry they develop pervasive *feelings of inferiority and inadequacy*. We can further recognize that the trait of industry is encompassed on the one side by the danger of habitual compulsive striving to excel in competition, and, on the other, by defeatist trends seen in an unwillingness to accept and face meaningful challenges. As striving to excel competitively is a highly valued American characteristic, its pathological aspects are readily overlooked.*

There are, however, other character traits that appear to have their roots in this period of life, and if not implanted firmly during it will never come to blossom. One is the *sense of belonging*, the assurance a child gains of being an accepted and integral part of the group and of the broader society,

---

* Ruth Benedict (1934) astutely realized that there may exist in every culture a group of abnormals who represent the extreme development of the favored cultural type, and whom the society supports in their furthest aberrations rather than exposing them. They are given license which they may exploit endlessly—yet from the point of view of another culture or another time in history they are considered the most bizarre of the psychopathic types of the period. One of the wealthiest men in the world, for example lived in total isolation because of a pathological fear of contamination and yet relentlessly sought after still greater wealth and power that could in no way improve his miserable life.

in contrast to feeling like an outsider. It involves more than social ease or anxiety; it concerns an identification with the society in which a person lives and a commitment to its values and ethics. Serious alienation usually reflects the transference of distrust of parents to the broader society, and although it usually becomes apparent during adolescence, it often has clear-cut precursors in a child's ways of acting in school and in relating to peers. A *sense of responsibility* must also develop at this stage. It involves a willingness and capacity to live up to the expectations one has aroused. It is insufficient for children to learn the technical skills and knowledge required to conduct their life tasks, for unless they can be relied upon their skills are of little value to their fellow citizens. To gain approbation, children need to be trustworthy in the sense of being reliable rather than simply honest. Traits such as a sense of belonging and of responsibility are also basic to the quality of *leadership*. It is now, in finding their places among peers, that children begin to assume their places in society. A child learns that he or she can lead and is expected to lead; that one is a supporter who helps the leader, or simply a follower, or one who is habitually alienated or rebellious. The child places the self in part, and in part is placed by others.

In finding their places in a society of peers, and through being evaluated by adults, by schoolmates and playmates, children develop more adequate evaluations of themselves than when relating primarily to family members, and form self concepts that serve to regulate their ambitions and ways of relating to others. The ego, so to speak, contemplates and evaluates the self, but in so doing the ego is considering the reactions of others to the self.* A boy, for example, realizes that some hold him in esteem and seek him as a friend, as a member of a team, as a birthday party guest. He evaluates who likes him and who avoids him and he notes how others respond to his critiques of these persons, and gains an evaluation of himself in the process. He recognizes that teachers praise his work, give him responsibilities, or consider him a dullard or a nonentity. He is learning who he is, and he is simultaneously learning his society's value system.

In the several environments in which school-age children live—the home, schoolroom, neighborhood play group—they begin to take on new sets of values and begin to view their social worlds from different perspectives, moving beyond the egocentric and family-centered orientations of

---

* G. H. Mead (1934) differentiates between the "I" and the "me" in his presentation of how a self concept arises through social transactions and recognition of how others evaluate the self. It is of interest that Josiah Royce also emphasized how we achieve self-knowledge only through contrasting ourselves in many ways with other selves—in other words, how self-consciousness depends on social contrasts.

early childhood. As we shall examine later in this chapter, the decline in egocentricity is of paramount importance to both the child's cognitive and ethical development.

Thus, even though the juvenile period has received little attention in classic psychoanalytic developmental theory, and few aside from Sullivan and educational psychologists have emphasized its importance, we shall here consider the critical significance of these years. It may be useful to realize that in most countries, though not in the United States, the sorting out of students for higher education occurs before adolescence, and thus children's personalities and performances in the grade school years will have a decisive influence upon their future lives.

THE EXPANDING ENVIRONMENT

As this chapter is concerned with a half-dozen years, we cannot describe with conciseness the change from kindergarten tot who has difficulty in differentiating play and fantasy from reality to junior high school boy or girl. Although at five and six the children's groups still are composed of both sexes engaged in playing "house" or "store" and in such activities as hide-and-seek and roller skating, between the ages of seven and eleven the two sexes are more completely separated than at any other time of life. Boys and girls may live as if in different worlds, coming together only within the home and in school.

The children's environments vary greatly and accordingly influence their way of life differently. Life is different on farms, in suburbs, and in the city, but it is almost always lived with playmates. The social environment may consist of a few girls caring for pets and riding their horses, or boys who get together when finished with farm chores to swim, play baseball at the town center, or turn the barn loft into a fortress. Or it may be a host of kids on a city street, seemingly a mixture of all ages and both sexes, but who are divided into subgroups within this agglomeration, and who, amidst the traffic of passers-by and cars, are in a world of their own, excluding adults from their awareness.

These years are often recalled as being among the happiest periods of life, particularly when the home is stable and relationships with parents are not a source of concern; but even when they are not, children can often forget their domestic woes while with their friends. It is a golden period of freedom marred only by school, when hours can be spent with friends away from adult interference. Children have become sufficiently independent to be on their own, exploring new interests and moving into real or imaginary ventures while burdened with few responsibilities. The parents still provide for their essential needs and furnish a haven in the home to which they can return when frustrated by their companions. Still, these years also encompass many woes—feelings of rejection by the group, the desertion of a best friend, the embarrassment caused by parents, the difficulties at school, the failures to be chosen for a team or a party—as well as the more significant anxieties caused by realization of parents' limitations as sources of protection.

THE SOCIETY OF PLAYMATES

Within the group of childhood companions many essential traits develop and many of the patterns for social living are learned or consolidated. Here, too, children are weaned from home, learning to feel comfortable and secure while interdependent with peers. The society of playmates has a socializing influence as a subculture of its own. It is not a haphazard assemblage of children occupied with random activities. It is a subculture with mores that are transmitted relatively independently of either the family or the school, passed on from one age group to the next in a constant succession and with a turnover that is much more rapid than the generational cycle of the family. Each child remains in the juvenile period for about a half-dozen years, and is replaced by another. There is constant movement of individuals into and out of the age group. The ways of the subculture are learned from the older children by the neophytes who hang on the periphery of the group, later assume fill-in roles, and then become members who gain increasing importance and responsibility over the next few years. The age roles are fairly well set and afford an opportunity to each child according to ability, and acceptance according to worth to the peer group. The task of learning how to get along with the group and be evaluated on one's own merits sets a very real challenge to the child.

Childhood peer-group activities and mores may remain more stable over generations than the mores of the larger society, and they are a force for conservatism. It is known that some games, and probably the customs that accompany them, go back to antiquity. The checkerboards and marble holes used by Roman children can be found scratched into stone floors in the Roman Forum. Two paintings by Breughel show sixteenth-century children engaged in games most of which are readily recognized from their similarities to contemporary games. The jokes which each child thinks are new and hastens to tell to parents are usually much older than the parents. The child is engaged primarily in the task of learning to live with peers, and the world of the juvenile group may change less than the adult world.

The Separation of the Sexes

The division of children into separate gender groups may be instigated by boys more than by girls. The exclusion of girls from the boys' juvenile peer group serves to help the boy become more secure in his gender identity and his masculine role. He is overcoming his dependency upon his mother but he is also divesting himself of residua of his identification with her and countering whatever envy he may have of the girl's prerogatives, particularly her socially ascribed right to remain more dependent.* He adopts a contemptuous attitude toward girls and whatever is girlish. He convinces himself that being a girl is something he would want less than anything else. Indeed, there may be nothing he fears more—nothing that he fears wishing more because the wish is not far from the surface. Repressing such wishes into the unconscious is one task of the "latency" period. He does not reject all girls; girls who behave as boys—that is, who act out their wishes to be boys—may be acceptable to him, for they reinforce the idea that no one would wish to be a girl. Still, he is very likely to feel attracted to girls—in secret—or at least to a particular girl, and finds roundabout ways of gaining her admiration.

The exclusion of the opposite sex is, however, not a one-sided matter. Both boys and girls are likely to feel at ease with and admire others who are more like the self. Both boys and girls who have siblings of the opposite sex who are close to them in age are usually freer to associate and play with agemates of the opposite sex. Then, too, as girls do not need to differentiate so completely from the mother and are likely to have stronger affectional ties to the father, they tend to remain closer to the home and become less rebellious than boys. They will, perhaps in retaliation, become

* Further, in order to achieve the capability of eventually taking care of a wife— even if not, as in the past, assuming a more dominant role in relation to a wife—the boy begins to assert his independence of women.

scornful of boys' boisterous behavior and reject them as smelly and dirty. They, too, must convince themselves that they would not wish to be boys.

Girls' Activities

Girls tend to spend more of their free time at home than boys, and may remain closer to their parents. While the society of children is important to them, the groups tend to remain small and the relationships more personal and intimate than group oriented. As the play of the two sexes differentiates, hop scotch, rope jumping, and jacks seem to be the prerogatives of girls. They do not tend to participate in group sports as much except under supervision; but basketball, field hockey, and soft ball can arouse great interest and enthusiasm and competitiveness in them as they grow older. Still, skating, riding, swimming, and other such activities, which are less team oriented, seem to be preferred. A significant part of young girls' play, in contrast to that of boys, bears a relationship to future activities. Play with dolls and at sewing and cooking is apt to turn into similar real activities around the home as years pass. The girl tries on mother's dresses, jewelry, and makeup, pretending to be grown. Girls also may become enamored of horses and horseback riding, sometimes developing a passionate interest in one horse: they seem to enjoy the feeling of power that comes with a sense of unity with the animal as well as the erotic stimulation of riding. As the girl passes ten and is almost prepubertal, desires for intimacy with other girls increase. Cliques that are formalized into clubs or secret societies afford opportunities to exchange knowledge or fantasies about menstruation, sex, and crushes. The approaching changes in physique and physiological functioning can be faced more securely when fears and hopes are shared. Now a girl may have a need for almost constant companionship. She may leave her girl friends after several hours of chatter but find that by the time she reaches home there is so much to say that she must continue on the telephone. Girls usually remain closer to the home than boys and find a prime interest in people and their interactions. Their value systems remain more like that of their parents. The girl may feel that her mother is her best friend. Her self-image depends greatly upon her girl friends' evaluations of her, but it will develop more definitely later in relation to boys. Some girls will become boyish for a time, and gain acceptance by the boys and inclusion in their games. Boys, in contrast, rarely participate in girls' games. The boyishness and the desire to be accepted by boys because of prowess at their sports usually fade in the prepubertal period, when the girl begins to desire a different type of acceptance from boys. Sometimes, of course, the tomboyish behavior reflects profound dissatisfaction with being female and forebodes serious gender-identity problems. A girl who learned to relate to boys as another boy eventually found herself married to a man who was unconsciously seeking a close relationship with another man, and who insisted that she go on extreme diets and exercise regularly to make her figure more masculine.

Girls today can still be very feminine when their competitive fantasies of becoming a figure-skating or tennis champion can lead to hours of practice each day in the search for fame, wealth, and the admiration of millions. Such fantasies concern personal achievement rather than simply gaining fame and admiration because of beauty or charm.

Boys' Activities

As boys move beyond hide-and-seek and other games shared with girls, they rather typically play "cowboys and Indians," which will turn into "cops and robbers" and various types of military games. They have a passionate interest in marbles, kite flying, bike riding, simple ball games; and then they begin to play games such as baseball, basketball, and football with poorly organized teams, countless fights about rules, arguments about cheating, and lopsided scores. Hours indoors are spent playing checkers, cards, and other games or in constructing models and collecting almost anything. There is the fondness for wrestling and body contact; the dares to fight, the chip on the shoulder; the avoidance of the bully, the teasing of the poor sport. There are the quarrels between friends who will never talk to one another again but seek one another out within the day. There is the boasting, the importance of winning, the complete exhaustion by bedtime. As they near the end of the period they may tend to form into larger groups that resemble gangs in order to have sufficient members to form real teams.

The term "gang" often has a bad connotation to parents. It conveys a vision of gang fights on city streets; of stealing, gambling, and narcotics peddlers. However, except in delinquent neighborhoods the gang is not an antisocial influence, nor does it provide a chaotic environment. It has organization and rules and customs which have been transmitted by the juvenile subculture and which somehow are suited to the specific society to which the subculture belongs. Partly because of the erroneous conception of the children's peer groups conveyed by the term "gang," adults often seek to minimize peer-group influences by organizing Cub Scouts and Boy Scouts, and baseball teams supervised by adults in competitive leagues. Parents may send their children to private schools primarily to have them engage in the supervised play in the afternoons. Some supervision can be helpful, particularly in activities that require adult direction such as scouting or sailing, and there can be a pressing need for proper guidance in disorganized neighborhoods where children may readily come under delinquent influences; or a need for substitute father figures or "big brothers" for boys who lack fathers. However, it is very important for peer groups to work out their own hierarchy and to set their own standards of behavior, learn to handle fights, deal with cheaters, and cope with less adaptable children. It is here that children gradually work out patterns of social interaction free from adult authority.* They will make mistakes but they gain essential experience. It is here that they learn who they are, independently of adult evaluations.

There is the good life of the protected and happy child, both boy and girl, but there are other lives that children lead as well. There is the slum child who returns to the empty flat after school with an empty stomach and an empty heart, who then ventures forth to find some companionship, looking at shop windows, snitching fruit from a stand, sharing a cigarette with a friend. There is the child of the migratory sugarbeet worker who never goes to any one school for more than a term, lives in a trailer or a series of shacks supplied by the farms, and works in the fields with parents to help eke out a livelihood. There are the black children who must watch that they not overstep a thousand intangible boundaries and who are having inferiority woven into them. And then, of course, there are the children who for emotional reasons cannot move beyond the family into the peer group and remain very much to themselves, lonely and embittered.

THE DEVELOPING SELF-CONCEPT

The manner in which juveniles gain a clearer concept of the self in peer groups or neighborhood gangs is complicated and often subtle. They learn to see themselves as others see them and often according to rather relent-

---

* The recent trend fostered by women's liberation groups to insist that girls be permitted to participate in sports such as juvenile baseball leagues organized for boys is a questionable maneuver. The tendency of boys to get away from girls at this age seems, as we have noted, to be an important part of the process of gaining a male identity and overcoming wishes to be female. Further, as girls mature more rapidly, they will, for a time, have a height and weight advantage. The notable tendency of fathers to be the major competitors in such juvenile leagues is also unfortunate. Many fathers act and feel disgraced if their young sons strike out or make errors in a baseball game, making such competition more a source of anguish than fun for the boy.

less standards. As we shall examine, at this age children have rigid standards of what is right and wrong, for they consider ethical values as fixed rather than suited to the circumstances, and believe individuals should be judged according to egalitarian standards and punished in an expiatory manner. The peer group has standards of what makes a good companion and a good member. They are based upon the achievements and attitudes of the child and they are not concerned with exonerating reasons. At this age the children are concerned with how good a playmate or companion another makes, not with the reasons why she is or why he is not. Important to the group are loyalty; a willingness to compromise and not insist on having one's own way; being a good "sport" in defeat; being able to keep a secret; not being a "bully" who picks on smaller or weaker children; not being a "sorehead" who quits when decisions go against one, or a "crybaby" who runs home for parental help when teased or hit; not "snitching" even if a friend does something one thinks wrong. Honesty is a virtue, but the standards do not always agree with those of adults: "Finders keepers, losers weepers" is usually an acceptable guide for minor items; and "swiping" inexpensive objects from carts or chain stores, while considered dishonest, may not be deemed a real infraction by the older children. Such behavior is often a testing of limits, a response to taking a dare, a way of showing off; if one never goes beyond parental restrictions one is apt to be considered a "baby."

The threat of being called a "sissy," "baby," or "chicken" can force a child to take a dare in order to prove himself or herself to the gang. Children are in the process of learning what challenges they can accept without coming to physical harm or suffering moral discomfort. Exclusion from the group brings intense unhappiness to most children, and a child will often prefer ridicule to being ignored, and will be the low man on the totem pole rather than feel unwanted. A boy will wear such nicknames as "Stinky" or "Dopey" in order to belong.

Athletic prowess can be a very marked asset for both boys and girls; but the best athlete is not necessarily the leader. Even at this stage of life the leader must be able to forgo his or her own interests for those of the group, and be fair in rendering judgments in order to preserve intragroup harmony. Initiative, often requiring imagination, attracts other children, but boastfulness rather than action, and self-serving fabrications soon lose friends for a child. Reliability and responsibility—important assets in school—are also valued by the peer group, particularly when it reaches the stage of forming clubs and more permanent teams. Not only may such peer evaluations be of greater importance to the child than those of teachers, but peers may also be more perceptive than teachers of values that count in the long run.

Modification of Values

In these children's groups new sets of values are learned which may or may not fit with those of the family. The children now come into intimate contact with the value systems of friends. They enter other homes and see how they are conducted. They learn how friends are treated by their parents and note the different ways in which families behave and compare the differing degrees of calm or friction within other households to the atmosphere in their own homes. They acquire a basis on which they can judge their parents as individuals. Children may learn better to appreciate their own parents or may come to develop bitterness toward them, but these experiences permit them to develop a perspective and more realistic values and judgments. There is often a de-idealization of parents, and sometimes an idealization of friends' parents. After all, a friend's mother and father are unlikely to fight with one another when a visiting child is around.

There are limits to the broadening influences exerted by the child's "gang." As the peer group is usually formed in the neighborhood it is apt to be constituted of children from families who are relatively homogeneous economically and socially. The childhood peer groups thus continue to help pattern and prepare the child for the type of life expected from persons of a given family type. Even in heterogeneous neighborhoods children are surprisingly selective in the choice of companions, tending to pick friends who come from similar backgrounds and with similar levels of intelligence because they understand one another better. For such reasons the influence of the family upon the child's values is often difficult to differentiate from that of the peers. Still, the juvenile group has different ideals from those of the family, and children idealize new models whom they would like to emulate. One can say that the child's "ego ideal" becomes modified by incorporation of these new figures, or the term "ideal ego" can be used to signify the image of the person one would like to become. The new models are taken from life, TV, and books: the adolescent athlete in the neighborhood whom the child glorifies; the teacher, coach, scout leader, whose achievements or kindness make that person seem a more desirable model than a parent; the baseball hero or comedian one watches on TV; inventors, scientists, storybook heroes. A girl is likely to develop a crush on a teacher whom the girls all admire or on a girl friend of an older sibling who seems so glamorous. Occasionally one sees abrupt changes in a child's behavior when the boy or girl takes on a role as if donning a new garment and begins to act the part. More conventionally a boy will begin to eat and sleep baseball, insist on wearing the baseball cap and shirt, and mimic the gait of his hero, for this is a time of hero worship. The girl may assume the characteristics of a woman tennis star or the woman reporter on TV. The models are apt to disappear almost as rapidly as they are taken on, for the child is subject to the fads and whims of the group.

The Special Friend

At about the age of ten the center of the child's life moves from the group of peers to a special friend, the "chum" in Sullivan's terms, who is distinguished from all other friends by a special intonation when the child refers to "my friend" (Sullivan, 1953, pp. 227–262). It is an intense and important experience, for the relationship usually constitutes the child's first major realistic attachment outside of the family. The friend is of the same sex because sharing feelings and experiences with another and thereby achieving empathy can usually occur only with a person of the same sex at this age. The intimate exchange helps diminish feelings of uniqueness, enables each to learn how another person feels about and manages similar problems. It is an expansion of the self beyond one's own boundaries. There is a constant need to be with the chum, and an altruistic attitude develops in which the friend's welfare is almost as important as one's own.

The child begins to think in terms of "we" instead of "I" and thereby develops a sense of altruism. The special friends are likely to share many intimate thoughts and feelings, and thus learn how another feels about parents, crushes, disappointments. Girls are likely to become even more intimate than boys in exchanging experiences and feelings and real girl friends are likely to spend hours confiding romantic fantasies and talking on the phone about what they have learned about other girls. The friendship is the first movement toward intimacy that develops on the basis of common personality traits and ideals rather than through family relatedness. As psychoanalytic psychology has shown, this first close friendship contains homosexual components—a narcissistic quality of loving and sharing with someone like the self—but it is not an indication of homosexuality but of movement toward learning to relate intimately beyond the family. If a fixation occurs at this stage, it is more likely to indicate disturbances in the family relationships rather than that something is wrong in the friendship.

THE CLASSROOM AS A SOCIALIZING AGENCY

Whereas the peer groups' tasks of socializing children and influencing their moral values are informal, the school has the express function of teaching the children the knowledge and skills they will require in order to function as reasonably self-sufficient adults in society. It is a major socializing agency, taking over from the family and supplementing the family's functions. However, the school does not function simply through its expertise in educational matters. Because of the nature of the classroom as a social system, the school can carry out socializing functions different from those with which the parents are concerned, a process in which both teachers and classmates play a part (Parsons, 1959).

The Teacher's Role

The school serves as the first significant institution which differentiates children on the basis of achievement. The parents have accepted the children simply because they are theirs—an acceptance and affection through ascription which children continue to need in order to feel emotionally secure. Status in the classroom is established by differences in performance on tasks set by the teacher, who is acting for the community's school system. This shift to being evaluated through achievement rather than ascription is fundamental to how children learn who they are and what they can expect of themselves. Although children may by now be old enough to start finding their way in the world, they are far from ready to lose parental affection and protection if they cannot live up to expectations. Further, the parents are emotionally unsuited to evaluating their children on merit alone. They have a strong investment in them, and their children's well-being is a major factor in their own lives. The teacher, in contrast, has an obligation to evaluate each child fairly and serve as the agent for bringing about a differentiation of the children in the class on the basis of how well they can learn and assume responsibilities. The ethical development of the children, their willingness to accept the teacher's authority, and the children's evaluations of themselves depend upon the teacher's objectivity and fairness.* Now, of course, the difference between parental and teacher roles is not as sharp as has been stated. The teacher, particularly in the

---

* The tendency of some educators to keep such evaluations minimal lest they discourage some children or penalize children for their poor natural endowment or deprived backgrounds thus has serious limitations as well as advantages for the children.

early grades, often treats the children in a somewhat motherly manner and will take individual shortcomings into account; and the parents reinforce the school's influence by rewarding children's school achievement and through conveying expectations that they will strive to do well. Many children soon learn that their mothers' happiness and satisfaction with them fluctuate with their grades and class standings. Serious emotional problems and blocks to learning can follow when a child finds that the affection and acceptance received from parents depend largely upon the child's school grades. A mother whose only way of feeling adequate and comparable with her peers had been to be the leading student in each grade became very upset when her son had difficulties in learning to read and was in the lower half of his first- and second-grade classes. She sought to coach him, but became intolerant of his "stupidity" and conveyed rather directly that she could not love a poor student; and before long the boy had developed a serious learning block as well as a reading problem.

The Classmates' Role

The child's classmates also enter into the socialization process and the reorganization of the child's personality. Not only is the child evaluated by teachers in relationship to fellow students and thus placed in competition with them, but each child is also evaluated by classmates according to different standards. The schoolchild learns to balance adult and children's values, seeking approval from both. Children now also identify with their age group in contrast to the identifications with parents and teachers. It is a step that dilutes the intrafamilial identifications and starts a new group loyalty in which children will identify with leaders of their own genera-tion.* The peer group in school usually has a less personal relationship to the child than does the neighborhood group, and also differs in that it is supervised by an adult authority rather than being on its own. Children's personalities gain complexity by the children's having to find ways of relat-ing to three or more groups of which they are members and still maintain an identity: to the family group; to the school group, both as student and as classmate; to the neighborhood peer group, free of adult presence.

* Freud, in "Group Psychology and the Analysis of the Ego," considers the unity of the group in terms of such common identifications. The English "upper classes" fos-tered strong generational loyalties to agemates who would share responsibilities for running the Empire by the "public school" system. Among the Indigenes of New Guinea, where the safety of each village depends on an almost constant defense against neighboring hostile villages, the initiation rituals and lengthy apprenticeship in the men's group reinforces bonds between agemates to such an extent that they almost replace kinship loyalties.

The Stresses of Starting School

As eagerly as the child has looked forward to becoming a schoolchild, the new situation commonly places the child under considerable emotional strain. The new student does not know how to respond to the teacher, who, though a woman much like mother is very different from her. The child is not accustomed to being judged on merit and being graded in relation to a large group of other children. Individual needs are often ignored, and sometimes a trait that parents have considered lovable or a reason to be lenient—such as a speech defect—is only an embarrassing handicap that the teacher strives to correct. Rules cannot be evaded by the child's being cute or crying. A child who finds himself or herself in a secondary role to brighter children may feel inadequate or stupid. The uneasiness reactivates wishes to regress, and behavior can become more babyish for a time. The child may seek reasons to avoid going to school, and as illness may become the only acceptable way out, the child may use hypochondriacal complaints, which need not be feigned, for anxiety creates feelings of dis-ease, and physical symptoms are a simple way of expressing a need for help. The problems usually pass as the child gains familiarity with the situation and makes friends with classmates. When a school phobia develops, the child is usually responding to the mother's anxiety that her child cannot manage without her; but sometimes to fears that the mother will desert while the child is in school, or to jealousy of siblings still at home.

The Family Social Background and School Achievement

Children from deprived homes and even children from the lower socio-economic levels generally enter school with serious disadvantages; and, unless special efforts are made, the disadvantages can increase in school. The teachers are assessing and rewarding the child for cognitive abilities and for "citizenship"—reliability in meeting obligations and commitments as well as class conduct. Despite their efforts to evaluate and reward children on an egalitarian basis, teachers are human and usually become more involved with the intelligent, knowledgeable, and better-mannered children. The teacher's interest in a child and her expectations for higher performance levels appear to stimulate the development of intelligence as well as improve learning.* However, quite aside from the teacher's interest, the

* R. Rosenthal (1966) found that when teachers were told that certain students had

school system favors children who have been prepared in the home to be verbal, curious, motivated to learn, and to control distracting impulsions.

Children from families of the higher socioeconomic levels, which are also usually the better educated, have been exposed to more diverse information and to much more verbal interchange, although they often have had less experience with diverse situations. The exposure to more varied experiences in the inner city can foster greater self-sufficiency and knowledge of the "world," but such advantages are commonly offset by the instabilities of the family, the meager verbal communication in the home, and the emotional tensions that are antipathetic to learning. The intensive studies of white inner-city children in Boston (Pavenstedt, 1967) revealed that by the time they started nursery school many were seriously handicapped by impulsivity, inability to delay gratification, retarded cognitive development, distrust of adults, etc. Teachers felt frustrated in their efforts to establish meaningful relationships because the children did not clearly differentiate between various teachers. Some inner-city black children may find that they must virtually learn a new language, as "Black English" is often found unacceptable, and later will be unsuitable for reading texts and literature. Fluent verbal abilities were once considered to reflect good innate intelligence, but it now seems fairly clear that habitual exposure to good verbal communication in early childhood fosters higher intelligence. How much intelligence level depends upon innate endowment and how much upon experience remains uncertain. Nature and nurture are both important. Many intelligence tests tend to reward high verbal abilities and therefore help select out children from educated homes as having better potential. Although tests can be utilized that minimize the influence of language skills and give a better index of the deprived child's potential capacities, they cannot eliminate the effects of early education completely.* It is becoming

---

unusual potential, these students showed a rise in I.Q., whereas a control series of matched students did not show a rise.

* The Intelligence Quotient, or I.Q., is determined by giving tests that measure a person's mental age—how the problems he can solve match the median of an age group. The mental age, divided by the chronological age, multiplied by 100, yields the I.Q. (M.A./C.A. $\times$ 100 = I.Q.), which is supposed to remain fairly constant throughout life. If a child is ten years old and solves problems that a twelve-year-old is expected to solve, the I.Q. is 120. As the mental age does not increase very much after the age of fifteen or sixteen, an arbitrary upper limit of fourteen, fifteen, or sixteen is set for the chronological age (differing according to the standardization of the specific test) in calculating I.Q.s of older adolescents and adults. As the I.Q. usually remains fairly constant throughout life, its use to predict the child's future potential for learning has

increasingly apparent that early experiences within the family strongly influence school achievement.

Intelligence and Family Background

The correlation between children's intellectual abilities and their parents' educational level or social status had formerly been widely accepted as an indication of the overriding importance of heredity in determining intelligence. Schooling was offered to all and the children would use as much of it as they were capable. There was concern that economic or emotional factors prevented some bright children from gaining as much education as they could utilize. Currently, however, there is a strong trend to consider that providing equal educational opportunity means instituting measures to develop the latent intellectual abilities of deprived children. Changes in the polity of the nation are involved. Efforts to raise the socioeconomic and educational level of impoverished groups relate to the rapidly diminishing need for unskilled labor as well as to democratic ideals. The task cannot be accomplished within a few years, and faces the difficulty that underprivileged families do not provide the necessary background.

Underprivileged children often enter school with other disadvantages. Unfamiliar with middle-class standards, they may be perplexed by the value systems they encounter. Their parents do not provide models of intellectual achievement with whom to identify, and sometimes have little interest in their children's school achievement.* Children from minority groups have difficulty fitting into the peer group and identifying with it. Neighborhood schools tend to lessen the impact when neighborhoods con-

---

been very successful despite occasional errors. Thus, I.Q.s determined in the early school grades often influence teachers' appraisals of the child and advice given concerning the child's educational prospects. However, the child's I.Q. can often be modified by special educational efforts, particularly in the preschool years. The improvement may sometimes be maintained because of the child's improved abilities in school, but it may also be necessary to maintain a stimulating home environment or provide continued special tutoring.

I.Q.s between 90 and 110 are considered normative. Children with I.Q.s below 80 will have considerable difficulty keeping up with a normal class or in moving past the eighth grade. Children with I.Q.s above 125 are apt to be bored with routine class work. Children who are idiots, due to a congenital abnormality or brain damage that affects cerebral functioning, fall outside of the bell-shaped distribution curves for intelligence found in the general population.

* In postwar Japan, where the rise of a new middle class increased the importance of a youth's acceptance into Tokyo University or some other major university on the basis of school grades, many relatively uneducated mothers learned their children's school work before it was assigned to the child in order thus to be able to help their children (Vogel, 1963).

tain families of similar economic and ethnic backgrounds, but a school filled with children from deprived homes does not constitute a suitable environment for efforts to raise the cognitive level of the students. In any event, unless the school serves a very homogeneous community, children now must come to grips with status problems based on social class and ethnic backgrounds. Attitudes toward the underprivileged children and their ethnic group enter into each child's self-concept, into children's evaluations of their parents as models, and into their commitments to the values of the society.

BOOKS AND TELEVISION

One type of companionship is available to virtually all children who have had some schooling. The companionship of books and the characters who people them can fill the emptiness of lonely days and can transport the child from the isolated farm or fishing hamlet, or replace the dingy slum airshafts and alleys with prairie or castle. Books have furnished the vision of a different and more hopeful life that has motivated many; and have brought into a colorless or disorganized home the heroic models for identification that displaced the disheartening real models. They have taught the use of imagination and opened eyes to visions of beauty and ears to the sounds of beauty. The love of books and even the craving for books usually develop during the juvenile period. For most it is not a love of great literature, which is almost always beyond the child's comprehension of his limited world, and for many it starts with books of little merit beyond their inspirational and narrative values. The delight in reading and the enthusiasm for discovering new worlds in books is what counts. If children keep reading they will become bored with the tawdry and commonplace, and in proportion to their understanding progressively seek out books that provide new vision and perspective.

Of course, television has become a far more pervasive influence than books upon most children. Between the ages of three and sixteen, the average child in the United States spends about one-sixth of his or her waking hours watching television—an activity (or lack of activity) that reaches its zenith (or nadir) between the ages of twelve and fourteen, when some twenty-three or twenty-four hours a week are spent with eyes fixed on the TV screen. At this age, almost eighty percent of the time is spent watching adult programs (Schramm et al., 1961). Excellent programs for young children have been provided by public television, and many programs expand children's horizons in felicitous ways. We cannot, however, consider here the quality of the vast majority of television programs intended to provide an escape from reality for adults, and attempt to weigh the effects of the envelopment of the child in violence and sex as well as banality. Television clearly influences children's cognitive and moral development by providing them with awareness of lives happier and more placid than their own, or, on the other hand, more unfortunate and chaotic than theirs. It provides figures real as well as fictitious whom they may wish to emulate. Unfortunately, it makes commonplace much that had once been unusual in children's lives, whether violence and death or the opportunity to watch big league baseball games. And experience has been made passive. Children's lives have been changed profoundly by television; but, as with many other changes in the way of life, evaluation is difficult, and one must consider what children would be doing if they were not watching television.*

COGNITIVE DEVELOPMENT

Under the impact of the new influences and perspectives that enter their lives and the formal education they receive in the school, the maturing children enter a new stage of cognition when about seven. They move beyond the preoperational or prelogical ways of thinking described in Chapter 7 and enter the period of concrete operations or concrete logic. They will gradually become able to reason systematically about situations that confront them, or which they can imagine in a visual, tangible form, but will still not be able to think in propositions or utilize abstract concepts. According to Piaget, concrete ideas are "internalized actions." Two major elements enter into the cognitive growth—the *diminution of egocentricity* and the capacity to carry out the operations of *conservation* and *reversability*, as we shall examine.

The Transition from Preoperational Thought to the Period of Concrete Operations

The transition to logical ways of thinking occurs slowly. It is difficult for adults to realize the limitations of the juvenile's cognitive capacities and

* A review of the literature up to 1964 can be found in E. E. Maccoby, "The Effects of the Mass Media."

ethical evaluations, and unrealistic expectations by teachers as well as parents can be the source of many serious difficulties for children. Second or third graders continue to confuse their fabulations with reality and are amazingly unconcerned about obvious contradictions in their statements and reasoning. Furthermore, they may make false statements or answers with a conviction that seems to derive from the belief that something is so because they believe it so. Efforts to have children explain just how they sought to solve a problem indicate that they still cannot think about their thinking.

Thus, many eight- and nine-year-olds explained that placing a stone in a glass of water raised the level because the stone is heavy. However, to cite one example, when an eight-year-old boy was asked if wood was heavy, he said it was light. Still, he expected it would make the water rise—because it was light, and knew that it would make it rise more than the stone because it was bigger. Yet, when asked why a stone made the water rise, he again responded, "Because it is heavy." He cannot handle the several factors of heaviness, lightness, and size at the same time (Piaget, 1947, pp. 181–182). We have noted that preschool children not only do not realize that points of view other than their own exist, but also do not realize that a person looking at an object from a different vantage point sees the object differently. Although problems of egocentricity are now fading, they still present notable difficulties. A child of nine or ten may have trouble realizing that if he traveled abroad he would be a foreigner, or that an American can be an enemy. As Piaget (1947, p. 75) noted, even family relationships that seem so obvious are not altogether clear to a nine-year-old—"She has two sisters, she is not a sister" is a common type of confusion.

Piaget has emphasized the preoperational child's inability to carry out the essential operations of *conservation* and *reversibility*. Thus, after two identical glass beakers are filled with water to the same level, the water from one is poured into a wider beaker. The child is then asked which beaker, the wider or narrower, contains more water. The child either says that the wider beaker has less water because it does not rise as high in the beaker; or, focusing on the width, that it contains more water. Children do not appreciate that if the operation were reversed the water would be at the same level in the two original beakers. They do not retain the original image in deciding the issue, or mentally reverse the procedure. They also are still unable to utilize two factors at a time. If they consider the width of the beaker, they do not simultaneously consider the height. Similarly, when a ball of plasticine is molded into a sausage shape, children may not realize that it still contains the same quantity of the material. Piaget has tended to

emphasize the importance of reversibility in analyzing this type of failure.*
School-age children will gradually master problems at this level. At least
some of the children's increased cognitive capacities on such tests relate to
improved linguistic abilities which help them remember the earlier state
and to keep one factor constant while considering the others, and so on.

The Capacity for Concrete Operations

Piaget has analyzed several of the juvenile's new cognitive capacities
which are basic to other achievements. Children become able to classify
objects in groups according to one or another attribute, such as shape,
color, or size. They can carry out such simple classifications by inspection
without having words to designate the categories but the process is helped
by having terms to use. More complex classifications require the use of
appropriate terms. Children also become capable of arranging objects in
series, according to increasing size, weight, or depth of color, etc. At a
somewhat older age they become able either to classify objects or to seri-
alize them using two attributes such as size and shape simultaneously.
Piaget terms these three operations *classification, seriation,* and *multiplica-
tion* and has devoted considerable effort to analyzing their development.

A critical aspect of many of these abilities seems to lie in the fact that
children gradually learn an increasingly integrated cognitive *system* into
which they can fit their experiences. They become less likely to fall into
contradictions or even to judge things egocentrically when they can fit
things into an organized approach to understanding experience.† Now the
children go to school to learn just such organized approaches to mental
activities. They learn the meanings of the words that are the culture's labels
for its categories—that is, its ways of classifying objects or experiences.
They learn syntax—the rules for logical operations. They learn mathematics—an approach to concrete and formal operations. They are also
taught in more explicit fashion various ways of solving problems, and to
think causally—that is, to seek determinants in precursors of events.

In an earlier chapter we considered the difficulties imposed upon children when they had to assimilate experiences, not only to the schemata that
each had gradually built up, but also to the schemata that the culture had

---

* See J. Flavell (1963), Chapter 5, and J. Piaget, *The Psychology of Intelligence,* for
further discussion of a complex topic that is not essential to this presentation.

† Representational acts that Piaget terms *operations* are an integral part of an organized network or system of interrelated acts. See also B. Inhelder and J. Piaget, *The
Growth of Logical Thinking from Childhood to Adolescence,* Chapters 1, 2, and 3, for a
systematic study of the schoolchild's developing intellectual abilities.

built up and conveyed to them through language. School-age children are, as we have examined, acquiring an ever increasing knowledge of the world, and the gap lessens between what they experience themselves and what they hear or read. Their schemata and those of the culture are being integrated. However, as we shall see, it is not until about the end of the grade school period that major confusions drop out, as the adolescent enters the period of formal operations that we shall examine in the next chapter.

THE DEVELOPMENT OF MORAL JUDGMENT

The juvenile's moral and ethical values also change profoundly. The school influences the child by introducing different and more impartial standards than the home, and through being a more formalized representative of community values. However, as we have seen, the juvenile culture also begins to exert a profound effect upon the child's value systems.

Adults commonly have difficulty appreciating the limitations of the children's understanding of right and wrong and the way in which they judge others as well as themselves. Although moral behavior develops early, and although at the time they enter school most children know the basic moral rules and conventions of our society (Kohlberg, 1964, pp. 383–431), judgment does not appear to become "moral" until early adolescence. Contrary to an impression one might gain from Freud's concept of the origins of the "superego," superego directives do not emerge like Pallas Athena, full-grown and fully armed, out of the father's head at the closing of the oedipal period. Ethical development, very much like intellectual growth, depends upon gaining experience and relating to different people in various settings, which gradually diminishes children's egocentricity, and, as Kohlberg has shown, depends very greatly upon cognitive development. Young children have neither the experience nor the intellectual capacities to use judgment rather than adhere to rules as they understand them. They tend to follow superego edicts in the form of internalized adult commandments, which they reify into immutable rules much more than they follow ethical values about which they can reason. The entire subject of knowledge of ethical values, moral behavior, and moral judgment is complex, difficult to study, and unsettled.* Here we are interested primarily in

* The reader is referred to L. Kohlberg's review of the topic in *Review of Child Development Research* and to Martin L. Hoffman's "Moral Development."

how children learn to make moral evaluations suited to circumstances rather than following relatively inflexible superego dictates.

Children at a very early age learn within their homes that ethical values do not follow the "pleasure principle" but often require them to rescind immediate gratifications for future goals or to maintain the affection of parents. Desires are sadly not a criterion of what is "good" or "just." Later, they must move beyond simply accepting parental values as infallible guides. It is through interacting with adults whose values differ from those of parents, and whose edicts children are less likely to consider immutable, and by learning to relate to peers and accept their very different perspectives that children gradually learn to consider a person's intent and the specific circumstances in making moral evaluations.

Children of three or four do not have a real appreciation of rules when they try to play games: they imitate using rules but are apt to bend them to their need to win. Children of seven or eight not only learn rules and adhere to them reasonably well but are likely to consider the rules of a game immutable. Rules are inherent in the game, or imposed by a higher authority, and cannot be changed by mutual agreement. Thus, a boy of eight who moved to a different town complained bitterly that the neighborhood boys were stupid because their rules for playing marbles differed from those used in his former community. To the youngster, his new friends did not have different rules; they did not know the rules. A child at this age is also likely to judge culpability in terms of the damage done. The boy who accidentally bats a baseball through a store-front window is considered guiltier than a child who spitefully throws a stone through a windowpane in his friend's house. The child of eight or nine does not clearly know the difference between a lie and a mistake, and will judge the guilt of a falsehood according to its magnitude. A "whopper" may be deemed a worse offense than a small lie told to cheat someone. The very young child decides what is right or wrong by whether it elicits punishment. Consequences rather than intent are what is important, so that "what is punished is bad" rather than "what is bad is punished."* By the age of seven, however, most children will say that a child is good even though punished in error. By the onset of puberty children consider rules as a type of contract capable of being changed by consent, and that intent is important in evaluating guilt (Piaget, 1948).

---

* In a study of delinquents and their parents, the author and his colleagues noted that parents often had the attitude that a delinquent act was reprehensible only if the adolescent was caught at it; and they seemed to teach their children that what one says is more important than what one does. These adolescents seemed to regard laws and rules as arbitrary, and therefore a focus of rebellion against parents.

From Morality of Constraint to Morality of Cooperation

Schoolchildren exhibit what Piaget terms a *morality of constraint*. They usually have rigid standards about punishments, considering that the same punishment should be meted out for the same infraction regardless of circumstances. They believe that a four-year-old who breaks a dish should be reprimanded or punished in the same way as a ten-year-old; or that a hungry little nursery school girl should be expected to await her turn for food just like her older brother. This type of morality develops because the immature and egocentric children accept their position as inferior to the adult and accept the adult's value system though they do not properly understand it. They usually must accept the adult edict or risk punishment. The adult, if challenged, is likely to bolster the rules by referring to essentially impersonal superordinate authorities such as the Deity, the police, or the school principal. As children pass the first decade, they begin to attain a *morality of cooperation* according to which the motivation and social implication of acts are appreciated. They also move beyond seeking expiatory punishments in which the punishment fits the crime—a child is deprived of candy in proportion to the size of the dish broken. They begin to comprehend punishment by reciprocity—for example, a boy who refuses to help his mother wash the dishes can expect his mother to refuse to drive him to the store when he wants to buy a comic book (Piaget, 1948).

School-age children tend to base their moral judgments largely on the basis of what will be punished and what will gain rewards or favors in return, but these criteria decrease in importance; whereas conforming to conventions to gain approval or to avoid censure and the ensuing guilt becomes increasingly important. However, higher forms of morality based on self-accepted ethical principles—forming judgments in terms of social contract and democratic principles, or on the basis of individual conscience —do not emerge until adolescence, perhaps with the onset of the cognitive stage of "formal operations" (Kohlberg, 1963).

The progression from a morality of constraint to a morality of cooperation depends upon the social environment in which the child lives. Whereas parents, teachers, and peers all seem to play significant roles, it does not seem possible to separate out just what each of these influences contributes. The total social world seems important, and children's perceptions of the values of parents, peers, teachers, and the law all influence the total effect upon the child. A child's moral judgments at any stage in their development "may represent spontaneous efforts to make sense out of his experience in a complex social world" (Kohlberg, 1964, p. 402). However, children's positions in society influence how they will make sense out of their experiences, and their level of cognitive development will be an important factor in the level of moral judgment achieved.

Sexual Interests

All juvenile peer groups are likely to carry out some activities which adults consider undesirable. The children will start using scatological words and engage in sex talk, progressing to telling stories that none of the group will admit not understanding. This is in part a penetrating into the mysteries of the adult world, in part a token of flaunting parental prohibitions as an indication of growing independence, and a means of gaining admiration by being more in the know than others. It is also a way of trying to share the fantasies of sex that the child experiences in private. The boys may have contests to see how far they can urinate, and compare the size of their genitals, an activity that may help overcome feelings of inadequacy derived from seeing adult genitalia. Some indulge in masturbation in one another's presence or with one another. Such sex play between boys or girls does not relate to homosexuality, as parents often fear, but is usually a movement from narcissistic preoccupations to heterosexual interests through a phase of sharing with someone like the self. Some visual or physical exploration of children of the same or opposite sex is fairly common during the so-called latency period, but it is just as likely to happen in the home with siblings of the opposite sex or the friends of siblings as in the gang. At any rate, the boy who is not accepted in the neighborhood gang may have difficulty progressing to relate to girls in adolescence, or may gravitate to less desirable groups composed of outsiders who are likely to indulge in more marginal sexual and social activities. However, such undesirable activities usually form a very minor part of the juvenile's life. The children are too absorbed in all the new experiences available to them to become engrossed with sex. As girls approach puberty, they are likely to share with the clique of close friends secret knowledge, or information given to one of the group by her parents, as well as concerns about when they will menstruate and how their breasts will develop, but we shall wait until the next chapter to consider these prepubertal sexual interests.

Growing Up Without Playmates

Although the peer group and special friend are usually very important to the schoolchild's development, they are not a vital part of every childhood.

Not all settings provide groups of peers as playmates; and some children are constrained from joining in the collective activities for reasons of health, because of parental restrictions, or because they are, for various reasons, "loners." The son of the school principal or the clergyman may feel that he is different and is treated as an outsider by his peers. The child from a minority group that is unwelcome in the community can be left very isolated though potential playmates abound. Such conditions are often trying for children but they are not necessarily injurious to their development, particularly if they can maintain pride in themselves and their families. The child does not learn to conform as rapidly or learn how to evaluate the self in comparison with peers so readily, but most children can find ways of keeping occupied by themselves, utilizing their imagination and developing active fantasy lives, and perhaps special skills and hobbies. After all, it is difficult for persons to become truly creative if they have learned to be highly conventional and are so thoroughly grounded in the society's ways of regarding things, that all uniqueness of perception or reasoning is repressed early in life in favor of the societal norms. Fantasy is a precursor of creativity, and though fantasy activities can be shared by two or three it is not a group activity and usually flourishes on loneliness or isolation. Many creative persons feel that they had been outsiders as children because they had been subjected to two sets of cultural directives that prevented them from being as ethnocentrically oriented and as set in the cultural norms as most of their peers. Children who grow up without peers may have to lose their egocentricity later than other children; but they may not lose it to a degree that eliminates their individuality, which may flourish as originality or be noted as eccentricity. Still, only an occasional parent will purposefully promote a child's isolation for such reasons, as it entails some risk of leading to unhappiness and emotional instability, and instability occurs all too readily without being fostered.

Rescue Operations

It is also during these grade school years when the child has gained a modicum of freedom from home and family that some type of "rescue" operation may alter the life of the child who has been raised in an unfortunate and distorting family environment. The child now comes under the sway of new influences in school, in the neighborhood, and in reading which can offset even though they cannot supplant the pervasive influence of parents and home. The child may be included in the activities of a friend's family; a teacher, a social worker, a camp counselor takes an interest in the child and becomes an ideal and a model. The child spends summers with his grandparents or with an aunt or uncle.* In one way or another the child learns that some path into the future exists, and confining gates can be opened to permit entrance into a more hopeful world. The family is the most important influence upon the child's development, but it is not the only influence and others can become increasingly significant.

NEW SOURCES OF ANXIETY AND DESPAIR

Although late childhood is so often remembered nostalgically as a time of freedom and of outgoing activities, it contains ample sources of anxiety and discomfort. There are, of course, the problems that derive from unresolved difficulties at early developmental stages, such as the residues of the intrafamilial oedipal conflicts and sibling rivalries, but the juvenile period in itself contains sources of anxiety and sometimes of depression. The child wishes independence but can readily suffer from the insecurities of having responsibility for one's own welfare. Whereas children become angered at parents who limit their activities, they still need to be dependent. Now they can become more upset than previously over their conflicting emotions toward parents and need to find a way of resolving them. Further, it now becomes apparent to children that even with the best will in the world parents cannot provide complete security. They are not omnipotent or omniscient, and the child now knows that they may die. Death wishes, conscious and unconscious, become more frightening and anxiety provoking. God is now often regarded as more all-knowing than parents and misdeeds and evil thoughts cannot be hidden from God. The girl is often still caught up in her oedipal problems and as she grows older may become more guilt ridden by her rivalrous feelings toward her mother as well as her fantasies about possessing her father. Then, too, the parents have expectations concerning children's achievements, expectations which children also

---

* Samuel Butler, for example, after being pushed out of the frying pan of a rigid home with ununderstanding parents, was thrown into the fire of a boarding school that was intolerable to him; he was rescued by an aunt who happened to live near the school and who fostered his interest in music and playing the organ and engendered in him a confidence in himself that his parents had seemed bent on destroying under the guise of breaking his willfulness.

hold for themselves; and there are inevitable failures when self-esteem may be seriously threatened. There are bitter days when a child feels left out by the gang for reasons he or she cannot fathom; or days of shame and self-reproach when a girl feels that she has behaved in ways that are unacceptable to her friends, or when a boy has let his best buddy down. Even though it is a time of transition and trying out, the juvenile may become despondent about his or her prospects.

Juvenile Defenses Against Anxiety

Just as at other phases of development, juveniles are apt to defend against anxieties by regressing. They seek ways of being cared for by parents by being ill, suffering injury, or invoking pity because no one seems to want them. They may spend more and more time at home, giving up efforts to become members of the peer groups, where they must be responsible for themselves. Most children will more or less consciously avoid some stresses at school or with peers by finding ways of staying home on occasion, but some retreat more permanently and will then be confronted by adolescence without adequate preparation in relating beyond the family. The common defensive patterns used at this time of life are those related to obsessive-compulsive patterns. Ritualistic behavior carried out to ward off harm and undo unacceptable wishes appears in almost every child. It is a resort to magical thinking in order to control exigencies beyond the child's control. The child must avoid stepping on cracks in the sidewalk, or must touch every lamp post, or get up on the same side of the bed every morning, put on the right shoe before the left shoe. If the child fails, some harm will befall the self or one's parents, or if the ritual is carried out correctly some wish will be granted—the home team will win or the examination will be easy. Children also seek means of controlling impulses and controlling nature, just as a primitive person seeks to control the weather or the outcome of a hunt by practicing a ritual which cannot be altered in any detail. The ambivalent feelings toward parents and siblings and the fear that harm may come to them because of hostile feelings are of particular importance. Reaction formation, undoing, and isolation are the mechanisms of defense used in such obsessive ritualization. *Reaction formation,* we may recall, concerns the tendency to repress an unacceptable impulse or wish and manifest its opposite—as when a boy becomes oversolicitous of his father's health after having hostile feelings toward him. *Undoing* consists of rituals or prayers that have the magical property of undoing a wish. *Isolation* has to do with the separation of affect and idea; the idea is somehow deprived of its emotional impact, often by keeping ideas from linking up which would force recognition of consequences and therefore arouse anxiety. Thus, when combined with undoing and reaction formation, prayers that the father not be killed in an auto accident prevent recognition of wishes that the father be killed in an accident.

The rituals may seem less strange when they are a component of prayers. The child may say prayers in a set sequence as part of the effort to achieve magical control. However, there is also a strong tendency to depend upon God who can omnipotently control and protect from illness and death, from failure to develop properly, and from other such matters that the child now knows that neither the child nor the parents can control. At this age children may gain solace from severe anxiety by feeling that God will take care of them if they behave, believe, and pray properly.

This is also a time when fantasy helps compensate for feelings of inadequacy and paucity of achievement. Fantasy also plays the more positive role of providing an imagined future greatness that spurs the child to achievement. The daydreams are not subjected to much reality testing and are often formed on the basis of the child's growing hero worship, but as the child grows older they either reflect some real assets or serve more clearly as compensations for feelings of inadequacy. The boy has his "Dreams of Glory," which have been pictured so ably in cartoons by Steig. He is the football player who arrives just in time to dash onto the field and score the winning touchdown before the final whistle blows; he is the general who saves the war by flying an old decrepit plane to shoot down the enemy plane carrying an H bomb; he is the first man to land on Mars. The girl may be the medical scientist who discovers a new drug just in time to save the dying president; the gold medal winner in the Olympics; the dazzling beauty queen who is also an atomic physicist. *Identification* is also helpful and blends with fantasy. The boy or girl identifies with a hero or a greatly admired person and feels capable of becoming as able and thereby more secure in facing the future, or more able to stand present inadequacies. Somewhat similarly, the juvenile may gain security and comfort in the reflection of a leader and willingly follows and becomes subservient to an older child who is much admired; or gains self-esteem from being a member of a group—a club, a team, a school with prestige.

Fixation at the Juvenile Level

The juvenile period also has importance because of the tendency to regress to it—a tendency which may be particularly common in the United

States, where children are permitted to lead relatively carefree and independent lives. Later, when one must do well in order to gain admission to college or find advancement in an occupation, the competitions of childhood seem gratifying. When sexual problems occur in adolescence or when marital difficulties create anxiety, the old days before members of the opposite sex were so important are idealized. Adults retain some of the pleasures of the period by spending their free time in sports, competing for fun rather than for keeps; or in still glorifying the athlete and identifying with him or her. Some of the brutality shown in films and on television, some of the ever-present interest in westerns and in whodunits may not be so much an outlet for unconscious sadism as a fixation at playing cowboys and Indians, or cops and robbers—a regaining of the pleasant feelings of childhood. Some individuals will, of course, remain fixated in the period of late childhood and early adolescence, seeking to maintain life as it was, occupied with games and with the members of their own sex.

The juvenile period ends with the new spurt in physical growth that precedes the onset of puberty when the child begins to turn into an adolescent. In the half-dozen juvenile years the relationships within the family and the personality integration achieved with the closing of the oedipal period have had time to consolidate and defenses have become strengthened, enabling the child to be better prepared for the emotional upsurges which accompany puberty and which threaten the established equilibrium. It is erroneous, however, to consider such consolidations as the major task of the juvenile period. While children's lives still center within the family, their environment is broadening as they venture off to school and into play groups consisting of peers. Adapting to these new environments and finding a place in them have required a substantial reorganization of the personality.

The children have been faced by the difficult reorientation of having their status determined by their achievements rather than through ascription. In their teachers they have been confronted by significant adults who have related to them very differently from parents. They have become part of a group of student peers and learned to identify with them and to measure themselves in relationship to peers. In the neighborhood peer groups they have begun to learn ways of living and relating as members of the society and with its ideals and value systems. In these broader environments children have had the opportunity to strengthen their gender identities, to become less dependent upon parents and their values, to learn how others evaluate their capacities and how much others care for them as individuals. In the process they move a long way in forming self-concepts on which their own evaluations of themselves and their future potentialities will rest. They have learned that status rests heavily upon industriousness and reliability; and have learned to be industrious, perhaps becoming compulsively competitive, or they may have tended to withdraw and no longer accept challenges.

Usually the child has formed his or her first intense extrafamilial relationship to another child, which, although it is with a member of the same sex, forms an important step toward ultimately forming an intimate heterosexual relationship. Toward the end of the juvenile period, perhaps at a time when the girls are prepubertal, boys and girls may again gladly find companionship in mixed groups. The boys feel more secure in their male identity and will be able to enjoy girls with whom they are not competing. The groups can still be fairly spontaneous and provide an opportunity to gain some familiarity with the ways of the opposite sex before the shyness and tension that come with adolescence disrupt the ease of the situation. The experiences beyond the family, both in school and with peer groups, enable children to overcome their egocentric and family-centered orientations, an essential step in both intellectual and ethical development; their ego capacities are greatly increased and they become prepared to be able to guide themselves when they enter adolescence and begin really to emerge from their families, and to utilize their judgment when beset by sexual impulsions that urge toward immediate gratification.

REFERENCES

BENEDICT, R. (1934). *Patterns of Culture*. Penguin Books, New York.

ERIKSON, E. (1950). *Childhood and Society*. W. W. Norton, New York.

FLAVELL, J. (1963). *The Developmental Psychology of Jean Piaget*. Van Nostrand, Princeton, N.J.

FREUD, S. (1921). "Group Psychology and the Analysis of the Ego," in *The Standard Edition of the Complete Psychological Works of Sigmund Freud*, vol. 1. Hogarth Press, London, 1955.

HOFFMAN, M. L. (1970). "Moral Development," in *Carmichael's Manual of Child Psychology*, vol. 2. 3d ed. Paul H. Mussen, ed. John Wiley & Sons, New York.

INHELDER, B., and PIAGET, J. (1958). *The Growth of Logical Thinking from Childhood to Adolescence*. A. Parsons and S. Milgram, trans. Basic Books, New York.

KOHLBERG, L. (1963). "The Development of Children's Orientations Toward a Moral Order: I. Sequence on the Development of Moral Thought," *Vita Humana*, 6:11–33.

———. (1964). "Development of Moral Character and Moral Ideology," in *Review of Child Development Research*. M. L. Hoffman and L. W. Hoffman, eds. Russell Sage Foundation, New York.

MACCOBY, E. (1964). "The Effects of the Mass Media," in *Review of Child Development Research*. M. L. Hoffman and L. W. Hoffman, eds. Russell Sage Foundation, New York.

MEAD, G. H. (1934). *Mind, Self, and Society: From the Standpoint of a Social Behaviorist*. University of Chicago Press, Chicago.

PARSONS, T. (1959). "The School Class as a Social System: Some of Its Functions in American Society," *Harvard Educational Review*, 29:297–318.

PAVENSTEDT, E., ed. (1967). *The Drifters: Children of Disorganized Lower-Class Families*. Little, Brown, Boston.

PIAGET, J. (1947). *Judgment and Reasoning in the Child*. M. Wardin, trans. Humanities Press, New York.

———. (1948). *The Moral Judgment of the Child*. M. Gabain, trans. Free Press, Glencoe, Ill.

———. (1960). *The Psychology of Intelligence*. M. Piercy and D. E. Berlyne, trans. Littlefield, Adams, Totowa, N.J.

ROSENTHAL, R. (1966). *Experimenter Effects in Behavioral Research*. Appleton-Century-Crofts, New York.

SCHRAMM, N., LYLE, J., and PARKER, E. (1961). *Television in the Lives of Our Children*. Stanford University Press, Stanford, Calif.

SULLIVAN, H. S. (1953). *The Interpersonal Theory of Psychiatry*. W. W. Norton, New York.

VOGEL, E. (1963). *Japan's New Middle Class*. University of California Press, Berkeley.

SUGGESTED READING

PARSONS, T. (1964). "The School Class as a Social System: Some of Its Functions in American Society," in *Social Structure and Personality*, pp. 129–154. Free Press, New York.

PIAGET, J. (1948). *The Moral Judgment of the Child*. M. Gabain, trans. Free Press, Glencoe, Ill.

SULLIVAN, H. S. (1953). *The Interpersonal Theory of Psychiatry*, pp. 217–262. W. W. Norton, New York.

CHAPTER 10

❀

Adolescence

INTRODUCTION

IT IS A DIFFICULT TASK to attempt to convey what transpires during these years in which the child blossoms into an adult beset by conflicting emotions, struggling to maintain self-control and to achieve self-expression under the impact of sensations and impulses that are scarcely understood but insistently demand attention. It is a time of physical and emotional metamorphosis during which the adolescent feels estranged from the self the child had known. It is a time of seeking: a seeking inward to find who one is; a searching outward to locate one's place in life; a longing for another with whom to satisfy cravings for intimacy and fulfillment. It is a time of turbulent awakening to love and beauty but also of days darkened by loneliness and despair. It is a time of carefree wandering of the spirit through realms of fantasy and in pursuit of idealistic visions, but also of disillusionment and disgust with the world and the self. It can be a time of adventure with wonderful episodes of reckless folly but also of shame and regret that linger. The adolescent lives with a vibrant sensitivity that carries to ecstatic heights and lowers to almost untenable depths. For some, the emotional stability achieved in childhood and the security of the family attachments contain the amplitude of the oscillations and permit a fairly steady direction; whereas others must struggle to retain a sense of unity and a modicum of ego control.

Adolescence can be defined as the period between pubescence and physical maturity. However, in considering personality development, we are concerned with the transition from childhood, initiated by the prepubertal spurt of growth and impelled by the hormonal changes of puberty, to the attainment of adult prerogatives, responsibilities, and self-sufficiency. It involves the discrepancy between sexual maturation with the drive toward procreation and the physical, emotional, and social unpreparedness for commitment to intimacy and for caring for a new generation. In industrial technical societies, in particular, the movement from childhood to the adult generation requires many years of experience. Although adolescence currently covers the teenage period, its onset varies with constitutional differences in times of sexual maturation and its duration is influenced by socioeconomic and other cultural factors. The youth whose father is a laborer and who leaves school at sixteen to take a semiskilled job and marries at eighteen has a brief adolescence. In contrast, graduate students who still have another three or four years of study ahead of them may be considered adolescent in some respects, for they are still unprepared to assume adult responsibilities at the high level for which they are preparing. We shall, however, somewhat arbitrarily, consider that adolescence ends around the age of nineteen, when most persons have completed their physical growth, and have become legally responsible for themselves; we shall therefore leave the life of older youths to the next chapter.

The passage through adolescence forms a critical period. At the start children are still at play, dependently attached to their parents and with futures unshaped; and at the end they will be responsible for themselves, their personalities patterned, their future direction indicated. The period leading up to the closure of adolescence is particularly important, for now the personality must gel into a workable integrate. Achieving a successful integration depends upon a reasonably successful passage through all prior developmental stages, but also upon the solution of a number of tasks specific to adolescence which leads to a reintegration and reorganization of the personality structure to permit the individual to function as a reasonably self-sufficient adult. One of Erikson's major contributions to psychoanalytic developmental psychology was his emphasis upon the crucial importance of late adolescence. Now, the young person must gain an ego identity, an identity in his or her own right and not simply as someone's son or daughter, an identity in the sense of a unique consistency of behavior that permits others to have expectations of how the person will behave and react. The person will have, in a sense, answered the question "Who am I?" and therefore others will know who the individual is. The achievement of an ego identity usually requires the concurrent attainment of the capacity to move toward interdependence with a person of the opposite sex: an intimacy that properly encompasses far more than the capacity to have sexual relations, or even to enjoy orgasmic pleasure in the act. It concerns an ability to dare to form a significant relationship without fear of loss of the self.* But adolescence is contemporaneously a lengthy developmental stage, and there are various other developmental tasks that must be carried out before an ego identity and a capacity for intimacy can be attained.

Whatever equilibrium had been established that permitted the relative calm of the "latency" period is upset by the biological changes that usher in puberty. First, children find themselves growing away from their childhoods as the prepubertal spurt of growth places an increasing distance between their eyes and feet, and size alone begins to bring them nearer to the adult world. Then, the maturation of secondary sexual characteristics tends further to estrange children from their bodies, and soon thereafter an upsurge of sexual feelings that intervene in fantasy, dreams, thoughts, and behavior alters young persons' feelings about themselves and those close to them. Even as the adolescent's self-image and perspective of the world is changing, and as emotions and sensitivities come under the impact of new sensations and compelling drive impulsions, equally profound changes in intellectual capacities occur, for the adolescent becomes capable of conceptual thinking or, in Piaget's terms, enters into the stage of *formal operations*. It is important that the tasks and conflicts imposed by biological ripening are usually accompanied by an increased intellectual potential to help cope with them.

Adolescence is a period during which children can prepare for self-sufficiency and independence while still gaining support, protection, and guidance from parents. The need to gain increasing independence from one's parents creates serious difficulties both for adolescents and for their families. The teenagers' situations become increasingly paradoxical, for even as they are becoming members of the adult generation, they remain

---

* Erikson (1956) considers the gaining of an ego identity as the primary task of adolescence and an essential precursor of the capacity for intimacy. For reasons that will be presented in the discussion of late adolescence, I consider these two tasks as interrelated, moving ahead in steplike phases that alternate or provide support for one another, with the final phases of gaining a capacity for intimacy following the achievement of an independent identity. By the end of adolescence, although the person has achieved an identity, he or she may still be caught in a conflict between fidelity to the self and the society's ethos and mores—problems common to post-adolescent *youth*.

members of the childhood generation within their families, where they lack certain adult prerogatives and opportunities for self-completion. The movement beyond the family gains impetus from the upsurge of sexual drives. In contrast to the erotized and sensuous longings and desires of childhood, sexual feelings are now driven by hormonal impulsions and are not easily repressed. The thoughts and feelings instigated by the drive naturally tend to attach to those who have been sources of love and affection, but run up against the generation boundaries, the incest taboo, and the guilt and fears that had been evoked earlier and brought closure to the oedipal phase. Now, however, repression cannot be as successful as earlier, and the sexual feelings must be redirected out of the family circle.

It seems essential to emphasize that the genital sexuality of adolescence is very different from prepubertal sexuality. Freud tended to obscure the difference in order to accentuate his discovery of the pervasive influence of sexuality throughout childhood. Prepubertal sexuality concerns erotic and sensuous aspects of affectional attachments, including the influence of stimulation of erogenous zones, upon general attitudes, thoughts and behavior, but it is not drive-impelled in the same sense as adolescent and adult sexuality; it does not involve increased hormonal secretions, a need to discharge sperm and semen, shifts in the menstrual cycle, or the increased erogenous sensitivity that follows the maturation of sexual organs at puberty. It is essential to any coherent theory and description of personality development to differentiate between pre- and postpubertal sexuality.

Both the move toward independence from the family and the control and redirection of sexual impulsions require reorganization of superego directives. Although the youth may continue to accept and adhere to parental standards in many areas, they should become one's own standards rather than rules imposed by parents; they should become more completely internalized and, as far as some directives are concerned, become more ego functions rather than superego edicts (Loewald, 1951). The superego directives must also change to become suited to help direct adult rather than childhood behavior and to permit sexual gratification and intimacy.

An important aspect of finding an adult identity and becoming capable of intimacy involves the clarification and strengthening of gender identity. Gender identity, as we have noted, becomes established within the first few years of life and is strengthened by the resolution of the oedipal phase and by peer-group identifications during the juvenile period. However, during adolescence the choice of a love object of the opposite sex helps to settle residues of identifications with the parent of the opposite sex and desires for the physical attributes and social prerogatives of the other sex. The process involves a reworking of the adolescents' oedipal attachment to the parent of the opposite sex and often renewed struggles concerning identification with the parent of the same sex now that the sexual impulsions of adolescence rekindle these old problems. The dynamics of these vicissitudes in the choice of love objects, and their impact on the achievement of a firm sexual identity will be discussed more fully below.

The essential tasks of adolescence lead to some conflicts with parents that are, in our society, almost an inherent part of adolescence. Readjustments are required of parents as well as the child, and a child's adolescence can provoke turmoil within a parent and conflict between parents as well as between parents and child. We shall seek to examine the relationship between the conflicts with the parents and the conflicts that rage within the adolescent. In considering the changes in the adolescent's personality according to the *structural concept*, we must recognize the profound reorganization required because of the increased force of the sexual impulsions; because of the development of new intellectual resources; and because of the changes in the superego injunctions as well as the new ability to gain directives from ideals and ideologies. The inner conflicts between the new, intensified id drives and the supergo injunctions provoke anxiety as the ego, so to speak, is squeezed between them, requiring new defenses. Anxieties also arise because adolescents must sort out variant potential organizations of the self and come to grips with how and where they will direct their lives.

Adolescence is a time of particular significance to psychiatry, for it is then that the severe emotional casualties appear in appreciable numbers. Even though much of the damage may have occurred earlier in life, it is at this period that those severe failures of integration that we term schizophrenic withdraw from social participation, cease trying to live confined by the culture's logic and language, and retreat into fantasy, guided by delusion rather than reality; and other adolescents rebelliously turn away from the restrictions required for social living and seek to live without the law.

Now, as these introductory comments indicate, the essential tasks of adolescence are complex and not readily summed up under the rubric of the attainment of an ego identity. The several requisite achievements are precursors of a person's integration into a reasonably independent individual about to launch on a course through life and to become intimately interdependent with another in order to gain completion as an adult man or woman. However, these complex tasks cannot be mastered rapidly. Adolescence is, currently, a lengthy period, lasting from five to ten years, and sometimes even longer. Properly, it is still a period of dependency, when teenagers are still trying out ways of living and of relating to others, testing capabilities and emotional limitations; they can still assume and shed roles, and bestow love without expectation that it will lead to permanent attachments. The period involves considerable trying out, with an implicit understanding that one is not yet playing for keeps. Adolescents are exploring their worlds and learning to know themselves, but the parents are still available to offer protection and guidance, and periods of regressive dependency upon them remain possible during recuperation from defeat or disappointment.

THREE SUBPERIODS OF ADOLESCENCE

To bring some order to the description and discussion of the dynamics of this lengthy period, we shall divide it into three subperiods. However, these divisions cannot be considered as definitive separations because adolescents vary considerably in how and when they work through various aspects of adolescence. It is clear enough that the pubescent twelve-year-old differs markedly from a college sophomore, but there is considerable variation in how one turns into the other. Even though it has been fairly customary to focus separately on the prepubertal preparation for adolescence, and then divide adolescence proper into an early and late phase, we shall make different subdivisions. Three overlapping phases will be considered. *Early adolescence* will include the prepubertal phase when the spurt in growth initiates developmental changes and the onset of puberty which does not usually provoke a marked shift in orientation. Early teenagers still continue in many patterns established earlier, remaining in monosexual groups and with home still very much the center of their lives. Then, about twelve or eighteen months after pubescence, an expansive period of *mid-adolescence* sets in, when movement toward the opposite sex begins to break up peer groupings and intimate friendships. It is then that the period of revolt and conformity, so characteristic of adolescence, is apt to start— revolt from parental and adult dictates and conformity to peer-group standards, loyalties, and ideologies. There is often a beginning of sexual exploration, which is often concerned more with breaking through inhibitions and testing one's own limits rather than with an interest in intimacy; and love and sex may be kept quite separate. New horizons open which the adolescent wishes to explore. It is also a time of marked ambivalence and mood swings. Sooner or later a period of delimitation, *late adolescence*, sets in when the young person becomes concerned with the tangible tasks of coming to grips with the future. The boy becomes concerned about his career, and currently the girl may become caught up in the difficult problem of how she will reconcile a career and marriage. The reorganization of adolescence comes to an end; delimitation is accepted and guidance may be welcomed. The period of late adolescence carries the individual into occupational and marital choices which consolidate the ego identity and capacities for intimacy; and even though these are often partly adolescent problems they will be left for discussion in the chapters on the young adult period.

EARLY ADOLESCENCE

The gradual progression of children toward maturity and independence is disrupted by the transformation of puberty which changes physique, drives, intellectual capacities, and social milieu and requires profound intrapsychic reorganization. Children become impelled toward becoming adults by the change in their size and contours; they must cope with a new inner pressure that creates strange feelings and longings, and adds an impulsivity and irrational force with which they have had little experience but with which each must cope very much on one's own—for as it is an intensely personal matter that involves the ties to the parents, the child finds it difficult if not impossible to seek their help. It is a metamorphosis that brings about a new and definitive physical differentiation between the sexes, but also increases the attraction between them and prepares the individual for a search for a new type of intimacy and gratification which becomes a keystone in happiness and a loadstone in motivation.

THE PREPUBERTAL SPURT IN GROWTH

The adolescent readjustment is set off even prior to pubescence when the gradual increase in size and weight that had prevailed since the age of two abruptly shifts into high gear. The child had been gaining approximately four to six pounds a year, but about two years before the onset of puberty girls start to gain about eleven pounds and grow three to four inches a year; and boys gain thirteen to fourteen pounds and grow four to five inches a year for the next five or six years. The boy's muscle mass and strength double between the ages of twelve and seventeen, which has a profound influence upon his behavior and his self-image. Children's orientation and view of life begin to shift simply because of their change in size; they are growing away from childhood and children, and adults are becoming less distant and awesome. Two factors in this upsurge in growth are important in changing the nature of the childhood society, and they are factors which carry over into puberty: girls mature about two years earlier than boys; and there is considerable variation between individuals in the time of onset of the spurt in growth. In girls the median age of pubescence is at about twelve and a half, between eleven and fifteen in eighty percent, "normally" between ten and seventeen, and with only rare exception between nine and eighteen.* In boys the onset cannot be determined as readily but puberty occurs about two years later with a median age of about fifteen. Thus, the upsurge in growth starts between ten and eleven in most girls and between twelve and thirteen in the majority of boys. In the sixth to eighth grades the girls tend to tower over the boys, some beginning to look like young women; while most of the boys are still immature. Movement of the two sexes toward one another is first impeded by the differences in size and then by the differences in the sexual maturity of boys and girls of the same age and educational level.

The Reshuffling of Peer Groups

The child can be upset when the spurt in growth and onset of puberty occur either particularly early or late. The girl who develops precociously worries about becoming a giant, and then may become embarrassed by her difference from friends and classmates as well as by her sexual feelings for which she has had little time to prepare. A mother described how she found herself becoming infuriated at men whose eyes lustfully followed her ten-year-old daughter whose bust and buttocks were rapidly taking on womanly proportions: "I want to scream at them that she is still only a little girl." The tardy girl starts to wonder if she will ever become a woman and worries about her endocrine system. Early maturation is usually more pleasing to a boy than late development. This is a time of maximal interest in competitive sports, and late maturation may force the redirection of interests. Still, it is often the disruptions of close friendships due to differing rates of maturation that may be most upsetting to some children. The girl

* Figures vary from country to country: menarche had been found to occur in the United States at a mean age of 12.7 ± 1.2 years (Reiter and Kulin, 1972); in Florence, Italy, at 12.5; and in France at 13.5 (Duche et al., 1966). The age of menarche has become lower, by about four months every ten years over the past one hundred thirty years, possibly as a result of improved nutrition. The mean body weight at menarche is 48 kg. (105 pounds) (Frisch and Revelle, 1970). However, recent studies indicate that currently menarche occurs at a mean age of 12.8 years in girls in the United States, the same age as in their mothers. The lowering of the age may have leveled off (L. Zacharias, 1976).

who has already started to menstruate and feels a physical attraction to boys has new interests and secrets that she does not confide in her former inseparable girl friend who is still "a child." In the reshuffling of groups and the formation of new close friendships, the less mature girl may be left feeling lonely and neglected. She may, however, remain more popular with boys of her age who are not yet ready to relate to more sexually mature girls. Prepubertal girls tend to have a greater interest in sexual matters than boys perhaps because they undergo a more profound physical trans- formation in becoming a woman. They are likely to form small cliques in preparation for the coming transition within which they exchange knowl- edge, beliefs, and misconceptions of menstruation, breast development, procreation, and childbirth and perhaps compare their changing physiques. Many form an intimate friendship with other girls with whom private feel- ings and fears, and even family troubles, are shared. The prepubertal boy having some friends who have matured also seeks knowledge, and is often fascinated by scatology which has a sexual connotation to him, and in telling stories he must pretend to understand to be one of the gang. More or less accurate information about sexual intercourse becomes common knowledge, but adult indulgence in erotic pleasures is difficult to compre- hend for the child who does not yet know the drive of intense sexual urges. They may find it difficult to believe that their own parents indulge in such unseemly conduct and fight off disillusionment in them.

The onset of puberty does not upset the monosexual peer groupings very noticeably. The shift in interest to the opposite sex that is driven by sexual impulsion usually lags a year or two behind pubescence. To some extent, the young adolescents' attentions and energies are absorbed narcissistically, as they are directed toward gaining a new self-image by the rapid altera- tions in their bodies and feelings which lead to comparisons with friends of the same sex and to a need for a close attachment to a friend of the same sex. As the development of secondary sexual characteristics starts earlier in the girl and alters her more markedly than the boy, we shall consider her first.

PUBERTY IN THE GIRL

Adolescence in the girl properly starts with an enlargement of the ovaries and the ripening of one of the Graafian follicles that will later produce an ovum, but the first visible manifestations are the elevation of the areola surrounding the nipple to form a small conical protuberance, or "bud," and the rounding of the hips due to broadening of the bony pelvis and the deposition of subcutaneous fat. The breasts also enlarge by disposition of adipose tissue and then by the development of the mammary glands and their ducts. The legs lengthen, changing bodily proportions, and the thighs approximate one another. During mid- and late adolescence pubic and axillary hair appears, the labia and clitoris develop, and the clitoris becomes erectile. The skin secretions change, becoming more sebaceous and contributing to the development of that bane of most adolescents, acne. Sweat glands become hyperactive with ensuing hyperhidrosis, which creates an odor which can embarrass the girl. Although seemingly trivial, acne and perspiration become matters of considerable moment to adolescents of both sexes.

Then, some time after the first changes in her physique have occurred, the girl starts to menstruate and she feels herself a woman. A few periods of spotty and almost unnoticeable discharge may precede menarche, and the periods are apt to be scanty and irregular for a year. Although ovulation may not occur during the first few months following menarche, it does take place almost half of the time and pregnancies can and do occur. Variability in the menstrual cycle is common. Even between the ages of seventeen and twenty, fewer than twenty percent of adolescent girls menstruate every twenty-eight days.

Currently, most girls are prepared by their parents and schools for menstruation. The schools show fifth-grade girls a film and distribute booklets. An examination of these materials (Whisnant *et al.*, 1975) has revealed marked shortcomings. While they assure that girls are not taken by surprise and have some knowledge of what menstruation is about, they cannot be considered adequate sources by either the girls or their parents.* Menarche forms a critical moment in a girl's life and it is probably unfortunate that much of the emphasis of instructional materials is upon casual acceptance. The first menstrual period is usually a very meaningful time for the girl and her parents, particularly her mother. Even though many pre-

---

* Most of these films and pamphlets are provided by industries to gain consumers for sanitary products. They are careful not to offend parents. The materials minimize the girl's subjective experience and convey how a girl should feel and behave rather than help her to explore her feelings. They draw the girl's attention away from her interest in the changes in her body and feelings and focus on cleanliness, daintiness, and ways of concealing menstruation from others. The information provided about internal and external sexual organs is inadequate and misleading. Many girls are led to believe that the bleeding comes from the ovum rather than the uterine lining. Girls are told that they are about to become "women" rather than adolescents, which can confuse them (Whisnant *et al.*, 1975).

pubertal girls say that the onset of menses will be "no big thing" they await the moment as an indication that they are developing normally, and when it comes they feel a sense of deep gratification and relief. Even though prepared, some feel terrified and bewildered and may start to sob—a reaction that may be primarily a release of pent-up anticipation and concern. The girl may have promised her best friend to tell her immediately, but most girls will first tell their mothers and elicit their congratulations, advice, and help. Commonly, menarche leads to a new closeness between the girl and her mother. Now the girl may for the first time really feel herself to be a woman like her mother. Reverie turns to what sort of woman and mother she will become in comparison with her mother. Girls who are sensitive to their feelings may not be able to express themselves in words, but are aware that something deeply meaningful has happened to them.

Occasionally, despite preparation and precautions, a girl may be seriously embarrassed when her first period stains her dress at school, or blood drops to the floor in the dining hall or at a party. Then, too, not all girls are properly prepared, and one occasionally finds a girl who was terrified by the flow of blood, and some who concealed it believing that it was a sign of some dread disease or a result of masturbation. The term commonly used by women for their menses, "the curse," tends to express, however jocularly, the notion that menstruation forms a symbol of woman's burden and inferior status.* Despite such feelings, however, it is also an important badge of womanhood. When the author engaged in a study of a group of women who had a virilizing pseudohermaphroditic syndrome at a time when the condition first could be reversed by cortisone therapy, he found it of interest that these women who had no breast development or other secondary sexual characteristics, and had deeply pigmented skins and kinky hair, expressed the hope that the new treatment would enable them to menstruate, even if it could do nothing else for them.

Menarche, and in some individuals each recurrence of menstruation, can reactivate a girl's dissatisfactions and concerns over being a female. The secret fantasy of really being a boy, which occurs with varying force in some girls, must now face the challenge of reality. A young woman described previously who was seriously ill with ulcerative colitis considered that her menarche formed a trauma she had never been able to assimilate.

---

* It is important to realize that before disposable menstrual pads were invented by army nurses during World War I, and their commercial introduction in the 1920s, the care of menstrual cloths or "rags" was a somewhat time-consuming and rather messy affair—and often difficult for a young girl—and that it was probably not as easy for women to remain as mobile and as free from menstrual odor as now.

Throughout childhood she was her father's "pal" and insisted that she was really a boy, and that she had only been a girl because her mother insisted on dressing her as a girl. With menarche she finally capitulated, but experienced bitter hostility toward her mother for having made her a girl. She later tried to achieve a compromise with her sexuality and overcome her feelings toward her mother by becoming a nun.

Acceptance of Femininity

How the girl accepts the change in her physique and menstruation depends, of course, on the stability of her gender identity: upon the firmness of gender allocation by her parents within the first few years of life; upon passing through childhood in a manner that leads to a firm identification with her mother; upon the group identities she achieved during the juvenile period. But during early adolescence when she is learning to feel at home with her woman's body and with woman's role in society, the parents' attitudes are particularly important—their attitudes toward their daughter but also toward one another. When a mother not only accepts her life as a woman but finds challenge if not fulfillment in it, and when a father admires and appreciates his wife, a girl can welcome the signs that she has become a woman and feel secure that she will be loved and find satisfaction in life as a woman. However, acceptance of being a woman is not the same as acceptance of the place and roles that have been given women in society. Even though a girl need not feel confined and limited because of her sex as in former eras, she may still resent the imbalance in opportunities for a career, and boys' superior attitudes.*

Currently, there is less dissatisfaction with being female and more about the prejudices that block opportunities. Whatever potential dissatisfactions there may be about having been born a girl are usually overshadowed by the adolescent's pride in her new status as a woman, the acquisition of a physique that attracts attention, and the value of the capacity to bear children, and in having the opportunity to be creative through bearing children and following a career, or to be able to choose one way or the other. Although many, if not most, girls have at some time had regrets at

---

* Whereas cultural change has greatly modified the feminine position in society, conferring advantages over the male in some areas, it has also diminished the tendency toward fatalistic and unconscious acceptance of being a member of the "second sex," and has opened the way for more conscious ambivalence and for more acceptable strivings toward active careers, thus bringing new sources of dissatisfaction and unhappiness into the lives of some women.

being female,* most will recognize some of the advantages and gain contentment through building upon these potential assets. In recent years it has become clear to many psychoanalysts that many men have deep but more hidden wishes to have been a woman, and in the past decade the dress and behavior of many adolescent boys has made this rather obvious.† As Bettelheim (1954) has noted, children of both sexes have some envy of the attributes and advantages of the other.

THE INFLUENCE OF THE MENSTRUAL CYCLE

With the menarche the girl's life comes under a new influence that is often puzzling to her as well as to those who live with her. The cyclic changes in the hormonal balance each month either directly or indirectly influence her mood and behavior. Benedek and Rubenstein (1942) carried out hormonal studies of women who were in psychoanalysis, and followed the nature of their dreams at various phases of the menstrual cycle. They reached the conclusion that during the first phase of the cycle, when the ovarian follicle is ripening, estrogen secretion mobilizes heterosexual tendencies and outgoing behavior, the sexual desires reaching a height at the time of ovulation—usually about twelve days after the start of the last menses; then, following ovulation, the progestin secretion favors a more passive receptive attitude and an inner-directedness, as if preparing the woman emotionally as well as physically for pregnancy; then, shortly before the start of the next period, progestin secretion drops sharply and the woman is apt to feel empty, irritable, and moody.**

---

* Whereas the "penis envy," which psychoanalysis believed all women must overcome or come to terms with, may not form a significant unconscious concern in all, it clearly has dynamic moment in the lives of some girls, particularly at menarche.

† It has been fairly acceptable for a woman to wish to be a man, but shameful for a man to wish to be a woman. Nevertheless, many more men seek to be turned into a woman operatively than vice versa. The Plains Indians institutionalized the "berdache"— men who chose to live as women, but who were also unusually brave in battle as members of the Crazy Horse societies. We have already commented on the elaborate rituals required to assure that New Guinea boys will relinquish early feminine identifications and develop into warriors.

** Although, as far as the author knows, there has been no attempt to replicate the Benedek-Rubenstein studies, a number of studies have confirmed the premenstrual tendency toward depression and anxiety. Ivey and Bardwick (1968), in a systematic study of twenty-six college students, found that anxiety scores on a test were significantly higher premenstrually than at the time of ovulation, and that death-anxiety, hostility, and feelings of inability to cope were much more prominent premenstrually. Premenstrual changes in the direction of anxiety and lowered mood and confidence could be found in virtually all subjects.

Although in very many women the cyclic changes in behavior and mood are scarcely noticeable, in some they almost dominate the women's life and the shifts in their behavior are almost incomprehensible without regard to the cycle. Thus a woman in intensive psychotherapy, albeit a very disturbed woman, exhibited very different attitudes toward the therapist as well as toward her husband and children in the different phases

Such cyclic changes have long been considered as an inner tide that influences the woman's life and exerts some degree of control over her conscious and unconscious behavior and thought. It is apparent that many women are profoundly affected by the course of the menstrual cycle—both by its physiological influences and by the unconscious attitudes provoked by menstruation. Among other influences, the increase in interstitial fluid premenstrually, which is quite marked in some women, can produce discomfort and irritability, but this is not usually an adolescent problem. The girl's attitudes toward her menses may reflect her mother's warnings that a girl must remain inactive during her period and put up with this burden in life, but more often will reflect her mother's own behavior. It is natural enough for a girl who has seen her mother become incapacitated for several days each month to anticipate her menarche with foreboding, and then perhaps to utilize her periods in order to obtain a secondary gain of attention and concern from those about her. Incapacitation during menses often runs in families. Even without such disturbances, the menstrual cycle provides a periodicity to a girl's life and an awareness of the passing of months accompanied by changes in mood and activity which form a major distinction between male and female psychology.

Her Changing Appearance

Concern with the continuing transformation of her figure naturally preoccupies the adolescent girl. She feels that her popularity and her chances of attracting a desirable husband will be markedly influenced by her changing facial configuration and her emerging bodily contours. Only an occasional girl can appreciate that attractiveness is not primarily tied to physical configurations, and if she is not pretty seek to become attractive through fostering other assets. To a very large degree the girl, despite her careful attention to what she sees in the mirror, and despite her constant comparisons of her own physique with those of friends and movie starlets, does not achieve an estimate of her charms by what she sees as much as through how she perceives others regard her; and at this age her father's reactions

---

of the cycle, month after month. In the postmenstrual phase she dressed carefully and tended to be seductive and outgoing—striving to please her therapist by what she brought to the sessions; during the second half of the cycle she would neglect her dress, become very discontented with life, and carry a chip on her shoulder, often attacking the therapist verbally; then premenstrually she would feel despondent and express her hopelessness, at times thinking of running away to find a new life, at others behaving like a helpless child and becoming dependent upon her husband and children as well as her therapist.

to her are particularly significant. The father is very likely to draw away from a daughter entering her teens, feeling that he should no longer be as physically close as previously, and he is often withdrawing from the sexual feelings she induces in him. The daughter often feels that her father now finds her unattractive or is actually repelled by something about her.* When the father separates from the mother and seeks a divorce, which seems to occur with particular frequency just when the girl becomes adolescent, the situation is aggravated. It requires considerable tact on the part of a father to convey somehow that he considers that his daughter has become attractive and likes the way she looks and yet assume a proper distance. The changes in the way in which boys and men relate to the girl can also cause anguish, embarrassment, or pleasure. A girl may become flaming red when boys emit low whistles as she walks by, or become upset when they look at another girl but not at her. A typical feminine dilemma sets in. The girl will be upset if boys do not seek her out because of her appearance but becomes angered because they like her for her looks and not for "herself," and later because they are interested or not interested in her sexually rather than in that indefinable self.

PUBERTY IN THE BOY

The physical maturation of the adolescent boy is also striking, even though it does not involve as much of a metamorphosis as the girl's. The alterations in size and muscular strength prepare him for the role of guardian and hunter. It would appear that such changes move him into a period of heightened athletic activity and competitiveness in contemporary society, and contribute to his difficulties in remaining a child in relationship to his parents. The size of the genitalia remained unchanged throughout childhood, but now at about the age of twelve or thirteen the testes begin to increase in size and the scrotal skin to roughen and redden; these changes are soon followed by an increase in the size of the penis. The appearance of pubic hair is followed by growth of axillary hair. The prostate and seminal vesicles mature, and spermatozoa form. The beard and body hair appear

---

* Women in intensive psychotherapy or analysis are often astounded when they develop the insight that their father's withdrawal was in reaction to attraction and sexual stimulation rather than because of disappointment in their daughter's appearance—an insight that sometimes marks a significant turn in therapy.

and the voice deepens, usually about four years after the first pubertal changes and when bodily growth is almost completed. The indentation of the temporal hair line is among the very last changes and indicates that adolescent maturation has been completed. Most boys are fully mature at seventeen or eighteen, but some complete maturation at fifteen and others not until twenty (Schonfeld, 1943).

Many boys have been masturbating before adolescence, but the activity generally increases after puberty.* Ejaculation occurs after maturation of the prostate and seminal vesicles, but spermatozoa are neither numerous nor motile, so that the adolescent remains sterile for a year or longer after ejaculation first occurs. Nocturnal emissions usually start between fourteen and sixteen and can cause considerable concern if the boy has not been properly prepared by his parents, though most youths will have learned about the phenomenon from friends. A boy may think that something is drastically wrong, perhaps that masturbation has damaged him. However, even the informed may experience anxiety because of the nature of the vivid dreams which precede and accompany the nocturnal emission and which seem more real than most dreams. The repressed sexual wishes of the adolescent may find undisguised expression in the accompanying dream and, at this time of life, are likely to contain homosexual and incestuous elements.

The force of sexual drives begins to exert its potent influence upon the thought and behavior of the adolescent, and whatever innocence existed in childhood requires strong defenses to maintain, and gives way in thought and fantasy if not in action before the internal pressures that refuse to be completely denied. In general, boys seem to experience urgency concerning sex sooner after puberty than girls and must find ways of coping with it. Stimulation from the seminal vesicles adds to the hormonal influences. Genital sensations cause restlessness, direct his thoughts to sexual objects, and urge him toward relief. Although he has experienced erections since infancy, they now occur with greater frequency, heat, and even pain; and unexpected erections can cause embarrassment. The thoughts that come unbidden and the fantasies in which he finds himself lost also cause embarrassment and feelings of shame which contribute to the frequency of blushing during this time of life.

* According to Kinsey et al. (1948, p. 500) the percentage increases from forty-five at the age of thirteen to seventy-one at fifteen. The study by Robert Sorensen (1973) finds a much lower percentage of boys who have masturbated, but despite the care with which his study was conducted, his figures seem too low and run counter to the experience of psychiatrists.

Masturbatory Concerns

Masturbation is practiced by almost all adolescent boys and, indeed, psychiatrists consider the absence of masturbation during adolescence a cause for concern, as it indicates a need for intense repression—or self-deception. However, in some social groupings masturbation is so frowned upon that early premarital intercourse is fostered.*

Although masturbation is not as common in the adolescent girl, Kinsey's (1953) as well as Sorensen's (1973) figure that forty percent of girls masturbate during adolescence seems a low estimate; many girls can masturbate by pressing their thighs together, and some are unaware that they are masturbating. Girls have less immediate physiological tension that drives them toward relief, as there is no female equivalent to local pressure from the seminal vesicles. The girl is more likely to be aroused by external stimuli and may not masturbate until after she has been sexually aroused by actual experiences with another person. However, in recent years some girls have masturbated regularly following the advice in some sex manuals that it will help them achieve orgasm during intercourse. Such advice filters down to young adolescent girls; and in some groups, peers urge one another to enjoy masturbation. Whereas, in 1970, a study indicated that thirty-five percent of freshman college women masturbated with some regularity, the percentage had doubled by 1974 (Sarrel and Sarrel, 1974).

Masturbation often provokes guilt and concern, particularly in the young adolescent. Such feelings may derive from the fantasies that generally accompany the act, but also from the spoken and unspoken indications from adults and peers that it is shameful and harmful. Although the belief, strongly held during the Victorian era, that masturbation caused insanity, blindness, impotence, and debility is no longer fostered, such ideas fade slowly and masturbation continues to be a source of much anguish to many adolescents.† Boys, perhaps because of the loss of semen, are more apt to be troubled than girls. A cycle may develop in which the boy determines to renounce the practice, struggling with himself to overcome the urge for relief and gratification, but fails to abide by his vow and suffers a loss of

---

* Kinsey has pointed out the marked differences between social classes in the United States at the time of his study. A policeman stemming from the lower class might arrest a boy he finds masturbating, but the judge would not consider it a notable offense—whereas finding youngsters having intercourse might provoke reverse judgments. (See Chapter 10 in Kinsey et al., *Sexual Behavior in the Human Male.*)

† S. M. Woods reported in 1973 that a survey of senior medical students revealed that twelve percent of them still believed that masturbation could cause insanity or homosexuality.

self-respect, considering himself a weak person and a wastrel; this can have a notable effect upon the youth's personality development and character. Still, such concerns are usually weathered and only contribute to major difficulties when other forces lead to asocial behavior. On the positive side, the ability to gain relief from sexual impulses through masturbation often permits the relative quiet needed for study or for delaying marriage in order to prepare for a career.*

Within a year or two after puberty the sexual urges have added a new force to id impulsions and are consciously and unconsciously beginning to become an urgent directive force with which the young person must learn to cope in some manner or other. We shall return to a discussion of some of the influences of puberty upon the family relationships and social life of the teenager and upon the reorganization of his psychic structure, but first we must note the changes in intellectual capacities which are occurring concomitantly.

THE ADOLESCENT'S COGNITIVE DEVELOPMENT

It is of particular interest that at just about the time children are beset by an awakening of sexual drives that demand attention and can lead to impulsive activity that disrupts a life pattern, they also acquire a new scope in their intellectual functioning that enables them to cope with their drives and feelings more effectively. Not only do they become capable of reasoning more logically and abstractly, and to consider imaginatively the effect of what they do upon their future welfare, but they also begin to evaluate their behavior in terms of ideals and ideologies. Of course, we might consider the matter conversely—that is, to note that just as children become capable of thinking far more effectively and directing their lives reasonably toward future goals, a new force that invites irrationality and fosters impulsivity enters their lives. The body's demands for sexual fulfillment that must be contained and at least partially repressed increase the domain and power of unconscious processes and motivations. It has been said that an adolescent boy is a person with two heads and it is often the head of the penis that guides his behavior.

* Kinsey found that whereas masturbation is more common in children from educated circles, even lower-class children who manage to gain a higher education have masturbated more than peers from their social class. (See Chapter 14 in Kinsey *et al.*, *Sexual Behavior in the Human Male.*)

Piaget's Period of Formal Operations

The change in the adolescent's cognitive abilities is not simply a matter of increased intelligence. As Inhelder and Piaget (1958) and Vygotsky (1962) have clearly demonstrated, the gradual increase in intellect leads to a qualitative change at about the time of puberty and the individual enters into a new stage of cognitive development—the period of *formal operations* in Piaget's terms. The stage starts at about the age of eleven or twelve but the capacities to think conceptually and hypothetically develop slowly over the next six or seven years and remain a potentiality attained only partially by most and fully by some (Dulit, 1972).

What is the nature of formal operational thought and why can it change the child's way of life so profoundly? The cardinal change derives from the new-found potentiality for manipulating ideas in themselves and not being limited to manipulating ideas of objects as previously. The adolescent becomes capable of understanding and building abstract theories and concepts. In contrast, the child can have coherent ideas, but does not construct theories. Whereas the child lives essentially in the present and in the domain of concrete reality, the adolescent can become involved in future projects that transcend mere continuities of the present, and can develop a passion for ideas in themselves and for ideals and ideologies. Perhaps the basic differences between the child's and the adolescent's cognitive capacities lie in the adolescent's ability to reason on the basis of hypothesis, that is, on propositions that need not be either true or false, but are formulated in order to try out all possible consequences, which are then checked on the basis of facts (Piaget, 1969). The capacity for hypothetical-deductive thinking is, then, the ability to make logical deductions from imagined conditions. The adolescent can reason "If x is true, then y must follow," and also "Had x been true, y would have been a possibility." The use of language develops to a point where concepts can be abstracted from reality and then be manipulated imaginatively—not simply as fantasy but with concern about figuring out solutions to real problems and the course of future events. Inhelder and Piaget emphasize that the critical attributes of formal operations are both the ability to think about thoughts and a reversal of relationships between what is real and what is possible.*

* Inhelder and Piaget have carefully analyzed the nature of formal operations in terms of symbolic logic and in terms of the mathematical logic of lattices and groups. These contributions to both formal logic and mathematics as well as to epistemology go beyond the scope of the present book and the reader is referred to their joint study, *The Growth of Logical Thinking from Childhood to Adolescence*, and also to Piaget's *Logic and Psychology*.

One of the most characteristic traits of adolescents and youths derives from the newly acquired cognitive faculties. They tend to overestimate the value of their cognitive solutions of problems. They fantasy or carefully develop imaginatively ways in which football teams, families, religions, nations, could be made to function better, ways in which poverty could be wiped out, warfare ended; and they cannot understand why such measures are not adopted. This overevaluation of the subjective over the objective Piaget has termed the *egocentricity of formal operations*. It involves the difficulties in seeing that one's own conceptualizations differ from those of other persons, as well as a neglect of all of the tangible measures that must be taken before a concept involving others or seeking to change institutions can be brought to actualization. Herein lies a source of much of youth's intransigence and argumentativeness but also of its inspiration and idealism. The egocentric orientation will gradually diminish as the adolescent hears others defend opposing points of view, becomes involved in discussions, learns to regard matters from various perspectives before reaching conclusions, and encounters the need to carry out carefully planned actions as well as to formulate the plans.

The extent of the development of formal operations varies greatly from individual to individual and particularly from social class to social class, depending notably upon the educational level achieved. It is uncertain whether the people in some preliterate societies ever reach the level of formal operations, but it is also clear that there are many persons in our society, particularly those who do not have more than a grade school education, whose capacities for formal operations, for concept formation, and for the proper consideration of future goals, are but feebly developed.*
As Piaget (1969) has noted, formal operations may develop differently, if at all, in persons without scientific and literary training, and many problems remain to be solved concerning the development of formal operations.†

---

* They may lack the conceptual tools needed for much hypothetical-deductive thinking, but the areas in which they think conceptually may simply be more limited in accord with their more limited experience in solving problems instrumentally rather than through ritual or magic (Lidz, *et al.*, 1973).

† Inhelder and Piaget (*The Growth of Logical Thinking from Childhood to Adolescence*, p. 337) consider that the transition to the stage of formal operations is made possible by a further maturation of the central nervous system at about the age of eleven or twelve, but they recognize that the relationship is "far from simple, since the organization of formal structures must depend on the social milieu as well. . . . A particular social environment remains indispensable for the realization of these possibilities. It follows that a realization can be accelerated or retarded as a function of cultural and educational conditions. . . . The growth of formal thinking . . . remains dependent on social as much as and more than on neurological factors." Actually they produce

Ideas, Ideals, and Ideologies

Adolescents then move beyond childhood in their capacity to think beyond the present. They can orient themselves to thinking about and directing their lives toward futures they have conceptualized. They also begin to form systems and theories into which they fit their perceptions and conceptions of reality. They become interested in ideas, ideals, and ideologies, and these serve to lift them beyond the present moment, their body's demands, and desires for hedonistic gratification. They can be motivated by goals that even surmount their lifetimes. They may well walk through these years of adolescence with eyes riveted on an unattainable star even as the body is demanding relief from the sexual tensions that possess it. Adolescents conceptualize social systems as well as logical systems. Behavior can be directed by the values of the social systems rather than simply through interpersonal relations and values, and they begin to place their families, their parents, and themselves in a broader social context in which the societal values are superordinate to the family value systems. The new abilities enable youths to embrace ideologies, to challenge the status quo, to envision a better world, to gain gratification through fantasy while waiting to become able to achieve in reality, and in general to soar above the prosaic world with its plodding inhabitants. The development of higher moral judgments and values clearly depends upon the development of formal operational thinking. As Kohlberg (1964) has shown, a morality of individual rights and communal welfare, and a morality based on individual conscience rather than laws or rules, does not begin to develop until the onset of adolescence, and even then in only a small minority of persons.

In early adolescence the new cognitive abilities are just beginning to develop and the potentialities opened by them are not yet striking, for they are still emergent and young adolescents are still only preparing to develop their own ideas and to try them out. Nevertheless, the new intellectual resources are important in increasing the ability to cope with the heightened aggressive and sexual impulses, to consider future objectives, and to enable them to become interested in new adventures into the world of

---

no evidence that the capacity for formal operations depends upon a further maturation of the cerebral cortex rather than upon the steplike development of the intellectual processes, the stage of formal education achieved, and the demands of moving toward adult responsibility. A similar line of reasoning would lead to the conclusion that the type of scientific thinking that started during the late Renaissance had awaited the further genetic evolution of the brain, rather than cultural evolution and the acquisition of some new and essential tools for thinking, such as the decimal system and algebra.

imagination that offer alternative as well as substitute activities and gratifications. The young adolescents' intellectual development is part of the entire process of adolescent awakening in which new horizons open before them and they begin to see the world in which they are going to live with an exciting and poignant freshness.

SEXUAL DRIVES

Early Adolescent Crushes

The onset of adolescence does not produce any striking changes in behavior or way of life for a year or longer. It is a time of inner stirring from sexual arousal, but the boy or girl is not yet ready to act upon the impulsions and much of the sexual arousal is absorbed by fantasy and by preoccupations with the changes that are occurring in the body and in one's own feelings. The adolescents continue to go around in the same monosexual groupings as they did but with the group membership shifting because of the differing rates of maturation and as close friendships give way to crushes. This is a time of intense crushes, some of which are directed toward persons of the same sex. In general, girls have more intense and outspoken crushes than boys, feel freer to manifest them, and talk together about a boy with whom one or several of the group have "fallen in love." There are also crushes on an older person of the same or the opposite sex. The adored person is often someone very much like the self or someone whom the adolescent would like to be. The differentiation between an object of identification and a love object is still not clear. In the process of moving from self-love to the love of another person, the love of someone like the self is a way station. Boys, in particular, are not yet sure enough of themselves to move toward a person of the opposite sex and the attachments are part of the process of self-completion. Girls are apt to have crushes on boys earlier than boys seek after girls, not only because they become pubescent at an earlier age but also because the boy is still fighting against his dependency upon mothering figures and fears losing his identity through engulfment by a female.

The crushes on older persons—a teacher, camp counselor, scoutmaster, older sibling of a friend whom the teenager at first admires from afar—can be extremely embarrassing and difficult for the older person. Girls find it romantic to have a crush and can unwittingly or intentionally embarrass a young male teacher or counselor to whom the postpubertal girl can be tempting and attractive. The young adolescent can find all sorts of ways to seduce the teacher or counselor into bestowing special attention and affection on him or her, and then becomes hurt and even depressed when the older person either purposely or unknowingly rebuffs the advances. Sometimes, the young teenage girl becomes seductive in nymphet fashion, having found power in her attractiveness and, perhaps, having a great need to displace her sexual attraction for her father. However, the tendency to have such intense feelings for older persons contains as much or more danger of homosexual than heterosexual seduction, because persons who are homosexually attracted to the young adolescent—that is, to a person who is not too definitively either a boy or girl—often take up occupations or activities that permit them to have close relationships with youngsters of this age group. However, the adolescent's crushes at this time generally are benign and fill important functions in personality development. They are part of the process of movement away from dependency on parents, and the new object of attachment forms an ideal that the youth seeks to emulate, and in the process the youth gains new ego ideals that modify the superego originally based on parental models, directives, and dictates.

Sublimation of Sexuality

The sexual impulses of boys are largely drained off into other activities, or at least efforts at sublimation of sexuality are pursued intensively. The boy seeks to gain repute among his friends and to emulate his heroes by means of his athletic prowess. His efforts to achieve security as a man and prestige as a masculine figure are still more important to him than the pursuit of love objects. He is still seeking recognition and admiration from his male peers to affirm his own worth, and only later will he perform athletically in order to gain the admiration of girls. The girls who are physically and often emotionally more mature are usually still not ready to go out with older boys. Dating is primarily a matter of going to parties together, and at such parties kissing games, perhaps with the opportunity for tentative but exciting fondling, are a means of approaching intimacy while safe because of the presence of others.

There is, of course, considerable daydreaming about the other sex, and often there are important secret crushes. The girl, in particular, may begin to spend hours by herself daydreaming of an older boy whom she admires from afar and about whom she constructs a wealth of fantasies, even transforming herself and her hero into a knight and lady reenacting tales of chivalry.

Society usually provides means of strengthening ethical standards as children approach and pass through puberty. The scouts mobilize idealistic strivings and provide a code of ethics while seeking to interest the young adolescent in nature, as well as providing a favorable group setting to offset antisocial group formation. Religious feelings become important and churches provide confirmation ceremonies with preparatory classes that reinforce ethical values. Adolescents with their new interests in ideals and ideologies can now find an interest in religion, although it may have only bored them previously. They not only need strengthening of superego directives but are also beginning to seek reasons and meanings in life. Confirmation ceremonies seek primarily to designate to adolescents that they have reached a time of life when they must become responsible for their moral and religious behavior. Adolescents now often experience a closeness to a Deity and feel that they have support and guidance in countering the temptations that are besetting them. The attachment to the church will form an indirect continuing bond to the parents, whom they may now be starting to deny.

The Resurgence of Oedipal Feelings

Although adolescents' relationships to their families are beginning to change, they are still very much family centered, accepting their positions as members of the childhood generation even though they are beginning to feel uneasy in them. Along with the upsurge of sexual feelings there is some reawakening of oedipal attachments. The sensuous and affectional attachments to the parent of the opposite sex, even though under the ban of repression, are the obvious channels into which the sexual feelings can flow. The oedipal attachments have to be resolved once again but at a different level, and this time the sexual feelings will not be repressed so much as redirected away from the parent. The boy may now begin to idealize his mother and find nothing wrong in commenting on how beautiful she is and seek ways to please her and gain her affection. He may feel that his father does not appreciate her enough and fantasy being her defender, or flare up at an older sister who carps at their mother. The girl's situation differs, as has been previously noted, for either just prior to the onset of puberty or early in adolescence she turns from her father and her father turns away from her. It usually constitutes the primary renunciation of her attachment to her father rather than a repetition of an earlier situation, and it can leave the girl feeling deserted, lonely, and even empty.

Then, as the real upsurge of sexual feelings gets under way, adolescents begin to turn away from their attachments to a parent, unconsciously and sometimes consciously concerned by the sexual aspects of the attraction. They begin to find fault with the parent, criticizing him or her, convincing themselves that the parent is not attractive and not an object worth seeking. The criticism also spreads to the parent of the same sex, for they begin to try to free themselves from the domination of superego injunctions based in large part on internalizations of the parents and their dictates. They do so by devaluating the worth of the parent. This process will pick up intensity as adolescence progresses and we will examine it in greater detail in discussing mid-adolescence. The girl is apt to dream of being a woman more capable than her mother, a person more attractive to her father, and may begin to talk to her mother in rather condescending tones, sorry for this "has-been" who has passed her prime. It is generally helpful to the girl and her development if the mother is not angered by the condescension and can allow her daughter to indulge in such fantasies of being a more desirable female and potential sexual partner than her mother. It helps the girl gain self-esteem and enables her to feel capable of relating successfully to boys.

Young adolescents are about to start the process of emancipation, to begin to experience feelings that are difficult to contain, and to relate to people more as adults than as children. It is a difficult time, and during the beginning of adolescence they are not yet ready to assume responsibility for themselves and to be capable of containing their drives and fantasies on their own. They still require direction and protection; and even though they may be beginning to be rebellious, they are apt to feel unloved and unwanted unless the parents place limits upon their behavior and provide safeguards against their venturing beyond their depth.

MID-ADOLESCENCE

OVERCOMING FAMILY ATTACHMENTS AND CONTROLS

Mid-adolescence is a pivotal time of life when youths turn away from the family that has formed the center of their existence for some fourteen or fifteen years. A year or two after pubescence the increase in sexual drive adds impetus to the movement toward adulthood. After the brief recrudescence of oedipal attachments, the intensity of the feelings creates a need for adolescents to gain emotional distance from their parents. They will be motivated to form and maintain affectional and sexual relationships to persons outside the family; to have, for the first time, both affectional and sexual strivings consciously focused upon the same individual. They cannot continue to regard themselves as children dependent upon their parents and must begin to feel capable of directing their own lives. The change requires a profound inner reorientation as well as a change in the actual relationships with parents. As the tasks of this phase of life primarily concern gaining independence from parental supervision and from the youth's own emotional attachment to the parents, it is natural that the family commonly becomes an arena of conflict. However, even though arguments with parents occur, when relationships between parents and children have been good, and the adolescent respects his or her parents, the conflicts are often minimal.* Although adolescents may need to overcome their parents' concerns about granting them sufficient latitude, much of the conflict involves their own ambivalences as they are caught between a need to free themselves and their longings for the security and affection they are leaving behind.

The security to begin the separation from the family depends as always not only upon the successful and harmonious passage through the earlier developmental phases but also on having a stable family base from which to venture. In a sense, the child now goes through another "practicing stage" (see Chapter 6) but now for a third and final phase of separation and individuation. As infants and toddlers, children differentiate and establish boundaries between the self and the mother and then find their places as boy or girl members of the family; then school-age or "latency" children move into peer groups and school; and now in mid-adolescence they try out and work out ways of becoming reasonably independent from their families. This is not yet the time for definitive separation, and if separation occurs serious problems are likely to ensue. Teenagers, no matter how grown up they feel, still need guidance, support, and a haven from which to venture and to which they can return. Not only will they be overcoming the repression of sexual expression, loosening their oedipal ties, and modifying superego injunctions to provide reliable inner directedness when they be-

---

* There is little justification for Anna Freud's (1962) statement, "The closer the tie between child and parent has been before, the more bitter and violent will be the struggle for independence from them in adolescence." Indeed, various investigators have shown that the serious adolescent disturbances and conflicts with parents reflect psychopathology in parents or pathology in their parental functioning. See H. Stierlin, *Separating Parents and Adolescents*; R. Shapiro, "Adolescent Ego Autonomy and the Family"; and N. Ackerman, "Adolescent Problems: A Symptom of Family Disorder."

come free of parental supervision, but they also must be gaining a knowledge of their own capacities and limitations in terms of the adult world,
and a familiarity with the ways of the opposite sex in order to overcome
residual inhibitions to sexual intimacy. The odyssey is rarely calm; it includes passages between Scylla and Charybdis, times when the youth need
lash himself to the mast to resist the sirens' singing, and when he can be
bewitched by Circe and turned into a swine.

Revolt and Conformity

It is a time marked by revolt and conformity—a strange and interesting
admixture that characterizes the height of the adolescent period. The parents and their standards must be denied as adolescents try things out in
their own ways. The parents, with their conservative concerns for their
children's future, do not seem to understand them; adolescents have never
been able to believe that parents can grasp the problems of the new generation. Indeed, the conflict between generations is inherent in social living
and essential to social change. However, the differences between parents
and child are usually not explosive, nor as marked as either parent or child
may believe.* Still, the turn from the parents as models may spread to
relationships with teachers and even to most adults, and creates uncertainty
and a degree of recklessness as the adolescent tests his or her own capabilities and limitations.

Even the more rebellious adolescents are, in general, among the most
consistent conformists, conforming to the ways of the adolescent group
from which they fear to deviate lest they find themselves outcasts and
isolates. It may even be a conformity to a pattern of nonconformity that
proclaims a freedom from, and even a contempt for, the useless conventions of society while also displaying loyalty to the youth group. The
adolescent society provides standards that furnish considerable guidance as
well as the milieu in which individuals can feel that they belong, while
seeking to renounce their attachments to their families. Youthful adolescents are likely to conform rigidly with the outer tokens that proclaim
membership. The way they dress, talk, flirt, become identification marks

---

* Psychiatrists and others interested in troubled young people have probably overestimated the rebelliousness of the mid-adolescent because they are involved primarily
with disturbed adolescents. Still, many parents find their adolescent offspring to be
contrary and difficult very frequently. However, Offer and Offer (1975) as well as
Elkin and Westly (1955), who have carried out systematic studies of middle-class
adolescents, have found relatively little overt parent-adolescent conflict, or even any
marked disruption of the developmental process. We should note that even during the
difficult years of the Vietnam war, which led to rebelliousness in many youths, their
parents were often sympathetic toward their feelings if not toward their actions.

for the person who still has no secure inner identity. Customs and clothing vary for differing socioeconomic and ethnic groups and from decade to decade: there are "hoods" who may indulge in gang fights and flaunt a degree of sexual promiscuity along with their black leather jackets that mark them as tough characters; there are youthful "hippies" prematurely following or aping older alienated adolescents and becoming involved with drugs; and various other adolescent subgroups, including those headed for admission to superior universities, who consider themselves an elite but who may seek to eschew upper-middle-class status by wearing shabby clothing, even if with studied carelessness. As other subcultures, the adolescent culture tends to have a distinctive language with many terms that are understandable only to themselves; they are contemptuous of those who do not understand, but discard expressions as they become known to younger groups or to adults. Fraternities and sororities also provide places where adolescents belong and feel accepted, conveying status and self-esteem simply through the fact of belonging, making the youth a member of an "in" group who can look down on those who do not belong. There are also the unorganized fraternities with less formal initiation procedures that hang around certain street corners where regulars can always be found for a game of cards or pool; or the more demanding city gangs in which membership requires participation in antisocial activities in preparation for later membership in criminal and semicriminal groups, though fortunately most will withdraw after a few brushes with the law and not progress to criminal careers. However, most youngsters, as during grade school (see Chapter 9), join together with others from similar backgrounds, and the group or gang, as we shall examine later in the chapter, may test limits but in general promotes a continuation of the family mores and standards.

OVERCOMING SEXUAL REPRESSION

The individual's inner equilibrium as well as the family homeostasis is upset by the intense impact of libidinal drives with which the child has had little experience. The urgency and autonomy of the sexual impulsions are strange and can be frightening. In contrast to other needs provoked by basic drives the parents cannot help their offspring very much in managing or satisfying the sexual needs. The parents may prepare, discuss, and advise them, but a great deal must remain intensely personal, particularly because it involves separating and differentiating from the parents. The early childhood erotic strivings had been directed toward a parent but had been repressed through fear of loss of love and retributive hostility, and sometimes in the boy through fears of castration. Now, the repressive ban on the expression of sexuality must be raised while the interdict on linking sex with affection for family members is retained; and the fusion of erotized and affectional feelings toward companions of the same sex disconnected in order to permit the fusion of sex and affection in heterosexual attachments.

During later childhood the repression of sexual impulses had been sweeping and was reinforced by many ego defenses. The prohibition cannot be raised simply by turning away from parental injunctions or even by parental permissiveness, because it has become firmly incorporated in the individual as superego directives. The lifting of the repression requires both changes in attitudes toward parental authority and modification of the superego standards to permit more latitude for sexual expression. We can conceptualize the situation by saying that the strengthened id impulses push the "ego" to challenge the superego restrictions and standards that were suited to the less driven child. However, much of the ego's strength and security in the ability to take care of and direct the self was gained by identifying with the parents and accepting their authority. Attempts to deny superego restrictions mean turning away from identifications that had provided strength and stability. A precipitous break with the source of identification can undermine the self, provoke intense guilt, and a loss of self-esteem in this process of achieving greater freedom for expression. Efforts to turn from superego directives can provoke severe anxiety that ego functions will completely give way before the force of the id impulses. After years in which children have accepted if not admired their parents, and during which they have felt guilt when disobedient, achieving success in surmounting either parental authority or their authority internalized as superego directives can provoke intense feelings of guilt and depression.

There are, however, other significant reasons that often retard the development of sexual relationships. The process of separation-individuation from the mother had been long and painful and the boundaries between the self and the mother—indeed, between the self and the parents—long remained tenuous. Now the adolescent is involved in becoming reasonably self-sufficient and in gaining security as an individual discrete from parents and family. The teenager fears losing his or her shaky identity in sexual intimacy. Symbolically, as sometimes reflected in dreams and fantasies, sexual intercourse is feared by the boy as reincorporation into the womb. Not until late in adolescence, when problems of ego identity are resolved, will most adolescents be ready to lose themselves in real sexual intimacy.

Of course, a considerable number of mid-adolescents engage in sexual intercourse. A recent study indicates that thirty-seven percent have at least experienced sexual intercourse by the time they become sixteen (Sorensen, 1973). An occasional couple will pair up and form a meaningful and enjoyable sexual relationship and spend considerable time in one another's company. Others will simply have tried out having sexual intercourse to feel themselves initiated or, perhaps, to vent anger against parents. It is difficult to generalize but probably many mid-adolescents who have sexual relationships are seeking to fill non-sexual needs that are not met in their families. The girl whose father has separated from her mother—and whose depressed and needy mother seeks solace and support in affairs and can give little to her daughter—finds an equally needy boy and seeks to spend all of her time with him to fill the unbearable emptiness she feels. In such instances sex and drugs, like food, assuage "oral" needs for affection. As sexual intercourse is likely to be unsatisfactory to such immature persons, they may settle upon the simpler gratification of oral sex. The inner-city adolescent without a father and with a working mother also needs to feel wanted. The boy may need to prove his masculinity by making his girl-friend pregnant, and the girl may wish a baby to have someone who loves her, or at least to whom she is important. However, most adolescents, before they can feel free to enjoy sexual intercourse, must slowly build up their security and confidence in their abilities to cope with the sexual drives, gain standards to protect themselves realistically, test their own limits of tolerating anxiety and guilt, modify their superego directives through interacting with peer groups with similar problems, and learn in actuality that sexual expression will not lead to dissolution of the self. Perhaps they unconsciously know what parents often fail to convey, that it is not so much a matter of morality as of immaturity; that they are un-likely to consummate the sexual act properly until they are sufficiently mature and ready, and that unsatisfactory attempts might endanger later, more meaningful relationships.

Reactivation of Oedipal Attachments

In moving away from the family, which had formed the matrix of their lives, it is natural for adolescents to become involved in numerous conflicts with parents; but many of the expressed causes of conflict are but surface manifestations, rationalizations, and displacements of the sexual struggle that simultaneously attracts and repels the adolescent from them. Since much of what is going on is under the ban of repression and is carried out unconsciously and therefore contains irrational and contradictory trends, any effort to discuss the developments of the period in reasonable and logical terms cannot convey the ambivalences, vacillations, and contradictions so characteristic of mid-adolescence.

With the onset of puberty, as has been noted, the former oedipal attachments become reactivated and the adolescent may indulge in considerable fantasy that is but thinly disguised about gaining the parent of the opposite sex and somehow gaining ascendancy over or being rid of the parent of the same sex. The fantasies usually concern parent substitutes or fictional characters but the youngster's behavior may clearly reflect the renewed attraction to one parent and the resentment of the other. Sometimes an awareness of the sexual attraction breaks through the repression or the clear revelation of a sexual dream creates alarm, but usually it is an inchoate awareness of discomfort aroused by the sexualized feelings toward the parent that leads the adolescent to seek to construct a barrier and to place distance between the self and the parent. There are many similarities with the earlier resolution of the oedipal desires, and the manner in which the young child resolved the intense attachment to a parent established a pattern that tends to be repeated in adolescence. However, the adolescent is not a five-year-old child and knows that children cannot marry parents but must find partners in the outside world. Nevertheless, the extent of the fantasies that seek to circumvent such realistic considerations can be extensive, and an adolescent's behavior may be directed toward living out such fantasies. Thus, an adolescent girl not only fantasied that she could stop her father's alcoholism by being more understanding than her mother and more interested in his work and hobbies, but she began to pattern her life to become her father's savior after her mother divorced him. A boy prepares for the day when he will be able to support his mother and thus enable her to throw his philandering father out of the house. The youth's physical development since childhood also leads to differences from the oedipal period. The adolescent boy may not only fear his father's retribution but may also fear his own hostile feelings toward his father now that he is as strong or stronger than his father. Both the girl and her father can be aware of the dangers of their mutual attraction and seek to desexualize the relationship. In one way or another the oedipal attraction is again repressed. Temporarily the need for repression creates guilt over sexuality and reinforces the ban on sexual expression, but ultimately it is the attraction to the parent as a sexual object that is repressed. However, serious problems can arise when parents cannot contain their own seductiveness. An adolescent boy whose divorced mother would come in the nude to kiss him good night, letting her breasts fall on him in the process, began to bring a girl home to sleep with him. A girl whose mother had run off with a lover was taken to Europe by her lonely father, who, to save money, registered them in hotels as man and wife. She soon had considerable difficulty in sorting out her feelings and began to select homosexuals as boyfriends. In reasonably normal circumstances, freedom of sexual expression will eventually be gained after sexuality is directed toward persons outside of the family and the erotic components of the attachment to the parent are again securely repressed, which is often a lengthy process. When it is necessary for family members to more or less consciously move away from one another in reactive efforts to escape from their sexual feelings from one another, the spontaneity of family life suffers and the totality of the intrafamilial relationships is apt to become seriously strained. Optimally a stable coalition between parents who maintain proper boundaries between themselves and their child guides adolescents to an unconscious and satisfactory resolution of their attraction to parents even as it had helped bring about the earlier oedipal resolution. Then the acceptance of the impossibility of finding sexual fulfillment in the family or of becoming a parent's primary love object helps direct the adolescent to seek a more complete and permanent love relationship outside the family.

OVERCOMING FAMILY DEPENDENCY

Needing to free themselves from their attraction to a parent, adolescents usually begin to deny the attractiveness of the parent by devaluing the parent's attributes, but they have other unconscious reasons for derogating parents. Movement toward adulthood requires them to overcome their desires to remain dependent, as well as their feelings that parents are more capable than they of directing their lives. They must prove to themselves that they are capable and do not need to rely upon their parents' judgment and advice. Nevertheless, their own inner directives derive largely from internalizations of their parents and their standards and directives. Such inner restrictions must be overcome as much as, or more than, the actual limitations set by the parents. The superego restrictions must be reconstituted in order to become suited for directing adult rather than childhood behavior; loosened to permit greater latitude but at the same time strengthened to become capable of directing the self with less supervision from parents.

Although modification of the superego is an intrapsychic matter, it usually involves altering the perception and evaluation of the parents whose value systems had been internalized. Adolescents set out to establish that their parents neither always know what is correct nor are paragons of virtue beyond emulation. They have sinned and they have erred. Even if their values and standards were once correct they were suited to some primordial era when the world was inhabited only by squares. Adolescents are in the process of convincing themselves as much as their parents that both parents and adolescent are very different from the way they were when he or she was only a child. The adolescent sometimes begins to talk and behave as if nothing the parents do is acceptable. Beset by ambivalences, both wanting the parents and wanting to be rid of them, teenagers are trying to convince themselves. The pendulum swings from one side to the other and episodes of denial of the parents are countered by periods of regression, during which the adolescent seeks surcease from turmoil through regaining peace with the loved and needed parents. The force of the turmoil may indicate the violence of the wrench necessary for the adolescents to free themselves rather than any basic hostility toward the parents. Arguments can become blindly irrational in order to help overcome the contradictions and the longing to remain attached. The inability of parents to understand are magnified; grudges are reinstated. The turmoil is within; the pulls are in both directions. Adolescence is the proper time to want to be—and to be—both dependent and independent.

Typically, adolescents begin to search out flaws in their parents. The process may start with a basic disillusionment in learning about their sexual life—their hypocrisy in practicing what they have forbidden—but youths are apt to seek shortcomings that they can attack openly and resent rationally. The criticisms of the parents' behavior and even more the attacks upon their character constitute a serious blow to the parents' authority and self-esteem. They may turn upon the ingrate upstart with a vindictiveness that leads into a cycle of misunderstanding and bitterness. Now, although teenagers wish to free themselves from their parents' domination and direction, they do not wish to demolish their parents. They still need them as objects of identification and as objects whose admiration and affection are worth seeking. Adolescents' own self-esteem remains closely linked to the esteem they have for their parents. Late in adolescence, after they have divested themselves of constricting inner controls and begin to see their parents from a more adult perspective, they will again return to accepting many of the parental standards as part of their own.

Adolescents are apt to have unusually severe standards. In trying to contain their importunate sexual impulses and their impetuous outbursts, which are forcing abandonment of their former ways of maintaining security, adolescents often magnify superego injunctions in order to bolster the forces of repression. They tend to judge their parents by the same standards that they create for their own defenses, and no one is able to live up to such expectations. Still, when teenagers later become more tolerant of themselves, they will become more tolerant of their parents. The criticisms of parents and the misunderstandings with them usually diminish as adolescents find themselves capable of independence and when their perceptions and judgments of others become less egocentric.

Real Disillusionment with Parents

Unfortunately, serious and permanent difficulties between parents and child sometimes develop when the adolescent's search for flaws in a parent's behavior and character leads to the discovery of a disillusioning reality. The youth gains a pyrrhic victory, so to speak, that shatters the image of the parents and concomitantly disturbs his or her own development. A girl of fifteen was brought for psychiatric help after becoming promiscuous. She had tended to idealize her mother, who had seemed a model of both glamour and efficiency. Her mother had provided her daughter with winter vacations in Florida and unusually fine clothing by her earnings from a flourishing insurance business that supplemented her artist husband's meager income. The girl came to realize that the mother's business was not what it seemed to be. The trips that kept her mother away from home one or two nights each week were spent with a wealthy industrialist who was her sole insurance client. When the girl had accompanied her mother on two vacations, it had just happened that the industrialist was staying at the same hotel. She also realized that her father, who could not maintain the family in the manner in which his wife expected him to, was managing not to realize that his wife was being unfaithful to him, even though it was obvious to many others in the small community. The inevitable and necessary loss of unrealistic childhood idealizations, or the failure of parents to live up to the excessive standards of the adolescent, is very different from the disillusionment that cracks the parental image and with it the adolescent's identifications with them.

At this developmental stage, when the oedipal resolution must be reconfirmed, and when the young person needs tangible models to follow into adulthood, who the parents are and how they interrelate is particularly important to their child's harmonious development. The adolescent is becoming aware of the parent as a real person and model rather than as a fantasied image; and who the parent is, influences whom the child seeks to become. The coalition between the parents, the support they give one another, the admiration they have for one another greatly influence the youth's transition through the adolescent period.

PARENTAL TRIBULATIONS

Adolescence is a time of considerable difficulty for the parents as well as for the developing child. Their trust in the child they have raised and in their own capacities to raise a child undergoes its most severe test. The child in whom they have invested so much love and effort is moving away from them. They can no longer supervise and fully protect but must place their reliance on what they have already inculcated in the child. Yet they know that their offspring lacks experience and their child's judgment cannot be fully adequate to new situations that will confront him or her. They fear that a single careless moment or a rash judgment will undo their years of effort and permanently blight the child's life. Excessive parental concerns are apt to reflect a desire to prevent a child from repeating the parent's own tragic youthful mistakes. Still there are few parents who do not experience restless nights when their son starts driving a car, or when they must first entrust their daughter to some oafish-looking, pimply-faced boy over whom she has lost whatever sense she had formerly possessed. However, parents now need to *confirm* their offspring by indicating their belief in their children's trustworthiness as well as in their capacities to assume responsibility for themselves. Still, limits must be set somewhere, but where are the boundaries? Adolescents are bound to resent delimitation and restrictions, considering them indications of lack of confidence if not an absence of trust; but they are just as likely to resent failures to set limits, taking such permissiveness as evidence that the parents are not sufficiently concerned or interested. Adolescents may begin to test their parents' limits and in the process move beyond their own. The indecisiveness of parents in the face of a changing morality can increase their children's uncertainty of what they are supposed, permitted, or expected to do—a situation that may be overcome by frank discussion of the dilemma between parents and children. Adolescents are not yet adults, and when the parents rescind their parental responsibilities prematurely, the adolescents are left without the support and protection they need—albeit sometimes from their own desires and impulses.

Adolescents are apt to take out their unhappiness upon their parents, vent their dark moods upon them, express irritation over trivia. When parents try to offer the affection their child seems to need, they may be rebuffed angrily, for it is at just such times that youths cannot let themselves continue to be babied and must tear themselves away from what they would like so much to have. They need something to rebel against and, at times, life seems to go easier for an adolescent if the parents become more strict and thus provide something to be angry about. Wide mood swings may occur that puzzle adolescents as well as their parents. They feel expansive and elated after having proved to themselves that they do not need their parents, only to plunge into despair when they become unconsciously concerned about surpassing a father or when feelings of hostile resentment toward parents create remorse—the youth reacting as if hostile wishes toward them were equivalent to murder. It is part of the crucial struggle to come to terms with superego directives and reestablish an equilibrium between the "id," "ego," and "superego."

It is unfortunate but often an inherent part of the life cycle that the crisis of adolescence in the child occurs contemporaneously with a critical period in the parents' lives. The child's adolescence in itself tends to create a crisis in the parents' lives because of the impending change in the family composition, the loss of the child's admiration, and an awareness of the child's sexual attractiveness and vigor at a time when their own sexual powers are waning. However, most parents have problems of their own in facing middle age and the realization that their own lives have reached a climax; that they must come to terms with what they will be able to achieve in life, with menopausal problems, with declining abilities. Mothers may be resuming careers of their own, or seeking ways of having a career, and may envy a daughter's opportunity to start early in life. As Stierlin (1974) has noted, many middle-age parents would like "to fly the coop" themselves and, in one way or another, involve the child. They may gain gratification from a child's exploits, they may displace their own desires onto the child and therefore distrust the child, they may delegate the child to fulfill their ambitions, etc. Such problems will be considered in the chapter on middle life, and here we can only note that the teenager is markedly affected by how the parents as individuals and as a couple are coping with the very consequential problems in their own lives. It may be of particular significance that the parents are coming to final terms with the limitations imposed by the "realities of life" just at the time when an adolescent offspring's imagination is beginning to soar and the adolescent is becoming impatient with the limitations that adults and their society impose by their stodginess and conservatism; the differences between the generations and the age-old ideologic conflict between them reach their zenith.

THE YOUTH GROUP AND IT'S CULTURE

As adolescents move away from their parents, the adolescent peer group gains in importance. The peer group changes into a youth group that carries the youth culture, and differs from the childhood peer group in having something of an anti-adult orientation and in becoming heterosexual. It is no longer simply a neighborhood group and may even span several high schools and communities, tending to be composed of youths with common interests and ambitions who, therefore, usually come from reasonably similar backgrounds. Thus, it is not usually a "counterculture" but rather an age-appropriate subculture. They band together for mutual support as well as companionship. The core is formed by a few close friends— pairs and small groups of individuals who are extremely important to one another. Here youths feel accepted because of friendship and find some respite from judgment and the acceptance on the basis of achievement that is becoming increasingly important in school and to the self as well as to the parents. Within the group they feel free from parental controls and can try out more adult behavior, which at first may mean daring to carry out things that had been forbidden in childhood. Here they find others who admire them and in a sense replace the loss suffered in withdrawing from parents. The others are in very much of the same situation and they support one another and learn to manage without parental supervision. The group serves an important function in modifying superego controls, for through observing others in the group, the group's reaction to the self and others, through accepting its standards and by means of constant discussions with these friends, the adolescents alter their guiding principles.

The adolescent group at first continues to be formed of members of the same sex, and throughout mid-adolescence friendships with members of the same sex will, for many, continue to take precedence over heterosexual attachments. Identification and object choice are still intertwined, and teenagers can be closest to those with whom they can identify. There is still considerable narcissism in the admiration of another. Recently the diminution in the differences in male and female gender roles leads to an earlier and perhaps less self-conscious mingling of the sexes, and similarity in dress helps diminish feelings of difference. Still, banding together helps adolescents to cope with feelings of strangeness in moving toward the opposite sex. Friends are sought not only for support and in order to like and be liked by them, but also to have someone whom one respects to measure oneself against. There is considerable rivalry in most adolescent friendships, for even though direct competition for the same objectives is avoided, there is competition in collecting achievements. Who one is, is partly a matter of whom one has for friends. Adolescents feel that they are not so well defined by family name, for they simply happened to be born into the family, but they have formed their friendships and have been accepted by the group. It is an important aspect of being confirmed as an individual independent of one's family. Here, in the group, adolescents learn to know who they are in the world beyond their families, to judge their own capacities; then, from the security of the group, they will begin to gain experiences with the opposite sex. Such needs for self-definition and for finding security take precedence over desires for actual sexual outlets. This process of freeing oneself from the family in order to find oneself and of moving into the proper group as a step toward independence is usually a more important task of mid-adolescence than forming love relationships and finding heterosexual outlets.*

The Youth Group Mores

The "gang" increasingly becomes the arbiter of appropriate behavior, a transition that often causes the parents considerable concern. Although the group's mores are likely to move toward the limits of what is acceptable to the parents, it usually serves as a modifying and restraining influence upon the individual while fostering a less family-centered orientation and an expansion of activities beyond what parents might condone. The peer group usually has a code that does not differ greatly from the basic mores of the families of its members, even though it fosters adventuresome be-

* The youth group and its culture probably plays a more important role in the life of the adolescent and his development in the United States than in European countries. Perhaps nowhere else is there such definite preparation in childhood peer-group activities for autonomous youth groups. Peer-group activities both in childhood and in mid-adolescence are under much closer family supervision among the middle class in European countries, perhaps leading to a more definitive and precipitous break from adult guidance when independence is finally gained in late adolescence. Moving away from the family at an earlier age, the American adolescent tends to be more dependent upon being popular to maintain a modicum of self-esteem. Even though the emphasis on group loyalty and decision making in the youth groups may well be part of the preparation for democratic living, it also contributes to a marked dependency upon the opinion of peers to provide motivation and direction for behavior.

havior that might be imprudent. Although in this rebellious period individuals might well engage in activities that they consider unacceptable to parents, they will hesitate to risk serious censure from friends, or do something that could lead to ostracism from the group. Thus, they may smoke marijuana at a party, but would not use heroin; or a boy may gamble but not cheat; or a girl may go with a boy of whom her parents disapprove but would be reluctant to be seen with a type of boy who would lower her friends' esteem for her. The need for conformity is a major safeguard, though, of course, it can also lead to experimentation with drugs. Although delinquent gangs are most commonly found in slum areas, even here the core members come from seriously disturbed families. When youths living in better neighborhoods or from "good" homes join together with others who have delinquent tendencies, they almost always come from homes that somehow foster antisocial tendencies, or in which rigid demands for obedience permit no latitude for a boy's instrumental behavior appropriate to his age, which is necessary for him to develop into an adult.

The movement toward the opposite sex generally starts from the security of the monosexual adolescent peer group. The boy and girl must first become more secure in their own sexual identities before daring to engage with the opposite sex. The interest does not arise from sexual drive alone; the narcissistic supplies needed to maintain and increase self-esteem are not as likely to come from friends of the same sex as from the opposite sex; and prestige with friends of the same sex depends on prowess with members of the opposite sex. At first the activity patterns do not change markedly but tentative brief meetings take place with groups of the other sex. They engage in a collective teasing banter which seeks to hide interest while still showing it. "Whom one teases, one loves." At first, neither boys nor girls are likely to show more than a casual interest in the person who is actually the center of their daydreams.

In the insecurity concerning their worth, adolescents seek attributes that make one enviable or popular. There is an increased consciousness of the neighborhood one lives in, the prestige of a sporty car, etc. Security comes with wearing just the right shirt or hairdo. Both sexes may spend considerable time in front of a mirror examining their faces, the girls working on their makeup, but also in practicing the proper face to wear under certain circumstances, and how to shift facial expressions in a sophisticated manner. The boys now wish for athletic prowess to be a hero to the girls. They join clubs and run for office in high school. To know that one is someone requires recognition by others. A teenager is also likely to seek recognition from some adult, usually a teacher. Mid-adolescents, individually and as a group, are not altogether anti-adult. Aside from the adult upon whom one has a crush, adolescents also appreciate those rare individuals who listen, seek to understand, and can share in some ways rather than remain at a different level.

MALE AND FEMALE PATTERNING OF THE PERSONALITY

Although the differences in interests and attitudes of boys and girls have diminished considerably, some differences in patterning remain. Girls have matured earlier physically and, in general, are more mature emotionally. Both sexes are likely to be following patterns noted since early childhood: boys are more apt to be into motor activities and competitive games, whereas girls are often more occupied and preoccupied with people. In the past, it had been noted that the ways of thinking of the male and female begin to diverge more definitely during the middle of adolescence, when the girl is less likely to deal with abstract topics or to be an innovator. Some such differences probably persist despite the changing orientation of women concerning careers. The greater amount of time spent in fantasying how she feels about others and how other people may feel in various situations ultimately leads to the development of "feminine intuition" and an ability to empathize with others. Of course, such attributes are not limited to girls, but we may say that boys who have such tendencies have a quality that softens their edges and their ways of relating, which has in the past been considered more "feminine." Currently, girls require capacities to think more abstractly and instrumentally, and boys to be more "intuitive" and interpersonally receptive, in order to become capable of sharing marital and parental roles more readily.

THE MERGING OF THE SEXES

The movement toward openly falling in love proceeds slowly, and achieving real sexual intimacy takes even longer. At first the male and female peer groups are apt to mingle primarily in reasonably public places, often in some hangout frequented by older mixed groups whose ways they watch and mimic. Then the groups may grow smaller, offering opportunities for couples to pair off in the dark but with the protection of having other couples close at hand, while starting tentative explorations of the mysteries of the other sex. The "necking" or "petting" at this age is as much a matter of exploring one's own feelings and learning to relax one's boundaries without fear of loss of the self or of control of one's impulses as it is a matter of gaining sexual gratification. It is a matter of exciting exploration and stimulation rather than a means of gaining release from sexual tensions. It may have very little to do with being in love and be much more an expression of eagerness to begin to live out fantasies and enter into the mysteries of sexuality. Usually the more complete loss of the self in sexuality that leads to sexual intercourse awaits late adolescence, when a person feels reasonably secure with the self, understands the desires of another, and feels certain that limits can be set when necessary.

The group parties will change into double dating, which permits each person to feel more secure with another couple around to provide sanctions concerning what is permissible. Many boys are likely to gain their first experiences in sexual relations with casual acquaintances such as a blind date or with a girl from another community who is more experienced and will take the initiative. The need to get away from girls whom they think about in more personal terms can be very great. The girl may first overcome her inhibitions on a date with an older boy who is more daring and whose attraction to her arouses assurances that she can be attractive to a boy in sexual terms. Of course there is no set pattern, and how persons overcome their inhibitions and repressions is a very individual matter. In all eras and cultures, some youths are unable to contain their impulses and have sexual intercourse at an early age. We have already noted that some seek close and fairly constant relationships with another person in early or mid-adolescence to fill the emptiness of their lives, and that some who had never developed proper boundaries between the self and a parent now seek to fuse with someone to replace the parent. Television as well as movies and sex manuals has made adolescents more knowledgable and has lessened the mystery. The absence of parents from the home has increased opportunities for sexual exploration and activities, but, perhaps more pertinently, has left many youngsters feeling lonely when they return home from school. The mores have changed, so that, for many, sexual activities are not a matter of morals but of the wishes and well-being of the participants. Nevertheless, it seems as if such matters—or even the availability of secure contraception—have not greatly changed the sexual behavior of boys, and the differences that have occurred over the past several decades may be in large part due to the larger proportion of girls who are now

having some type of sexual intercourse. Although it is difficult to generalize, it seems as if attitudes of mid-adolescents toward sex have changed
more than their behavior: they discuss sex more openly, particularly with
members of the opposite sex, some flaunting rather than hiding what they
do, and more may experiment once or twice with intercourse; but sexual
behavior may have changed less in recent decades for this age group than
for their elders.

Blocks to Early Sexual Relationships

It usually takes a number of years before the sexual drives that have
started soon after puberty can achieve expression and fulfillment, particularly among middle-class adolescents. Well over half of the students who
arrive at college are still virginal. It is more than morality that is involved
in creating the delay between the capacity for sexual relationships and their
realization.

The adolescents of both sexes must overcome the repression of sexuality
that had become so firmly entrenched and they must disengage the drive
from their earlier intrafamilial love objects. Although psychoanalysis has
emphasized the boy's need to overcome unconscious fears that sexual activity can lead to castration by his own father or the girl's father, or at least
arouse dangerous hostility in his or the girl's father, there is reason to
believe that it may be still more of a problem for him to overcome his
feelings that females in the image of the mother are powerful and enveloping and he will be lost if he gives in to his need for them. He may find the
expectations of girls of his own age frightening now that girls feel freer to
take the initiative. Confusions of castration fears and fears of mothering
figures can also arouse unconscious concerns that the boy may lose his
penis in the vagina, unconsciously considered as a biting organ with teeth
—a fairly widespread fantasy that sometimes emerges into consciousness.
The girl, too, has special fears to overcome: fears of penetration and
injury, fears of annihilation that come with orgasm, and sometimes feelings
of shame with her own genitalia, which she feels must be repulsive to any
male. Superego controls also gain support in repressing the id impulses by
marshaling the dangers that can come from sexual indulgence. There are
more or less realistic fears of pregnancy and venereal disease which have
become less important only during the past decade or two. Even though
venereal disease has become common among adolescents to cause concern,
gonorrhea no longer imposes a threat of sterility, nor does syphilis mean
years of treatment and perhaps a need to forgo marriage and having children. Although it has been thought that the "pill" has been responsible for

more adolescents having sexual relations, the majority of mid-adolescents who have sexual relations do not use the "pill" or any reliable form of contraception (Sorensen, 1973). The girl usually pauses before losing her virginity, perhaps torn between her desire to wait for her true love and the wish to have the experience behind her. She may have fears, too, of becoming a lost woman, unable to control her impulses and lust after she has once given way to her desires; and the boy may also take pause in feeling that the intensity of the experience will be overwhelming and more than he can contain.*

The intermingling of the sexes may be more important in expanding adolescents' social awareness than their sexual knowledge and experience. Members of the other sex are perceived in more realistic terms of appreciating that they have similar problems, uncertainties, and desires. Desires for recognition shift more definitively to the opposite sex; and behavior becomes directed toward being more attractive to the other sex. There is a constant building up of illusion and return to reality. The more basic patterns of the personality characteristics of each sex begin to interrelate, and complement the other. The girl does not form a direct rival to the boy and can provide him with satisfaction and assurance by enjoying his achievements and sharing them with him; she thus bolsters his narcissistic needs while she spurs him onward. Although circumstances are changing, the girl may still hesitate to outshine boys intellectually lest she become unpopular. The girl who had felt rejected when her father withdrew from her as she became pubescent now finds that boys can like her and love her as she is—as a girl—and gain a moratorium during which she can pursue other objectives as well.

Early Love and Sexual Identity

Sometime during late mid-adolescence or early in late adolescence the young person is likely to fall in love. It is quite likely that the first heterosexual love will contain narcissistic components. The boy may well fall in

---

* There are also more irrational fears that are utilized to buttress the superego. We have already observed that the male's fear of a vagina with teeth has been noted in virtually all parts of the world. Less obviously, the adolescent is also apt to be fascinated by fictitious stories of couples who were unable to separate after having intercourse and had to be taken to the hospital in the embarrassing position in which they were locked. It is of interest that this myth was utilized to preserve the sanctity of the dark medieval church, in the lore that this situation would occur when couples had sexual relations in the church. It was further fortified by the legend that such unions would lead to the birth of a werewolf. Perhaps a werewolf would be the proper product of the "black mass," an anti-Christian witchcraft rite during which couples copulated on the altar.

love with a girl whom he unconsciously recognizes as someone he would like to have been, had he been a girl. The girl may fall in love with the boy she might have been. These early loves can be important in fostering a more secure gender identity. While there are still some narcissistic and homosexual components in this type of object love, for it is a stage in the movement from narcissistic love to heterosexual love, something significant happens for identity formation; the boy is placing the feminine components of himself—the residua of his identification with his mother—onto the girl he loves. He no longer needs to contain these elements in himself because he can have them in the girl he loves and whom he seeks to possess. His masculinity is solidified and confirmed and he becomes ready to achieve an ego identity of his own and to move toward intimacy with another. The same process is likely to happen with the girl and perhaps in an even more dramatic manner. In falling in love with a boy and finding herself lovable to a boy, she need no longer regret not being a boy or having the prerogatives of a male. She can be satisfied with loving the boy who has the penis and who may be all too willing to share it with her. She again feels complete and is ready to progress toward interdependence with another.

Unfulfilled Sexuality and the Unconscious

Being in love, a state which cannot be fully explained or analyzed, seems to be a state of existence in which the boundaries between the self and another are again loosened and one's sense of well-being depends on being of utmost importance to the chosen person. It is a condition that will be discussed again in later chapters. During these years, even though the physiological drive toward sexual expression is probably as intense as at any time in life, particularly in the male, in our contemporary industrial society—at least in the middle and upper classes—it does not usually lead to fulfillment in heterosexual love. The adolescent is going through the necessary phases in preparation for later fulfillment. Some relief is gained through masturbation, which in turn is apt to cause considerable conflict in some and little if any in other youths; and there is a greater or lesser amount of sexual play, which often serves to heighten tension rather than relieve it. Even though sexuality often preoccupies adolescents, much of the sexual thought and fantasy takes place at the borders of consciousness when the person is somewhat cut off from the world of reality, as when in bed falling asleep or awakening in the morning—at times when ego functioning is in abeyance. Even more is censored, repressed, and remains unconscious, becoming manifest only in dreams but still exerting a powerful influence upon behavior. The high school boy who barks at his mother and criticizes her bitterly and somehow finds a reason why he must be away from home whenever his father has to spend an evening in his office has no awareness that he is combating his attraction to his mother. The girl who has started running around with a fast crowd and lets it be known that she can be had sexually realizes only during psychotherapy that she has been trying to demonstrate her heterosexuality to others as well as prove it to herself, whereas her most fundamental attachment and the subject of her half-waking fantasies is a female teacher.

The new force of the sexual impulsions, together with the repression necessary to keep the sexual urges under control, increases the scope of unconscious mental processes considerably. The increased drive, so to speak, directs the individual's perception and interests toward sexual objects and sexual matters, and like a magnet among iron filings draws more and more associations into its sphere of attraction. Further, the earlier childhood pregenital erotic and sensuous strivings that have long been banned from consciousness join together with the new unconscious sexual motivation. Oral and anal erotic desires and fantasies, masochistic and sadistic imaginings, voyeuristic and exhibitionistic strivings, homosexual attractions and concerns, imagining of the parents in the primal scene, etc., are reawakened during this period of unfulfillment as if the strivings motivated by the sexual impulsion flowed into all of these old outlets in the search for some way of achieving gratification.

ADOLESCENT MECHANISMS OF DEFENSE

The newly gained capacities for conceptual and hypothetical thinking not only increase the intellectual control of ego functioning but also make possible a greater elaboration of the mechanisms of defense. At this age the adolescents may not gain much sexual gratification in reality, but their active fantasies help them ward off impulsive activity that might create realistic dangers or generate "instinctual" anxiety of complete loss of control in the sexual act. Masturbation is usually accompanied by fantasies that relieve the emptiness and the loneliness of the act. Such fantasies can serve a variety of purposes such as permitting a safe linkage of genital activity with the desired love object, providing a mental preparation for future activity, and affording an imaginary outlet for pregenital or polymorphous perverse erotic strivings that are residues from earlier developmental phases. Other fantasies which are less directly connected with sexual stimulation can help drain off the unconscious associations through the elaboration of romantic daydreams of loving and being loved as well as of future achievements that will bring greatness and renown and thereby admiration and love.

Fantasy formation relates to the defense of *sublimation*, in which sexual impulses are redirected into less earthy and more "sublime" activities. Sensitive adolescents who cannot yet fall in love with a specific person on a realistic basis, or at least gain sexual release through such love, can experience a more diffuse love of nature or of mankind in which there is a vague seeking for expression and fulfillment of the feelings that are surging within them. They seek to lose themselves in nature or find ways of giving themselves to the service of mankind. Poetry bubbles within them and flows from their lips, and they record daydreams as well as events in diaries. These and similar activities are pushed by the sexual drive, and the expansiveness that comes with capacities for abstract and formal operations.

Adolescents are also beginning to *intellectualize*, utilizing their capacities to think and reason in order to control impulses, not necessarily by reasoning out rational solutions of problems, but through diverting interests into intellectual channels. The common manifestations of such intellectualization are the prolonged discussions and arguments about the nature of things, the purpose of life, the errors in the parents' ideas. Adolescents are also likely to attach themselves to an ideal or an ideology in order to find an outlet for their energies, including their sexuality and aggressivity, but also to achieve new guidelines through having a more meaningful way of life. The ideology may now take precedence over parental teachings and modify the examples of parental behavior that have guided them. Young persons may embrace a new ideology with a fervor that consumes their energy and directs their attention, forcing aside any ideas that conflict with it as well as any personal needs that interfere with its pursuit. They are, in Piaget's terms, in the egocentric phase of formal operations, in which they do not appreciate that other persons can start from different premises or can reasonably believe that other ideals have even greater importance. There can be a touch of fanaticism in their behavior which both political and religious movements have often utilized. The Children's Crusade, the Hitler Youth, and the Chinese Red Guard are examples of how the ideological selflessness of youth can be mobilized into mass movements.

Asceticism, related to such abnegation of the self for ideologic purposes, is another common means used to control the upsurge of sexual and aggressive impulsions. It is as if the strength of the erotic drives were turned against themselves and the superego injunctions that the id seems on the verge of overthrowing were strengthened to deny any pleasures. The ascetic

adolescent denies all types of sensuous gratification and through such mortification of the flesh seeks to bury the erotic needs and be rid of the difficulties they are causing. Still the eroticism in this mortification of the spirit
and flesh is often apparent even when it leads to the extreme of masochistic
flagellation.

Although adolescents need to find means of containing the sexual drives
until better prepared to cope with them realistically, the drives help push
them toward seeking and gaining adult prerogatives. They are moved to
explore their worlds and those in it and to expand their horizons. This is a
time of expansion and expansiveness. They need to try out, to toy with
ideas, to put their ideas into action, and to begin to gain recognition.

Although many adolescents are now beginning to help the family earn a
living even if they continue at school, this is by and large still a time when
responsibilities are not too great. Adolescents do not yet need to confine
their restless energies to the prosaic step-by-step surmounting of realistic
problems that later will limit daydreams, bring pause before risk, and lead
them to understand the adult's inability to change the world into what the
youth thinks it should be. It is still difficult for the young person to understand why people do not "do" things about injustices; why their lives are so
prosaic; why they refuse to take a chance. It is a time in which the youth
can float above the world, secretly glorying in beauty, being in love with
love, and dream of future greatness. There is also the loneliness of feeling
deserted by friends who have now found new loves. The world at times is
too much to bear. The adolescent is filled with potentiality and hovers in it.
Whether a person will continue to expand in late adolescence or begin to
pull in his or her antennae and start to consolidate efforts depends on many
contingencies.

LATE ADOLESCENCE

The major tasks of late adolescence concern the achievement of an ego
identity and capacities for intimacy. When young people have liberated
themselves from their families sufficiently and gained enough latitude and
security to permit sexual expression, they pause before undertaking definitive commitments. The expansiveness of mid-adolescence gives way to the
need to consolidate and to try out imaginatively and realistically various
ways of life, including trials at relating meaningfully to persons of the
opposite sex. It is often an uneasy pause, for they may feel that time is
running out in that they will soon be expected to assume adult status,

commit themselves to a specific way of life, and find ways of supporting themselves. Persons require a more definitive integration than previously so as to provide them with an identity as persons in their own right and to enable them to move beyond independence to gain completion in intimate interdependence with others. For a minority of persons, these tasks will continue into the young adult period in a somewhat different form that we shall examine in the next chapter.

In the United States many adolescents of both sexes, approximately forty percent, will gain some college education. The proportion increases with social class and wealth, but community colleges and state universities provide opportunities for the underprivileged. Although college settings and educational standards vary widely, the student's horizons will widen to a greater or lesser degree and his or her outlook will become less egocentric. The process both helps and complicates the achievement of an ego identity.

Whether or not they live away from home, adolescents at college move away from parental influence and usually become very much responsible for themselves. They now come under the tutelage and influence of teachers whose standards, beliefs, and ideas are considered as valid as those of parents, if not more authoritative. Many students experience life in a very different setting from the one at home: students who grew up in small towns enjoy the stimulation of large cities, with their theaters, museums, admixture of social classes; or those from a megalopolis learn the advantages of life in a college town. Students learn that others with interests that may seem strange to them are even respected because of them. A boy who scarcely knew that classical music existed has a roommate who listens only to Bach and when his annoyance wears off begins to appreciate that baroque music can be more exciting than rock and roll. A girl whose roommates must remind her to eat meals and to change her clothing occasionally turns out to be a mathematical genius whom the university had recruited almost as avidly as it had a renowned prep school quarterback. Students who had been outstanding in their secondary schools may have difficulty readjusting when they find themselves surrounded by equally exceptional students.

Here inner-city blacks meet and associate with well-to-do whites, causing as much uneasiness in one set as in the other. Students sort themselves out in fraternities, eating clubs, tables in the dining halls, cliques according to social backgrounds, and ethnic groupings. Forty years ago Jewish students often formed an uncomfortable minority who felt unwanted, whereas currently blacks and Chicanos from deprived backgrounds are likely to group together at meals and may even lessen their discomfort by aggressively turning away whites who seek to be friendly. Despite such difficulties the university setting has become one of the principal equalizing agencies. As the college years pass, the exclusiveness of the group diminishes. By the time of graduation, the influences of family and social backgrounds on individuals have diminished markedly. Whatever the student's original background, graduation from one of the academically elite universities opens the way for a person to become a leader in his or her community or the nation.

As they grow older, college men and women tend to mingle more freely, finding real companionship rather than simply going on dates with members of the opposite sex. Students are exposed to very different sexual standards from those they knew at home. A student, male or female, may strongly believe in premarital chastity, and find it difficult to live with a roommate who uses the room to have sexual relations rather than for study. Couples sleep together casually or only in a lasting relationship. Adjustments are made and readjustments of ideas develop. Parietal rules have become minimal at most universities: if students can vote and go to war, they are capable of defining their own morality. It is not simple for all. Life at the university differs markedly for the various students. For some who enter in order to become doctors or lawyers, it has become a highly competitive affair, often with interests already focusing if not narrowing; for others, these are relaxed years of socializing and play, with studies only a secondary matter. However, the first years, at least, provide many with an opportunity to broaden and learn new ways of living and thinking. Students may first appreciate that they cannot yet find an identity, learn who they are, because they had never before known who they might become. The agriculture student could never have thought of becoming a botanist before he learned of the influence of gravity on the shape of trees, or the prelaw student have considered becoming an art historian before she heard a series of brilliant lectures on Chinese painting. Some students will become indecisive about who they are. They may begin to realize that it is a matter of who they wish to become rather than of deciding who they are. Still, in one way or another, it is at college that many students reach critical decisions about themselves, and that adolescence will come to an end.

THE IDENTITY CRISIS

"Who am I?" is a theme repeated in countless variations by late adolescents. It is a question that troubles them unconsciously even more than consciously. Young persons are in the process of finding themselves even when they give it little thought. The boy now needs to know what to do with his life in order to give it cohesion, and the girl, who formerly was more concerned about whom she would marry, wonders whether she will direct herself toward a career or to marriage and motherhood, or undertake the difficult life of combining the two. But neither the boy nor the girl can answer such questions without knowing who he or she is—yet such decisions will influence who a person becomes. In some, the recognition that a turning point in life has been reached when decisions of a fairly irrevocable nature must be made precipitates a crisis. The individual realizes dimly or with anxiety-provoking acuteness that if he or she does not make decisions the passage of time will make them instead. Friends move on, move past, embark on careers, prepare to marry. The pause can lengthen into a paralysis of indecision. The responsibility of independent choice and its consequences can bring a period of perplexity, turmoil, and sometimes profound despair. Adolescents may fly from their surroundings, leave college, leave home—as if distance will resolve their problems. The change may bring respite, and though it is unlikely to solve intrapsychic problems, a moratorium during which an adolescent can gain additional experience, a broadened perspective, or increased emotional maturity can help one find direction. Some will seek to transcend their conscious abilities to find their identities, and become "seekers" who use drugs to "expand consciousness" and somehow reveal unknown abilities; or search out a "guru," who in cryptic, oracular fashion can provide guidance; or become involved in one or several consciousness expanding groups; or enter therapy with an analyst who will help probe their "unconscious."

Identity crises of late adolescence have received considerable attention both in novels and in psychiatry. Novelists have frequently passed through serious identity crises themselves, and psychiatrists are involved with patients many of whom had difficulties in emerging from adolescence. Most individuals, however, manage the transition with reasonable calm as a natural progression into an acceptable identity. The college student who knows that he will enter his father's business is only disturbed intellectually by the various problems aroused by his studies but they have not altered his tangible objectives. The girl who has found her future spouse has no doubts about entering teachers' college to learn to teach, in order to be able to support herself until her husband finishes his education, but she knows that a teaching career will be secondary to marriage. The "jock" who finds that he is not good enough for the freshman football team, and has no other reason to continue in college, joins the police force at Christmas vacation, content to have realized a life-long ambition. A girl who cannot remain in her large and very unhappy family after completing high school but who is too insecure to venture forth on her own, enters nursing school where she will be financially independent in a protected environment. Nevertheless, with increased education and with rapid social change, there has been an increasing need for individuals to find their own identities relatively independently of their families; the young adult is less likely to remain somewhat dependent upon the family or to follow in a family tradition than in previous eras, or to remain in the family home after leaving college. As a result, identity problems have become increasingly common and difficult.

Identity Formation

The transition from adolescent to adult involves becoming a person in one's own right, not simply someone's son or daughter, and a person who is recognized by the community in such terms. It involves the drawing together and resynthesis of a process that has been going on since birth and the crystallization out of an individual who will tend to preserve his or her identity despite the vicissitudes of life that are yet to come. The individual has passed through a series of developmental phases, and at each level there has been an identity and there has been a relatedness between the identities at each phase. Still, these identities always had a tentative quality, for each was a phase in becoming; but now it is time to be. The concept of ego identity was formulated by Erikson to emphasize that the developmental phases of childhood are not ends in themselves but stages in the progression toward developing into an integrated and reasonably self-sufficient person capable of filling an adult role in life and fitting into the social system in which the person lives. The integration is not achieved simply by passing through successive stages of psychosexual development without traumata and undue fixations, but depends on constant reorganization during the process, and then, during adolescence, a reintegration to permit moving from childhood dependency to adult responsibility.* It is concerned not simply with inner organization but also with how that organization permits the individual to move properly into the social roles permitted and expected of an adult in a given society and its subsystems.

* "The process of identity formation emerges as an evolving configuration, a configuration which is gradually established by successive ego syntheses and resyntheses throughout childhood; it is a configuration gradually integrating constitutional givens, idiosyncratic libidinal needs, favored capacities, significant identifications, effective defenses, successful sublimations, and consistent roles" (E. Erikson, "The Problem of Ego Identity," p. 116).

The concept of ego identity is not definable in very precise terms and a degree of vagueness is preferable, for it is still simpler to delineate the area of interest than define it in terms of critical attributes. It concerns the consistency that characterizes individuals despite the changes that occur over time, and as they move into the many different roles they fill at any one period in their lives.* We might say that by the end of adolescence the individual's name—as should be the case with all nominal words—provides a degree of predictability concerning how its bearer will behave and what others can anticipate from that individual under a variety of circumstances. Equally important is that the person also has some idea of how he or she will behave, relate, and feel under varying conditions. Of course, human behavior is so complex and subject to so many contingencies, as well as conscious and unconscious influences, that prediction of how a person will react and interact in unfamiliar situations remains limited (except, of course, to a psychiatrist).

Identity formation has much to do with the person's past identifications and their fusion into a new integrate. The identifications with the parents remain basic despite the many vicissitudes they have undergone, but to them have been added the identifications with various ideal figures and both friends and enemies,† for something remains of all. Various significant persons who have been lost—or more or less abandoned—particularly the parents, are preserved within the self. Identity formation also involves

---

* The concept of ego identity also implies the attainment of a homeostasis of the self or the personality which absorbs the impact of influences upon the personality and tends to resist radical change and perpetuate itself, so to speak. The homeostatic mechanisms within the personality are extremely complex, and involve matters beyond current knowledge. While the sorting out of identifications is very important, it involves many other matters, some of which I shall indicate here: (1) What a person perceives and how the person perceives it influences markedly the further development of personality traits; yet it involves a process that is circular, for perception depends in part on the projection of personality characteristics—as we know from the utility of projective personality tests. (2) Patterns of relating within the family now come to a closure, but will continue to influence all further interpersonal and group relationships. (3) Parental directives have now been internalized as superego directives; but even more important, many have moved closer to the ego "core" and become ego rather than superego functions and thus are fundamental and rather spontaneous determinants of behavior. (4) The patterns of the defensive mechanisms utilized to avert anxiety and depression as well as cognitive styles and patterns of emotional reactivity have become fairly set. (5) The individual has assimilated into the self both cultural instrumentalities and norms as well as much of the social system in which he lives, and thus gains a stability in behaving, perceiving, relating, according to these norms. (6) The assumption of a major life role—such as the role of a physician or future physician, lawyer, or even profligate—contributes to consistency and resistance to change.

† Identification with the aggressor is often an important defense in which one takes on strengths and attributes of a feared and hated object. Thus, some sage warned, "Select your enemy carefully, because you will end up resembling him."

identifications with groups as well as individuals: the family as a unit with its traditions and specific mores; the social class into which one is raised; ethnic and religious groupings; and one's nation and time in history, which are usually taken for granted, as well as one's gender, which, as we have emphasized, forms a keystone in stable identity formation. To gain coherence of personality functioning and a sense of unity, aspects of identifications that are inconsistent with the total pattern, which are ego-alien, must be discarded or repressed. "Identity formation," as Erikson has pointed out, "begins where the usefulness of identification ends. It arises from the selective repudiation and mutual assimilation of childhood identifications, and their absorption in a new configuration, which in turn, is dependent on the process by which a society (often through subsocieties) identifies the young individual, recognizing him as somebody who had to become the way he is, and who, being the way he is, is taken for granted" (Erikson, 1956, p. 113).

Adolescents are seeking consistent ways of relating to others, for finding their way through life and for solving problems. They need and seek reference points. They feel, like Archimedes, that, if given a place on which to stand, they can move the world—or at least they can face it. Although finding guidance into the future depends upon the stability of previous identifications and their resynthesis, it also requires standards for judging behavior and directives. We have seen that the adolescent moves beyond superego injunctions taken from the parents; the parental injunctions have been modified through fusion with ego ideals, and through the assimilation of standards of peer groups and the mores of the community. In an effort to find a definite way of life, adolescents are likely to embrace a cause which not only tells them what to do with their lives, but also provides standards for judging what is right and wrong, what is pertinent and what irrelevant. Still, only a small minority find that their major problems will be solved by joining a political party, a religious movement, or a social movement. Politics is not a way of life for most, nor is religion. Joining an all-encompassing religious movement, whether an Eastern sect or fundamentalist Christian, usually lends direction to a life for but a few years. Direction is more apt to come from reaching a decision about a career. When young persons make a choice about their future occupations, they settle many problems, for they can then direct their attention and exert their energies in preparing for it. What an adolescent will do with his or her life helps answer the query "Who am I?"*

---

* A topic that will be expanded in the chapter on occupational choice.

Identity and Delimitation

Yet, one of the functions of adolescence is to keep pathways into the future open, to prevent premature closure before a youth has gained sufficient experience to judge properly what to do with one's life. *Identity foreclosure*, the failure to develop beyond the juvenile period or early adolescence, limits both opportunity and the ability to guide one's own life. There are many social, educational, and intrapsychic reasons for such foreclosure that cannot be considered here.* Adolescents have been expanding and sampling, so to speak, but now in late adolescence matters change as they realize that they must consolidate, weighing whether or not they wish really to pursue some particular field of endeavor. They may find it difficult to renounce one potentiality to follow another, yet they know that each person has only one life to lead. Now, more than ever before, they must delimit themselves in order to gain organization. Some will flee from such closure, hating the idea that they must become someone in particular, and in so doing may find settings in which "doing one's thing" —which may mean being nothing but simply oneself, an indefinite if not an amorphous self—is prized. But most become weary of the indecision, and seek a future objective which will do away with vacillation and the constant need to make decisions. They may feel, and believe correctly, that everything hangs in the balance—and that if, by chance, they take a left turn rather than a right, it will decide much of their future. This is a time when a single decision can greatly influence an entire life, whereas later, after a person has embarked on a set course, it will require a major reorientation to alter a life pattern. The young person can become paralyzed with indecision when any decision seems so important. A college senior had entered the university some three years before, fairly certain that he would follow his father and become a physician. He had been responding to expectations for him rather than his own interests. He became increasingly engrossed in courses in literature and history, and found that the natural sciences were tolerable but uninteresting to him. His father died, and soon thereafter he decided not to become a physician; but now he found himself torn between following an academic career or entering the government's foreign service. He did not have difficulty finding something he wished to do with his life,

---

* *Identity foreclosure*, including the assumption of a *negative identity*—the commitment to identification with persons who are shunned, despised, or hated—is a common outcome of development in white or black slums, but particularly black inner-city slums. Such pathological developments, even though all too common, are beyond the scope of this book. The reader is referred to S. Hauser, *Black and White Identity Formation*.

but rather found himself unable to decide what not to do with it. Some in this predicament can, like Goethe, decide that it does not really matter whether they make pots or pans, or plant peas or beans, but can trust to their genius to make whatever they do turn out well, or that it matters little just what one decides to do—what matters is the commitment and endeavor that will make whatever one does interesting.*

The achievement of an identity includes recognition by others, and such recognition, even when tentative, often helps the youth find a place in society that he can occupy without inner conflicts. The recognition by a teacher who suggests or persuades him to enter a given field can help settle problems of finding an identity. Finding a mentor does more than provide guidance, the youth obtains *confirmation* of his or her worth from someone who matters. The mentor may then turn into a sponsor who provides actual help in starting a career. To some, such experiences come quietly and unexpectedly while they still consider themselves junior dependent members of society. A college sophomore spends his summer vacation working as a surveyor, enjoying the work with a crew in the woods. When the foreman becomes ill, the student takes charge of the crew and gains their respect despite his youth. At the end of vacation the head of the engineering firm suggests that he remain in a more responsible position, assuring him that he can have a good future with the firm. Although he continues college, he has definitely decided to become a civil engineer and has the assurance of an excellent position after he is graduated. He had started the summer still carefree and without feeling pressed to decide about a career; his life and future were still amorphous, but when he returned to college he could envision a pattern of life and he had a plan to follow that solved many problems for him.

Identity Crises

The youth seeks outward to find a way of life that will satisfy, and also turns inward seeking resources and weighing liabilities. What are the talents, and what are the desires that need fulfillment? Comparisons with others are searching, and older adolescents may mercilessly take into account only the strongest assets of the persons to whom they are comparing themselves. They cast aside attributes they possess that will not lead to perfection. They hold up a mirror to the soul and unconscious processes

* Developmental novels—*Erziehungsromane*—usually deal with the crisis the author passed through in finding a way of life and are of particular interest to the study of personality development. Noteworthy examples are Goethe's *Wilhelm Meister*, Samuel Butler's *The Way of All Flesh*, Somerset Maugham's *Of Human Bondage*, Strindberg's *The Red Room*, and James Joyce's *A Portrait of the Artist as a Young Man*.

well up and threaten to bring chaos. When the forward flow of the stream is halted, much old debris can float to the surface. A boy may recognize and become disturbed by the erotic nature of his love for his mother, by sadistic impulses, or by worries about his masculinity that make him wonder if he might be homosexual. The girl may realize that she is still sexually tied to her father, or is fleeing any identification with her oppressed and suppressed mother. Adolescents may achieve profound insights into unconscious processes, but they are often of little help at this juncture of life. For many adolescents, the solution to many sources of anguish, to much of the self-doubting, lies in finding direction and starting toward a goal rather than in further introspection. Such problems are so common at the end of adolescence that they are often considered an inherent part of the period. However, identity crises are often more severe in those adolescents who reject following patterns familiar to them, or expected of them, as well as for those who resist closure by accepting a secure way of life. Currently, women pursuing careers are likely to face identity crises, as we shall consider below. Such persons often do not finish with their identity problems in late adolescence, as we shall discuss in the section on *Youth*.

Ego Diffusion

As late adolescence is so often a time of conflict, some neurotic suffering is almost inevitable. However, more difficult problems occur and the seriousness of these may be difficult to assess. The dangers lie not in failing to reach an immediate solution and find an identity and way of life—for many persons will take several years until they find themselves—but in finding a negative solution: adolescents give up, feel defeated, and suffer "ego diffusion," in which they virtually cease trying to direct their lives consciously, leaving themselves prey to unconscious motivations, and they drift, perhaps becoming more or less schizophrenic; or they become embittered about the ways of society and the adults who inhabit and direct the Establishment, and become alienated, refusing to become committed to a way of life; or they embrace alienation itself as a way of life, "dropping out," or becoming perpetual "seekers" after an inner light.*

Although the inability to find a positive identity and a way of life may seem to be a matter of decision, insofar as it depends upon decision rather

---

* The recent trend toward the use of marijuana and LSD as a means of finding oneself and discovering a new truth and meaning through more immediate access to the unconscious is clearly related to the Dionysian religion in ancient Greece. Dionysus was the "liberator"—the god who through the use of wine and the ecstasy of the bacchanal enabled a person to stop being himself for a brief period, thereby setting the person free from feelings of responsibility and the burden of being himself. It was a flight from the

than chronic indecision the choice rests upon unconscious determinants that reflect profound problems. A bright college student who "drops out" to join counterculture groups in Greenwich Village or Berkeley, experimenting with cocaine or even with heroin, not only is unable to identify with his father—or any paternal figure—but must prove to himself that he is different from his father; he may also be unable to relate to women, who are experienced as engulfing, overwhelming figures who are untrustworthy, and he may be moving into or reactively fighting against a homosexual identity. Study reveals serious family and developmental pathology. As Keniston has elucidated through his studies of alienated students,* the young man may have been profoundly disillusioned in his mother, who had been seductively close to him, when she betrayed him by adhering to his father; and disillusioned in a father who despite external appearances turned out to be weak, relatively ineffectual, and perhaps effeminate. Others have been disillusioned in recognizing that one or both parents are dishonest, promiscuous, deceitful toward spouse and child.

The Girl's Identity Problems

Achieving a firm ego identity has become increasingly difficult for many girls, particularly, though not exclusively, for liberated, intellectually competent girls. They are caught up in the historical crisis—brought on by the planned limitation of childbearing, women's increased education, the altered structure of the family, etc.—that has been changing women's place in society and thereby the adolescent girl's image of herself and her future

---

Apollonian spirit, which sought self-understanding through experience, an attempt to gain insight through revelation. Dionysus was thus a god of illusion with a welcomed way of release from planning and control. He appeared at a time when the individual began to emerge from the solidarity of the family for the first time, and "found the burden of individual responsibility hard to bear." The aim of the cult was the achievement of ecstasy, a losing of oneself, and its psychological function was to "satisfy and relieve the impulse to reject responsibility, an impulse that exists in all of us and can become under certain social conditions an irresistible craving" (Dodds, 1951, pp. 76–77). LSD is used for similar purposes, primarily by late adolescents and young adults who find the burden of achieving an ego identity too great. The illusion of profound insight into the self and the meaning of the universe so often experienced under the influence of the drug makes it particularly tempting and dangerous. The taker has the illusion of finding the self through losing the self. The use of the drug is often bound to group ritual in which individuals feel freed from responsibility for their own behavior and can be carried away as were the participants in the bacchanalia. It is of interest that some devotees seek to ritualize the use of LSD into a religious rite (Lidz and Rothenberg, 1968).

* See K. Keniston, *The Uncommitted.* Such tragic situations are dramatized effectively and realistically in Arthur Miller's *Death of a Salesman* and Eugene O'Neill's *Long Day's Journey into Night.*

self. She is very likely to realize that women's traditional roles are providing and will provide less satisfaction than in the past, but the new roles for women are still far from clear. Entering the highly competitive arena like men and with men can leave some very basic needs unsatisfied; even many men would like to be able to get away from the constant pursuit of prestige and power. Still, many girls feel strongly that their mothers have been left with rather empty lives now that their children are grown, even though they had found gratification in being mothers. The new models that are just beginning to appear may seem conflicted and difficult to follow.

The college woman is becoming highly educated—indeed educated beyond the level of all but a limited number of men in other industrial nations—but what is she to do with her education? Use it to raise educated sons, or to provide backing for an educated husband? Many college women are clearly as competent as, or more competent than, their brothers or male classmates, and see no reason why they should not seek fulfillment and realization by taking on instrumental roles in society and become business executives, lawmakers, professors themselves. Some are secure in their capabilities and since mid-adolescence have been certain that they would pursue careers. These girls often either follow in the paths of mothers who have had careers or decide that they will realize the potentialities their competent mothers had sacrificed to become wives of highly capable men (Keniston, 1971); or they have had some other such guiding principle. Thus, a college freshman decided, as soon as she assured herself that she could obtain good grades in the sciences, to follow her mother's sister and become a pediatrician, thereby making certain that she would not become a person like her mother, who catered to the needs and whims of her dominating and thoughtless father. However, even most of these girls will also expect to marry and have children sooner or later, and they are aware that combining a real career—and pinning one's future happiness on its success —with marriage requires finding a man who will consider his wife's career on a par with his own, and that having children will very likely interfere with a career and even disrupt it. They wish fulfillment through their own special abilities and not only through being women with innate capacities to create children; and yet they wish to have a basic identity as women who have children and can be nurturant at home, no matter how impersonal and competitive they may be at work. They may be haunted by the fear of growing incapable of intimacy, warmth, and tenderness, and remaining unloved and lonely whatever their achievements. Their abilities to stick to their resolve may depend on their being able to find a man at college, with whom they can have a warm companionship and sexual intimacy to assure themselves that they can give of themselves and can be desired. Of course, finding other young women at college who feel reasonably at ease in competing with men also helps.

Still, even those adolescents who have the primary objective of becoming a wife and mother (who, we should remember, still constitute the large majority of adolescent girls) are now beginning to realize that caring for children will adequately occupy only ten to fifteen years of their seventy or more years of life; and that marriages are not as permanent as formerly. Some will wish to lay the foundations for a part-time or full-time career or avocation before marriage, or at least before having children. Here, too, an identity based on being a wife and mother alone may be felt to be insufficient. Further, female classmates and professors at college may urge a college sophomore who looks forward to marriage but is highly competent to be true to herself and make the most of her capabilities by pursuing a career. Even an adolescent who believes deeply that for her a sense of fulfillment and creativity will come through complementing a man's life and nurturing children may today feel a traitor to her sex if she follows her felt needs and intuitive convictions. Such girls may realize that for them there can be a very basic inner conflict between having a career and being a mother. For some girls to achieve the autonomy necessary for a successful career, they must establish very firm boundaries which may include renunciation of remaining identifications with their mothers, and then later will find it difficult to relax the boundaries sufficiently to form a symbiotic union with an infant, or to permit a child to become sufficiently dependent upon them (Keniston, 1971). They may also fear that once they permit themselves to begin to compete for prestige, particularly with men, they may never be able to withdraw from the race and have children.

Currently, the problems of the girl's ego identity are very complex. Those who pursue careers will have not only many identity problems similar to those of men but also those related to the changing positions of women in society, problems which also involve new attitudes toward intimacy, sexual behavior, marital choice, and career choice. We shall consider such problems further in this and subsequent chapters.

INTIMACY AND LOVE

Even though young adolescents may have had various sexual experiences, usually they are not ready to become involved in intimate relationships until late adolescence; and even then, they are apt to be tentative. They have been seeking release, knowledge, excitement, and have been engaged in exploring their feelings and those of persons of the opposite sex, more than in seeking completion of the self through a lasting relationship with another. Indeed, a stable love relationship in the mid-teens often indicates an inability to tolerate separation from parents and can block the development of a firm ego identity. Even though the sexual drives are as imperative as earlier, late adolescents are often less upset by them. They have usually found some means of coming to terms with their sexual needs, even though on a temporary basis, and superego dictates are less restrictive. They feel more certain of their capacities; they have strengthened their defenses against being overwhelmed by drives, and they permit themselves some outlets without too much conflict.

Gradually adolescents begin to have a less self-centered and narcissistic orientation to their sexual and affectional needs. They become involved in love relationships in which the welfare of the partner is also important, and the satisfaction that the other obtains becomes a source of pleasure to the self. They feel, even if they do not consciously realize it, that they are incomplete alone and that a member of one sex cannot feel complete without joining with a member of the opposite sex. They wish to share and find someone whose roles and ways of loving are complementary to their own, who gains satisfaction from what they do, who is not a rival, and to whom they are necessary. They are no longer seeking someone like themselves, or even someone of the other sex in whom they find attributes they might have liked to possess, but someone who completes them and admires them. When an adolescent persists in pursuing an unrequited love, the romantic striving has a pathological character as if the boy or girl feels fated to repeat the frustrations of the oedipal situation rather than to find situations that can bring fulfillment.

Now that persons have begun to come to terms with who they are, and have fairly definite ego identities, they often fall in love in a serious fashion. The meaning and intensity of being in love varies with the maturity of the person. Now couples are drawn together and the life of each encompasses the other. They think and talk in terms of "we," emphasizing their mutuality of interests, feelings, future lives—often temporarily overdoing the romantic belief in their unity. There is an impelling need to be together and share experiences. Things done separately are carried out with thoughts of the partner. Separation can be painful, and thoughts of being replaced by another engender real suffering. The lover invests the representation of the loved one intensely, and even though it may be painful at times, the experience of being drawn beyond one's own confines and beyond one's own life into such intimate concern and involvement leads to a loosening of boundaries of the self, to a release that is ecstatic. Now, an intense attachment to another that combines the affectional and erotic can for the first time replace the intense attachment to a parent that had to be renounced. The psychic intimacy usually blends with a physical and sexual intimacy, but the emotional and psychic investment can become more irresistible than the sexual urges from which such feelings may derive.

I cannot don the poet's mantle to write of the bliss of early love when the self is partially lost in devotion to another, and when the awkwardness of self-consciousness shifts into a grace of being desired. Even though most early loves break up sooner or later, they form important omens for the future. They indicate that disappointments over frustrations within the family can be overcome, that repressions of sexuality are not too great, that defenses are not too rigid. The relationships may be disrupted because the choice resembles a parent too closely or, conversely, is too dissimilar; or because the boy and girl are not yet ready to relinquish their newly gained independence; or because too many tasks toward achieving security and a career remain. Sexual frustrations may produce too many frictions. Sexual intercourse between inexperienced persons, even when they are in love, may be unsatisfactory, and the couple may not be ready to seek advice, or know where they can find help. Such relationships are an important part of developing into an adult, a proper trying out of how one relates to another on intimate terms. They are part of the expansion of adolescence but also a coming to terms with the need to delimit and share, and such courtships should be trial periods rather than firm commitments.

The Changing Sexual Mores

The changes in adolescent sexual mores have permitted many in recent decades to include sexual intercourse as part of their experimentation with intimate relationships. However, it is erroneous to believe that most teenagers are having sexual relations. It has been estimated that fewer than fifty percent of girls and about sixty percent of boys have had sexual relations as teenagers (Sorensen, 1973) and that about fifty percent of college students have sexual relations (Sarrel, personal communication). It is possible that there has not been a great change in the number of late adolescents who currently have intimate sexual experience in comparison with previous generations, but there is probably more intercourse than petting to orgasm than earlier in the century,* and more openness about cohabitation. There is probably considerably greater freedom, particularly for the girl to have sexual relationships without a serious commitment to the partner; sometimes with only sufficient commitment for her to assure herself that she is not promiscuous. A great effort has gone into making premarital sexual relationships more casual and less focal. The desire for intimacy and closeness may be more important than sexual release, and the practice of couples sleeping together without having intercourse has become common among college students. The "double standard" by which parents expected sons but not daughters to have sexual relations before marriage is disappearing and parents are now more likely to be concerned about a daughter's becoming pregnant than about her losing her virginity.

It is also apparent that adolescents can permit themselves to feel bolder and require less protection by parietal rules because the sexual act encompasses far less danger and is far less threatening to the continuity of development and career than formerly, as there is less threat of being forced into an undesirable marriage. Improved contraception, the legalization of abortion, and a decrease in the seriousness of the consequences of venereal infections are important factors in producing this change; but fewer than twenty percent of adolescent girls use a reliable mode of contraception regularly, if at all. One out of six teenage girls becomes pregnant without being married, and fifteen percent of college women have unwanted pregnancies, most of whom have abortions.† Venereal diseases have again become common because condoms are used relatively infrequently, the male expecting the girl to take the necessary contraceptive precautions.

---

* It should be realized that university students in many other countries had prolonged sexual affairs even prior to World War II, and, in particular, Scandinavian sexual mores have long differed markedly from those of the United States. The practice of "heavy petting" that had been considered more permissible in contrast to sexual relationships has something of a perverse character, in that forepleasure becomes the goal, and this seemed very bizarre to many Europeans.

† In 1974 teenagers accounted for about one in five births—about 617,000 babies and a quarter of a million abortions. It has been estimated that out of every ten teenagers who get pregnant, three are married, three get married, and four have abortions or babies without getting married. The "unwanted" pregnancies are often consciously or unconsciously desired. The boy, particularly among groups where "machismo" is important, may need to prove his masculinity. In some settings boys—or men—feel cheated if the girl uses contraception and their sperm is wasted. Girls—particularly fatherless, neglected girls—may wish to have a baby as a "doll" to love them and to love; or to assure themselves that they can be fertile. Girls may wish to show their parents that they are not the only ones who can have affairs. College students may need to prove their masculinity or femininity when threatened by homosexual temptations. Somewhat older students can settle problems concerning marriage and career by becoming pregnant, or when they feel uncreative and stymied in their work, they can fall back on their natural creative capacities, etc. (Sarrel and R. Lidz, 1970).

Many progressive religious leaders no longer equate sexual abstinence with morality, and some even believe that greater freedom of sexual expression may lead to a lessening of unconscious motivations toward unethical behavior. The concept, stemming originally from psychoanalytic teachings that sexual repression can be harmful to the harmonious development of the individual, has had considerable influence upon teachers, clergy, doctors, and parents. The greater acceptance of sexuality by elders permits more open discussion in adolescence; and it is the openness of sexual behavior as well as the freedom of discussion that represents much of the change over the past few decades. Victorian standards are considered ludicrous rather than providing a guide for sexual behavior. Abstinence is not defended as a virtue, though a large number abstain because they do not feel ready, or perhaps because it may be easier to abandon old standards verbally than in actuality. However, it is natural enough for the boy to desire sexual release with a girl whom he likes rather than with either a prostitute or someone who does not matter, and for the girl to wish to share sexually with her boy friend rather than have him turn to another for gratification.

Identity and the Capacity for Intimacy

The discussion of the problems of achieving an ego identity separately from the consideration of gaining a capacity for intimacy has been arbitrary, required for clarity, for the two processes are closely interrelated. The answer to the query "Who am I?" depends, in part, upon knowing that one can love and be loved as an individual, and even more specifically upon whom one loves and from whom one desires love. Ego identity involves the feelings of completion that come from feeling loved and needed, from being able to share the self and the world with another. Still, the capacity of intimacy can develop only as feelings of self-assurance and of being an integrated and reasonably independent individual gradually consolidate. Concerns over sexual capacities, over gender identity, and then over the ability to be close and gain closeness markedly influence the adolescent's developing ego identity.

Traditionally, the capacity for intimacy has been more of an inherent part of gaining an ego identity in girls than in boys. Those girls who enter late adolescence seeking completion through finding a husband will still find a large measure of their self-concepts in terms of exploring their own attributes and finding out which boys or young men can engender a sense of completion in them. However, for many male as well as female adolescents, just who can provide a sense of completion depends on who one believes one is or wishes to be, and not simply on the capacity to be intimate with the person. A college freshman had an excellent relationship, including a sexual relationship, with a high school classmate whom she believed she loved dearly. However, she increasingly felt a disparity between their intellectual capacities, cultural interests, and ambitions. Determined to become a tax attorney—her father was an accountant—she could not believe she could continue to share interests with a physical education instructor. In contrast, adolescents' ambitious plans for the future may vanish when they fall in love. The girl may begin to appreciate the satisfactions her mother gained in loving and being needed by others, something that previously had seemed so burdensome to her. She may learn from her experience that sex, instead of being anxiety provoking and not particularly gratifying, is extremely exciting and enjoyable, and perhaps even more enjoyable and necessary for her than for her boyfriend.* The young man who had expected to become a neurosurgeon decides that entering his uncle's business on graduation in order to marry his love will provide greater happiness.

It makes sense to many to explore and try out how things work with different partners; and not to feel impelled to marry in order to have a sexual relationship. Part of women's liberation concerns the abandonment of the double standard, and as late adolescent girls are often more mature than their male classmates, they are as likely as a boyfriend, if not more likely, to desire sexual intercourse as part of a relationship. Serial monogamy, in which couples confine their sexual behavior to one another but do not thereby make lasting commitments, has become common among older adolescents as well as young adults. The new freedom can have the

---

* The comparison of the relative satisfaction gained by each sex in the sexual act is, of course, impossible. The only person who has ever been deemed capable of so judging was the mythical Tiresias. According to legend, Tiresias had been turned into a woman when he saw snakes copulating, and had then lived as a courtesan for many years, but eventually regained his masculine anatomy. It seems that once when Hera was upbraiding Zeus for one of his many infidelities, he told her not to complain for as a woman she gained far more pleasure when they did have sexual relations. Hera did not accept her spouse's infinite knowledge and insisted that the remark was ludicrous, that everyone knew that the man gained more pleasure from the act than the woman. The quarrel thus turned from the particular to the universal, but neither one could convince the other. Finally they remembered Tiresias and called upon him to settle the argument, admitting that for once a mortal could know something hidden even to a god. Tiresias stated that if the pleasure of the sexual act is divided into ten parts, nine parts are the woman's. This assertion so angered Hera that she struck Tiresias blind. Zeus could not undo Hera's act, but sought to compensate Tiresias by conferring upon him inner sight, thus making him the greatest of all seers; and he bestowed on him seven life spans, which accounts for the appearance of Tiresias in myths that took place in different eras.

salutary influence of lessening the import of sexual desire as a dominant motivation for marriage and the choice of marital partners; and in diminishing sexual repression during late adolescence to permit more rational decisions concerning other matters aside from marriage, including career choice.

There are, however, some difficulties inherent in the contemporary situation. They devolve from problems of emotional maturity more than from questions of morals or ethics. Adolescents of both sexes tend to engage in sexual relationships of either a transitory or more involved nature before they are ready. The group mores no longer tend to support refusal or delay, and the individual must be willing to maintain a stand concerning what is right for himself or herself. Indeed, a college woman may find herself under pressure from her friends "to go on the pill." When a young person, whether male or female, behaves sexually in ways alien to his or her own values because of a partner's desires or demands, or because of group pressures, sexual problems are very likely to ensue. The girl may feel obligated to have sexual relations with her boyfriend, just as his last girl-friend did; and a boy may not be ready to admit his inexperience. A very popular young man on the campus became upset after his first sexual intercourse. He had gone to study in the room of a girl he liked and found interesting. Late in the evening, she started to undress and he started to leave, but it became clear from the conversation that she believed that he, a much-sought-after young man, was very experienced and would be pleased to sleep with her. He found that he was unable to tell her that he was still virginal and felt that she would take his refusal as a rebuff.

Girls today, in keeping with much of the literature on sex, consider it important to have an orgasm each time they have intercourse, and couples feel that simultaneous orgasms are evidence of a good relationship; and yet a girl is not likely to have an orgasm the first several times she has intercourse, and couples may need considerable experience before relations are fully satisfactory for both.

When a young couple has a sexual relationship, one member is apt to invest more of the self in it than the other, and not be able to accept the other's casualness; or when the affair is serious, one will be hurt when it breaks up, despite promises that neither would expect it to be permanent. Actual sexual difficulties are apt to occur more commonly among adolescents who are still not properly disengaged from their oedipal attachments, and who cannot cope with the dependency needs of a partner when they are far from independent themselves. Of course, similar problems occur in young married couples. It is not a matter of age but of readiness, and couples are more apt to be ready when they must also consider the life-long involvements of marriage. The solutions are not readily available, for there cannot be generalized answers. Here we are simply noting that the adolescent often considers such matters in terms of standards of morality and propriety, which they are willing to change, when questions of maturity may be more pertinent.

Variant Uses of Sexuality

The adolescent may start to use his or her sexuality for purposes other than either gaining sexual release or moving toward intimacy. Compulsive sexuality that enables the boy to believe that he is a real man, or the girl to think that she is irresistibly sensuous—or at least to lead others to believe so—is often a defense against fears of homosexuality or deep feelings of worthlessness, or a flight from loneliness and emptiness. Some will use sexuality as a means of sadistically dominating the partner, or of humiliating the opposite sex; or to make the other feel sexually inadequat or worthless. Then, there is the potentiality that the pleasures of the sexual act can lead a person with a shaky identity into finding solace and diversion through it, and sexuality becomes something of a game. The use of sex as a game or a diversion in late adolescence and early adult life is common enough; it can be part of a competition with peers of the same sex, as when cliques of college men keep tabulations of their "box scores." Seduction through various tactics and strategies can become a game in itself. Some consider such activities an inherent part of late adolescence and early adulthood in the male, and even some girls are attracted by men with many conquests. Such diversion need not be deleterious unless it ultimately becomes a substitute for seeking after real intimacy.

THE END OF ADOLESCENCE

Sooner or later adolescence ends for most (but not all) persons, and it can end in many different ways. Still, we may generalize and consider that persons become adults after they feel independent enough and have explored the horizon sufficiently. They begin to feel that the world is too large and they can become lost in it. They realize all too keenly that success in a chosen career depends upon the effort they put into it, for they are competing with others who seem as capable as they are. An obsessive quality may develop in youths who formerly had been carefree; it is an obsessiveness deriving from efforts to overcome anxiety about the future through thinking through and working out solutions in advance, mingled with compulsive strivings to satisfy expectations. They cannot afford to fail after finally making a decision about their futures. Such concerns can lead to over-delimitation, to a constriction of interests and of the personality. It is the danger opposite to that of ego diffusion—an outcome that is not so devastating and chaotic, but narrowing if it becomes more than an expedient to gain a good start and becomes a way of life.

Now the loss of bonds to the family is no longer pleasing, particularly as newer relationships are being cut into as friends pair off and marry. The need for interdependence with another and for intimacy asserts itself and gains dominance as a motivation. The youth cannot keep seeking after some indefinite ambition but must settle down to conquer a specific section of the vocational world. The young person begins to believe, albeit often unconsciously, that striving after fame or wealth, or the pursuit of some ideology, is less important than coming to mean something to some specific individual. The youth realizes that life will gain in meaning through being meaningful to another person and having the other person need him or her. Thus the strivings for intimacy and identity come together, for much of the feelings of having a specific identity will come from being needed and wanted by another person, and from the meaning one has to the other person. Even as the self first took form in childhood through a feedback from significant others, now one particularly significant person helps define the self. Intimacy comes when an individual is capable of balancing giving and receiving and can seek to satisfy another rather than simply seek self-fulfillment and achievement.

It is now, at the end of adolescence, that youths often move beyond the egocentricity of "formal operations," when they could not really appreciate that solving problems subjectively is a very different matter from solving them in actuality. They realize that to change the nation, or even the university, will take years of effort, and may have doubts whether it is worth devoting one's life to a task that is so likely to fail. However, some highly motivated and idealistic youths will resist closure and find themselves only when they come to terms with the social system in which they live, as we shall consider in the next chapter. Now adolescents begin to see themselves moving through a complex world and a maze of people rather than having others pass through their world.* They realize that they are living in a brief span of history isolated in an infinity of space. If they are fortunate they find meaning in what the world is, and do not get lost in their insignificance. They appreciate that there are ways of regarding the world which are very different from their own. Reluctantly, they may decide that although ideologies are worth pursuing, they must first look out for their own futures. They also begin to see their parents as individuals with lives of their own, caught up in their own marriage and occupations, rather than simply as parents. They now begin to understand their parents' foibles and deficiencies and sometimes even to hope that they will be able to do as well. They may begin again to accept components of parents as conscious objects of identification and their standards as part of their own superego directives. As they leave adolescence, they may have lingering regrets that they have not dared more or that they have not been able to stick to the ideals that but so recently fired their lives. In a way, it is always regrettable when youths become as conservative and conventional as their parents at an early age. Fortunately not all do.

* A nineteen-year-old, after revisiting the town in which he had spent his first summer vacation during college and where he had made many friends, recalled his thoughts and feelings while walking to the railroad station when he left. "I was in something of a daze; the people hurrying through the streets looked different to me than people ever looked before. I realized in a way that I had never before that all of this had remained while I had come and gone: my friends were pursuing their lives, falling in love and out again, changing their studies, finding new interests, and I was only peripheral to it, indeed scarcely mattered. Of course, I had *known* this before but I had never *felt* it."

REFERENCES

ACKERMAN, N. (1962). "Adolescent Problems: A Symptom of Family Disorder," *Family Process* 1:202–213.

BENEDEK, T., and RUBENSTEIN, B. (1942). "The Sexual Cycle in Women: The Relation Between Ovarian Function and Psychodynamic Processes," *Psychosomatic Medicine Monographs*, vol. 3, nos. 1 and 2. National Research Council, Washington, D.C.

BETTELHEIM, B. (1971). *Symbolic Wounds*. Rev. ed. Collier Books, New York.

DODDS, E. (1951). *The Greeks and the Irrational*. University of California Press, Berkeley.

DUCHE, D., SCHONFELD, W., and TOMKIEWICZ, S. (1966). "Physical Aspects of Adolescent Development," in *Psychiatric Approaches to Adolescence*. G. Caplan and S. Lebovici, eds. International Congress Series, no. 108. Excerpta Medica Foundation, New York.

DULIT, E. (1972). "Adolescent Thinking à la Piaget: The Formal Stage," *Journal of Youth and Adolescence*, 1:281–301.

ELKIN, F., and WESTLY, W. (1955). "The Myth of Adolescent Culture," *American Sociological Review*, 20:680–684.

ERIKSON, E. (1956). "The Problem of Ego Identity," *Journal of the American Psychoanalytic Association*, 4:56–121.

FREUD, A. (1969). "Adolescence as a Developmental Disturbance," in *Adolescence: Psychosocial Perspectives*, ed. G. Caplan and S. Lebovici, Basic Books, N.Y.

FRISCH, R., and REVELLE, R. (1970). "Height and Weight at Menarche and a Hypothesis of Critical Body Weights and Adolescent Events," *Science*, 169:397–399.

HAUSER, S. (1971). *Black and White Identity Formation: Explorations in the Psychosocial Development of White and Negro Male Adolescents*. Wiley-Interscience, New York.

INHELDER, B., and PIAGET, J. (1958). *The Growth of Logical Thinking from Childhood to Adolescence*. A. Parsons and S. Milgram, trans. Basic Books, New York.

IVEY, M., and BARDWICK, J. (1968). "Patterns of Affective Fluctuation in the Menstrual Cycle," *Psychosomatic Medicine*, 30:336–345.

KENISTON, K. (1965). *The Uncommitted: Alienated Youth in American Society*. Harcourt, Brace & World, New York.

——— . (1971). "Themes and Conflicts of 'Liberated' Young Women." The 1971 Karen Horney Memorial Lecture. Unpublished.

KINSEY, A., POMEROY, W., and MARTIN, C. (1948). *Sexual Behavior in the Human Male*. W. B. Saunders, Philadelphia.

———. (1953). *Sexual Behavior in the Human Female*. W. B. Saunders, Philadelphia.

KOHLBERG, L. (1964). "Development of Moral Character and Moral Ideology," in *Review of Child Development Research*. M. Hoffman and L. Hoffman, eds. Russell Sage Foundation, New York.

LIDZ, R. W., LIDZ, T., and BURTON-BRADLEY, B. (1973). "Cargo Cultism: A Psychosocial Study of Melanesian Millenarianism," *Journal of Nervous and Mental Disease*, 157:370–388.

LIDZ, T., and ROTHENBERG, A. (1968). "Psychedelism: Dionysus Reborn," *Psychiatry*, 31:116–125.

LOEWALD, H. (1951). "Ego and Reality," *International Journal of Psycho-Analysis*, 32:1–9.

OFFER, D., and OFFER, J. (1975). *From Teenage to Young Manhood*. Basic Books, New York.

PIAGET, J. (1957). *Logic and Psychology*. Basic Books, New York.

——— . (1969). "The Intellectual Development of the Adolescent," in *Adolescence: Psychosocial Perspectives*. G. Caplan and S. Lebovici, eds. Basic Books, New York.

REITER, E., and KULIN, H. (1972). "Sexual Maturation in the Female: Normal Development and Precocious Puberty," *Pediatric Clinics of North America*, 19:581–603.

SARREL, P. (1975). Personal communication.

SARREL, P., and LIDZ, R. W. (1970). "Contraceptive Failure—Psychosocial Factors: The Unwed," in *Manual of Family Planning and Contraceptive Practice*. M. Calderone, ed. Williams & Wilkins, Baltimore, Md.

SARREL, P., and SARREL, L. (1974). Unpublished data.

SCHONFELD, W. (1943). "Primary and Secondary Sexual Characteristics: Study of Their Development in Males from Birth Through Maturity, with Biometric Study of Penis and Testes," *American Journal of Diseases of Children*, 65:535–549.

SHAPIRO, R. (1969). "Adolescent Ego Autonomy and the Family," in *Adolescence: Psychosocial Perspectives*. G. Caplan and S. Lebovici, eds. Basic Books, New York.

SORENSEN, R. (1973). *Adolescent Sexuality in Contemporary America: Personal Values and Sexual Behavior, Ages Thirteen to Nineteen*. World Publishers, New York.

STIERLIN, H. (1974). *Separating Parents and Adolescents: A Perspective on Running Away, Schizophrenia and Waywardness*. Quadrangle Press, New York.

VYGOTSKY, L. (1962). *Thought and Language*. E. Hanfmann and G. Vakar, eds. and trans. MIT Press and John Wiley & Sons, New York.

WHISNANT, L., BRETT, E., and ZEGANS, L. (1975). "Implicit Messages Concerning Menstruation in Commercial Educational Materials Prepared for Young Adolescent Girls," *American Journal of Psychiatry*, 132:815–820.

Woods, S. M. (1973). Cited in unsigned article, "Sex Counselling and the Primary Physician," *Medical World News*, March 2, 1973, pp. 35–49.

Zacharias, L. (1976). Cited in the *New York Times*, March 27, 1976.

SUGGESTED READING

Blos, P. (1962). *On Adolescence: A Psychoanalytic Interpretation*. Free Press, Glencoe, Ill.

———— (1970). *The Young Adolescent*. Free Press, New York.

Caplan, G., and Lebovici, S., eds. (1969). *Adolescence: Psychosocial Perspectives*. Basic Books, New York.

Sze, W., ed. (1975). *The Human Life Cycle*, pp. 217–361. Jason Aronson, New York.

"Twelve to Sixteen: Early Adolescence." *Daedelus*, vol. 100, no. 4, of the Proceedings of the American Academy of Arts and Sciences.

CHAPTER 11

❁

The Young Adult

THE LENGTHY developmental process as a dependent apprentice in living draws to a close as individuals attain an identity and the ability to live intimately with a member of the opposite sex, and contemplate forming families of their own. They have attained adult status with the completion of physical maturation, and, it is hoped, they have become sufficiently well integrated and emotionally mature to utilize the opportunities and accept the responsibilities that accompany it. They have reached a decisive point on their journeys. They have dropped the pilot and now start sailing on their own—but they have been taught to navigate and they have been provided with charts, albeit charts that can be but approximately correct for the currents and reefs change constantly. They have practiced under more or less competent supervision, taken trips in sheltered waters, and now they assume responsibility for themselves and must accept the consequences of their decisions. Usually couples decide to share the journey, and soon others join them, bidden and unbidden, whose welfare depends upon their skills and stability.

However, some will still tarry undecided about where they will journey, or the course they will take to an unfamiliar place, or whether to try out partners imaginatively or in actuality before setting forth. Some are still uncertain about where they will find their place in the scheme of things, whether they wish to find a place in the scheme, or whether there is a scheme of things at all. Those who delay are a minority, but include among them many who will be innovators, creators, and leaders, and therefore they require that we, too, pause to consider their transition through a period that Keniston (1970) has designated as *youth*, during which youths seek to reconcile potential conflicts between their emerging identities and the social order.

Still, the energies and interests of most young adults will now be directed beyond their own growth and development. Their independence from their parental families motivates them to achieve an interdependence with others and find their places in society. Through vocation and marriage they become united to networks of persons, find tasks that demand involvement, and gain roles into which they fit and are fitted and which help define their identities. They are virtually forced to become less self-centered through the very pursuit of their own interests.

The time when adult life starts is not set chronologically, for persons may have entered upon their vocations and selected spouses some time in adolescence, and others will remain tentative in their commitments through their twenties and may, in some respects, be considered still adolescent. If persons are still uncommitted, most make their occupational choices early in adulthood. Most individuals will also give up their much sought independence to share with another in marriage. Then the life cycle rounds to the point at which young adults are again confronted by the start of life, but now as members of the parental generation, and they often undergo profound personality reorientations as they become involved in the unfolding of a child's life. The period ends at a somewhat indefinite time, approximately when children's needs no longer form a major focus of attention, usually between thirty-five and forty, when persons have attained stable positions in society, or, at least, when they realize that they must come to terms with what they will be able to make out of their one and only life.

Young adults are at the height of their physical and mental vigor as they launch upon making their ways in the world; and their energies are usually expended more effectively than they were during adolescence. The expansiveness of adolescence had usually given way to efforts at consolidation in late adolescence, but young adults must focus energies and interests even more definitively as they commit themselves to a specific way of life; to marriage, with its libidinal investment in a single significant person; and to producing and nurturing a new generation. Now, more than ever, alternative ways of life must be renounced to permit the singleness of purpose required for success and to consolidate one's identity; and intimacy becomes reserved for a single person to make possible meaningful sharing with a spouse. Although commitment to another person entails the danger of being carried along in the other's inadequacies or misfortunes, its avoidance carries the penalty of lack of opportunity to be meaningful to others and have others become meaningful to the self.

Vocational choice and marital choice are two of the most significant decisions of a lifetime. Although they are sometimes made easily and even seemingly casually, they are both extremely complex matters that are resultants of the individual's entire personality development. They are two cardinal resultants of the lengthy process of achieving adulthood that we have been tracing; and now these decisions will become major determinants of the course of the individual's further personality development, of the satisfactions that will be gained from life, and of the trials and problems that will ensue and strain the integration of the personality and perhaps even warp it. The individual's own capacities and integration markedly influence the choices of occupation and spouse, and then influence how the person can cope with and gain fulfillment from both—and subsequently from being a parent. We shall, in the following two chapters, scrutinize the choices of vocation and spouse and then consider the tasks involved in adjusting to marriage and being a parent, but we shall first consider the period of youth and the integration of persons as they start adult life.

YOUTH

Keniston has suggested that a new stage in the life cycle, *youth*, has emerged with the growing complexities of postindustrial civilizations.* For many, the commitments of adult life do not follow directly upon adolescence. Indeed, in periods during which the assumption of adult status is

---

* Much as Ariès (1962) contends that prior to the industrial revolution "childhood" did not exist, and the idea that adolescence as a stage of life first developed at the start of the present century (Demos and Demos, 1969). There are, however, reasons to challenge these contentions. In most nonliterate (primitive) societies, though children may be expected to help with adult tasks, they are treated differently from adolescents and adults. The participants in the "Children's Crusade" were neither under six nor adults. As R. W. Beales (1975) has clearly documented, children were not considered competent to decide on conversion or fully responsible in seventeenth- and eighteenth-century New England. Jonathan Edwards placed the upper limits of childhood at fourteen; Thomas Hooker believed that a child of ten or twelve lived "the life of a beast" and could not consider the mysteries of salvation; etc. In the early days of Massachusetts only a person who was over sixteen could be executed for striking or cursing a parent.

Similarly, there is evidence of recognition of an adolescent period in nonliterate societies and in the early New England settlements. Among the Stone-Age peoples of

delayed, there may be a prolongation of adolescence, and late adolescents and unmarried young adults are grouped together as "youth."*

Youth, in Keniston's usage of the word, does not designate such prolongation of adolescence, but rather a distinct stage in the life cycle through which only a limited number of people pass. These are persons who, having gained an ego identity or self-concept, become caught up in tensions between the self and society. "The awareness of actual or potential conflict, disparity, lack of consequence between what one is (one's identity, values, integrity) and the resources and demands of existing society increase. The adolescent is struggling to define who he is, the youth begins to sense who he is and thus to recognize the possibility of conflict and disparity between his emerging self-hood and his social order" (Keniston, 1974, p. 405). A central problem of the period is to find ways in which the self and society can become more congruent; and a critical task in personality development lies in achieving *individuation* (Jung, 1926)—the capacity to acknowledge reality and to cope with it, either through acceptance or through revolutionary opposition, but preserving a sense of "self," of intactness and wholeness of self—distinct from society, even if engaged in fostering social reform or in revolutionary activity. *Individuation* is a psychological process or an "intrapsychic" matter in which one's ego identity is differentiated from the social system in which one lives. Failure to individuate properly leads to conformity to societal norms, which is, of course, simply the lot of most persons, but which can be scorned by youth as "selling out" or being "brain washed," and becomes a denial of the self when it is a matter of

---

Papua/New Guinea a boy does not become an adult after going through the pre-adolescent or adolescent initiation rituals, but spends many years learning the skills a man requires as well as the myths and rituals essential to the society; not until around the age of nineteen is he considered a man and ready to marry. A distinction is made between prepubescent and post-menarchal girls everywhere, and in Papua/New Guinea the postpubertal girls have special privileges until they marry. In early New England the period of apprenticeship, which did not end until the age of twenty or twenty-one, was, in a sense, equivalent to the period of adolescence. Beales (1975) notes that elements of a "youth culture" existed in colonial New England. In the early eighteenth century elders bemoaned the licentious ways of youth who frequented taverns, participated in lewd practices, frolics, and company-keeping. The term "youth" seems to have been applied to older adolescents and unmarried young adults.
* We find that in colonial New England "youth" for Benjamin Coleman (1720) was a "chusing time":

> NOW O Young People is *your chusing time*, and commonly your *fixing time*; and as you fix it is like to last. Now you commonly chuse your *Trade*; betake your selves to your business for life, show what you incline to, and how you intend to be imploy'd all your days. Now you chuse your *Master* and your Education or Occupation. And now you dispose of your self in *Marriage* ordinarily, place your *Affections*, give away your hearts, look out for some *Companion* of life, whose to be as long as you live. And is this indeed the work of your Youth?

overconformity. The antipodal danger is *alienation*, in which efforts to preserve autonomy lead to the withdrawal from the social matrix that gives life substance, and perhaps even from interpersonal relations that give life meaning. A variant of alienation occurs when meaning and fulfillment are sought through psychedelic drugs.

It seems rather clear that *Youth* is not an altogether new stage of development. Over the ages many persons who were visionary, creative, or revolutionary passed through some such stage. In times of stress and change—as during the Great Depression of the 1930s—some young persons, because of their accurate perceptions of societal deficiencies, have been reluctant to enter into the adult world, for that seemed to be the way to stagnation if not simply an acquiescence in society's inequities and corruption. However, these were youths of superior cognitive capacities which permitted them to develop high ethical standards and to view matters from a perspective different from that of most of their contemporaries, and therefore they were usually, though not necessarily, persons who were highly educated. As currently about seventeen percent of young people in the United States complete college, a much higher proportion than heretofore, it is possible for a significant number of persons to experience the conflicts between self and society that lead to the developmental stage we are calling *youth*.

When we consider, the characteristics of *youth* depend upon the attainment of the stage of *formal operations* in cognitive development and then moving on to appreciation of the *relativity of social systems* and of the social roles and mores they encompass; to recognition of the *malleability of persons*, and how greatly who they are and what they become depend on how and where they are brought up; and to *transcend conventional morality* and even the postconventional morality of the social contract to attain a higher universal justice about which individuals can and must make their own judgments. The concepts of social relativity, developmental malleability, and universal abstract morality are not new, but they are interrelated matters that have of late taken on new pertinence. Becoming caught up in them opens new horizons for a youth, but in so doing creates developmental problems that can demolish the individual and not just one's individuation.

Relativism

The theory of relativity has affected thinking outside the physical sciences. We are concerned with the relativism that has arisen from gaining perspective through the study of other times, other civilizations, and other cultures that enables some persons to overcome their ethnocentricities and recognize the validity and utility of the ways of other peoples, even though they are very divergent from our own; and, consequently, that the ways and standards of our own society are more or less arbitrary. Persons may then believe that they have no obligation to adhere to societal norms, and claim that members of the society are simply indoctrinated or "brainwashed" to conform and preserve its constricting if not iniquitous ways. Particularly in times when societal ways run counter to a person's self-concept and ideals and lead to disillusionment in the society—as in the United States during the Vietnam war and the Watergate scandals—youths feel the schism between self and society intensely. The conflict need not lead to political activism to change society, or to a rejection of society with a dropping out into an "alternate culture" such as a communal way of life, but may lead to rejection of the self, with concomitant despair or even suicide, or to efforts to transform the self through study, meditation, Zen, psychoanalysis. Youths may also find a solution of the dilemma by choosing a career, such as medicine, that will permit them to preserve their ethical values within a social system they reject, or to embrace a legal career that will enable them to help correct injustice or change society.

Another consequence of relativism may be even more threatening. Recognizing the relativity of values as well as mores, youths may find themselves without a sense of meaning or purpose. The query "What difference does anything make if there is no meaning, no purpose, no God?" can lead to paralyzing existential anxiety or to an empty hedonism to counter despair, but for some it can open the way to a new freedom in directing their lives. A young man who was uncertain about his decision to study for the clergy took a moratorium of a year to reach a decision and spent much of it reading in a university library. His search after the nature of God led to a conviction that there could be neither a Deity nor a hereafter. However, after a period of personal disorientation and anxiety, he decided that if there were no general scheme of things and no meaning to the universe, that if he did not wish to be miserable, he would have to give meaning to his life. As he had no interest in bowing out of life, he decided that he could, as an American, make a game of his life and see what score he could make; or he might make a work of art of his life and strive to live an interesting tale of adventure, or a well-balanced introspective novel; or he might seek to help others live less troubled lives. He found that new ways of thinking about life had opened before him. He had, in a sense, learned that his life need not be empty because the world lacked purpose; it was up to him to provide meaning for his life. He had, in a sense, achieved what Perry (1970) has termed "commitment within relativism."

Human Malleability

The increased awareness of human malleability—the recognition of how greatly what persons become depends upon how and where they are brought up—has brought about a major social revolution that has greatly affected youth. Young people have been major movers in the civil-rights movement, the Peace Corps, Head Start, women's liberation, and other activities that seek to enable people to develop more fully and have better opportunities in life. It has also led some youths to believe in their own *omnipotentiality*—of their own capacities to change themselves and the direction of their lives. They need not follow in their parents' footsteps, or even in the patterns provided by the past; and they can, if they persevere, achieve beyond their earlier expectations for themselves. A young person may even believe that complete self-transformation is possible without regard to prior upbringing, education, and innate capacities. A college student, having learned that people can make of themselves whatever they wish, decided to become a harpsichord virtuoso, ignoring his lack of any musical training up to the age of twenty-one and his lack of any particular musical aptitude. Such persons have not yet overcome the egocentricity of formal operations and fail to differentiate between cognitive solutions of problems and the actualization of the imagined solution. However, at a more realistic level, young people have delayed, studied, and worked to change the direction and scope of their lives. Occasionally, the multiplicity of potential futures can virtually paralyze. A college student caught up in several divergent interests engendered by her courses and her extracurricular work in the inner city could not decide between them, and then came to realize that she might also be interested in areas in which she had not yet had experience. She spent hours asking friends why they had decided on one career or another. Eventually, she decided it mattered little what career she chose as long as it interested her and could be of benefit to others, and she then decided to study journalism because it could encompass many of her interests.

Abstract Morality

The attainment of the highest and most abstract level of morality also contains dangers. It will be recalled that according to Kohlberg's (1964) conceptualization of moral development, a limited number of persons move beyond conventional morality to define right and wrong in terms of the well-being of all members of a society, and of these some transcend such considerations to embrace more universalistic standards in which individuals must judge for themselves whether laws conform to higher principles such as the "golden rule." Persons can then become caught up in the relativism of laws and "justice," and reach idiosyncratic standards in which they take the law into their own hands; or even decide that, as everything is relative, the entire system of conventional morality is meaningless. They forget that societies have, at least to some extent, gradually developed moral systems that help preserve the integrity of the society and its members.* As Keniston (1974) has commented regressions from this highest form of morality can occur and lead to the amoral behaviors that are sometimes encountered in countercultures, and give license for orgiastic sex and unbridled drug usage; or to anarchy as the highest form of political morality.

Having entered into a relativistic world, youths can find it difficult to find solid footing, guidelines for their behavior, and directions for their future lives. They are apt to question if not distrust conventional roles, values, and mores; and to turn their backs against lessons that can be gained from the past and seek to start afresh and make a new world. Clearing new trails through the jungle is a difficult task that does not get a person very far quickly. The youth makes forays into society and at commitments to other persons, seeking a workable way to relate to society and within society; or toward finding or founding a new and more congenial society; or searching for the right companion and to learn whether one is ready to form a permanent and exclusive relationship with another.

Many youths find direction, at least temporarily, by participating in movements that allow them to exercise their higher morality by combating some social ill. Marxism, antiwar movements, and civil rights have engaged generations of American youth. At a more individual level, they may decide on careers that will help lessen the woes of others or can enable them to improve society. They help bring about changes in society and its mores. Currently, the belief that sexual practices are the concern only of the individuals involved, rather than a matter of general moral values, has enabled young persons to live experimentally with one or more partners and delay marriage. During the Vietnam war, the youth in the United States were caught between their self-concepts and their country's unjust posture,

---

* In questioning conventional morality, some even see no reason for the incest taboo, not realizing how important it is to the emergence of the child from ties to parents and the family, as well as to the maintenance of the family. Many major dramatic works—*Hamlet, Oedipus Rex,* Aeschylus's *Oresteia*—concern the woes that follow upon incestuous behavior.

and the young men found themselves in a dilemma concerning whether or not to avoid military service.

At present, young women may be having greater difficulties during *youth* than men. They are very apt to be caught up in tensions between their emergent ego identities and society's expectations and delimitations of women. Their conflict is further aggravated by their own ambivalent desires to achieve in careers and also to devote at least part of their lives to motherhood—a desire which, if not deeply rooted in women's biological makeup, has been deeply ingrained in most women during their formative years. As we have considered (Chapter 10) adolescent girls are entering womanhood at a time when women's roles in society have been changing profoundly. Most women now work before they have children, but do not become seriously engaged in pursuing careers: although they may be involved in the Women's Liberation movement, they are largely concerned with equal opportunity and pay at work, the condescending or sexual attitudes of employers toward them, having the freedom to pursue a career should they so wish, etc., but their basic orientation continues along traditional feminine lines of becoming a wife, helpmate, and mother. However, the highly educated women who move into and through the period of *youth* find a real conflict between their self-image as highly competent persons who wish to pursue careers and societal expectations for them. Their achievement orientation has conventionally been considered more masculine than feminine; and they may feel caught between their strivings to achieve and their own images of themselves as women. With relatively few models to follow, they are involved in changing both the way society regards and treats women and the way women regard themselves. They believe that women can be achievement oriented and still retain expressive characteristics, and that men should incorporate expressive as well as achievement-oriented instrumental characteristics. Women's liberation for them encompasses fundamental changes in the ethos of the society rather than simply the practical matters concerning equality of opportunity and treatment. However, as Martina Horner has found, bright, highly competent college women have feared success, considering that achievement requires competition, that competition is aggressive, and that aggression is unfeminine. She further found that two-thirds of college men did better in competitive than noncompetitive situations, as compared with fewer than one-third of the women subjects.* It is hoped that such anxieties concern-

---

* In a type of projective test given to ninety female and eighty-eight male first- and second-year college students, fifty-nine of the women but only eight of the men made up stories that reflected fear of success. The main trend of the women's stories indicated

ing achievement have diminished under the impact of Women's Liberation movements, but it is unlikely that they will become extinguished in the near future.

The problems of female youth are also accentuated because they have greater freedom than men in the choice of future roles. They can decide to be primarily wives and mothers, and gain considerable gratification from it; but being a husband and father has not yet become a career for men. Here, as elsewhere, the ability to choose opens the way for inner conflict.

The awareness of the *relativism* of societal standards and roles as well as the feeling of *omnipotentiality* that is so much part of *youth* enables young women to move beyond the stereotypes of male and female roles, of the concept that instrumental functions are male and expressive functions essentially female, and to consider themselves doing almost anything that men can do. They can also go beyond objectivity and insist that sexual equality means the absence of any differences between the sexes,* and in the process deny the advantages of being a woman—rejecting any desire to have a child. They may also turn away from any need for a man, and find that they can gain sexual fulfillment through lesbian relationships. Perhaps, more unfortunately, they may become aggressively overcompetitive, identifying with the enemy, so to speak, and forgetting that they had objected to such aggressive competitive behavior in men.

Seeking new ways of being women, female *youth* usually remain away from home after college. They need the companionship of others who share their aspirations and encourage their strivings. They may live with a man while at college, encouraged to learn that there are men who find them attractive because of their abilities, but they must be certain that it is not that they are attractive despite their abilities. If they are to have a career they must find the proper man who will help them manage both career and marriage. They may also wish to be certain that having a career will continue to be more important than motherhood, or find ways of combining the two. It is important that they become aware of the difficulties of dual-career marriages from other colleagues, or at least recognize that a

---

fear of being rejected, losing marital opportunities, and losing friends as a consequence of being at the top of the class. Others gave evidence that such success might mean they lacked femininity and might be abnormal. Some even denied that it would be possible for a woman to head a medical school class; and one woman gave the bizarre response "She starts proclaiming her surprise and joy. Her classmates are so disgusted with her behavior that they jump on her in a body and beat her. She is maimed for life" (Horner, 1968).

* As reflected in some writings of proponents of radical Women's liberation. The ultimate was seen in a first-year medical student (not at Yale) who called a professor of anatomy a male chauvinist and left the lecture hall when he sought to demonstrate (on a skeleton) the differences between the male and female pelvis.

woman must be extremely well organized to manage it. We shall return to consider such matters in the chapters on occupational and marital choice.

We have been considering *youth* as a stage in the life cycle of some particularly well-endowed and sensitive young people. We must, however, also realize that a period between the end of adolescence and the firm commitments of marriage and serious occupational involvement exists for graduate students and single persons in their twenties. It is often a time of trying out, trying occupations and partners, often an enjoyable time without serious responsibilities. Today, with the more or less socially approved practice of living with a member of the opposite sex in trial marriage or simply for convenience and enjoyment, the pressures to marry have diminished, and the duration of the period of youthful living is increasing.

THE INTEGRATION OF THE YOUNG ADULT

What does the young man or woman require within the self to make the essential decisions concerning career and marriage and have a reasonable chance of gaining strength and finding satisfaction from them? Fortunately, perhaps, psychiatrists are not required to sit in judgment and only very few persons seek their opinion and permission. We have followed the phasic preparation since birth for the assumption of adult status, and we shall not attempt to summarize here the steps by which a person integrates, achieves an ego identity and a capacity for true intimacy. We shall but attempt to state briefly some of the essential and some of the desirable aspects of a person's integration at this stage of life—concepts which will be amplified in subsequent chapters. Although it is simple to illustrate how deficiencies in achieving such capacities can lead a person into serious difficulties, we hesitate to call them requisites rather than desiderata, for few, if any, persons have all of these attributes, and the attainment of any of them always remains a matter of "more or less." We are considering an ideal, so to speak, to convey how a mature young adult might be integrated.

Young adults have, as we discussed in the preceding two chapters, become reasonably independent of their parents. They have established fairly clear boundaries between themselves and their parents; properly, they have not been burned in the process and become wary of ever relating intimately again, but they recognize that their paths and their parents' now diverge because they are moving toward different goals. If their early development went well, the revolt through which they gained their own identities has subsided and they can appreciate their parents on a fairly realistic basis. They no longer need their parents as essential objects who support and direct them, for parental figures have been internalized and are thus a salient part of their identities, and they do not need to attach themselves to another person immediately to ward off feelings of emptiness when they leave their parents, nor seek sexual relations primarily to counter loneliness. As they become spouses and parents themselves, they will continue to take on characteristics of their parents, but their identities will now also include derivatives from other significant persons. When the early family environment has been unfortunate, later relationships with teachers, friends, or friends' parents may have furnished stabilizing forces, more suitable objects for identification, and more hopeful objectives. In the process, they have learned to separate themselves and keep away those persons, including a parent, who are injurious to them, and perhaps even malignant if internalized as part of themselves. They do not confuse new significant persons in their lives with parents or siblings to the extent of repetitively reenacting old intrafamilial problems. A man does not, for example, awaken at night uncertain whether he is sleeping with his wife or mother, as did the son of a highly seductive woman; or a woman repeat with her daughter and husband an old rivalry with her sister for their father's affection.

As a result of the reorganization accomplished during adolescence, those components of the superego derived from internalization of the parents and their directives are less important. The individual may still follow parental dictates, but because they have been incorporated into the person's own ethical system rather than because of fear of displeasing the parents. Indeed, as we have previously noted, much of what had been reasonable and useful in the superego now becomes part of the ego, and becomes more and more fully incorporated into the core of the ego—that is to say, into the basic orientation upon which decisions are made. The directives which help the individual to decide what is acceptable and unacceptable behavior now concern social and cultural norms and ideologic standards that are superordinate to parental dictates. The parents are no longer seen from the perspective of the child. They are no longer regarded as omnipotent figures who could take care of all difficulties if only they would, nor are they "split" into good parents who take care of one, and bad parents who do not. They are recognized as having both capabilities and inadequacies and more or less ambivalently as promoting both affection and anger; and concomitantly the superego now permits latitude for sexual outlets which, in turn, can help diminish the urgency of id impulsions. Although certain impulses, desires, and behavior arouse guilt, shame, or anxiety, these emotions are more likely to become signals to alter behavior or attitudes rather than leading to self-punitive depressions.

The ego tends to have greater control, considering one's ultimate well-being before giving in to immediate gratifications. A mass of data garnered from personal experience as well as from the person's cultural heritage can be utilized in reaching decisions. It can be manipulated imaginatively in an effort to try out alternative courses and their probable consequences, and also for fantasied gratifications; but the person distinguishes between pure fantasy and what it might be possible to realize. Magic and wishful thinking have given way before the need to turn fantasy into action so as to be able to gain the realization of wishes. Individuals appreciate that others perceive and experience events differently from the way they do, and both the limitations of their own views and the different ideas and feelings of others must be taken into account in seeking to bring ideas to fruition. Young adults now know enough about themselves and the world to decide whether the realization of a wish or a fantasy is a possibility worth pursuing.

A major aspect of a person's ability to carry out adaptive behavior concerns the capacities to tolerate tensions and the inevitable anxieties of life and still adhere to objectives and work through difficulties. The ability to adhere to commitments is usually taken as an index of "character," for it permits consistency and the avoidance of distraction by each attractive opportunity—whether it is an opportunity at work extraneous to one's own goals or a sexual distraction. Whereas at some periods in adolescence or young adulthood each fork in a road seems to require a decision, as the course of a life may be changed by following one path rather than the other, after commitments have been made, the objectives determine the ultimate direction and it matters little if one route or the other is followed for a stretch in progressing toward the goal.

Tensions and frustrations create anxiety and depressive spells but do not lead too often to a search for regressive solace in sensuality, in sleep, or in loss of self-awareness through the use of alcohol or narcotics. Frustrations are recognized as a part of life and, although avoided, they are accepted when necessary without mobilizing undue hostility and aggression—and such aggression as is aroused is directed toward overcoming the frustration rather than in vengeance or in hurting the self or those whom one needs. Various mechanisms of defense help control anxiety, but they are not called into play to an extent that markedly distorts the perception of the world or blinds one to realistic difficulties which must be faced and managed.

Now that problems of dependency and symbiotic strivings have been worked through, the boundaries of the self are secure enough for young adults no longer unconsciously to fear losing their identities when they seek after intimacy. They do not fear that a needed person will devour, engulf, or annihilate them, or that the loss of the self in orgasm will lead to obliteration; nor will they confuse themselves with a child, as does a mother who feeds her child when she is hungry. The young woman, however, needs to keep her boundaries sufficiently fluid to accept having a fetus within her, and to form a symbiotic bond with an infant.

A person is now secure enough in his or her gender identity not to need to prove his masculinity or her femininity to the self and others by repetitive compulsive sexual activity, or in undue masculine aggressivity or feminine seductiveness. And both men and women will realize that being a member of one sex or the other has both advantages and disadvantages, and are ready to make the most of the advantages rather than deplore their fate.

It has been customary in psychoanalytic literature to evaluate the stability and maturity of the progression to adult life in terms of the capacity for genital sexuality—properly, not simply the capacity for pleasure from orgasm in heterosexual relationships, but to enjoy sexuality in a meaningful intimate relationship. It is apparent, however, that some persons lead satisfactory and highly productive lives, even though they never achieve such genital sexuality, and that a person's maturity, including emotional maturity, may better be considered in terms of the achievement of a firm ego identity as well as the capacity for intimacy, recognizing that the capacity to come to terms with frustration or one's inadequacy can be a major aspect of maturity.

The developmental achievements that we have been considering as necessary for proper behavior in early adult life have been presented in rather black and white terms. In actuality, no one fully outgrows childhood needs and dependency strivings; no one progresses to adulthood unscarred by emotional traumata and more or less injurious relationships; no one manages to avoid being caught up in trying to solve some old problems; everyone continues to be somewhat motivated to gratify residual pregenital strivings; and we all utilize defenses of our ego that are no longer really necessary, and transfer characteristics of parents onto other significant persons. These are the things that color personalities and provide a distinctiveness and human frailty to all.

Still, such deficiencies, to sum up, should not lead persons to invest too much energy and effort in repetitively seeking after solutions to old problems poured ever again into new bottles, and should not prevent them from seeking completion in the present and the future rather than through the impossible task of remaking the past. Adults should also be capable of accepting the realization that many of the ways and rules of society are arbitrary, but that people need such regulations in order to live together— and they do not feel deceived and cheated by the arbitrariness of the rules; and they find their places in the social system, accepting it while hoping to improve it. Nor are they so readily disillusioned by other people, for faced by the difficulties in living they have become more tolerant of the failures and even deceptions of others.

Whatever their preparation, the time has come for young adults to make their own way in the world; they can delay and linger in the protection of the homes, or in the halls of their alma maters, where the storms of the world are filtered and refined, but they cannot tarry too long without commitment and the direction it provides. The choice of an occupation and the choice of a mate are the decisions that start them on their way. While both of these choices are often made as a rather natural progression in the path that a life has been taking, they are both highly *overdetermined*, tending to be resultants of the total developmental process together with the realistic opportunities available at the critical time of life. Although a single factor may clearly predominate in leading to a decision, a variety of factors virtually always enters consideration; and the conscious motives are often only rationalizations of unconscious forces that are exerting an indirect and disguised but powerful influence. The decisions may be no less useful and no less wise because of such unconscious influences, for unconscious motives may direct a person to significant and essential needs that are neglected or denied consciously, and because unconscious decisions can include repressed memories and intangible and nebulous perceptions and associations that may have considerable importance.

REFERENCES

Ariès, P. (1962). *Centuries of Childhood*. Alfred A. Knopf, New York.
Beales, R. W. (1975). "In Search of the Historical Child: Miniature Adulthood and Youth in Colonial New England," *American Quarterly*, 27:380–398.
Coleman, B. (1720). "Early Piety Again Inculcated . . . ," p. 33. S. Kneeland for D. Henchman and J. Edwards, Boston.
Demos, J., and Demos, V. (1969). "Adolescence in Historical Perspective," *Journal of Marriage and Family*, 31:632–638.
Horner, M. (1968). "A Psychological Barrier to Achievement in Women—The Motive

to Avoid Success." Symposium presentation at the Midwestern Psychological Association, May, 1968.
—— (1969). "Fail: Bright Women," *Psychology Today*, 3:36 ff.
JUNG, C. G. (1926). *Psychological Types: The Psychology of Individuation*. H. G. Baynes, trans. Harcourt, Brace, New York, 1961.
KENISTON, K. (1970). "Youth as a Stage of Life," *American Scholar*, 39:631–654.
—— (1974). "Youth and Its Ideology," in *American Handbook of Psychiatry*, vol. 1. S. Arieti, ed. Basic Books, New York.
KOHLBERG, L. (1964). "Development of Moral Character and Moral Ideology," in *Review of Child Development Research*. M. L. Hoffman and L. W. Hoffman, eds. Russell Sage Foundation, New York.
PERRY, W. G. (1970). *Forms of Intellectual and Ethical Development in the College Years*. Holt, Rinehart & Winston, New York.

SUGGESTED READING

Group for the Advancement of Psychiatry (1975). *The Educated Woman: Prospects and Problems*. Mental Health Materials Center, New York.
KENISTON, K. (1974). "Youth and Its Ideology," in *American Handbook of Psychiatry*, vol. 1. S. Arieti, ed. Basic Books, New York.

CHAPTER 12

❀

Occupational Choice

AN OCCUPATION REPRESENTS much more than a set of skills and functions; it means a way of life. It provides and determines much of the environment, both physical and social, in which a person lives; it selects out traits that are utilized most frequently and strengthened; and it usually carries with it a status in the community and provides social roles and patterns for living. Through determining with what sorts of persons one spends much of one's life, a vocation markedly influences value judgments and ethical standards. Occupation and personality traits are intimately related.

We find ourselves forming judgments about people according to their vocations. Physicians ask their patients, "What do you do?" and the response not only helps decide what sort of person they are taking care of, and what sort of fee they can charge, but also may help them reach a diagnosis and formulate a plan of therapy.* Taxi drivers and long-haul truckers, though both vehicle drivers, tend to have very different personali-

* Jeremy Morris (1953), for example, in his epidemiologic studies of coronary occlusion found that London bus drivers were significantly more vulnerable than conductors. Was this because of differences in the amount of physical activity, of emotional stress, or was it a reflection of the different personalities of drivers and conductors?

ties and are even prone to different ailments.* Even though we have difficulty in defining the reasons for our anticipations, we expect a woman
lawyer to be more aggressive and intellectual than a woman trained nurse
and we are apt to relate differently and present different aspects of ourselves to them. Such preconceptions aroused by the name of an occupation
are usually tentative and are sometimes erroneous, but there are good
reasons for such "snap judgments" that psychological studies tend to vali-
date.† Is it that similar personalities tend to select given occupations, or is
it that the pursuit of a specific vocation leads to the development of certain
traits? Both factors operate. Occupational choice is usually a function or a
reflection of the entire personality; but then the occupation plays a part in
shaping the personality by providing associates, roles, goals, ideals, mores,
and a life-style.

Despite the importance of occupational choice in determining the further
course of personality development and of the functions of an occupation in
the emotional and physical well-being of those who pursue it, relatively
little can be found on the topic in the psychiatric literature.** The neglect
of the topic is even more surprising because people's choice of vocation
brings into focus much of their developmental dynamics as well as many unconscious forces influencing their lives. Perhaps the topic has received so little attention because it has been only in recent years and in a relatively few
countries that the opportunity to select an occupation has been available to
any sizable proportion of the population. In most countries well over fifty
percent of the people are engaged in farming; the differences between
laboring jobs available to the poorly educated are scarcely worth considering; and skills, crafts, and small shops are traditionally passed from parent
to child.†† Then, too, not until after World War II did occupational
choice present much of a problem for any sizable proportion of women. In

---

* In my experience taxi drivers in large cities are often attracted by a job requiring
minimal skills in which they can be reasonably independent. Subjected to constant
stress, they often suffer from gastric disturbances including peptic ulcer. The long-haul
truck driver is more fiercely independent and aggressive, often carries a chip on his
shoulder and finds an outlet in driving his huge truck. Severe and intractable headaches
related to the tension of driving and his aggressivity are not uncommon. The cab
driver is also subject to frequent sexual stimulation by the behavior of passengers and
by suggestions to male cab drivers from women that coming into the apartment for a
few minutes will be more rewarding than finding another passenger. There are as yet
few women long-haul truckers.

† See, for example, E. K. Strong, *Vocational Interests of Men and Women.*

** The first dynamically oriented study, which still remains one of the most significant,
combined the efforts and skills of an economist, psychiatrist, and other social scientists
(Ginzberg *et al.*, 1951).

†† In the Middle Ages, parents placed their children as apprentices with another
family at the age of seven (Ariès, 1962).

most countries the type of schooling a child will follow is decided early in adolescence, or even earlier, in accord with expectations of the occupation they will pursue. In many societies, perhaps in most, parents believe it rather foolish to consider that children or even youths can make a career decision for themselves better than can their more experienced parents.

OVERDETERMINATION OF VOCATIONAL CHOICE

Currently in the United States, vocational choice constitutes a major problem for adolescents and young adults. Young people have probably never been so conscious of how much their future welfare depends upon the length and quality of their education, and of how the maintenance or advancement of their social and economic position involves their pursuing a suitable vocation. The extent of choice increases with educational level and lack of higher education tends to foreclose options both in adolescence and in later life.* Late adolescents, particularly college students, often live with the problem as a background against which they sample courses, try out jobs, and evaluate people they meet as models they might wish to emulate. Youths worry and cogitate about their future vocation and although their conscious evaluations and decisions are important, they are often motivated to make the decision by determinants of which they are unaware; not that unconscious factors are all important but rather that they are frequently the decisive element in a matter that is so highly overdetermined.

If, for example, we consider a class of medical students, we find that the reasons for their selection of medicine as a career are not only varied but often very private. Indeed, there is probably less frank discussion even among close friends about career choice than there is about sexual problems. Many students have considerable difficulty thinking through and conveying the reasons for the decision or how it was reached, and many of the reasons they give and accept themselves are clearly only part of the story. One is emulating her father; another is living out his pharmacist father's thwarted ambition; someone is responding to his mother's idealization of the obstetrician who delivered him—influences of which the student

---

* Although many high school graduates earn as much as, or more than, many college graduates, the value of a college education is measured properly not in monetary terms but by the quality of life it permits.

is only partially aware because they were simply part of the atmosphere in which he or she grew up. There may be a student who has secretly vowed to herself to combat cancer, which robbed her of a mother, and another to learn to treat schizophrenia, which permanently removed his sister to an institution. Some consider medicine as a means of earning a secure livelihood that assures prestige in the community, and some as a means of social advancement. Others may have in childhood feared death and decided to meet the problem counterphobically, head on, as a foe to fight and at the same time to learn to tolerate death as a familiar. Another may have simply agreed with Philip Carey in Maugham's *Of Human Bondage*, who decided that if he could not be great he could at least be useful. Indeed, students may find it difficult to admit that they are following their idealism and finding a meaning in life by seeking to help others. These are all acceptable motivations, but rarely the only significant influences. Although it has been said that a surgeon may be a sublimated sadist who might have been a butcher if he had been less well educated, or that a psychoanalyst is only a refined variant of a voyeur, such sorts of pseudoanalytic statements are usually oversimplifications of characterologic influences that will be discussed later (see Chapter 19). Still, the author once studied three prizefighters and could not fail to note that all three had brutal fathers whom they had vowed to beat up when they were old enough and strong enough. And it appears fairly obvious from his autobiographical narrative that one of our greatest explorers almost lost his life seeking to overcome once and for all his childhood anxiety over separation from his mother (Byrd, n.d.).

To convey something of the complexity that can enter into a vocational choice, let us turn to a specific example which may serve to illustrate the fusion of childhood residues, characterologic factors, and realistic determinants that contributed to a decision. It is somewhat atypical, at least in being concerned with an unusual person whose capacities permitted a fairly wide choice.

A young internist, R., consulted a psychiatrist on his return from military service. He had been assigned to Japan, where he had enjoyed the aesthetic properties of the country and of many of its inhabitants, but found himself becoming depressed and increasingly dissatisfied with his life as a physician. At the age of thirty-five, R. had already published several significant contributions to science and success in his career seemed assured. After he had been in Japan away from his practice for a year, he began to doubt that he was gaining satisfaction from medicine, resenting the demands of practice that required him virtually to forgo other interests. R. had shown considerable talent as a painter while in college, and was now wondering whether he should abandon medicine and enter upon some artistic career; but as he had a wife and child, a radical shift in vocation would be difficult.

To clarify his predicament, R. reviewed the steps that had led him into medicine, recalling incidents and determinants that he had virtually forgotten until he had reviewed his life while relatively inactive in Japan.

During his junior year in college R. had been unable to decide what to do with his life. His father, a successful architect, had suggested that R. follow in his footsteps, as had his older brother, and join the flourishing family firm. R. had expected to become an architect but had been reluctant to abandon his hopes of becoming an artist; though on the other hand, he was concerned about risking his future on his artistic talent. Raised amid reasonable affluence, he would not enjoy penury. He decided to leave college for a year to study at an art school in New York, both to gain a better estimate of his abilities and interests and to get away to think things out on his own. Although he enjoyed painting and the life he was leading in Greenwich Village, R. found himself becoming even more indecisive as the year passed, and he became intensely anxious and somewhat depressed. Then, at the end of the year, much to the surprise of his family, R. announced that he was going to study medicine.

Now, some fifteen years later, R. was trying to reconstruct with a psychiatrist the events of that year in New York and examine how he had reached his decision. When he had left home to go to New York he had no thoughts of studying medicine. Indeed, had he been asked what he might become, he would not even have included medicine among the potentialities. He had, however, determined to reach a decision by the end of the year, for he feared that endless vacillation could lead him to drift into an unsuitable vocation.

In reviewing his early connections with medicine, R. recalled that he had suffered from an episode of rheumatic fever just before starting school which had kept him in bed for some months and had left him with a slightly damaged heart valve. For several years his parents had limited his activities and been overprotective whenever he had a respiratory infection. He remembered how close he had felt to his mother during his incapacitation. During high school, he had experienced some envy when the family physician had suggested to his studious older brother that he study medicine and eventually take over his lucrative general practice—but this had been envy that his brother had been preferred rather than due to an interest in medicine.

During the year in New York, R. had shared a couple of rooms with a fraternity brother who was doing graduate work in physiology. He became intrigued by a subject about which he had been completely ignorant, fascinated by the intricate and complex balance of the human organism. A fellow art student contracted jaundice, and having little money became a patient on the public wards in a municipal hospital, where R. visited him and deplored the circumstances. R. recalled how as a child he would wonder how grownups could manage when ill without a mother to care for them; indeed, he had dimly considered the ability to care for oneself alone when ill as a sort of measure of maturity. As he talked, R. recalled his pervasive concerns about illness throughout his childhood and adolescence, which may have reflected his parents' unexpressed anxieties concerning his rheumatic fever. Perhaps, he reflected, learning that physicians received free medical care from their colleagues had influenced his choice of a career.

He had first consciously thought of studying medicine during a discussion of physiology when his roommate had talked about a friend who, after two years in law school, had changed his mind and was taking premedical courses. He realized that he, too, could still make a radical shift in his plans and perhaps escape from his indecision concerning the choice of art or architecture.

When Easter came and went, he started to experience episodes of acute anxiety and found himself worrying that he might have cancer. He could not decide about his future—but slowly he reached the conclusion that it did not really matter what he did, provided he pursued it enthusiastically. He could learn to like and even enjoy anything that really challenged him. The next step carried the matter further when he decided, masochistically, that perhaps he should do what he liked least and prove that aptitude and liking for a particular occupation made little difference. Such ideas virtually led to the choice of medicine, but there were other influences, too, several of which will be mentioned. R. felt, in retrospect, that he had been rebelling against his parents' expectations that his artistic abilities would define his future, and that he had been reacting against the praise he received for his paintings which let him doubt that his parents loved him "for himself."

Then, with considerable embarrassment and uneasiness, R. suddenly remembered something he felt certain had been of considerable moment in his shift to medicine. When he was fifteen, he had gone camping with friends, his first extended stay away from home. He had become ill, suffering from nausea and feelings of malaise which may only have been the resultants of fatigue and nostalgia. Still, he had been convinced that he had cancer, probably because a cousin had died a lingering death from leukemia a few months earlier. His concerns mounted, and in his anxiety R. prayed and made a vow that if God would let him live for another twenty years, he would devote his life to the welfare of mankind. As usually happens, after he recovered, his pact with God was forgotten. But during the year of decision in New York when he became anxious, depressed, and hypochondriacal, his vow returned to plague him. He doubted that the life of either artist or architect would redeem his pledge of self-sacrifice; one would be too enjoyable and the other too lucrative. The recurrent anxiety contained fears that he might soon die and recalled his earnestly given pledge, which helped explain his curious decision to launch into doing what he least wanted to do. It was a means of redeeming his vow and saving his life. R. was further shaken when the psychiatrist pointed out to him that the twenty years of life he had sought from God had been completed just at the end of his stay in Japan and that now he was again uncertain about his future.

The negation of a specific talent in making an occupational choice and the appeasement of God through altruistic choice may be somewhat unusual, but the complexity of the decision-making process may not be so extravagant as it seems. The residua of childhood anxieties over separation from the mother; the concerns over trying to compete with a father and older brother whom R. felt he could surpass; the influences of a serious childhood illness; the control of impulses through ascetic strivings are among the influences that coalesced to guide this individual into an acceptable path into the future.

THE DEVELOPMENTAL HISTORY OF OCCUPATIONAL CHOICE

The choice of an occupation does not usually take place abruptly, but tends to be the product of a long process that starts early in childhood and changes as the individual develops, and it reflects the nature of the personality integration, and, as we shall consider, the choice in adolescence or early adulthood frequently is not final, as persons change careers throughout life. The earliest considerations of a future vocation are diffuse and unrealistic, reflecting the little child's preoperational thinking and his egocentric, narrow view of the world. The three-year-old boy may state that he will be a mommy when he grows up; the little girl will have skaty-eight

children and live with her mommy and daddy. The boy may wait in sus-
pense as someone counts the buttons on his clothes to find out whether he
will be a "doctor, lawyer, Indian chief," or less fortunately "poor man,
beggarman, thief."

As children enter into dramatic play with peers, their fantasy choices are
abundant and shift from hour to hour. They not only decide to become a
figure skater or a doctor, but become one in their imaginative activities.
The play contains elements of trying out various occupational roles, but
possibility, feasibility, ability, or the steps that must be taken to achieve the
occupations in reality are not considered. Occasionally, a role that is
somehow reinforced sticks, becomes a favored game and fantasy, and may
eventually lead to an occupation, as when a little girl plays nurse with
dolls, progresses to helping an overburdened mother care for younger siblings, and thereby gains approval and attention that offset the shift in her
mother's attention to the babies and establishes a pattern for gaining praise
and affection that eventually leads to a choice of nursing as a career.

In the juvenile period children plan to follow in the paths of various
idols and heroes: space pilot, tennis player, movie star, probably more
often someone known through television or reading than a person in their
own environment. Gradually, consideration of ability and realistic limitations enter the picture; the baseball star becomes a sports announcer, the
woman president in the image of Indira Gandhi or Golda Meir, a high
school principal.

As children reach high school they may have some awareness of whether
they will seek to emulate a parent or seek some parent surrogate or other
ideal figure to follow. Tentative choices are made that may guide them for
a time but youngsters know neither themselves nor the world well enough.
During high school vacations, they may take jobs to see whether they like
them, steps that can be decisive in finding a vocation if education does not
go beyond high school. During the period of adolescent expansiveness, as
previously noted, there is often both a turning away from parental models
and guidance and an upsurge of idealistic goals.

A college education brings new careers into consideration as the students' horizons broaden and they come in contact with teachers with whom
they may identify. Here, they also find opportunities to measure themselves
against others with similar aspirations. Eventually, a *realistic* phase starts
in which young persons take stock of their capacities, their needs, and the
potentialities that open before them. They are now all too aware that the
realization of ideals and aspirations will require time and effort. They may
carefully gauge where the winds are blowing and what careers will be apt to
flourish in the years ahead.

In a general sense, there are two major ways of thinking about a career. Some consider it most important to seek out an occupation which will provide satisfaction and enjoyment and from which they can hope to gain a full and interesting life. Others will consider an occupation primarily as a means of earning a living to gain security or to achieve power, whereas satisfactions will come from a family, prestige in the community, sports, an avocation, or from something made possible by money, such as collecting paintings or girlfriends. A shift from the first of these approaches to the second is likely to occur as the time approaches for reaching a definite decision. Realistic decisions for women will include considerations of whether they will have children and when and the importance of their own careers in comparison with their husbands', and other such critical matters already broached in Chapter 10 and which we shall discuss below.

To *crystallize* goals and firmly commit oneself to a vocation, one must find a way of entering upon the career and gain a pattern to follow. The absence of a known pattern, usually in the form of one or more persons with whom to identify, can divert the youth from a field of interest. Crystallization requires commitment with acceptance of the ensuing uncertainties, but firmness of commitment is essential to prevent veering into new attractive areas that appear en route: some premedical students may be tempted into biochemistry or physiology through fascination with such fields or through identifications with teachers, whereas others will shed such temptations, having committed themselves to medicine. Although the attainment of goals requires commitment, objectives also change as individuals gain experience and also as new opportunities are appreciated or open before one, and malleability can be an asset in pursuing a career.

The final phase in occupational choice concerns the *specification* of interest within a field through the acquisition of specialized skills. It means further renunciation of diversified interests and activities, and often a willingness to delay gratifications such as income, children, and recognition. On the other hand, it can also permit the utilization of specific assets and personality traits as well as the cultivation of special areas of interest. A young woman who is fully committed to being a psychologist can through specialization make use of her aptitude for mathematics by concentrating on statistical methodologies; or return to the humanistic considerations which had led her into psychology, but which had been caught in the blind alley of a rat-maze, by moving into clinical psychology or school counseling; or bring into her occupation her knowledge of art by studying the creativity or the visual imagination of painters. Such increased delimitation and specialization is often essential for reaching the higher levels of achievement and recognition, but it may come simply as an outgrowth of an occupation on which a person has already embarked, as when an attorney gradually moves into a specialized field such as dealing with corporate tax matters. Often, of course, the crystallization of a vocational choice is but the first of a series of specifications. Medicine, for example, is a field of interest that requires certain basic training, but further decisions must still be made: medicine; surgery, specific field of surgery; length of training; private, group, institutional practice; teaching; research, area of research; etc. Even after specification or specialization, further occupational decisions will be required throughout life which can markedly influence personality functioning: will the investigator accept a promotion that turns one into an administrator; will the clinical teacher turn from the care of patients to try to solve some puzzling problem in the laboratory?

Although the young persons' choice of an occupation usually influences their subsequent way of life and personality development profoundly, the decisions are not irreversible (Ginzberg, 1975). The time required to prepare for some careers, such as psychoanalysis or nuclear physics, diminishes the likelihood that those engaged in them will move far from them; yet persons of all levels of education may change occupations at almost any time in their lives. Community colleges, special schools, rehabilitation programs, help persons who had stopped their education at an early age to enter more skilled occupations. Women often change occupations when they resume work after their children are in school. Even the commitment to the Catholic priesthood is no longer regarded as irreversible. Some persons who perceive that they have gone as far as they can in a given occupation will prefer to take a chance in a new occupation in midlife rather than experience years of frustration. Retirement at sixty-five will simply lead some individuals to move into a new field of endeavor. Then, too, many changes occur within individuals' original vocation that lead them into new orientations, as when an attorney enters politics, moves from corporation counselor to executive, or decides to teach in a law school. The choice of a career, which is so often made only after prolonged soul-searching, may not decide the future as definitively as a youth is apt to believe.

WOMEN'S OCCUPATIONAL CHOICE

Women constitute approximately forty percent of the work force in the United States, excluding those whose full-time occupations as housewives and mothers are among the most arduous. They have the potential for succeeding at virtually any occupation except for a few that require a masculine physique,* though the number of women in some occupations has been limited by custom, prejudice, gender role allocation and training, as well as women's own preferences. The proportion of women in medical and law schools is increasing rapidly. Although the number of women in high administrative positions is low, and women may not have been raised to be sufficiently aggressive and competitive, it has become apparent that women can head governments as successfully as men.† However, as we have already noted, women usually take other matters into account in choosing a career in addition to some of those, or all of those, considered by men. Even though many young liberated women believe that marriage and child rearing should not interfere with women's careers any more than they do men's, that is not the way it has been or is likely to be for most women in the near future, or the way many women wish it to be.

For those women who place success in a career foremost and decide to remain unmarried, or to marry but not have children, the special problems are few though often still significant. For example, they will have to decide, if admission to, or advancement in, a field is closed to women, whether to eliminate it from consideration or to try to enter it and combat the prejudice. They may judge whether they have overcome or can overcome the fear of success discussed in the preceding chapter, or whether they can continue to accept the self-image of a single or a childless woman, or whether they can find a husband who will give his wife's career sufficient consideration when moving to a new location is required by one of their careers, etc.

About ninety-five percent of American women marry, and although the age at which they marry is increasing, particularly for educated women, it seems unlikely that the proportion will decrease appreciably in the near future. A very large proportion continue to desire children, though far fewer children per family than formerly. Dual-career marriages with children almost always present problems for both spouses but particularly for

---

* It is highly unlikely, though not impossible, that a woman could become a linesman on a professional football team, and any such opportunity would be limited to women with unusual physiques. However, the absence of women from some occupations that require considerable strength is only a matter of custom. Women in the Soviet Union clean and repair roads. In New Guinea women carry the heavy loads. When asked why men do not, at least, share these tasks, the indigenes are taken aback and say that everyone knows that women are built so that they can carry more than men. There is no reason why women cannot be bomber pilots, and, sorrowfully, they probably will be.

† Moreover, at the time of writing, both the governor and the secretary of the state of Connecticut and the provost of Yale University are women.

the wife. The couple may decide that the homemaking tasks and the child rearing will be shared equally, but at least in times of crisis, as when a child is ill, the woman usually carries the major responsibility. Despite decisions and determinations prior to the arrival of a child, many women find that taking care of the child becomes a major source of gratification to them which they are reluctant to cede to a husband. Even when the children are properly cared for by a housekeeper or in a nursery, mothers who work full-time wonder whether their absence is having a deleterious effect upon their children. Many women who have managed to continue their careers while their children were very young express doubts that it has been worthwhile. Some of the difficulties and concerns may be due to the manner in which the mothers had been raised to accept the primary responsibility for child rearing rather than to innate maternal tendencies, but the mother's feelings are still very important—as are the father's.

In planning a career, a woman may have to decide how to implement it and still have children. One solution is to finish the necessary preparation before having a child, but defer embarking on the career, while nevertheless keeping abreast of it, until the children have entered school. Some may decide instead to wait until they are sufficiently far along in their careers to enable them to have adequate full-time domestic help before having a child, or to rely upon a mother or mother-in-law to care for the child, so that they can return to work soon after the child is born without disrupting their careers. The woman, indeed the couple, who decides on a dual-career marriage does well to recognize at the time the decision is made that for most the relaxation upon returning home from work will be limited, and that the couple's expectations must be sufficiently malleable to allow for a change in plans as opportunity permits or necessity requires. Among women who planned a career are some who, after a hiatus to care for young children, will prefer to remain housewives and devote time to local politics, volunteer or part-time work, a hobby, or study. Women have an option, not available to men, of deciding to relinquish a career to become housewives and mothers. Many a graduate student, confronted by difficulties in completing a thesis, has slipped up in her contraceptive practices and had her immediate future decided for her, and others consciously opt out of pursuing a career. Educated American women whose husbands provide adequately for their families are in a position to foster a cultural blossoming among womankind.

Many young women, rather than planning a career after finishing their schooling, consider work as a temporary activity until they marry, or until a husband can support a family. They consider that much of their future and their position in society will depend upon their husbands' careers, and they consider their own occupations as supportive of their husbands. They may enjoy work and even find life as a housewife and mother confining and look forward to returning to work when the children are grown, but they feel little urgency to hurry back in order to gain advancement. The jobs that are conventionally women's jobs—secretary, telephone operator, retail clerk, and, recently, bank teller—are not positions that usually open the way for great advancement. However, with the decreasing size of families, the majority of women now work.* It seems likely that more women would become involved in gratifying occupations in midlife if, when they were young, they had prepared for their lives after children no longer kept them occupied.

In keeping with their upbringing, which tends to foster the expressive or affiliative aspects of women's personalities rather than the more aggressively competitive, many young women continue to seek affiliative types of occupations. A secretary may seek a good wage but she is not as concerned with achievement in a career as with aiding the person for whom she works. Nursing, teaching, and social work are conventionally women's career jobs, and medicine is increasingly becoming a woman's as well as a man's career in the United States, as it has been in Europe—and all have a nurturant or affiliative quality. Although more women are becoming bus drivers, bank clerks, editors, accountants, lawyers, than heretofore, many women will continue to prefer affiliative occupations, even though new opportunities become open to them.

PERSONALITY AND OCCUPATION

Occupational choice reflects the development and integration of the personality. It is often difficult to follow just how specific career choices are determined, but personality traits which we term characterologic play a significant part in the selection of a type of occupation. We can note that fixations in psychosexual development will contribute to the decision:

---

* In 1970, sixty percent of women between the ages of twenty-five and sixty worked at least part-time, and of women between forty-five and fifty-five, sixty percent were still working or again working. Further, seventy percent of separated and divorced women below the age of sixty-five worked, and, as we have seen, a sizable proportion of marriages now break up.

"oral" characters may be attracted toward becoming chefs or dieticians, or may seek security by becoming wealthy in order to be assured that oral supplies will always be available; "anal" characters with tendencies to obsessive meticulousness are likely to enter careers that deal directly with money, such as banking, bookkeeping, accounting—or with collecting and assembling; "phallic" characters may seek some occupation in which they can assert power, or gain admiration for their physiques.

It is apparent that certain types of personalities are better suited for some occupations than others, and that some are unsuited for certain occupations. The human race can be categorized in various ways to take note of such compatibilities and incompatibilities (see Chapter 19). Occupational counselors and psychologists utilize such characterologic groupings as aids in placing persons in suitable occupations.* Such categorization is usually made on the basis of expressed occupational interests, personality traits, including intelligence and aptitudes, and noting whom a person would like to emulate.

The Influence of Occupation on Personality Development

We have been examining how the personality enters into the choice of an occupation, but we must now turn to consider how people's occupations become a major influence in the sort of adults they become. In selecting their vocations—if they can select—individuals tend to choose a social environment in which they feel comfortable, composed of persons with whom they like to associate and whose regard they seek. It will act to preserve personality traits they have developed or it creates strains that provoke change. Persons' identities gain solidity through their identification with a group of people pursuing similar objectives and with its group mores. Although occasional individuals maintain their own standards relatively independently of what those around them believe and do, most persons' superego standards bend toward the group values and to the ideals

---

* Holland (1966) has found it most useful to divide persons into the following categories: realistic, intellectual, social, conventional, enterprising, and artistic, or into combinations of these categories; but some are virtually exclusive of another, such as realistic and artistic. He has also placed occupations in the same categories. He considers that inventories of interests are personality inventories; that members of a vocation tend to have similar personalities and developmental histories; that persons in a vocational group having similar personalities will create characteristic interpersonal environments; and that vocational satisfaction, stability, and achievement depend upon the congruency between one's personality and the environment in which one works.

and demands of the group leaders, as became apparent during the 1973 Senate Watergate hearings. Persons who enter the advertising business may not be overscrupulous about truth, but they find themselves in an environment in which the truth is slanted for sales. They come to value the capacity to conceal and mislead and their personalities alter,* for they gain the esteem of those they esteem by their ability to mask the truth.

In contrast, some occupations support more conventional superego standards and may, of course, be selected for such reasons. The clergy, police, and others attach themselves to the maintenance of ethical standards. Physicians select a profession in which their own welfare is supposed to be secondary to the well-being of their patients. Value systems and goals are reinforced or redirected.

In the process of learning a trade or profession, novices learn a way of life along with the knowledge and skills of the occupation. It will shape or help shape many facets of their personalities. First-year medical students may wonder how physicians behave under a variety of circumstances and how they will reach decisions concerning life and death, and they unconsciously gain the answers from observing their teachers and colleagues and assuming their ways of behaving and styles of living before the end of their training. Whatever their traits before entering medical school, they develop a degree of obsessive meticulousness; assume a benevolent, protective way of relating to people; expect a type of deference from patients; intellectualize as a defense and learn to hide feelings or even repress them to a marked degree.

One can note how friends or brothers who have been close friends because of common interests, traits, and ideals begin to change and differ after more or less chance—or seemingly arbitrary—selection of different occupations. The factory worker spends his evenings out at the corner tavern, playing cards and spinning yarns, while his wife stays at home tending the children; but his brother who has become a priest acquires a very different set of interests, standards, and ways of relating to people. They have developed very different ego functioning—different intellectual assets, areas of competence, ways of relating—and they also have different outlets of id impulsions, with the priest requiring sublimation and asceticism to satisfy his superego. Here is a banker's wife in a small New England community, a pillar of conservatism, married to a puritanical husband; she gains little sexual gratification in her marriage and expects little but would not consider divorcing her husband, who is a "pillar of the

---

* A recent study suggests that such traits also influence their children, who learn that what they say and can get away with is more important than what they really do.

community." Her childhood neighbor, who had similar beliefs and ways in childhood, lives among her Madison Avenue public relations colleagues a little farther west in New England, and now considers that her life would be blighted were it not sexually exciting, and tries analysis and divorce, or, more likely, divorce and then analysis, after her second marriage also proves not fully satisfying. Such comparisons cannot be made properly because no individuals are alike, and there are no "ifs" in life, but it appears from experience that the way of life dictated by a career influences personality functioning very profoundly.

The physician whose occupational choice was discussed earlier in the chapter might have become an artist or an architect except for certain chance occurrences that tipped the balance when the decision was being weighed. Life is aleatory and contingencies can make a difference. The life and personality of R., the physician, is different from what the life and personality of R., the artist, would have been. He leads a more regular life; he is a member of a medical school faculty; he has tended to suppress his fantasy and shift his creative urges into disciplined research; he has learned scientific ways of thinking that permeate his domestic life and child rearing; he has married a social worker who also has a highly developed sense of social responsibility, etc. R., the artist, would seek gratification through what he painted, and acclaim through his paintings. If he were properly creative, he could innovate at the behest of his fantasy, unconcerned with the impact of his experiments on the future of science. He could and probably would work at irregular hours, and follow the direction of his creative impulses rather than his sense of responsibility. The people with whom he associated would cherish free spirits who lived as they liked without too much concern for social conventions. Success would not depend as much upon effort alone as upon his creative capacities. His ways of thinking would be less organized and scientifically trained, and perhaps free from intellectualizations that might hinder his artistic creativity. The occupational roles, the institutions to which one belongs, the style of life, the education in preparation for the occupation, the ideals and ideal figures one follows, the values of one's peers—all will greatly influence who one will be in later years.

The Mores and Morals of Various Occupational Groups

The understanding of the ways in which people of varying occupations lead their lives, and the perspectives and goals they are likely to hold, is essential to therapists, who must overcome tendencies to understand patients in terms of their own mores and morals. An illustration may serve to indicate how such understanding can increase a therapist's skills. During World War II two young officers were promoted to the rank of captain and sent to an anti-aircraft weapons unit defending a beautiful South Sea island well away from combat. One was delighted by his good fortune and thoroughly enjoyed the life on the island of his dreams. The other soon complained of intractable headaches that led to hospitalization until an experienced army physician sized up the situation. The second officer was a West Pointer whose life ambition was to become a general. His chances of ever becoming a general were minimal unless he found an opportunity to display his abilities—and preferably also his heroism—and become a colonel by the end of the war. He felt that he had been sidetracked into an unimportant position by a prejudiced senior officer and he could scarcely contain his hostility toward that officer and the army. In contrast, the captain who was pleased by the assignment was a reserve officer who, though a conscientious, patriotic citizen, had little interest in military life or in becoming a hero, preferring the life among the Polynesian girls—which he had never really hoped to experience.

Occupational choice, then, forms one of the crucial decisions of a lifetime. Such choices are usually highly overdetermined, reflecting much of the entire prior personality development, and the conscious reasons usually are but part of the determinants of the decision. The occupation selected and pursued may, then, become a major influence in the subsequent personality development, the persons with whom one interrelates, and the type of life that is led. The problems of occupational choice faced by women differ in some respects from those of men, because most women have wished to include time and opportunity for rearing children in their plans. In a reasonably affluent society, the choice of occupation made as an adolescent or young adult is no longer as decisive as formerly, as people often change careers at any time in the life cycle.

REFERENCES

Ariès, P. (1962). *Centuries of Childhood*. Alfred A. Knopf, New York.

Byrd, R. (n.d.). *Alone*. G. P. Putnam's Sons, New York.

Ginzberg, E. (1975). *The Manpower Connection*. Harvard University Press, Cambridge, Mass.

GINZBERG, E., GINZBERG, S., AXELROD, S., and HERMA, J. (1951). *Occupational Choice: An Approach to a General Theory.* Columbia University Press, New York.
HOLLAND, J. (1966). *The Psychology of Vocational Choice.* Blaisdell Publications, Waltham, Mass.
MORRIS, J., HEADY, J., RAFFLE, P., ROBERTS, C., and PARKS, J. (1953). "Coronary Heart-Disease and Physical Activity of Work," *Lancet*, 265:1111–1120.
STRONG, JR., E. (1943). *Vocational Interests of Men and Women.* Stanford University Press, Stanford, Calif.

SUGGESTED READING

GINZBERG, E., GINZBERG, S., AXELROD, S., and HERMA, J. (1951). *Occupational Choice: An Approach to a General Theory.* Columbia University Press, New York.
HIESTAND, D. (1971). *Changing Careers After Thirty-Five: New Horizons Through Professional and Graduate Study.* Columbia University Press, New York.
HOLLAND, J. (1966). *The Psychology of Vocational Choice.* Balisdell Publications, Waltham, Mass.
SMUTS, R. (1971). *Women and Work in America.* Schocken Books, New York.

CHAPTER 13

❀

Marital Choice

THE COUPLE who are about to marry realize, as on few other occasions in their lives, that they are making a decisive commitment. The ceremony culminates their lives to that moment, and their choice of a partner is a resultant of their total experience. It marks the start of a new way of living and the achievement of a very different status in life. They are aware that their future happiness will depend in large measure upon the relationship being established. They may also feel, though they usually do not consciously recognize it, that the direction of their future personality development and their entire manner of adapting to life hang in the balance. While the marriage ceremony has been considered by some primarily as providing permission and social sanction for sexual intercourse, such views when not facetious are alarmingly superficial. The union that is formed changes, or at least should change, the ego structure of both persons, so that it henceforth concerns the direction and welfare of two lives rather than one; and new superego directives are taken over from the partner which together with id impulses and basic drives of the spouse will henceforth influence behavior. Along with the hazards and the need for realignment of personality functioning, the marriage brings with it new opportunities for self-fulfillment and completion.

The bride and groom have reason to experience anxiety for, as with any commitment, consequences must be accepted in advance. It is, however, a special commitment to intimate interdependence. In their relationships with their parents, they had no choice of the objects of their dependency, but now a voluntary choice is being made and the responsibility for consequences must be accepted. The potential sources of disturbance and danger are overshadowed by the recognition of marriage as a new source of strength and support. In finding an occupation or career, individuals gain solidity through the pursuit of a definite goal, by limiting their strivings, by taking into themselves the way of life, the roles and value systems that accompany it. In marrying, one gains a partner who shares and supports and upon whom one can rely, for the well-being of each is bound up with the fate of the other. Further, persons assume the pattern of living of a married person for which there are traditional directives, and they also acquire a definite place in the social system. Again further delimitations of the numerous potential ways of living have occurred; and while limitations may seem onerous, they also promote cohesiveness and can open new ways of expressing one's potentialities.

The problems of marital adjustment and family living are of paramount importance in understanding the emotional difficulties of people, and cannot be considered separately from the choice of the partner. While this may seem a platitude, many marital problems are largely dependent upon the personality characteristics of one member which might well create difficulties no matter who was the spouse. One might consider, for example, a man who appeared to have made an excellent choice of a beautiful and very wealthy young woman who understood his difficulties with his own family and was willing to help him overcome a number of anxieties that interfered with his ability to work. However, even though his wife bore no noticeable resemblance to his mother, he was so fearful of all women because of his experiences with an overbearing, directive, and demanding mother, that any proximity to women that might lead to sexual relationships provoked intense anxiety in him. He could scarcely remain in the same house with his wife after supper, and was soon too removed from her to enable her to try to be helpful to him. Still failures of complementarity create many other problems.

It becomes apparent during the psychiatric treatment of many married persons that the choice of the spouse for neurotic reasons ties the individual to an untenable way of life which leads to the mobilization of deleterious traits and prevents the development of more favorable characteristics. While it is usually true that the partner selected fills some basic need and in some respects forms a suitable choice, the concept can be overemphasized, as will be considered later in the chapter. It is quite apparent that many people do not really know the person whom they are marrying and do not realize how greatly the partner's personality will influence their own. In considering marital problems, one is no longer concerned with an individual but with a dyad, and how the marriage works out relates clearly to the question of the partner selected. It must also be recognized, however, that even pathological needs may properly be managed if a suitable partner is selected, as when a woman who has a morbid fear of childbirth finds a man who wishes to be the center of his wife's life without any interference from children.

We wish to consider why people marry, whom they marry, and when, examining how the decision to marry and the choice of a mate fit into the pattern and sequence of the life history and influence further development. The emphasis upon the family as the primary socializing agency for the child means that particular consideration must be given to the marital union that forms the milieu in which the children will be raised. There is also the practical everyday need of the therapist who, when he becomes aware of it, finds that marital problems often form a focal point in the unhappiness and the emotional disturbances that bring many patients to him. While patients at times come directly seeking advice about marital situations, more commonly the resultant distress has produced physiological dysfunctioning that creates symptoms or leads to displaced substitutive complaints. It is a common experience that the complaint of chronic backache in a woman may relate to her wish to refuse sexual relations that she finds repulsive; or the obesity that complicates a medical ailment depends upon the need for a person who feels starved for affection to gain satisfaction from overeating, etc. A man complaining of intractable headaches soon vents his rage which arises because he believes his wife married him only for his money and constantly expresses contempt for him because of his lower social status. He also expresses his feelings of hopeless frustration because she is unapproachable and unresponsive to his sexual needs, considering them an imposition and making him feel he is being indecent.

Although interest here does not lie in the pathological but the unfolding of the personality through marriage, any discussion of marital choice and adjustment must take into account shortcomings and failures, for these pertain to the majority of marriages rather than the exception in contemporary society. Although the majority outcome cannot be considered as the norm, it indicates the difficulties of attaining a satisfactory marital choice and adjustment. Approximately one out of three first marriages formed at the present time in the United States will terminate in divorce, if current

divorce rates continue.* About half of the divorces will take place during
the first ten years of marriage and fortunately about one half before there
have been any children. Such figures must not be taken as an indication
that marriage is becoming less important. Ninety-six to ninety-seven percent of all Americans marry, and, of those who divorce, eighty percent will
try again (Carter and Glick, 1970).†

Divorce rates in general reflect the ease of obtaining a divorce ɪ ᵗher
than the success or failure of marriage in general. On the other hand, they
do not indicate the extent of marital unhappiness, for many marriages that
formally remain intact are seriously disturbed. There are various figures
concerning successful marriage and they are difficult to interpret. Perhaps
the optimal estimate has been that somewhat less than twenty-five percent
of marriages are fully satisfactory to both partners, but other studies cut
the figure to anywhere between five and twenty-five percent. It has also
been estimated that considerably less than half are deemed reasonably
adequate by the couple. Still such figures do not mean that many more
marriages do not subserve some essential functions for both partners who
might be even unhappier if unmarried or married to someone else.

MARITAL CHOICE: LOVE AND UNCONSCIOUS PROCESSES

The basis of marital choice in the United States today reflects the individ-
ualistic, democratic society in which decision and responsibility rest primarily upon the two persons who are marrying. While the reasons for the
specific selection of a partner are elusive, the reason usually given and
generally though not always believed is that they have fallen in love; and
love is a state that has eluded philosophic and scientific definition throughout the ages. Freud (1914), like others, drew an analogy between being in

---

* The annual divorce rate reached a high of about eighteen per thousand marriages
in 1946 and then fell to approximately nine per thousand in the late 1950s, but
has been rising steadily in recent years and again approximates, and may now exceed,
the post-World War II levels.

† There has been an increase in the proportion of persons under thirty-five who are
single since 1960, a change thought to indicate that people are now marrying a few
years later than previously; but the change may reflect a slight diminution in the percentage of people who marry. In Sweden, which has often antedated American trends,
first marriages decreased fifty percent between 1966 and 1972 and illegitimacy rose
about twenty-five percent.

love and being sick when he said that "this sexual overestimation [of the love object] is the origin of the peculiar state of being in love, a state suggestive of a neurotic compulsion," but he did not underestimate its importance, calling love "the highest form of development of which object —libido—is capable," and he defined normality in terms of the "ability to love and to work."

Falling in love is largely an irrational matter, dependent upon unconscious determinants that trail back into infancy. However, as has been noted in other connections, the unconscious processes may be more suited than intellectual assessments for drawing together the diffuse needs of an individual, the incoherent judgments of people, the feeling-tone memories, the pleasing and displeasing in the expression, vision, feel, smell of another, and many other such factors that enter into personal attraction. The intellect could scarcely cope with so many variables, even if they were consciously available to weigh. While the unconscious processes designate whom one loves, they are apparently less capable of judging properly with whom one can live in harmony. It is of more than passing interest that one of the most decisive steps in a person's life rests largely upon unconscious processes which are at best checked by logical appraisal of the chances for success or failure.

Anyone who has had the unpleasant task of suggesting to a couple who are prepared to marry that they at least postpone a marriage which seems unwise because of the serious emotional instability of one of them, has learned that reason has little chance against the erotically driven impulsion with its capacities to blind. It is also important to note that the choice of partners by the couples themselves on the basis of romantic love forms a custom that is fairly unique to modern civilization and is probably more prevalent in the United States than anywhere else. Indeed, some authorities consider that romantic love in itself is a phenomenon of Western culture which only started with the troubadours, who even then were not singing of love in connection with marriage. Although ancient literature from many countries appears clearly to negate this theory and indicate that "love," whatever this connoted at the given time and place, has always tended to draw people together, and lead them to desire marriage, still it has usually not been a major determinant of marital choice: partners have been chosen by parents, by kin groups, according to prescribed relationship patterns, and for economic and social reasons.

There is little, if any, evidence that the contemporary freedom to select partners has led to happier marriages; but the functions that marriage seeks to fill today are vastly different and are not easily equated with marriage under different traditions. Attention here can only be directed to the contemporary scene, with recognition that the nature of marriage and the way in which partners are chosen is an integral part of the society in which it exists. While young people in particular are apt to confuse a passionate attraction for mature love, it must be recognized that a number of young adults have become wary not simply of marrying early but of conventional marriage as a way of achieving happiness.

ALTERNATIVES TO MARRIAGE AND NUCLEAR-FAMILY FORMATION

Although in this chapter we are considering the influence of the choice of a spouse on personality development, it seems necessary to comment briefly on the choice of a type of marriage, or, as some would prefer to say, of the type of "bonding." Some persons, still a small minority, see no reason why they require the legal or religious sanction to live together, or why they should be impeded by legal ties if they decide to separate. Some wish to have their respective rights and privileges as well as the terms for separation or divorce in the form of a contract before entering into a "bonding" or marriage. Concerned about the isolation of married couples and families, a couple may decide to live as part of a group, with or without being married, in one of a variety of arrangements. They may live in a cooperative home in which household tasks, expenses, and child rearing are shared. Even though it is sometimes hoped that the group will live together and develop into something resembling an extended family, couples usually leave after a few years. Many find that whereas it is difficult enough to adjust to a marital partner it is still more difficult to adjust to living intimately with a number of couples. Many persons have joined communes, not simply as a means of living with a partner or satisfying sexual needs with a group rather than a single person, but to form a small alternate culture which turns away from our highly competitive industrial society. They seek self-actualization through making the most of their innate abilities, enjoying social interaction in the group, eschewing future goals, eliminating sex-linked roles, and, perhaps, seeking sexual pleasure with various partners in various ways. Very few such communes have lasted long enough to permit their evaluation, particularly their effect upon children.* As many communes seek to form alternate cultures, if not a part of the

---

* However, as noted previously, the survey reported in *Children of the Counterculture* (Rothchild and Wolf, 1976) indicates that in many communes the effects on children are disastrous.

counterculture, they have difficulty in gaining the approval of the larger society, and in rearing children to live in the general society. Which, if any, of the variations of married life or alternatives to marriage can fill the needs that lead people to marry will not be considered here, but the consideration of why people marry and of the functions of marriage in people's lives may help the reader make such judgments.*

THE PLACE OF MARRIAGE IN THE LIFE CYCLE

The understanding of why people marry and, perhaps, the meaning of the intangible but very real and pertinent force of love appear to require a scrutiny of the place of marriage in the developmental sequence of a person and of the biological and social forces playing upon the young adults when they decide to marry. While we cannot hope properly to define love and explain why a specific person is selected, the whole process may be clarified if we view it in the total developmental setting rather than as an isolated phenomenon. The fusion of biological and social determinants demands attention, for reference to only the sexual drives or the societal functions of marriage leads to an inadequate and confusing view of the institution.

We have followed young adults as they achieved reasonable emancipation from parental control and started on a search for a way of life of their own. The unmarried young man and woman find themselves in anomalous positions in the parental home. They are adults, no longer requiring care or wishing to be children, but they are still members of the childhood generation. The attachment to the home derives largely from former needs and abiding affections, but the home is no longer the real center of their lives or the focus of their hopes and desires. The family must function as a unit and requires a leader, and it becomes increasingly likely that clashes will occur between the parents and the adult child who has different attitudes, goals, and desires. The erotic bonds and dependent needs that helped foster

---

* It is, of course, limiting for persons to focus on self-actualization in the present, for a person's actualization usually involves "becoming" rather than simply "being," and it runs counter to the essential human attribute of foresight. A common problem in communes and cooperative groups of couples that is not inherent in the concept has been the tendency of many persons who join such groups to wish to remain dependent. The difficulties in eliminating or radically changing gender-linked roles and personality attributes has been considered in previous chapters. Communes, of course, differ markedly from extended families, or primitive villages, because of the very different backgrounds of the members and the absence of kinship loyalties and bonds that start in early childhood.

harmony have been severed or negated. The path toward fulfillment as an adult does not lie in the parental home. In particular there can be no fusion of sexual and affectional needs or completion of generative desires within the family of origin. Emotional independence has been gained but freedom does not bring fulfillment, it simply opens the doors to permit the individual to seek it. Young adults are likely to feel at loose ends as part of a home in which they no longer fit: they are adults with few prerogatives, and without their own domain. Waiting will not suffice, for a son cannot inherit his father's family, or a daughter her mother's, though the desire to do so can gain the upper hand and lead to a frustrated life.

Usually the major attachments that provide direction to the person's life and the meaningful relationship now lie outside the family. There are a group of friends of the same sex who have common interests and with whom activities and confidences are shared. The occupation and activities related to it gain prominence whether a person is already started on a career or is still a student. The wish and need to satisfy and please the boss or teachers become as important as satisfying parental wishes. There are friends of the opposite sex who provide passing or more permanent companionship, partial or complete outlets for sexual drives, perhaps one or more trials at living with another in an intimate relationship, admiration that bolsters self-esteem, and from whom one seeks and may find affection and love.

The variations are manifold, but usually the peer group, including members of the opposite sex, forms the major source of interpersonal satisfaction. Customarily for the man, and in recent decades for young women, life as an unmarried young adult is considered a period during which he or she can enjoy freedom before assuming the responsibilities and restrictions of matrimony. Adults who have been away from home during the transition from adolescence attending a university, employed in a different community, or in military service often find it difficult to return home to live. They move out of their family homes to establish their own quarters, alone or with a friend. Often this is a time of sexual adventure that is more direct and less hesitant than it was during adolescence and a time when sexual excitement and the challenge and intrigue of conquest become ends in themselves; or of living in serial monogamy to have real companionship until ready to marry. Others give up this period of freedom, having found the right partner with whom they may live while waiting to marry, or until they are certain they wish to marry. The freedom from parental edict permits a freer and more conscious pursuit of sexuality. The intensity and extent of the occupation or preoccupation with sexual conquests relate to such factors as inability to tolerate loneliness, the need for physical contact to feel desired or desirable, and the search for reassuring experiences concerning sexual capacities, rather than to any quantity of sexual drive. The man may tend to experiment more because of the need to overcome residual fears of losing his individuation in an intimate relationship with a woman and of again becoming dependent on a woman, whereas the young woman is frequently more consciously appraising future husbands.

Of course, life as an unmarried adult may not exist at all, marriage following the closure of adolescence, or with the marital choice already made and simply awaiting consummation, and the period may terminate abruptly any time when the person falls in love and decides to marry. For some, the hesitancy concerning marriage may be overcome only as friends pair up and marry, leaving the single individual feeling out of place with friends whose major emotional investments now lie in their own homes and their young children. The pressures of parents and married friends, who feel that life can be completed only in marriage, increase. Loneliness becomes a greater problem and persons begin to wonder about their own rationalizations for not marrying. Even though living with a partner, persons are apt to feel very vulnerable without a permanent relationship. The partner may find a more attractive partner, educational or career needs may lead to separation; relationships between parents and the partner are somewhat tenuous—even if cordial, not those of family members;* and persons do not have the right to expect that their welfare is as important to the partner as the partner's own well-being, for they are not yet bound to a life in common. The entire social system pushes young men and women toward marital status, for the life of a single person, particularly for a woman, becomes increasingly limited. Motives other than romantic love gain more importance in the decision to marry and in the choice of a partner.

THE NATURE OF THE IMPULSIONS TO MARRY

The impulsion to form a lasting marital union rests upon the biological nature of humans and the requisite lengthy period of nurturance in the family setting. The two sexes are obviously different and have different

---

* Parents have difficulties in knowing how to relate to an offspring's "friend" and, unless communications between parents and child are unusually good, can be uncertain how their child wishes them to regard the relationship. It differs in many respects from that of parents-in-law to the child's spouse. They also have some problems in referring to the partner, difficulties that have given rise to such terms as my "sin-in-law" or my "daughter-out-law."

biological functions and are suited to each other for satisfactory release of sexual tensions and attainment of the complete orgasmic pleasure on which nature through the evolutionary process has set a high premium to assure perpetuation of the species. Sexuality in itself, however, does not explain the institution of marriage nor does sexual attraction suffice as a reason why people marry. Sexual gratification is scarcely considered a primary function of marriage in some societies, occurring independently of marriage, particularly for men, and it may be pertinent to marriage only in regard to procreation. Currently, for the majority of young adults the satisfaction of sexual drives does not wait upon marriage. However, it must be recognized that whereas much premarital sexual activity can provide release, excitement, and pleasure, it may not afford much emotional satisfaction and a sense of completion.

The desire to propagate, which may well have instinctual components, particularly in women, but which also arises in both sexes through the desire for a sense of completion through parenthood, more clearly fosters a reasonably permanent relationship. The children require protective nurturance for many years. As discussed in previous chapters, it is difficult for single parents to raise a child, and a child properly requires a parent of each sex. From the parents' standpoint, one of the major gratifications of having children is the sharing of the child and the child's development with another, and preferably with the other parent.

We have noted throughout the developmental process the preparation, which is often unconscious and unnoted, for males and females to fill divergent roles, to possess different abilities, and to focus on different interests. In all societies children have been reared in a manner that leads to a need for interdependence with a member of the opposite sex to carry out properly the activities of life, particularly child rearing. Though the differences in the way girls and boys are brought up are diminishing, whether each sex will become essentially self-sufficient, and whether it will be deemed desirable, remains to be answered in the future. The differences extend beyond tangible matters to differing ways of regarding and relating to people, and to finding different sources of satisfaction so that neither a man nor a woman has a rounded approach and grasp of life alone. Although adolescents and, at times, young adults may be more at ease with members of their own sex whose ways are more familiar because they resemble their own, when adults become independent it is far more likely that a man and woman will complement one another and fill out each other's interests and needs than will a person of the same gender, quite aside from the sexual needs.

The incompleteness of the individual, however, is particularly telling because each person grew up as a member of a family in which tasks and roles were shared, which provided support during immaturity and which formed a place where a person was accepted for affectional reasons rather than for abilities or achievement. During infancy and childhood intangible bonds to others were formed that provided warmth and security, and gave meaning to life. Within the family children could feel secure that their well-being was as important to the parents as to themselves. We have seen that the child starts life in symbiosis with the mother and gradually gains an independent self. The movement toward separation and increasing independence had always been ambivalent, containing an urge toward freedom for self-realization and a regressive pull toward dependent relatedness with its comfort and security. Throughout development there had been a strong impetus, largely unconscious, toward regaining a total relatedness with another person.

It has also been noted, particularly in the discussion of the resolution of the oedipal attachment, that the sensuous or erotic components of the relatedness to parents had to be frustrated within the family in order to foster proper independent development. The upsurge of sexual feelings at puberty not only remained unfulfilled but led to further movement away from the parents. A major aspect of development, the strong attraction to the parent of the opposite sex, after having been formed and having served a useful purpose, was frustrated and left hanging. It was sublimated and displaced, but unconsciously left a sense of incompletion that required closure. These structured but unsatisfied longings and patterns provide the foundation for the later love relationships.

Young persons had to overcome a variety of feelings of inadequacy before being ready to lose themselves in a total relationship again. The unconscious memory of the disappointing frustration remained in them. The boy needed to gain security against being overwhelmed and lost in a relationship with a woman. The forbidden incestuous connotation of sexuality had to be overcome in both sexes, the dangers of rivalry with parents set aside, and independence from parents achieved. The independence from family, however, increases the feelings of incompletion and aloneness. The sexual drive, however, now is free to find expression and adds compelling moment to the forming of a new union which will more fully, sexually as well as affectionately, complete the strivings and pattern that had been forcibly renounced in childhood. Persons who fall in love again transcend themselves, but this time as adults who can take care of another as well as be cared for. The welfare of the other becomes synonymous with one's own welfare. The libidinal strivings are again focused on a specific person but now they are reciprocated. Though the two persons are still physically separate, the act of falling in love forms a union between them.

The libidinal drives play a major role in the finding of a love object. The passionate needs pervade intellect and color perception. The wish for the desired object transcends reality. It attaches to some desired and needed fragment in another person, to a physical characteristic or behavioral trait, and around it fashions the idealized person of one's desires. In a sense, every lover is something of a Pygmalion.

It is a time-worn adage that love is blind. It is blind in proportion to the intensity of one's needs. There is an old story told by Petrarch of a youth who fell in love with a one-eyed girl and was sent away by his parents who opposed the marriage. After he returned several years later, when he asked his former love how she had lost her eye during his absence, the girl replied, "I have lost none, but you have found yours."

What is the image the lover sees? Some trait produces a resonance of the primary parental love model. It may be quite apparent or because of residual incestuous fears be hidden under markedly different characteristics such as a different physical appearance or divergence of race or religion, a fairly common factor that has been termed "neurotic exogamy," because of the resemblance to the taboo against marrying persons from the same clan or village in many primitive societies.* Although an attempt by Hamilton (1929) to trace a similarity between marital partners and parents led to a negative conclusion, psychoanalytic work is more likely to uncover one. It is not always present or at least not observable even with careful scrutiny, and it would seem that women tend to marry a man more obviously related to the father than a man is likely to choose a wife resembling his mother. The person in love also sees an admiring person, noting in the eyes of the other the devoted attraction which may well relate to the infant's fixation on the eyes of the loving and admiring mother. Lovers find someone who supports and increases their own self-esteem and turns the admirer into the person whose admiration and love they wish. While a person is desired who will complement the self, the loved one may be selected narcissistically in the image of the self whom one loves. However, the resemblance between spouses, which is often noticeable, is not this simple; as the choice is apt to fall on someone who resembles a parent; and as a person is apt to resemble a parent, the spouses may bear resemblances to one another. The

* However, about three-quarters of the marriages in the United States in 1960 were between persons of similar national origins, and about the same proportion of Protestants and Catholics married within their faiths; a significantly smaller percentage of Jews married persons of other religions.

choice of a love object seen as the source and possessor of total erotism which re-creates fantasy images of adolescence is apt to be based on an evaluation even less close to reality than other types. There are, of course, many other specific determinants of the choice of the precise partner which are elusive and can be traced only in extreme instances when the determining factors are unusually clear.

Readiness for Marriage

In some respects the question of whom a person chooses to marry must be related to the question of when a person becomes ready to marry, for when conscious and unconscious preparation for marriage has been completed the proper person often mysteriously appears. While it is romantic to believe that true lovers will eventually meet though separated by continents, the facts show that twelve and a half percent of five thousand couples in Philadelphia lived at the same address prior to marriage and over fifty percent within twenty blocks of one another.* Proximity of residence is clearly a major factor in selection, while attendance at the same schools and churches accounts for another large proportion. The choice is basically not of one person from among the inhabitants of the world but from the relatively small number of persons met under favorable circumstances at a very specific time in life.

THE DEVELOPMENTAL HISTORY OF MARITAL CHOICE

The process of marital choice has a developmental history much like that of occupational choice and this history influences the outcome, for the choice may take decisive form at different stages in the process. The various phases have already been noted as we followed personality development from early childhood. The earliest choice is the incestuous wish to

---

* See J. Bossard, "Residential Propinquity as a Factor in Marriage Selection." The topic has been reviewed by A. M. Katz and R. Hill, "Residential Propinquity and Marital Selection: A Review of Theory, Method, and Fact." The figure given for similar address is higher than that found in other studies, perhaps because it did not take into account a tendency for engaged couples to move close to one another, even before the days when they were likely to live together.

marry a parent which occurs before the child recognizes that the parent also grows older while he or she grows up, a choice retained until the resolution of the oedipal attachments takes place, when it is banished into the unconscious where it continues to exert its influence. There is a period when fantasy choices are fairly clearly parental substitutes, friends of parents, teachers, and the like, who can approximate a realistic choice as the child's age comes closer to that of the parental substitutes, as when a high school student falls in love with a teacher, or the student nurse with the physician who teaches her. Eventually, the possibility of marrying an older person who remains something of a parental figure becomes realistic. It is a common pattern of marriage in some countries where the woman marries an older, paternal man. More commonly, the adolescent moves from the fantasy of a romantic storybook ideal divested of sexuality to form a crush on an older adolescent who is an idol of the peer group. During adolescence there may be considerable daydreaming of the perfect person one will find, and, for the girl, of a man who will pursue her and sacrifice himself for love of her. In late adolescence desirable sexual characteristics more clearly become part of the image.

Eventually fantasy choices give way to courtship experiences which involve the actual trying out of the suitability of potential partners. At present, the trying out starts long before actual courtship through the gaining of familiarity with members of the opposite sex and the sorting out of what types of persons one likes. In contrast to societies where the girl cannot go out unchaperoned, the courtship will usually include "going steady" or a period of living together as a trial of compatibility in consideration of future marriage, or simply as an experimental run. The couple may try out their sexual compatibility, unfortunately often under circumstances that are far from favorable. Even among those who live together sexual difficulties are fairly common. One or both frequently hide their lack of satisfaction from the other, trusting that the difficulties will eventually disappear as they often do; but where facilities are available many seek counseling, even though neither engaged nor married.* There may also be a preengagement understanding between the couple that is a semiformal consideration of future engagement and marriage. Such pledges accompanied by the exchange of significant tokens have varying degrees of meaning, but are more readily broken than a formal engagement which usually involves the meeting, if not the approval, of the two families.

With the achievement of adult status, repeated dating often assumes the

---

* Early difficulties in achieving sexual satisfaction and compatibility will be considered briefly in the next chapter.

significance of courtship. By then persons have had an opportunity to take stock, not only forming opinions concerning the type of spouse desired but also what sort of persons they are likely to attract. Who has shown serious interest provides some measure of prospects. Still, the chance meeting or unexpected interest of a person may upset fantasies, expectations, and self-assessment at any time. Thus a young woman of twenty who became engaged to a man twelve years her senior tried to explain her decision which was as unexpected to her as to her family. She said, "I had always expected to marry someone who I was sure would amount to something, but also liked to have fun, to go dancing, play tennis, and enjoy the things I did. Then suddenly he came along and asked me to go out with him. I didn't think I'd be interested and I wasn't sure I'd know how to behave with an older man. I made excuses several times until I didn't know what to say. Then on our first date I found I was comfortable with him and felt taken care of. It was clear he wanted to get married. He isn't what I'd thought I wanted, he's just an insurance salesman and doesn't want to be anything else, he just wants to have a good home and a nice life. Still now I know I love him and want to be with him as I never wanted anyone before." Indeed, in falling in love seriously the young adult is apt to descend from romantic dreams to reality, but through falling in love he or she magnifies the reasonably prosaic choice into the most important and wonderful person in the world. The shift involves the more mature realization that the other need only be the most wonderful person in the world for the self.

THE ENGAGEMENT

The decision to marry is conventionally marked by the formal engagement. Although in some societies the engagement or betrothal is virtually a contract to marry, it currently forms a period prior to marriage that permits the couple to associate intimately and fairly constantly and to make certain that they are suited to one another. However, many couples now become very close and intimate to varying degrees without becoming engaged. An engagement for some still involves obtaining parental approval, but at present it often amounts to little more than telling the parents that they intend to marry and establishing a convenient date. Nevertheless, the decision brings realistic considerations to the forefront. The prospect of confronting parents with someone to whom they will certainly object gives pause and may even deter an agreement to marry. The compatibilities of the families, economic and geographical considerations, and desires to retain close relationships with parents may enter into consideration. Despite the insistence on self-determination by the couple, parental opinions as well as those of friends are often heeded and probably serve as a useful check against impulsive or inappropriate marriages.

The engagement is more than a trial period. It provides time prior to the definite commitment and the assumption of responsibilities to fuse interests and identities and for each to accommodate to the other in a movement away from the romantic attraction to a more conjugal relationship. It is usually a period of freer and more intense sexual activity, during which they may feel easier about obtaining contraceptive advice or sexual counseling.* Some couples, particularly younger ones, decide to wait until marriage to have sexual relations, which often makes the engagement period a difficult and frustrating time, for the sexual play and intense attraction heighten the desire for immediate consummation. When a couple evaluate their compatibility on the satisfaction of sexual relationships, or, as is now often the case, on the woman's ability to have an orgasm each time they have intercourse—if not on the ability for both of them to experience stimulaneous orgasms—difficulties are likely to ensue, for a good sexual adjustment frequently requires time, experience, familiarity, and confidence in the self and the partner.

It is clear from various sources that a reasonable engagement period safeguards against later divorce. Impulsive marriages without any waiting period are notably unsuccessful, which forms one reason why many states require a waiting period between obtaining a license and the actual wedding ceremony. Trends concerning optimal length of engagements cannot be clearly established. Some couples, particularly childhood sweethearts or college couples, may have a brief formal engagement though they have been informally engaged for many years. Three different studies indicate that the chances for excellent marriage adjustment are greatest when the engagement has lasted more than two years, but few advisors would suggest such prolonged formal engagements. As a survey of married college graduates indicated that about one third of the women and one fourth of

---

* Figures concerning premarital intercourse between engaged couples have become outdated and have been more a measure of the reliability of statistics gained from questionnaires than facts. A study made some years ago, in which members of married couples were separately asked whether they had engaged in premarital intercourse with the spouse, revealed that approximately fifty percent of the husbands, but only sixteen percent of the wives, had done so.

the men had previously been engaged to another person, it is clear that engagements serve a useful purpose as a trial period (Burgess and Locke, 1945).

Aside from testing the compatibility of the couple, and permitting closer assessment by each of the other, the engagement also provides persons time to ascertain their own readiness for marriage. As the actual event approaches, concerns about one's ability to accept responsibility, about sexual competence, and about less conscious fears of genital injury promote anxiety. The narrow margin between anxieties which will blossom into incapacitation in marriage and those which will fade when the period of waiting is over may be difficult to assess. Those who approach the psychiatrist, clergyman, or marital counselor may wish someone else to make the decision for them, but usually they come too late for anyone to help them work through an adequate assessment of themselves and the partner, and only under extreme conditions can a third person assume responsibility. It is of interest that a notable proportion of those who break an engagement will break more than one.

VARIOUS MOTIVATIONS TO MARRY

There are many reasons for marriage and the choice of a partner other than falling in love. They may be ancillary and only contributory factors or they may be dominating motivations, adequate in themselves; or they may, because of their force, almost preclude a lasting, satisfactory marriage. Some are clearly negative motivations in the sense that they cause a person to seek marriage in order to compensate for some unhappy life situation rather than because of strong desires for married life with the partner. It would be naïve to consider marital and family problems on the assumption that the marriage arose through love, and without being ready to hear and understand what led each spouse into the unhappy bond. Yet, as with many other life situations, what might be favorable or unfavorable for the success of a marriage can rarely be stated in categorical terms, for the chances of success depend upon the balance of factors involved in the specific situation. Some reasons aside from love of the specific partner that enter to a greater or lesser degree into any marriage are the desire to have a home of one's own, to gain completion and complementation with a person of the opposite sex, to find sexual outlets and settle problems of sexuality, to have children, to gain security, to acquire status and a place in society. Yet each of these may contain distortions that will interfere with the relationship.

While the desire for a home of one's own properly emerges with the change in the young adults' relations with their families, it can also arise primarily as a need to get away from unhappiness in the parental home. The parents' quarrels, their domination, the breakup of the parents' marriage after the children have grown, and countless such reasons can impel a young person to seek a spouse hastily. Statements that one hears from unhappily married people, such as "After that fight with my father, I would have married the first man that came along, and I suppose I did," may overlook the fact that the young woman seduced the first man she went out with and made him feel obligated to marry her. In a different context, the youth who is away from a small community for the first time, as for example after he is inducted into the army, feels intense loneliness without a home and may find a girl in the nearby town who behaves much more forwardly than any he knew before to be most desirable, and he cannot wait to marry her.

Sexual attraction and the impulsion of sexuality form a desired component of the decision to marry. Marriage not only provides an outlet for sexual expression but it permits a settling of sexuality so that finding a partner need no longer be a preoccupation or a constant occupation. Still, sexual need can lead to impetuous choice or unwittingly into a relationship that has few if any other virtues. The selection of a partner simply because of his or her sexual attractiveness to others not uncommonly derives from a need to gain prestige or bolster self-esteem through having an enviable partner. Anxieties concerning sexual adequacy can lead to a marriage undertaken primarily to assure the self of one's adequacy as a man or woman, or occasionally simply to conceal impotence or homosexuality from the world. A young woman who has considerable guilt over masturbation and who has some intermittent concerns that she might be homosexual because she recognizes her competitiveness with men and her jealousy of their friendships with each other, starts having casual affairs. Before long she compulsively sleeps with any college classmate who makes advances to her. When she finds a passive young man whom she can dominate and with whom she assumes a masculine role in intercourse, she leads him into marriage in the hope that it will stop her promiscuity. She does not recognize that he seeks to marry her because of his need to find a boyish girl in order to feel aroused, and soon after marriage she resents being treated as a boy rather than a woman. A college professor finds that his homosexual interests are creating suspicion on the campus and seeks to shield himself. He selects a woman he meets at a religious conference whom he believes has no interest in anything but spiritual matters. His inability to tolerate any physical closeness becomes unbearable to the wife, particularly as she married largely to have children. Such conscious use of marriage for self-protection or for selfish motives is not a rarity among disturbed persons.

The wish for security and to have someone who will provide support financially and emotionally is not only an appropriate part of marriage but can be an acceptable reason in itself, particularly when it is openly or tacitly understood by both persons, as when a widower with children marries a woman who wishes a home and to make a home for someone. It is less favorable when a girl becomes so fed up with her work in a factory or with being the target for the foreman's expectations that she sleep with him that she decides that marriage to the young man she has been trying to avoid is preferable to the insecurities and burdens of unmarried life. Ambition also often takes precedence over other motivations; and sometimes it is the ambition of the parents rather than of the person who is marrying. After all, marriage for wealth, career, opportunity, or social advancement has the sanction of ages when such motives were considered natural and proper, with each family or individual seeking the best opportunity and with love a secondary factor. While such reasons in themselves need not be injurious to a good marriage, when they are clearly the dominant motive partners whose wealth or prestige is being acquired may all too readily feel unwanted for themselves, or the spouses may feel obligated to act deferentially.

The wish for children, too, can form a primary rather than an adjunctive reason for marriage, with the choice of the spouse a secondary matter, and may eventually leave the spouse feeling neglected after the arrival of the child. A woman in her thirties who has had little opportunity to marry because she is contemptuous of men spends much time in fantasy about a son who will become a great musician such as she would have been if she had been born a male. She is intensely rivalrous with her sister, and when the sister has a child she attaches herself to a younger man and for the first time in her life becomes very seductive. The man's personality matters little except that she rightly feels she can lead him to the altar. Soon after the birth of the son this woman became very discontented with her husband's passivity and sought a divorce, feeling she had no need for him and resenting his attachment to her son.

Marriages are often enough precipitated by pregnancies, particularly in teenagers, only a small proportion of whom, as has already been pointed out, use reliable contraception, and who tend to seek abortion later in a pregnancy than older women. Reliable contraception and the availability of abortion lessen the need for such marriages, many of which soon end in divorce. However, in many instances the pregnancy only determines the time of a marriage between a couple who have already decided to marry or simply serves to chase away the last hesitancies of one or the other partner. Pregnancy has been a more or less customary—for one cannot say conventional—way for a girl to secure the man she wants but who avoids proposing or ignores her proposals. While surely leading to some satisfactory marriages when the girl knows her mind and perhaps her boyfriend's better than he does, the resentment or shame over being forced to marry can place a lasting blight over a marriage.

The Hostile Marriage

The expression of hostility through the act of marrying forms a common source of disastrous marriages. It is usually as destructive to the person who is being hostile as to the relatively innocent partner who has become involved. The hostile persons use themselves as weapons for gaining revenge, wishing others to suffer because they suffer. In the process they become the targets of their own animosities. The most obvious instances are marriages on the rebound, after the desired partner rejects or marries someone else. The hasty step may be carried out in order to regain self-esteem by feeling wanted and needed by someone, but it usually contains the intention of showing the rejecting person that he or she is not needed; and it contains the fantasy that the true love will realize his error and dash in at the last moment and insist he cannot live without her. The hostility over being rejected takes precedence over love and the person punishes the self for the hostility by making an inappropriate marriage, in a sense wishing the true love to suffer because the person is unhappy. Even when hostility does not dominate the picture, the marriage made hastily, before the disappointment has been worked through and assimilated, leaves the person dissatisfied with the spouse, and often involved for years with fantasies of the first true love whom the spouse can never match. A young woman who married hastily primarily to get away from home after her fiancé was killed in combat, insisted on wearing the engagement ring from her first fiancé until the moment she entered the church for her wedding. She lived through her first pregnancy fantasying that the dead man was the father of her child.

A different type of hostile marriage involves the expression of diffuse antagonisms toward members of the opposite sex, often provoked by envy. The person marries a dependent person and seeks to treat a subservient spouse sadistically. The marriage takes the form of a misplaced triumph over the hated enemy. A young woman had been aggressively homosexual during adolescence and in her early adult years. Her homosexuality had been determined in large part by her envy of her brothers who were obviously preferred by her mother. She eventually learned she could seduce and dominate some men by being a sexual tease just as easily as she could dominate certain women. She married a masochistic man whom she constantly teased and belittled sexually and she gained pleasure in being able to humiliate him in sexually perverse acts. In a somewhat similar manner a man who was bitterly hostile toward his mother became a specialist in wooing many girls until they seemed desperately in love with him and were willing to abase themselves sexually, and then rejected them. When he finally married he repeatedly stimulated and frustrated his wife sexually but expected her constantly to derogate herself and admire him.

Rescue Fantasies and Sadomasochistic Marriages

It may be useful to note the place of rescue fantasies in the choice of a partner, for they are particularly pertinent to the medical, nursing, and social work professions. Eliciting sympathy because of unfortunate life circumstances engenders in the other the fantasy that one can undo the harm and save the person from an unfortunate fate. A man feels impelled to rescue a girl from a home that is miserable because of an alcoholic father. He sees the girl's faults but believes that they are not really part of her and that he will change matters by providing love and care. Doctors are apt to confuse caring for patients with the desire to take care of them personally. A nurse may seek to marry a schizophrenic patient in the belief that her care will cure him. Such desires may often grow out of a lack of security in one's own attractiveness or sexual ability accompanied by the feeling that he or she has a right to marry only if it is a sacrifice to save the spouse.

Some of the types of marital choice that we have been discussing in the past few pages are often designated as sadomasochistic. The spouses unconsciously select partners whom they can hurt and who, in turn, will hurt them. They may argue, quarrel, fight, repeatedly injure each other's self-esteem and be chronically unhappy, but because of the interdigitating psychopathology they could not live intimately in any other type of relationship—one might almost say could not be happy in any other sort of marriage. In most such marriages, a sadist does not select a masochist, but rather both are sadomasochistic in varying proportions. One may behave sadistically under certain circumstances, and the other under different conditions. Each has vulnerabilities which the other rapidly uncovers and uses as a target for barbs and sallies. Frequently each is preoccupied with hurting the other to get even. The patterns usually do not involve sadistic perversions, and need not include physical violence, and the sadistic pleasure can even be gained through moral righteousness. A fundamentalist minister brought his wife to a psychiatric clinic because of her drinking. It soon became apparent that the minister habitually and sanctimoniously caused his wife to consider herself a sinner because of her sexual desires, and because she had not been "saved" by an inner revelation as he had been. He had, indeed, treated her very much like a servant. The wife, in turn, hurt him and gained vengeance by being "ill" with "alcoholism," which she manifested primarily by attending services and church socials in an intoxicated state. Her behavior permitted her husband to feel even more pious and self-sacrificing because of his tolerance of her illness, which he dealt with, however, as if it were a visitation of Satan that marked his wife as selected for damnation whereas he had been elected for salvation.

Largely because of such sadomasochistic marriages, in which the conflict and hurt really serves the unconscious needs of both partners, there has been a strong tendency on the part of psychiatrists to consider that virtually all such marital choices serve some fundamental personality needs of the persons who make these seemingly unfortunate selections. The partners find their complementary mate intuitively; through their interaction during courtship; or perhaps most commonly because of resemblances to parents who had been involved in such sadomasochistic relationships throughout the person's childhood. Indeed, one may gain the impression that for some persons marriage means a sadomasochistic relationship because of the homes in which they were reared, and that they seek a spouse who will fill the necessary role to create a marriage similar to those of their parents. Nevertheless, as noted earlier in the chapter, the concept that all unhappy marital choices serve the unconscious needs of the spouses can be overdone and applied inappropriately. The marital choice serves a purpose, but as we have been saying, there are factors other than unconscious needs that can lead into an unhappy marriage.

Young people, in particular, are apt to disregard the family of the intended spouse, insisting that they are not marrying the family. While this is true enough, it is also clear that one of the best indicators of a future happy marriage is whether or not the person comes from a stable and happy home. Divorce runs in families as much as certain hereditary illnesses. In a sense, of course, one is marrying the family insofar as the spouse is the product of the parents and the way in which he or she has been raised in the family.

The choice of the suitable partner clearly presents difficulties, and it has been possible only to indicate the importance of a suitable choice and some of the types of difficulties that commonly arise. The choice of the partner constitutes the major decision of a supposedly voluntary nature that can complement and alter the personality makeup and afford opportunities for self-completion before the production of a new generation. In contemporary society the marriage leads to the fusion of two persons necessary to produce offspring and to furnish the family milieu in which they grow up. While offering opportunities that should help them to mature, the decision and selection rest upon the outcome of each person's development in a family. They are impelled by sexual feelings and other needs for affinity. The frustrations of the oedipal bonds in the family of origin lead to the search for completion in marriage, and the marital choice is apt to reflect the many unconscious problems of the intrafamilial oedipal situation. It turns backward as well as into the future and thus is particularly prone to regressive or neurotic determination. It can include such motives as the effort to undo and redo childhood unhappiness; to live in the present in terms of infantile and childhood situations that are no longer appropriate; the holding of expectations from a spouse that are more suited to a parent; the search for narcissistic gratification as an admired child rather than wishing to share and to direct the marriage for mutual satisfaction. The entire matter of choice of a marriage partner is so closely linked with the entire personality development that the choice forms a distinctive measure of the total outcome of the process. Perhaps it was simpler when the decision did not rest upon the individual partners and less was expected of marriage and the blame for its shortcomings did not fall so heavily upon the couple itself.

REFERENCES

Bossard, J. H. S. (1932–1933). "Residential Propinquity as a Factor in Marriage Selection," *American Journal of Sociology*, 38:219–224.

Burgess, E., and Locke, H. (1945). *The Family: From Institution to Companionship*, p. 390. American Book, New York.

CARTER, H., and GLICK, P. (1970). *Marriage and Divorce: A Social and Economic Study.* Harvard University Press, Cambridge, Mass.

FREUD, S. (1914). "On Narcissism," in *The Standard Edition of the Complete Psychological Works of Sigmund Freud,* vol. 14. Hogarth Press, London, 1957.

HAMILTON, G. (1929). *A Research in Marriage.* Boni Publications, New York.

KATZ, A., and HILL, R. (1958). "Residential Propinquity and Marital Selection: A Review of Theory, Method, and Fact," *Marriage and Family Living,* 20:27–35.

ROTHCHILD, J., and WOLF, S. (1976). *Children of the Counterculture.* Doubleday & Co., New York.

SUGGESTED READING

BURCHINAL, L. (1964). "The Premarital Dyad and Love Involvement," in *Handbook of Marriage and the Family.* T. Christensen, ed. Rand McNally, Chicago.

SUSSMAN, M., ed. (1975). "The Second Experience: Variant Family Forms and Life Styles." Special issue of *The Family Coordinator,* Journal of Education, Counseling and Services of the National Council on Family Relations, vol. 24, no. 4 (October).

CHAPTER 14

✿

Marital Adjustment

THE TOPIC of marital adjustment is often taken to refer to the couple's sexual adjustment. Even though the sexual adjustment is of vital moment to the future of the marriage, the subject has much broader ramifications. It involves the requisite shifts within each person— within the personality of each—that make possible the necessary interrelationship that proximates a coalition; it concerns the finding of reciprocally interrelating roles that permit the meshing of activities with minimal friction; it includes the reorganization of the family patterns which each spouse learned at home, and which may involve differing ethnic and social class patterns, into a workable social system; it concerns how the childhood family romance of each partner can find consummation. The achievement of a sexual union that satisfies the erotic needs of both partners fosters mutuality and can lessen the tensions that mount in each partner and the strains in the relationship that must inevitably arise. In general, it can be the lubricant that eases friction. It often serves as a sensitive indicator of the maturity of each partner and of their capacity to interrelate on an intimate and adult level. Yet it is but part of the total relationship, and it will pall if it is not emergent from a satisfying and fulfilling interpersonal relationship.

When a marriage gets off to a good start, it forms a stabilizing influence for both spouses and a new opportunity for self-realization. Life becomes a new adventure filled with opportunity to live out what has long been imagined. Both partners relish having the other so interested in their well-being and feel secure in being the center of the spouse's interest and love. Activity, thought, and fantasy have a new tangible and legitimate focus which gives a new coherence to one's life. The companionship banishes loneliness, and sexual satisfaction beings a sense of release and fulfillment that mobilizes energies for the pursuit of incentives derived from the marriage. Many new tasks provide novelty. During separation between breakfast and supper, which can seem very long, the thoughts of each turn toward the other, sharing in fantasy until rejoined. The freedom of sexual intimacy and mutual exploration lends excitement which, in turn, leads to a new-found calm. Each partner makes mistakes and is apt to misunderstand, but evidence of love negates any intent to hurt. The glow of the first months of marriage, with its romantic and even unrealistic overassessment by the spouses of each other, can provide an opportunity for the couple to gain a true familiarity with one another, to gain reciprocal roles, to learn how to share their lives.

However, even the best-matched couples encounter difficulties in adjusting to the new life together. The harmonious transition from honeymoon to ordinary life is often hampered by various disagreements and disappointments that can mount to resentment and regrets over the commitment. Most couples are well aware that such difficulties are likely to arise and feel determined that they will not happen in their marriage. The potential sources of friction are legion, and there seems no reason to try to catalogue these common sources of irritation which can mount to chronic disappointment or discord when one or both partners feel the other is selfish and does not reciprocate in investing effort and showing concern for the other. Topics that the couple have difficulties in discussing because they seem so intensely personal, such as sexual desires and dissatisfactions (which will be discussed later in the chapter), personal hygiene, or jealousies of parents-in-law, can become serious sources of resentment. These early months can contain periods of trial when each spouse may wonder about the wisdom of the marriage and experience anxiety about the future.* Even when things go very badly the newlyweds are reluctant to let others know

---

* J. Landis (1946) classified the major areas that are likely to be divisive as "religion, social life, mutual friends, in-laws, money, and sex relations," which seems fairly inclusive; but W. Goode (1956) also considers as important: drinking, triangles, gambling, helling around, value differences, etc. Many of these are symptomatic difficulties—either of the emotional instability or immaturity of one or both partners or of failure to achieve compatibility and a mutually satisfactory reciprocity and sexual adjustment.

of their plight, and will suffer in quiet resentment and despair before falling back on parents or friends for advice as they might desperately wish to do.

The marriage ceremony is not the end of the story as it is in so many romantic novels, and most couples are very aware that it only marks the beginning of a new stage of life in which happiness or contentment must be achieved rather than simply expected as a consequence of the marriage. However, those adolescent girls and young women for whom finding a suitable husband has been a major goal may forget that it is but a means toward achieving a rounded life. Relatively few women now stop their vocational and educational activities simply to live as housewives, and those who do may soon become bored, irritated that their husbands do not continue to provide excitement, and worried about the emptiness of their days; those women may decide somewhat prematurely to have a child to bring meaning to the marriage rather than as a product of marital fulfillment.

THE EFFECT OF MARRIAGE ON PERSONALITY STRUCTURE

A successful marriage will usually both lead to and require a marked reorganization of the personality structure of each partner that will influence the further personality development of each. The marriage necessitates forming a union in which certain functions are shared, others undertaken by one spouse, and in which some aspects of individuality are renounced. Certain facets and traits of the personality will be developed further and others fade as the personality configuration changes in relation to a new most significant person. The nature of such personality reorganization is difficult to state coherently but may be elucidated through considering the changes somewhat schematically in terms of the *structural concept*.

The ego functioning of each spouse must expand in marriage to consider the other as well as the self, and also the marriage as an entity. Optimally, the spouse becomes an alter ego whose desires, needs, and well-being are considered on a par with one's own, and whose opinions and ideas are taken into account in reaching decisions affecting spheres of common interest. Many wives continue to place their husbands' occupation before their own, but compromises must be made when both are pursuing careers. If a working couple adhere to a traditional division of tasks in the home, the wife will have far less free time than the husband; and many couples now seek a more equitable division of roles and household work. Consideration of the spouse involves small matters as well as major decisions, and indeed becomes an inherent part of a way of life. The wife cooks the hamburgers her husband likes rather than the artichoke salad she would prefer. The choice of a movie involves weighing the intensity of the preferences of each. The purchase of a house and the selection of a neighborhood in which to live cannot be the sole decision of one partner without creating difficulties. The couple realize that they have become interdependent in many areas and that the well-being of each is bound up with the contentment of the other. It is not a matter of the willingness of one to sacrifice for the sake of the spouse. Self-sacrifice leads to masochistic attitudes that can slip over into punishment of the other through suffering. In the intimate relationship of marriage, each member finds a major reward in the comfort, absence of tension, and warmth of affection achieved when the spouse feels relaxed and happy; and each strives, consciously and unconsciously, for this reward. The situation is analogous to the process through which the infant and mother achieve mutuality, discussed in Chapter 5. The process requires more than intent and the desire to please, for it cannot transpire without an understanding of the needs and preferences of the other, recognition of what is crucial to the happiness of the other as well as to one's own, and an ability not to confuse the other's preferences—which can be set aside—with the other's needs. As women have usually become more attuned than men to interpersonal relations as they grow up, the wife is usually more sensitive than her husband to the other's ways and needs; but men, too, can learn the rewards of meeting another person's needs. It is when one or both partners give up efforts to achieve such satisfaction from the marriage that difficulties become serious; and when efforts to gain one's way through bargaining, the use of various wiles, gamesmanship, or deceit become prominent (Bernard, 1964).

The superego directives of each partner also change to meet the superego standards and cope with the id impulses of the spouse. Each partner grew up with differing parental and societal directives that have been internalized as superego directives. A husband may be placed under new standards by his acceptance of his wife's aspirations for him; or modify his drinking patterns because of his wife's attitudes about alcohol which she assimilated from her mother; or his wife's superego may permit him to overcome repressions fostered by his own superego restrictions and engage in sexual behavior which previously had been barred even from his fantasy. We may note that the tragedy of Macbeth unrolls as Macbeth's superego injunctions against regicide are overcome by his wife, who has fewer conscious scruples in the way of her ambition; and her taunts of his weakness and cowardice vanquish his conscience. Indeed, a spouse's value system will usually markedly modify the value systems derived from parents which initially formed the foundations of the superego directives. Discrepancies between these two major sources of behavioral guidance can create considerable conflict within the individual, between spouses, and between a spouse and in-laws.

Alterations in the expression permitted to id impulses follow as a consequence of modification of the superego; but other influences are also effective. Consideration of the partner's sexual urges are clearly basic to a satisfactory sexual adjustment. Persons will, at times, be motivated to sexual activity by their spouses rather than by their own urges. A new freedom in giving vent to sexual drives follows the availability of a sexual outlet that is not only permitted by society and parents but is even an obligation. The release of interests tied up in conjunction with sexual repression extends beyond the area of sexuality and provides new energies that can be turned to constructive uses and permit the development of a more harmonious and rounded personality. The aggressive and self-preservative drives of the spouse are also important; it is obvious that efforts to keep a spouse's aggression minimal are important aspects of marital adjustment. The *ego defenses* that the partner utilizes in order to control id impulses must also be respected lest the partner's ensuing anxiety create serious problems. Of course, certain defenses—such as a wife's obsessive cleanliness that restricts her husband's activities, or a husband's projections of blame onto his wife—can create considerable marital difficulty. Still, a husband or wife frequently accepts a spouse's peculiarities as well as defenses as perfectly reasonable in order to maintain harmony. Thus, a young wife was willing to adhere to a rigidly restrictive diet even though she was not obese in order to placate her husband, who needed her to have a boyish figure to stimulate him sexually. Many married persons rapidly learn what they must do or not do in order to avoid angering the partner, even if the partner's need seems very unreasonable.

The personality may also change gradually after marriage because of a shift in identification models, notably by taking on characteristics and standards of a parent-in-law. A young attorney whose father had been a farmer married the daughter of a federal judge. He soon began to resemble his father-in-law in many ways, in his gestures and intonations as well as in his politics and ambitions. His admiration of his father-in-law may have been a determinant of his marriage, but his wife had probably been attracted to him because she saw in him characteristics that resembled her father's—and she unconsciously fostered the development of these traits in her husband. In the process the young attorney acquired an identification that began to direct his career. Indeed, the German adage that a man's career is commonly continued by his son-in-law recognizes the woman's tendency to fall in love with a man who is like her father.

Some women, however, ambitious for themselves through having competent husbands, may have had to compromise and marry men who do not live up to their aspirations; and others, who wish to shape their husbands, marry less forceful and more malleable men. Difficulties can then ensue because the wife sets out to remake her husband in the image of her own ideal, which may be difficult for the husband to tolerate, for directly or indirectly his own sense of adequacy is being undermined, and his potency may decline as well, either because of his feelings of inadequacy or as a means of passive rebelliousness.

THE TRANSFERENCE OF PARENTAL TRAITS
TO THE SPOUSE

Almost everyone tends to "transfer" parental attributes to a spouse because the relatedness to the parents forms the foundations for relationships with other intensely significant persons. These transferences lead to some blurring of the marital relationship when spouses are seen more in the image of the parent than as they really are. Indeed, herein lies the source of many neurotic marital conflicts, and it is often complicated by the choice of a person who actually fills the shoes of the parent. On the one hand, a person may be upset when the spouse does not remain true to the needed image and breaks the illusion; on the other, undesirable traits of a parent are attributed to a spouse erroneously. A newly married woman, for example, became upset and punitively withdrawn whenever her husband took a cocktail before dinner and infuriated when he took two. She expected her husband to become abusive after a few drinks, drift away from home after dinner, and come home intoxicated late at night. Only during psychotherapy did she realize that nothing in her husband's past or present behavior warranted her fears and anger. She had married a man who had some resemblances to her father, and who she thought had her father's good traits without his tendency to go on alcoholic sprees that had created many anxiety-filled nights for her family during her childhood. The husband's taking of a cocktail had mobilized concerns about the imminence of divorce that neither she nor her husband had been able to understand. A common source of impaired communication lies in such misinterpretation of even minor signs in terms of parental behavior. A man accustomed to his mother's resentment whenever he was late for supper, enters his own home with a chip on his shoulder whenever he is late and starts counter-attacking as he opens the door. He has no chance to find out that his wife has been awaiting him calmly and cheerfully, for as the daughter of a general practitioner whose hours were very irregular she did not, like his mother, expect her husband to appear on schedule.

The narcissistic needs of a husband or wife for unceasing admiration also usually reflect ways of relating to a parent of the opposite sex. A husband may need his wife to support his masculinity by admiring his athletic prowess or his charm with women as had his mother. A wife who had been her father's favorite, who had been pampered and praised for her beauty, and had usually been able to "twist her father around her finger" by her seductive behavior, expected her husband to continue to admire her beauty and stop whatever he was doing to fondle her whenever she flirted with him, as he had done during their courtship. She felt hurt when he criticized her poor cooking and lackadaisical housekeeping and when he could not be sidetracked by her pouts and seductive twirls. Further mis-understandings arose when her husband failed to realize that his wife's display of her nude body before a mirror was for her own admiration or to elicit praise from him rather than an invitation to have sexual relations.

The Parental Roles of Spouses

Such examples of difficulties that may result from transferring parental attributes to a spouse should not be misconstrued to indicate that the wish for a spouse to fill something of a parental role is necessarily neurotic or detrimental to a marriage. Indeed, a marriage encompasses desires to complete the family romance that had to be frustrated in the family of origin. Even mature persons seek something of a parent in a spouse. It is a matter of the proper balance of such needs. Even a husband who can be decisive on his own and unhesitatingly accept the responsibility for his wife and family will welcome a maternal nurturant attitude from his wife when he is ill or disheartened. The capacity of a spouse to be protectively and affectionately parental and conversely to be able to permit the other to provide solace can be particularly important during times of stress, disappointment, or loss, when the disturbed spouse can feel troubles dissolve through receiving tangible evidence of being loved or wanted. The ability of a couple to sustain one another and give of themselves during times of difficulty is a critical aspect of any marriage.

We have been examining how the personalities of persons alter in marriage and how their "structures" change through the interrelationship. The changes involve something of a fusion of the personalities in which each gives up some aspects of independence for the benefits of a new interdependence. Of course, unless individuality and individual interests remain, there can scarcely be a meaningful and lasting interrelatedness. Still, in forming the coalition both spouses leave themselves vulnerable to feeling incomplete if the other is lost, and they accept the risk of giving themselves in expectation of receiving in return—a commitment that can lead to profound hurt.

MECHANISMS OF DEFENSE OF THE MARRIAGE

The coalescing of personalities and the dependency upon a spouse often lead to a remarkable inability to perceive a spouse's faults and mistakes. We frequently find one partner constructing defenses to cover a spouse's weaknesses rather than to defend the person's own ego. When the attachment is needed greatly one partner may construct a whole array of defenses against the recognition of something that could disrupt the relationship. A woman who had waited three years for her husband's return from overseas combat duty during World War II blossomed when she had news that he was finally en route home. Yet within two weeks of his return she was suffering from an agitated depression and was profoundly delusional. She had been orphaned early in life and had fallen in love with her husband and idolized him while still in her early teens. She had never recognized that he could be difficult, stubborn, and insensitive, even though he was brilliant, competent, and a strong father figure. In the hospital she castigated herself for not feeling adequate love for her husband. She could think of no sources for her current unhappiness until she was urged to re-create in detail just what had happened upon her husband's return. Then she recalled that his first words when they met on the pier were "My, but you've grown older," and after their first sexual union he remarked, "Is this what I've been waiting three years for?"

The need to defend the partner and accept his beliefs can extend to become a *folie à deux*, which in minor forms is far from uncommon among married couples. An attorney, after losing a local election which he considered critical to his career, believed that the mayor who had been his close friend was responsible for his defeat. His friends and relatives could not persuade him that the mayor had extended himself to try to secure his election. His bitterness reached delusional proportions when he believed that the mayor was sabotaging his legal practice. His wife, otherwise a very sensible woman, shared his animosity and became enraged at her relatives when they tried to convince her that her husband was in error and that they were being unjust and hurting themselves in defaming the mayor.

THE FUSION OF THE FAMILIES OF ORIGIN

The interrelationship of two persons to form a marital unit involves the reorganization and fusion of the influences of both of their families of origin. The families in which they were reared have been incorporated into their personalities and all persons retain many attitudes originating in their families concerning marital roles, marriage as an institution, and the value of family life. Further, the family of origin incorporated the values, mores, and sentiments of its ethnic, religious, and social class origins and each spouse carries such cultural values and mores into the marriage. Such considerations are particularly important in the United States where marriages often cross the various cultural boundaries and where the new family gains cohesion and form through the blending of the two personalities rather than through merging into a network of kinfolk (see Chapter 2). The greater the divergency of backgrounds, the greater difficulty the couple may find in achieving a satisfactory reciprocal relationship.*

The couple share the tasks of the marriage and the roles they fill according to their own dispositions, particularly before they have children, but they have expectations of how to move into reciprocally interrelating roles that derive from the patterns in their families of origin, which each may

---

* However, in some respects persons from educated backgrounds from different countries and cultures may have more in common than persons of widely differing socio-economic classes within the same country.

believe are the natural and proper way of doing things. When couples decide to share household tasks between them, they are unlikely to have any models to follow and must make conscious shared decisions about what each partner will do. As tasks such as housecleaning, laundering, and cooking are still not carried out with much spontaneity by many men, wives may resent their husbands' dilatory, if not refractory, participation in their agreement. However, even when the couple adhere to more or less conventional patterns, there can still be marked discrepancies that lead to conflict. Many personality clashes in marriage are basically clashes between such role expectations. A marriage between a Midwestern Lutheran man and a Catholic woman of Irish and German extraction encountered serious difficulties from its inception despite the husband's premarital agreement not to interfere with his wife's Catholicism and to permit their children to be raised in her faith. He later insisted that having grown up in a small farming community composed entirely of Protestants, he had no idea that Catholicism was a way of life as well as a religion. In seeking to follow his own Germanic family pattern in which his father had completely dominated the family, he became infuriated when his wife placed the dictates of the Church above his wishes. He was angered when she went to confession, considering that their life was no concern of the priest's, and he resented her insistence on attending morning Mass when he expected her to be serving breakfast to him. Even though the wife was willing to modify her religious practices, she soon found that she felt uncomfortable and insecure when deprived of the pattern.

Reciprocal Versus Collateral Marital Roles

There are some fundamental differences in families that can be very difficult to bridge, particularly if the spouses are unaware of the great differences in their orientations to family life. In somewhat simplified form we may consider that the contemporary urban American family tends to rest upon companionship between the spouses and finds its stability from the couple's finding reciprocal interactional patterns agreeable to both; but other families, including many in lower socioeconomic groups, tend to find stability in an institutional pattern common to many cultural groups in which the roles of husband and wife are parallel or collateral rather than interactional. In the collateral type of family the husband and wife each have sets of functions and roles to carry out, and the marriage is more concerned with a way of sharing the tasks of life and having a home in which to rear children than with providing companionship for the spouses. Such nuclear families are likely to be part of a more extended family system (see Chapter 2 and Bott, 1955). In these families the spouses gain support and definition for their lives by having rather clear-cut roles to fill and tasks to carry out and from interrelating with the larger family group rather than from the companionship and personal support of the spouse. Even when persons who have emerged from collateral families have modified their views by contacts with the more common companionship type that is portrayed in motion pictures and stories, residues are likely to remain that can interfere with their finding harmonious relationships with spouses raised in isolated nuclear families. Thus, a young woman from a New England Protestant family married a man of Greek Orthodox extraction who considered himself liberated from the old traditions. However, the wife became upset when he took it for granted that he would spend much of his free time in coffeehouses with male friends, whereas he objected to her passing an evening with a bridge club rather than with his sisters.

Autonomy of the Family

The highly mobile self-sufficient family made necessary by contemporary industrial society requires that the primary allegiance of each marital partner shift from the parental to the marital family; that the center of gravity, so to speak, be established within the nuclear family; and that decision-making functions be assumed by the couple. However, the interference of parents in a marriage and the use of parents as a major source of security are common disruptive forces in marriages. A New York family had not really become a unit even after fifteen years of marriage and the birth of three children. The husband complained that his wife placed more importance on her mother and sisters than on him. She refused to move away from an apartment house in which her mother and married sisters lived, even though this required the husband to travel two hours to work each morning. The sisters spent a large part of the day together and it was a rare evening when one of the sisters was not in the apartment. The wife discussed each family quarrel with her sisters and consulted them before any major family decisions were made. The wife agreed with her husband's account but insisted that his devotion to his mother was largely responsible for the situation. He spent two evenings a week with his mother and usually expressed his mother's views rather than his own when they argued. She complained that because of her husband's neglect she could not have tolerated the marriage without her family's company and help in raising the children. Fortunately, with professional help, both managed to see that their attention and loyalty to their original families had never permitted their own marriage to become firmly established.

EQUITY IN MARRIAGE

As we have noted, a large proportion of young married women continue in the occupations outside the home, at least until shortly before the first child is born. Many husbands, in turn, seek to help with the household work; and increasingly agreements are made concerning a reasonably equitable division of tasks. We must realize, however, that the majority of working wives, perhaps seventy-five percent or more, do not desire their husbands' help with domestic work. They continue in the tradition which gives precedence to their husbands' emotional needs and satisfactions with their marriages. Women's expectations are changing, but up to now problems of redistribution of roles and tasks exist largely among college graduates, and particularly in dual-career marriages. Women who are pursuing careers almost always expect a reasonably equitable sharing of domestic tasks, and marry men who expect to help them with household work, if not share it with them.

Even when the couple can decide just what each will do in carrying out the essential tasks of a married couple—earning money, cooking, cleaning, ironing, etc.—problems are very likely to arise. As the Rapoports (1975) point out, even though great strides have been made toward political, economic, and ideological equality of the sexes, the issues surrounding equity in the family sphere have only begun to be touched. Relatively few men have been brought up to be efficient housekeepers or cooks; or to consider dusting or sewing as their jobs or as men's work. Proper housekeeping requires considerable skill. Many men do not know where dust collects, or note the scuff marks on the flooring. It takes time to learn and a desire to learn. Husbands are apt to help their wives with domestic chores rather than take the active responsibility for specific tasks, as is necessary for equitable division of labor. Many prefer to mow the lawn, wash windows, make repairs, etc., but leave the daily repetitive nitty-gritty to their wives.

Even if an equitable distribution is carried out, some husbands who consciously are willing and conscientiously do the cooking, sewing or ironing find themselves losing their self-esteem—in some instances to the extent of affecting their potency—when they occupy themselves with tasks that they and society have considered feminine. Similarly, some wives, even though they ardently wish to have a career, may become unhappy when their husbands measure them in terms of grades, completing a thesis, promotions, or earning capacity. Such emotional strains may require conscious recognition in dividing up the tasks of living to achieve equity in marriage. The Rapoports (1975) have found the concept of "identity tension–line" useful in understanding how far a couple can go in establishing and assuming identities that differ from sociocultural definitions of male and female identities. When discomfort and irritability in carrying out a role or task arise, the spouse may be expressing the sentiment "this is as far as I can go in experimenting with a new definition of sex-roles without having it 'spill over' into my own psychological sense of self-esteem" (Rapoport and Rapoport, 1975, p. 428). It may be dangerous to an individual's emotional health or to the integrity of a marriage to push oneself beyond such limits or for the husband or wife to insist that the spouse do so. The balance between the couple can be redressed in some other way, or at some later period in the marriage. Indeed, when tit-for-tat bargaining must be carried out and young spouses are each defending their rights rather than seeking mutuality, other areas of married life are usually very unsatisfactory.*

The problems related to equity between marital partners can, with a modicum of good will, usually be solved even in a dual-career marriage as long as the couple are childless. More difficult and realistic problems arise when there are children, which concern what kind of offspring the couple wish to produce as well as the continuity of both careers—but we shall consider such difficulties in the next chapter.

MARRIAGE AS A SUPPORT

The capacities to adjust to marriage and the potential for growth through marriage depend upon the successful passage through prior development stages, particularly upon having gained during adolescence a suitable iden-

---

* An extreme was seen in a young couple who sought therapeutic help. They had argued vehemently over which of them would carry out each household task and had reached an impasse over carrying out the garbage. They had then both kept their own garbage in a separate container, and carried out their own garbage cans.

tity as an individual reasonably independent from parents, and capacities for intimacy. Nevertheless, many marriages between persons who have not had an unblemished passage through prior developmental stages, and who may even be rather seriously impaired, are adequately successful. "An arch," wrote Leonardo, "is a strength built out of two opposing weaknesses." Couples who are fortunate have unconsciously sought out and found partners with complementary needs. A woman who feels unable to empathize with babies and make decisions about children's needs finds a man with strong maternal tendencies and who, as an oldest child, has had considerable experience in helping raise his younger siblings. Some partners know that they each have shortcomings and try to help one another manage. Indeed, even marriages between mature persons are helped when each knows that he or she is far from perfect and does not expect perfection from the spouse. Some persons marry knowing that the marriage will be difficult, but believe that it will be better than life alone. Marriage provides an integrating force, not only because of support from the partner, but also because it provides tangible tasks to cope with, rather definite roles to take on, and a position within society. However, even though personality problems can be helped by marriage, they more commonly create difficulties, for marriage presupposes reasonable independence, a secure ego identity, and capacities for intimacy from each partner.

THE SEXUAL ADJUSTMENT

A mutually satisfying sexual relationship, while not essential to a satisfactory marriage, is usually critical to marital happiness. Currently, in marriages that rest on the interaction between spouses and on companionship, the sexual goal of both partners is to experience orgasm, which not only offers relief from tension but ecstatic pleasure enhanced by providing a similar experience for the spouse. The release and enjoyment of a good sexual relationship smooths away the rough edges of the minor incompatibilities that occur in every marriage and the frictions that arise in daily living. Sexual incompatibility will usually reflect disturbances in other areas of the marriage that have engendered resentments, anxieties, fears, and even loathing that virtually eliminate the potentialities of achieving sexual harmony. Various personality disturbances may interfere with participation in the sexual act or enjoyment of it; some of these problems have been discussed in previous chapters under the following topics: achievement of capacities for intimacy, attainment of a secure gender identity, and the gaining of adequate independence from parental authority.

Early Sexual Problems

As many, if not most, persons who now marry are no longer virginal and many couples have attained a satisfactory sexual relationship prior to marriage, a discussion of problems of sexual adjustment may have more properly been placed in the chapter on adolescence. However, many couples still wait until marriage to consummate their relationship sexually, and still others have married despite sexual difficulties, or because one partner has concealed the lack of satisfaction from the other. In any case, it is convenient to be old-fashioned and imagine that the couple are relatively inexperienced sexually, at least with one another, when they marry or decide to form a permanent relationship.

Some difficulties in sexual adjustment frequently occur in the early days of the marriage as reflections of inexperience, ignorance, sensitivities, and difficulties in communication that can be overcome by collaborative effort when pertinent advice is available. If uncorrected, such early maladjustments can freeze into chronicity or deepen into serious incompatibilities, spilling over and blighting any chances for a happy marriage. The husband who has had difficulty with his potency becomes fearful of rebuff, resentful of his bride who does not or cannot help him, and worried about his masculinity, withdraws; the bride who is tense and finds intercourse painful and disappointing seeks to avoid coitus. The topic of sexual adjustment in marriage has endless ramifications; here, we shall be concerned only with difficulties which frequently arise early in marriage and which are not necessarily due to severe individual personality disturbances or which are reflections of notable incompatibilities in other areas of the marital relationship.

The physician, nurse, clinical psychologist, and social worker require knowledge of the sexual act and the problems that interfere with its satisfactory consummation. People may go to the clergyman or the attorney with other problems arising in marriage, but they tend to turn to the physician, nurse, or marital counselor for help with sexual problems. Further, alert physicians find that many physical complaints that bring patients to them are essentially displacements of sexual problems. All too frequently physicians are not authorities on sexual matters, and may give advice according to stereotyped concepts, or according to what their particular socioeconomic and ethnic groups deem proper and satisfactory. Sexuality in practical, everyday marital terms has only recently become part of the medical curriculum, yet patients are very likely to regard the physician, and particularly the gynecologist, as someone who has learned all about such matters. But gynecologists, with some exceptions, are notably uninterested in patients' personal problems, or in their sexual difficulties, except those stemming from anatomical and endocrine pathology.

The Victorian Heritage

I have some hesitancy in writing about sexual adjustment in marriage, which has been the subject of many popular treatises, because recent studies have made it clear that even widely recognized authorities have offered considerable erroneous and even harmful advice based upon folklore and pet preconceptions rather than upon scientific foundations. Sexuality is not a topic that benefited greatly from the scientific revolution, until the studies of Masters and Johnson (1966), remaining under the extensive repression that had been our heritage of the Victorian period. Havelock Ellis and Freud sought to sweep away the barriers, but even they promulgated erroneous concepts which their reputations have helped perpetuate.* Residues of this morality still linger in current mores; and though it still influences the formal ethics, it has been pretty well shattered as far as upper-middle-class society is concerned. However, white lower socioeconomic groups still are affected by it. Sexual mores vary widely with socioeconomic class and ethnic grouping.

Intimacy and Sexuality

Sexual compatibility forms a critical measure of two persons' capacities to achieve true intimacy. It forms a test of the security and stability of personality development. Here, individuals must perform very much on their own and achieve without the support of their parents. They may

---

* The emergence from the peculiarities of Victorian morality has taken over half a century—and we now find that even much of the enlightenment that started in the 1920s continued many errors that arose in reaction to the excessive prudery of the Victorian. The Victorian mores were probably unusual with their notions that a proper "lady" would not be interested in sex: that she would not think about it and certainly would not talk about it. Indeed, there was the connotation that enjoyment of sex would be improper. She would accommodate herself to her husband and would wish to have children, but she would not expect fidelity from him but be relieved if he had a mistress who provided for his sexual needs. Ibsen's *A Doll's House* and *Ghosts* cannot be understood out of the context of this morality, nor Strindberg's *A Madman's Defense*. It is also inherent in Shaw's early play *Misalliance*.

blame parents for difficulties, but it will help little; but the ability to turn to the spouse for help, or for both to work through problems together, can be decisive. People feel that sexual abilities are somehow a reflection of something very basic in them; and each spouse feels revealed as well as naked before the other.

The proper carrying out of the sexual act and the enjoyment of it involves an ability to give way to the irrational, the timeless, the purely animal in one: it includes a loss of individuality in a temporary fusion with another. It contains the potentiality of leaving behind the tensions of civilization as one loosens the bonds to reality to float again in the purely sensuous. Here, one needs to be unabashed by the nakedness of impulse and drive, by recrudescence of the infantile and the revealing of much that one has sought to hide from others. The woman requires a capacity to rescind control and give way before an ecstasy that seems to threaten to overwhelm and annihilate her by its very intensity. The man needs to have moved beyond fear of reincorporation into the mother, a fear of engulfment by the womb. The sexual act contains a definite and direct relationship to infantile relatedness to the mother, with a renewed interest in sucking, in odor, in skin eroticism; and a reawakening of old forbidden desires to explore and play with orifices. So very much that has been learned needs to be undone; much that has been forbidden and long repressed and kept unconscious but that haunted dreams and masturbatory fantasies needs to be released to permit sexual intimacy and enjoyment and to allow fulfillment rather then provoke shame and guilt. The very good sexual adjustment demands such abilities to reverse the socialization process—and yet to permit the individual to be secure in the feeling that the regression and reversal will be only temporary and not reclaim the self.

Fortunately, the strength of the sexual drive is great, and to some extent the movements used in the sexual act are inherent, firmly built into the organism. When the partners are reasonably mature and desire one another, they can usually work through the difficulties and with patience find a unique source of profound pleasure as a shared experience that heightens their love. It provides relief from tensions and a total absorption that obliterates concern and can lead a couple to believe that no other pair has experienced similar pleasure and that they are uniquely matched. The fulfillment binds them closer, whereas frustration tends to separate them as their urges crave satisfaction.

A college education and even a modicum of sexual experience premaritally are no assurance that the individual is knowledgeable or has had any experience that was remotely satisfactory; and sometimes a person who has functioned well premaritally experiences difficulties with a spouse. A couple who had lived together before marriage for two years among Bohemian friends and had a highly enjoyable sexual relationship encountered difficulties almost immediately after legalizing the relationship when the husband frequently was unable to have an erection with his wife, and then sought to reassure himself about his masculinity by having extramarital relationships. He could no more consider his wife as a sexual object than he had been able to think of his mother as having sexual relations.

The Marriage Night

The bridal bed of the marriage night is frequently far from an optimal place for the consummation of the marriage. The long anticipation, the fatigue, intoxication, and anxiety can interfere with the act, and set off a chain of unfortunate consequences. According to medical and psychiatric tradition, the bride may be so pained and shocked by the trauma of having her hymen ruptured that she can become bitterly resentful toward her husband and fearful of further sexual experiences.* Such concerns have led virginal brides to have dilatations prior to marriage—sometimes upon the urging of the gynecologist from whom they sought contraceptive advice. However, other factors are more likely to impede adequate performance and undermine the confidence of either in his or her capacities.

The husband's concerns over his adequacy turn toward his ability to have an erection and maintain it sufficiently long to satisfy his wife, and often, about whether or not he will be able to have coitus frequently enough. Stories of impotence and premature ejaculation may trouble him, particularly as many men have had such difficulties on some occasions. The wife will be concerned with her responsivity—with whether or not she will be frigid, whether she will be able to have an orgasm and even if she will behave in a proper manner, not knowing just what a proper manner should be. At present, she may be more concerned about not seeming adequately

---

* A Greek epitaph reads:

> At the bridal bed of star-crossed Petale
> Hades, not Hymen, stood: for as she fled
> Alone through the night, dreading love's first stroke
> (as virgins will), the brutal watchdogs seized her.
> And we, whose morning hope had been a wife,
> Found scarce enough of her body for burial.
>   Antiphanes the Macedonian

(Translated by Dudley Fitts in *Poems from the Greek Anthology* [1938].)

passionate or free to engage in variant sexual acts than about whether she will seem "ladylike."

Physical Sources of Sexual Frustration

Indeed, an inexperienced couple may have difficulties with penetration; and even if they do not fail, the coitus may be painful to the wife and afford neither any satisfaction. Let us consider the sources of such difficulties.

The young male becomes fully aroused sexually more rapidly than the woman, even without actual physical stimulation. With an erect penis and concerned about carrying out the act, he may seek to penetrate his wife before she is physically ready. The woman has the task, which may at first be difficult, of being able to relax her perineal musculature in the time of excitement. She may experience spasm of the muscles at the orifice and in the lower third of the vagina, that will block penetration or cause pain. While she may become sexually excited, proper preparation for an orgasm often requires considerable physical stimulation, particularly until she has learned or becomes enabled to experience orgasm readily. Indeed, women rarely experience orgasm the first time they have intercourse, and frequently not even during the first weeks of marriage.

Arousal in the Woman

Although the woman can experience an initial sexual excitement almost instantaneously by either psychic or physical stimulation, it does not prepare her for intercourse. A secretion in her vagina by transudation is the source of the wetness women feel and recognize as an indication of psychic stimulation, and the nipples and clitoris may become erect and more sensitive. These phenomena can serve as a signal that stimulates desire for arousal or form the first phase of progressive arousal. Only with some further psychic or physical stimulation does the vagina become lengthened and widened and open into a receptive organ by vascular engorgement of the vaginal walls, very much as the penis expands and hardens by vascular engorgement. Only somewhat later, and in most women only after there has been physical stimulation and the entire perineal area becomes congested and highly sensitive, does the external third of the vagina become markedly congested and narrow through its thickening to form what Masters has termed the "orgasmic platform" (Masters and Johnson, 1959), a soft but firm and lubricated canal that properly envelops and stimulates the penis during its thrusting movements; and simultaneously permits the penis indirectly to exert mechanical traction on the clitoral hood that stimulates the clitoris and heightens the woman's excitement. Until the vagina and perineal region are thus prepared, intromission of the penis will not only be difficult, but may also be unpleasant, if not painful, to the woman and unsatisfactory to the man. Now although there are many similarities between the male and female preparation for coitus and orgasm, the man is more likely to attain a full erection from psychic stimulation and be prepared for the act sooner than his wife. In many couples, the man learns to delay and becomes capable of greater delay with relaxation, security, and experience; and the woman becomes capable of more complete arousal with less physical stimulation, and may gain an ability to reach orgasm more rapidly.

The wife, particularly early in marriage, may be unable to achieve orgasm unless she has experienced considerable physical stimulation; her arousal is heightened by precoital play with her breasts, kissing, caressing of her body, and stimulation of her mons and clitoris prior to intromission. She may be fully prepared for intromission only after considerable stimulation of her external genitalia. Then, after intromission, she may not be able to have an orgasm unless her mate can delay—or continue his thrusting movements after his orgasm. A discontinuance of the stimulation is very apt to disrupt the progression to orgasm; and even though the man's erection may diminish after orgasm, the penis will usually stiffen again if he does not withdraw. However, when the husband cannot continue intromission, stimulation of the mons area or perineal region in general can rapidly revive the arousal and lead to orgasm unless strong psychic factors cause repression of the excitement.

Clitoral or Vaginal Orgasm?

The clitoris serves as the primary center for sexual arousal in the woman; and it is necessary specifically to negate several common misconceptions that have gained wide acceptance. The most drastic and widespread misconception concerns the notion that there is a difference between a clitoral and a vaginal orgasm, and that one of the difficult developmental tasks of the woman is to progress from immature clitoral orgasm to experience vaginal orgasm and that childhood and adolescent clitoral masturbation serves to fixate the clitoris as the focal area of libidinal excitement. Freud (1905), for example, considered that the vagina displaced the clitoris as the focus of libidinal excitement after puberty unless fixations occurred or a congenital abnormality existed. Indeed, many women have continued in psychoanalysis or psychotherapy because they considered their orgasms remained "clitoral."*

The studies of Masters and Johnson appear to have demonstrated conclusively that the orgasm is essentially the same, no matter where the stimulation is applied, and that during coitus it is still the clitoris that is the major site of stimulation and sexual excitement. When the vaginal mucosa is thoroughly engorged to form the "orgasmic platform," the engorged clitoris has retracted against the symphysis pubis and is covered by its "hood" or prepuce. The labia minora are also engorged and highly sensitive. When the penis distends the vaginal outlet it also distends the labia minora which, in turn, pulls upon the clitoral hood. The thrusting movements of the penis thereby indirectly cause the clitoris to be rhythmically stimulated by its hood, which leads to heightened excitation and properly to orgasm. Sensory sexual excitation within the vagina does not occur. The failure of sexual arousal by the penile thrusting during intercourse occurs when the clitoris is not stimulated indirectly because of lack of proper vascular engorgement of the vagina and other perineal tissues—a failure that usually is due to emotional blocking, but sometimes to inadequate preparation. Damage to the area in childbirth can impede the necessary mechanical traction, but this is not usually a problem of newlyweds. The intensity of the orgasm does not depend upon whether the clitoris or vagina is stimulated: some women experience more intense orgasm through clitoral masturbation and others through coitus; and for many women it is the circumstances rather than the site of stimulation that makes the difference.

---

* It is difficult to know just how this concept arose and just what it was supposed to mean. It properly meant that a woman who was able to have an orgasm only through direct stimulation of the clitoris and not from penile stimulation within the vagina was not able to experience or enjoy intercourse properly. However, it also seems to have meant that some women could not experience a generalized, deeply felt total bodily orgasmic response but only a rather localized erotic heightening of tension and release that left her incompletely satisfied. But beyond this it often led women to believe that because they required preliminary stimulation of the clitoris to become properly aroused, or because excitement was felt primarily in the clitoral area rather than intravaginally, they were not experiencing a proper orgasm; and women have completed psychoanalysis resigned to the fact that they would simply have to make do with a "clitoral orgasm," which even though it seemed fully satisfying was just not the real thing that more completely feminine and mature women experienced.

Although doubts were expressed that the vagina could properly become the primary erogenous zone as it does not have genital corpuscles (sensory nerve endings of a type found in the clitoris and labia minora and in the glans of the penis), the idea was so firmly entrenched in psychoanalytic theory that even major investigators of female sexuality have had difficulty in discarding it. The first decisive disagreement was presented by Marmor in 1954, who insisted that the clitoris must remain the major area of sexual excitement and that this function could not transfer to the vagina.

The Female Orgasm

The orgasm properly involves a general bodily response for both sexes. For the woman after a period of mounting muscular tensions that may involve involuntary contortion of the face and spasms of the long muscles of the arms and legs, the orgasm starts with a sensation of intense sensual awareness in the clitoris that radiates upward into the pelvis followed by a sensation of warmth spreading from the pelvic area through the body. The woman then experiences a feeling of involuntary contraction in the lower vagina, followed by a throbbing that unites with the heartbeat. At the onset, the outer third of the vagina may or may not go into a brief spasm; there are then rhythmic contractions at 0.8 second intervals for the first three to six contractions (the periodicity is the same as that of the penile emissive contractions), and then another three to six contractions occur somewhat more slowly and less intensely. The uterus also undergoes spasmodic contractions during orgasm, as do the rectal and urinary sphincters. The attainment of the orgasm requires a continuation of the stimulation— in coitus, of the penile thrusting. Cessation or interruption of stimulation will disrupt the heightening of excitement to orgasm.

The Male Orgasm

The male orgasm starts with the expulsion of the contents of the seminal vesicles, prostate, and ejaculatory duct into the prostatic urethra, giving the man the feeling that ejaculation is now inevitable: but it will take several seconds before ejaculation occurs (an interval utilized in the practice of coitus interruptus). Then, in the second phase of the orgasm, the semen is propelled through the penile urethra by the perineal muscle contractions and expelled in forceful spurts into the vagina. After several ejaculations the force lessens and the timing lengthens for several more contractions. During the experience, the extended penis is exquisitely sensitive, which tends to impel the man to seek further stimulation and leads to a pleasure-pain tension for which relief is sought (the continued intense erection can even be painful while simultaneously pleasurable); and during coitus the man, usually together with the woman, is impelled to move the penis in rhythmic thrusts in the vagina, which heightens the excitement of both— and eventually leads to the intense orgasmic release. The phase leading to orgasm is usually accompanied by increased muscular tension in many parts of the body, with considerable involuntary contractions as well as voluntary, which heighten during the ejaculation, after which relaxation occurs abruptly.

There are many similarities between the male and female orgasmic behaviors and, as would be expected, they are suited to one another and to foster preservation of the species by placing a high sensuous reward on seeking copulation rather than masturbatory gratification. Aside from the male's more rapid preparation for the act, one other difference requires comment. The wife can experience multiple orgasms during a single sexual act, or after a brief interval, whereas the husband has a longer refractory period, requiring at least several minutes between acts, and he has a more limited capacity to have repeated orgasms within a given period.* This discrepancy, however, has little practical significance in marriage, where the quality of the experience is what matters and rapidly repeated sexual intercourse is not usually deemed necessarily desirable.

Women's Potential Difficulties

As we have already noted, a woman is unlikely to experience orgasm during her first coital experience, and should not become disappointed until she has experienced several weeks or months of fairly frequent intercourse. However, if she chronically continues to become excited and physically prepared without progressing to orgasm, she will usually feel tense and irritable from the frustration of unresolved sexual excitement. The condition can, of course, be relieved by masturbatory activity, unless the woman is also psychologically blocked from achieving orgasm under such conditions. The danger is that the couple gives up trying to have the wife experience coital orgasm. According to the Masters-Johnson studies, the woman is more likely to reach orgasm when her tissues are thoroughly engorged because the indirect stimulation of the clitoris will then be more successful; and they also believe that learning to have an orgasm is necessary for many women; and that after a woman has experienced an orgasm several times,

---

* Masters and Johnson have found that below the age of thirty many males may be able to ejaculate several times after relatively brief refractory periods of a few minutes. Some young men may also be capable of experiencing orgasm ten times during a night, but few would have any urge to do so except upon some special occasion to prove or test their capacities. Whereas women may be capable of virtually unlimited orgasms, this is merely a technical matter because a woman will not desire such unlimited experience after participating fully in the sexual act. Discussions of far-reaching effects upon society of the recognition of woman's unlimited capacities to experience orgasm, such as can be found in M. Sherfey, "The Evolution and Nature of Female Sexuality in Relation to Psychoanalytic Theory," are unrealistic and confuse what is possible for a woman with what she would desire and enjoy. Sherfey seems to confuse satisfaction, satiation, and exhaustion.

she will progressively have less difficulty and reach it more quickly, thereby increasing the physical compatibility between the couple.*

Women may also experience problems because of the use of contraceptives. Although the "pill," which affords a woman virtual certainty that she will not become pregnant accidentally, has been a boon to many, its reliability is not appreciated by all. Numerous women become depressed or develop headaches when on the pill, others become concerned about the increased danger of phlebitis, which is almost negligible in young women, etc., and approximately fifty percent of women discontinue its use. However, as R. Lidz (1969) has found, women who use intrauterine devices for contraception also may become depressed or develop other symptoms that have been attributed to the "pill." Those women who feel that sexual intercourse is meaningful only if they can become pregnant, or that they are depriving their husbands of the opportunity to impregnate them, etc., are likely to develop some reason to stop taking the pill, and may also have difficulties enjoying sex when using a highly reliable method of contraception.†

Rainwater's studies of women of lower socioeconomic status showed that many of the women had little or no sexual experience at marriage, and that many husbands taught them only enough to gain their participation but with little or any regard for the wife's satisfaction. The investigation indicated that when the husband was solicitous and interested, the wife was far more likely to enjoy the act and share it, whereas those wives whose husbands taught only "the bare essentials necessary to perform the act" (Rainwater and Weinstein, 1960) are apt to regard coitus as something for a husband's pleasure alone, feel used, and resent it. Thus, the husband's way of proceeding and the effort that goes into making coitus a mutually

---

* Thus, the following measures may be helpful. Although the husband obviously cannot continue the single act indefinitely, repetition several times over a few hours may help because the wife's genital area becomes increasingly engorged with repetition of frustrated excitation. Then, too, the husband often can continue the act longer after his initial orgasm has relieved the acuteness of his desire and because of the decrease in volume of the seminal fluid that enters the prostatic urethra prior to ejaculation. As the woman's pelvic organs tend to be engorged during a week or so prior to her menstrual period, efforts to produce orgasm may be more successful during this phase. Finally, relaxation of concern can be extremely helpful—it is difficult for a concerned woman, but perhaps more possible if the problem can be shared with her husband and his cooperation in overcoming it gained.

† Problems also arise because of monilia (yeast) infections of the vagina, which can cause spasm of the muscles around the entrance of the vagina, and even cervical irritation and pain. Why such infections have become common is not altogether clear. The use of antibiotics is a common cause, but frequent vaginal douching to assure proper "feminine hygiene" probably also contributes. Sarrel (1975) reports that in a study of two hundred adolescents over a four-year period, fifty-five percent developed monilia vaginitis.

satisfying experience can be very important. However, many women who are essentially frigid have profound blocks to the enjoyment of intercourse because of the intensity of the repression, oedipal fantasies, fears of damage or of pregnancy, resentment of male prerogatives, etc., that may require skilled psychotherapy, but skilled sexual counseling that recognizes that sexual difficulties usually involve both partners and provides them with active guidance has enabled many couples to overcome their difficulties (Kaplan, 1974).

Common Problems of Young Men

The young husband not infrequently has difficulties early in the marriage. He may find that his erection fails when he tries intromission, or that he ejaculates so quickly that neither his wife nor he can enjoy the act. He is usually aware that he is expected to delay until his wife is prepared and becomes overly preoccupied with efforts at control. He may have unrealistic ideas of how potent he is supposed to be. It is not uncommon that the wife may be the more sexually experienced person, and he becomes concerned with how he will measure up to her previous partners. An understanding and patient wife can help overcome difficulties before they become set or even multiply. Efforts to enter the vagina prematurely greatly increase the difficulties, for not until the woman has become properly aroused can the penis move into the vagina easily. Even then, the husband may need his wife's help in guiding the penis properly. When there are difficulties in maintaining the erection, stimulation by the wife will usually correct the situation. Premature ejaculation tends to become less of a problem as the man gains confidence. Repetition of coitus for a second or third time within an hour or two can help the man gain control and confidence in his performance. Here, the ability to discuss problems rather than conceal them, and planned efforts to better the sexual relationship, help a great deal. It may be useful for the man to stop, for a time, thinking about providing pleasure and simply consider his own feelings. Concerns over loss of the penis or damage to it when it is in the vagina, fears of damaging the wife's internal organs, fear of impregnating her, residual incestuous concerns, and other such difficulties can all create problems. Some such concerns are usually present, consciously or unconsciously, and when not profound are likely to vanish or become relatively unimportant when confidence is gained and as familiarity with the wife develops.

Many men are concerned with the size of their genitalia—perhaps often as a carry-over from childhood, when the father's genitalia by comparison seemed enormous to the child, and concern was heightened by the many remarks boys and young men make about genital size as an index of virility and of desirability to a woman. Although the size of men's penises in the flaccid state varies notably, Masters' measurements show that the size of the flaccid penis makes relatively little difference, for small penises expand more than large ones—and even though differences may remain they are relatively slight. Further, the vagina, unless damaged in childbirth, accommodates itself to the penis, and size is rarely a factor in a man's ability to satisfy his spouse, and it is no indication of his virility or sexual capacities.*

The husband's abilities to satisfy his wife should not depend upon a capacity to have sexual relations with great frequency, but more upon the way in which the sexual act is carried out. When the wife experiences a deeply felt orgasm during coitus, she can feel relaxed and satisfied. Her potential capacity to have many more orgasms is not particularly pertinent. Desire varies from person to person and according to circumstances. Differences in frequency of desire, however, are one of the most commonly reported problems of sexual adjustment (Bernard, 1964). It is likely that the frustrated male is less able to set aside feelings of arousal and tension than the woman. However, such matters are difficult to judge as they have been influenced greatly by the cultural tradition. Couples who are interested in one another's happiness can almost always manage to regulate the sexual relationship so that it is mutually satisfactory.†

Achieving Mutual Sexual Gratification

The communication of desire can, of course, present problems, particularly to the inhibited. For most couples most of the communication of desire is nonverbal and wives rapidly learn to recognize when their husbands are desirous, but husbands are less likely to be as sensitive to their wives' signals. Wives also learn how to refuse to recognize signals when they are not feeling responsive or to find means of sidetracking the hus-

---

* A woman may also be concerned that her vagina will not be large enough. The vagina can distend enormously—as is required in childbirth. The size of the penis or the vagina is important in cases of developmental failure when the organs remain infantile or anomalous—but these are very uncommon.

† Of course, a variety of difficulties or misunderstandings can arise. Thus, a woman who had been married for ten years consulted a psychiatrist because her husband still sought to have relations three to four times each day and returned home from work at lunchtime primarily in order to have intercourse. Such frequency of the need for intercourse is not a matter of unusual potency but an indication of a sexual compulsivity, often to reassure the self against concerns about homosexuality.

band's demands (Rainwater and Weinstein, 1960). An ability to talk about desire can help the adjustment, and discussion may be essential to the improvement of the act to attain mutual gratification. However, some couples, particularly well-educated couples, engage in considerable discussion prior to each sexual experience or during it, which often indicates some lack of proper mutuality. Talk about desire is often kept minimal because it can only be accepted or openly refused, and a spouse may wish to feel out the situation rather than impose his or her own wishes on the other, or risk rebuff. Still, in some marriages, the failure to discuss lack of satisfaction leads to continued misunderstandings.

The desirability of simultaneity of orgasm has also received considerable attention in literature on sexual adjustment, where it has sometimes been considered a major measure of a satisfactory marital adjustment. Most couples find that such simultaneous experience heightens the pleasure of both partners and the feelings of unity and loss of boundaries, but some persons may prefer to have an orgasm and then more quietly enjoy the spouse's pleasure in orgasm. In any event, such simultaneity is not something that must preoccupy a couple, for it is likely to occur after the spouses are familiar at a preconscious level with the way in which the partner acts and reacts—and the signs of impending climax in one serve as a trigger for the other.

Some Common Misconceptions

The occurence of menses can also lead to some minor difficulties. Some husbands will wish to have intercourse during their wife's menstrual period, but the wife feels that it is dangerous. Some women are not only more sexually excited during the menses but find coitus more satisfying, yet find their husbands reluctant for aesthetic reasons. In any event, there are no reasons, other than aesthetic or religious, why couples cannot have coitus during the menses.

Norms for marital sexual behavior do not exist, and indeed what is considered normal or abnormal behavior varies widely among ethnic groups and socioeconomic classes, and from couple to couple. As discussions of sex are not only apt to promote misconceptions but often contain much boasting and banter, young persons may have marked misconceptions of what might be considered abnormal or perverse. Young men listening to their confreres may consider themselves inadequate if they do not have intercourse four or five times a night, or their wives to be cold if they do not wish to participate on retiring and awakening each day. One such young man had serious qualms about his right to marry and experienced great surprise and relief when he learned from his fiancée that she thought sexual relations once or twice a week would be more than adequate and hoped that he would be tolerant of her efforts to learn to participate properly. It is not uncommon to hear among laboring groups in particular that intercourse is regarded by both husband and wife as something the man needs to have nightly for his health, very much as he is supposed to move his bowels, and it is carried out in a routine, perfunctory manner without any relationship to affection. The wife who considers intercourse little more than a duty expresses her satisfaction with a husband who is thoughtful and "doesn't bother me too often." Alert physicians and therapists are aware that a woman who responds to inquiries about her sexual life with "It's all right" or "He's pretty considerate" is getting little, if any, enjoyment from it.

Divergent Sexual Mores

Sexual practices vary greatly. Some couples raised in certain European traditions or as members of fundamentalist religious sects may never have seen one another in the nude in many years of married life (Komarovsky, 1964). Others will consider any masturbatory foreplay as shameful or disgusting, and some will be shocked at the idea of deviating from the customary face-to-face position with the man above the woman.* Many will maintain that whatever a couple wish to do in the privacy of the marital bed that is mutually satisfactory and injurious to neither is acceptable. For many persons, in any case, the private and shared intimacy of the sexual act is a time when various repressed fantasies and desires are indulged. Various types of precoital play are considered proper preliminaries. Some couples, encouraged by various sex manuals, devote time and energy to making an "art" of their sexual activity, or make new means of excitation a central aspect of their marriage. According to various surveys and on the basis of psychiatric experience, it is clear that many couples practice oral-genital relations on occasion without causing concern to either partner. In some respects what occurs during or before sexual intercourse bears a resemblance to preconscious fantasy life and tends to be

---

* It may be of interest that according to Malinowski (1955) the Trobriand Islanders find it a source of great amusement to mimic this position, which they term the "missionary position" and which they find very unsatisfactory.

dissociated from what occurs in the workaday world or even from what goes on between a couple at other times. It involves a sort of sharing of preconscious and unconscious strivings as part of the intimacy and fusion. However, the insistence of one partner on a practice that is repugnant to the other, such as anal or oral relations or some other deviation, can create difficulties, and can cause symptoms such as vomiting or intestinal upsets that a person has difficulty revealing even to a doctor.

The physician and marital counsellor must not be naïve about marital practices. They will encounter newly married women who consider their husbands perverts for trying to have normal coitus; women who believe it indecent to have an orgasm; couples who have never consummated the sexual act searching for a physical cause of their sterility; men or women who soon wish to invite another man or woman to share the marital bed; men who rarely if ever wish to have relations. The variations and permutations of sexual desires and practices are so great and concerns about them are so frequently displaced onto other complaints that it is necessary to be able to hear what patients may have difficulty in conveying, to listen without personal prejudice and with emotional equanimity. The therapist must also recognize that sexuality can be used as an expression of hostility as well as love, and as a means of domination or degradation of the spouse, or to express deep resentments toward the opposite sex. Sex can also mean little to one spouse other than being a means of bargaining to have his or her own way in other matters—such as the right to purchase a new dress, or to go fishing for a weekend. It is also something that some spouses prefer to have the partner indulge outside of the marriage, and not all infidelity is motivated primarily by the unfaithful partner.

Marriages Without Sexual Relations

Marriages can survive without sexual activity and even provide satisfaction for both partners; and though usually one will feel seriously deprived if not cheated, other factors including deep admiration or love for the impotent or invalided partner may be compensatory. Marriage is a relationship that is broad enough to find stability on varied foundations. In some marriages both partners are happier when sex is not in the picture. In others, the couples find other interests that furnish adequate self-realization. However, difficulties that block sexual intimacy will usually affect other areas and, if they do not create friction, at least limit the mutuality the couple can achieve. Yet, when it is necessary and when a decision can be made that abolishes constant expectation, indecision, frustration, and self-pity, the marital bond can transcend disappointments in the sexual sphere.

Sex and Emotional Maturity

While the achievement of "genital sexuality" has been considered a major indicator of mature personality development in both psychoanalytic theory and practice, as discussed in the chapter on adolescence, it is a concept that confuses as much as it clarifies. If the concept is to be meaningful it must involve more than a capacity to achieve and induce orgasm in heterosexual coitus. In such terms it has often been pursued by immature persons and accepted as a reassuring token of normality. The concept of "genital sexuality" properly contains the implications of the capacity to relax defenses through having sufficient security in the self to let a truly intimate relationship develop that fuses affectionate and sensuous love in a lasting relationship; to be sufficiently autonomous not to fear the loss of boundaries in being joined to another, or being overwhelmed in giving way to id impulsions, or becoming lost amid unconscious fantasies of childhood years when indulging sexuality, or being dominated and used by another if one shows the intensity of one's needs.

Theoretically, at least, it helps the solidification of a marriage when the couple have time to learn to know one another intimately, find reciprocal roles, and achieve a satisfying sexual relationship before children arrive on the scene. Gaining satisfactory marital adjustment prior to parenthood helps the couple share the offspring, to enjoy them as a mutual product, and to maintain a coalition as parents.

The experience of marriage offers opportunities for more complete fulfillment and the rounding out of the life cycle. The living out of adult patterns in the relatedness to another as a mature man or woman, the experiences of producing a new generation and gaining a vital connection with the future, the giving of oneself to children and living as a parent are usually closed to the unmarried. The changes in the personality that develop as the intimate interrelationship forms, in themselves tend to stabilize the personality, establish firmer bonds to others, provide a completion through complementarity with another, and lessen the sharp edges of egocentricity. The sexual interchange permits reasonable mastery of libidinal strivings that may otherwise be primarily diverting, in both senses of the word, and turns them into a force that promotes unity and cohesiveness.

THE SINGLE LIFE

As close to ninety-seven percent of Americans marry, and about eighty percent of those who are divorced remarry, it seems clear that living through adult life in marriage is considered the desirable course. Nevertheless, some persons remain unmarried, through either conscious or unconscious choice and only rarely from lack of opportunity. When we consider the chronically ill, invalided, and mentally ill, it would seem that the proportion of the population who can marry but do not is surprisingly small. However, there are indications that currently a larger proportion may remain unmarried. There has been, since 1960, an increase of fifty percent in those persons between the ages of twenty and thirty-four who are still unmarried, and similarly the proportion of divorced persons who do not remarry has also increased by about fifty percent (Glick, 1975). Women are no longer as economically dependent on men as formerly, and neither men nor women have to marry to live for prolonged periods with a member of the opposite sex. Homosexual liaisons or "marriages" have become more acceptable. Some groups in the Women's Liberation Movement foster an independence from men, and even a hostility to men, as if the two sexes were enemies rather than complementary. While the single life closes many doors, there are still countless ways available that can lead to a rich and meaningful life. Though many persons will prefer to venture into a marriage that offers little chance of happiness rather than remain single, others can rightfully feel that an unhappy and conflictful marriage is more confining than completing and can be destructive of such integrity as the person has obtained. The life development of many persons does not lead to the potentiality of further growth through marriage or for the assumption of the intimate relatedness and the responsibilities of parenthood. Many such persons correctly realize that their future will be more secure and complete if it is pursued in some other direction. It may be salubrious if it becomes more acceptable for such persons to remain unmarried, and for those who have tried marriage and found that they are not suited for marriage or that marriage is not suited to them, not to involve others in another marital failure.

The formation of a stable and satisfying marriage is probably the most crucial factor in assuring the emotional stability and security of the next generation, as well as a favorable subsequent personality development of the spouses. The outcome of the marriage depends to a very great extent upon the choice of the spouse, as has been explained in the preceding chapter. What the ultimate success of a marriage depends upon goes beyond the objectives of this chapter and the capacities of the author. Spouses can complement one another and live together harmoniously in a wide variety of ways. Some of the requisites for married life as parents will be discussed in the next chapter. In general, a good marriage in our contemporary society usually depends upon the achievements by both spouses of sufficient independence and firm integrations as individuals to enable them to live interdependently rather than with one partner dependent on the other; and upon the ability of both to continue to grow after marriage and develop new interests so that the marriage is constantly being renewed. Such continued renewal is important to the stability of the marriage and the satisfaction of both partners, and goes beyond settling down and trying to find a way of living together harmoniously. Children and interest in their constant change is one important means by which such renewal can be achieved.

REFERENCES

BERNARD, J. (1964). "The Adjustments of Married Mates," in *Handbook of Marriage and the Family*. H. T. Christensen, ed. Rand McNally, Chicago.

BOTT, E. (1955). "Urban Families: Conjugal Roles and Social Networks," *Human Relations*, 8:345–384.

FITTS, D., trans. (1938). *Poems from the Greek Anthology*. New Directions Paperbook, New York.

FREUD, S. (1905). "Three Essays on the Theory of Sexuality," in *The Standard Edition of the Complete Psychological Works of Sigmund Freud*, vol. 8. Hogarth Press, London, 1953.

GLICK, P. (1975). "A Demographer Looks at Marriage," *Journal of Marriage and the Family*, 37:15–26.

GOODE, W. (1956). *After Divorce*. Free Press, Glencoe, Ill.

KAPLAN, H. S. (1974). *The New Sex Therapy*. Bruner-Mazel and Quadrangle/New York Times Books, New York.

KOMAROVSKY, M. (1964). *Blue Collar Marriage*. Random House, New York.

LANDIS, J. (1946). "Length of Time Required to Achieve Adjustment in Marriage," *American Sociological Review*, 11:666–677.

LIDZ, R. W. (1969). "Emotional Factors in the Success of Contraception," *Fertility and Sterility*, 20:761–771.

MALINOWSKI, B. (1955). *Sex and Repression in a Savage Society*. Meridian Press, New York.

MARMOR, J. (1954). "Some Considerations Concerning Orgasm in the Female," *Psychosomatic Medicine*, 16:240–245.

MASTERS, W., and JOHNSON, V. (1959) "Orgasm, Anatomy of the Female," in *The*

Encyclopedia of Sexual Behavior, Vol. 2. A. Ellis and A. Abarbanel, eds. Hawthorn Books, New York.

———. (1966). *Human Sexual Response*. Little, Brown, Boston.

RAINWATER, L., and WEINSTEIN, K. (1960). *And the Poor Get Children*. Quadrangle Press, New York.

RAPOPORT, R., and RAPOPORT, R. N. (1975). "Men, Women, and Equity," *The Family Coordinator*, 24:421–432.

SARREL, P. (1975). Personal communication.

SHERFEY, M. J. (1966). "The Evolution and Nature of Female Sexuality in Relation to Psychoanalytic Theory," *Journal of the American Psychoanalytic Association*, 14:28–128.

SUGGESTED READING

KAPLAN, H. S. (1974). *The New Sex Therapy*. Bruner-Mazel and Quadrangle/New York Times Books, New York.

MASTERS, W., and JOHNSON, V. (1966). *Human Sexual Response*. Little, Brown, Boston.

RAPOPORT, R., and RAPOPORT, R. N. (1975). "Men, Women, and Equity," *The Family Coordinator*, 24:421–432.

SPIEGEL, J. P. (1957). "The Resolution of Role Conflict Within the Family," *Psychiatry*, 20:1–16.

CHAPTER 15

❁

Parenthood

THE ARRIVAL of the first child transforms spouses into parents and turns a marriage into a family. The endless drama has curved around to face again the beginning of life; but now the players are taking the parents' nurturant and supportive roles that they learned while they were ingénues playing the children's parts; but the old lines do not quite fit and constant improvisation is required.*

In becoming parents, the marital partners enter into a new developmental phase (Benedek, 1959). The tasks with which the parents must cope, the roles they occupy, their orientation toward the future alter profoundly. They are offered opportunities for new satisfactions, to achieve a greater sense of completion, and to live through experiences which had been fantasied but frustrated since early childhood. They need no longer play at being "mommy and daddy"—they are. However, this simple step into parenthood, so often taken as an inadvertent misstep, provides a severe test of all

* Many aspects of parenthood have been discussed elsewhere in this book. The requisites that a couple must fill to provide a family proper for raising reasonably well-integrated children have been presented in Chapter 2; some of the changes that take place in the wife when she becomes a mother in Chapter 4. The parental tasks of coping with the child's changing needs have formed a major portion of the chapters on infancy through adolescence. This chapter does not attempt to repeat such material. It is concerned with how the transition to parenthood influences the personality of the parent.

467

preceding developmental stages and the consequent integration of the individual parents as well as of their marriage. The inevitable changes in the husband and wife will, in turn, alter the marital relationship and place strains upon it until a new equilibrium can be established.

The birth of a child, perhaps actually the awareness of conception, changes the marital partnership by the need to make room—emotional room—for a third person. The product of their unity can be a strong bond, a source of common interest and shared identification, but children are also a divisive influence—in varying proportions in each marriage, a unifying and separating force. The spouses who properly have transferred their major object relationships to one another, and each of whom wishes to be the focal point of the partner's emotional and affectional investment, now find the other intensely investing a newcomer. Further, a family unit is not as plastic as a marital union. A childless couple can relate to one another in a great variety of ways and the marriage remain adequate if both partners are satisfied or even if they simply believe it more satisfactory than separating would be. The preservation of the equilibrium of a family, however, and even more clearly the adequate rearing of children, requires the achievement and maintenance of a dynamic structuring of the family in which each spouse fills definitive responsibilities. Deficiencies of the marital partners in filling the tasks and roles they have accepted or agreed upon lead to conflict and family imbalance. On the other hand, the increases in structure and shared responsibilities which are an inherent part of family life can provide greater security to the spouses and greater stability to the marriage.

Let us first consider the capacities of the individual spouses to move into the phase of parenthood, because it is the immaturities, fixations, and regressions uncovered by the need to be a parent that usually interfere with a spouse's acceptance of his or her respective parental functions or with the capacity to fill them adequately.

PARENTHOOD AND PERSONALITY DEVELOPMENT

Speaking of the ideal which reality occasionally approaches, the partners who married have both achieved individual identities, shown themselves capable of intimacy, and have given up their independence for the benefits of interdependence with its security of knowing that the welfare of each is extremely important to the other. They have found the completion that could not be gained within their own natal families where sexual union could not be permitted and in which they remained children. The spouses seek resolution of their particular version of their frustrated and incompleted family romances. The incompleteness of the male and female roles and skills is balanced by those of the partner. The task of self-creation is more or less over for most. The energies that went into sexual repression or in seeking ways of satisfying sexual drives, and into the search for the partner who could bring completion to the imbalance of being a man or a woman, are released for investment in a creativity that transcends the self. While the child does not always oblige and wait, persons properly become parents only after they are reasonably launched as adults, when they are at the height of their physical and intellectual capacities and well settled in their marital relationship. They can feel themselves adults because the incompleted oedipal strivings which indicated their junior status—their membership in the childhood generation—have now found indirect expression and fulfillment. The spouses have been freed from the basic restrictions of childhood, and are ready to become parents themselves.

The conception of the child is an act of mutual creativity during which the boundaries between the self and another were temporarily obliterated more completely than at any time since infancy. One can grasp the symbolic validity of the common but erroneous notion that a woman must have an orgasm in order to conceive. The infant is a physical fusion of the parents, and their personalities unite within the child they raise. As their common product, the child can become a continuing bond forged by that creativity, a focus of mutual hopes, interests, and responsibilities. Whereas each parent grew up a product of different family lines with differing customs and identifying with different parents, they are now united by a child whose experiences they will share and with whom they both identify. We must also recognize that whether they have willingly or unwillingly been turned into parents, here as in other spheres of life many persons grow through finding the abilities to meet responsibilities thrust upon them.*

---

* We are, in this chapter, concerned primarily with the effects of parenthood on young adults when they become parents after achieving fairly firm integrations as adults and marry. Many young unmarried adolescents also become parents, but many if not most of these hand over much of the parenting to others. There are also many immature married adolescent parents who are still too preoccupied with their peer groups and their own pleasures to be parental, and some whose marriages are too chaotic to provide a setting in which they can be very parental.

THE WOMAN AND PROCREATION

Although some women will prefer to remain unmarried, and some who marry recognize that having a baby will interfere with their careers or marriages and remain childless, most married women wish for the sense of fulfillment that comes with the creation of a new life. Strong sociocultural directives have added impetus to a woman's feelings—which may or may not be correct—that she possesses an innate drive that requires satisfaction through conceiving, bearing, and nurturing children. Her generative organs seem meaningless unless her womb has been filled and her breasts have been engorged, if not suckled. Women's sexuality is more complex than men's, more closely tied to nature through the menstrual cycle and with a monthly uncertainty about fertility or reminder of infertility; and it encompasses conception, the incorporation of a fetus within her, childbirth, and nursing as well as sexual passion and copulation. Only recently have the sexual act and childbearing become disconnected for those who so wish, and the decision made available concerning whether to have children.* Fewer babies need now be born because of the parents' recreational rather than procreational desires. With the choice given them, perhaps fewer women will wish to disrupt their careers, or take the risk of becoming a single parent through divorce, or overcome various residual fears of pregnancy and parturition; but for many women, creativity as a mother becomes a central matter that provides meaning and balance to their lives. Any sense of incompletion or deprivation because they had been born girls has been offset by the realization of their innate capacities for creativity, but the realization has required actualization. Vestiges of envy of the man lead some women to desire strongly to have a son through whom they can unconsciously live out a life closed to them because they are women.

---

* Although the pill and intrauterine device are extremely effective contraceptive methods, studies in a family planning clinic clearly show that many women become depressed or anxious on virtually "fool-proof" contraception. Many women feel that intercourse makes no sense if they cannot conceive, and lose their sexual desire. Some women never feel as well and as satisfied with life as when pregnant. Being fertile not only raises their self-esteem but also increases the respect and attention they receive from their husbands. Women who crave to have "something alive inside" of them are unlikely to adhere to contraception even if they know that they cannot properly care for another child for reasons of health or finances. Some women also feel guilty about having sex without the risk of pregnancy; or feel it wrong to fool around with nature; or feel that they are not cleaned out properly because their menses are scanty when on the pill; or fear they are being unfair to their husbands who will not be able to impregnate them, etc. It becomes clear that many deeply held wishes and needs to become pregnant can interfere with rational decisions about fertility control (R. Lidz et al., 1976).

Childhood fantasies of displacing mother and providing a child for father are now symbolically realized. The birth of a child turns a wife into a woman by setting her on a par with her mother. Her love for the husband who has made such completion possible deepens. She does not wish the child just for herself but as a meaningful outcome of her relatedness to her husband, pleasing him with a gift that is something of him that he has placed in her to nurture but also something of herself that the husband will cherish. To some extent, the baby is herself loved by a benevolent father. The process carries residua of the little girl's envy of the mother who could produce a child with and for the father. The husband who is loving permits the woman to complete an old but very important fantasy.

The strength of some women's drive to procreate is shown most clearly by those who prefer to risk death rather than remain barren. A physician who observes such situations gains the impression that the desire to produce a new life forms a drive that takes precedence over self-preservation. A woman in the days prior to antitubercular chemotherapy became ill with tuberculous pneumonia shortly after her marriage and verged on dying for several months. The disease was finally arrested after several years of sanatorium care but a threat of breakdown of the healed lesions remained. After continuing in good health for several years after resuming married life, she insisted the time had come for her to have a child. Her physician sought to dissuade her lest the pregnancy and delivery reactivate the disease, and her husband reassured her that she was more important to him than a child. Eventually both husband and physician realized that she would never be content without a child. Perhaps the strong maternal desires were a good omen, for she blossomed during her pregnancy and neither the delivery of the child nor caring for it affected her tuberculosis.*

In the past, at least, most women who decided that they were better off without children, or that children were better off without having them as mothers, experienced some regrets, some sense of lack of fulfillment as women. The compunctions have been fostered, at least in part, by cultural pressures and values. Alice Rossi (1968) notes, "On the level of cultural values, men have no freedom of choice where work is concerned; they must work to secure their status as adult men. The equivalent for women has

---

* Even though a woman's desires to have a child are firm and decisive, they are often mixed with concerns, some conscious and many unconscious. Some are residual from early childhood fantasies about oral impregnation, fears of the baby's growing as a parasite in the stomach, fears of being mutilated when the baby is delivered, etc. Some derive from her having observed the martyrlike suffering of her pregnant mother, or from listening to old wives' tales from her grandmother or from not so old wives of her own generation.

been maternity." The young woman has been under considerable sociocultural pressure to consider that her fulfillment as well as her status as a
woman depends on having children. With marriage and sexuality open to
her without maternity, and with greater opportunities for fulfillment
through a career, such pressures seem to be diminishing, and as pronatal-
ism diminishes because of overpopulation, perhaps fewer babies will be
born for prestige reasons rather than because they are deeply desired.

THE MAN AND PATERNITY

The husband usually also has strong desires for an offspring and can be
transformed by it. The child provides a continuity into the future that
mobilizes ambitions. An offspring forms an important sign of virility—even
though it does not require much virility to impregnate a wife (one father
replied on being congratulated, "Don't congratulate me, it was the easiest
thing I ever did—and besides I wasn't even trying"). Among some ethnic
groups, in particular, the ability to father children is an essential indication
of masculinity, and "machismo" can be a major impediment to birth control. Paradoxically, even as paternity secures and heightens a father's
masculine self-esteem and permits realization of his instrumental functions
of protecting and providing, it also affords him with an opportunity to
express the nurturant qualities derived from his early identification with his
mother that previously had few acceptable outlets and required repression.
The child's admiration and adulation of him will provide him with narcissistic supplies, and he now gains the position and status of "father" that he
had envied and desired to attain since his earliest childhood.

There are also forces that promote jealousy of a child, and antagonisms
to a child, particularly a son, that are held before us in myth.* The
husband may resent his wife's attention to the child, and old sibling rival-

---

* Some of the earliest Greek myths concern this cycle of fathers seeking to be rid of
their sons, and indicate impulsions or wishes that are subject to the strongest taboos.
The myths serve as reminders of the hideous penalties that follow infractions of the
taboo. Uranus, the primeval Greek deity, having married his mother, Earth, banished
his sons, the Titans, to Tartarus, but the youngest, Kronos, aided by his mother Gaia,
eventually castrated Uranus. Kronos ate his first two sons, but the third, Zeus, saved
by his mother Rhea, eventually overthrew him and started the era of the Olympian
gods. The legend of the accursed House of Tantalus which eventually led to Agamemnon's death and then to the slaying of Aegisthus and Clytemnestra by Orestes who
became mad after the matricide, started when Tantalus fed one of his children to the
Gods. The myth of Oedipus also unfolds from the same theme. Laius in seeking to
save himself from the prophecy that his infant son would grow up and slay him, ordered

ries may thus be rekindled. There may exist more deeply buried fears that his son will grow up and wish to get rid of him, just as, in the oedipal phase of his childhood, he had fantasies of killing his father. Such fears are less frequent in societies and families in which the father fills a more nurturant and less dominating role in the family.

THE REORIENTATION OF PARENTS' LIVES AND MARRIAGES

A young wife's readiness to become pregnant is often marked by "nesting procedures" which signal that she feels settled in the marriage and is ready for the next major event of her life. If the couple have been living with parents, or in some transient manner, she wishes a home of her own. If she is employed, the job begins to pall. There may be a flurry of interest in fixing up the home with thoughts of preparing a room and play space for the baby. Sexual intercourse now carries a context beyond love and passion. Her thoughts may focus more on the possibility of conceiving than on the mutuality with her husband. The husband, noting the change, may feel hurt, believing that he is no longer sufficient for his wife. Menstrual periods bring disappointment and feelings of emptiness. If the woman has difficulty in becoming pregnant, she may stop work and focus her interest on the home, believing that it will help her conceive—and it may.

The knowledge that she is pregnant changes the woman's life, for she now feels free to indulge her fantasies about a tangible future with the child. She daydreams of the baby, plans her future in terms of the child, and makes provision for his or her care. Her life has found a new center which is within her and she enjoys feelings of self-sufficiency. For many years to come the center of her existence will be her children. She requires the capacity to include both husband and children as her major investment rather than dividing her interest and affection between them.

The mother, as discussed in Chapter 4, forms a bond to the baby as it develops within her. The father's tie to the infant differs but he, too, can develop strong nurturant feelings through sharing with his wife and providing emotional support for her.

---

the infant Oedipus exposed on a mountain side. Such fears and antagonisms can perpetuate themselves from generation to generation, and removing such dangers to family life required the emergence of myths that emphasized the penalties—the myths serving as something akin to a cultural superego.

When the spouses are both emotionally ready for parenthood, the arrival of an offspring stabilizes and deepens their relationship, and different ideas about family and parental roles, or of child-rearing techniques, are not likely to become disruptive. The child provides new sources of interest which both share, and which no one else will find as absorbing. Any slack in their lives that permitted boredom now disappears; and doubts about the marriage, which may have arisen after the initial ardor had passed, vanish. They are aware of the deepening of their commitment. Marriages can be undone, but parenthood is irrevocable as long as the child lives.*

Some young married couples are surprised to find that the birth of the first child changes their lives even more than did their marriage. There are many satisfactions in watching the baby change from day to day, and in having such a tangible focus to one's life, but there are also tribulations. The carefree days of early married life are gone, and the young mother spends most of her time at home. As much as she loves her baby, the need to care for it constantly becomes wearisome as a steady regimen. The daily routine is arduous, and can require real management skills when there are two or more small children. She experiences frustration as she does not know how to cope with some developmental problem that inevitably arises. Her self-esteem suffers when a child is not responsive to her efforts.† There are days of anxious concern when a baby is ill. The mother who had worked misses adult companionship. She begins to count the days until the weekend when her husband can share the duties, and she begins to await the time when a child can be off to nursery school or kindergarten. It may not be a good omen when a mother feels too guilty to admit that she feels burdened at times and would like an occasional respite from the household chores and care of children.

Whereas the wife who has been working primarily to provide additional income will usually give up her work gladly and devote herself to the baby and her home, the woman who is pursuing a career can find her situation difficult. Some will have selected the time to have a baby and suspended their careers for several years, but others will wish to return to their studies or work after a few weeks or months. Unless a grandmother assumes the care of the baby or a good nursery is available—the two common solutions in the USSR but both infrequent in the USA—or unless a reliable, full-time

---

* Even when the infant is given for adoption, the existence of the child and concerns over what has happened to the child usually continue to haunt the parents.

† Even though many parents have had little, if any, training, experience, or education in the care of infants and children, they are supposed to be competent—perhaps through reading a book. The mother's self-esteem, in particular, as well as the baby's future, rests heavily on their child-rearing capabilities. We have in earlier chapters noted various ways in which help can be provided to the parents.

nurse and housekeeper can be obtained, combining the care of very young children and a career becomes very hard, and life for the parents extremely difficult. Both husband and wife may attempt to work half-time, or one—usually the wife—will work part-time, relying on domestic help and her husband to enable her to be away part of the day and also to find time to study or work at home. The husband's way of life, which changes considerably even if his wife does not work, must change markedly as he assumes major responsibilities for the child and home rather than simply act as a helper. Unfortunately, but realistically, most of those men who have supported their wives' careers have done so—at least in the past—only when it does not disrupt their own careers and lives too profoundly. Even when the wife and mother manages to make satisfactory arrangements for the care of the baby while she is at work, she is likely to feel guilty whenever something goes wrong, or simply because she is not at home with the baby. There have been strong pressures for mothers to devote themselves to the full-time care of their small children, even though there is little, if any, evidence that such care is better for the child than a few hours of undivided parental attention each day. Nursery schools are more available than nurseries, and many mothers will feel free to return to their career activities away from home only when the child, or the youngest child, can attend nursery school.

Even when the mother does not work away from the home, the presence of a child also requires reorganization of the marriage and can upset the equilibrium that the spouses had established as a couple. In a marital relationship harmony depends essentially upon the couple's finding reciprocally interrelating roles, but roles usually must shift to care for the child properly. The wife may now be tied down to the home and its care more than formerly; the husband may need to find ways of earning more money to make up for the loss of his wife's income as well as to provide for the baby. One or both may not recognize the added strain upon the partner. Wives may expect their husbands to share the nurturant care of the child and the housework, and husbands may willingly do so. However, even though a wife has had little, if any, more experience with child rearing than her husband, the man does not usually develop the same bond to the small baby, nor is he likely to feel as much at ease in caring for a baby because of the way in which he had been brought up (see Chapter 14). As the child grows a little older, even if a father is able to fill most of the nurturant functions, there is reason to believe that it will influence the child's developing gender identity. There are many unanswered questions, and it may be a matter of what sorts of persons the parents and the society wish to raise. Usually, a couple, as described in Chapter 2, will continue to differentiate to some degree between what the father and the mother do, and each will establish a somewhat different relationship with the child that complements rather than interferes with the other. The mutuality of parenthood thus fosters a supportive interdependence between the spouses.

Still, the unexpressed but essential demands for parents to carry out role-bound functions can cause serious strains on the individuals and the marriage. The stresses can be particularly insidious as the spouses may be only dimly aware of the functions and obligations of their roles, and that the acquisition of a child has imposed a need for more definite structuring of their relationship. Indeed, the need to fill these parental roles in which demands are made by the child and the spouse while the rewards of parenthood are still nebulous can set a stern test of the marriage and the stability of the parents. A child can almost as readily provoke conflict as promote greater closeness and sharing. Whereas the wife usually wishes to share the child with her husband and feels hurt if he does not share her enthusiasm, her essential preoccupation with the baby and her own feelings about the baby can leave the husband feeling excluded.

The Impact of Children on Parents' Personalities

While the parental influences on children seem obvious and the relationship of parents' difficulties to the children's personality problems have been discussed in various contexts, the child, in turn, can profoundly affect one or both parents. The influences are reciprocal—a child's needs or specific difficulties uncover a parent's inadequacies. A mother can lose her self-esteem when she finds herself unable to cope with her baby. A woman who had been highly successful in business and had helped her husband in his career by her perfectionistic attention to detailed problems, became frustrated when she could not seem to help her baby. The baby developed colic at three weeks of age, and as a sophisticated person she knew that some pediatricians attributed such difficulties to the mother's way of handling the baby. Intensity of effort could not help, and feeling herself a failure she became angered by the infant who unwittingly frustrated her and she began to suffer from episodes of incapacitating migraine. A rather common pattern has been noted in men who develop peptic ulcer soon after the birth of a child. They had always been anxious about the security of sources of food and support and they married women who worked and provided additional security against poverty and starvation. When the wife can no longer work and there is an additional family member to provide for, the anxiety becomes serious and chronic.

The woman's capacities to provide maternal nurturance to her infant are related to the quality of the nurturant care she herself received in her infancy and childhood. If her needs then were met with reasonable consistency and she did not experience chronic frustrations and rage, she now has confidence that she can properly satisfy her own child. We might hazard that her own feelings and responses were properly programmed in her childhood and she can now empathize with and understand the needs and feelings of her children. The mutuality established between herself and the child increases her self-esteem, her pride in her motherliness, and her assurance of her femininity. She can transcend the inevitable difficulties and periods of frustration without self-derogation or distorting defenses against loss of self-esteem. In contrast, the woman who was deprived in early childhood responds to a child's dissatisfactions and refusals to be placated with increased feelings of inadequacy. Regrets at having married and hostile feelings toward the child are disturbing and must be undone. A vicious cycle sets in between a frustrated child and frustrated mother. The mother's inadequacies and despair soon spill over into the marital relationship; she may become depressed, place unrealistic demands upon her husband for support, or erect defenses, including projection of blame, that upset the family equilibrium.

A woman whose concerns about her capabilities as a wife were heightened by a long period of sterility, had her pleasure in having a baby turn into desperation when she found that she could not quiet her infant who would become rigid and shriek when she picked him up to try to comfort him. Her husband's attempts to be helpful were taken as criticism of her adequacy. Her mother had been an aloof woman who had avoided physical contact with her children and had never been able to convey a sense of warmth and protectiveness. The young wife now felt herself even more inadequate than her mother, whose attitudes she had resented. As becoming a more adequate wife and mother than her own mother had formed a major motif of her life, the foundations of her integration were being undermined. She turned the old hostilities toward her mother against herself—she had not rid herself of the resented internalized mother—and became convinced that her husband wished to be rid of her.

Although the topic cannot be discussed at this juncture, we must remember that the need for a parent to adjust and for the marriage to readjust is not confined to the time of the birth of the first child or to the first few years of its life. As we have noted in following the child's development, each transition into a new developmental phase requires an adaptation by the parents, and one or another of these required adaptations may disturb a parent's equilibrium. The child's going off to school may reawaken the fears the mother experienced in her own childhood when she was separated from her mother; a father's jealousies become aroused when his daughter starts dating; the parents have difficulty being left without children in the home, etc. A highly intelligent woman, who had been terrified in her own childhood that her mother would abandon her if her mother learned that she continued to masturbate despite warnings of dire consequences, could not tolerate her son's playing with his penis in his bath and would frantically warn him that he would become an idiot if he continued, even though intellectually she knew differently. As her own childhood had been lonely and she had felt unwanted by her peers—largely because her parents never remained in one neighborhood for more than a year or two—she would become very upset whenever her son had a quarrel with playmates, or if he were not invited to a party. She would scold him for not being more affable and more popular, which made him self-conscious and less able to seek companionship.

We have been considering how the personality changes, emotional difficulties, and regressions of a spouse that occur in response to some phase of parenthood can upset the marriage. The manner in which either one of the parents relates to the child can in itself create problems. A wife, whose beauty flattered the husband's pride and whose vivaciousness delighted him, turns into an ogress to the husband who empathizes with the daughter, whom she treats as a nuisance and mistreats when she feels annoyed with the girl's need for attention. Ethnic or social class differences in role expectations which had been inconsequential in the marital partnership become more troublesome when they concern child-rearing practices. A woman of Irish descent accepted and even admired her Polish-American husband's domination of her and his decision making for both of them; but she could not tolerate his expectations that their three-year-old son would be strictly obedient or else receive a thrashing, or his insistence that she docilely accept his decisions concerning the child's upbringing.

THE CHILD CONCEIVED TO SAVE A MARRIAGE

The stresses of being parents are great enough to challenge the harmony of a fairly secure marriage, yet many children are born in an effort to salvage one that is threatening to disintegrate. The very immature young wife who married after her first fiancé had died in combat and spent most of her pregnancy fantasying about him (see page 429) remained intensely bound to her mother and spent many evenings with her and even slept with her mother one or two nights a week. She resented her husband's refusal to take her dancing two or three nights a week as he had during the courtship. When he threatened to leave because he could not tolerate her immaturity and inability to stay home, she decided to have a second child, even though she could not properly care for the first, believing that two children would keep her so busy that she would not have time or energy for dancing and would certainly be unable to leave her husband. Although a child can help a marriage that is not working well by producing a new interest for one or both partners, it is not likely to repair a really unhappy marriage. The baby then simply binds the partners in a relationship they cannot tolerate and the child can be severely resented for holding them together.* However, the baby often dissipates boredom in a wife and dispels the feelings of emptiness that may come after the initial phase of marriage has passed and expectations that marriage would profoundly change her life are unrealized. The husband may also gain new self-esteem that changes his behavior and even modifies his personality. The man who married only after his girl-friend assured him that she did not expect great potency from him (see page 461) annoyed his wife by his lack of self-confidence and his desire for her to make the important decisions. The birth of a son set aside his insecurity, fired him with ambition to provide for his son better than he had been provided for, and he began to assert himself at work and with his wife—much to her satisfaction.

THE PARENTS' IDENTIFICATIONS WITH THEIR CHILD

Not only do children identify with parents, but parents also identify with their children. Babies are immediately part of their mothers' lives, for they have grown in them and only gradually separate from them. Some fathers will require time before they can spontaneously enjoy the baby, sometimes not until the child is old enough to be considered something of a person. The experience of parenthood makes possible a sharing of another life reciprocally to the way the parents as babies shared feelings with their

---

* A situation which can lead to a mother's phobia that she might hurt or kill the child if left alone with it—and, at times, to child abuse or infanticide.

mothers. Again, as in infancy and as in some fortunate marriages, there exists a type of unique closeness and pleasure that comes of being empathically related, with the boundaries between the self and another lowered in a positive rather than a pathological manner. The parents take pleasure in the child's joy and suffer with the child's pains more than in almost any other relationship. The child's development and achievements are experienced with pride and increase the parents' self-esteem. In certain respects the parent lives again in the child. The parent reexperiences many of the joys of childhood simply through observation and has permission to regress in time and behavior in playing with the child. The parents often live in the child, for whom they seek to establish more favorable situations than they experienced in childhood; such efforts are commonly overdone in an attempt to provide the child with what parents lacked in childhood, and usually fill the parents' needs rather than the child's. The son must have the carpentry set the father had wanted so badly and the father is usually so impatient that he gives it before the child is ready, which permits the father to indulge himself with the toy for a time, and the child to tire of it before he can use it properly. When overdone, such needs of a parent to live through a child interfere with the child's development, particularly when the child properly feels that he or she cannot become an individual but must live primarily to complete a parent's life. The converse also occurs. The parent who had been indulged in childhood and who resented the lack of direction and firmness may provide such restrictions for the child.

Through the process of identification the child can also provide one of the two parents with the opportunity to experience intimately the way in which a person of the opposite gender grows up. The sharing of the vicissitudes in the life of a child of the opposite sex, almost as if they pertained to the self, provides a broadening perspective even if it is not needed to fill some residual childhood wishes. The use of a son by the mother and occasionally of a girl by the father to live out a life the parent would like to have lived as a member of the opposite sex has been noted by many as a source of potential difficulty for both child and parent. However, one cannot consider such patterns to be detrimental or useful in themselves, for it is rather a matter of balance: a mother's inability to empathize and enjoy the experiences of a son as a son interferes with the development of the necessary reciprocal identifications between them. Parenthood also provides the opportunity to be loved, admired, and needed simply because one is a parent and, as such, a central and necessary object in the young child's life. The many potentialities for emotional satisfactions from parenthood manage to outweigh the tribulations and sacrifices that are required. It is unfortunate when parents cannot gain deep gratification from being needed by others and giving to them, the essence of being parents, and instead find children's needs and dependency simply burdensome (Doi, 1973).

THE CHANGE IN THE COUPLE'S POSITION IN SOCIETY

Aside from directly influencing the parents and their marriage, the child exerts an indirect effect through changing the parents' position in the society. New sets of relationships are established as the parents are drawn to other couples with children of the same age. The mother seeks out other young mothers with whom she can compare notes and exchange advice and admiration of the children. They are also drawn together to share supervision in order to gain some free time. As the child grows older the parents are brought together with other families through interest in nursery schools, parent-teacher's organizations, cub scouts, and in gaining suitable recreational pursuits for the children. They join organizations and clubs and plan vacations for the benefit of the children. The way in which the parents conduct their lives alters and may include a change in residence to assure the proper advantages, physical and social, for the children. A new impetus toward economic and social mobility often possesses the parents. The family's position in society becomes more definite and includes a general pattern of how parents should live in order to raise children properly. Frequently the couple's relatedness to their own parents improves and grows firmer once again. They have achieved a new status in their parents' eyes and in focusing upon their children have a new common interest and can bypass areas of friction which may have existed between the two generations.

THE CHANGING SATISFACTIONS AND TRIBULATIONS OF PARENTHOOD

Parenthood, the satisfactions it provides and the demands it makes, varies as life progresses; and changes with the parents' interests, needs, and age as well as with the children's maturation. There are phases in the child's life that the parents are reluctant to have pass, whereas they tolerate others largely through knowing that they will soon be over. The changing lives of the children provide many satisfactions that offset the tribulations, uncertainties, and regrets. The little girl that the mother nourished as a baby becomes a helper about the home, following the mother's model; she matures into adolescence and becomes a companion who shares and understands as well as requiring understanding; she becomes a wife and mother herself and has a new appreciation of her mother's life. The father finds his son experiencing many things that had long before absorbed the father, and he is fascinated to note how alike boys and their games remain over a generation. The children share interests in television, scouts, and sports with parents, but eventually they develop interests in matters that are more meaningful to the parents—hobbies, music, literature, careers. Although rivalries often pervade the father-son and the mother-daughter relationships, usually the parent can share with a child without rivalry, for children's achievements are regarded by parents very much as extensions of their own accomplishments.

The parents change. The young father, who was just starting on his career when his first child was born, settles into a life pattern. He becomes secure with increasing achievement and interacts differently with his youngest child and provides a different model for him than for his oldest. Or, he becomes resigned to falling short of his life goals, pursues them with less intensity, and focuses more attention on his children's future than on his own. The mother may have less time for a third or fourth child than for her first, but she may also be more assured in her handling of them. The birth of a baby when the parents are in their late thirties will find them less capable of physical exertion with the child and less tolerant of annoyances, but they are less apt to be annoyed. The parents become accustomed to the child's increasing independence; and though they are concerned because they provide less guidance, they are also relieved by the greater freedom from responsibility. Yet, according to an adage that is virtually a platitude, a parent's concerns about a child never cease but only change. Eventually the children marry and leave home. The couple do not cease to be parents; but with their major responsibilities for their children over, a way of life to which they had become accustomed and which provided much of the meaning to their lives comes to an end. They pass through another major demarcation line in life which we will consider in the next chapter.

THE CHILD-CENTERED HOME

Parenthood is something of a career as well as a phase of life. The consciousness that the children's personalities, stability, and happiness are influenced profoundly by how they are nurtured and reared has altered the tasks of parenthood profoundly. Parents could once turn over their children to wet nurses for the first year or two of their lives and to "nannies" to raise, or send them off to a school at the age of seven or eight. They believed that children's characters were born into them through the bloodlines they inherited, much as with the horses they rode. Then, too, parents' emotional investments in children were often held in check, for death gathered many before they grew up. Now most parents have only two or three children, and their belief that what sorts of persons their children will become depends so greatly on how they are brought up has made parenthood a very self-conscious activity.

The emphasis on improving the children's opportunities has contributed to the child-centered home, which has been or, perhaps, had been considered one of the outstanding characteristics of twentieth-century America. The term properly implies a home in which the ultimate welfare of the children takes precedence over the convenience and comforts of the parents. The child-centered home, however, becomes a travesty when the wishes and whims of the children dominate the home; or when parents fear to carry out the parental functions of delimiting and guiding their children's behavior. Teachings and misunderstandings of teachings concerning dangers that arise from frustrating a child's self-expression or "instinctual drives" serve to suppress proper parental functioning. The insecurity thus engendered in parents often offsets the potential advantages of their being parents who seek to adjust to their child's needs. Few things are as important to children as parents' self-assurance and security. Self-assurance does not mean rigidity or dogmatism. Perhaps only parents with self-assurance can properly elicit children's opinions and foster children's self-expression before reaching some decision pertaining to them. However, a home in which the parents can find no calm because of their children's "prerogatives," or in which the mother constantly feels harassed in her efforts to do the right thing without taking her own needs and desires into account, can be detrimental to the children through making the parents unhappy in their lot as parents. The parents require satisfaction if they are to be able to give of themselves to the child; and their happiness as individuals, and as a couple, is just as important as anything they may be able to do for a child or that they can give the child.

The American family may be becoming less child centered. Some young couples are more concerned with continued self-actualization through careers than through children, or with more hedonistic gratifications than those that come from having children depend upon them. Together with such reasons as overpopulation and the loss of faith in the future, they may also feel that their parents gained too little reward for their efforts, and, perhaps, that they are even less certain of how children should be raised than were their parents. It would seem as if in these precarious times parents are less willing to give hostages to the future than a decade or two ago. However, in such matters as elsewhere, trends are cyclic and it is difficult to foresee how the next generation will regard the rewards and disadvantages of parenthood.

Many things are required from persons to be competent parents and from a marriage to be suited for family life. Some of the most salient considerations have been discussed in the chapter on the family when we considered the requisites of the milieu in which the child develops. If one reviews these desiderata a central theme can be noted. The parents need to be persons in their own right with lives and satisfactions of their own, firmly related in marriage and gaining satisfaction from it, rather than having their individuality and the marriage become subordinated to their being parents. All too commonly child rearing is discussed in terms of techniques—of what parents do for a child and how it should be done; or in terms of the mother's nurturant capacities and emotional stability. Who the parents are and how they relate to one another, and the nature of the family they create are also fundamental influences upon the child. The parents as models for identification, their interaction as an example of mutuality, the importance of the family structure in integrating the children's personalities are among the topics that demand careful scrutiny if we are to learn what produces stable and unstable children. Perhaps, when parents learn that their behavior as individuals and as a married couple is of prime importance in determining their children's personality development, they will be less perplexed about how to raise children and in a better position to raise happy and stable children.

REFERENCES

BENEDEK, T. (1959). "Parenthood as a Developmental Phase: A Contribution to the Libido Theory," *Journal of the American Psychoanalytic Association*, 7:389–417.

DOI, L. T. (1973). *The Anatomy of Dependence*. J. Bester, trans. Kodansha International, Tokyo.

LIDZ, R. W., RUTLEGE, A., and TOURKOW, L. (1976). "Patient Motivation in Selection and Acceptance of Contraceptives," in *Regulation of Human Fertility*. K. S. Moghussi and T. Evans, eds. Wayne State University Press, Detroit.

ROSSI, A. (1968). "Transition to Parenthood," *Journal of Marriage and the Family*, 30:26–39.

SUGGESTED READING

ANTHONY, E. J., and BENEDEK, T., eds. (1970). *Parenthood: Its Psychology and Psychopathology*. Little, Brown, Boston.

BENEDEK, T. (1959). "Parenthood as a Developmental Phase: A Contribution to the Libido Theory," *Journal of the American Psychoanalytic Association*, 7:389–417.

DOI, L. T. (1973). *The Anatomy of Dependence*. J. Bester, trans. Kodansha International, Tokyo.

ROSSI, A. (1968). "Transition to Parenthood," *Journal of Marriage and the Family*, 30:26–39.

CHAPTER 16

❀

The Middle Years

IF WE THINK of life as a play, the middle years lead up to and away from the climax of the plot. The characters have all been on stage, and the theme and countertheme introduced; as the third act ends, the play reaches its denouement, and when the actors enter their forties their fates have been settled. The play then begins to move toward its inevitable conclusion. The critical transition may not be recognized at the moment, but some time around the age of forty, most persons gain insight into the way their lives are going to turn out. Can goals be achieved, dreams fulfilled, satisfaction attained? Will one's most significant relationships provide fulfillment and happiness? Must one come to terms with just getting by, or accept disappointment and disillusionment? Many persons refuse to be passive players, acting out the script of the Master Playwright. They will rewrite the ending. At the start of middle age there is still time to revise, time to start afresh or, at least, to salvage the years that are left—and many will try.

The middle years start when persons achieve maturity, usually in their early thirties, having gained the skills, knowledge, and assurance needed to settle into their careers and family lives. They are caught up in the challenge of making the most of their abilities and opportunities. They soon move into the period most people consider the "prime of life," the years between thirty-five and fifty-five, during which they reach the midlife transition or crisis—a period of stocktaking, and perhaps of reorientation, occurring around the age of forty—and become *middle aged*. Middle age is usually a period of fruition, but often a time of coming to terms with where one's life is going. Then, as persons enter their mid-fifties, the efforts and creative capacities of most, though far from all, persons diminish as they tend to coast on previously gained skills and accomplishments until they reach old age, which is rather arbitrarily considered to start at about sixty-five.

Our efforts to encompass almost half of the life span in this chapter will be rather inadequate and, in places, somewhat ambiguous. Although there are clear relationships between people's ages and the various critical turns during the middle years, landmarks vary with education and social class, and there are notable differences between the lives of men and women.* The middle years have been changing markedly for women, because they are usually occupied with being mothers for far fewer years than formerly, and because the two transitions in women's lives that had formerly been highly upsetting to many, the "empty nest" and the menopause, are now often welcomed.

MATURITY

People reach maturity in very different ways. When they were in their twenties they consumed much of their energies learning skills needed at work and for raising children. Some were still trying out jobs if not careers. Others felt they were just getting started and were not yet ready to make a major effort. Some changed occupations or spouses, having become dissatisfied with the results of decisions made before they knew themselves or the world. They were likely to believe that life belongs to youth and to consider anyone over thirty incapable of understanding what they sought in life. However those who went to work after completing high school may have become firmly settled and have come to terms with what they expected from life before they reached thirty.

* We must also recognize that relatively few intensive and careful studies concerning the middle years have been carried out in comparison with those of childhood and adolescence, and even of old age.

In their early thirties, most persons begin to settle down and make deeper commitments to their work and families. Now almost all women who have children are devoting a large part of their time to raising them. Although most couples have their first child when they are in their early or mid-twenties, there may now be a trend for women, particularly highly educated women, to marry later, or at least to delay having a child until they near the age of thirty. Now persons are likely to experience the pleasures of mastery. They have gained assurance and are "on top" of their work whether in an occupation or in taking care of the home and children. The work may be arduous but some tasks have become routine and experience provides answers to many problems. The mother can keep her little child engaged in helping as she cleans, or listening to a story while she washes the dishes, a story she had made up to tell an older child. The man at work has acquired ways of approaching various colleagues and no longer must prepare precisely what he is going to say at a luncheon meeting. However, though a woman now finds caring for a child easier, if she has several children the tasks of managing are multiplied, and if the man is moving up the ladder, he becomes confronted by more complicated problems.

It seems simpler to generalize about men's lives than women's as people move toward middle age. With his wife occupied with their children and employed only part-time, if at all, the man is now the main support of his family. He is now out to establish himself in his career. As Levinson *et al.* (1974) have noted, at the same time the man settles down he also becomes involved in "making it." He sets markers on the way to his goal and dates when he expects to reach them. He is in a race, the so-called rat race, toward success, and if not competing with others, he is timing himself. A fortunate person may feel sufficiently sure of his abilities to be able to disregard competition. A pharmacologist with a large pharmaceutical corporation could say, "I don't wish to sound conceited but I know what I do and can do, and I know the potentialities of most of the others in the laboratory. The firm would be foolish if they did not place me in charge of our division as soon as they could clear the way for me." Others enjoy the competition, some because it induces them to use all of their capabilities, some because it requires them to devise means of looking better than they are or of jockeying into a favorable position with the boss. The sorting out has started, even though definitive decisions concerning a person's future remain to be made. Seniors recognize the bright, the highly motivated, the creative, the leaders. A young adult may have had one or more mentors who taught and guided him and smoothed his way, but now he may acquire a sponsor who picks him out as a protégé, grooms him as a successor, backs him for promotions, or recommends him when a good position opens elsewhere.

Although the man in his mid-thirties is now a mature person capable of assuming responsibility, he is usually still a junior member of his occupation—a manager who carries out the plans of an executive, or an assistant professor who teaches required courses planned by others. At home, however, he is a decision maker and planner. Here, he carries the responsibilities together with his wife and seeks to provide a model for his children. Here, he gains self-assurance in his ability to look out for others. Of course, for the many who know that they will never gain acclaim or even very much attention in their occupations, the esteem and love of a wife and children may be particularly important. A telephone linesman who realizes that his pay will increase from year to year but that he will never advance beyond foreman feels that his children admire him for what he is, and some of his major satisfactions come from coaching the children's baseball team and taking the family on a trip in their camper each summer.

As men who expect to become successful approach the age of forty, they feel constrained in their junior status. They have abilities and ideas and wish to put them into operation. It is not simply a matter of advancement. It is time to become one's own man (Levinson *et al.*, 1974). The chief is a fine man but he is not always right. He is too conservative and does not see the opportunities. He holds on to the reins and does not realize that the younger man could do the job as well if not better. If there is no place in the organization in which the individual can do things on his own in his own way, he begins to look elsewhere. Other firms need young executives and heads of departments. The man who is ready to come into his own may now break with his sponsor (much as the adolescent separates from his family); he finds fault with his boss; feels unappreciated or misunderstood; and, unable to contain his resentments, breaks away in anger. He may seek to become a competitor who by his achievements shows that he has been unappreciated. An associate professor of internal medicine accepted the chairmanship of a department in a much less prestigious medical school in the same city, and set out to develop a superior department. He confided to a coworker that he was out to woo the best students from his former university to his department, as a way of getting back at his former chief who had promoted a rival to section chief.

The opportunity to be one's own man, to be relatively free to direct oneself and the organization, or some division of the organization, provides a sense of accomplishment and sets new challenges that mobilize energy and enthusiasm. New facets of the personality are utilized and develop as the individual assumes a leadership role. Some who feel that they have now reached their goals accept the prestige and diminish their efforts; but others become disappointed when they find that they are still limited by constraints that keep them from completely fulfilling their aspirations. The new chief of research for the corporation finds that he must compete with advertising, development, sales, etc., for funds to develop his new process; or that the president does not think the process will lead to increased earnings. It is a rare and fortunate man who finds his career strivings free of constraints by middle age, or at any age.

Even those who feel assured of success may change careers in mid-course. Indeed, some may feel free to change only after it has become clear to them and others that they are not giving up because of failure. A man who had demonstrated his abilities by planning and completing a large housing development for his father's corporation resigned to go abroad to study musical composition. His major interest had always been music, and he was an excellent pianist. But he had not pursued a musical career because his father considered his interest in the piano an effete activity, implying that he lacked the courage and stamina to make his way in the building industry. Only after he had demonstrated his ability to compete effectively in his father's industry could he feel free to follow his own interests. Another highly capable man surprised the heads of a multinational corporation by resigning in response to a major promotion. He had been placed in charge of a large manufacturing plant in a different part of the country. It was the fifth time in twelve years that it had become necessary to relocate his family to move along the path to the presidency of the corporation. His wife felt rootless and one son was in difficulty at school. He decided that, if he were so well thought of in one of the country's leading corporations, he could find a rewarding and useful position in the city in which they were living. A major university was happy to recruit him as its treasurer.

Women frequently change the course of their lives some time between the ages of thirty-five and forty. They may resume their education or careers when their two or three children are in grade school; or, if they wait longer until the children are more self-sufficient, they will become engaged in some significant activity outside the home when the last child is in school. A woman may know precisely what she wishes to do, and have kept preparing by study or part-time work while the children were small. A woman with a master's degree in psychology who had kept abreast in the field and gained experience by assisting at the university a few mornings a week started working for her doctorate as soon as her children were all in school. Many women will return to work to help finance their children's college education, or simply to improve the family's standard of living. There are many alternatives, and a woman may not be completely certain whether she is starting on a career or simply pursuing an interest, and may need time to find out. A woman who followed her youthful ambition to become a high school English teacher soon found that she had enough of adolescents at home, and became a magazine editor instead. For another, an evening course in photography, taken as a diversion when her two children were small, blossomed into a major interest and occupation. Whatever the precise course of action, these years are increasingly becoming a time of transition for women. They often embark on the new activity bursting with enthusiasm and interest after release from being tied to the home for years. Those who return to college, expecting to feel uneasy among young students and unable to compete with them, often find not only that their experience and maturity give them an academic advantage, but that young women seek their friendship and advice.

Women professionals—physicians, architects, musicians—who had been pursuing their careers in low gear, so to speak, while occupied and preoccupied with small children, now feel free really to devote themselves to their professions, even though motherhood will still remain a major activity. Some women, even some who had prepared themselves for professions, now seem ready to enjoy the benefits of being supported by a husband. They decide to pursue interests as amateurs, rather than pursue a career. They enjoy running charitable organizations together with friends; or, having been initiated through becoming a member of the school board, they find that politics can become a fascinating activity in which they can gain power and prestige even if they do not wish to hold public office.

MIDDLE AGE

Stocktaking

Middle age is properly a time of fulfillment, when years of effort reach fruition. However, it is commonly ushered in, around the age of forty, by an interlude of stocktaking and uneasiness—the midlife crisis or transition. As many women have already undergone a major transition, the crisis occurs more frequently in men. The turn into middle age involves a state of mind rather than some specific bodily landmark. It is initiated by awareness that the peak years of life are passing. Persons realize that they are no longer starting on their way; their direction is usually well set, and their present activities will determine how far they will get. James Baldwin (1967) wrote:

> Though we would like to live without regrets, and sometimes proudly insist that we have none, this is not really possible, if only because we are mortal. When more time stretches behind than stretches before one, some assessments, however reluctantly and incompletely, begin to be made. Between what one wished to become and what one *has* become there is a momentous gap, which will now never be closed. And this gap seems to operate as one's final margin, one's last opportunity, for creation. And between the self as it is and the self as one sees it, there is also a distance, even harder to gauge. Some of us are compelled, around the middle of our lives, to make a study of this baffling geography, less in the hope of conquering these distances than in the determination that the distances shall not become any greater.

A man had been occupied and preoccupied with making his way in a career, and with providing for his wife and children. A woman's life had centered around the care of her children and in making a proper home for them. Now it is time to look where their lives have been going, for new patterns of living are required. Then, too, parents have died or retired; and persons realize that they are now members of the older, responsible generation. They have moved to the center of the stage.* The consciousness of the critical transition is abetted by awareness that the body is slowing down. It is no longer the well-oiled machine that quietly responds to the demands placed upon it; it creaks and groans a bit. The woman sees the menopause looming before her when her generative capacities will come to an end. What has been achieved? And what do the years ahead still hold? Middle age is obviously not a bountiful time for all. For some the regrets and disillusion mount, often mixed with a bitter resentment that life has slipped through their fingers. Still, even for the fortunate, the balance of life is upset by awareness of the passing of time and the limits of life's span. There is a recrudescence of a type of existential anxiety, an awareness of the insignificance of the individual life in an infinity of time and space. Now, in middle life, a stock taking and a reevaluation occur. Two of the world's literary masterpieces start on this note. Dante opens the *Divine*

---

* I recall an occasion when several medical school professors in their mid-forties received the news that a department head had died of a stroke; it was the third death of a senior faculty member within the year. They sat silently, a bit stunned, and then one looked at the others and quietly said, "Now it is up to us."

Comedy with the line "Midway in the journey through life, I found myself lost in a dark wood strayed from the true path." Goethe's Faust finds that although he has studied philosophy, medicine, and law thoroughly, he is fundamentally no wiser than the poorest fool, feels his life wasted despite his achievements, and makes a pact with Mephistopheles in his attempt to salvage it. The lives of ordinary mortals beyond this juncture are more prosaic than the ways in which these two giants attained salvation; but in a personal rather than a universal context, the path often leads to pacts with the devil before a resolution can be found. For some, middle age brings neither fruition nor disappointment so much as angry bewilderment as they find that their neglect of meaningful relationships in the frenetic striving for success now makes life seem like "a tale told by an idiot—full of sound and fury, signifying nothing" (*Macbeth*, Act V, Sc. 5).

Although the usual course of life continues along a well-trodden path, with ample satisfactions and rewards found on the way, with hopes and ambitions tempered by experience, and doubts and concerns countered by religion or philosophy—summing up and reassessment are characteristic of middle age, even when they do not lead to any notable changes.

The stocktaking does not simply concern success or failure in achieving goals. It has to do rather with inner satisfactions, with considering whether what one has achieved is compatible with one's earlier dreams and ideals; with any disparity between one's way of life and what truly provides a sense of self-esteem (Levinson *et al.*, 1974).

Satisfactions of Middle Age

When life has gone well, when ambitions and expectations have not exceeded potential, or when modifications of goals either downward or upward have been made in accord with reality, the middle years can bring great satisfactions. Most persons are now at the height of their potential. They have passed their physical prime but they use their heads effectively and have learned to conserve their energies. They know what will work and what will be a waste of time and energy. The executive has learned which functions can safely be delegated and to whom, and he can make many decisions on the basis of past experience. The artisan now rarely encounters an unfamiliar job, directs assistants how to tackle a task, and reserves for himself those aspects that require special skills or involve risks. Now persons know their areas of competence and they have the satisfaction of feeling in control in them. Some enjoy the prestige and power and may feel impelled to seek after more and more power over others, but the sense of mastery provides pleasure to less driven individuals. The more successful persons have not simply acquired knowledge and skills but also wisdom in making decisions, in approaching tasks, and, particularly, in convincing others. A chemical engineer in his fifties managed to overcome a major crisis in his industry by inventing a totally new and highly complicated process and then putting it into operation, all within a few brief years. When reviewing how he had managed the accomplishment, he explained that, because of his intensive and prolonged experience with related chemical processes as well as his knowledge of the theory involved, he had been able to figure out, with considerable assurance, how various chemical reactions would turn out, even while lying in bed at night, simply by calculating mathematical formulae, thereby eliminating much trial and error. Less experienced engineers, or those without his special knowledge of theory, would have required many time-consuming and costly trials. He went on to point out that he had not only to convince himself that he dare eliminate trials, but also later to convince the president of the firm that it was worth taking the risk of spending a million dollars in constructing a model plant.

Persons are now established in their work. For some, particularly in executive circles, the period between forty and fifty, or even fifty-five, may involve intense striving to capture the elusive top positions or properly to climax a career by amassing the wealth or prestige that has come within grasp. Demonstrated capacities may lead to greater demands, expectations, and responsibilities, and open new opportunities. Others become involved in political jockeying to win out over a competitor. The strain of the competition can be wearing. However, as far as the vast majority is concerned, if individuals have not yet reached the peak of their achievements, they can see how far they will get, and move toward it as part of the career pattern. In the factory, they have become foremen or foreladies, or at least old and experienced hands, with security and some special prerogatives. In a profession, persons are established members whose experience is valued by younger colleagues. They are no longer in direct competition with younger members, but can take a parental attitude in guiding the next generation. They need no longer prove themselves from day to day, for they are credited with past accomplishments. Those whom they direct or supervise respect and seek to satisfy them. They see the realization of their efforts and can relax occasionally and depend upon their experience.

Adolescents or even young adults commonly consider that their parents' lives are over; that they have had their day in a remote past, but now, in their forties or early fifties, the "heyday in the blood is tame" (*Hamlet*, Act III, Sc. 4); that their lives are without passion and without a future. Some middle-aged persons feel the same way about themselves. But each period of life differs from the others, offering new opportunities and new ways of experiencing as well as new tasks to be surmounted. The more mature can accept the advantages and pleasures of middle life together with the limitations it imposes. Persons become pathetic and sometimes even ludicrous when they insist on seeking the pleasures and rewards appropriate to a younger age. Some fear displacement by the next generation; some now begin to live through their children; but others are still very much engaged in pursuing their own careers and life patterns and may well feel that with responsibility for children gone they have a new freedom to focus on their own lives and interests. As we have noted, many women find new interests and enthusiasms now that they can pursue their old careers again, or enter upon new vocations or avocations now that their children can look after themselves. The "empty nest" syndrome—the mother's depression after the children all leave home—is still fairly common, as we shall consider later in the chapter, but most women now find other satisfying interests. With parental functions largely completed, persons are likely to find related gratification in a different type of generativity. They have reached a stage of life when they can be the mentors. They wish to have heirs in their fields of endeavor to whom they can bequeath their knowledge, and who will carry their interests into the next generation. They are interested in the future of their firms, university departments, hospitals, towns, in which they have invested their energies, and they hope that these institutions will not only flourish after they leave, but continue along the lines they have pursued. Erikson (1959) has considered such *generativity* a crucial aspect of middle life, with *stagnation* as the negative outcome.

Some Critical Problems

A critical aspect of middle age concerns coming to terms with one's accomplishments: not only to accept the limits of achievement and not become embittered and depressed over what one considers inadequate recognition of what one has done, or of one's personal qualities, but also to be able to enjoy the prestige attained and to accept the responsibilities that accompany it. Soon after a much desired promotion or some specific recognition of their abilities some persons become depressed—the "promotion depression" that catches all by surprise. Classically, the man is caught in an outgrowth of a pattern that had its origins in his childhood—he feels vulnerable in surpassing his father. It is a version of the childhood fantasy of displacing the father with his mother; and old fears haunt him that father will take vengeance, and he punishes himself for his hubris. Commonly, however, persons resent being burdened with a new load of responsibilities. They had striven to reach the goal, but the goal turns out to be somewhat of an illusion. It is no haven but requires more work, more decision making, more responsibility. They cannot turn from it without loss of self-esteem, but they resent the expectations others have for them, the demands of the boss or the organization, or a spouse's ambition that carried them beyond their limits.

When most people become middle-aged they still have adolescent children. Although adolescents require less actual care, they usually require considerable attention and can become sources of great concern to parents. Memories of their own adolescent problems return to haunt the middle-aged parents. They struggle between wishes to set limits and protect, and their realization that each generation must gain experience on its own. They know that there is a way between control that is resented and protection that is desired, but how to find it? They seek to understand their children according to the ways and concepts of the young generation, but have trouble finding any sense in them. They may also feel envious of their children's vitality and their growing sexual interests and attractiveness, and relive the missed opportunities of their own youthful years. Now the parents must recognize the individuation of their children in order to foster their attainment of firm ego identities. However, some will seek to bind one or more children to them, feeling that their own lives will be meaningless without a child or needing completion through a child. Others may use a child as a delegate (Stierlin, 1974) to achieve what they could not achieve, or to live out the sensuous pleasures they could not permit themselves. Such usages of adolescent children are very likely to lead the children to revolt against the parents or into serious problems that can blight parents' lives, but they also assure the children that they remain central to the parents' lives.

When things go well, however, the children will eventually cease to preoccupy the parents—a time that may indicate the actual start of middle age for many parents. The change usually affects a mother more than a father. The nurturant functions, which have constituted her cardinal interest and shaped her activity for two or more decades, come to an end. Concerns for her children may remain a dominant interest, but they are in the form of thoughts and feelings and no longer take up much of her time and effort. Some mothers feel that their major life function has been completed. Though a mother may be pleased and even relieved at the release from so much work and responsibility, she usually also has regrets and feels an emptiness in her life. A mother may feel that the children to whom she has given so much have become neglectful and ungrateful, and misunderstandings can easily arise with children whose dominant interests are now their own spouses, children, and careers.* The capacity to shift cardinal emotional investments seems essential to a satisfying middle and old age. The withdrawal of a major "cathexis" or emotional investment from children may be the first such shift, but others will follow inevitably as parents, relatives, and friends die.

The Physical Changes

Middle age is a period of considerable significance both for medicine and for psychiatry. Whether persons admit it or not, although they may be in the "prime of life," they have passed the peak of their physical abilities. Hair is growing gray or sparse, wrinkles appear, the abdomen gets in the way when they bend. Slowly but surely, they realize that their bodies no longer respond to their demands without squeaking. The paper must be read at arm's length and then bifocals become a necessity. The wear and tear of life add up and begin to be felt. The knee injured in youth stiffens at times and aches in bad weather. A back injury may be incapacitating every now and again. The drink before supper is no longer taken simply to enliven, but to counter the dull fatigue felt after a day's work. The slow increment in weight requires reluctant attention to diet, for a gain in weight at this age is considered hazardous to health.

Changes in the various organ systems occur as processes of repair and renewal lag and lead to degenerative changes that increase the proneness to illness and dysfunction. For the man, the years between forty and fifty hold the threat of sudden death from coronary occlusion. Such heart attacks are less likely to be fatal later in life after a gradual narrowing of the coronary arteries leads to development of anastomatic arterial pathways by which the heart muscle can receive blood after a large vessel occludes. Malignancies take their toll and women are advised to check their breasts for masses regularly and have annual gynecological examinations. Even persons who remain healthy become familiar with hospitals through visiting friends, and find that they can no longer avoid scanning the obituary columns if they wish to keep track of acquaintances. They may gain some secret satisfac-

---

* The "empty nest" syndrome can contribute to depressive illnesses in middle-aged women. The problem is likely to be most severe in divorced or widowed mothers, and particularly by immigrant or first-generation women who have not become well acculturated and whose families were, therefore, particularly important to them (Deykin et al., 1966).

tion from surviving enemies, or from noting that they are outlasting acquaintances or that one's own obituaries will read better than those of a colleague. Middle-aged individuals become aware that ill health and even death are potentialities that hover over them and those close to them. Such awareness consciously or unconsciously influences the pattern of life. Some slacken the pace of their activities to keep in step with the body's capacities or infirmities, whereas others are provoked to renewed exertions in order to get more or further before it is too late. Psychologically disorganizing illnesses become less common, for the personality has become more firmly integrated and an ego identity established; but depressive reactions become more frequent, and they are related to regrets over the way life has gone, accompanied by resentment toward those who have caused frustration and by anger against the self for failing to meet expectations.*

The Menopause

The woman's loss of nurturant functions is compounded by the loss of generative capacities, another function that has been so much a part of her existence and so fundamental to her self-esteem. Even though most women are prepared for it, and may even welcome it, the menopause forms a major landmark in women's lives, and a woman is likely to feel, perhaps only unconsciously, that she will be elderly after it occurs, and an empty woman. The menopause occurs at a mean age of forty-eight or forty-nine; but often in the mid-forties and occasionally even earlier. Most women are psychologically preparing themselves for it as they turn forty. It is common for women to believe that the menopause comes in the early forties or even the late thirties, and some women oblige by suffering from appropriate symptoms ten or fifteen years ahead of time. The difficulties may ensue

---

* Concerns over the meaningfulness of life in general, and of the course of one's own life, are not confined to intellectuals. A coal miner who was hospitalized because he was becoming increasingly incapacitated from arthritis expressed some suicidal ruminations. He was deeply disappointed because he realized that his life's strivings would amount to nothing. Raised in poverty by immigrant parents, he had entered the pits at twelve. He had become resigned to spending his life in the mines but swore that his children would become educated and lead a better life. Both his wife and he had scrimped and taken extra jobs whenever any were available. Now, at the age of forty-five he was an old and disabled man and had not saved enough to send his two sons to college. Even more disappointing, neither of his boys wished to continue beyond high school; neither was interested in their father's ambitions for them—that one become an engineer and the other a doctor. In actuality, it seemed apparent that neither had the capacity for a higher education; but the hopes that had given meaning to the miner's life had collapsed. He was resentful toward his sons, but he also blamed himself for having been an inadequate father.

both from the physiological changes that occur with the cessation of estrogen secretion and from the emotional impact of the "change of life."

The changes in hormonal secretions, with a marked decline in estrogen
secretion as the climacteric starts, upsets the physiological homeostasis and
produces an array of physical discomforts that varies in degree and duration
from individual to individual. The menses may cease abruptly or taper off
over a year or longer, with periods missed or coming irregularly; the flow
may be sparse or unexpectedly profuse. The woman may become uneasy,
for the irregularity can interfere with plans, lest she be caught unawares.
Although an occasional woman may experience no discomfort during the
climacterium, vasomotor instability often causes considerable trouble during the menopause and occasionally for some years thereafter. Waves of
hot feelings that sweep over the woman, termed "hot flashes" or "hot
flushes," are most common, but unexpected sweating, blotching of the skin,
and feelings of being unpleasantly warm much of the time can also be
annoying. Episodes of faintness or dizziness make some women feel insecure, and headaches can become troublesome. Most women are simply
uncomfortable and uneasy, but a few become severely upset. Although the
emotional lability may be provoked by the hormonal changes, for some
women the menopause requires a realignment of attitudes about the self
that cuts deeply into the personality and its defenses. It is a time of emotional vulnerability when neurotic difficulties can flare into symptoms,
particularly depressive symptoms. However, such difficulties were more
common when large families were desired or when a woman's prestige and
self-esteem were closely related to her generative capacities. Now, when a
few children are sufficient and women have other gratifications in life,
relatively few women suffer from notable menopausal problems. Most are
pleased to be free of the bother of menstruation and of the possibility of a
late, undesired pregnancy. Nevertheless, even though a woman experiences
only mild physical discomfiture, she will feel changed by the event and will
have readjusted her inner balance.

Although attitudes concerning the menopause have changed greatly in
recent decades in the United States, old traditions persist among some
ethnic groups. Folklore has engendered the belief that the menopause
causes serious emotional and mental instability and that a woman is fortunate if she does not become seriously depressed or insane: the physical
symptoms are amplified into an almost unbearable suffering, another
burden to which the deprived sex is subjected. Another common belief,
held by men as well as women, that the woman loses her sexual responsivity and ability to enjoy sex with the menopause, may lead a woman to feel

that she will become an undesirable old woman whose husband may properly seek gratification elsewhere. Such concepts have no basis in fact.
Indeed, there is now ample evidence that, in general, the woman's potential
for sexual responsivity throughout middle age is greater than the man's.

We noted that menstruation, even though resented as a burden, constituted a desired symbol of femininity (Chapter 10). The woman feels the
loss of this badge of womanhood—an indicator of her capacity to reproduce—that has provided feelings of worth. In contrast to the situation in
childhood, she now has no prospects of a future flowering to offset feelings
of emptiness and deprivation. She knows, indeed, that she will lose more
than her menses and fertility: her breasts grow flabby, the subcutaneous
adipose tissue that softens her contours gradually disappears, her skin
becomes wrinkled and sags, and pouches appear under her eyes. Ultimately
she will again assume a rather sexless appearance which she may be better
able to conceal from others than from herself. Her narcissism suffers, for
she will no longer be able to use her physical charms to attract. She may
mourn for the person she had been. Helene Deutsch (1945) believed that
"almost every woman in the climacterium goes through a shorter or longer
period of depression." It may be scarcely noticeable in a woman who feels
that her life has been productive, who finds new sources of fulfillment and
pleasure in middle life, or it may be apparent only in bursts of frenzied
activity utilized to ward off recognition of the changed status; but many
women will experience a downswing before they reorganize themselves.*

Fortunately, the physical discomforts of the menopause can be largely
dissipated by replacement therapy with estrogens. The woman no longer
need fear distressing symptoms. At the present time the medical management of menopausal symptoms varies according to the opinions of the
gynecologist or internist: some prefer to let mild or moderate symptoms
continue without replacement in order to permit a new balance to become

---

* The relationship of a woman's pride and self-esteem to the intactness of her body
and particularly to her generative organs is often overlooked by gynecologists who can
cause considerable unhappiness by expecting patients to assume a logical attitude toward
the removal of the uterus or the ovaries in middle life. When the gynecologist finds a
benign uterine tumor that requires removal, he may insist upon removing one ovary at
the same time: the woman does not need it, one ovary supplies sufficient hormone,
and the chances of developing cancer of the ovary is halved. However, many women
cannot take this attitude and feel that they are being mutilated. All too often more
radical procedures are carried out when they are not absolutely essential; the woman is
"cleaned out" of her uterus and both ovaries, the gynecologist assuring her that menopausal symptoms can be avoided by estrogen replacement therapy. Somehow male surgeons tend to have relatively little regard for ovaries because in contrast to testes they
are not visible. A rational approach recognizes how much a woman's uterus and ovaries
are related to her feelings of worth (R. Lidz, 1974).

established as soon as possible. However, discomforts can easily be checked if deemed necessary.

Currently, an increasing number of gynecologists institute permanent estrogen replacement therapy at the start of the climacterium. They not only consider that it is unnecessary for women ever to experience menopause, but that various other manifestations of aging can be prevented. The subcutaneous tissues do not atrophy, protein loss is countered, the breasts remain firm, the genital tissues do not atrophy, and the loss of calcium from the bones that leads to bowing of the spine and loss of height is slowed. As such measures have been undertaken only in recent years, the long-term results and possible dangers cannot yet be assessed.* At present, it appears that the increasing longevity of women can be accompanied by preservation from many aspects of aging.

The Security of a Good Marriage

A good marriage provides great security, for both partners are certain of the affection of the person most important to him or her. They do not have to pretend, or extend themselves, or find new meaningful relationships but can feel settled with one another. The children are now more likely to be sources of pleasure than concern. If the spouses have one another, the disappointments of life are buffered. If others do not regard the husband as a successful man, at least his wife appreciates what he has done or tried to do. If the children seem to neglect their mother or have become hostile during their adolescence, her husband still loves her. Even if there had been friction earlier in the marriage, middle-aged spouses often come to terms with one another. Each knows that his or her way of life and well-being depends upon the other. Each has become accustomed to the ways of the other, and would feel uneasy with another. For many couples the sexual adjustment is more satisfactory than when they were young; perhaps it is less frenzied but they know the other's needs and tacit signals, and have found ways of satisfying each other. With greater control, skill, or artistry, the sexual act can bring more subtle pleasures.

However, some problems in sexual adjustment can arise. The wife may experience a heightening of sexual drive with the menopause; particularly if concerns over impregnation had interfered with her spontaneity she now feels a release to enjoy sex without worry. Then, too, the relative freedom

* There seems to be a possibility that such replacement therapy may increase slightly the chances of developing cancer of the uterus.

from concerns about her children and from the fatigue caused by looking after them permits relaxation and renewed interest in sexual pleasures.* The husband whose sexual drive has been declining may not respond to the wife's increased interest. After the age of fifty or fifty-five, the man's sexual adequacies may decline rather notably, but he remains interested and capable under proper circumstances. However, the failures of potency that occur on occasion may upset him considerably and lead him to avoid further attempts except when he feels certain of success, and because of the psychic factors involved in male potency, self-consciousness can augment his difficulties. Such problems can lead a husband to seek extramarital relations in which he finds new stimulation. But a harmonious and affectionate married couple can usually manage the shifts in sexual interests and capacities between themselves.

Restitutive Efforts

The man who is satisfied with where he is getting in his career, the woman who feels that she has provided a good home for her husband and children and has found stimulating interests to fill her life, the husband and wife who enjoy a harmonious marriage and have the affection and respect of their children—such persons can meet their middle age wisely and complacently and seek simply to round out a full life in the years that lie ahead. Still, the person who has few regrets or who has acquired sufficient wisdom to absorb the disappointments must be considered fortunate. It is not so simple to continue to meet life with dignity and integrity when envy, regret, and bitterness gnaw at one. Life is a one-time matter and it is difficult to cope with the feeling that the chance has been wasted. There may yet be time before old age brings infirmities, time to realize the life dreamed of in youth, to love and be loved, to gain the pleasure one has had to forgo, to win the fame and fortune one has envied—or, perhaps, simply to feel wanted by someone who cares, or to be free of carping criticism and blame for past mistakes. Middle age is notably a time when restitutive efforts are made. For some the grasping after the gold ring succeeds, but more often impetuous attempts bring further unhappiness. The final fling

---

* In contrast, as Masters and Johnson (1966) have noted, a woman who has never gained pleasure from the sexual act may use the menopause as an excuse to avoid frequent sexual relations. These investigators have also found that sometimes the postmenopausal woman will experience pain on urinating after intercourse—a result of the thinning of the vaginal wall. They note that unless replacement therapy is used, a woman must have intercourse with some regularity after the menopause to maintain an adequate vaginal outlet and to prevent shrinkage of the vagina.

before the gates close* can disrupt a family and fill the last half of life with bitterness. The spouse becomes resentful and the children become disillusioned and unforgiving. The wife who is striving to ward off feelings of emptiness after the children have left and after her menopause becomes hostile and depressed when her husband has an affair with a younger woman. More marriages would be wrecked if many wives did not anticipate such behavior from their husbands in middle age and managed to forget or pretend to forget when their husbands realized that another woman does not provide the answer.

The narcissistic person, whose equilibrium has rested upon the admiration of others and in pride in youthful attributes, seems most prone to seek to regain adolescent capacities. A woman who was admired for her beauty and whose self-esteem derived largely from the glow of desire she could light in men's eyes felt displaced when her daughter was pursued by many suitors and when her praise now came for having an extraordinarily beautiful daughter. The mother had her face lifted, spent long hours at the beautician's, and began to dress more and more youthfully. She intruded upon the young men who called upon her daughter, and sought to captivate them with her wit and physical charm. At times, it was hard to tell whether the young men were courting the mother or the daughter.

Strains upon the Marriage

These years can present a severe test to a marriage. With the children no longer a major focus of attention, the spouses are on their own again, largely dependent upon one another to keep their marriage alive and their lives meaningful after a lapse of twenty or thirty years. The children no longer provide diversion or activity, or serve as scapegoats for the conflict between the spouses. The spouses have more time together, which can be either a burden or an opportunity for increased closeness. Boredom comes easily after all these years together, and a number of persons will return to adolescent and early adult patterns of using sexual adventure as a way of averting ennui and loneliness. There is some increase in the divorce rate in middle age. However, a fair number of such divorces are not caused by new infatuations, or middle-aged flings, but rather because the couple had

---

* *Torschluss* is a syndrome recognized in the German language and literature in which a middle-aged person seeks gratification while it is still possible, and the term *Torschluss-panik* is used to describe the frenzied anxiety-driven efforts of a man to make the most of his waning potency by pursuing young women.

decided to wait until their children were grown before dissolving an unsatisfactory marriage. Although friends are often reluctant to see a marriage
that had endured for so many years break up, and though it usually causes
considerable unhappiness for one of the partners, such shifts of marital
partners in midlife work out well for many. One or both partners have
matured sufficiently to select a spouse with better judgment than he or she
used in the impetuousness of youth. A person may even find that the
second marriage is the real thing, the second choice being more suitable,
and both partners are able to get off to a better start the second time.
However, the tendency for repetition in the marital choice is striking. Often
friends observe that the new spouse has characteristics very similar to the
first. Then, too, the older man who finds a young wife whom he feels
appreciates his virility, may well be marrying a woman who is seeking a
father figure and who is relatively disinterested in the sexual aspects of
marriage. Because of the imbalance caused by the higher death rate among
men than women in middle age, more divorced women than men are likely
to remain unmarried, particularly as they are much less likely to marry a
younger spouse. A man is also less likely to remain unmarried after a
divorce—or the death of a wife—because he is less capable of taking care
of himself and a home.

Vocational Problems

People continue to change jobs throughout middle age, and the shifts
can create difficulties in readjustment. The more satisfactory changes usually occur within a career rather than through shifting careers. Careers
properly consist of a succession of related jobs, arranged in a hierarchy of
pay and prestige through which persons move in a reasonably ordered and
predictable sequence (Wilensky, 1968). Persons are usually prepared for
the next job in the hierarchy when they move into it. However, as persons
move through middle age, their responsibilities are likely to increase as
their energy and malleability begin to diminish; they are passed over for
promotion and become resentful, or are promoted into positions that lead
into blind alleys.

There are some careers that come to an end in middle age, and those
who pursue them are in difficulty if they have not prepared themselves for
new careers. An opera singer became a voice teacher and gained considerable gratification from the success of her students. In contrast, a tennis professional who became a coach began to find his days too arduous as he
turned fifty, and marital troubles developed when he became reluctant to

take his wife out evenings and ceased having sexual relations in order to conserve his strength. Others lose jobs because of increasing automatization or shifts in industrial needs, and the middle-aged are not welcomed into fields in which they are untrained; and middle-aged skilled workers tend to resist retraining.

In early middle age there is still time to shift vocations. As we have noted, many women not only change from their primary vocations as mothers and housewives, but enter new careers. Some men also decide that they can still start anew; but as the years pass, such changes become increasingly hazardous, for they come at a time in life when persons should be getting settled in what they have been doing rather than moving into a spot where they must prove themselves anew. There are many opportunities, of course, for successful persons. There is always a need for good, experienced executives. The successful corporation attorney is offered a position as head of a government agency; a university professor is made head of a foundation, etc. "Head hunters," agencies that pirate executives for other corporations, may find an excellent opportunity for the competent but frustrated successful businessman. But there are few good places available for those who have not yet made the grade. As middle age passes, most persons, whether executives or laborers, become concerned more with maintaining the position and security they have attained than with seeking a better opportunity. Workers rely upon the union to protect them from displacement by younger persons and to defend their seniority rights when unemployment threatens. They learn to control feelings of resentment toward employers, to swallow their feelings when they are passed over for promotion, and find virtue in patience. As age increases, future security progressively takes precedence over opportunity. Other sources of self-realization must be found. Still, not all are wise or able to contain themselves. To some who have sought wealth, the stock market beckons—or the races or gaming table where luck may succeed when effort has failed.

Although when all goes well a person experiences relief from the need to prove himself constantly, success does not necessarily bring surcease from striving. Indeed, many successful persons tend to be compulsive, becoming anxious when they are not giving their best, while others have succeeded because they find and enjoy challenge in what they are doing. Still, it is easier to continue strenuous efforts when they are not taken as a test of worth. Some cannot accept being bested by youth or admit that age brings some limitations. A man who was invalided by a heart attack, and soon died of a second, described how his first heart attack occurred. He was a sandhog, extremely proud of his strength and his independence since early adolescence. He had been unable to accept the banter of the young crew he supervised and who referred to him as Grandpa even though he had just passed forty. He felt that to retain their respect as a foreman he must show himself as capable as any. When his crew was confronted by a particularly difficult task in moving a boulder in a tunnel, he insisted on showing how it could be done. Their entreaties to him to desist and let them do it only infuriated him. As he tugged and shouted directions, he experienced a sudden sharp pain in his chest and collapsed. In the hospital he vowed that he would never live as an invalid and rely on his wife's support—and he never did. The industrialist may continue to expand his business as if his livelihood depended upon it. Indeed, some "oral" characters can never feel that their future supplies are secure. At first, they feel they will be haunted less by the specter of insecurity after they have made a million, but the million then seems peanuts and not security, and failure of an important business venture creates as much anxiety as if they could no longer feed the family. However, the pursuit of unnecessary riches even to the hurt of others brings high esteem in Western civilization.

Ill Health

The problems that arise from ill health in middle age form realistic difficulties often enough to require at least passing comment. Illness can temporarily disrupt the course of a life or require reorganizations of a life plan. The blood pressure rises insidiously and indicates a need to slow the pace; diabetes that starts after forty is relatively common and not usually serious but requires attention to diet. Some such moderate incapacitations can bring compensations. Sir William Osler is said to have remarked that one of the best ways of assuring a long life is to suffer a mild heart attack in middle age. The man gains a sufficient reason to cease driving himself and permit himself to enjoy living. He may have played golf only for the companionship, and now he can limit himself to a few holes and then sit at the "nineteenth hole" sipping a highball while he chats with friends. The wife of a man who had once been a prominent attorney considered that a mild heart attack had saved him from a serious depression. His practice had fallen off precipitously after the death of his partner, but he could not admit his inability to manage the firm and gain new clients. The family lived largely on his wife's inherited wealth, but without openly recognizing the situation. Her income would not have been able to offset his business deficit much longer, but he had been unable to give up his office and disclose the poor state of his practice to his friends and colleagues. His wife had helped maintain the pretense lest he become depressed and suicidal. The heart attack brought relief for both of them. His physician agreed with his wife that he was unable to continue his work, and he retired, occupying himself with legal research at home. The tendency to fall back upon ill health, either real or imagined, as a means of resolving serious difficulties presents a very real problem to physicians. The prop of ill health should not be removed incautiously. The reasons why a person needs it must be ascertained, evaluated, and removed before a physician insists that there is no need for the patient to refrain from his usual activities. On the other hand, persons can be made to despair and feel that their lives are worthless by overcautious efforts to preserve life.*

Children and Grandchildren

Even though children cease to be a major responsibility for the middle-aged couple, they are usually not lost to the parents and continue as a major center of interest. The parents who have given of themselves while fostering their children's growth and gradual emancipation from them now have children who feel free to return to them, and even to turn to them for help, for they have no reason to fear losing their independence when they do. Relationships change as children become adults with whom parents discuss problems and from whom they may seek advice. Readjustments of relationships must be made when children marry, and it is unfortunate when parents feel that they have lost a child rather than gained one in the process. The arrival of the first grandchild will usually evoke some feelings of strangeness and perhaps something of a shock at becoming a member of the third generation. Grandparents are supposed to be old, but middle-aged grandparents do not yet feel old. The grandchildren furnish a new major source of interest; and if the grandparents can participate in raising them, they often behave differently from the way they did in rearing their own children. They feel more free to give and indulge, for they seek to be loved and needed by the grandchildren—sometimes to their children's despair.

---

* The point is illustrated by a story which, I believe, was told originally about the distinguished Baltimore internist Dr. Louis Hamman. A patient consulted with Dr. Hamman after recovering from a coronary occlusion. After Dr. Hamman had examined him thoroughly, the patient said, "My doctor told me that I must give up smoking, business, golf, sexual relations, and go to bed each night before eleven—is that correct?" Dr. Hamman agreed that it was sound advice. "If I follow it," the patient then asked, "will I live longer?" "That," Dr. Hamman replied, "I can't say, but it will seem longer."

Middle Age for the Unmarried and Single

However, not all persons marry. Some consciously prefer to remain single and others remain single unwillingly but, as we considered the matter in an earlier chapter, they usually have unconscious deterrents to marrying or unadmitted reasons for remaining single. There are many ways in which a single life can be satisfactory and even happy; but as the middle years pass, the advantages are apt to diminish. The daughter who has been the dutiful child and remained unmarried to look after her parents may have persevered in the hope of becoming the most favored child who would be properly appreciated after her siblings all married and left home; or perhaps the strength of the oedipal attachment prevented marriage: her parents absorbed her entire emotional life and she seems content to remain with them. Eventually, she finds herself saddled with the care of infirm or even senile parents who can no longer give her anything in return. The reward for being a dutiful child turns into a resented burden. When the parents' deaths eventually sever the relationship, she is unprepared to live on her own. Although it is easier for a bachelor to find a wife in middle life, he has often become too set in his ways to share his life with another. Moreover, according to Kinsey about fifty percent of men who have never married by the age of thirty-five are actively homosexual, in the sense that they have had some homosexual relationship within the year—a finding confirmed by clinical experience—which makes it even less likely that a middle-aged bachelor will be able to make a satisfactory adjustment to marriage.

The widowed and divorced increase in number, and fewer women find new spouses. Between the ages of fifty-five and sixty-five, twenty to twenty-five percent of women become widowed; and because of the greater longevity of women, far fewer women than men remarry or find companionship with members of the opposite sex. Quite aside from matters of affection, middle-aged women have good reason to be concerned about their husbands' health. Widowhood usually brings a decline in the woman's social and economic status. People's social milieu is established in part by occupational status, and wives in general do not have the occupational status of their husbands. As the proportion of widows increases with age, intact couples find it difficult to include many of their widowed and divorced women friends in their activities. To find male companionship, many women discover that they must take the initiative, if not become aggressive and seductive, attitudes that are strange to them. Both men and women may find it difficult to remarry in their fifties and sixties. Ways of interacting with a spouse have become set; children often consider them faithless to their dead spouse. Yet life is far from over in the fifties—or early sixties—and the single life can be very lonely.

The passage over the crest of life is a particularly critical period, a time of summing up in preparation for the second half of adulthood, and, as such, a time of further integration or reintegration. Women commonly change their way of life markedly as they return to vocations or start careers. In the transition from adolescence to early adulthood, individuals had become committed to a way of life. They have now lived it and are now mature—or are unlikely ever to become mature. Now, approaching the divide, they look back and also try to prognosticate on the basis of their experience. A man may try to climb still higher, change course while he still can, or decide which path of descent is safest. Whether persons make the most of the opportunities available or whether they begin to die slowly depends upon a wide variety of personality factors, but they continue to include attitudes related to the confidence, trust, and initiative inculated in the earliest years. The realization that the turn toward the end of life has been rounded awakens anxiety and despair in proportion to feelings that one has never really lived and loved. The capacities to become mentors and sponsors, to become *generative* in developing social and occupational heirs, gain increasing importance.

As the middle years pass, the likelihood of reorganizing and reorienting diminishes. It becomes time to make the most of the way of life that has been led. Regrets cannot be waved away but they are futile: what life has brought must be accepted if the closing years are not to be wasted or become unendurable. Dignity, perhaps shaded by resignation, protects an individual against despair. When not caught up in efforts to undo or redo, or to search after what has been missed in earlier years, persons can usually find and use the benefits that come with maturity, enjoy the opportunities it presents, and move toward bringing closure and completion to their lives in the years that still lie ahead.

REFERENCES

BALDWIN, J. (1967). From a review of *The Arrangement*, by Elia Kazan, in *The New York Review of Books*, vol. 8, no. 5 (March 23), p. 17.
DEUTSCH, H. (1945). *Motherhood*, vol. 2 of *The Psychology of Women*. Grune & Stratton, New York, p. 473.

DEYKIN, E., JACOBSON, S., KLERMAN, G., and SOLOMON, N. (1966). "The Empty Nest: Psychosocial Aspects of Conflicts Between Depressed Women and Their Grown Children," *American Journal of Psychiatry*, 122:1422–1426.

ERIKSON, E. (1959). "Growth and Crises of the 'Healthy Personality'," *Psychological Issues*, vol. 1, no. 1, Monograph No. 1. International Universities Press, New York.

LEVINSON, D. J., DARROW, C. M., KLEIN, E., LEVINSON, M., and McKEE, J. B. (1974). "The Psychosocial Development of Men in Early Adulthood and the Mid-Life Transition," in *Life History Research in Psychopathology*. D. F. Ricks, A. Thomas, and M. Roff, eds. University of Minnesota Press, Minneapolis.

LIDZ, R. W. (1974). "Woman and Her Womb," *Connecticut Medicine*, 38:559–560.

MASTERS, W., and JOHNSON, V. (1966). *Human Sexual Response*. Little, Brown, Boston.

STIERLIN, H. (1974). *Separating Parents and Adolescents: A Perspective on Running Away, Schizophrenia, and Waywardness*. Quadrangle Press, New York.

WILENSKY, H. L. (1968). "Orderly Careers and Social Participation: The Impact of Work History on Social Integration in the Middle Mass," in *Middle Age and Aging: A Reader in Social Psychology*. B. Neugarten, ed. University of Chicago Press, Chicago.

SUGGESTED READING

LEVINSON, D. J., DARROW, C. M., KLEIN, E., LEVINSON, M., and McKEE, J. B. (1974). "The Psychosocial Development of Men in Early Adulthood and the Mid-Life Transition," in *Life History Research in Psychopathology*. D. F. Ricks, A. Thomas, and M. Roff, eds. University of Minnesota Press, Minneapolis.

NEUGARTEN, B., ed. (1968). *Middle Age and Aging: A Reader in Social Psychology*. University of Chicago Press, Chicago.

CHAPTER 17

❁

Old Age

SHORTLY BEFORE they reach the age of sixty-five, persons in the United States visit the social security office, where they present their birth certificates and answer a few questions about their employment and marital status. Though their visit is brief, polite, and painless, they are likely to experience a slight inner chill, for they have gone through a rite of passage. They have entered "old age." They have not even joined a very select group, for there are now twenty million Americans, ten percent of the population, who are in their "golden years."* Nevertheless, many of their agemates have already died, and, even more than the middle-aged, the elderly tend to measure time in terms of years left rather than years lived. There is still time left: life expectancy is thirteen years for men and sixteen years for women; but those who pass the age of sixty-five know that they will be fortunate if their remaining years are relatively healthy and untroubled.

* In contrast to four percent in 1900. Life expectancy is now sixty-eight for men and seventy-six for women. The increase in life expectancy derives largely from the decreased mortality of young children. After the age of sixty or sixty-five there has been little increase in life expectancy over the past fifty years. As has often been pointed out, the best way of having a long life is to select long-lived parents and ancestors. Whereas the life expectation of nonwhites is lower than for the white population probably because of the latter's better nurture, after the age of sixty-five the life expectancy of nonwhites is greater.

For many persons, however, little has changed significantly when they tuck the social security card into their wallets, aside from the realization that they have passed a major landmark. The critical transition comes at the time of retirement, or, for the housewife, at the time of her husband's retirement. Retirement may mean a well-earned surcease from work, which permits individuals to enjoy their declining years, or it may connote being discarded, worn out, and useless to industry and society. The difference is conveyed, in part, by the contrast between the active "I am retiring" and the passive "I am being retired." People have, however, changed over the past several decades and now increasingly welcome retirement as an opportunity to live in leisure, and they accept and anticipate retirement as part of their life cycle. Whether retirement can be enjoyable—an autumn of deep but brilliant hues—depends greatly, as we shall consider later, upon income and health; whether it will be enjoyable depends greatly on the personality of the individual—and upon contingencies.

OLD AGE AND THE LIFE CYCLE

Erikson (1968) has designated the achievement of *integrity* as the critical task of old age: "the acceptance of one's one and only life cycle and of the people who have become significant to it as something that had to be and that, by necessity, permitted no substitutions." *Integrity* requires the wisdom to realize that there are no "ifs" in life; that one was born with certain capacities, a set of parents, into specific life circumstances, in a particular time in history, encountered various conditions and made numerous decisions, etc. Whether any of these circumstances could have been changed is questionable, but the past cannot be altered, though one's attitudes toward the past can be. It is too late to start out on a new life journey, but persons can use their experiences, accumulated knowledge, mature judgment, to round out their own lives and to improve the path for those who follow. Some will seek to add to the heritage of their culture, to leave the world changed for the better because they have lived. The negative outcome of life at this stage is *despair*—despair that the one and only lifetime has been wasted, with bitterness toward others or self-hatred filling the person's days, excluding the wise and constructive use of the experiences of a lifetime.

In old age persons are moving toward completion of the life cycle; they seek to bring a sense of *closure* to their lives and to complete their affairs.

Efforts are usefully spent in rounding out what they have accomplished. In the process, most, if not all, elderly persons review where they have been. Achieving closure may keep some persons rather fully occupied, but there is usually time for leisure; and many will enjoy leisure as acceptable, in a sense as a reward for their many years of work and striving. Although Freud defined normality as the "ability to love and to work," we might well add, "and to utilize and enjoy leisure" (Kimmel, 1974, p. 271).

Although I would not wish to push the analogy too far, the aged person goes through a reversal of some of the critical developments experienced during adolescence. The force of the sexual drives diminishes, lessening the id impulses; although some desires motivated by hormonal secretions remain, a major portion of the sexual strivings again arise from desires for affectionate and sensuous sharing and from dependency needs, as in childhood. Then, as women lose the subcutaneous padding of fat that rounded their contours, and as women's secondary sexual characteristics and men's muscularity diminish, the physical differences between the sexes lessen. Instead of being future oriented, the aged turn increasingly to the past and to what they have done rather than what they will do. They will again become increasingly dependent, but now upon their children or other members of a subsequent generation.* Concomitantly, the aged at times must again become virtually obedient to the caretaking persons or they will be rejected, as in childhood. If persons live long enough their capacities for ego control gradually diminish as the abilities to conceptualize gained in adolescence fade with the senile changes in the brain. Finally, whereas adolescents move toward sharing their lives intimately with another, the aged must sooner or later absorb the loss of the person with whom they shared their lives.

After a paragraph that conveys so distressing a picture, it may be useful and necessary to remind the reader that old age is also a time of contentment and pleasure for many. Contentment comes with the lessening of passions and with relief from impassioned striving and struggle—as well as with acceptance of, or even resignation to, the way things have turned out. Pleasure derives from leisure-time activities, the rewards of fulfillment, the happiness of children and grandchildren, the successes of spiritual heirs or of the institutions one helped create. There is time, finally, to enjoy and experience what had to be put off or renounced during periods of greater demand. The period of aging as a whole may be considered by persons to

---

* In the Fijis, where terms can have different connotations, the aging man who ceases to be head of the family is no longer called "father" by his children, rather he addresses his eldest son, who has taken over the family responsibilities, as "father."

be the end of the line, where they are left standing at the outskirts of life, waiting at the edge of nothingness, or as a time of relaxed closure of life that still contains much to experience and enjoy.

It seems useful to consider three phases in the latter years of life, even though they may neither be discrete nor occur in all persons. The *elderly* remain essentially unchanged from their middle years, except for the differences in their way of life that may be created by retirement. They consider themselves capable, complete, and competent to take care of their needs and affairs. However, sooner or later changes in their physical condition or life circumstances force the elderly to become reliant on others and they are then considered *senescent*. We shall follow a convention and refer to the period past the age of seventy-five as *advanced old age*, although many are not yet senescent. The last phase, which many are spared and which may not occur even in advanced age, is *senility*, when the brain no longer serves in its essential function as an organ of adaptation and persons enter their second childhood or dotage, during which others must look after them almost completely. The process of aging varies greatly and some will be senescent and occasionally even senile by the time they reach sixty-five, whereas others will remain reasonably independent at ninety. However, in almost everyone physical decline begins to cause appreciable limitations by the age of seventy-five.

RETIREMENT

The lives of the elderly in the United States have been changing markedly during the past quarter century because of the development of social security measures and various pension and retirement plans. In 1950, forty-six percent of males over sixty-five were in the labor force, but in 1971 only twenty-six percent were. In 1950, sixty percent of the auto and steel workers in Detroit and Pittsburgh who were eligible were unwilling to retire at sixty-five (Friedman and Orbach, 1974). Their reluctance seems to have been related to the serious diminution of income that would have accompanied retirement, but many also felt they were being discarded on the industrial slag heap. Retirement and social security benefits and, consequently, attitudes toward retirement have changed considerably. By 1965, Harris (1965) had found that three-quarters of American adults would like to retire at sixty-five or earlier; and almost half thought they would prefer to retire at sixty or earlier. Only about a third of retired persons found retirement less than satisfactory, and most of these were dissatisfied because of financial troubles, poor health, or loss of a spouse. Fewer than ten percent of the retired men were unhappy because they missed working. When retirement benefits are good, as they are among the auto workers, whose standard of living usually does not decrease after retirement, the proportion of persons satisfied or pleased with retirement is high (Barfield, 1970). It seems likely that certain occupations are attractive in part because they offer opportunity for early retirement. Increasing numbers of civil servants and members of the military are selecting to retire early; and the majority work only occasionally following retirement.

Some professionals do not retire at all, at least not until forced to do so for reasons of health. Many physicians find it difficult to distinguish themselves from their profession, for they have assimilated an orientation that has thoroughly permeated their lives. Some scientists gladly accept retirement but remain absorbed in their field, finding ways of teaching or continuing to make a contribution, or at least they keep up with the developments in their respective fields by reading extensively and attending professional meetings. The quest for knowledge has become a way of life that persists. Social workers, because of their interest in people, are likely to find part-time employment or volunteer work, if paid positions are unavailable.

The transition from work to retirement contains numerous sources of potential difficulty. The retired persons can find that time hangs heavily; they miss the friends at the place of employment; they feel empty without the prestige that accompanied their lost position; they brood over failures to achieve goals or to gain adequate recognition. Further, the realignment of tasks in the home creates frustration, and old difficulties with spouses become magnified. Such matters can and do create difficulties but far fewer than had been thought twenty-five years ago. Poverty, with the restrictions it imposes, and poor health are the major sources of unhappiness. In 1971 approximately one-quarter of the aged lived below the poverty level as defined by the government * (and at least a third, by more reasonable standards). Indeed, in 1971 half of the elderly were living on less than $75 a week, a marginal level at best.

Many observers have been struck by the apparent frequency with which deaths occur shortly after retirement, yet statistics do not confirm such impressions.† Nevertheless, persons whose entire way of life has been

---

* At that time, $1,852 a year for a single person and $2,328 for a couple. In 1976, $2,387 and $2,984 respectively.

† Increases in the death rate following retirement are probably due to the fact that a common cause of retirement is poor health. Fifty-four percent of those who retire early report health as a reason, in contrast to twenty-one percent of those who retire at sixty-five (Reno, 1971). Statistics do not, however, tell us anything about individual instances.

bound up in a particular occupation and who have found little satisfaction in other areas of living may well run a risk of becoming depressed, if not dying. A physicist, X, had dominated his department and intensely pursued the solution of a critical problem for many years. His retirement came at an unfortunate time. During the preceding year the problem had been solved by another physicist, who received wide acclaim, with relatively little credit being given to X for posing the problem and laying the foundation for its solution. Though he hid his feelings, he deeply resented those who neglected his contributions. He wished to drive onward to recoup, but he no longer had a department he could direct, and he felt that his former students were moving in the wrong direction. In retirement, he started to build a stone wall, and despite his wife's pleas, insisted on lifting heavy stones into place. He soon suffered a heart attack and died.

Depressive reactions that last until a new equilibrium is established are fairly common; but some persons continue to brood, feeling displaced, their ideas neglected, the organization they had built up over many years changed. They identify with the firm, department, hospital, they developed, and cannot trust others to carry on properly. The new ideas introduced are not seen as progressive but simply as the products of inexperience that endanger the organization. Such unhappy outcomes, however, usually occur in persons who had been unable to let others share responsibilities sufficiently to prepare successors, and thus had failed in a major aspect of their careers.

The readjustment to retirement is usually greater for men than it is for women. Only ten percent of women over the age of sixty-five are employed, and the percentage has not changed appreciably over the past twenty-five years. Until recently, relatively few women's lives assumed meaning through their careers, and the retirements of such women have not been studied. Most women's lives have been changed by their husbands' retirement, but the changes have required little readjustment of roles and activities.*

Persons who are approaching retirement have usually been urged to plan for it, lest boredom, depression, illness, and marital discord follow. However, various studies indicate that, if planning makes a difference, the benefits do not extend much beyond the first year. The attitudes persons have toward retirement and the realistic nature of their expectations seem

---

* However, women have been hardest hit economically. In 1969, fifty-one percent of old women who lived alone, and seventy-seven percent of nonwhites, had incomes below the poverty level (Kreps, 1970). In 1973, rules were changed so that a widow could receive one hundred percent of her husband's social security benefits.

more important. However, conscious planning may be less important than formerly, now that retirement is anticipated as a desirable stage of life, and persons are more or less consciously planning for their years of retirement long in advance.

THE ELDERLY

The ways in which people adjust to retirement usually reflect their personalities and the styles of life that go along with them. In general, men seem to become less aggressive and women more assertive as they enter old age, and both tend to diminish their activities and become less involved with people. Formerly, some authorities believed that gradual disengagement was salutary, reflecting the elderly person's decreasing emotional investment in others, rather than being imposed by social conditions. Others maintained that continuing activity and social engagement preserved feelings of worth and usefulness that seem essential to contentment: but such broad generalizations cannot be made (Havighurst *et al.*, 1963). Some persons are happy with time for reading and contemplation, whereas others need to be involved with other people in various activities to function well.* Many will spend increasing amounts of time watching television, whereas others are happy reviving pictures of their past years stored in their minds. The reasons why the elderly spend time in reminiscence can be generalized in several ways. People seek to bring closure to their lives and pick up strands from earlier days to perceive how they have become woven

---

* Reichard and her collaborators (1962) have identified three personality types among men who adjust well to retirement, and two types among those who do poorly. The largest group is termed *mature*. They are reasonably capable of accepting themselves realistically and find satisfaction in relating to others and in various activities. They are not unduly blocked by neurotic conflicts. They consider that their lives have been rewarding, take old age for granted, and make the best of it without notable regret. The *rocking-chair men* welcome the opportunity to be free of responsibility and indulge their passive needs in old age. Because of their passivity, old age brings them compensations for its disadvantages. The *armored* group ward off their dread of physical decline and death by keeping active, and their strong defenses permit them to adjust well.

Among the poorly adjusted, the largest group are the *angry* men, who are bitter about failing to achieve their goals in life and blame others for their disappointments. They are unable to reconcile themselves to growing old. Another group are *self-haters*, who turn their resentments over feelings of failure in life inward and blame themselves. They feel even more inadequate because they are old.

The investigation did not study women.

into the fabric and pattern of their lives. They become intrigued by the vitality of an experience forgotten during busier days—the summer of a youthful love and what life might have been if . . . ; the way the children looked when small, and the feel of their tiny hands; the years in the army, the landing in France, and the buddies who were lost; etc. The memories bring back poignant, bittersweet feelings of happiness and regret. Some persons will, at times, wish to make the evanescent past live once again, experiences that have no tangible existence and remain only in them, for if there were others who once shared them, they either have forgotten by now or are dead. Soon, the experience, the relationship, that had meant so much will have vanished forever, as if it had never been. Thoughts are also turned to the past by obituary columns, where a name will revive a host of memories. Then, too, the elderly realize that although the future can still bring them much, it cannot be as vital as the past. Those were happy times, they think; and even if they were not, past sorrows can have a touch of glamour.

There are many ways of adapting to old age. Varying degrees of disengagement may be helpful and sooner or later become necessary. But, by and large, those elderly persons seem happiest who find that there is still more to do than time permits, and for whom old age is not just a period of decline and idle waiting. A satisfactory adjustment requires an acceptance of one's limitations; that physical capacities are diminished, that income has fallen off, that one is no longer central to the affairs of others. Nevertheless, it can still be a period of growth when the experience and wisdom accumulated can be used to the advantage of others—in community affairs, in talks with younger colleagues, in picking up interests that had to be set aside during busier years. And there is time to contemplate, observe, and join the many strands together.

One gains an impression that persons who continue some sort of productive activity remain alert longest. Some persons, either because of their inner capacities or because of their fortunate heredity, seem to go on forever; Chief Justice Holmes, for example, remained a brilliant and active jurist into his nineties, even as his father, Oliver Wendell Holmes, the physician and poet, had remained a productive writer. Some persons, such as Titian, Frank Lloyd Wright, and Picasso, seemed to become more productive as they aged, perhaps because they felt freer to express themselves. Winston Churchill and Golda Meir first really came into their own and achieved greatness at an age when most persons are retired. Even in old age there can be no standing still, for waiting and failing to utilize one's resources lead to stagnation and regression.

Change of Residence

Many elderly persons will change their residence around the time of retirement. The home in which they have lived for years is too large, too costly, and too difficult to maintain. It is more convenient to move into town or the city, where access to stores, movies, and friends is easier. Many elderly who live in the north migrate to the sun belt, where they are less limited by wintry weather and respiratory infections, and where aches and pains may diminish. The well-to-do may be attracted to retirement villages, where activities are available, new friends can be found, and special provisions are made for the needs of the elderly. Poorer persons may find it convenient or financially necessary to move into special subsidized housing for the elderly. Moves to new locations often have advantages and attractions, but by and large the maintenance of close contact with relatives and old friends is usually more important. As people age, capacities to make new friends diminish, and new friends are not likely to have the same involvement as old friends and relations. Social activity may depend on one's being among people one knows well; and then, too, sooner or later the help of others will be needed.

Indeed, as persons move through old age, relatives become increasingly important, not only children but also relatives of the same generation. The common backgrounds furnish topics of interest and form stronger bonds as the number of friends diminishes. An elderly woman who felt very lonely after her husband died told the social worker that it was difficult to live alone after all their years together. Not only did she miss the companionship, but so many things she did that kept her busy no longer needed doing. But she also missed her older sister and sister-in-law, both of whom had died. She had spent much of her time caring for each of them in succession during their terminal illnesses. It had been difficult and depressing, but they were reliant on one another, and she had been happy to be needed and to feel their love for her. Her children were good and attentive enough, but they had other interests; she felt herself a burden to them when she was ill, and they could not understand what being a widow, or being old, or being ill—or all three together—was like, as her sisters could.

The Marriage Relationship

The marital relationship usually becomes increasingly important to the elderly as their lives become more restricted. While it is true that spouses can become more irritating to one another now that they spend more time together, and even little things, such as a favorite expression or a tone of voice, may prove infuriating, couples usually grow closer and more tolerant of each other as they become more interdependent. They *care* for one another, accept each other's help, and hope that they will never need the help of any other. The passionate love of their youthful days may have quieted during middle age into a less romantic acceptance of each other, but now their lives are thoroughly intertwined by countless shared experiences, and days are spent together. An upsurge of deeply felt and rather romantic love often occurs. Their sexual life may be less impassioned and active. The comfort of sensual closeness may become more important than orgasmic pleasure. However, contrary to the beliefs of the young, they can and often do remain sexually active into advanced old age. The husband becomes less potent but not impotent, although clear-cut orgasms may become infrequent; but the wife can usually continue to achieve orgasm readily. However, the urgency diminishes or leaves, and the elderly are no longer under the sway of sexual impulsions unless they have need to reassure themselves and counter feelings of aging by the sexual act.

The elderly couple are all too aware that their life together will end, and they often hope that they will die at the same time. The wife, knowing that women outlive men, becomes solicitous of her husband's health. She has good reasons aside from affection, for she has had ample opportunity to witness the plight of her widowed friends. The imbalance in the longevity of men and women means that far more women than men have lost their spouses by the time they become old. Thirty-eight percent of women between sixty-five and seventy are widows, whereas only ten percent of men are widowers.

When both partners continue into old age, sooner or later the invalidism or death of one brings the need for another major adjustment. It often forms a critical juncture, for the couple have managed through their interdependence upon one another, and their familiarity and devotion have eased the way. The old person not only must assimilate the loss of a partner who has become an integral part of his or her life, but must often also adjust to becoming dependent on others. The loss of a spouse provokes a period of stress, when an elderly person is particularly prone to incapacitation or death. The woman is usually better able to manage by herself than the man who has not learned domestic skills; but her social life is likely to become more restricted. Men are in relatively short supply; they are therefore sought as partners for widows at parties and are commonly invited out by elderly women who reluctantly learn that they must take the initiative if they wish to be accompanied.

Life as a single person can be particularly lonesome for the elderly because of their limitations and loss of friends. Remarriage, though often opposed by children, has become more acceptable to them in recent years, and sometimes even brings the first real marital happiness a person has known. Marital mores have changed for the old as well as the young, and increasingly elderly couples choose to live together without marrying—eschewing marriage for sentimental reasons, to avoid difficulties in breaking off the relationship if it does not work out, and for tax and inheritance reasons.

Advanced Old Age

As the elderly reach their mid-seventies they may have mixed feelings about their prospects of attaining a very advanced age. Their hopes for the years ahead are usually modest. They wish to live out their lives with dignity, to remain capable of caring for themselves and their spouse, to continue managing things between themselves. They hope to find ways in which they can still be useful even if not essential, but particularly that they will not become a burden to anyone. As they grow still older they hope to find serenity and contentment. They are concerned that they may become invalided or senile, and hope that death will intervene before such eventualities occur. Completing life in an old-age home or a mental hospital, separated from family and friends, is a dreaded possibility, but even this often seems preferable to burdening those one loves.

Those who enter late old age are a somewhat select group. Those who survive to reach eighty will still have an expectation of living another ten years. Although nearly all are beset by infirmities, some still remain very vital. A medical school dean and scientist kept busy with national medical affairs for fifteen years after his retirement. When he was almost ninety the dean assured a colleague who had not seen him in several years that his health was good, adding that, of course, he had suffered a small coronary occlusion and had a bit of cancer removed from his gut in the interval, but that a few things remained to be done before he would be ready to call it quits. Adolf Meyer, the doyen of American psychiatry prior to World War II, suffered a severe stroke just before reaching eighty, but soon wrote to a former student describing some unusual aspects of his incapacitation, and expressed his regrets that distance kept the colleague from coming to study his condition with him. A retired museum curator in his late seventies continued to write articles about his major interest, and walked a long distance to comply with a request for some of his papers by delivering them in person, delighted that they would be of use to a graduate student.

Such persons have lived fully and continue to make the most of what life offers until the end. However, they form a tiny minority, for very few have their assets and inner resources. Yet many who are less well endowed will still seek to experience life actively and enjoy it rather than fall into despair. Others without such resources accept what comes and seek to make the most of it, even when it is little. An elderly woman recently responded to the receipt of a Christmas package, apologizing for her handwriting but reminding her niece that she was now past ninety. She knew that she had to accept her shakiness, her sleeplessness, her various aches and pains. "Goethe," she wrote, "had once said that it takes no art to grow old, but it is an art to endure it." Still, she was pleased to have friends, letters, occasional visitors, and quarters that were suited to her needs. She felt fortunate to be old in the present rather than a hundred years ago—what would she have done without telephone, television, radio, and taxicabs? She could, thankfully, still enjoy sitting out on warm days and viewing the beauty of the garden. And she had her beloved cat to care for and sleep with.

The elderly eventually become increasingly dependent on others; and the change in status is difficult for many to assimilate. Persons who had provided for their children and guided them now become dependent on them. Self-esteem derived from self-sufficiency is undermined. While little difficulty arises when firm family relationships exist, the dependency can provoke anxiety and friction. The old person may react by increasing assertiveness, or with feelings that the children are ungrateful, and is eaten by resentments. Some become so insistent upon not becoming a burden that the family worries about their well-being. Indeed, as persons progress into advanced age, their care becomes a burden, even though it may be willingly accepted by children who provide for a loved parent. It can, however, be a time when old injuries are consciously or unconsciously repaid. Not all children feel devotion to their parents and many give grudgingly and gain satisfaction from dominating a parent who once dominated them. Children who were glad to get away from home because of unhappiness with their parents will not be pleased to have the parents rejoin them. Shakespeare's keen portrayal of the problems of advanced age in *King Lear* offers a dramatic example of the woes that can follow dependency upon hostile children; and of how the failing judgment of a proud and rigid man can lead him into such dilemmas. Elderly persons are rightfully concerned over losing their autonomy and becoming financially dependent. When independence goes, some individuality soon follows.

The change toward a more restricted, conservative, and rigid pattern of living is complicated by the increasing limitations imposed by the changes in the brain that are part of the process of aging. When the loss of cortical cells and brain tissue occurs gradually, it imposes limitations but it also helps protect the individual against the impact of the inevitable misfortunes that come with age and the concerns over the approach of death. In a way, the dropping out of the brain cells parallels the dropping out of the ties to important persons that had made life meaningful and helps life taper off gently.

Improved living conditions and advances in medicine, particularly in the use of prosthetic aids, have made it possible for an increasing proportion of the elderly to enjoy their remaining years. Physical deficiencies eventually occur in everyone. The presbyopic diminution in visual accommodation that occurs in the forties is offset by eyeglasses. The cataracts of old age can be removed and adequate vision restored. Some loss in auditory acuity occurs in all, and deafness can become an extremely serious problem. In some respects, deafness is a greater handicap than loss of vision, as it cuts off communication, turns the person more and more inward, and increases misunderstandings. Deaf people can be particularly troublesome to others and arouse more annoyance than the blind. The person feels left out and, characteristically, any tendencies toward suspiciousness increase. The electronic hearing aid has provided a major advance in maintaining pliability in the aged and in permitting them to relate to others. Still, it is not simple for an elderly person to adjust to a hearing aid, and it properly requires education before the hearing impairment becomes severe and while the person is not too rigid to accept the new appliance. The use of dentures has become so widespread that currently it is difficult to realize how the absence of teeth can not only impair the pleasures derived from eating but also affect health by provoking nutritional deficits. The prostatic enlargement that led many men to end their lives in misery can now readily be remedied by surgery even in advanced age. The common occurrence of osteoarthritic changes in the joints brings some limitation to virtually all elderly people and in some becomes a source of invalidism which unfortunately cannot be helped appreciably and thus becomes a major cause of dependency on others.

SENILITY

Health can fail in many ways and can provoke rather striking changes in the person who finds limitation difficult and dependency hard to bear. Still, it is the inevitable changes that occur in the brain that are most pertinent here because of their impact upon the critical integrative functions.

Senile and arteriosclerotic changes lead to a gradual loss of cells in the cerebral cortex. Large blood vessels may occlude, causing apoplexy or a "stroke"; and if an area essential to symbolic activities is damaged, intellectual capacities are seriously affected. Indeed, some decline in intellect begins in the thirties, but it is relatively insignificant until the sixties and becomes marked only in the seventies. However, the extent of the decrement varies widely; some individuals suffer appreciable deterioration even before reaching sixty, whereas in others special tests must be used to demonstrate the deficits even in advanced age. Knowledge learned in the past and even habitual ways of solving problems tend to be retained, whereas abilities to think out new solutions to problems and new techniques are more clearly impaired.* As many persons in their prime seldom learn new ways of solving problems and tend to rely on what they learned earlier in life, the intellectual impairment in old age may not be apparent. Suggestions that a person in advanced old age is mentally limited are often angrily refuted by relatives. One may note, though, how a man in his seventies who can take care of himself capably is unable to help his six-year-old grandson piece together a simple jigsaw puzzle. The child finally masters the task while the grandfather finds means of hiding his failure. The difficulties are usually most apparent in memory functions. Although it is often said of elderly persons that they are intact except for memory failures, careful testing will demonstrate a more general limitation even before memory deficiencies become obvious.†

Memory Impairments

We have already noted how elderly people spend an increasing amount of time thinking and talking about the past. However, some very old persons live only in the remote past and misinterpret the events around them. The person becomes unable to recall recent events and lives more and

* Kurt Goldstein (1963), in explaining why certain capacities are retained and others lost in brain-damaged persons, including many aged persons, considered that the brain-damaged person can no longer take an abstract approach to problems but can still think concretely.

However, a more clear-cut difference exists between retention of what was previously learned and the diminution in abilities to solve problems at the present time. The general vocabulary and general information tend to be retained and form a measure of former intellectual capacities, and new tasks that must be solved with minimal reliance on past learning (such as the block design test or digit symbol test) offer a measure of current intellectual capacities (Lidz et al., 1942).

† The Wechsler Adult Intelligence Scale (WAIS) takes this anticipated decline into consideration in providing a measure of what an elderly person's intelligence level had been.

more in the remote past, as if a shade were being pulled down over recent happenings, until eventually nothing remains except memories of child- hood. This type of memory failure depends on senile changes in the brain and is perhaps the most characteristic feature of senility. We do not prop- erly understand why earlier memories are retained while more recent happenings are lost.

If persons live long enough, the time may come when they not only live in the past but act as though they are in the past, and then are no longer capable of caring for themselves and must be considered psychotic. A man in his eighties talked about little except events of his boyhood in a rural community. The failure of his memory was obvious. When a friend who had been a history professor visited him, the old gentleman, remaining a proper host, turned the conversation to the American history he had learned in a one-room schoolhouse. However, he would stop and ask the former professor, "You know who Abe Lincoln is, don't you?" and "You have heard of Ben Franklin, haven't you?" He could not put together his appreciation of his visitor's profession and his realization that the professor obviously knew the rudimentary facts he could still recall. Yet, after his guest departed, he was able to take a bus to another part of the city, get a haircut, buy his cigars, and find his way home without difficulty. In con- trast, an ancient lady in a mental hospital behaves very differently. A doctor who has looked after her for several years visits her. She greets him by offering him a chair and saying, "My father will be right down. Yes, he is the minister and will be glad you've come to talk about building the new church." She sits down, waits, and wonders whether her visitor would like some tea. After he declines, she waits a few minutes longer, goes to the door and says, "I don't know what's keeping Father. I'll go and call him again." She walks out and with the change in scene completely forgets about her physician, who must fetch her from another room, where she sits looking at a magazine. This woman does not just talk about the remote past but lives in it and is therefore disoriented as to time and place and requires constant supervision.*

The failing intellectual abilities may also become manifest in diminished

---

* However, one may be fooled by one's preconceptions. An elderly man of seventy- six was brought into the hospital in heart failure and was completely disoriented. After the heart failure had subsided and his brain again received sufficient oxygen, he ap- peared to be oriented and rational. However, since he kept insisting that as he was ready to return home his mother would drive over and pick him up, his physicians de- cided to keep him a few weeks longer to see if his mental state would improve further. Then one day, somewhat to their chagrin, his mother of ninety-five drove over from a town some hundred miles away, accompanied by her ninety-seven-year-old sister, and took their little boy home.

control over impulses and emotions; frequent displays of anger or distrust may make it difficult for others to get along with the aged person. The old person may indulge in masturbatory activity, which can embarrass others. Occasionally, an old man makes sexual advances to women, perhaps more frequently to young children. Though such sexual activity usually has a childlike character consisting of exhibitionism, voyeurism, or attempts to be masturbated, it can create serious difficulties. Elderly women may also be troubled by sexual sensations and avoid situations that arouse them. Such feelings may be heightened by irritation in the vaginal area that comes with senile atrophy of the mucous membranes. Their sexual urges are rarely expressed aggressively, but may create shame and concern over masturbation.

The change from old age to senility, if it occurs, may take place gradually as brain cells drop out, or the break may come suddenly. During an illness such as pneumonia or heart failure the diminished oxygen supply to the brain, which would have no permanent effect upon a younger person, sounds the death knell for degenerating brain cells. Or a drug given for an illness affects the brain but instead of causing a transient toxic dysfunction destroys cells and the person never recovers; or the margin of adjustment had been so narrow that once mental disorganization takes place persons cannot regain their equilibrium. Such senile breaks are often precipitated by an emotional crisis or a change in the life situation that requires readjustments beyond the old person's capacities. A man's wife dies and he cannot care for himself and grows confused in the attempt; or after moving into a new home he cannot orient himself to the strange surroundings; or the children with whom he lives quarrel, or turn against him and blame him for their difficulties, and he cannot cope with the conflict and emotional turmoil around him. Kurt Goldstein (1963) has emphasized the importance of "catastrophic reactions" in the behavior of brain-damaged persons, including the senile. When such persons are confronted by a task beyond their capacities, the resultant frustration causes mental disorganization that carries over into subsequent efforts. The confusion can perpetuate itself as the disability spreads to other capacities. The reaction can be halted by simplifying the environment and the tasks demanded of the person.

An old person requires a reasonably stable environment in which he feels secure; and as he grows still older, calm and simplicity in surroundings where things remain in familiar patterns. Shakespeare recognized such factors in his portrayal of King Lear's insanity. Although Lear displayed poor judgment, he functioned reasonably well until he was cast out of his home by the daughters he had favored and trusted. When he became enraged and found himself in strange surroundings, he became disorganized and behaved in a senile, confused manner. Typically, when the weather turned fair again and he found shelter in the love of his faithful daughter, Cordelia, he again became reasonably well integrated.

INTACT FINAL YEARS

It seems necessary to emphasize again that not all persons become senile, even at very advanced ages. Persons of ninety can be alert and keep themselves usefully occupied, even though they can rarely remain self-sufficient. Still, those who are mentally intact are likely to grow somewhat depressed as the relationships to others that made life meaningful are broken by the deaths of relatives and friends, and they come to feel unnecessary, even if not unwanted. However, not all such feelings that death would be welcome are indications of depression. Death is usually less feared by the very old, who may regard it as a haven from the efforts required to continue enfeebled living, and preferable to the senescence that looms ahead. A man of eighty, who started to distribute his possessions in expectation of dying, was still alert and cheerful. At the family's request, his physician reassured him about his health and advised him that as he might well live another ten to twenty years he should not give away so much of his wherewithal. He told his doctor that were it not sinful he would pray to die soon: he was not downhearted but he had led a full life, his children were all married, and as almost all of his generation were dead, he could wish for nothing more except to escape becoming a burden to himself and those he loved.* With

* A young physician, social worker, or clinical psychologist may believe that very little can be done to help persons of advanced age with emotional or social problems. However, because many elderly persons expect so little and because their needs are limited, a great deal can often be accomplished briefly. Such efforts are not directed toward profound personality changes. Thus, a seventy-six-year-old man who was hospitalized for intractable bronchial asthma was found to be sensitive to dog and cat dander. When he was told that he would be able to return home if he got rid of his two dogs and four cats, he exploded and insisted on seeing a psychiatrist. He told the psychiatrist that the recommendation was nonsense. He had known he was allergic to cats and dogs for many years, always had these animals in the house, but had not suffered from asthma since he was fourteen. At fourteen he was allergic to horses but more to the riding master who was having an affair with his widowed mother. He stopped being asthmatic when he left home and went to live with his aunt. Now he was allergic to alcohol—to his wife's drinking, for when intoxicated she would start cursing him, make suicidal attempts, and leave him feeling desperate. He was too old

advancing age, an increasing number of elderly move into homes for the aged, or to nursing homes because of their infirmities. Although only four to five percent of the elderly live in institutions, ten to twenty percent of the aged have been residing in institutions at the time of death (Kastenbaum and Cundy, 1972). Approximately a quarter of these persons no longer have any living children; and many can no longer be kept at home because of their illnesses and infirmities.

SOCIETY AND THE AGED

Different societies have dealt with the aged in various ways (Simmons, 1945). Economic considerations are a potent factor in shaping the traditional position of the elderly in a society. The Eskimo of the far north, who live an arduous existence in an environment that scarcely supports their small, isolated families, cannot afford to provide for the infirm. When the aged—and people age early under the demanding conditions—feel that they have become useless, they go off by themselves to freeze to death on the ice.* In the tropics, where nature's abundance makes the care of an additional person no hardship, the society can afford to be more benevolent. The elderly can lead a simple life helping to care for the young children. The Chinese have—or had—tended to revere the aged, who carry the responsibility for making the important decisions for the extended family. They have learned in their ancient civilization that they cannot afford to neglect the accumulated experience and knowledge of how life should be conducted, particularly during periods of stress. In the United States we have done rather poorly with our aged, and only recently have begun to make provisions for them. The wisdom of the past is less valuable in our

---

to cope with her, and too old to live by himself. He needed her. It turned out that his wife, who was twenty years younger than he, was now very upset because she feared her husband's death and being left alone, even as she had felt abandoned when her father had died shortly before she married. Some psychotherapeutic work with the wife, but also bringing a housekeeper into the home, changed the entire situation.

* An anecdote related in the book *The Top of the World* (Ruesch, 1959) indicates that the stoic measure is not carried out gladly. The grandmother in the story goes out to sit on the ice when a grandchild is born and there is another mouth to feed. Just after she leaves, the parents, who had never before seen an infant, as can well happen in their isolated existence, came to believe that their toothless newborn was defective and incapable of survival. They ran out to give the infant to the grandmother to take along with her. She realized that she was still necessary to the naïve couple and, telling them that she knew how to make the child get teeth, returned to live a few years longer.

changing society, but the family structure with the isolated nuclear family that is geographically and socially mobile leaves little room for the dependent aged. Homes have little surplus space and rents are often paid in terms of the number of rooms. It is also important that there are few clear-cut roles for the elderly to provide them with a sense of being useful. Still, before we blame ourselves too readily we must recognize that no society has previously been confronted by an equivalent problem. In 1970 over twenty million, or about ten percent of the population, were over sixty-five, and about ten million were over seventy-five. The responsibility for those below sixteen and over sixty-five falls to just about the equivalent number of persons between these ages.

The increasing size of the aged population presents one of the major social problems of contemporary society, a problem created largely by the advances in medicine. Medical science has not only changed the nature of the practice of medicine but the structure of society itself. Still, organized medicine has been more than reluctant to turn its attention to the problem it has created, either through preparing physicians to care for the aged patient properly, or through supporting measures to provide suitable medical care for the aged as a group. Although the major interests of students who enter medicine continue to be in curing patients, they find that they are engaged in a task of caring for more and more patients whom they will not cure but must seek to help. Medicine has become increasingly caught up with problems of invalidism, disabilities due to chronic illnesses, with problems of the aged and the prevention of the infirmities that come with age.

The elderly will increasingly form one of medicine's and society's major problems. The preservation of life and lengthening of the life span by medical science become dubious achievements unless the added years can be reasonably satisfactory. The task, of course, transcends the problems of medicine, and many liberal policies of government concerned with social security measures have not been brought about by increasingly liberal beliefs on the part of politicians but through the need for measures to cope with the changing age distribution in the population. The older voter, who has never been considered radical or even liberal, has managed to mobilize the collective power of the elderly to make it possible for retired persons to have a means of living without having to fall back on family or institutional charity. Many measures have been instituted to help alleviate the situation; and an understanding of the elderly person's assets, needs, and difficulties can help guide the expansion of such measures. Retirement insurance, private, industrial, and governmental, has started to alter the situation. It is no longer necessary for the employed to support the retired as completely as formerly. Although social security measures lag, with about one-third of the elderly living close to or below the poverty level, a start has now been made. In providing for the later years while still working, a person helps assure security and future independence from charitable help. Part of the current plight of the aged exists because industrial and governmental plans did not exist or were inadequate in their younger days; because many industrial retirement plans were not transferable when a person changed employers; and because of the rapid monetary inflation in recent decades. However, the low level of social security payments received by many couples results, in part, because the years housewives spend in raising children and keeping house are not counted in the social security system. They are thereby pushed into paid employment not simply to augment the family income but to help provide for their old age. There is, however, increasing awareness that along with providing financial security for later life, it is also necessary to foster interests while one is still young that will enable life to be more meaningful in old age. Still, if it is difficult to interest educated groups and executives in such preparation, it is far more difficult with the factory worker whose life has been narrowed by performance of rather routine work over many years.

Several developments that increase the opportunities of the elderly will serve as examples of future potentialities. Cities like St. Petersburg, Florida, have found it economically advantageous to make special provisions for the aged, and furnish examples of how to foster their comfort and happiness. The hotels and the community as a whole find ways of keeping these guests or residents active and well occupied. The hotels provide movies and entertainment, foster collective activities, and see that the guests are introduced and brought together. Doctors in attendance can be readily obtained at night. The sidewalks are built without curbs, benches are provided for those who tire, and wheelchairs are readily available. New friendships develop to replace those that have vanished. As lessened mental agility also means less initiative, stimulation to activity needs to be provided by others. There is good reason, aside from the climate, for the elderly to move to St. Petersburg.

Golden age clubs exist in many communities. Here elderly persons have a meeting place where they find companionship which does not require individual initiative to establish. Hobbies and various activities are fostered and taught. Many old people, unfortunately, are reluctant to give in and let others assist them in finding friends and activities, or to admit that they have reached a stage where they need to change their habitual patterns. Many who do find new sources of interest and an escape from increasing loneliness.

Retirement villages offer older people a new start in a somewhat protected and sheltering environment where socialization and activities are fostered, transportation to urban centers is provided, and new friendships can be made. Government-subsidized urban housing for the aged, designed with suitable facilities, is now developing rapidly. However, the congregation of elderly people into special homes or communities has at least two major shortcomings. It tends to separate them from their children and other relatives who form their strongest link to a meaningful life, and it segregates them from younger people. The elderly can carry out many useful functions if they are not segregated. They baby-sit, or care for the homes, animals, and plants of people who go away for weekends; or help cook or garden, make children's clothes, etc. However, living in special facilities for the aged is far better than in rundown tenements, seedy "hotels," and bleak old-age homes. However, a good modern home for the aged can be turned into a welcome haven for those who can no longer fend for themselves. It need not be a last resort of outcasts. A modern home provides room in which individuals or couples can retain some of their own possessions and have a place of their own. As long as they are able, the elderly people participate in housekeeping and cooking, which gives them a sense of being useful; and recreational and occupational activities are provided that are suited to their abilities. When they become ill or bedridden and must be removed to an infirmary, they are not cut off from the friends they have made in the institution. Such homes find that they need send few to nursing homes or to mental hospitals.*

L'ENVOI

For a large proportion of the aged, life will finally end after some years that are neither happy nor unhappy. Many will move beyond feelings of despair at critical losses. Their lives narrow as relatives and friends die and they feel themselves anachronisms without a proper place or purpose. Thoughts

* The allocation of thousands upon thousands of the aged into mental hospitals forms one of the more disgraceful chapters in American social history. Although it is probably correct that few, if any, were sent to mental hospitals who were not seriously depressed or disorganized, many became incapacitated largely because of lack of suitable places to live and of means of support. Once they are hospitalized, the lack of personal attention, the barren surroundings, and the depressing atmosphere impede recovery, and often lead to apathy and progressive deterioration. In contrast, in a good home for the aged in which socialization and activity is carefully fostered, only a very occasional person has to be sent to a mental hospital, even when many are in their nineties.

and interests increasingly become directed backward into the past. A new egocentricity develops as concerns over security and prestige engender pettiness and miserliness. Without interests that draw outward, concerns over bodily functions increase in importance. Health becomes a major topic of conversation, and feelings of being neglected can lead to an increase in complaints over failing health. Release from striving turns into stagnation in those who were not prepared when they were younger to pursue interests of their own. Even as life draws to a close a person still requires self-esteem and a purpose that provides meaning beyond the day, week, or month. An ability to look forward to a meaningful future, for others if not for the self, helps counter apathy and promotes alertness. The time-honored means of finding purpose in age has been offered by religions. They teach either hope in a life after death or the subordination of the individual to a higher and ultimate good. Religion, when meaningful, has provided solace, hope, and a way of life in old age; but if it is mere form rather than a vital part of a person's life it may do little more than teach resignation to an unhappy lot. Religion appears to serve best, even in old age, when it continues to be a way of life rather than becoming a way of dying.

The way of life of the elderly reflects the personality configurations established in earlier years, but it is greatly affected by how adaptive capacities are reduced by physical infirmities and mental limitations, as well as by the potentialities afforded by the society to persons as they age and become less able to manage for themselves. The aged have passed the stage of being procreative and are often beyond being creative, but the type of life they lead and is afforded them by others will still profoundly influence those who come after them. Their well-being causes concern to their children and grandchildren. Their presence in a child's home may cause disturbances and conflict that create stresses in the child's marriage and affect how grandchildren are raised. They may serve as a beneficent figure for identification to grandchildren; and liaisons between grandparents and grandchildren frequently form important influences that convey traits and interests over an intervening generation. The way in which they lead their last years provides an example and a warning to their descendants and influences how they provide for their own later years. Further, how the old people are treated by their children commonly furnishes an illustration to grandchildren of how persons treat parents. The aged may be close to the end of life, but the way in which they live and let live will continue to influence life.

REFERENCES

BARFIELD, R. F. (1970). *The Automobile Worker and Retirement: A Second Look*. Institute for Social Research. University of Michigan, Ann Arbor.

ERIKSON, E. (1968). *Identity: Youth and Crises*, p. 139. W. W. Norton, New York.

FRIEDMAN, E. A., and ORBACH, H. L. (1974). "Adjustment to Retirement," in *American Handbook of Psychiatry*, vol. 1., 2d ed. S. Arieti, ed. Basic Books, New York.

GOLDSTEIN, K. (1963). *The Organism*. Beacon Press, Boston.

Group for the Advancement of Psychiatry (1965). *Psychiatry and the Aged: An Introductory Approach*. Report No. 59.

HARRIS, L. (1965). "'Pleasant' Retirement Expected," *Washington Post*, November 28.

HAVIGHURST, R. J., NEUGARTEN, B., and TOBIN, S. (1963). "Disengagement and Patterns of Aging," in *Middle Age and Aging*. B. Neugarten, ed. University of Chicago Press, Chicago, 1968.

KASTENBAUM, R., and CUNDY, S. (1972). "The 4% Fallacy: A Methodological and Empirical Critique of Extended Care Facility Population Statistics." Paper presented at meeting of Gerontological Society, San Juan, Puerto Rico.

KIMMEL, D. (1974). *Adulthood and Aging: An Interdisciplinary Developmental View*. Wiley, New York.

KREPS, J. (1970). Cited in D. Kimmel, *Adulthood and Aging: An Interdisciplinary Developmental View*. J. Wiley & Sons, New York, 1974.

LIDZ, T., MAY, J. R., and TIETZE, C. (1942). "Intelligence in Cerebral Deficit States and Schizophrenia Measured by Kohs Block Test," *Archives of Neurology and Psychiatry*, 48:568–582.

REICHARD, S., LIVSON, F., and PETERSON, P. (1962). *Aging and Personality*. J. Wiley & Sons, New York.

RENO, V. (1971). *Why Men Stop Working at or before the Age of 65*. Report No. 3. U.S. Department of Health, Education, and Welfare, Social Security Administration Office of Research and Statistics, Washington, D.C.

RUESCH, H. (1959). *The Top of the World*. Pocket Books, New York.

SIMMONS, L. W. (1945). *The Role of the Aged in Primitive Society*. Yale University Press, New Haven, Conn.

SUGGESTED READING

BUTLER, R. N., and LEWIS, M. I. (1973). *Aging and Mental Health: Positive Psychosocial Approaches*. C. V. Mosby, St. Louis, Mo.

FRIEDMAN, E. A., and ORBACH, H. L. (1974). "Adjustment to Retirement," in *American Handbook of Psychiatry*, vol. 1, 2d ed. S. Arieti, ed. Basic Books, New York.

GITELSON, M. (1948). "The Emotional Problems of Elderly Persons," *Geriatrics*, 3:135–150.

Group for the Advancement of Psychiatry (1965). *Psychiatry and the Aged: An Introductory Approach*. Report No. 59.

NEUGARTEN, B., ed. (1968). *Middle Age and Aging: A Reader in Social Psychology*. University of Chicago Press, Chicago.

CHAPTER 18

❁

Death

IT MAY SEEM STRANGE for an unconsidered moment to conclude this guide to the life cycle with a chapter on death. But death is part of the life cycle, an inevitable outcome of life that brings closure to a life story; and, because humans from early childhood are aware of their ultimate death, it influences their development and their way of life profoundly. Then, physicians—as also nurses and medical social workers—have intimate relationships with death: they confront Death as the immortal antagonist against whom they shield their patient for a time; but when the outcome becomes inevitable, physicians again turn midwife to ease the passage through the gate of life, this time to return patients into the dark womb of oblivion, where they will find surcease from pain and striving.

The topic is large, the subject of countless religious and philosophic treatises and, of late, of psychological and sociological studies (Becker, 1973; Feifel, 1959; Kubler-Ross, 1969). Here, we shall but briefly direct attention to the importance of considering death when seeking to understand a person's life. Traditional psychoanalysis has considered concerns over dying as manifestations of either separation or castration anxieties; and Freud (1920, 1933) believed that a death instinct draws people toward death and the cessation of all striving. He came to consider the struggle between Eros and Thanatos fundamental to understanding behavior—a view that attained limited acceptance.*

CHANGING ATTITUDES TOWARD DEATH
THROUGH THE LIFE CYCLE

Death has a different meaning and impact on a person at different periods of life. Children usually become aware in a meaningful way of death as the end of life at about the age of four or five. Their concerns are clearly an aspect of separation anxiety; and fears that their mothers will die arouse as much concern as their own deaths. It is a fear of being isolated without a protecting and nurturing person and reflects the child's incompletion and the lack of clear boundaries between the self and the mother. It can mount to become a serious problem in the insecure child, perhaps particularly in children whose mothers have left them for a prolonged period in their second or third years. But many children will also puzzle about death, and experience an uncanny feeling in trying to grasp its essence—the beginnings of an "existential" anxiety.† Many children find solace or release from such anxieties through belief in a life after death in which they will continue to have their parents. A patient recalled what he believed was a milestone in his maturation. Shortly after his marriage, war had broken out and his native country was attacked; on his way into combat he found himself wishing to believe in a life after death but not, as in childhood, from anxiety, but rather because of his love for his wife and the intensity of his desire to be certain he would again be with her.

The interpretation of fears of death and dying as a form of castration anxiety seems, at times, an attempt to handle a pervasive source of concern by changing it into an immature and needless childhood oedipal fear, to consider an ultimate reality by saying, in effect, "Death is no more real than fears that father will castrate you and you are really only suffering

---

* An excellent discussion of the confused concepts of aggression, destructiveness, and the death instinct in psychoanalytic theory can be found in Robert Waelder's chapter "Destructiveness and Hatred" in his *Basic Theory of Psychoanalysis.*

† Thus, a patient recalled how at the age of six he suddenly stopped playing with a construction set while his mother was singing a melancholy tune; he felt confronted by an intangible but impossible something as he suddenly thought to himself, "Death— what does it feel like, what happens?" After a time he asked his mother, but felt that her remarks about God were simply evasive, and he went about in something of a daze, seeking to avoid thinking about it. Similar episodes returned upon occasion later in childhood and still had repercussions in his adult life. The interpretation of these episodes in terms of an earlier separation anxiety does not explain away the phenomenon.

from guilt over wishing that your father were dead." Of course, such wishes are sources of anxiety that one will be castrated or die, but they do not explain why death is feared. Death can also seem like castration when a person is cut down in the prime of life, thereby rendered impotent to carry out strivings and hopes, or to find fulfillment in love. Death is the reaper with a scythe who cuts off life. Death also provides a challenge and a test, particularly to men who must prove to themselves that they can face death and not run or flinch—the essence of bravery. Perhaps persons feel that they must conquer death through flaunting it, or at least through looking straight into its hollow eye sockets before they can feel secure enough to live.

With marriage and parenthood, concerns over death transcend the self, even as do concerns in other areas. Parents will be concerned over what will happen to a spouse and their children should they die, and take precautions for the sake of the family as much as for themselves. We also see how, despite self-preservative drives, parents readily give up their lives to save their children. Indeed, anyone with combat experience soon realizes that men will die for their group; and many will seek to preserve their group's good opinion of them at the risk or sacrifice of their lives. Moreover, many men are willing to fight in wars because they consciously or unconsciously believe that preserving a way of life takes precedence over preserving a life.

Persons' attitudes toward death usually change as they age. To old persons Death becomes a familiar. They have had much experience with it, have thought a good deal about it, and eventually expect the final visitor and may even await his call. Whether the desire for death can be considered an "instinct" is a moot question. The elderly often tire of life and simply wish to drop out of the circle of the dance.*

THE CHOICE OF LIFE AND DEATH

Of the essence is that human beings alone among all living things are aware of death and can make the decision whether they wish to live or die.

---

* Freud (1915) believed during World War I, when life was growing burdensome, that although people could desire the death of an alien, and even unconsciously wish for the death of someone they love, they have profoundly repressed ideas of their own mortality. He asked if it would not "be better to give death the place in actuality and in our thoughts which properly belongs to it—it has the merit of taking somewhat more into account the true state of affairs, and of making life again more endurable for us. To endure life remains, when all is said, the first duty of all living beings. Illusion can have no value if it makes this more difficult for us . . . If you would endure life, be prepared for death." A somber note and view of life, but one that can fortify.

Indeed, they repeatedly face the decision unless they make it once and for all as part of an abiding ethic, as most persons do. Still, human behavior and attitudes can never be comprehended properly unless one realizes that death is often tempting, and that fears of giving way to the desire despite wishes to live are a source of anxiety and various neurotic defenses.* When life grows burdensome, particularly when significant persons are lost, or when resentments become pervasive, death can be tempting.† Religions have dealt with the problem in various ways. Christians and Mohammedans are assured of a heavenly life after death if they live properly or if they die protecting the religion; but they are threatened by far greater torment than they can possibly suffer in this life if they commit suicide. Some, like the Swedenborgians, consider that we are living through purgatory in this life, and must endure it for the sake of the salvation that assuredly follows—for how else can the torments on earth have meaning? Hindus are tied to the wheel of life, and will be punished for their sins, including suicide, by having lower status in human or animal form in future metamorphoses. They hope ultimately to achieve Nirvana, an oblivion of absence of stimulation and striving which is akin to our concepts of death. Some consider that the essence of Judaism concerns the affirmation of life despite suffering and tribulations.

The Influence of Death on Ways of Living

The belief in some type of existence after death clearly influences how most persons live. Man is directed by future goals as well as impelled by drives—the carrot motivates as well as the stick. The ethos of Christian beliefs blends with superego dictates and heightens conflicts over giving in to unacceptable impulses by stretching the punishment into eternity. The converse attitude which accepts the death of the mortal body as the end of

---

* The fear of giving in to suicidal impulses as a source of anxiety is perhaps seen most clearly in combat situations where the temptation to have it over with and no longer suffer the anxiety, deprivation, anger, and loss of comrades can become great. The temptation is usually repressed but the wish reappears in nightmares—or is projected in the form of heightened danger from the enemy (Lidz, 1946). Similar conditions arise in civilian life. Suicide is the tenth leading cause of death, and accidental deaths which are not always so "accidental" are another leading cause of death.

† As the most popular soliloquy in the greatest Western drama reflects:

> To be, or not to be, that is the question;
> . . . 'tis a consummation
> Devoutly to be wish'd, to die, to sleep;
> But that the dread of something after death,
> . . . makes us rather bear those ills we have . . .
> (*Hamlet*, Act III, Sc. 1.)

the individual leads some to "take the cash and let the credit go" and seek what pleasure they can while there is still the chance; or to learn to fortify themselves stoically against inevitable contingency. Although which religious or philosophic attitude a person embraces is determined partly by the culture, the family, and the formal education, it is also influenced by basic attitudes concerning trust and distrust, anxiety and security, hopefulness and pessimism, passivity and aggressivity, etc., established in the early years of life. Nevertheless, religions and philosophies, either explicitly or tacitly, usually concern mortality and contribute to a way of life and personality development.*

The desire for some type of continuity into the future is pervasive, particularly in societies in which the person is an individual rather than primarily a member of a collectivity.† Individuals seek many ways "to cheat drowsy death" and somehow perpetuate themselves—that is, one's name, ideas, ways of doing things, one's "flesh and blood"—from oblivion. The desire for descendants in whom one lives, who will carry the name or keep alive even a spark of memory of one's existence, has been a significant directive in virtually all societies, and influences marriage and divorce as well as extramarital procreation. Some seek to leave their tangible imprint on the world through the structures they build, be they indestructible pyramids or more useful bridges, dams, or buildings; some leave behind the children of their fantasy in poems and story; some strive to insure that posterity will know that the course of history changed because they lived and conquered, and some because of what they discovered or invented. Others will seek a type of immortality through joining their lives to a more abiding organization, a church, philanthropic movement, or library or orchestra; or by playing an active part in the conquest of a specific disease or some other scientific problem. The infinitesimal grain in the cosmos becomes part of a visible body and a significant force. The ways of seeking some semblance of immortality are diverse, but how individuals strive for it provides a key to understanding many aspects of their behavior. Some individuals clearly and loudly proclaim how they seek to perpetuate themselves, but others almost hide it from themselves, yet still it can be detected from their actions and from what they hold most high.

The realization of mortality also influences the life pattern by provoking a desire to give it closure. The sense of closure may involve finishing a

---

* As Montaigne expounded in his essay "To Study Philosophy Is to Learn to Die," and concerning which Freud comments in "Thoughts for the Times on War and Death."

† In more collectively oriented societies, the continuity and reputation of the family, the city, or the nation may take precedence over individual life.

single important job or a more general life task such as building up an estate for one's children or completing an area of scientific investigation to which much of a lifetime has been devoted. It may concern achieving some final years of relaxed living in order to observe the world or enjoy the fruits of a lifetime of effort; or the conscious rounding out of a life story as if it were a novel being told. The finite lifetime provides delimitation that directs an individual toward specific and limited objectives and counters diffusion and unbridled strivings. Death hangs as a reminder to persons of their limitations—which they may strive against but with which they must somehow come to terms. It provides the foil for contrasting classical and romantic approaches to living. Life, we may consider, is provided with a frame by death. Death not only influences how the course of life is run, but it lends incisiveness to the meaning of events, sharpens our appreciation of the transitory and of the beauty we would like to hold. Perhaps, above all, it heightens the preciousness of those we love because of their mortality.* It requires of each a willingness to risk pain in committing the self to a meaningful attachment to another, but it also augments the value of such relationships.

To those who reach old age and have attained some wisdom in the process, death often assumes meaning as the proper outcome of life. The world and those who inhabit it have changed. The loved ones are dead or scattered. New ways of doing things have replaced the familiar. The new generation places little value on what is most important. The government piles up debts, encourages the idle, forgets the heroes of the war before the last. Girls act like boys and men dress like women. Life can never contain a moment of inertia, but the ways of the individual begin to congeal. The need to understand differently from earlier in life and to alter standards, ideas, and techniques is resented. Then, too, life brings sorrow and tribulations which are apt increasingly to outweigh the happy occasions. It is time for others to take over, and old persons feel in the way. They have had their run of it, now it is time for others to take the field. They may appreciate life and living, and their hours may be crowded with fond memories that block new experiences, but they grasp that death is nature's way of making possible much life and assuring constant renewal.

Then, too, there is a significant reversal from the child's anxiety about death as some unknown state of separation from parents which would leave the child isolated and intensely alone. Aged persons become increasingly lonely as they are separated from those who have been most meaning-

---

* Freud (1915) considered that people invented ghosts in their desire to preserve loved persons who die.

ful to them. Death now is no longer perceived as an ultimate loneliness, but rather as an assurance that sooner or later they need no longer feel alone—whether because they believe they will be reunited with others or because it will simply bring an end to all experience.

However, people for the most part and under most circumstances do not wish to die, but cling to life as their most precious possession. They will face death and accept it for the sake of what they cherish—for companions and to preserve honor; but they may also cling to life in concentration camps as long as the faintest glimmer of hope remains. Paradoxically, but understandably, it is those who have never been able to live, either because others have restricted them or because of their own neurotic limitations, who may fear death the most. There are some, even some elderly persons, who not only suffer anxiety but become agitated when they know they are going to die, and who may not only suffer but cause others to suffer with them. Still, people are almost always able to accept the inevitable. It is uncertainty that creates anxiety. Few who know that their death is inevitable and close do not accept the knowledge with resignation.

The Dying Patient

It is an integral part of being a physician to face the dying and to help patients and their families meet the situation. By and large, physicians have in recent years sought to protect the dying from becoming aware that their fate is sealed. Perhaps, as has been suggested, many who enter medicine are particularly afraid of dying and transfer their own concerns to their patients. A considerable literature has appeared to point out that physicians, in seeking to protect patients, often overprotect them and create serious difficulties, and may sometimes be protecting themselves rather than patients from unpleasant and painful situations.

The care of the dying patient is a large topic that is not really germane to the subject of this book, but it seems worth devoting a few paragraphs to it because of its importance to physicians and paramedical workers, and because of the pathological way in which it is so frequently carried out. The physician cannot find a general rule about whether to inform patients that they have a fatal illness,* for each patient is an individual. Physicians cannot properly cope with patients' problems in terms of their own fears or of their own religious (or nonreligious) beliefs. An alert physician can

---

* Physicians usually have greater difficulty telling patients that they have a malignancy—that is, a neoplastic illness—than other, even more definitively fatal conditions. Perhaps cancer seems more final and seems to conjure up greater suffering.

usually tell when patients wish to know that they have a fatal condition, and if uncertain, can test out the patient's defenses against recognizing the fact or hearing it. Patients can have strong mechanisms of defense against perceiving what may seem obvious.*

However, all too frequently, attempts to protect the patient have unfortunate and sometimes disastrous effects. A wall of deception is constructed between patients and families and friends that keeps them from really communicating at a time when they may wish to be closer than ever before. Patients are kept from setting their affairs in order, and commonly they are more concerned about the continuing welfare of a spouse and their children than about whether they live for another few years. Some dying persons also feel that efforts to hide their condition almost succeeded in depriving them of properly experiencing their last experiences, and of understanding what dying is like—something they had wondered about since childhood. Even more unfortunate, the insistence to patients with terminal illnesses that they are not so ill and will recover can confuse the patients, provoke profound distrust, and even lead to disorganization and delusion. Patients are not permitted to believe what they consciously and unconsciously know to be a fact. A middle-aged woman who was suffering from metastases in her bones from cancer of the breast was told that she was suffering from severe arthritis; and when she asked if she did not have metastases, the truth was denied. Eventually, she developed delusions of persecution—in part because she was being persecuted in having the extent of her suffering denied and her knowledge negated, supposedly to spare her unnecessary suffering.

Patients with terminal illnesses can usually accept what those around them can accept—albeit sometimes with periods of depression and unhappiness—but they wish to be assured that they will not undergo prolonged suffering, and this is an assurance that can almost always be given honestly today because of the availability of tranquilizers and narcotics.†

---

* Thus a young physician who had caught a very serious infectious illness from a patient verged on dying for a week. He was aware that he had relatively little chance of recovery but fortified himself by preparing himself for the next week when, he convinced himself, the illness would first reach its height. After recovering, he wondered why he had never been afraid he was about to die. He then recalled that one night when he was most ill, he had been afraid that someone was going to come through the window and shoot him. He had projected the danger from the illness within him to the environment that could be controlled; and at the same time it was a regression to early childhood when he had had such fears of burglars coming in the window to kill him.

† Currently many persons fear going to a hospital when in the last stages of a fatal illness because patients are often kept alive by desperate measures, and even after they can no longer regain consciousness. Persons fear they will become hopeless and helpless burdens to relatives and society, exhausting funds they would like to leave to heirs, or

The author recently had an experience that will serve to close the discussion of this involved topic. I was asked by friends to see their mother, aged ninety-three, who was slowly dying of a malignancy. They asked that she not be told the diagnosis because their aunt, her favorite sister, had died a slow and painful death from cancer some forty years earlier, and their mother had for many years feared a similar end. The relationship between the mother and her children had been unusually good, but now she was angry and did not even wish to see them. I requested permission from both the family and the attending physician to use my own judgment in managing the situation.

As soon as the amenities were over, and the old lady realized my visit was professional, her anger toward her children burst out. She had thought that she had been a pretty good mother and had always considered her children before her own wishes—but now that she was really helpless, her children had abandoned her. Not one of the three had offered to take her into his home! What would she do? She was well-to-do but how long could she spend hundreds of dollars a day for room, nurses, physicians! Apparently they thought she might live for years, but she wished she could die now and have it over with.

This was a sorry ending for a congenial family. The patient was told that her children had not abandoned her, but that she had but a month or two to live and they knew that she could not leave the hospital. She could feel certain that we would not let her suffer unduly, and it was time to prepare for her end. The patient calmed down immediately and asked why in the world her doctor or her children had not told her. Did they think she was a child? She knew she would soon die even if she were not ill. Why not now? Her relationship with her children and grandchildren changed immediately, as they could again talk about their past days together, and about plans

---

wasting public funds that could be spent usefully. Hospitals and physicians fear malpractice suits unless they keep patients alive, if it is in any way possible—though such practices are, in essence, malpractice. Physicians had formerly assumed, and still covertly assume, responsibility—usually with consultation—for allowing persons to die rather than letting them suffer when recovery is impossible and living has also become impossible.

The author, when a house officer, asked the great neurosurgeon Harvey Cushing to examine a patient with numerous metastases from a malignancy whose pain could not be adequately controlled and to advise whether a cordotomy—an operation severing the nerve tracts in the spinal cord that conduct pain—should be performed. After Dr. Cushing examined the patient and assured himself that the patient was suffering great pain and could not live very long, he looked me in the eye admonishingly and said, "Young man, in conditions such as this you give the patient morphine, more morphine, and more morphine." He meant enough morphine so that the patient slept deeply and stopped taking fluids and would soon die peacefully.

and hopes for the future. I stopped in to see the patient from time to time during the month she lived. She would tell me tales about New York in the 1880s and 1890s, about her travels in various parts of the world, and about interesting people she had known. She enjoyed reminiscing, as if she were going through a final review of a reasonably happy life.

During one of my visits, she fell asleep for less than a minute and awakened with a start and a puzzled smile. She had been dreaming, a vivid and realistic dream. In the dream her aged mother was living with her, and she was sitting in her rocking chair just as she had sixty years before. Her mother had a set of false teeth for appearances but they were not good for chewing. In the dream the patient and her husband were going to dine at her sister's house. She told her mother she would prepare supper for her and in the dream scraped an apple and made a gruel for her—perhaps just as she once had done in reality—and then she had awakened. The patient was not asked to associate to the content of the dream; but it seemed clear it was the manifestation of a wish, a wish fulfillment. Perhaps it was a wish to be young, or to have her mother again; perhaps it was a wish to be treated by her children as she had treated her mother; but I think it also expressed a desire to be able again to be the useful, nurturant woman she had so long been. In any event, it is the only dream I have heard from a ninety-year-old, and it is a very important and informative dream to me.

REFERENCES

Becker, E. (1973). *The Denial of Death*. Free Press, New York.

Feifel, H. (1959). *The Meaning of Death*. McGraw-Hill, New York.

Freud, S. (1915). "Thoughts for the Times on War and Death," in *The Standard Edition of the Complete Psychological Works of Sigmund Freud*, vol. 14. Hogarth Press, London, 1957.

———. (1920). "Beyond the Pleasure Principle," in *The Standard Edition of the Complete Psychological Works of Sigmund Freud*, vol. 18. Hogarth Press, London, 1955.

———. (1933). "Why War?" in *The Standard Edition of the Complete Psychological Works of Sigmund Freud*, vol. 22. Hogarth Press, London, 1964.

Kubler-Ross, E. (1969). *On Death and Dying*. Macmillan, New York.

Lidz, T. (1946). "Nightmares and the Combat Neuroses," *Psychiatry*, 9:37–49.

Montaigne, M. E. de (1958). "To Study Philosophy Is to Learn to Die," in *Complete Essays of Montaigne*. D. M. Frame, trans. Stanford University Press, Stanford, Calif.

Waelder, R. (1960). *Basic Theory of Psychoanalysis*. International Universities Press, New York.

SUGGESTED READING

BECKER, E. (1973). *The Denial of Death*. Free Press, New York.
FEIFEL, H. (1959). *The Meaning of Death*. McGraw-Hill, New York.
Group for the Advancement of Psychiatry (1965). "Death and Dying: Attitudes of Patient and Doctor." Symposium No. 11.
KUBLER-ROSS, E. (1969). *On Death and Dying*. Macmillan, New York.

PART III

Patterns and Perspectives

CHAPTER 19

❀

Life Patterns

WE HAVE FOLLOWED the human life cycle, examining the critical tasks of each developmental stage, and how different persons tend to be confronted by similar problems at the same phase of life. We have sought to emphasize the continuity of the process in which progression depends upon how the preceding developmental tasks were surmounted; but also the continuity that arises because the mastery of the tasks of each stage is not an end in itself but subordinate to the goal of the development of a reasonably self-sufficient individual capable of living cooperatively with others and properly rearing offspring while assuming some responsibility for the welfare of the society. In focusing upon each phase of the life cycle in turn, we have noted that themes or patterns develop in each individual that color and sometimes virtually determine the way in which a person responds to the phase-specific tasks and tries to cope with them. In the inordinately complex task of seeking to understand an individual, we can be guided by finding such repetitive patterns and leitmotifs. We strive to grasp their origins and to perceive the variations in the themes as they recur in differing circumstances.

Out of the multiplicity of factors that enter into the shaping of a life, resultant patterns of living and relating emerge. A theme, or a group of interrelated themes, appears that can be modified and adapted to the stage-specific tasks or to the exigencies that arise. Sometimes the dominant theme results from an early childhood fixation and reiterates itself, unable to develop and lead onward, remaining in the same groove like the needle on a flawed phonograph record. The basic themes are more readily detected in emotionally disturbed persons because they are more set, more clearly repetitive, and perhaps more familiar to the practiced ear that has heard similar themes so often before. Still, repetitive ways of reacting and relating occur in all lives. The meaning of an episode in a life can often be grasped properly only through understanding how it furthers, impedes, or disrupts essential themes.

UNDERSTANDING A REPETITIVE PATTERN

Let us consider a woman's behavior that seems absurd as well as pathetic. She had grown up in a home that was miserable as well as impoverished because of her father's severe alcoholism. In late adolescence, she had married an older man, an alcoholic. Just as she was about to divorce him after ten unhappy years he was killed in an automobile accident. Now she spends her evenings trying to take care of a man who flees from her into the oblivion of an alcoholic stupor every weekend. She cleans him, bathes him, nurses him back to face the work week, and she is distressed because she has failed to convince him that he needs her and should marry her. She knows that she is foolish, but she feels certain that she can make him happy, satisfy his needs, and wean him from the bottle.

We can seek to understand her repetitive involvement with alcoholic men in a variety of ways. In terms of the structural concept, we might consider that she needs punishment by a strict superego because of her rivalry with her mother for her alcoholic father. In terms of fixation of libidinal investment, we might consider her masochistic behavior to be a reaction formation to anal-sadistic impulses against her father, or we might weigh the oral components of her fixation and emphasize that she identifies with the oral addictive behavior of her alcoholic men and provides the care that she would like to have received from a mothering person. However, focusing upon oral or anal character traits, or upon an abstract balance between superego, ego, and id, provides little specific understanding of this woman and why she is seriously upset because an alcoholic man will not marry her. The term "masochistic" is useful in summarizing some of her basic characteristics, but it is also necessary to note that she behaves masochistically only in the fairly specific context of her need to be made unhappy by alcoholic men.

The woman's compulsion to repeat an unhappy experience with a second alcoholic husband becomes specifically meaningful when the theme is traced back to its childhood origins in her family. In psychotherapy, she recalled the hours she had spent as a little girl with her father, who would tell her wonderful stories of his childhood and of leprechauns while he was repentant and sober between alcoholic bouts; these wonderful hours were disrupted by her mother's scoldings of her father for his idleness and unworldly dreaming. As a girl she had believed that her father was an alcoholic because of her mother's coldness and shrewishness. Her late oedipal fantasies dwelled on what her father would have been like with a different wife: herself, grown up into a sensuous and sensitive woman who could care for his needs. She came to despise her mother as an embittered harridan. Differentiation from her mother became a major developmental motive. She sought to be warm and nurturant, the only person who understood and appreciated her father. In therapy she recalled having had vague fantasies in early adolescence in which her mother would desert the family and leave her to care for it; but her mother remained while her father became a hopeless invalid. The theme developed through her marriage to a man who resembled her father both emotionally and physically. She would prove in the marriage that, had she been her father's wife, her father would have been a very different person. She would demonstrate to herself that she was unlike her mother. Despite her efforts and resolve, she found that her nurturant, protective, and sensual efforts failed. Indeed, in retrospect, she thought it likely that her attempts to be particularly close and protective precipitated her husband's episodes of drinking.

Shortly before her husband's death, she had been forced to recognize that she could no longer tolerate the situation. Her husband was neglecting and mistreating their children, and when drunk he often turned against her and struck her. She was not even as capable as her mother, who had managed to remain with her father and nurse him during his years of chronic illness. Much of the hostility she had felt toward her mother was now directed against herself. She had not only mourned her husband but had become depressed after his death, tending to blame herself for his hapless life and premature end. She emerged from her depressed and somewhat apathetic state when she again became involved with an alcoholic whom she hoped to marry and sought to save. She entered therapy in part because she found herself becoming upset because he avoided marriage, and in part because her priest sized up the situation and urged her to seek help. The priest had recognized her compulsion to repeat a pattern that would lead her into another hopeless and desperate situation. She would continue to try to solve the old problem of proving to herself that she, in contrast to her mother, could have prevented her father's alcoholism. A primary task of psychotherapy was to release the patient from her bondage to such unconscious repetitive and frustrating efforts to solve old problems in the wrong generation, and, through viewing her parents from a more adult and realistic perspective, enable her to gain a new self-image and more mature motivations. The therapeutic task was to overcome a fixation involving a failure to resolve the oedipal situation adequately, but the designation of the problem in such terms means little without the more specific knowledge of the repetitive pattern, how it arose, and how it re-appeared in new situations.

REPETITIVE PATTERNS AND THE
NATURE OF TRAUMA

Without an appreciation of the nature and force of the life pattern, it often is difficult to grasp the emotional impact of events on a person, or even what is beneficial and what traumatic. A brother's marriage is usually considered a happy event, but a young woman became severely upset when her older brother's marriage upset her lifelong pattern of security opera-tions. As a child of six she had suffered from desperate anxiety when her mother died and the family almost broke up. She had thrown herself into the task of helping her father care for the home and her brothers in order to make it possible for the family to remain together. She feared that unless she constantly proved her usefulness she would be unwanted and sent to an orphanage.

As she grew older she developed little faith in obtaining security through marriage—for as a black woman she had seen many men desert their wives. She felt that only relationships between a parent and a child pro-vided security that could be trusted. Her father would never desert her because she was essential to him, caring for him and his household. Still, her father was growing old and death would eventually take him from her. She developed two safeguards against feeling lost and deserted after he died. Marriage was not one of them. Indeed, she refused to marry a persis-tent suitor, for marriage would take her away from her home. But she sought to have a baby by him out of wedlock, a child to whom she would give so much love that the child would never leave her. In addition, she made a home for her older brother and worked to supplement his income.

She filled all of his needs, other than sexual, so that he had no reason to marry. He needed her and would remain with her after her father died. However, her plans went awry. She failed to become pregnant by her boyfriend; and while considering finding another who might be more fertile, she had herself examined and found that it was she who was sterile. Then, soon after her father's death, her brother decided to marry—perhaps because her intense solicitude, which included unconscious seductive behavior, frightened him into marriage. Suddenly, the pattern she had developed to insure against the recurrence of being deserted collapsed, in part because of the intensity of her defense.

Repetitive Patterns, Personality, and Ego Functioning

Freud's major contribution, among his many contributions to the understanding of human functioning and malfunctioning, was his elucidation of the limits of people's conscious decision making and of the rationality of their behavior. He clarified the force and scope of unconscious determinants in the service of sexual and aggressive impulses and desires, and demonstrated how the avoidance of anxiety leads to the construction of mechanisms of defense that limit or distort the perception and understanding of reality. The directive capacities of the self that we term ego functions are never free from repressed unconscious influences. At times, the ego functions seem to serve primarily as a front to maintain self-esteem by transforming underlying irrational motives into an acceptable form. For a time during the development of psychoanalytic theory and practice, the pendulum swung far in the direction of underestimating the role of rational, reality-oriented decision making. Currently, a new theoretic balance has been achieved by an assimilation of studies of cognitive development into psychodynamic theory. However, in studying the limits of reality-oriented behavior—of the capacity of the ego to direct the self by balancing reality needs, id demands, and superego injunctions—we must be concerned with the limitations imposed by the personality configurations and life patterns that emerge during the developmental years.

PSYCHOSEXUAL FIXATIONS AND CHARACTER

Psychoanalysis has developed two interrelated approaches to the study of personality types and how such personality patterns limit the adaptive range of individuals but at the same time make their ways of reacting and relating more comprehensible and predictable. The first approach is based upon fixations of psychosexual development—originally conceived in terms of libidinal fixation at one or another erogenous zone. Failures to work through the essential developmental tasks of the period result in fixation of interest and attention on these tasks or regressively on those satisfactions gained in an earlier period before the frustrations occurred. Fixation can be taken to mean, as in this volume, that when the tasks of a developmental phase are not mastered adequately the child is unprepared to cope with subsequent developmental tasks and continues to seek fulfillment of the frustrated needs in a repetitive manner. Such fixations can be major determinants of basic life patterns. The major traits of "oral" characters were discussed at the end of the chapter on infancy, and of "anal" characters in the chapter on the toddler. Some shortcomings of the concepts of "oral" and "anal" characters were also discussed. These are the two best-developed categories, but a "urethral" character and a "phallic" character have also been described.* The concept of the "genital" character is not used to describe a personality type but rather to designate more or less normative development in which no serious fixations occur at pregenital phases. Originally the term connoted that the libido was free for mature investment in a gratifying sexual relationship, with pregenital investments subserving forepleasure to sexual intercourse rather than remaining a goal of sexual desire. In terms of Erikson's concepts of psychosocial development, the attainment of genital sexuality is approximately akin to the capacity for intimacy after an ego identity has been achieved. The concept of the genital character emphasizes the deficiencies of a characterology based on phases of libidinal development. It pays little, if any, attention to the developmental

* The concept of the "urethral" character is not well developed. It is related to fixation at a level of urethral erotism—the sexual excitation felt when urinating, perhaps accentuated by irritation from chronic childhood masturbatory play. It relates such burning sensations to burning ambition, and also to the excitement of lighting fires and wishing to extinguish them by urination. Bed wetting is thus related to sexual excitement. The "phallic" character, whose development is related to fixations at the oedipal period, is overmasculine, tending to be a Don Juan, boastful and reckless. The reactive nature of the masculinity becomes apparent after a little study. Incestuous drives are not far beneath the surface, and perverse activities or fantasies are common. The character configuration has been related to fixations caused by castration fears which block the proper resolution of the oedipal conflicts; but it seems more clearly related to a boy's relationship with a mother who focuses her admiration and love on her son's genitalia, which she prizes highly. The penis, so to speak, remains the mother's possession, and the man repetitively seeks admiration through overmasculine behavior, considering his penis a prize that women cannot resist. Women may be termed "phallic" when they habitually use their bodies exhibitionistically as a substitute for the penis they lack; or sometimes the term is used for aggressive women who fantasy and act out fantasies of being dominant masculine persons, either subjugating men or dominating other women homosexually.

tasks of adolescence, and it has required profound modifications to include interpersonal and intrafamilial influences on character formation.

Characterologic Syndromes

The second common way of characterizing persons used in psychoanalytic psychiatry is borrowed from clinical syndromes. A person is termed "hysteric," "narcissistic," "phobic," "obsessive," "schizoid," "paranoid," "sadomasochistic," "depressive," etc., but these terms do not necessarily designate obvious psychopathological conditions. The usage rests upon the recognition that there is no sharp line of demarcation between the normal and abnormal, and that psychopathological syndromes are essentially aberrations of personality development rather than discrete illnesses. Each of these terms derived from pathological states also designates a characteristic combination of mechanisms of defense that gives a particular pattern to the person's ways of thinking, relating, and behaving —a pattern which is found in more exaggerated and more rigid form in persons suffering from the clinical syndrome. The way in which these designations are used depends somewhat upon the user's conceptualization of the psychiatric disorders. A proper discussion requires careful consideration of psychopathology, and thus extends beyond the province of this book; but we shall define several terms briefly, simply to illustrate the usage of terms which not only is common in the psychiatric literature but has entered the general vocabulary of the language.

Paranoid personalities utilize *projection* as a major defense against recognition of unacceptable impulses and motives. There is a failure in establishing proper boundaries between the self and others, and one's own motives are ascribed to others. Persons who constantly feel belittled, and misjudged, and who bear grudges because they feel thwarted by others who they believe are against them, are often termed paranoid. *Hysterical* personalities readily *repress* upsetting situations and impulses, particularly sexual desires, and bolster the repression by *conversion* into some physical symptom and through *displacement* of affect. The failure to recognize motives that seem obvious to others may create an impression of prevarication or malingering—as in a soldier who emerges from a harrowing combat experience without awareness of having experienced any fear but suffering from an inability to walk. The term "hysterical" is often used to refer to women who are unaware of their habitually seductive behavior and who are upset or insulted when men respond and make advances to them. Such personality traits are related, with some justification, to fixations at the oedipal phase. The term may also refer to persons who are emotionally labile because of uncontrolled outbursts of repressed feelings or impulses in a disguised or displaced form. *Obsessive* personalities tend to seek to control their impulses and also the contingencies of the future by being meticulous, by carefully following routines and perhaps by being particularly neat and orderly, and by the use of the defenses of isolation, undoing, reaction formation, and intellectualization. The relationship to the "anal character" has been noted in the chapter on the toddler. The term *compulsive personality* is sometimes used almost as a synonym for "obsessive personality," but it may also indicate persons who need to satisfy or placate the needs of others in order to feel secure though unconsciously resenting the demands they believe others place upon them. The relationship to rescinding initiative in order to comply with parental demands during the period of ambulation can be noted. The use of these terms in categorizing persons is approximate, and in general they serve primarily as means of communicating some concepts about a person's characteristic ways of behaving and relating.

The term *narcissistic* character or personality, now widely used in discussing sociopathic, addictive, borderline, and schizophrenic patients, does not derive from a definitive clinical syndrome; and the use and abuse of the term vary greatly. In general, narcissistic refers to persons with a fundamental disturbance of self-esteem, and who may seem self-satisfied, haughty, and even contemptuous of others, but who require constant admiration or praise from others and therefore develop various ways of gaining admiration. Their relations to others are superficial because their interest in others is almost wholly in what they can gain from them in the way of admiration and protection. They are apt to become hostile when others do not fulfill their unrealistic expectations and take care of all their needs. The origin of the character disorder seems to relate to failure to individuate adequately and to establish suitable boundaries between the self and others; but it probably also involves deficiencies in the nurturing persons.*

There are many other ways of categorizing personality types, all of which have serious shortcomings.†

* The concept of the narcissistic personality is unusually complex and the source of many controversies. The reader is referred to Otto Kernberg's *Borderline Conditions and Pathological Narcissism* and Heinz Kohut's *The Analysis of the Self* for further consideration of the topic.
† Some seek to relate personality types to some physiological process or to physique. Thus, Hippocrates divided people into choleric, sanguine, phlegmatic, and melancholic types, a personology which brought various body fluids into the language as adjectives

LIFE PATTERNS AND FIXATIONS

In the study of life patterns or basic life themes, we are concerned with a type of fixation, but not a fixation that can be defined in terms of developmental stages alone. The fixation is to a way of gaining security that is more specific and usually relates to a way the child found security within the family. The fixation may, however, be to a life pattern that was developed in order to defend against the recurrence of a situation that caused severe or intolerable anxiety or depression—as in the case of the woman who found a major guide and motivating force in securing her relationships to her father and brother in order to prevent a reexperience of the unbearable separation anxiety that followed her mother's death. Such clearly defensive patterns will usually have their origins in the family because that is where the immature child is usually most vulnerable. A life theme may be basically adaptive, in the sense of being concerned with the development of assets, or defensive—that is, adaptive in defending against a trauma. Perhaps adaptation and defense, in this context, are never clearly separable.

Defensive Life Patterns

Defensive life patterns are not the same as patterns of mechanisms of defense of the ego against anxiety. The mechanisms of defense operate by repressing awareness of a disturbing impulse or experience or through altering the proper perception of it. The defensive life pattern seeks to avoid the recurrence of an unbearable threat. It will usually include mech-

---

describing persons and states of emotion. Kretschmer (1926) related personality characteristics to body structure, classifying individuals as leptosome (asthenic), pyknic, athletic, or dysplastic types—a typology that gained a considerable following in both medicine and psychiatry. Sheldon and Stevens (1942) pursued a related but more complex classification based on physique. Jung's (1938) division of people into extroverts and introverts has probably been the typology most widely followed. In brief, the extrovert's energy and interests are directed toward activities, interpersonal relationships, and objective facts and actions, whereas the introvert is more interested in ideas, subjective states, spiritual values, etc. Such classifications have some utilitarian value, but most persons refuse to fit clear-cut categorizations. Their usefulness has also been limited because of the attempts to link character or personality with some inborn physical characteristics in a rather simplistic manner. As Stern (1938) pointed out, most typologies tend to divide persons on the basis of inward and outward directedness. Riesman's (1954) use of inner and outer directedness has become an integral part of the American intellectual scene. A different approach to classifying people can be found in Chapter 12. The reader is also referred to the review of the topic of personality types by D. W. MacKinnon, in Chapter 1 of Volume 1 of *Personality and the Behavior Disorders*, and to A. A. Roback, *The Psychology of Character*.

anisms of defense, but the pattern may sometimes prevent the establishment of satisfactory defense mechanisms. Thus, persons who find means of always remaining dependent upon a parental figure may not develop defenses against experiencing separation anxiety or gradually gain confidence in their capacities to manage on their own. Then if the defensive pattern is undermined—as occurred when the woman's father died and her sibling substitute for him married—the person is left relatively defenseless and prey to severe anxiety.

The satisfactory development of defensive life patterns enables many persons to compensate for serious traumatic occurrences in childhood or chronically disturbed childhood environments and lead satisfactory lives despite them. The outstanding assets of some individuals are developed as part of such defensive or compensating patterns. An exceptional trained nurse entered her vocation as a continuation of a pattern of helping her mother take care of her numerous siblings. She had felt rejected by her mother in childhood as an additional burden, but learned to gain appreciation and praise by becoming a "little mother." The psychiatrist, however, is likely to see people as patients after the defensive patterns of their lives have been undermined and collapsed, or when frantic restitutional efforts are being made. Indeed, the understanding of the nature of an emotionally traumatic occurrence requires a grasp of how such life patterns are threatened or demolished by the occurrence. The topic will be elaborated further in the next chapter when we discuss physiological functioning, for the disruption of defensive life patterns can place serious strains on the body's physiological defenses.

The Family and Life Patterns

The family occupies a central position in the understanding of life styles and life patterns because the family is everywhere the essential agent that provides the nurture, structure, and enculturation needed by infants to survive and develop into persons capable of adapting to their physical and social environment; but also because children develop through internalizing their parents' ways and their interactions with each other, and because they gain motives and directives by the need and desire to relate harmoniously within the family. It is in the family that patterns of emotional reactivity develop and interpersonal relationships are established that pattern and color all subsequent relationships. The family is also central because for most persons, if not all, it is the intimate relationships in both the natal and marital family that provide much of the fulfillment and meaning in life— and because, as we have considered elsewhere, individuals' satisfactions with themselves and their sense of self-esteem continue to depend to some degree upon internalized parental values, even though the parents may be dead for many years.

In Chapter 7 we examined how children's transition through the oedipal phase and how their coming to terms with what Freud (1909) called "the family romance" help to crystallize their personalities and to establish basic patterns of interpersonal relationships. The oedipal situation sets a basic pattern for the human condition, not because it is "instinctual" but because it is an inevitable consequence of the human condition. The oedipal transition concerns more than the boy's repression of his erotized attachment to his mother and his identification with his father in order to be rid of his projected fear that his father will kill or castrate him; or the girl's libidinal attachment to her father and subsequent repression of it. All children start life symbiotically attached to their mothers, and soon develop an egocentric understanding of the relationship with her; as the mother necessarily frustrates the attachment, they suffer narcissistic injury, and learn that others are also important to her. In essence the oedipal transition has to do with the child's movement out of a mother-centered world to find his or her place as a boy or girl member of the family unit. The child must progressively learn the prerogatives and limitations of parents and children and of males and females. Reluctantly, the child gradually gives up the special closeness to the mother to gain increasing autonomy and the security that derives from belonging to a sheltering family.

It is not a quibble to maintain that the oedipal transition is a consequence of the human condition rather than instinctual: it is essential to understand that how it transpires differs from individual to individual, depending upon the circumstances—how the parents relate to one another as well as to the child, the personalities of the persons involved, and the sibling relationships. Minimally, a triangular relationship exists between parents and child that affects each of them, and usually other children are present or will later enter into the arena; and relationships with members of the extended family—either in actuality or as internalized in the parents— are also always significant. The manner in which the oedipal resolution occurs sets a basic pattern that may later be modified, but which will never be completely undone. Although it will differ for each person, common patterns recur and lead to similar life patterns. A major task in becoming a psychiatrist lies in gaining familiarity with these various ways of resolving the oedipal situation and the ensuing life patterns, and then from knowledge of developmental dynamics and familiar themes to be able to formulate useful conjectures about new and unfamiliar patterns.

The term "oedipal situation" is used with varying degrees of specificity.

Children establish life patterns not only through how their attachment to the parent of the opposite sex is resolved, but also through how they find or seek to find a place within the family, with parents, siblings, and any other significant persons in the home. They are reacting in response not only to their own egocentric appreciation of the situation and their fantasies about it, but also to the way in which the other family members relate to them— which very often is far different from the more or less ideal circumstances presented in the chapters on childhood in this book. The ways in which the parents relate to the child and to each other guide the child into various patterns. Thus a boy or girl may be led to identify strongly with the parent of the same sex in order to gain the affection of the parent of the opposite sex, and later become capable of marrying a person like the parent of the opposite sex to form a union in which each supports the other and both have a major interest in rearing the next generation, etc. Or it may, as in the case of the woman with the alcoholic father and husband, lead to efforts to be very different from the parent of the same sex—to differentiate rather than identify. Or it may foster a reversed oedipal resolution in which the child identifies with the parent of the opposite sex and seeks a love object of the same sex. It may lead to efforts to relate to two parents who differ so profoundly that the child has an impossible task. There are many such general patterns, and the common variants are too numerous to designate here, for they are properly learned in work with patients.*

The sibling patterns within a family may be regarded as offshoots of the oedipal situation, and they can also be fundamental in establishing life patterns. Sibling rivalries can establish a pattern of relating to peers in a hostile, aggressive competition for supremacy. In contrast, when siblings provide strong support to each other, in extrafamilial settings they may tend to rely on teamwork in sports and seek cooperative coalitions in occupational ventures. An oldest daughter may develop maternal attitudes toward younger siblings that virtually direct her life efforts into teaching and then toward having a large family of her own. Though they have not been emphasized particularly in this book, sibling relationships can be almost as profoundly influential as the relationships with parents, and a person's relatedness to a brother or sister is often closer and more meaningful than the relationship to parents.†

* Not only because the topic is beyond the scope of this chapter and book, but because many such patterns have not been specifically delineated in the psychiatric literature—and still remain part of the more or less conscious knowledge of the experienced clinician.

† Freud, in "Totem and Taboo," postulated that brothers in the "primal horde" envious of the father's prerogatives with their mother banded together to kill the father. Although there are no indications from anthropological studies that a primal horde ever existed, the idea may be taken as symbolic of the rivalry between genera-

A parent's favoritism for one child over another, preference for one sex over the other, or unfavorable identification of a child with a disliked parent or spouse, and other such matters, can heighten the rivalry between siblings to bitter and lasting animosities.* On the other hand, the rivalry between siblings, which is also a virtual consequence of the human condition, fades—or is repressed and replaced by reaction formation—when parents balance the attention and affection they give their children, and when they teach through their own behavior that the well-being of others in the family is part of their own welfare.

Myth and Life Patterns

Legend and myth are important to the psychiatrist and to the understanding of people because tradition filters out and deposits into such tales significant and commonly experienced patterns; and they are often patterns that can be considered only in myth or dream because they deal with drives and wishes that have been taboo in the society and repressed in the individual. The myth may deal with ancestral figures who lived before cannibalism, incest, parricide, matricide, and the like became taboo, and it may concern fantasies of such behavior that are repressed in the developing child. The myth holds before us, as a sort of cultural superego, the horrors that follow upon such unthinkable behavior.† The Greek tragedies and the plays of Shakespeare and Strindberg survive in part because they are con-

---

tions. The Joseph saga of the Old Testament suggests another basic configuration in which the youngest son of an elderly father does not become involved in clear-cut oedipal rivalry but is favored by the father and identifies with him. The older siblings become resentful and seek to be rid of the favored intruder who is identified with the father and seek to kill him. The story also suggests how a younger child may be able to fare well in a distant land where he is free of the danger of the envy of the older siblings.

The Joseph story is also a story of death and rebirth that relates to the Adonis and Tammuz myths—as well as to the story of Jesus, in which the favored son of God is killed and resurrected; the Joseph story is also, in essence, the story of the "chosen" Jewish people who are repeatedly being exterminated and reborn.

* We may note that in Genesis, Abraham sent Ishmael into the desert to placate Isaac's mother, Sarah. Similarly, Rebecca had her favorite son, Jacob, steal his father's blessing from Esau. The ensuing conflict between the symbolic descendants of Ishmael and Esau who intermarried, and those of Jacob continues into the present.

† The myths of the accursed house of Tantalus, for example, move across the generations to tell of the punishment of Tantalus by the gods because he fed them his son, an act which once may have been the essence of piety; of the punishment of Thyestes for seducing his brother Atreus's wife; of that of Atreus for serving a stew of Thyestes's children to Thyestes in vengeance; of the fate of Agamemnon because of his father Atreus's vengeance and for sacrificing his daughter Iphigenia to help recover his sister-in-law from Troy; of the death of Clytemnestra, Agamemnon's wife, at the hand of her son, Orestes, for killing her husband and virtually abandoning her son; of the insanity of Orestes that followed his matricide.

cerned with variations on basic life themes or patterns that transcend individual experience and even eras and differences in cultures. *Hamlet* is not simply the story of an oedipal conflict; it is rather a particular variant of the oedipal situation that followed on a mother's infidelity to a father and therefore also to a son who identified with his father, and sheds light upon the emotional consequences of many variants of the theme. It is related not only to the Oedipus saga through Hamlet's parricide (Jones, 1949; Murray, 1914; Wertham, 1941) and incestuous preoccupations about his mother but even more closely to the Orestes myths, in which Orestes kills his mother because of her infidelity to his father and collusion in his murder. Because he committed matricide, Orestes becomes insane, whereas Hamlet, who has an impulsion to kill his mother upon which he cannot act, verges on insanity and is preoccupied with suicide. Freud gained some of his most telling insights from Shakespeare and Sophocles, and these writers' works remain excellent sources from which understanding of various basic life patterns can be gleaned.

REFERENCES

FREUD, S. (1909). "Family Romance," in *The Standard Edition of the Complete Psychological Works of Sigmund Freud*, vol. 9. Hogarth Press, London, 1959.
———. (1912–1913). "Totem and Taboo," in *The Standard Edition of the Complete Psychological Works of Sigmund Freud*, vol. 13. Hogarth Press, London, 1955.
JONES, E. (1949). *Hamlet and Oedipus*. W. W. Norton, New York.
JUNG, C. (1938). *Psychological Types*. Harcourt, Brace, New York.
KERNBERG, O. (1975). *Borderline Conditions and Pathological Narcissism*. Jason Aronson, New York.
KOHUT, H. (1971). *The Analysis of the Self*. International Universities Press, New York.
KRETSCHMER, E. (1926). *Physique and Character*. Harcourt, Brace, New York.
MACKINNON, D. W. (1944). "The Structure of Personality," in *Personality and the Behavior Disorders*, vol. 1. J. McV. Hunt, ed. Ronald Press, New York.
MURRAY, G. (1914). *Hamlet and Orestes: A Study in Traditional Types*. The Annual Shakespeare Lecture of the British Academy. Oxford University Press, New York.
RIESMAN, D. (1954). *The Lonely Crowd*. Doubleday Anchor Books, Garden City, N.Y.
ROBACK, A. A. (1927). *The Psychology of Character, with a Survey of Temperament*. Harcourt, Brace, New York.
SHELDON, W., and STEVENS, S. (1942). *Varieties of Temperament*. Harper & Bros., New York.
STERN, W. (1938). *General Psychology from the Personalistic Standpoint*. Macmillan, New York.
WERTHAM, F. (1941). *Dark Legend*. Duell, Sloan and Pearce, New York.

SUGGESTED READING

DEUTSCH, H. (1965). *Neuroses and Character Types*. International Universities Press, New York.

LIDZ, T. (1975). *Hamlet's Enemy: Myth and Madness in Hamlet*. Basic Books, New York.

RANK, O. (1952). *The Myth of the Birth of the Hero*. E. Robbins and S. E. Jelliffe, trans. Robert Brunner, New York.

CHAPTER 20

❀

Personality Development
and Physiological Functions

IN THIS PENULTIMATE CHAPTER we must direct
our attention, albeit but briefly, to what has been called "the mysterious
leap from the mind to the body." Despite the obvious influence of thought
upon the body's functioning—the sudden cold sweat, the pounding heart,
the penile erection, the urgent defecation—it has been difficult for the
philosophically oriented to pass beyond the barrier of the mind-body dichotomy to grasp how the intangible idea or emotional state can influence
something real and composed of matter such as the heart or the even more
prosaic intestines. We are not, however, primarily concerned with the resolution of an age-old metaphysical dilemma, but enter upon the topic because we cannot understand human functioning without a clear appreciation of how emotions and physiology are inextricably interrelated, and how
individuals' personality development influences their body structure and
can even determine what constitutes stress for them and creates strains on
their physiological apparatus.

The student of medicine's primary interest in personality development
may properly derive from the impact of personality functions on physiological functioning, and on the etiology and treatment of disease. Good physicians have always been aware that the majority of patients come to them
because of emotional disturbances. It has become increasingly apparent

that personality and emotional disorders not only are a major factor in the etiology of the so-called diseases of stress—such as peptic ulcer, ulcerative colitis, asthma, essential hypertension, hyperthyroidism—but may also contribute to the causation or chronicity of almost any illness.* Nonmedical persons who are involved in the care or treatment of personality disorders need to be constantly aware of the physiological concomitants and potential bodily repercussions of emotional disturbances. The topics of psychophysiological disturbances and psychosomatic medicine form disciplines in themselves.† As the reader is not expected to be versed in physiology and neuroanatomy, we shall seek to present here merely a general orientation that will permit a grasp of the essentials of the topic and of its importance.

Personality development influences the physiological processes in many different ways. There is essentially nothing different about the gastric apparatus of a Hindu and a Mohammedan, and yet the appetite of the Hindu may be stimulated by pork but not by beef, whereas a Mohammedan neighbor who has inadvertently swallowed some lard may even become sick.

Although the sight of a friend at mealtime may stimulate gastric secretions and improve the appetite, it is not expected to cause one to drool. Yet the author encountered some persons in the South Seas for whom the sight of a stranger entering their village started them salivating even as the ringing of a bell stimulated Pavlov's dogs. Such changes in appetite are, of course, not simply ideas but also alterations in the physiological functioning of the stomach, which is very sensitive to the emotional state of the person who possesses the stomach.**

---

* Including fractured bones because of "accident-proneness," and acute infectious diseases such as pneumonia through style of life, unconscious neglect of reasonable precautions, etc. Thus, a man who suffered from lobar pneumonia three times in one year had almost courted such illnesses after serious family arguments. He would emerge from the very hot furnace room in which he worked all day, go to a bar, and take three shots of whiskey, which dilated his peripheral blood vessels still further as well as dulled his feelings about his enraged wife, then would walk for hours in freezing weather rather than go home, occasionally stopping for another drink of whiskey, which would interfere further with his body's ability to conserve heat.

† At least three journals in English are specifically devoted to studies in the field, *Psychosomatic Medicine, Journal of Psychosomatic Research,* and *Psychosomatics.* For a more physiologically oriented introduction, the reader is referred to the author's chapter in the first edition of the *American Handbook of Psychiatry. Psychosomatic Medicine,* by Franz Alexander, furnishes a good general approach to clinical problems.

** Scientific studies of the effects of emotion on gastric physiology started when one of the heroes of American medicine, William Beaumont (1833), made direct observations of the interior of the stomach and of its secretions; he concomitantly demonstrated that a good scientist can function under almost any circumstances or find material for study wherever he may be. As an army surgeon stationed on the frontier in 1829, Beau-

PERSONALITY AND PHYSIQUE

Persons' physiques are commonly considered a product of their heredity, their physical environment, and their nutrition during their developmental years. Yet personality development is also involved. A critical study that changed the conceptualization of Fröhlich's syndrome provides an excellent illustration. The syndrome, which consisted of obesity and small genitalia in boys often accompanied by sluggishness or somnolence, had usually been considered to result from some unknown dysfunction of the pituitary gland. Bruch and Touraine (1940) noted, however, striking similarities in the personalities of the mothers of these children and in the ways in which they reared their sons. These mothers were unable to bestow any real affection but gave their sons food instead. To these mothers, who had grown up in deprived homes, food formed a symbol of affection and security. They felt insecure and inadequate as mothers unless the child overate and appeared healthy and well provided for by being obese. In addi-

---

mont saved the life of a trapper, Alexis St. Martin, who had suffered an accidental gunshot wound in the abdomen. St. Martin was left with a fistula between the stomach and the exterior abdominal wall, which permitted direct observation of the interior of the stomach, its activity, and the sampling of its secretions. Beaumont hired St. Martin and carried out careful studies of his unique subject for many years, which included observations of the effects of emotional states on gastric physiology.

Another series of classic studies of the stomach, carried out by Stewart Wolf and Harold Wolff (1943) on another man with a gastric fistula, was directed specifically at elucidating the effect of emotions on gastric functioning. The experimental subject, known only as Tom, suffered from atresia of the esophagus—not from ingestion of lye as is usually the case, but, as a good Irishman, from inadvertently swallowing a cup of scalding chowder. Since he was unable to eat, a fistula into his stomach was created surgically. The researchers gave Tom a job doing chores around the laboratory so that they would have him available for their studies. They observed their subject's stomach as he spontaneously experienced a variety of emotional states and they learned how to induce various emotional states in him to further their studies. The proper digestive functioning of the stomach depends upon the harmonious integration between acid and pepsin secretion, motility, the degree of dilation of the blood vessels in the mucosal lining, and the proper opening of the entrance to the duodenum. In brief, they found that when Tom was anxious or fearful the motility of the stomach decreased, the mucosal lining of the stomach became pale, but acid secretion continued; when he was angry the mucosa became engorged, the acid secretion might double, and the stomach which could be overactive was also friable and easily injured. Both patterns disrupted the harmoniously integrated patterns of motility, acid and pepsin secretion, and vascular engorgment of the mucosa conducive to proper digestion. Other investigators disagree with these precise findings, but all have found significant alterations in motility, secretions, and vascularity with various types of emotional stress.

Another highly significant study has been carried out by Engel and Reichsman (1956) on a young child, Monica, who was born with an esophageal atresia and had a gastric fistula made surgically. The study has particular importance in relating the effects of apathy and depression to gastric functions.

tion, these women were reactively concerned about their sons' safety and needed to keep them in the home and away from play with other children lest they get in trouble or danger. The combination of stuffing a child by making him feel guilty if he did not overeat and preventing expenditure of energy was sufficient to explain the obesity and sluggish inactivity; the genitalia were in fact not small but only appeared so because of the child's obese abdomen and thighs.

The syndrome of anorexia nervosa, in which the person is chronically emaciated, sometimes to the extent of being a "living skeleton" of fifty or sixty pounds, was once thought to be due to a pituitary deficiency. It is, however, due to self-imposed starvation of emotional origin; and, when it starts in early adolescence, the person often fails to develop secondary sexual characteristics. Oskar Mazareth, the hero, or antihero, of Günter's Grass's *The Tin Drum*, who stopped growing at the age of three, is only a fictional symbol, but in recent years clear evidence has been found of emotionally induced dwarfism (Blodgett, 1963). Somewhat less dramatic but more common are the decrements in rates of growth and weight gain in children after they are institutionalized, despite the availability of ample nourishment and excellent physical care.

The development of an athletic physique can also depend upon the individual's self-concept and mechanisms of defense. A youth of seventeen was slight, with poor muscular development and a small frame, when he entered college. He sought psychiatric help early in his freshman year because of phobic symptoms. During his therapy he soon became aware of intense feelings of rivalry with his father and his wishes and fears of attacking and injuring him. As he worked through his hostile feelings toward his father, and in seeking some expression for his aggressive impulses that previously had been repressed, he became a member of the college wrestling squad. Exercising daily with various apparatus in the gymnasium as well as wrestling, he became one of the strongest and most massive students in the university by the time of his graduation.

PERSONALITY DEVELOPMENT AND PHYSIOLOGICAL FUNCTIONING

Let us turn now to consider the influence of personality development on physiological functioning. It will be recalled that in discussing the endowment with which the infant enters this world, we noted that relatively early in the evolutionary process the organism developed automatic means of spontaneously preparing for flight or fight when confronted by danger. These emergency responses are part of the organism's patterns of fear and aggressivity. They are not simply emotional states but pervasive changes in the functioning of the entire organism in preparation for coping with the danger and to minimize the effects of any consequent injury. Although the neurophysiological mechanisms that set off and mediate these reactions are very complex, for our present purposes it will suffice to note that they involve secretion of the hormones epinephrine and norepineprine by the adrenal medulla, and the activation of the autonomic nervous system—of which the adrenal medulla is, in a sense, a part.* Almost instantaneously, the person becomes more alert and sensitive to stimuli because of changes in the reticular activating system in the brain; blood flow is shunted to the muscles and brain from the peripheral vessels and digestive organs, and the heart rate increases to supply more oxygen to the muscles and brain, and to remove waste products; the coagulability of the blood increases to counter bleeding; the peripheral blood vessels constrict not only to shunt blood to the muscles but also to lessen blood loss; sweating helps dissipate the heat generated by muscular activity and makes the body slippery; the pupils dilate, either the better to see in the dark or to make the animal appear more frightening—the list of physiological changes is great and still not fully known. They include mobilization of blood sugar from depots in the liver to provide energy; changes in kidney function to lessen blood volume; alterations in respiration to increase the oxygen-carbon dioxide exchange; a series of changes in the stomach and intestines, including a tendency for immediate evacuation of the bowels; and changes at the synapses in parts of the brain. In addition the adrenal medullary secretions may trigger secretion of andrenocorticotrophic hormone by the pituitary that sets off another major defense system of the organism that will be considered later in the chapter.

Now all of these responses can be highly useful and life-saving when animals, including human animals, confront an enemy from which they must flee or engage in mortal combat, or when all possible resources must be marshaled in overcoming some environmental hazard as in running from a

---

* It has often been considered that epinephrine primarily prepares for flight and norepinephrine for fight. It has been suggested that animals who tend to flee secrete more epinephrine than norepinephrine and the opposite occurs in those more apt to fight than flee. Some evidence as summarized by Engel (1962) suggests that epinephrine is the major secretion during the period of alarm and anxiety without action; but that with action, be it either flight or fight, norepinephrine secretion becomes greater, automatically shifting the physiological patterns for action.

forest fire, but they are not always useful in mastering the enemies and hazards of a civilized world, such as in combating a business opponent, or the need to make a good impression when being interviewed for admission to a graduate school. The physiological responses to danger contribute little toward countering the hostility of a rival for promotion, or to finding a job by means of which a person can indirectly feed his or her family. These physiological responses are of even less value in situations that arouse anxiety, anger, or resentment. Yet, anxiety, as noted in Chapter 8, is related to fear, and anger and resentment to aggression, and these emotions are accompanied, to a greater or lesser degree, by the same fundamental bodily defenses against impending danger. The more acute the anxiety or severe the anger, the more likely that the physiological changes will be severe and diffuse. But anxiety occurs in relation to danger from one's own impulses, or to concerns over loss of significant persons, or to apprehensions about future contingencies—and these can rarely be solved by either flight or physical combat. Similarly, hostile feelings and resentments can rarely be overcome by fighting and vanquishing the person with whom one is angry. Still, these physiological states create unpleasant and even unbearable feelings, and anxiety impels individuals toward ridding themselves of its source. These states serve useful functions primarily in motivating a person toward changing the conditions that may be inducing them—if the person consciously knows what they are. As anxiety is most commonly brought about by unconscious factors, it can serve only as a very diffuse type of motivation.

FUNCTIONAL SYMPTOMS

The physiological concomitants of anxiety and hostility, however, particularly when they are chronic, are major sources of so-called functional symptoms. These psychogenic complaints are not imaginary but usually have a firm physiological basis. Persons who suffer from severe headaches for which no "organic" cause can be found—no brain tumor, eyestrain, sinus infection, arthritic vertebrae, or migraine—are not imagining the pain. They usually suffer from "tension headaches" caused by the tensions of the muscles that accompany increased alertness. The pain from the tense neck muscles is felt over the occiput, and from the frontal and oculomotor muscles in the forehead. A pounding heart, sudden abdominal cramps, drenching sweat, can all be part of the physiological response to danger. A syncopal attack—a faint—can occur when the blood vessels in a person's muscles dilate suddenly in preparation for flight; but when the person merely stands instead of running or fighting, the muscles do not pump blood as they do during activity, and insufficient blood reaches the brain. In a state of inaction the individual becomes aware of such physiological responses and may consider them to be symptoms.*

It will be recalled (Chapter 9) that the mental mechanisms of defense may be unconsciously brought into operation at the first physiological signal of anxiety. Either the signal leads to cognizance of the threat of danger and directs the person to do something about it, or a mechanism of defense such as repression, isolation, projection, prevents perception of the threat or changes it into something that does not threaten self-esteem or require self-punishment. The mechanisms of defense, then, do not simply help a person to maintain self-esteem—or to alter id impulses into a form acceptable to the superego—but also help to keep the body from responding to potential anxiety-provoking situations. These responses would serve little but would disturb the body's physiological equilibrium and thus produce unnecessary strains on the organism. They are thus a means of protecting the body's integrity from the physiological concomitants of anxiety, anger, and resentment.

EMOTIONS AND BODILY DAMAGE

Although the physiological responses to anxiety are usually brief and produce discomfort rather than damage to the organism, an inability to resolve the anxiety-provoking situation or failures of the ego's mechanisms of

* Although the physiological responses to anxiety and hostility are diffuse, individuals usually become conscious of one or more specific manifestations, and these seem to become the primary symptoms of anxiety or fear for the individual. It is not clear how this occurs. In World War I, for example, many soldiers, particularly in the British Army, were incapacitated by the "effort syndrome" or "neurocirculatory asthenia"—the heart beat very forcefully and rapidly and the soldier became short of breath with very slight exertion. Considerable attention was paid to the syndrome. In World War II, during the Solomon Islands campaign, numerous soldiers had similar symptoms but together with the full gamut of physiological responses to danger—hyperalertness, sweating, diarrhea, slightly elevated blood pressure, etc.—and when special effort was made to prevent them from focusing on their heart symptoms rather than on their anxiety, only a very few developed the "effort syndrome," which clearly seemed a residue of the more diffuse anxiety state and could be relieved by blocking the sympathetic nerves to the heart.

defense to conceal the threat can lead to untoward effects. A clear and dramatic though unusual example was provided by a twenty-year-old college student who was admitted to a general hospital for intensive study because of a puzzling, life-threatening ailment. Although his blood pressure was generally normal, on three distinct occasions it had soared to extremely high levels and had remained elevated for several days. On one of these occasions a hemorrhage of a retinal blood vessel had temporarily blinded him in one eye. Such abrupt and transitory episodes of hypertension can be caused by a tumor of adrenal medullary cells that pours epinephrine or norepinephrine into the blood stream when the tumor is squeezed by an abrupt change in posture, as in bending. However, very careful studies eliminated the possibility that the patient had a tumor of this type. He was referred to a psychiatrist, and was pleased to have an opportunity to discuss some serious personality problems and the situations in which his hypertensive episodes had occurred.

He related that he had been engaged in a homosexual relationship with a classmate for five or six years; but during the past year they had both determined to terminate the sexual aspects of their relationship. His home life had been unfortunate. His parents, who had been markedly incompatible, had divorced when he was ten, and he had been sent to boarding school. During his vacations he was shifted from one parent to the other, feeling happy with neither. His father was a highly successful surgeon who held rigid and high expectations for himself and his son but who was given to violent rages, during which he sometimes broke furniture and windows. The patient recalled imagining his father's surgery as brutal and sadistic assaults on people. His mother was oversolicitous and worrisome, and conveyed a lack of confidence in herself and her son. Without attempting to portray his complicated and unhappy childhood, it will suffice to say that he was not averse to homosexual seduction in boarding school, and after indulging in such activities with several boys he formed an intense relationship with a classmate who became the only important person in his life.

The first episode of high blood pressure occurred when he was eighteen. When he was examined for induction into the military service, his blood pressure was found to be so high that he was hospitalized immediately. No cause could be found for the elevation, which disappeared after a few days. The patient knew that he had been extremely upset at the time, indeed had been suffering from almost unbearable anxiety. He did not believe, in retrospect, that he had been anxious about induction but rather was intensely fearful of being separated from and eventually losing his homosexual partner. The second episode might seem humorous were it not for the dire consequences. The patient and his friend, having become concerned about their homosexuality, had decided to end the sexual aspects of the relationship and make heterosexual adjustments. When resolve did not lead to results, they made a substantial wager about which one would first have sexual relations with a girl. The college year ended with the wager unclaimed. During the summer vacation the young man met a girl who gave ample indication that she was not averse to going to bed with him. After vacillating for several weeks, he mobilized his courage and decided upon a specific date and place. During the day prior to the chosen night, he suffered from severe tension, was unable to eat and occasionally felt faint. He was determined not to back down from his resolve, and he forced himself to drive to the girl's home even though he felt nauseated and unbearably anxious. Just as he rang the doorbell he lost the vision in his left eye. A physician found his blood pressure to be extremely high and discovered a hemorrhage in his retina. He went to the hospital instead of to a motel and once again his blood pressure receded after two or three days, and he soon regained his vision.

The student then made no attempt to win the bet for several months, but when he returned to college in the fall his friend also could not claim the money. Then the young man noted that a park near his college was frequented by women of a professional character, and he decided that he might be able to "make out" with one of them. He again steeled himself for the venture, and finally sat down on a park bench with a woman and arranged to go to her room. When he stood up he became acutely dizzy and could scarcely walk. He took a taxi to his doctor and was again placed in the hospital. On this occasion his pressure was extremely high and his condition became even more serious when his kidneys shut down and did not produce any urine for several days. Once again his blood pressure returned to normal, but then, partly his suggestion, a psychiatric consultant was asked to see the patient.

The genesis of this young man's homosexuality need not be considered here beyond noting that it constituted a pattern established to ward off fears of being overwhelmed and engulfed by women but which also partly masked his incestuous fixations which were terrifyingly dangerous because of his fantasies of mutilating reprisals by his violent father. His homosexuality eventually became socially unacceptable and threatened his self-esteem. His attempts to change to heterosexuality by determination and his refusal to be stopped by his anxiety and symptoms of fear, and his failure to overcome the problems and fears that had directed him toward homosexuality, left him prey to an intense physiological concomitant of anxiety.

Such devastating effects of the physiological responses to fear, anxiety, or hostility are uncommon.* The more lasting bodily disturbances related to these emotions usually occur when the physiological defenses against threat and danger chronically interfere with the homeostatic functions mediated by the autonomic nervous system.

THE DUAL FUNCTIONS OF THE AUTONOMIC NERVOUS SYSTEM

Let us look at the problem a little more closely. The reader will recall that the entire evolutionary process has had to do with finding new ways to preserve the cell and assure its reproduction (Chapter 1); and that when higher and more complex forms of life arose, complex mechanisms were required to make certain that the tissue fluids surrounding the cells retained their chemical composition with the remarkable constancy needed for maintenance of the cells. It may seem eccentric and even cynical to suggest that all of the complexities of personality development and the human life cycle that form the subject of this book are concerned with a unique way of preserving the germinal cell—at least when regarded from an evolutionary perspective. The body fluids must remain very constant, for slight change in the acidity of the blood, the oxygen and carbon dioxide tensions, the concentrations of sodium, potassium, calcium, and other ions, or in the body temperature are incompatible with proper physiological functioning and the survival of cells, tissues, and the life of the individual. The internal environment is maintained relatively constant by means of complicated chemical buffering systems and various checks, balances, and feedback systems. Humans must rely upon what Walter Cannon (1963) termed "the wisdom of the body" to handle itself, for it far surpasses conscious human

---

* How uncommon remains uncertain. In any event, hyperthyroidism sometimes follows directly upon a terrifying experience about which the person can do little (Lidz and Whitehorn, 1950). Thus, a black man who was raised in the deep South was terrified after he killed a white man in an auto accident. He had nightmares of a lynching he had witnessed as a child and soon became hyperthyroid. Another man became hyperthyroid after watching his farmhouse burn with his wife and child in it, being restrained from attempting to rescue them because it was hopeless. The thyroid hormone sensitizes to epinephrine and has something to do with mobilization for severe chronic stress as well as the regulation of metabolism. Sudden death after acute fright has also been reported by various observers. The author believes that he knows of coronary occlusions, including several deaths from such heart attacks, that followed upon the patient's experiencing unbearable anger and frustration.

intellectual abilities. Now what concerns us here is simply that a great deal of the nervous control of these homeostatic mechanisms is mediated by the autonomic nervous system, the same system and pathways that are involved in the preparation of the body to flee or fight when the person is confronted by danger or, as we have seen, when the person becomes anxious or hostile.* When, for example, the body temperature begins to fall, the autonomic nerves carry impulses that cause constriction of the peripheral blood vessels to conserve heat loss from radiation. If the carbon dioxide tension in the blood rises, respiration automatically deepens. Heart rate and constriction of various blood vessels vary in accord with the needs of exertion and the maintenance of a proper blood pressure. The secretions of the digestive juices in the stomach, the state of the blood vessels in the lining of the stomach, and the motility of the stomach are influenced by the autonomic nervous system. There is no need to attempt to convey the sweeping and important homeostatic functions of the sympathetic and parasympathetic nervous systems.

What ensues when these two functions of the autonomic nervous system conflict? As the reactions to danger are emergency functions, they are usually short-lived and usually do not interfere for long. When fear, anxiety, aggressivity, or hostility become chronic, or occur repetitively, then the smooth regulation of the body's maintenance of its homeostasis can be impaired. Under some conditions such disturbances can lead to more permanent changes, including illnesses such as peptic ulcer, hyperthyroidism, or bronchial asthma.† A middle-aged woman is sent into the hospital with a severe skin condition, an atopic dermatitis, that has affected her face particularly severely. The condition started a month after her second marriage and steadily worsened over the ensuing two months despite various therapeutic regimens. She is clearly depressed and when the resident physi-

---

* A great deal more is involved than the autonomic nervous system, of course, including virtually all of the endocrine glands, but the secretion of epinephrine plays an important role in triggering some of these secretions, and the autonomic nervous system is intimately connected with the various visceral centers in the brain.

† In some of the diseases of stress it is clear that other factors are essential. Peptic ulcer, for example, occurs predominantly in persons who constitutionally tend to have high levels of pepsin secretion—as well as emotional problems. Most persons with bronchial asthma are severely allergic, yet some are not allergic at all but have only a certain type of emotional difficulty; many will have asthma only when exposed to the proper allergen, and the severity of the asthma depends on both the severity of the exposure to the allergen and the degree of emotional upset. Asthmatic patients often cease being asthmatic when they are removed to the hospital, away from a difficult home situation. Similarly, the blood pressure of patients with essential hypertension usually becomes lower after they are placed in the hospital and without any other therapeutic measures.

cian, in seeking to learn what might be disturbing her, inquires about her recent marriage, the woman begins to cry. She reluctantly relates that she made a serious mistake in marrying again. Soon after the marriage, it became clear that her new husband was interested only in a type of perverse sexual relationship. When she had refused to participate, he had asked why she would not, saying that her sister had always enjoyed it. The patient had complied but felt humiliated and ashamed—and perhaps even more ashamed and angry to learn that her sister, who was married, had been having an affair with her new husband for many years. She did not know what to do or how she could even continue to see her sister. As she discussed her problem and eventually decided on what she might do about it, her skin healed and remained normal. The vascularity of her skin apparently had been chronically affected by her reactions of shame and buried rage.

LIFE PATTERNS AND PHYSIOLOGICAL IMBALANCE

The life pattern of a person and particularly the repetitive ways of reacting and relating can have much to do with creating a state of physiological strain or imbalance. It will be recalled that in our discussion of the influence of oral fixation on character formation at the end of the chapter on infancy, we presented the problems of a man suffering from peptic ulcer. He had remained closely tied to his mother, insecure of his capacity to support and feed himself, and afraid of reexperiencing a traumatic episode in his childhood, when his family had been threatened by poverty and starvation. He was an obese man who habitually overate when he felt insecure and suffered from frequent episodes of heartburn. He had married a motherly woman when he realized his mother was getting old. He suffered his first attack of bleeding from a peptic ulcer while awaiting induction into the army, and a second serious episode when his wife unexpectedly became pregnant. The theme that ran through his life, and which was repeated in many variations according to his age and the specific circumstances, concerned the need for assurance of "oral supplies" of food and nurturing protection. Never able to venture beyond his dependency on maternal figures, this man found even the ordinary course of life to be filled with threatening, anxiety-provoking situations that could upset his physiological functioning—and perhaps because of his oral fixation his gastric functioning in particular.* Any threat of separation from his mother and any need to become self-reliant provoked anxiety which he never overcame because a phobic defense against traveling kept him from leaving his small native town. He needed to earn more money as a married man in order to feel secure. He had the intelligence and training to hold a far better position than the one he had; he often thought of changing jobs or starting a business of his own, but when he did he became anxious and suffered from stomach upsets and convinced himself that his health did not permit him to change jobs. But then he would resent that his boss did not appreciate his abilities and promote him, and he would suffer from indigestion again. A new job could not offer him an enjoyable challenge and a sense of accomplishment; going into the army could not provide new adventure; his marriage provoked as much anxiety as it did happiness, despite his having found a considerate and nurturant wife; the prospect of becoming a father was an ordeal rather than an anticipation of fulfillment. The minor, almost daily upsets that helped keep his gastric functioning disturbed can readily be imagined. As the defensive pattern of his life was concerned with an unrealistic and unattainable search for complete security, it contained in it the sources of repetitive episodes of anxiety and frustration.

Sometimes the defensive pattern of life opens the way for serious emotional trauma that can have a devastating effect upon the person's emotional stability and physiological functioning. The impending induction into the army of the man we have been discussing was more than an anxiety-provoking episode. It threatened the core of his security operations. He would no longer be able to have a mother or mothering wife at hand; his phobia of traveling would be unable to protect him from being removed from them; he would be cast out on his own into a hard world that did not supply sustenance. As he had neither gradually gained confidence in his ability to care for himself, provide for himself, and survive on his own nor had he developed various mechanisms of defense that could serve to buffer the anxiety and perhaps change the perception of the danger into a more containable form, he reacted to the threat of induction with all of the

---

* The influence of life patterns, particularly defensive life patterns, is particularly important in the study of the "psychosomatic disorders." Many investigators in this field strongly believe that each of the major psychosomatic disorders occurs in persons who are sensitized to similar types of problems and perhaps whose life patterning leads to specific types of conflict. The patient being discussed is rather typical of many patients who suffer from peptic ulcer. Patients with ulcerative colitis are even less mature and more childishly dependent and have grave difficulties in making decisions; hypertensive patients may well show a different configuration which leads them to feel chronically enraged but rarely able to express their feelings, and so on. The "specificity" of such configurations is a matter of considerable dispute. A good presentation of this general orientation can be found in Franz Alexander's *Psychosomatic Medicine*.

physiological intensity of a child who loses his mother or who is faced by some overwhelming danger. It was at this juncture of his life that he developed his peptic ulcer and bled from it. Similarly, a woman who seeks security against feelings of abandonment by her mother by becoming the essential loyal child who will care for her mother after the other children leave eventually loses her mother by death or finds herself resentfully burdened with a helpless old person. If, as a part of the pattern, she seeks to bind a son to her by lavishing on him an overprotectiveness she believes she would have liked as a child, then the son is likely to rebel in a desperate effort to gain his freedom and his own identity, and flee from his mother rather than remain in a filial relationship to her. Then, when this trauma that has been feared since childhood occurs, she, too, responds with a profound and even devastating physiological reaction as if to an overwhelming danger: perhaps as she did in childhood when the sensitizing event originally occurred. Indeed, it was at this juncture in her life that a woman in this situation developed hyperthyroidism.

Misfiring of Mechanisms of Defense

We must note, too, that, although the mechanisms of defense usually serve to lessen the physiological impact of situations that are potentially anxiety-provoking, they can also increase the person's vulnerability. If, for example, a defensive mechanism prevents awareness of a situation that is actually dangerous, reality may eventually force recognition of the serious dilemma and the physiological response to the shock of recognition of danger can be profound. A man whose entire way of life rested upon his devotion to his wife and children managed to forgive his wife when she confessed to having an affair, but stated definitely that any further infidelities would lead to a divorce. Several years later he managed to use various mechanisms of defense to keep himself from realizing that his wife was proving La Rochefoucauld's epigram, "There are many wives who have never been unfaithful but none who have been unfaithful once." When he was abruptly and unexpectedly forced to recognize the actual situation, he suffered a serious coronary occlusion.

Furthermore, mechanisms of defense can go astray, so to speak, and become sources of severe anxiety. Thus, a woman managed to repress her hostility toward her husband and her wishes to be rid of the child who tied her to the marriage with the aid of various mechanisms of defense including undoing, reaction formation, and obsessive oversolicitude for her child. She eventually worked herself into an unbearable position. She became fearful of ever leaving her child alone, unable to sleep unless the child was sleeping beside her, fearful when he walked to school, and she could scarcely bear the anxiety of waiting for his return, fearing some harm had befallen him. She was unable to tolerate any prolonged separation from her son, which led to difficulties with her husband. When it became necessary for her to remain in the hospital, she insisted on leaving to accompany her son to a picnic, for he might drown while swimming unless she were present to watch, even though she could not swim. Such decompensated defenses are not uncommon, and when chronic they can become a major factor in the etiology of psychosomatic disorders.

THE ALARM REACTION AND THE GENERAL ADAPTATION SYNDROME

There are various other ways in which adverse life situations and serious emotional disturbances affect physiological functioning and the integrity of the body which do not depend so greatly upon dysfunction of the autonomic nervous system. One major set of interrelated physiological responses to severe stress involves the defensive activity of the adrenal cortical hormones. Rather than preparing the organism for action against danger as by flight or fight, these hormones provide a strengthening of physiological defenses against bodily injury, but the reactions also come into play following emotional stress, at least after severe emotional trauma. Epinephrine triggers the secretion of adrenocorticotrophic hormone (ACTH) by the pituitary, which in turn stimulates secretion of the adrenal cortical hormones (cortisone and related hormones). A continuation of the trauma can overstimulate the physiological defenses and lead to permanent changes in various organ systems, or exhaust the defenses, which can also cause profound structural damages. The physiologist Hans Selye, who has been a primary investigator of these types of responses to stress, has termed one set the *alarm reaction* and certain of its more continued physiological consequences the *general adaptation syndrome*.* The changes that

* Selye (1946) became interested in the physiological responses that are common to many illnesses and may also accompany injury: such as the shifts in the number and types of white cells circulating in the blood, fever, changes in blood pressure and volume, changes in vascular permeability, etc. Many such responses hinge upon the secretion of adrenal cortical steroids. In a general way, a primary response to trauma is the alarm reaction, in which increased corticoid secretion decreases vascular permeability and diminishes fluid loss from blood vessels into the tissues, which together with other measures helps prevent shock. Following the alarm reaction, a state of resistance follows,

occur seem to help explain the etiology of some illnesses such as rheumatoid arthritis, some types of kidney ailments, and various types of "collagen disease." Although the adaptation syndrome may primarily be a defense against physical injury, it can also occur in response to severe emotional trauma. Thus, Selye found that the entire reaction leading to death from adrenal cortical exhaustion could be produced in rats by tying their legs—a procedure which produces extreme fright in these animals. Death ensued with typical changes in many organ systems, even though the animals were carefully shielded against injuring themselves during their struggles. The endocrine, neuroanatomic, and neurophysiological interrelationships involved in the adrenal cortical defenses are under intensive study by many investigators.

Although emotional factors appear to influence the individual's resistance to illness, including infectious illnesses, the area has been very difficult to investigate carefully.

PHYSIOLOGICAL RESPONSES TO HOPELESSNESS AND HELPLESSNESS

Engel and his coworkers (1962) have focused their investigations upon physiological reactions accompanying a person's withdrawal of emotional involvement, particularly following the loss of a significant person, and have sought to differentiate between the reactions of helplessness and those of hopelessness. These are considered means of conserving energy and preventing the emotional and physiological impact of unbearable loss or overwhelming threat. The patterns are related to those of apathy and depression. At present, most of the evidence of profound physiological change is indirect, and the nature of the changes remains uncertain.

We have been considering the impact of emotions on physiological functions and how personality development influences the physiology of the

---

accompanied by tissue changes, and when trauma is severe may eventually lead to death. The type and extent of these defensive tissue changes depend upon such factors as severity, spread, and duration of the trauma as well as constitutional factors. However, even relatively early in the adaptation response, growth can be inhibited, the gonads can undergo involution, lactation in nursing mothers ceases, and ulcerations occur in the gastrointestinal tract. Later, tissue changes such as are found in the various "collagen diseases" occur. The total reaction involves a profound shift in balance of the entire neuroendocrine system and cannot be presented here.

individual. Although it is but one aspect of the involved and highly technical subject, we focused attention particularly on the automatic defenses
against danger mediated by the autonomic nervous system, and on how
such emergency functions can conflict with the homeostatic functions of
the autonomic system and produce a variety of dysfunctions. The individual life patterns, particularly a defensive life patterning, can lead to
repetitive triggering of the physiological defenses against danger, and under-
mining of the life patterns can create overwhelming emotional stress
accompanied by severe strains on the integrity of the organism. The mental
mechanisms of defense serve not only to defend the ego and maintain self-
esteem but also to protect against anxiety which triggers the physiological
defenses against danger; but at times, such mechanisms can go astray and
provoke emotional states that create strains on the physiological defenses.

REFERENCES

ALEXANDER, F. (1950). *Psychosomatic Medicine: Its Principles and Applications.*
W. W. Norton, New York.
BEAUMONT, W. (1833). *Experiments and Observations on the Gastric Juice and the
Physiology of Digestion.* F. P. Allen, Plattsburgh, N.Y.
BLODGETT, F. M. (1963). "Growth Retardation Related to Maternal Deprivation," in
Modern Perspectives in Child Development. A. J. Solnit and S. Provence, eds. Inter-
national Universities Press, New York.
BRUCH, H., and TOURAINE, G. (1940). "Obesity in Childhood: V. The Family Frame
of Obese Children," *Psychosomatic Medicine,* 2:141–206.
CANNON, W. B. (1963). *The Wisdom of the Body.* Rev. ed. W. W. Norton, New
York.
ENGEL, G. (1962). *Psychological Development in Health and Disease.* W. B. Saunders,
Philadelphia, Pa.
ENGEL, G., and REICHSMAN, F. (1956). "Spontaneous and Experimentally Induced
Depressions in an Infant with a Gastric Fistula: A Contribution to the Problem of
Depression," *Journal of the American Psychoanalytic Association,* 4:428–452.
GRASS, G. (1963). *The Tin Drum.* Pantheon, New York.
LIDZ, T. (1959). "General Concepts of Psychosomatic Medicine," in *American Hand-
book of Psychiatry,* vol. 1. S. Arieti, ed. Basic Books, New York.
LIDZ, T., and WHITEHORN, J. C. (1950). "Life Situations, Emotions, and Graves'
Disease," *Psychosomatic Medicine,* 12:184–186.
SELYE, H. (1946). "The General Adaptation Syndrome and the Diseases of Adapta-
tion," *Journal of Clinical Endocrinology,* 6:117–230.
WOLF, S., and WOLFF, H. G. (1943). *Human Gastric Function.* Oxford University
Press, New York.

SUGGESTED READING

ALEXANDER, F. (1950). *Psychosomatic Medicine: Its Principles and Applications.* W. W. Norton, New York.

Association for Research in Nervous and Mental Diseases (1950). *Life Stress and Bodily Disease.* Williams & Wilkins, Baltimore, Md.

CANNON, W. B. (1963). *The Wisdom of the Body.* Rev. ed. W. W. Norton, New York.

LIDZ, T. (1959). "General Concepts of Psychosomatic Medicine," in *American Handbook of Psychiatry,* vol. 1. S. Arieti, ed. Basic Books, New York.

SELYE, H. (1956). *The Stress of Life.* McGraw-Hill, New York.

CHAPTER 21

✿

The Therapeutic Relationship

THIS CHAPTER will move beyond the dynamics of personality development to consider some essential aspects of the therapeutic relationship. The practice of medicine or psychotherapy, or relating properly to a patient or "client" as a nurse, social worker, or clinical psychologist, requires profound knowledge of people, and this book has sought to provide a guide for studying people and learning from relationships with them. Knowledge about persons and their development, however, does not assure a capacity to relate effectively and therapeutically with them. A major difficulty in the practice of medicine, and particularly in the related disciplines concerned with the treatment of people's problems in living, is that the therapist's major instrument is the self. Good physicians, even before their differentiation from medicine man or priest, relied upon their personal powers to help promote healing, and have needed to be students of people. The advances of scientific medicine that have eradicated so many diseases during the past century have not diminished the importance of the physician as a person; and they have made possible the turning of more time and attention to problems of living rather than to the preservation of life. The focusing of increased attention on personality functioning and malfunctioning during the past decades permits a more rational attitude in working with the irrational, and has provided guidelines for assuring more useful therapeutic relationships. As we are not here concerned primarily with pathology or its therapy, attention will be directed only toward an essential aspect of the therapist's relationships with patients that rests upon the understanding of personality development. We shall consider the *transference* relationships between patient and therapist and how they are critical to clinical work in all fields of medicine and form the core of psychotherapeutic activities.

"TRANSFERENCE"

The term "transference" refers to the unconscious tendencies to relate to another person in terms of a prior relationship, basically in terms of a childhood relationship with a parental figure, transferring to the other person attributes of the parental figure or another significant individual with whom he or she is being identified. Although such transferences occur in all important relationships, coloring and obscuring the characteristics of the person with whom one is interacting, they are of particular moment in medicine where the physician has a unique importance to the patient, and in relationships with any therapeutic figure upon whom a person depends and toward whom the person is apt to feel dependent.

Before discussing the transference relationship, let us consider some rather typical and clear-cut episodes that occurred on the medical service of a university hospital. A third-year medical student has just started his clinical clerkship in internal medicine. His position, in essence, is that of assistant to the intern, learning through active participation under close supervision in the work of the medical service. He is assigned a young woman patient, he elicits a detailed history of her current illness and past health record, and he performs a physical examination. Like all students at the start of their clerkship experience, he is uneasy and rather insecure because he is still hesitant and awkward in carrying out his duties. Nevertheless, after a few days he notes, or others remark, that his young woman patient seems to have improved; at least she has perked up and gained sufficient energy to apply eye shadow and lipstick and arrange her hair carefully each morning. She has her sister bring in her silk nightgowns and a new dressing robe. She always greets the student with a pleasing smile, and recalls some additional information to impart to him. She asks his advice concerning the operation on her heart that is being considered. When the student asks her what the professor has advised, the patient imparts her lack of confidence in the professor's opinion because he is so very busy that he can have little time to think about her and her heart; she places the most weight on the student's judgment. The student tries to stifle his joy at having been assigned a patient who is so astute as to recognize ability when she encounters it. He sits down and offers his considered opinion, based on his experience with one other similar case and his reading in the textbook (written by the professor).

Another student is not so fortunate in the assignment of patients. He helps with the care of a truck driver with severe liver disease admitted late in the evening. The student stays up most of the night with the house staff testing urine specimens, drawing samples of blood, helping to give intravenous fluids, holding the patient's head when he vomits, etc. The next morning he wearily drags himself from bed after a couple of hours' sleep and rushes to the ward, where he is pleased to hear that the patient is doing nicely. He happily walks into the patient's room to draw some blood, and is taken aback when he is assailed by a series of choice invectives from the patient, who wishes to be left alone, and who accuses the student of having collected sufficient blood during the night to support himself for a month. Every friendly approach is met by a renewed outburst in which the patient makes it clear that he despises the student and his canine forebears. The student begins to feel that the efforts of the previous night had been a mistake, for the man was not worth saving, and he lets the patient know it.

Although these examples may seem to gild the lily, they are actual occurrences that may perhaps have become a bit polished in the telling. It is sometimes difficult for physicians to follow Osler's (1963) advice and retain their equanimity, but recognition of the transference nature of both the young woman's admiration and the truck driver's hostility could have helped both students to keep their feet on the ground and use such situations to gain better understanding of the person they were treating. Neither of these patients knew much about the students, and the woman had little reason to become enamored of one or the man to hate the other. They were relating primarily to symbolic figures in terms of earlier relationships to some significant persons. The young woman with the damaged heart valve was unconsciously seeking security, when she was dependent and rather helpless, by seductively wooing a man to look after her much as she had learned to gain her way with her father. The truck driver carried a chip on his shoulder, for he felt that if he had to be dependent and rely on any man he would be used and victimized just as his father had forced him to work when he was a boy and had appropriated his earnings until he ran away from home. Neither of these patients' responses was suited to the students' behavior, but being sick and dependent had provoked old patterns of reactivity. If therapists recognize the tendencies of patients to identify them with earlier significant figures in the patients' lives, they need not take such reactions personally, but can more dispassionately observe the patients' ways of relating to them and utilize the understanding they gain in the management of their patients.

The ability to utilize the self as an instrument for comprehending and gaining insight into the patient's ways of reacting and relating and for influencing treatment, requires an objectivity about one's own feelings and behavior and knowledge that comes only with experience. It is among the most difficult skills required of a therapist. Still, in the illustrations we have used, it was fairly obvious to anyone other than the students involved that the woman had no logical reason to consider her student-clerk the best physician available, and the student should have been able to realize that he was neither Rex Morgan nor Sir William Osler; and that the man had no grounds for such violent antipathy toward a person seeking to help save his life.

All relationships, particularly new relationships, contain elements of earlier ones. Our judgment of a new acquaintance is based upon experiences with others of whom they remind us. We size up new persons by consciously and even more unconsciously fitting them into the pattern of someone we have known, or a class of persons we have known. Stereotypes can, of course, save considerable energy and even keep us from knowing persons as individuals. However, an astute observer may gain considerable knowledge about a person by recognizing subtle similarities to others. Transference situations are usually more loaded emotionally. The intense relationships with parental figures in childhood become an integral part of the personality and influence the entire behavioral pattern of a person. Various childhood distortions of the relationship with parents and feelings about them are usually partially corrected as an individual gains maturity and a secure ego identity; but some childhood feelings and perceptions remain, and others are very likely to become reactivated during periods of intense emotional insecurity. The life patterning established by the transactions within the family of origin strongly directs an individual toward fitting new significant persons into the pattern, changing them to fit, or persons are selected to be significant who fit into the life patterning. As has been discussed in the two preceding chapters, there is a fundamental tendency throughout the course of life to pour the new into an old mold; to deal with persons according to past experiences. Such repetitive tendencies are usually more prominent in emotionally disturbed persons or during times of emotional disturbance.

The Therapist's Position and Role

Patients do not consider the therapist simply as another person, and the relationship is not a casual matter to them. Patients come to physicians with needs they cannot manage by themselves, no matter how mature and self-sufficient they may be about nonmedical matters; and persons come for psychotherapeutic or casework help because they can no longer cope effectively. The difficulties are usually worrisome, interfering with patterns of living and threatening the person's well-being. Patients expect that when they place themselves in a therapist's hands, their health and welfare will be of primary importance to the therapist. The therapeutic relationship rests upon the tradition of the doctor-patient relationship; and physicians long held an especially prestigious place in society because, along with the clergy, they were expected to place the patient's welfare on a par with their own. Indeed, they were expected to risk their lives regularly in caring for the sick; and until the serious infectious diseases were brought under control during recent decades, they could give but little thought to their own safety while caring for the ill. They continue to do whatever they can for a patient—whatever lies within their abilities—not because of their own needs, or because of some personal relationship to the patient, but simply because patients come to them in their role as physicians. As other professions have moved into the healing arts, or become adjuvants to medicine, they have to a greater or lesser degree assumed a similar role. One of the problems has been that few such professions, aside from nursing, have been taught in a similar life-and-death setting which emphasizes the difficulties and burdens of assuming responsibilities. Patients, however, expect any therapist to consider their well-being as a physician would—or should.

THE TRANSFERENCE RELATIONSHIP

The conventions inherent in the physician's role and status help predetermine the nature of the transference relationship in therapy. Patients must place their therapists in positions of authority if they are to feel secure, and they tend to make a therapist as omniscient and omnipotent as possible. They seek to endow the therapist with the qualities of a parental figure who will care for them and protect them. Thus, to a much greater extent than in most relationships, the therapist is regarded as a parental person and the characteristics of one or both parents are often transferred to the therapist, a process which reactivates patterns of interrelating that were used with a parent. The age and sex of the therapist make relatively little difference. The most virile physician may be perceived by a patient very much in terms of the patient's mother, and an aged woman may regard the young intern as she would a father figure. Recognition of such general trends which so often enter into the therapeutic relationship provides therapists with an orientation that guides them in using themselves helpfully. Blindness to the nature of the relationship engenders trouble.

Let us consider an example that is not so gross as the problems encountered by the medical students. A woman who is seriously ill requires considerable attention from the physicians and nursing staff. She is appreciative and complains little despite intense suffering. Then, as her illness comes under control, her complaints increase rather than subside. At times she resembles a whining child and the ward personnel have trouble containing their annoyance and begin to avoid her. The physicians become concerned and repeat several expensive procedures to make certain that she is recovering properly. The head nurse, however, notes that her complaints fluctuate during the day in a way that relates to changes in personnel rather than in her fever chart. One particular older staff nurse had spent much time with the patient during the critical phase of her illness. If, when this nurse comes on duty, she first sees the patient and spends a few minutes with her, everything goes well; but if she carries out some procedure with another patient first, the woman has many complaints by the time the nurse reaches her. The circumstances become fairly apparent to the perceptive head nurse when this patient occupies a double room with a very ill patient. If the particular nurse pays more attention to the roommate, difficulties arise and the patient becomes petulant and childish. Indeed, she reacts badly when she receives less attention than the other patient from any of the staff, but it is most obvious with her favorite nurse. The patient, as subsequent discussions with the psychiatrist revealed, had again become a child, having regressed markedly as do many seriously ill persons. She again had in the nurse a benevolent mother who was concerned about her and carefully nursed her; she became an envious child as she had many years before when her mother seemed more interested in her younger sister who had been in bed for many months with a chronic illness and required considerable attention. The patient now as in childhood sought to regain maternal attention by emphasizing her own needs in a hypochondriacal manner.

Misuse of Transference Phenomena

Knowledge of the transference aspects of patients' behavior, particularly a little knowledge about transference phenomena, can lead to its misuse by therapists in order to protect themselves from a patient's criticisms. Not all of a patient's misapprehensions, antagonisms, desires to change therapists or to leave treatment, derive from transference problems. Transference difficulties should not be blamed for resentments induced by failures to understand, thoughtlessness, mistakes, or neglect. Hospitals, for example, can provoke considerable aggravation in the bedridden patient. A patient can become annoyed by senseless hospital routine, lengthy waiting for a bedpan, cold and scarcely edible hospital food. A therapist may usefully wonder with the patient why these inconveniences produce such excessive reactions, but time and aggravation can usually be spared by reserving consideration and discussion of transference problems for significant situations for which the therapist's behavior or current circumstances are probably not responsible and the patient's reactions seem inappropriate. In most situations in medical practice, transference difficulties are considered primarily when a patient's behavior appears out of place, exaggerated, or based on misunderstandings.

Transference in Psychotherapy

In medical practice, general social casework, and other situations where the therapist is not specifically trained in the utilization of transference phenomena, they serve primarily as a guide to more effective use of the therapist-patient relationship. But in psychotherapy, transference serves as a major means of gaining understanding of a patient's basic attitudes and ways of relating, and often as a major therapeutic lever in bringing about changes in the patient's attitudes and ways of understanding others.

A psychiatrist who practiced psychoanalytically oriented therapy became ill and canceled his appointments for a day. The following morning, his first patient told him that she was glad to have had the extra hour, for she had been extremely busy at her job and would have needed to remain overtime had he kept the appointment. In fact, she continued, missing the session may have been more helpful as it gave her time to talk to her boss about some of her difficulties and he was very understanding and gave her some sound advice. As the psychiatrist had returned to his practice before he was fully recovered because he believed that this particular patient might become upset if he were ill, he could have become annoyed to hear her say that she was glad he had missed an hour with her and that her boss was able to give advice that the psychiatrist withheld or could not give. However, he simply listens and it soon becomes apparent that the patient is trying to tell herself and her psychiatrist that she will not let herself be hurt by needing someone badly and then be left in the lurch by him. She will make it clear to her psychiatrist that he is not so very important to her. This is an old pattern that has kept her from forming any close relationships and one of the reasons she is still single and turning into a spinster. The psychiatrist eventually comments in an offhand way that he recognizes that she is not angry because he stayed home on the preceding day and it does not matter if he or anyone else is really interested in her or not. Tears begin to trickle down the patient's cheeks, and when she tries to talk she finds herself sobbing that she did not really mean that; and, now, she feels for the first time the importance of her denial of her wishes and needs to be cared for and to be taken care of, a recognition which she has managed to evade in therapy except in intellectual discussions which were kept isolated from emotional context. She then goes on to consider her loneliness as a child and how her father was only interested in her brothers, with whom he could fish and hunt.

Another patient had heard that the psychiatrist had been ill. She starts her hour by expressing her concerns about his health and then tells of a fantasy she had that morning in which she told the psychiatrist that she loved him. In her daydream the psychiatrist was very ill, worried about dying, and needed the solace of the love she could express for him. The psychiatrist does not believe that the patient really loves him, nor does he think he must reassure the patient that he had been home with a relatively inconsequential viral infection. He notes to himself that although the patient has been in treatment for over a year, only in these circumstances has she been able to let herself fantasy being close to her therapist. It is only when she feels she is needed and can be useful because the man is weak and helpless that she can dare to experience affection. As she is married to a semi-invalid, the psychiatrist wonders whether this is a repetitive pattern and just how it had originated. He becomes alert to how the situation may be utilized and simply asks, "You felt that I needed you?" which starts the patient talking about her need to be needed before she can feel affectionate.

As elsewhere in psychotherapy, insight into a patient's misapprehensions or unconscious motives does not call for immediate interpretation; indeed, many experienced therapists rarely give intellectual interpretations at all, but seek to guide patients to reach understandings themselves, and largely through feelings and thoughts engendered in the transference relationship with the psychiatrist. Transference misconceptions may be utilized most effectively by letting them be worked through against reality.

A psychiatrist who had his office in his home received an urgent call from a woman graduate student who asked for an emergency consultation because of her suicidal preoccupations. Although it was evening, he arranged to see the patient immediately. When she arrived, the psychiatrist's sixteen-year-old daughter opened the door and showed her to the waiting room. After several sessions, the patient started psychoanalytic therapy with him. Somewhat to his surprise, the patient referred to his daughter as his beautiful young mistress. He did not correct her misapprehension, which of course led to a rather distorted view of the psychiatrist and his way of life. The references to the imagined mistress gradually became more frequent and central to the young woman's problems. They were transferred from her disillusion in her father, her envy of her father's mistress, her disappointment in her mother, and many other such matters that had long directed much of the patient's fantasy life and distorted her image of herself. After about eighteen months, she suddenly realized that her idea that her analyst had a young mistress was without basis and she began to understand how profoundly a central theme from her childhood was affecting her life.

COUNTERTRANSFERENCE

The patient's transference affects one side of the therapeutic relationship; the *countertransference*—the therapist's tendencies to react to the patient in terms of his or her own earlier significant relationships—is, in many ways, even more important. Clearly, therapists need to view their patients as realistically and as free from distortion as possible. Patients properly must be treated for their own problems and not for some other person's difficulties, including the therapist's. If, for example, a therapist had an alcoholic father who made the therapist's family life miserable, old resentments toward the father may deleteriously color the relationships with alcoholic patients. If a male therapist has idealized his mother and mother figures and been willing to sacrifice himself to gain a token of affection from motherly women, his judgment in his treatment of older women may be faulty.

Countertransference phenomena enter into therapists' attitudes toward patients in many ways simply because therapists are human and their early interpersonal relationships can never be fully excluded from them. Insofar as countertransference enters the relationship, the actuality of the situation is obfuscated. Yet, some countertransference feelings are advantageous, for without such connectedness to prior significant relationships, the therapist might be too aloof and unable to empathize with patients. Psychoanalysts must be thoroughly analyzed themselves, in large part to gain sufficient insight into their own lives and to become aware of the unconscious components of their ways of relating to and understanding others in order to provide assurance that countertransference problems will not seriously influence their work with patients. Knowledge of the self, however gained, is of the essence to anyone engaged in treating people psychotherapeutically. Whether analyzed or not, good therapists continue to learn something from virtually every patient they treat about their own foibles and their tendencies to misperceive patients and what they communicate. Psychoanalysis is purposely carried out in a manner that seeks to heighten the use of the transference attitudes and to minimize the distortions stemming from the countertransference. Patients on the couch do not see their analysts who sit behind them, and patients do not receive cues from their analysts' expressions or comments, which are, particularly during the early phase of analysis, sparse and nondirective, seeking to increase the free flow of associations from the patient. Patients, thus, with little knowledge about their analysts, tend to transfer to their analysts ideas and feelings derived from earlier significant relationships, which eventually become the topic of analytic scrutiny. The analyst's minimal activity lessens the impact on the therapy of countertransference, for after the patient becomes a more distinctive individual to the analyst, countertransference phenomena are less likely to interfere.

Relatively few analysts, however, adhere rigorously to the style of making themselves a "blank screen" for the patient's transferences and projections. Many analytically oriented therapists seek to serve as what Sullivan (1953) termed a "participant observer," listening to the patient's associations and past and present experiences, while trying to guide the patient into more objective and less distorted perceptions and understanding by commenting briefly and inserting questions or questioning sounds at appropriate moments. Such psychotherapeutic interventions as a participant observer properly require even greater self-knowledge and ability to manage countertransference phenomena than do more classical psychoanalytic techniques. Perhaps, most analysts work in a style between these two models, varying their techniques to suit the patient and the phase of therapy.

Whereas a thorough psychoanalysis is the most effective way for a therapist to gain self-understanding, unfortunately it does not assure it; and there have been gifted therapists, including Freud and many of the early analysts, capable of proper empathy and with deep insights into their own natures and foibles who were not formally analyzed.

Countertransference phenomena cannot be completely avoided or excluded. In customary relationships between a physician, nurse, or social worker and a patient, it is the countertransference excesses that require checking. Therapists become alert when, for example, they find the patient's difficulties provoking strong emotions in them; or when they realize that they are strongly involved emotionally, as when falling in love with a patient or when feeling hostile to a patient. At such times, the danger arises that the treatment will be influenced or even directed toward alleviating the therapist's feelings rather than the patient's problems. Equanimity does not mean disinterest, but it implies that the therapist can maintain a suitable perspective, and that the patient's problems rather than the therapist's emotional needs will guide their relationship.

Countertransference phenomena are, in a sense, part of the larger problem of therapists who are caught up in their own needs while treating patients. They may involve the reasons for the choice of a career. Physicians, or any therapists, may seek power and an opportunity to display it and be unable to countenance any interference with their decisions; or they may seek the love of their patients, leading them to sacrifice themselves excessively; or they may unconsciously seek to make their patients feel dependent upon them and indebted to them, thus interfering with the goal of fostering patients' development of autonomy. They may desire the plaudits of colleagues more than the well-being of patients; or they may make authoritarian use of their positions in order to gain vengeance on mother or father figures. Good therapists strive constantly to achieve reasonable equanimity and objectivity that permit optimal use of their knowledge and skills for the benefit of their patients. They require ability to learn not only to know their patients as specific individuals and to recognize patients' transference problems, but also to know themselves, their strengths, weaknesses, needs, and repetitive patterns, as well as they can.

It is often difficult for physicians to keep their feet on the ground when they hold the responsibility of dealing with life and death, and also for any therapists who can rightly believe that they can often change the course of a life. When patients idealize them, they can lose perspective and begin to believe they are the persons whom patients think they see. Such exaltation of the self can rebound and bring therapists misery if they expect the impossible from themselves and find it difficult to forgive their own errors. The failure to recognize the transference attitudes of patients breeds trouble, but when therapists see themselves in terms of their patients' transference reactions to them, they are courting disaster.

Although the ability to assess countertransference attitudes competently is essential for psychotherapists, such insights concerning the self cannot be expected from other physicians or from those in related professions. Still, an illustration of how countertransference can be kept from interfering excessively with a therapeutic relationship may be useful. A resident psychiatrist, well along in his training, started to treat a new patient under supervision. He spent a considerable portion of the first supervisory hour discussing his initial encounter with the patient and the feelings and memories it had aroused in him. When he first saw the patient, he felt his heart start to speed up. He noted the reaction and realized that her appearance had surprised him. He had expected a young woman who was seeking help because of marital difficulties, but he had not anticipated the pretty, vivacious, and extremely well-dressed woman who stood before him. He realized that she was a type he had liked to date while in college and bore some resemblance to his wife in the way she walked and talked. When he contemplated his reaction to her, he realized that a connection existed between something in her appearance and his older sister, whom he had idolized in his early childhood. But he also recognized that something in the patient created an unpleasant feeling in him which he could not fathom, but which he believed would eventually lead him to dislike her. In retrospect he thought it had to do with a smug self-satisfaction which conveyed an assurance that everyone admired her beauty and that any person would be lucky to have her about. The resident felt annoyed, because he did admire her appearance and feel attracted to her. The details are not as important as the therapist's awareness of the feelings that had been aroused in him, and his efforts to alert himself from the very onset of the therapeutic relationship to potential sources of countertransference distortion, of both a positive and a negative character.

The Use of Transference Relationships Outside Psychotherapy

In the practice of general medicine and in other relationships that contain a therapeutic intent or implication, transference relationships are not used so pointedly and purposefully as in psychotherapy; but they often influence the relationship for better or worse even though the therapist may not realize it. Clearly, therapists can use themselves and the relationship more effectively when they are aware of its importance and how it can affect a patient. The simple recognition by therapists that they are, or can be, parental authority figures and potential sources of support to the dependent, often regressively dependent, patient can help the patient to surmount crises. As persons who are capable of countering the internalized superego, therapists, by the power vested in them by patients' transference, can help offset patients' losses in self-esteem. When illness fosters regressive needs for dependency, physicians can permit patients to gain security through dependency upon them until the circumstances change. A patient confronted by a serious operation may feel far more secure if the general practitioner whom he or she has known for years is present in the operating room. The patient may know that the surgeon and the surgeon's assistants are far better equipped than the general practitioner, who could do little, if anything, to help, but the practitioner is a parental figure who, the patient feels, will be personally concerned and protective. It may be irrational, but it is an understandable and an emotionally useful irrationality. Persons who become dejected because they are invalided and no longer self-sufficient may regain self-esteem because of a therapist's interest in them and respect for them. The ramifications are many, and it is such transference phenomena, whether evoked purposefully or accidentally, that account for many unexpected transitions back to health akin to those documented by faith healers.

Sometimes a patient's needs can be met by the controlled use of a transference relationship when little more specific can be done and with unexpected salutory results. A young woman with severe acute arthritis lay in the hospital feeling hopeless and lost without any family to whom she could turn. Her father, if she had a legal father, had abandoned her mother when the patient was still an infant. Her mother had been a prostitute, but a rather unusual woman with an interest in literature that she had conveyed to the patient, but she was now in a mental hospital, chronically psychotic. The patient had spent her adolescence in foster homes and institutions, but because of her attractiveness, superior intellect, and drive, she had been provided with a college education by a church group. She had repeatedly sought to attach herself to one or another mothering woman attempting to become the favorite child by working inordinately hard to become essential to the mothering person. However, she either became too involved in the woman's family or involved with homosexual women whose advances she rebuffed, so that she never managed to find a permanent home. She had become ill with arthritis while working in a missionary school in the southern mountains after she had been displaced as the woman missionary's favorite and was no longer permitted to live in her home. It had been a severe blow, as she had believed that she had finally found a haven, a mother, and her proper calling.

The attending physician took an interest in the patient and suggested that she become an occupational therapist or nurse. He visited her daily and would chat briefly with her about her life and her many interesting experiences. A rapid shift occurred in the course of the illness, and somewhat to the surprise of the hospital staff she made a complete recovery without any residual deformities. The physician then fostered a long-term relationship in which she came for "checkups" at regular intervals, during which she told him about her progress in nursing school and discussed her plans with him. He was demonstrating that someone was interested in her, and indeed he had become interested in her. As he had consciously developed the relationship to foster the patient's self-sufficiency rather than to permit her to become permanently dependent upon him, he was surprised neither by her seductive efforts to attach herself to him nor by her suggestions that she could be very useful to his wife if permitted to live with his family as a mother's helper. He could retain interest without being frightened away by her attempts to become part of his life, for he had anticipated such efforts from her life story; and he could seek gradually to redirect her energies into channels that held promise for her future.

Indeed, physicians or any other therapists can sometimes be very helpful because of their transference positions, even when they do little more than permit persons to come to the office, where they listen attentively and empathically to what patients wish to convey. A man who finds little understanding from his wife and children, or an aged person who no longer has any significant person left, may gain much from a therapist's interest, and from being able to talk to someone who listens dispassionately and does not place blame vindictively. All too often physicians believe that they are wasting their own and their patients' time when they simply listen and think that they must *do* something—prescribe medicine, a diet, a vacation, or stop a patient from wasting money on unnecessary visits. Physicians may feel uncomfortable because they cannot offer useful advice concerning a patient's insoluble problems. The patient, however, knows that the problems cannot be resolved and is grateful for the opportunity to ventilate feelings that must be hidden from others, and regains self-esteem because the therapist considers him or her a person to whom it is worth listening.

An understanding of transference and countertransference phenomena provides directives that can greatly improve the therapists' relationships with their patients, but more precise guidelines are gained through interviewing skills with which the therapist helps patients tell about themselves. Patients' anamneses—their accounts of their illnesses and relevant material from their past lives—constitute the most important diagnostic tool in medicine, and form the foundation of most types of psychotherapeutic relationships. The various techniques that help elicit information from patients form a major topic in themselves, and are not part of the subject matter of this volume. However, the capacity to listen to and understand what persons seek to communicate and to note what they do not or cannot say is a major aspect of skillful interviewing. Patients' recognition that the therapist listens, hears, and understands provides an incentive to them to communicate what they consider meaningful. Such capacity to hear and understand what is meaningful in an individual's life rests upon knowledge of psychodynamics—upon knowledge of the epigenetic nature of personality development, of the crucial tasks of each phase of the life cycle and what is likely to be most significant to persons at their stages of life, of the critical importance of interpersonal relationships to everyone—and upon the ability to detect life themes and repetitive patterns. This book has sought to provide a guide for gaining such knowledge; but it cannot be learned from books alone, for it requires responsible involvement with people and a readiness to learn to know the self. What therapists hear from patients about their lives can be disturbing because some of it will surely also apply to the therapists. Yet much of the satisfaction gained from the practice of medicine and from conducting any type of therapy derives from a willingness and ability to hear and understand. It enables the therapist to gain and grow from each relationship, which in turn makes each patient a new adventure. As the therapeutic relationship ceases to be something given to the patient but rather a situation in which the therapists also receive, they can give of themselves without feeling resentful or drained.

REFERENCES

OSLER, W. (1963). *Aequanimitas and Other Papers*. W. W. Norton, New York.
SULLIVAN, H. S. (1953). *The Interpersonal Theory of Psychiatry*. W. W. Norton, New York.

SUGGESTED READING

BALINT, M., and BALINT, E. (1962). *Psychotherapeutic Techniques in Medicine.* Charles C Thomas, Springfield, Ill.

BIRD, B. (1973). *Talking with Patients.* J. B. Lippincott, Philadelphia, Pa.

BRUCH, H. (1974). *Learning Psychotherapy.* Harvard University Press, Cambridge, Mass.

NAME INDEX

SUBJECT INDEX